Center for
Creative Leadership®

THE CENTER FOR CREATIVE LEADERSHIP HANDBOOK OF LEADERSHIP DEVELOPMENT

Top row from left to right: Mary Lynn Pulley; Keith A Caver; Michael H. Hoppe; E. Wayne Hart; Craig T. Chappelow; Christopher T. Ernst; Patricia J. Ohlott; David M. Horth; Wilfred H. Drath

Bottom row from left to right: Marian N. Ruderman; Sara N. King; Ancella B. Livers; Sharon Ting; Russ S. Moxley; Victoria A. Guthrie; Cynthia D. McCauley; Jennifer W. Martineau; Ellen Van Velsor

Not photographed: Kerry A Bunker; Maxine A. Dalton; Christina A. Douglas; Patricia M. G. O'Connor; Charles J. Palus; Laura Quinn

THE CENTER FOR CREATIVE LEADERSHIP HANDBOOK OF LEADERSHIP DEVELOPMENT

SECOND EDITION

Cynthia D. McCauley

Ellen Van Velsor

Editors

Foreword by John Alexander

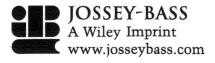

JOSSEY-BASS
A Wiley Imprint
www.josseybass.com

Center for
Creative Leadership

leadership. learning. life.

Published by Jossey-Bass
A Wiley Imprint
989 Market Street, San Francisco, CA 94103-1741   www.josseybass.com

Jossey-Bass books and products are available through most bookstores. To contact Jossey-Bass directly
call our Customer Care Department within the U.S. at 800-956-7739, outside the U.S. at 317-572-3986
or fax 317-572-4002.

Jossey-Bass also publishes its books in a variety of electronic formats. Some content that appears in print
may not be available in electronic books.

Library of Congress Cataloging-in-Publication Data

The Center for Creative Leadership handbook of leadership development / Cynthia D. McCauley,
Ellen Van Velsor, editors ; foreword by John Alexander.—2nd ed.
    p. cm.
    "A joint publication of the Jossey-Bass business & management series and the Center for Creative
Leadership."
    Includes bibliographical references and index.
    ISBN 0-7879-6529-4 (alk. paper)
    1. Leadership. 2. Creative ability in business. I. Title: Handbook of leadership development.
II. McCauley, Cynthia D. (Cynthia Denise), 1958- III. Center for Creative Leadership.
IV. Van Velsor, Ellen.
HD57.C38 2004
658.4'092—dc22

                                                              2003017288

Printed in the United States of America
SECOND EDITION
HB Printing   10 9 8 7 6 5 4 3 2 1

A JOINT PUBLICATION OF

THE JOSSEY-BASS

BUSINESS & MANAGEMENT SERIES

AND

THE CENTER FOR CREATIVE LEADERSHIP

CONTENTS

CD-ROM: A LIBRARY
OF RELATED CCL PUBLICATIONS

Managing Across Cultures: A Learning Framework
Meena S. Wilson, Michael H. Hoppe, Leonard R. Sayles

Building Resiliency: How to Thrive in Times of Change
Mary Lynn Pulley, Michael Wakefield

Preparing for Development: Making the Most of Formal Leadership Programs
Jennifer Martineau, Ellie Johnson

Making Common Sense: Leadership as Meaning-Making in a Community of Practice
Wilfred H. Drath, Charles J. Palus

Should 360-Degree Feedback Be Used Only for Developmental Purposes?
David W. Bracken, Maxine A. Dalton, Robert A. Jako,
Cynthia D. McCauley, Victoria A. Pollman

A Cross-National Comparison of Effective Leadership and Teamwork:
Toward a Global Workforce
Jean Brittain Leslie, Ellen Van Velsor

FOREWORD

For more than three decades, the Center for Creative Leadership (CCL) has endeavored, in the words of its mission, "to advance the understanding, practice, and development of leadership for the benefit of society worldwide." During this period, through its well-known educational programs and extensive research initiatives, CCL has worked with hundreds of thousands of managers and executives from a broad range of organizations—from Fortune 500 companies to nonprofit and government organizations, including the military. As a result, our faculty, which now numbers more than a hundred at four different CCL locations, has created a substantial base of practical knowledge about what it takes to make people more effective leaders and how good leadership contributes to more effective organizations.

This handbook, now in its second edition, gathers that knowledge into one easily accessible source that will be useful to anyone who cares about leadership development, especially those who see a strong connection between personal development and leadership development.

Organizations today are facing unprecedented challenges that often seem to exceed the individual and organizational capacity for leadership. The only effective response to these circumstances is development, and we at CCL believe that this handbook can contribute significantly to the response. My sincere thanks to the editors and chapter authors whose efforts and expertise have made this volume possible. In it, we hope, will be found information that is valuable to scholars and practitioners alike—insights that will improve the understanding, practice, and development of leadership worldwide.

Greensboro, North Carolina   John R. Alexander
August 2003   President
                                                                              Center for Creative Leadership

PREFACE

As an institution, the Center for Creative Leadership (CCL) has devoted much of its energy and resources to understanding how to help people in their quest to become better leaders. We have approached this task from both research and practice perspectives; that is, we have tried both to study the process of leadership development systematically and to intervene in that process. In over thirty years of work, we have gained a wealth of insights; created leader development models, tools, and programs; and, we believe, had a positive impact on the learning and growth of leaders worldwide.

This handbook serves to summarize and integrate much of what we have come to understand about leadership development. Its goal is to provide you with both a conceptual understanding of the elements of leader development and practical ideas about how people can enhance their leadership capacity and how organizations can contribute to that process. It also introduces a broader concept of leadership development—one that we have only recently articulated and that views leadership development as requiring more than the development of individual leaders.

We have written this book for people in organizations who design and implement development processes. In many organizations, this responsibility belongs primarily to human resource and training professionals. But more and more, line managers are playing an increasingly active role in the development of leaders and leadership in their organizations. Although we have HR professionals in mind as our primary audience, we hope that line managers who want to be more sophisticated in their practice of leadership development find useful ideas in this book.

Roots of the Book

First, a word about the sources of the ideas in this handbook. Although all the authors brought their own experience and expertise to bear on their chapters, each was also influenced by and drew from numerous streams of research and practice at CCL. We would like to point out some of these streams.

One of our core activities at CCL is running weeklong feedback-intensive leader development programs for mid-level or senior managers. This activity began in the early 1970s with what has become our flagship program, the Leadership Development Program. About four thousand managers complete this program each year. In addition, our work has broadened to include other programs, including one designed specifically for top executives (Leadership at the Peak), another built around a behavioral simulation that challenges participants to run a company (The Looking Glass Experience), one that focuses on the strategic work of leaders (Developing the Strategic Leader), and numerous others customized for specific populations or organizations.

Because we wanted to evaluate and improve our feedback-intensive programs, we began studying their impact. What we learned not only helped us refine our programs but also gave us a window on how leader development unfolds over time and how to best assess learning and change. Evaluation studies continue to be a central part of CCL's research activities.

We were also one of the first organizations to routinely use 360-degree feedback instruments in our leader development work. Providing organizations with these tools and training people in how to use them have become core activities at CCL. Not only did we put a great deal of research into developing these instruments, but we have continued to investigate the dynamics of the 360-degree feedback process as well.

Another outgrowth of our assessment work is formal coaching interventions. One-on-one developmental coaching with a trained facilitator was a feature of CCL's earliest feedback-intensive programs. These coaching sessions—often the highlight of a program—help participants integrate their assessment data and begin crafting development goals. To extend the learning process over time, we began offering a series of postprogram coaching sessions to our participants. Coaches support and challenge participants as they work on development goals back in their organizations. For many years, CCL has also provided individual feedback and coaching to senior managers in our Awareness Program for Executive Excellence (APEX).

Another stream of research that has greatly influenced this handbook started with a project that ultimately produced the book *The Lessons of Experience* (McCall, Lombardo, and Morrison, 1988). Through interviews and open-ended questionnaires, executives told the stories of their developmental experiences—the events and people that shaped them as managers and leaders. This study significantly influenced CCL's understanding of leader development in that we more clearly saw that the majority of leader development occurs on the job through assignments, relationships, and hardships. Formal development programs play an important and distinct role in leader development, but they are not a substitute for these other formal and informal experiences.

From this initial research flowed further study of developmental assignments and relationships, as well as research into people's ability to learn from experience. The original *Lessons of Experience* study was also replicated with more diverse managerial populations. We learned to integrate the tools and ideas from this stream by designing and delivering a program for human resource professionals, Tools for Developing Successful Executives. The participants in this program are a continuous source of learning for us as they work to apply the program's concepts to the leader development processes in their own organizations.

Another important research thrust looks at issues in developing women and people of color for higher-level management positions in organizations. CCL's history in this area (often referred to as "glass ceiling" research), as well as more recent research, is summarized in Chapters Nine and Ten. Again, on this topic we have connected our research to practice through our programs, such as The African-American Leadership Program and The Women's Leadership Program.

A more recent research emphasis focuses on cross-cultural differences in leader development and on leading effectively across countries and cultures. The issues of cross-cultural leadership and leader development are also encountered on a daily basis as we go about our educational work in Europe, Asia, and with the increasingly international mix of participants in our classrooms in the United States. We have learned much from these direct experiences.

Finally, we also draw on the latest focus of research and development at CCL: the leadership capacity of groups and organizations. This capacity is not just embedded in individuals in leadership roles but is also found in the relationships, systems, and cultures of the organization.

What the Handbook Does Not Cover

Although the word *handbook* in the title may suggest exhaustive and comprehensive coverage of a particular field, this book does not cover everything that could conceivably be examined in the domain of leadership development. Leadership and development are broad concepts that can be approached from many different perspectives. Because of our particular history of research and practice, we have gained a certain perspective on leadership development. It is this perspective in its various aspects that we cover in this handbook. Hence the handbook does *not* do any of the following things:

- It does not provide a comprehensive review of leadership theories. There are a number of excellent reviews of the various ways scholars have approached and understood leadership (see Bass and Stogdill, 1990; Clark and Clark, 1994; Hughes, Ginnett, and Curphy, 2002; Rost, 1991; Yukl, 2002). In the Introduction, we, the editors of this handbook, share a view of leadership development that has evolved within CCL. This view does not neatly fit into any of the classic categories of leadership theories (such as trait theories, situational theories, or transformational theories). Rather, we have tended to borrow ideas from various theories and integrate them.

- It does not present a definitive model of leadership. Unlike a number of our colleagues in the leadership development field (Bass, 1985; Covey, 1991; Kouzes and Posner, 1987), we do not present a single, detailed model of leadership that frames and delineates the practices, competencies, or behaviors of effective leaders. One reason for this is that we are trying to represent a collective perspective. In our work at CCL, we use numerous specific models to describe how effective leaders think and act. Recently, we have more closely examined the commonalities across these models. In the Introduction, we share a resulting framework that articulates a number of broad capabilities that people develop over time and that enable them to more effectively take on leadership roles.

- It does not cover all methods of leader development. In this handbook, we focus on the methods with which CCL has considerable experience and expertise. Therefore, you will not find much specific mention of knowledge-building educational experiences (used commonly in university settings with a heavy emphasis on case studies), sensitivity group experiences (developed and used extensively by National Training Laboratories), outdoor adventure experiences (popularized by Outward Bound), and team learning approaches (popularized by Peter Senge and his colleagues at MIT). However, in our work we do borrow from all these approaches, and there are individual CCL staff members who have considerable expertise with them.

Organization of the Book

We have organized the handbook into four major sections. The first is the introductory chapter, in which we summarize CCL's view of leadership development.

As we noted, there are various perspectives on leadership and on development, and it is important for you to know the perspective this book takes. Thus the Introduction is an important framing chapter for the book, setting forth our basic assumptions, a model of the key elements in leader development, and a framework for understanding the important aspects of leadership development beyond individual leader development. Because the remaining chapters all refer to these ideas, we strongly urge that you read the Introduction before moving on to other chapters in the handbook.

Part One focuses on individual leader development. This, the longest part of the handbook, conveys the essence of our knowledge about methods and processes of leader development. Each of the first six chapters in Part One describes a particular type of developmental experience: feedback-intensive leader development programs, 360-degree feedback, developmental relationships, formal coaching, job assignments, and hardships. The final two chapters in Part One look more closely at the leader development process. Chapter Seven describes the key components of the process: a variety of developmental experiences, the ability to learn from those experiences, and an organizational context that is aligned with and supportive of development. Chapter Eight provides insights on how to evaluate the impact of leader development initiatives in organizations.

Part Two contains five chapters that explore leader development in specific contexts. In the first part of the handbook, we draw on the broad array of our research and application experience, but in Part Two, we remind ourselves that although our experience in leader development has been in some ways broad, in other ways it has been narrow. Although we have operations and alliances outside the United States, CCL's staff is primarily from this country. Participants in our programs and in our research projects have been predominantly from middle or senior levels of management in U.S.-based companies; accordingly, the majority have been white males.

As we move from working mainly with white males to working more with women (Chapter Nine) and people of color (Chapter Ten), as we work with people from other cultures (Chapter Eleven), and as we work with leaders in global organizations (Chapter Twelve), we learn more about leader development. Finally, as we bring a lifelong adult development perspective to our work (Chapter Thirteen), we deepen our understanding of how leader development is intertwined with personal development.

Part Three provides two final chapters that highlight our shift from an almost exclusive focus on leader development to a more encompassing view of leadership development. Chapter Fourteen shares an emerging conceptual framework for understanding leadership as an organizational (rather than strictly individual) capacity. Chapter Fifteen examines the collective-level capabilities that enable organizational leadership capacity and methodologies for developing these capabilities. Both chapters argue that enhanced organizational leadership capacity is needed as organizations face increasingly complex challenges.

What's New in the Second Edition

To produce the second edition of the handbook, all authors updated their chapters from the first edition. CCL's research and practice in each of the chapter topics has grown markedly in the years since the first edition, and we wanted to revise the handbook to reflect that growth. This was particularly noticeable for leader development across race and across gender. Previously, these two topics had been combined into one chapter. We now had too much material for one chapter and therefore divided it into two.

Four chapters make their debut in this edition. A chapter on formal coaching was added—not only because our own coaching practice has been growing but also because the field has seen extraordinary demand in recent years for quality coaching. The chapter on lifelong adult development is partly based on research completed since the first edition was published. The final two chapters are also new. They represent our latest work on developing leadership as an organizational capacity.

Also new with this edition is an accompanying CD-ROM containing a library of publications from the CCL Press. Adding these publications allowed us to share more in-depth knowledge and expertise on specific topics addressed in the handbook.

As with the first edition, working on this handbook together has helped us clarify and integrate our knowledge and perspectives on leadership development. Our primary goal remains to present that knowledge in a way that others can use in their efforts to create developmental experiences and design leadership development processes and systems.

Greensboro, North Carolina   Cynthia D. McCauley
August 2003   Ellen Van Velsor

ACKNOWLEDGMENTS

It is impossible to name all of the colleagues and clients who have contributed to developing the knowledge contained in this book. The knowledge has developed over time through numerous projects and programs. We feel privileged to be part of the CCL community; we want to acknowledge the entire community as the source of our knowledge and thank them for their support in putting this handbook together.

There are particular colleagues to whom we do need to draw special attention, individuals who provided valuable input and feedback on various chapters and authors of chapters in the first edition of the handbook on whose work we built. Our special thanks go to Jennifer Deal, Lorrina Eastman, Kelly Hannum, Marcia Horowitz, Martha Hughes-James, Lily Kelly, Jean Leslie, Kathleen Ponder, Hallie Preskill, Byron Schneider, and Martin Wilcox. We are also grateful to the three anonymous reviewers who provided us with an external perspective and insightful critique of the first edition of the handbook. And we extend our thanks to Lisa Lee for working closely with us to achieve greater coherence and to make our ideas more accessible to readers.

Finally, we could not have put this handbook together without the help of Laura Ziino, who was instrumental in coordinating much of our work. Her ability to get everything into the right format, keep track of the latest version of each chapter, search out missing information, pull material together from all the authors, and stay on top of the work flow was a major asset to us in putting the manuscript together. Thanks, Laura, for the wonderful job that you did.

THE AUTHORS

Kerry A. Bunker is a senior faculty member at the Center for Creative Leadership. As comanager of the Awareness Program for Executive Excellence, he oversees and delivers an intensive assessment, feedback, and coaching experience designed to help the most senior-level executives enhance their effectiveness as leaders. Over the past eight years, he has also been manager of Leading Transitions, a family of custom interventions aimed at helping leaders respond to the challenges of ambiguity, change, transition, and downsizing. Prior to joining CCL in 1987, he spent eleven years in a variety of executive development roles at AT&T's corporate headquarters. He has published articles and chapters in numerous areas of management and psychology, including a recent publication in the *Harvard Business Review* titled "The Young and the Clueless." He holds a master's degree from Western Michigan University and a doctorate in industrial and organizational psychology from the University of South Florida.

Keith A. Caver is director of North American custom solutions at the Center for Creative Leadership. In this role he is responsible for the management of all custom business with respect to quality, design, content, and delivery for the region. Previously, he was responsible for all CCL client management activities and for testing and assessment services. He also serves as a senior faculty member, designing and training a variety of open enrollment and client specific programs. Prior to joining CCL, he spent twenty years as an officer in the U.S. Air Force.

He is also the coauthor of *Leading in Black and White: Working Across the Racial Divide in Corporate America,* as well as numerous articles on leadership. He holds a bachelor of science degree in management from Park University and a master of science degree in management from the Air Force Institute of Technology. He has completed postgraduate studies at the University of Alabama and the University of North Carolina at Chapel Hill.

Craig T. Chappelow is a senior manager of assessment and development resources at the Center for Creative Leadership. He divides his time between working with clients and managing CCL's 360-degree assessment instrument business. His area of specialization is in the interpretation and delivery of instrument-based feedback to senior executives. He is coauthor of *Keeping Your Career on Track,* a guidebook for managers published by CCL, and writes a regular column on leadership for the Jossey-Bass journal *Leadership in Action.* Originally trained as a chemist, his work experience includes technical positions at several major corporations. He is also a freelance writer and has published on a wide variety of subjects from business to parenting. He holds a bachelor's degree from MacMurray College and a master's degree from the University of Vermont.

Maxine A. Dalton is a senior faculty member at the Center for Creative Leadership. She earned a bachelor of science degree in nursing from Vanderbilt University, a master of arts in rehabilitation counseling from the University of South Florida, and master's and doctoral degrees in industrial and organizational psychology from the University of South Florida. She was a consultant with Drake Beam Morin for five years before coming to CCL in 1990. She has published on various aspects of leadership development, including 360-degree feedback, learning tactics, expatriate assignments, and global leadership. She is the lead author of *Success for the New Global Manager: How to Work Across Distance, Countries, and Cultures.* She has trained hundreds of feedback specialists, has given feedback to many individuals and groups, and has worked with human resource development professionals in a program designed to teach them how to implement development processes using CCL concepts and tools.

Christina A. Douglas is a former faculty member at the Center for Creative Leadership. She has conducted research on developmental relationships and has written *Formal Mentoring Programs in Organizations: An Annotated Bibliography.* She also served as a feedback specialist in CCL's Leadership Development Program. Prior to joining CCL, she worked for Xerox Corporation and managed projects related to development and validation of selection systems. She received her bachelor's degree in psychology from Cornell University, her master's degree in industrial and organizational psychology from the University of Maryland, and her doctorate in organizational behavior and human resources from Purdue University.

Wilfred H. Drath is an R&D group director and a senior fellow at the Center for Creative Leadership. He has worked with managers on their development and has participated in leadership development design for the past two decades. His current research and educational work focuses on the evolution of leadership and leadership development toward more inclusive and collective forms. He has written or collaborated on numerous CCL publications and journal articles on new frameworks for understanding and practicing leadership and leadership development. A recent book, *The Deep Blue Sea: Rethinking the Source of Leadership,* explores a relational-developmental framework for understanding leadership. He graduated from the University of Georgia and attended graduate school at the University of North Carolina at Chapel Hill.

Christopher T. Ernst is a faculty member at the Center for Creative Leadership. Since joining CCL in 1997, his work has centered on advancing the capacity for leadership in a global and interconnected world. His current interest is in understanding and developing the leadership strategies necessary when groups of people with very different histories, perspectives, values, and cultures work together. He is coauthor of the book *Success for the New Global Manager: How to Work Across Distance, Countries, and Cultures.* Prior to joining CCL, he was a visiting professor at the Asturias Business College in northern Spain. He holds a doctorate in industrial and organizational psychology from North Carolina State University.

Victoria A. Guthrie is a senior fellow at the Center for Creative Leadership. She is a designer of three of CCL's leadership development programs: LeaderLab, Leading Downsized Organizations, and Leading Creatively. In addition, she has designed and conducted custom programs for international organizations in Europe, Canada, the Caribbean, and the United States. She is author of *Leading with Purpose: Where It All Begins* and *Coaching for Action: A Report on Long-Term Advising in a Program Context* and coauthor of a number of other publications. Prior to joining CCL, she was with Xerox Corporation. She holds a bachelor's degree in management from Guilford College and a master's in business administration from Wake Forest University.

E. Wayne Hart is the coaching manager for the San Diego campus of the Center for Creative Leadership. He delivers keynote and motivational speeches on coaching in organizations; coaches senior executives; recruits, trains, and supervises executive coaches; and designs and delivers coaching and leadership training programs. He coached executives and entrepreneurs from 1975 until joining CCL in 1999. During those years he also cofounded and managed a large professional group, developed and sold a health care management organization and an outsource information management company, served as president of a small oil trading corporation, launched an environmental technology company, provided both clinical and forensic psychological services, and served on nonprofit and for-profit boards. He holds a master's degree in management from California State University and a doctorate in psychology from the Fielding Institute.

Michael H. Hoppe is a senior faculty member at the Center for Creative Leadership. A native of Germany, he has had extensive international experience in the fields of education policy, organizational behavior, and management development. He has lectured and published on leadership and intercultural communications in the United States and Europe. He holds a doctorate in adult education and institutional studies from the University of North Carolina at Chapel Hill. He also received a master of arts degree in clinical psychology from the University of Munich (Germany) and a master of science degree in educational psychology and statistics from the State University of New York at Albany. His current research activities revolve around the development of leadership effectiveness in multicultural environments.

David M. Horth is a senior faculty member at the Center for Creative Leadership. He is coauthor of *The Leader's Edge: Six Creative Competencies for Navigating Complex Challenges* and of Visual Explorer, a tool for facilitating dialogue and engaging diverse perspectives on complex leadership challenges. He is the senior architect of CCL's Leading Creatively program and has published a number of papers on the intersection of creativity and leadership. Known internationally as a creativity practitioner, he is Visiting Research Fellow at the Centre for Entrepreneurship at Greenwich University, London, and is a member of the board of trustees of the Creative Education Foundation. He began his career as an engineer, emerging twenty-one years later as a strategist specializing in creativity and innovation. He is also an accomplished musician on several instruments. He holds a bachelor of science degree from the University of Surrey in the United Kingdom.

Sara N. King is group director of global open enrollment programs at the Center for Creative Leadership. She has held several positions of leadership at CCL, including group director of the individual leader development practice area and worldwide director of the Leadership Development Program. She joined CCL in 1986 as part of the research team that studied executive women's career development in Fortune 100 firms. For most of her career at CCL, she has been a faculty member teaching in a variety of open enrollment and custom programs. Her expertise focuses on the development of individual leaders through feedback-intensive programs and processes. This experience led to her most recent publication, *Discovering the Leader in You*. She received a bachelor's degree from Wake Forest University and a master of science degree in educational administration from Cornell University.

Ancella B. Livers is a manager of open enrollment programs at the Center for Creative Leadership. She manages and trains the Leadership Development Program and The African-American Leadership Program. Prior to joining CCL, she was an assistant professor in the School of Journalism at West Virginia University. Earlier in her career, she served as acting business editor and Capitol Hill reporter for the Gannett News Service and appeared as a regular guest on the Baltimore public affairs television show, *Urban Scene*. She is the coauthor of *Leading in Black and White: Working Across the Racial Divide in Corporate America*. She holds a master of science degree in journalism from Northwestern University and master of arts degree and doctorate in history from Carnegie Mellon University.

Jennifer W. Martineau is the director of the design and evaluation center at the Center for Creative Leadership. In her ten years at CCL, she has focused on the evaluation of leadership development programs and initiatives. She serves as internal evaluation coach to CCL faculty and staff, CCL clients, and other leadership development professionals. She has worked with an array of client organizations, including international for-profit and not-for-profit institutions, school systems, and government agencies. Her work can be found in book chapters, peer-reviewed journals, and practitioner-oriented publications. She earned her bachelor of arts degree in psychology at North Carolina State University and her master of science and doctorate degrees in industrial and organizational psychology at Pennsylvania State University.

Cynthia D. McCauley is a senior fellow at the Center for Creative Leadership. During her two decades at CCL, she has held various positions in research and management. Her research has focused on leader development experiences (360-degree feedback, leader development programs, job assignments, and developmental relationships). She codeveloped two of CCL's management feedback instruments, Benchmarks and the Job Challenge Profile. She has written numerous articles and book chapters for scholars, HR professionals, and practicing managers. She received her bachelor of arts degree in psychology from King College and her master of arts and doctorate in industrial and organizational psychology from the University of Georgia.

Russ S. Moxley is local coordinator for Courage to Teach in North Carolina, an independent trainer and consultant who focuses on executive coaching and leadership development workshops, and the director of the Center for Leadership and Ethics at Greensboro College. Previously, he was a senior fellow at the Center for Creative Leadership. He is the author of *Leadership and Spirit,* coeditor of the first edition of the *Center for Creative Leadership Handbook of Leadership Development,* and contributing author of chapters for two edited leadership books. He has a bachelor of arts degree in social science and a master of theology degree from Southern Methodist University in Dallas.

Patricia M. G. O'Connor is a senior faculty member at the Center for Creative Leadership. Since joining CCL in 1995, she has worked with senior managers and executives in the design and facilitation of leadership development processes. Her client collaborations, publications, and presentations have addressed the organizational practices of corporate communication, 360-degree feedback in the development of learning cultures, systemic approaches to leader development, action learning, and other practices for developing organizational capacity for leadership. Her current work examines how the relationships among human, social, and organizational capital influence an organization's ability to address complex leadership challenges. She brought to CCL ten years of management experience in finance, sales, and human resource functions. She received a bachelor of science degree in human resources from the University of Illinois (Urbana-Champaign) and a master of business administration degree with honors from Bernard M. Baruch College (City University of New York).

Patricia J. Ohlott is a faculty member at the Center for Creative Leadership. She is coauthor of the Job Challenge Profile, a CCL assessment instrument that she and her colleagues have used to study the developmental impact of job assignments. Her other research interests include the career development of women managers and issues relating to the management of diversity and difference in organizations. She is coauthor of the book *Standing at the Crossroads: Next Steps for High-Achieving Women.* She has cowritten several CCL reports and has published articles in the *Academy of Management Journal,* the *Journal of Applied Psychology, Personnel Psychology,* and the *Journal of Management Development.* She has a bachelor of arts degree in psychology from Yale University and has completed graduate coursework in business administration at Duke University.

Charles J. Palus is a senior faculty member at the Center for Creative Leadership. He conducts research on how groups of people make sense of complex challenges. He is codesigner and lead researcher of the Leading Creatively program and the inventor of Visual Explorer, a tool for facilitating dialogue amid diverse perspectives. He has published widely on topics related to adult development and shared meaning-making and is the coauthor of *The Leader's Edge: Six Creative Competencies for Navigating Complex Challenges*. Prior to his coming to CCL, he was a research engineer for E. I. Dupont de Nemours & Co. and a leadership instructor and program designer for the Hurricane Island Outward Bound School. He earned his bachelor of science degree in chemical engineering at the Pennsylvania State University and his doctorate in adult developmental psychology at Boston College.

Mary Lynn Pulley is a senior faculty member at the Center for Creative Leadership. She is project manager for CCL's Blended Learning Initiative. She also designs and delivers custom programs to an array of CCL clients. Prior to joining CCL, she was based in Seattle, Washington, where she was founder and president of Linkages Workplace Consulting. There she helped organizations create systems using digital technology to enhance learning, communication, and resiliency. She has also researched, taught, and spoken extensively on the topic of resilient leadership. As the author of *Losing Your Job, Reclaiming Your Soul: Stories of Resilience, Renewal, and Hope*, she explains how individuals can be resilient and thrive in the face of corporate downsizing and restructuring. She holds a master's degree in counseling psychology from the University of North Carolina at Chapel Hill and a doctorate in human and organizational development from Vanderbilt University.

Laura Quinn is an assistant professor of communication at the University of Colorado at Colorado Springs. Prior to joining the university in 2002, she was a faculty member at the Center for Creative Leadership. Her research interests focus on the development of organizational capacities for leadership, sustainability, and corporate social responsibility. She has published in *Business Communication Quarterly* and the *Journal of Management Communication*. She has a bachelor of arts degree in business and a master of arts degree in communication from the University of Colorado. She received her doctorate in organizational communication from the University of Texas at Austin.

Marian N. Ruderman is an R&D group director at the Center for Creative Leadership. Her research focuses on the career development of women and the impact of diversity on management development processes. She has written widely on these topics in popular magazines and professional journals. She is coauthor of the book *Standing at the Crossroads: Next Steps for High-Achieving Women* and coeditor of *Diversity in Work Teams: Research Paradigms for a Changing Workplace*. She is also a coauthor of CCL's feedback instrument, the Job Challenge Profile. Her published work has been cited widely in the press and has been applied in The Women's

Leadership Program. In addition, she speaks frequently to corporate and academic audiences about issues relating to the career development of women. She holds a bachelor of arts degree from Cornell University and earned her master of arts degree and doctorate in organizational psychology at the University of Michigan.

Sharon Ting is a coaching manager and comanager for the APEX program, CCL's premier coaching experience for senior-level executives. In these capacities, she designs, develops, and manages a variety of coaching services as well as leadership programs for organizations. She has extensive international experience and personally coaches select senior executives. She has coauthored a number of articles, including "The Young and the Clueless" in the *Harvard Business Review*. Prior to joining CCL, she was executive vice president of a public authority that designed and constructed health care facilities throughout the state of New York and specialized in public and capital financing. She received her bachelor's degree in art history and English literature from the State University of New York at Albany and her master of business administration degree from Wake Forest University. She also sits on the board of trustees of the Rochester Institute of Technology in Rochester, New York.

Ellen Van Velsor is an R&D group director at the Center for Creative Leadership. She is responsible for the development of knowledge in the area of individual leader development and its conversion to programs, products, and services. She has expertise in the use and impact of feedback-intensive programs and 360-degree feedback, gender differences in leader development, how managers learn from experience, and the dynamics of executive derailment. She is coauthor of *Breaking the Glass Ceiling: Can Women Reach the Top of America's Largest Corporations?* and has written numerous book chapters, articles, and reports. She serves as associate editor of *Leadership Quarterly* and coedited a special double issue of the journal, focused on leadership and diversity. Before joining CCL, she was a postdoctoral fellow in adult development at Duke University. She holds a bachelor of arts degree in sociology from the State University of New York at Stony Brook and a master's and doctorate in sociology from the University of Florida.

OUR VIEW OF LEADERSHIP DEVELOPMENT

Ellen Van Velsor
Cynthia D. McCauley

A s in any discipline, the field of leadership development advances its understanding and practice by examining and reexamining fundamental questions. In leadership development, these central questions include the following:

- What does it take to be an effective leader?
- What aspects of a leader's talents are hard-wired, and what aspects are developable?
- How do people learn important leadership skills and perspectives?
- Do some people learn more than others from their leadership experiences?
- What are the necessary ingredients for stimulating development in leaders?
- What are the best strategies for enhancing leadership development?

Exploring these types of questions with our clients and colleagues has been the basis of the Center for Creative Leadership's efforts to advance the understanding, practice, and development of leadership. In the 1970s, CCL began experimenting with feedback-intensive leadership development programs—programs that provide participants with a heavy dose of feedback in a supportive environment. Over the years, we have refined these programs and added new components, developed more sophisticated feedback tools and methods, and studied the impact of our programs on the participants. We have also tried to understand how managers learn, grow, and change throughout their careers—not just from formal programs but also from the challenges in their working and nonworking lives, the relationships they cultivate, and the hardships they encounter.

We continue to invest energy and resources in efforts to understand and improve the leadership development process. For most of CCL's history, the essential question that has provided direction for both our research and educational activities has been, How can people develop the skills and perspectives necessary to be effective in leadership roles? Much of what we have learned from examining this question is contained in this handbook. More recently, we have broadened our research and practice beyond developing individuals to developing organizational capacity for leadership. What we are learning from this broader perspective on leadership development is also shared in the handbook.

In this introductory chapter, we present a framework for understanding what is to follow. We distill what we have learned into a model of leader development, and this model serves as scaffolding on which to place the concepts that are discussed in detail in the chapters that follow. We also discuss how and why our understanding of leadership development is expanding to include issues in addition to the development of the individual leader.

Assumptions and Model of Leader Development

We define *leader development* as the expansion of a person's capacity to be effective in leadership roles and processes. Leadership roles and processes are those that facilitate setting direction, creating alignment, and maintaining commitment in groups of people who share common work.

You should note three things about this definition. First, it is a definition of *leader development*, not of the more commonly used phrase *leadership development*. Most of our research and educational programs are directed toward developing the individual, so developing *leaders* is where we begin in describing our model. We will return to the broader concept of *leadership* development later in the chapter.

Second, we try to look at what makes any person effective in a variety of leadership roles and processes (rather than looking at the traits or characteristics of formal leaders). The assumption here is that in the course of their lives, most people must take on leadership roles and participate in leadership processes in order to carry out their commitments to larger social entities—the organizations in which they work, the social or volunteer groups of which they are a part, the neighborhoods in which they live, and the professional groups with which they identify. These leadership roles may be formal positions infused with authority to take action and make decisions (for example, a manager, an elected official, or a group's representative at a meeting), or they may be informal roles with little official authority (the team member who helps the group develop a better sense of its capabilities, the person who organizes the neighborhood to fight rezoning efforts, the whistle-blower who reveals things gone wrong). Leaders may actively participate in recognized processes for creating change (such as serving on task forces or project teams, identifying and focusing attention on problems or issues, or getting resources to implement changes) or more subtle processes for shaping culture (telling stories that define organizational values, celebrating accomplishments). Rather than classifying people as "leaders" or "nonleaders" and focusing our work on developing "leaders," we believe that all people can learn and grow in ways that make them more effective in the various leadership roles and processes they take on. This process of personal development that improves leader effectiveness is what we understand leader development to be about.

Finally, although it may go without saying, we should note that we do believe that individuals can expand their leadership capacities and that this effort to develop is worthwhile. A key underlying assumption in all of our work is that people can learn, grow, and change and that this learning and personal growth does enhance individual effectiveness. We do not debate the extent to which effective leaders are born or are developed. No doubt, leadership capacity has its roots partly in genetics, partly in early childhood development, and partly in adult experience. What we focus on here is what our experience has amply demonstrated: adults can develop the important capacities that facilitate their effectiveness in leadership roles and processes. People can use their existing strengths and talents to grow in their weaker areas and can significantly enhance their overall effectiveness through leader development work.

The core question, of course, is how to go about it. How do people acquire or improve their capacity for leadership? How do organizations help them in this process? A two-part model, illustrated in Figure I.1, reflects our attempt to summarize what we have learned thus far about the ingredients that go into leader development.

The three factors in part (a) of the model—assessment, challenge, and support—are the elements that combine to make developmental experiences more powerful. That is, whatever the experience, it has more impact if it contains these three elements.

We know that although leaders learn primarily through their experiences, not all experiences are equally developmental. For example, the first year in a new job is usually more developmental than the fifth or sixth year. Working with a boss who gives constructive feedback is usually more developmental than working with one who does not. A training program that encourages lots of practice and helps participants examine mistakes is usually more developmental than one that provides information but no practice. Situations that stretch an individual and provide

FIGURE I.1. LEADER DEVELOPMENT MODEL.

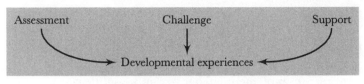

(a) Developmental Experiences

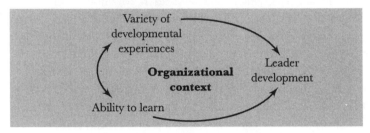

(b) The Development Process

both feedback and a sense of support are more likely to stimulate leader development than situations that leave out any of these elements. You can make any experience—a training program, an assignment, a relationship—richer and more developmental by making sure that the elements of assessment, challenge, and support are present.

Part (b) of the model shows that leader development is a process that requires both a variety of developmental experiences and the ability to learn from experience. The latter is an element that the individual brings to the development process. In the course of much of our work, we have noticed that people learn from similar experiences to differing degrees and in different ways. Although such variation is explained in part by the level of challenge that different people perceive in any experience, another factor is the individual's ability to learn from an experience. The ability to learn is a complex combination of motivational factors, personality factors, and learning tactics.

Part (b) of the model also shows that developmental experiences and the ability to learn have a direct impact on each other. Being engaged in a developmental experience can enhance a person's ability to learn, and being more readily able to learn can lead one to draw more development from any set of experiences. Thus although we conceptually separate the developmental experience and the learner in our model (the better to discuss them), they are in actuality closely interconnected: developmental experiences can enhance a person's ability to learn, and individuals with high ability to learn seek out and may benefit more from a variety of developmental experiences. This dynamic is examined in much greater detail in Chapter Seven.

Finally, part (b) indicates that any leader development process is embedded in a particular organizational context: the organization's business strategy, its culture, and the various systems and processes within the organization. This context shapes the leader development process—how it is focused, how well-integrated and systemic it is, and who is responsible for it.

Elements of an Effective Developmental Experience

Through CCL's research and educational programs, we have begun to gain a better understanding of the elements that are key drivers of leader development (assessment, challenge, and support). When we look at any type of developmental experience, from training programs to job assignments, we find that they are most effective when all three elements are present.

These elements serve dual purposes in the development process. First, they motivate people to focus their attention and efforts on learning, growth, and change. Second, they provide the raw material for learning: the information, observations, and reactions that lead to a more complex and sometimes quite different understanding of the world. To enhance the development of leaders, we need to help them find, create, and shape a wide range of learning experiences, each of which provides assessment, challenge, and support. Table I.1 summarizes the motivational role played by each element, as well as the kind of learning resource each provides. In the next three sections of this chapter, we look at each of these elements in more depth.

TABLE I.1. ELEMENTS OF A DEVELOPMENTAL EXPERIENCE.

Element	Role in Motivation	Role as a Resource
Assessment	Desire to close gap between current self and ideal self	Clarity about needed changes; clues about how gap can be closed
Challenge	Need to master the challenge	Opportunity for experimentation and practice; exposure to different perspectives
Support	Confidence in ability to learn and grow; positive value placed on change	Confirmation and clarification of lessons learned

Assessment

The best developmental experiences are rich in assessment data. Assessment data can come from oneself or from other people. The sources are almost limitless: peers in the workplace, bosses, employees, spouses, children, parents, friends, customers, counselors, and organizational consultants. The processes for collecting and interpreting the data can be either formal or informal, with many shades of variation in between.

Formal assessment from others includes such processes as performance appraisals, customer evaluations, 360-degree feedback, organizational surveys that measure employee satisfaction with managers, and evaluations and recommendations from consultants. Informal assessment data from others are available more regularly through less structured processes: asking a colleague for feedback, observing others' reactions to one's ideas or actions, being repeatedly sought out to help with certain kinds of problems, or receiving unsolicited feedback from a boss. Self-assessment can also occur through formal and structured means, as with psychological inventories or journaling, or through informal and often in-the-moment processes, such as monitoring of internal states, reflecting on decision processes, or analyzing mistakes.

Assessment is important because it gives people an understanding of where they are now: their current strengths, the level of their current performance or leader effectiveness, and what are seen as their primary development needs. So one important function of assessment data is that they provide a benchmark for future development. Another is that they stimulate people to evaluate themselves: What am I doing well? Where do I need to improve? How do others see me? In what ways do my behaviors affect others? How am I doing relative to my goals? What's important to me? Still another is that assessment data provide information that helps people answer these questions. In the context of their everyday work, people may not be aware of the degree to which their usual behaviors or actions are effective. In the face of a new challenge, they may not know what to continue doing and what to change. Even if they realize that what they are doing is ineffective, people may believe that the answer is merely to work harder; it may not occur to them to try a new strategy. But when an experience provides feedback on how one is doing and how one might improve or provides other means for critical self-reflection, the result can be an unfreezing of one's current understanding of oneself to facilitate movement toward a broader and more complex understanding.

Assessment information also points out the gaps between a person's current capacities and performance and some desired or ideal state. The desired level might be based on what the job requires, what someone's career goals demand, what other people expect, or what people expect of themselves. This gap is one of the keys to why developmental experiences motivate learning, growth, and change. If the area is something that is important to them and if they believe in the accuracy of the assessment data, people work to close the gap by improving their current capacities. If the assessment data indicate that there is no gap—that in fact someone is quite effective in a particular area—then the outcome of the assessment can be increased self-confidence. As a result, the person may seek out more opportunities to use and refine the strength.

Good assessment data also help people clarify what they need to learn, improve, or change. Having data not only motivates a person to close the gaps but also provides clues as to how those gaps might be closed. For example, if a leader learns that part of the reason for low morale in his work group is his pattern of not delegating important work to others (which, he comes to understand, is grounded in perfectionism), then improving morale involves learning how to let go of work, including how to be more in touch with his perfectionist tendencies so that they can be better managed. If a person's frustration at work is diagnosed as being partially caused by low tolerance for ambiguity, she can focus on ways to increase her tolerance or to shape situations so that they are less ambiguous.

Assessment enhances the power of leader development because assessment processes, whether formal or informal, help people fully understand their situation and become motivated to capitalize on the learning opportunities available to them.

Challenge

Developmentally, the experiences that can be most potent are the ones that stretch or challenge people. People tend to go about their work using comfortable and habitual ways of thinking and acting. As long as conditions do not change, people usually feel no need to move beyond their comfort zone to develop new ways of thinking and acting. In a comfortable assignment, people base their actions on well-worn assumptions and existing strengths, but they may not learn much from these opportunities. The same is true for a comfortable relationship, feedback that confirms, or training in skills that have already been mastered. In all such cases, comfort is the enemy of growth and continued effectiveness.

Challenging experiences force people out of their comfort zone. They create disequilibrium, causing people to question the adequacy of their skills, frameworks, and approaches. These experiences require that people develop new capacities or evolve their ways of understanding if they are going to be successful. For example, a task force assignment can be developmental when the task is critical to the business, success or failure will be known, and task force members must present a recommendation for action to the senior executives of the organization, because challenge is embedded in the assignment. However, it is particularly developmental for people who have not faced such challenges before.

People feel challenged when they encounter situations that demand skills and abilities beyond their current capabilities or when the situation is very confusing or ambiguous and current ways of making sense of the world no longer seem to work. For some people, challenge might mean being caught in the middle of a conflict where others are making demands that seem to call for resolution in opposite ways. For others, challenge might mean struggling to empower subordinates who do not take initiative and seem to resist taking a personal stake in their work. And for others, challenge might come in the form of work in a corporate environment, where it becomes less clear what "results" mean or how to achieve them.

So what are the elements of situations that can stretch people and motivate development? In other words, what are the sources of challenge? One common source is novelty. Experiences that require new skills and new ways of understanding oneself in relation to others can be the most challenging. These situations are often quite ambiguous, requiring much discovery and sense making by the newcomer. The power of new experiences is illustrated in Linda Hill's in-depth study (1992) of men and women during their first managerial assignment. Hill found that becoming a manager required more than learning new skills and building relationships. Rather, it was a profound transformation, one that caused them to think and feel in new ways—to actually develop a new identity.

Difficult goals, whether set by oneself or by others, are another source of challenge. People often respond to difficult goals by working harder. But they may also discover that extra effort is not enough, that they have to work differently in order to reach the goal. Executives report that some of the toughest assignments in their careers are starting-from-scratch assignments in which they have the difficult goal of building something from nothing—and usually have to do it quickly, with little structure in place and little experience (McCall, Lombardo, and Morrison, 1988). To succeed, they have to let go of normal operating procedures and learn as they go, using whoever and whatever is available to solve problems. Leaders who go through formal leadership development programs are often faced with the difficult goal of changing their own behavior or risking endangerment of their groups' performance or their own career goals. Again, this difficult goal is a source of challenge and thus is a potential stimulus for learning and growth.

Situations characterized by conflict, either with someone else or within oneself, can also be a source of challenge. Effectively dealing with conflict with a person or group requires people to develop an understanding of other perspectives, to become better able to differentiate others' points of view from their own, and perhaps to reshape their own points of view. People face similar challenges when they experience incompatible demands that cause conflict within themselves—for example, meeting work and family responsibilities, working satisfactorily for both the boss and subordinates, or meeting customer needs in ways that do not over-stress the organization. Ron Heifetz (1994), director of the Leadership Education Project at the Kennedy School of Government, Harvard University, sees the surfacing and orchestration of conflict as one of the hardest but most valuable tasks of leadership. In his view, conflict is the stimulus for mobilizing people to learn new ways. He gives the example of an industrial plant that was a major source of jobs for a community but was creating levels of pollution unacceptable to federal agencies. As community leaders were forced to deal with the conflict between jobs and health, they developed new ways of understanding the problem (namely, as an issue of diversifying the local economy), which implied new courses of action for them to take.

Dealing with losses, failures, and disappointments can also stretch people. Job loss, business mistakes, damaging relationships, and similar events can cause a great deal of confusion, often stimulating a search for new meaning and understanding. In CCL's work, we have found that these kinds of experiences, which we call *hardships*, startle people into facing themselves and coming to terms with their own fallibilities. Hardships also teach people how to persevere and cope with difficult situations. This is sometimes referred to as the "inoculation effect": undergoing stressful experiences may render similar experiences in the future less distressing, primarily because the person has developed better coping strategies.

The element of challenge serves the dual purpose of motivating development and providing the opportunity to develop. Challenging situations motivate by causing disequilibrium and then capitalizing on people's need for mastery. When the outcomes of the situation matter to people, they are motivated to work toward meeting the challenge. This means becoming competent in new areas, achieving difficult goals, managing conflicts, and easing the pain of loss and failure. Mastering challenges requires putting energy into developing skills and abilities, understanding complex situations, and reshaping how one thinks.

Challenging experiences also provide opportunities to learn. People do not learn how to negotiate without having places to practice negotiation, test out different strategies, and see how people react. They do not gain broader perspectives without coming face-to-face with people who have different perspectives or with situations that do not fit neatly into how they think about the world. People do not learn to cope with stress without feeling stress and figuring out how to decrease it. By engaging the challenge, people interact with the environment in a way that produces the information, observations, and reactions needed to learn.

Simply stated, people do not develop the capacity for leadership without being in the throes of the challenge of leadership work. Participating in leadership roles and processes is often the very source of the challenge needed for leadership development. Leadership roles and processes are full of novelty, difficulty, conflict, and disappointments. In other words, leadership itself is a developmental challenge. Leading is, in and of itself, learning by doing.

Finally, we also want to emphasize the importance of variety of challenge for developing the wide range of capacities that leaders need. We emphasize this because we have found that people learn different lessons from different kinds of experiences. From a "fix-it" job, leaders can learn toughness, the ability to stand on their own two feet, and decisiveness. From leaving a line job for a staff position, leaders have the opportunity to learn how to influence individuals over whom they have no direct control. From a formal leadership program, participants learn how to step back from the day-to-day routine and develop a deeper understanding of their preferences, strengths, and blind spots. From an effective boss, leaders learn important values such as fairness and sensitivity to the concerns of others. From a hardship situation, people can recognize their limits and learn how to deal with stress. All are important leadership lessons; each is learned from a different type of experience. Thus a variety of challenging experiences throughout their careers is an important ingredient for developing versatile leaders.

Support

Although developmental experiences stretch people and point out their strengths and weaknesses, such experiences are most powerful when they include an element of support. Whereas the element of challenge provides the disequilibrium needed to motivate people to change, the support elements of an experience send the message that people will find safety and a new equilibrium on the other side of change. Support helps people handle the struggle and pain of developing. It helps them bear the weight of the experience and maintain a positive view of themselves as capable, worthy, valuable people who can learn and grow.

Support means different things to different people. For some, seeing that others place a positive value on their efforts to change and grow is a key factor in staying on course with development goals. For others, having the resources and freedom to move forward on self-initiated goals is the needed support.

Perhaps the largest source of support is other people: bosses, coworkers, family, friends, professional colleagues, coaches, and mentors—people who can listen to stories of struggle, identify with challenges, suggest strategies for coping, provide needed resources, reassure in times of doubt, inspire renewed effort, celebrate even the smallest accomplishments, and cheer from the sidelines.

Different people may provide different kinds of support. For example, the new managers in the Hill study cited earlier relied heavily on peers to release their pent-up frustrations and find emotional support. Those who had developed close relationships with former bosses often turned to those individuals when struggling with difficult questions. We have also found that the support of one's current boss is particularly important when trying to change behaviors or learn new skills. Bosses can be a strong source of reinforcement for the desirability of the targeted development, and they can provide the needed resources for successful learning and change.

Support can also come from organizational cultures and systems, taking the form of norms and procedures. Organizations that are more supportive of development have a closely held belief that continuous learning and development of the staff are key factors in maintaining organizational success, and they tend to have systems in place that support and reinforce learning. They have systems for helping people identify development needs and work out plans for addressing them. They use a variety of development strategies, make resources available for learning, and recognize and reward efforts to learn and grow. Feedback, cross-group sharing of knowledge and information, and learning from mistakes are part of their organizational culture.

Support is a key factor in maintaining leaders' motivation to learn and grow. It helps engender a sense of self-efficacy about learning, a belief that one can learn, grow, and change. The higher their self-efficacy, the more effort people exert to master challenges, and the more they persevere in difficult situations (Bandura, 1986). Support also serves as a social cue that puts a positive valence on where people are currently and on the direction in which they are moving. They sense, "If other people support me in doing this, it must be something valuable to do."

Support mechanisms also provide learning resources. By talking to others about current struggles, openly examining mistakes, and seeing to it that the organization reacts positively to the changes they make, people have the opportunity to confirm and clarify the lessons they are learning. They get the sense that they are on the right track, that the feedback they are receiving is legitimate, and that the new ways in which they are making sense of their situations are shared by others or will work toward making them more effective.

If people do not receive support for development—that is, if their environments, coworkers, bosses, friends, and family do not allow and encourage them to change—the challenge inherent in a developmental experience may overwhelm them rather than foster learning. For a sales manager on a key cross-functional task force, beginning to understand and value the dilemmas of the manufacturing engineer on the task force may be the initial step in developing a broader perspective—but what if she is thwarted by a boss who constantly reminds her not to give in to "the unrealistic demands of those bozos in engineering"? Or, as another example, an organization that wants to develop more effective teamwork is unlikely to make progress if it continues primarily to reward individual contributions.

In summary, the key elements that make any experience more developmental are assessment, challenge, and support. Whether you are designing a training program, providing 360-degree feedback, putting someone in a developmental job assignment, or matching an individual with a mentor, you need to ensure that all three elements are part of the experience.

What Develops in Leader Development

Over the years, we have asked effective managers to identify what they have learned that has made a difference or a lasting change in how they manage. We asked them to think about experiences on the job, outside of work, and in formal leadership development programs and to isolate the critical lessons. The results are clear: development comes from many kinds of experiences. These managers learned from challenging assignments, from significant people, from hardships, from training and coursework, and from a miscellany of other events (Douglas, 2003; McCall, Lombardo, and Morrison, 1988; Morrison, White, and Van Velsor, 1987, 1992). The lessons they learned involved new skills, values, abilities, and knowledge. Over time, people who failed to learn became stuck—whether in their personal lives or in their jobs.

We also know, however, that some traits such as IQ and certain personality characteristics are more or less innate and appear to remain stable over time. Development work with adults cannot significantly improve IQ or provide a personality transplant, despite what some people hope and others fear.

Over time, we have begun to identify some of the individual capabilities that enable leadership and can be developed. We believe that when these capabilities are enhanced, individuals are better able to carry out the leadership tasks of setting direction, gaining commitment, and creating alignment. Some capabilities reflect how individuals manage their own thoughts, feelings, and actions. Other capabilities reflect how individuals work with others in a social system. A final set reflects how individuals facilitate the accomplishment of organizational work.

Self-Management Capabilities

People develop more effective ways to manage themselves—their thoughts, emotions, attitudes, and actions—over time. The capacity for self-management enables leaders to develop positive and trusting relationships and to take initiative—important aspects of roles that help people work together in productive and meaningful ways. Self-management capabilities include self-awareness, the ability to balance conflicting demands, the ability to learn, and leadership values.

Self-Awareness. A key aspect of understanding oneself is having awareness of personal strengths and weaknesses: what one does well and not so well, what one is comfortable with and uncomfortable with, which situations bring out one's personal best and which are difficult to handle, when one has a wealth of expertise to draw on and when one had better look for expertise elsewhere. But self-awareness also means that people must understand *why* they are the way they are: what traits, learned preferences, experiences, or situational factors have shaped their profile of strengths and weaknesses. Self-awareness means understanding the impact their strengths and weaknesses have on others, on their effectiveness in various life roles, and on reaching their goals.

Ability to Balance Conflicting Demands. In organizational life, people encounter conflicting demands. For example, boss and subordinates may have different priorities, internal systems may not match external client needs, and the joint demands of personal and work life may cause stress. People must learn to not let the conflicts paralyze or overwhelm them, to understand the natural roots of the conflicts, and to develop strategies for balancing or integrating them.

Ability to Learn. When we say someone has the ability to learn, we mean that the person recognizes when new behaviors, skills, or attitudes are called for, accepts responsibility for his or her own development, understands and acknowledges current personal strengths and weaknesses, engages in activities that provide the opportunity to learn or test new skills and behaviors, reflects on his or her own learning process, and works to develop a variety of learning tactics in order to acquire needed skills or behaviors. A person with the ability to learn does not deny or ignore the need for new approaches, does not get stuck using habitual behaviors or outmoded skills, and is not seduced by past success into believing that no change or development is necessary.

Leadership Values. We have found that people who project certain personal values are particularly effective in leadership roles. Foremost among these values are honesty and integrity, which engender trust and credibility in others. Strong personal initiative and drive are needed to persevere in the face of difficult organizational goals. A positive, optimistic attitude supports both individual and group efficacy.

Social Capabilities

People develop many interpersonal and social skills over the course of their lives. Because leadership roles and processes are by their very nature social (meaning that they require making meaningful connections to others), the ability to work effectively with others in social systems is a fundamental capacity of leaders. Social capabilities include the ability to build and maintain relationships, the ability to build effective work groups, communication skills, and the ability to develop others.

Ability to Build and Maintain Relationships. At the heart of social capabilities is the ability to develop cooperative relationships. In leadership roles, the ability to develop positive relationships with many different types of people is particularly important. The foundation of this ability is the capacity to respect people from varying backgrounds and to understand the perspectives that they bring.

Ability to Build Effective Work Groups. People in leadership roles need not only to develop their own relationships with others but also to facilitate the development of positive relationships among others who work together. Effective leaders help create synergy, motivation, and a sense of empowerment in work groups.

Communication Skills. Communication skills operate in two directions. In addition to being able to communicate information, thoughts, and ideas clearly in different media, individuals with effective communication skills are able to listen carefully and understand what others are saying, thinking, and feeling.

Ability to Develop Others. Leadership roles often call for the ability to develop others in ways that allow people to work together in increasingly productive and meaningful ways. This includes the ability to help others diagnose their development needs, to provide appropriate feedback and other learning opportunities, to coach and encourage changes in their behavior, and to recognize and reward improvements.

Work Facilitation Capabilities

People develop skills and perspectives that enable them to facilitate the accomplishment of work in organizational systems. Organizations consist of many individuals, groups, and subsystems that need to work interdependently to accomplish collective goals and outcomes. Individuals in leadership roles facilitate the implementation, coordination, and integration of this work. Work facilitation capabilities include management skills, the ability to think and act strategically, the ability to think creatively, and the ability to initiate and implement change.

Management Skills. Management skills encompass a broad range of competencies related to the facilitation and coordination of the day-to-day work in organizations, including setting goals and devising plans for achieving those goals, monitoring progress, developing systems for accomplishing work, solving problems, and making decisions.

Ability to Think and Act Strategically. Day-to-day work is accomplished in the context of broad organizational objectives that support the long-term vision and mission of the organization. People who can think and act strategically have a clear sense of the desirable collective future. They make decisions, set priorities, and support initiatives that will bring the current reality more in line with the desired future.

Ability to Think Creatively. Creativity involves seeing new possibilities, finding connections between disparate ideas, and reframing the way one thinks about an issue. Creativity yields innovation when novel ideas or perspectives are used to solve difficult problems. Implementing innovations also requires an element of risk taking, of going into uncharted territory and leaving the familiar behind.

Ability to Initiate and Implement Change. Leadership roles often require the ability to make major changes in organizational systems and practices. This includes establishing the need for change (for example, by demonstrating that current ways of working are no longer adequate), influencing others to participate in the change, and institutionalizing the new ways of working.

Although by no means exhaustive, our description of individual capabilities illustrates the breadth of capabilities needed to provide leadership in organizations. To develop any of these capabilities, people first have to realize that their current skills or perspectives are inadequate or are not being fully utilized. This alone can be a major step, sometimes triggered by a mistake or failure, a personal crisis, or a piece of feedback from an assessment experience. Next, people have to identify the skill or perspective that they want to more fully develop and begin to try it on for size. Finally, after an extended period of practice, they can begin to feel comfortable with the new skill or perspective and start to use it effectively. This cycle is repeated many times as people expand their self-management, social, and work facilitation capabilities. This is why we say that leader development takes time.

Enhancing Leader Development

We believe that leader development can be enhanced by intervening in the learning, growth, and change processes of individuals. This is a key assumption underlying our work. If leaders do learn, grow, and change over time, and if we understand the factors that contribute to that growth process, development can be enhanced by influencing these processes.

The leader development model suggests three main strategies for enhancing this process:

1. Create a variety of rich developmental experiences that provide assessment, challenge, and support.
2. Enhance people's ability to learn from experience.
3. Use an approach that integrates the various developmental experiences.

Creating Rich Developmental Experiences

There are many types of experience that develop a person's leadership abilities. Significant among them are the formally designed developmental experiences of 360-degree feedback, feedback-intensive programs, and coaching relationships, as well as the more naturally occurring experiences of job assignments, developmental relationships, and hardships. (Each is explored at length in its own chapter in Part One of this handbook.) The developmental potency of any one of these experiences depends on whether it contains a good mix of assessment, challenge, and support.

For example, although a feedback-intensive program focuses on assessment, it must also challenge the participants and at the same time support them. The element of challenge comes from exercises and simulations used in these programs, which are deliberately designed to take people out of their comfort zone, and from interactions with other participants, who often challenge participants' points of view. At the same time, these programs take great care to create a supportive environment in which people can be candid and hear negative information about themselves, while the positive information they get shores up their self-confidence.

Job assignments are another example. They can be particularly rich sources of challenge, but if people are to learn from assignments, they must have opportunities to receive ongoing feedback while struggling with the challenge. People in challenging assignments also need others they can turn to for support, as well as a feeling of being supported by the organization in general.

Enhancing the Ability to Learn

To repeat, learning from experience involves recognizing when new behaviors, skills, or attitudes are called for, accepting the responsibility for development, understanding and acknowledging current strengths and weaknesses, engaging in activities that provide the opportunity to learn or test new skills and behaviors, reflecting on one's own learning process, and working to develop a variety of learning tactics in order to acquire the needed skills or behaviors. The person does not deny or ignore the need for new approaches, does not get stuck using habitual behaviors or outmoded skills, and is not seduced by past success into believing that no change or development is necessary.

It is usually not easy to recognize when new skills or approaches are needed. Sometimes mistakes or failures serve to get people's attention. But often, even in new situations, people tend to stick with the skills and approaches that have worked for them in the past. The temptation to rely on existing strengths can be especially powerful when new situations demand a quick response or when one has had a long history of success with a particular approach.

Assessment and feedback are crucial if people are to recognize that current skills are insufficient and comfortable approaches are inadequate. Getting reliable information continuously about how they are doing is an important way for people to know that change is necessary; it is therefore an important component of enhancing the ability to learn. Assessment that includes feedback on strengths, as well as development needs, can work to build self-efficacy and help individuals face the difficult challenge of learning new behaviors.

Relying on comfortable approaches in new situations almost always limits effectiveness and learning. Yet it is possible to develop new learning tactics. When people are given a variety of challenging experiences, the novelty they face demands that they develop new learning tactics. Assessment of how they currently learn, understanding of other ways to learn (perhaps through reading or skill-based training), developing the practice of reflecting on their experience, and getting the opportunity to experiment with new behaviors and learning tactics (in the classroom or on the job) can help people develop the flexibility inherent in a strong ability to learn from experience. Chapter Seven looks in depth at what is involved in enhancing this critical ability.

Linking Developmental Experiences

Creating rich developmental experiences and equipping people to learn are two strategies for enhancing leader development. A third strategy is to design and implement developmental experiences so that they are more integrated and connected to one another.

For example, a training program can be preceded by open conversations about expectations of learning goals and can be timed so that it helps a leader rise to the challenge of a tough new assignment. The assignment is in turn supplemented by ongoing feedback and coaching, as well as opportunities to reflect—alone and with others facing similar challenges—on what and how the leader is learning.

Our major criticism of the approach of many organizations to leader development is that it is not systemic but rather events-based. How, they ask, should we develop a bright young engineer—clearly gifted, with high potential—who needs improvement in interpersonal skills? Too often the answer is to send the engineer to a training program, and the shorter it is the better. There is no question of determining readiness, no feedback prior to training, no planned support or reinforcement upon return. The hope is that this kind of training "fixes" people. As you will discover, we have found that training is a powerful intervention and an important part of a developmental system—but it is only one part.

The story is the same with multirater (or, as some call it, 360-degree) feedback. Again the frequent tendency is to use the feedback as an isolated event rather than as part of a process. Multirater feedback is an effective assessment activity, an experience that helps unfreeze people and prepares them to learn from other developmental experiences. But if you just give someone feedback from an instrument and stop there, little real development takes place.

From Leader Development to Leadership Development

In the first edition of this handbook, we focused almost exclusively on leader development. The hint of a broader framework was beginning to emerge, but we could not yet clearly see where we were headed. Five years later, we are much more on the "other side" of this shift in our perspective.

As we said earlier, we have begun to understand leader development as one aspect of a broader concept of leadership development. We define *leadership development* as the expansion of the organization's capacity to enact the basic leadership tasks needed for collective work: setting direction, creating alignment, and maintaining commitment. Traditionally, these leadership tasks have been carried out through a management hierarchy, that is, primarily by individuals in positions of authority in organizations. Yet it is getting harder and harder for formal leaders to enact leadership effectively on their own. The challenges that organizations are facing today, both internally and externally, are challenges that often overwhelm existing resources and defy known solutions. These complex challenges require new assumptions and methods yet to be developed. They require organizational and individual learning and change. Perhaps most important, today's challenges are often too complex for individual leaders to fully understand alone. To face these complex challenges, shared meaning must be created in the midst of seeming chaos and uncertainty. Individuals, groups, and organizations must work collaboratively to explore, set and reset direction, create alignment, and maintain commitment.

So to expand leadership capacity, organizations must not only develop individuals but also develop the leadership capacities of collectives (for example, work groups, teams, and communities). They must develop the connections between individuals, between collectives within the organization, and between the organization and key constituents and stakeholders in its environment. Developing connections means enhancing understanding and recognition of the interdependencies that exist between individuals and between groups within an organization, as well as between organizations in a supply chain, an industry group, or any other kind of network. It also means developing the individual and collective capacities to create shared meaning, to effectively engage in interdependent work across boundaries, and to enact the tasks of leadership (setting direction, creating alignment, and maintaining commitment) in a way that is more inclusive. For example, organizational leadership capacity is enhanced when the executive team is able to enact leadership effectively as a unit; when interdependent groups can identify an emerging organizational problem and pull together to effectively deal with it; when leaders and group members in various parts of the organization readily connect with each other about interdependent work, shared challenges, or shared expertise; and when individuals and groups engage in dialogue with one another rather than act in isolation.

Figure I.2 illustrates both the relationship between leader development and leadership development and the shifts this movement implies for practice. The figure is made up of two intersecting axes, the horizontal axis representing development that targets individuals, on the left, and development aimed at a collective (group or organization) on the right. The vertical axis differentiates between development that is focused on capabilities seen as existing *within* an entity (individual or group), at the top, and development that is focused on the interdependencies *between* entities (individuals or groups), at the bottom.

Traditional leader development practices, including much of the work done with participants in feedback-intensive programs, 360-degree feedback instruments, and formal coaching, focus on capabilities (skills, perspectives, and preferences) that are seen as within the individual. These leader development practices can be thought of as populating the upper left quadrant of Figure I.2. The work CCL has done on how managers learn, grow, and change from their experience can also be seen as captured here, because for the most part it has focused on how developmental events are understood by individuals and incorporated within a person's developing capability as a leader. This work has been a key influence on CCL research and practice and is discussed in several chapters of this handbook. In fact, the leader development model, discussed earlier, also fits in this upper left quadrant, as we have understood and used it thus far.

FIGURE I.2. LEADERSHIP DEVELOPMENT FRAMEWORK

Team development and organization development comprise the upper right quadrant of the figure. While both of these categories of practice move from focus on the individual to focus on the collective, the activities tend to remain focused within the entity, developing capabilities of the team, or focusing on intraorganizational processes, such as culture or systems change.

The lower two quadrants of the figure represent leadership development practices that focus on the interdependencies between individuals (lower left), between groups or teams, and between whole organizations (lower right). The practices we would imagine in these quadrants would be those that worked to develop the connections between individuals, between groups or teams, and between whole organizations so that the shared work of the organization could be carried out in a way that is most effective.

The figure also illustrates that the development of individuals, collectives, and connections is embedded in the organization's culture and systems and therefore shaped by them. Both culture and systems often reflect the assumptions being made by organizational members about interdependence, learning, and shared work, as well as the understood processes for enacting the leadership tasks. Thus culture and systems can support or be an obstacle to moving beyond the limitations of current ways of enacting leadership in the face of new challenges.

We believe that this kind of comprehensive approach to leadership development—engaging in developmental work that spans all four quadrants—is the surest route to sustainable leadership capacity for organizations. As we go forward with our research and practice, we will continue to use practices developed for work on capabilities within individuals and teams while expanding our work to focus on helping individuals, teams, and organizations develop enhanced connectivity between entities at all levels.

What stimulated this shift in our thinking? As we worked more with the same organizations over time and with multiple leaders in the same unit or organization, we became attuned to the limitations of an exclusive focus on individual development. Individual leaders can no longer accomplish leadership tasks by virtue of their authority or their own leadership capacity. Instead, individuals and groups need to carry out the leadership tasks together in a way that integrates differing perspectives and recognizes areas of interdependence and shared work. For organizations or other collectives to experience sustained leadership over time—to have a sense of direction and alignment, to maintain commitment to the collective work, particularly when dealing with difficult problems that require organizational change—they need more than well-developed individuals. They need well-developed connections between individuals and deeper and more meaningful relationships around shared work. They need to form and deepen relationships within communities and across the boundaries between groups and collectives. They need to develop the capacities of collectives for shared sense making and for learning from shared work and shared experiments in the face of challenge and change. They need to get better at integrating the learnings into a unified sense of purpose and direction, new systems, and coherent shifts in culture—that is, to enact leadership together through the connections between individuals, groups, and organizations. Certainly, individual development is still a vital aspect of leadership development. It is, in fact, a basis for enabling the other aspects of leadership development and will remain a key focus of our work. However, we believe that broadening our knowledge and practice of leadership development provides more avenues for improving leadership in organizations and more potential impact for the work we do.

We have been able to sustain this shift in perspective because we are part of a larger community of leadership scholars and leadership development practitioners who are experiencing and articulating the same shift. For example, David Day (2000) points out that developing social capital (that is, the networked relationships that enhance cooperation and resource exchange among individuals in an organization) is an important aspect of leadership development. Recent approaches to organizational sustainability have taken a more integrative approach to individual, team, and organizational development (Beer, 2001). And in *Relational Wealth* (2000), Leana and Rousseau focus on the idea that relationships are a key competitive advantage for a firm, rather than simply an outcome of its activities. We see our new work going forward as connected to the work of these others—that is, toward understanding how the unique properties of relationships, networks, and communities of practice can be seen and developed in any organization, public or private.

Conclusion

To sum up, let us return to the leadership development model and the assumptions behind it. First, we define *leader development* as the expansion of a person's capacity to be effective in leadership roles and processes. Second, we believe that developing the individual capacities needed for effective leadership—such as self-management, social skills, and work facilitation capabilities—is synonymous with what is often labeled "personal development." This development unfolds over time. It is maximized by a variety of experiences that challenge people, support them, and provide them with understanding of how they are doing. It also depends on their having an ability and willingness to learn from experience. Leader development processes that integrate various experiences and embed them in the organizational context are the most likely to be effective at developing leaders' abilities. But we realize that leader development and leadership development are not synonymous. We see leadership development as the expansion of the organization's capacity to enact the basic leadership tasks needed for collective work: setting direction, creating alignment, and maintaining commitment. And we are just beginning to develop knowledge and expertise in the aspects of leadership development that go beyond individual development.

Finally, if there is one key idea to our view of leadership development—an overarching theme that runs throughout our work—it is that leadership development is an ongoing process. It is grounded in personal development, which is never complete. It is embedded in experience: leaders learn as they expand their experiences over time. It is facilitated by interventions that are woven into those experiences in meaningful ways. And it includes, but goes well beyond, individual leader development. It includes the development of the connections between individuals, the development of the capacities of collectives, the development of the connections between collectives in an organization, and the development of the culture and systems in which individuals and collectives are embedded.

PART ONE

INDIVIDUAL LEADER DEVELOPMENT

CHAPTER ONE

FEEDBACK-INTENSIVE PROGRAMS

Victoria A. Guthrie
Sara N. King

Feedback-intensive programs (FIPs) represent a best practice in the work of the Center for Creative Leadership (CCL). At the heart of CCL's work for more than thirty years, feedback-intensive programs have incorporated research on effective leader behaviors and learning processes, enabling individuals worldwide to develop a deeper understanding of their leadership strengths and development needs as well as develop action plans to leverage that knowledge for greater effectiveness in their organizations.

The idea for a feedback-intensive program started at CCL with Robert C. Dorn, who had a vision for a program in which assessment center–type data would be fed back to participants in a safe, supportive environment for development purposes. He believed that development through a feedback-intensive program meant helping a person see significant patterns of behavior more clearly, make better sense of the attitudes and motivations underlying these patterns, reassess what makes the person more or less effective relative to the goals he or she wants to attain, and evaluate alternative ways of meeting these goals. He believed that the task of a creative leader is to envision and help bring about change which has positive long-term consequences, not only for a single part of the organization, but for the organization as a whole, and the society of which it is a part. An inseparable part of this task is to help each person in the organization develop to his or her fullest potential, not only as a contributing member but as a unique human being. CCL's Leadership Development Program was a realization of his vision and the first of many FIPs developed over time by CCL.

This chapter will acquaint people with the mechanisms and underlying principles of this particular development process so they can better understand what we see as the defining features of a feedback-intensive program. We use the concepts of assessment, challenge, and support to articulate how a feedback-intensive program works, and we describe what we know about the outcomes of a well-designed FIP. Finally, we discuss when and how to use an FIP for leader development. Our hope is that this information makes it possible for people to get the most benefit from this type of experience, and it provides some essential knowledge for organizations that want to design and conduct their own programs.

What Is a Feedback-Intensive Program?

A feedback-intensive program is a comprehensive assessment of an individual's leadership, generally in one or more sessions, using multiple lenses to view numerous aspects of personality and effectiveness. It is a blend of methodologies, combining assessment-for-development tools (such as 360-degree feedback), experiential interactions, direct teaching of practical content from leadership research, and peer and staff coaching. All of this occurs within a supportive learning environment, to maximize interaction among participants and faculty.

Unlike many other leader development programs, which focus only on knowledge acquisition, using lectures, case studies, and discussions, our feedback-intensive programs add assessment and guided experiences, using a process of active inquiry that is learner-focused. Ours is a holistic approach in which no formulas for success are given but a safe learner-centered environment allows individuals to examine their current situation, revisit their beliefs, take risks, and shift mental models.

We know from our classroom experience and research that behavioral change does not just happen, nor is it something that can be "done" to someone. To behave differently, people first need to recognize a need for change. Then they need to understand how to do things differently and to become comfortable with the new approaches. Doing all this takes time. Short programs (lasting three days or less) can do an excellent job of raising awareness of different perspectives and ideas, but they teach more at the cognitive level (knowledge acquisition and limited self-awareness change) than at the behavioral level (significant change in awareness and behavior) (Young and Hefferan, 1994). We have found that it typically takes at least five days to bring a person through the full process of self-awareness and even longer to effect significant behavior change.

Defining Features of CCL's Feedback-Intensive Programs

Our feedback-intensive programs have five defining features: feedback is rich and comprehensive, content is challenging and relevant, multiple methodologies and activities are used, a safe and supportive learning environment is established, and assessment, challenge, and support are integrated.

The feedback in an FIP is rich and comprehensive. It comes from multiple sources, such as boss, customer, peer, family member, and direct reports, and reflects many attributes, such as resiliency, innovation, and resourcefulness. We believe that people approach leadership with frameworks built on their past experience, their values, and their personality-based needs and preferences. Over time, people tend to develop skills in areas that are comfortable for them. As people are rewarded for what they do well, they naturally tend to rely on those strengths. Yet we know that new challenges often demand new approaches. As situations change, strengths can be overused, and new development needs can surface. The comprehensive multi-source feedback gathered throughout the program is consolidated and integrated into applicable action plans through one-on-one coaching during the program.

The models and content presented in our FIPs challenge participants to focus on the issues they face in their work environment and find solutions for greater performance. They also allow participants to focus on individual behaviors, styles, and values to enhance their leader effectiveness and life satisfaction.

Multiple methodologies and activities employed in a feedback-intensive program speak to the current strengths, needs, preferences, values, skills, and behaviors from the perspective of many different audiences, and they point the way to understanding what new strengths are necessary to meet the demands of rapid change. These combined tactics facilitate participants' understanding of how their behaviors are related to underlying personality aspects.

An FIP is classroom-based and structured to provide a safe and supportive learning community. It typically takes place away from work so that participants are better able to focus on learning from the experience and integrating that learning into their work behaviors. There is ongoing dialogue and discussion among participants and between participants and faculty. This is also balanced with opportunities for individual reflection.

Assessment, challenge, and support are integrated in preprogram and postprogram activities as well as throughout the program itself. This preprogram-program-postprogram approach allows an FIP to be a part of a longer development plan that provides a continuous process for self-directed personal growth.

Preprogram Activities

Preprogram activities are methods for preparing the individual for the program itself. At CCL, an FIP includes a set of assessment activities that are sent to participants prior to the program. Responding to these preliminary activities stimulates people to reflect on their own leadership behaviors—and thus their process of leader development begins. Participants frequently report that they gain insight as a result of filling out a particular questionnaire or answering a specific question on an essay-type survey. This process is similar to what McCarthy and Keene (1996) define as the heart of assessment. They describe assessment as the conversation that takes place first within the individual as he or she receives information from the world, then with others as they share their worlds, then between the teacher and the participant as the person learns the world of the "experts," and finally, between the individual and his or her work.

Preprogram activities can include virtual meetings to discuss the objectives of the upcoming program; the completion of a variety of personality inventories, attitude surveys, questionnaires about current leadership challenges, and self-ratings of skills and abilities; the beginning of a reflection process as participants describe their expectations for learning; an interview with the boss about how he or she views effective leadership in the organization; and preparation of a business case or project to be worked on during the program. (See Table 1.1 for more detail.)

The Program Itself

The art of designing a program lies in fully understanding the needs of the target population. The conceptual framework, content, and placement of exercises and assessments must match and reflect the complexity and turbulence participants face, be relevant to their leadership challenges, and be action-oriented (Burnside and Guthrie, 1992). With that framework in mind, the concepts, content, and outcomes can be chosen or developed to address the challenges faced by the target population. For example, a program for entry-level managers might be aimed at helping them learn to influence others and build credibility for their management skills. A program for mid-level managers may be focused on developing others and maintaining effective life balance. A program for senior executives might focus on enhancing strategic leadership skills or changing the ingrained behavior patterns that helped them move up in their organizations but are becoming less effective as they near the top of the ladder.

To develop the conceptual framework and content, program designers reflect on several questions. Given the audience and the purpose of the program, to what concepts and models do the participants need to be exposed? On what

TABLE 1.1. ACTIVITIES IN A FEEDBACK-INTENSIVE PROGRAM.

Phase	Assessment Activities	Challenge Activities	Support Activities
Preprogram	• Personality measures • 360-degree feedback • Leadership instruments • Open-ended, essay-type questions • Qualitative reports by participants about challenges • Interviews with boss • Preparation of business cases or projects	• Completing personality and leadership measures • Writing essays, doing interviews, and preparing cases challenge individuals to think about their views on self, organization, and leadership	• Staff contacts with each participant to provide information, answer questions, and clarify expectations
Program	Methodologies for assessment: • Reflection • Participant observations • Staff observations • Videotape	A variety of teaching tools and delivery methods: • Assessments • Lecturettes • Discussions • Simulations • Exercises • Different viewpoints and mental models • Nontraditional techniques (acting, music, collage, and so on)	Staff-created learning community: • Cooperative developmental environment • Appropriate self-disclosure • Respect and openness • Authenticity • Nonprescriptive and nonjudgmental commentary • No right answers • Respectful work with each person • Positive climate
Postprogram	• Repeat of multirater or 360-degree feedback • Instruments to assess behavior change • Feedback coaches	• Learning partners • Feedback coaches	• In-class learning partners • Feedback coaches • Back-home learning groups • Alumni groups • Blended learning • Succession and development-planning processes

dimensions will they need to be given feedback? And how will these concepts and models be linked to the overall program objectives and the reality of their leadership situation at work? This last question is particularly important, because it not only provides the developmental framework for organizing the program but also enables the participants to organize their own experiences as they move through the program. New managers are likely to need modules that help them understand and practice influence skills and that focus on similar issues challenging individuals in their first management assignments. Mid-level managers may engage in activities focused on coaching others, giving and receiving feedback, and issues such as life balance that are coming to the fore. Senior executives may need to explore the behaviors that can lead to derailment, such as inability to admit a mistake, inability to develop new strategic perspectives, and poor interpersonal relationships.

In an effective FIP, content is presented simply and directly. If the content is too complex, people may be overwhelmed and spend the entire program struggling to understand the material, rather than putting it into action. The challenge for program developers and staff is to determine how to take a complex topic and present it so that participants can make a connection between what they learn in the classroom, what they do in their jobs and in their lives, and how to put the new learning into action. If the content is not relevant to their work and if it does not tackle their highest priorities, participants will find the FIP less valuable.

At CCL, we design our programs to include assessment, challenge, and support (ACS) as the basic foundation. To give you a view of how ACS is woven into an FIP, we will describe a general design (summarized in Table 1.1). More detailed descriptions of activities associated with ACS are given later in the chapter.

The exercises on the first day of a program serve as both an icebreaker and a tool to catch the attention of participants. The individuals attending our programs are confident people with complex jobs. Their confidence stems from the fact that they are usually doing well in their current roles, and most of them know that they have potential for expanded leadership roles in the future. Because they are successful and busy people, participants often arrive at the program preoccupied with work back home. It is important to begin the program in a way that quickly forces participants to focus on the work at hand in the program and to realize that they have something valuable to learn. We frequently start a program with an exercise that challenges participants immediately and often build in assessment on the first day, to help participants gain the focus they will need for significant learning throughout the week.

At the same time, anticipating the feedback to come during the program can cause some stress for many participants. It is common for people to report feeling that they are about to be exposed: "I've made it successfully to this point, but this time, under this much scrutiny, I won't be able to hide my flaws." So in addition to reviewing the goals of the program and the schedule for the week, our faculty take time, on the first day, to begin the steps toward creating a learning community by building a climate for openness and support, including creating a process for participants to become acquainted. (We will elaborate on these activities later in the chapter, when we discuss how support is provided in an FIP.)

The exercises we use in our FIPs are of many types, including leaderless group discussions, targeted experiential exercises, and small-scale simulations (these and other assessment methods are discussed in more detail later). Placed early in the program, these exercises provide challenge, boost self-confidence, build relationships among participants, and serve as a valuable source of corroborative data to compare to the feedback participants will receive later in the program. As people work through the exercises, trained staff may observe and record their behaviors.

As the program continues, assessment becomes central. Participants receive feedback from assessment instruments, enabling them to establish benchmarks for their strengths and development needs. Frequently, an FIP is segmented into modules that address the objectives of the program and relate to various issues faced by people in leadership positions. Either the module itself has some form of assessment built in, or at some predetermined point, one of the questionnaires completed in the preliminary packet is brought into the discussion, and the feedback on the prework instrument relates to the content of the module. For example, in a module on decision making there may be a place for introducing the feedback collected earlier from the participants' direct reports (say, opinions on each participant's decision-making style). Or a module on ethical decision making might include an experiential exercise (observed and later debriefed by staff) that surfaces the trade-offs often present in decision making. The participants themselves also contribute feedback, reflecting on themselves and each other. Time is structured so that people learn how to give constructive, developmental feedback in small groups and discuss issues important to each individual.

In addition to modules that embed feedback in short, topical lectures, we allot a concentrated period of time for consolidating feedback and learning. This is often the most meaningful part of the program for participants, because they work with coaches one on one to integrate their various pieces of data and experience and begin to devise a developmental action plan. The structure of the coaching session varies, depending on the target audience and the program outcomes. Some coaching sessions occur during the program itself, perhaps a three-hour block near the end of the week. Sometimes coaching is provided as an ongoing follow-up between the participant and the coach over a period of months following the program.

In another program design, in which participants first work independently and then as learning partners with others, individuals use this time to consolidate and make sense of the information they have received from various sources: they summarize their current strengths and development needs and point themselves in the direction of setting development goals and devising action plans for accomplishing them.

Using all the feedback participants have received during the week and the discussions they have had with staff, their classmates, and their feedback coaches, our programs conclude with the participants establishing goals for their continued development and identifying the strategies they will use for attaining them.

Postprogram Activities

A feedback-intensive program that spans time—such as those conducted in several sessions over a six-month period, often with some form of coaching included—seems to have a greater impact than a single-session program (McCauley and Hughes-James, 1994; Young and Dixon, 1996). In a multisession approach, people are able to shift from maintaining cognitive frameworks to being able to effect change in their approaches and perspectives. Leader development takes time—a one-week program cannot do it all.

Yet even when leader development takes the form of a single feedback-intensive program, that FIP should not end when the participants leave the classroom. It is important to establish activities to help embed the new learning, provide support for change, and continue the development process. After all, the individual has invested a week or more in this development process, and the organization has invested time and money to develop this person. It is therefore important to supplement a single program, to turn it from an event into an ongoing development process by adding activities that reinforce action plans and provide support for change. (See also Chapter Seven.)

We know that change takes time. Research indicates that it can take more than a year to begin to perceive a behavior change as a result of a single FIP experience (Young and Dixon, 1996; Young and Hefferan, 1994). There are a number of ways to provide structured support to participants that will enable them to continue to reflect on what they have learned about themselves and to pursue goals and action plans. The process to continue assessment, challenge, and support can range from individual activities to organizational support. Some of these activities are discussed next.

Individual Activities

Individual assessment, challenge, and support activities include goal letters, goal-setting reports, formal coaching, and blended applications.

• *Goal letters.* Participants write a "goal letter" to themselves that will be mailed to them at a specific time in the future, generally two to three months after the program. This activity provides meaningful reflection on the learnings from the program and challenges participants to demonstrate actions taken and goals selected as a result of the program.

• *Goal-setting reports.* At the conclusion of the program, participants establish and commit to three or four goals and create action plans to achieve these goals once they are back in their organization. In three months, program staff follow up by writing participants about their goal completion or modification. The participants provide an assessment of how well they are achieving their goals. Staff offer another round of follow-up to give participants an opportunity to establish additional goals or motivation to continue pursuing the ones they have set. This process gives ongoing accountability for the actions set in a program.

• *Formal coaching.* A coach who has worked with a participant during the program provides a strong support mechanism for embedding developmental learning and using it more effectively. The role of CCL's coaches provides one example of the interactive nature of ACS during and following a program. From our research and in discussions with the coaches, we find that coaches serve a number of roles, including feedback provider, sounding board, feedback interpreter (assessment); dialogue partner, accountant, role model (challenge); and counselor, reinforcer, cheerleader (support) (see Chapter Three). After the FIP, the coach generally focuses on the action plan created during the program and the individual's current situation. This type of integrated coaching process allows the participant to continually refocus his or her action plan as the situation changes (Guthrie, 1999).

• *Blended applications.* Online tools enhance any of these methods for ongoing development. Depending on the participant, blended learning can be used as a source of development by providing various training cases, discussions, chat rooms, and further assessments online after the conclusion of the program.

Informal Coaching
Informal coaching is provided in an FIP through peer group discussions, learning partners, and alumni programs.

• *Peer-group discussions.* These small groups are formed during the program to provide feedback and support. Participants can choose to use these small groups for similar purposes after the program. Peer groups establish a constructive, developmental feedback process that enables participants to provide challenge, assessment, and support to one another as they work on their action plans back home.

• *Learning partners.* Learning partners are triads assigned to work on a specific challenge common to the partners either prior to, during, or following the program. Learning partners can also be extended to three colleagues at the work site.

• *Alumni programs.* These programs bring past participants together to network and share insights and developmental experiences since their FIP experience.

Usually one or two days in length, alumni programs afford people an opportunity to assess what is working well or not so well. Such programs reinforce previous learning, provide a boost (in both motivation and energy) to pursuing action plans, and present an opportunity for new learning and development.

Organizational Activities

Assessment, challenge, and support continue in organizational activities such as action learning, program debriefings, and extended use of 360-degree instruments.

• *Action learning.* Working on key business and leadership challenges during and following a program enables participants to apply classroom learning immediately. Following detailed assessment and scenario building around a challenge, participants share ideas, offer suggestions and experiences, and challenge one another's perspectives. This process becomes even more beneficial when it includes the participant's manager or human resource development person.

• *Program debriefings.* Meetings between participants and managers or between participants and human resource managers should occur after the program to debrief the experience and communicate goals. Debriefing questions might include ones like these: What was the experience like for you? What was a key thing you learned? What will you do more of? Do less of? Do differently?

• *Extended use of 360-degree instruments.* Another process uses a 360-degree instrument designed to assess behavior change as a result of the program. We have developed one such instrument, Reflections, based on our impact assessment research, and we often use this tool to follow up with participants, help them monitor their own development, and get feedback from others about perceived change.

Now that we have discussed what we see as the defining features of an FIP, we turn to an in-depth description of the ways in which assessment, challenge, and support are built in to our programs.

Elements of Assessment

Assessment is one of the key elements that drives leader development, and it is a major part of a CCL feedback-intensive process. Assessment provides participants with a picture of their effectiveness in their current role, an understanding of how their personality-based preferences play out in behavior, and a benchmark for their future development.

A Variety of Sources and Methodologies

To be of most benefit, assessment needs to come from a variety of sources and through multiple methodologies. Assessment sources can include feedback from the participant's boss, peers, direct reports, training staff, fellow participants, and feedback coach. The participant is also a source, in that he or she completes self ratings on assessments prior to the program and has opportunities to reflect on how he or she is doing during the course of the program. When norms are available for various instruments and exercises, participants can compare their scores or performance to a larger database of other executives who have completed the assessment in the past.

The variety of sources is critical because different rater groups may have different views of the individual. For example, direct reports may rate a manager's supervision skills differently than that manager's boss would. A boss or peers, on the other hand, might have a better view of the extent to which the manager works effectively across boundaries than the manager's direct reports might. And of course, any or all of these raters might not see the manager as they see themselves. When the messages across sources differ, this can be frustrating for the receiver (due to lack of clarity) but valuable as well; understanding that different sources interpret behaviors very differently or that a particularly negative issue is not widely viewed by others is an important insight.

When all sources of feedback convey a similar perspective, whether to praise a strength or reveal a development need, this can increase the force and clarity of the message. This clarity also helps point out next steps. In an FIP, it is very important that the participant have time with a coach to review assessment feedback patterns, to discuss both the consistencies and the inconsistencies.

In addition to the variety of sources, multiple assessment methods and techniques are critical. These methods include self-assessments, 360-degree feedback, peer feedback, and observations from trained observers. Particular assessment methodologies may be more or less valuable for individual participants, depending on their learning styles (see Chapter Seven). The variety of sources is needed both to maximize learning when participants are using their favored style and to challenge them to stretch when using a less preferred style. In addition, a variety of methods, like the variety of sources, can provide a more comprehensive assessment of the participant's strengths and development needs. Finally, receiving the same feedback or learning the same lessons again and again, in the context of different assessment methodologies, helps reinforce and deepen the impact of the learnings.

Key Issues in Assessment

One of the key features of an FIP is the delivery of a rich and comprehensive assessment. While the behavioral assessment focuses on what managers do and how they are perceived, the personality assessment gives insight into the deeper orientations and preferences that often underlie behaviors. For the assessment to have the desired impact, trust among the group (participants and staff) and trust in the data must be present. Trust among the group evolves from an effective learning environment that includes confidentiality. Being able to trust the data is an outcome of staff attention to confidentiality, the degree to which rater data in assessments is anonymous, and the reliability and validity of the assessments used.

Confidentiality is a major part of building a nonthreatening environment for assessment, and it happens in two ways. First, we set clear classroom expectations that participants should be free to explore issues and try out new behaviors with each other. What happens in the classroom will not be shared with others not involved in the program. Second, we tell participants that the assessment data belong to them and that no one other than program staff has access to those data without their permission. This is the key difference between performance assessment as conducted in most organizations and our assessment for development approach.

In performance assessment, an individual's boss views the results, and the individual is rewarded or disciplined accordingly (Dalton, 1998). Assessment for development puts the results in the participant's control. The participant can share the data with others or not, as he or she sees fit, and what is not shared remains confidential.

Rater anonymity when completing formal assessments is also important for valid data. When back-home raters know that their identities will not be revealed, they usually answer questions as honestly as they can, often providing feedback that they could not or would not give face to face, either because they know that their identities will not be revealed or because they understand that the data will not be used for performance appraisal purposes. We know that when ratings are used for appraisal, they differ significantly from ratings used for development. We also know that when ratings can be attributed to a source, the scores are often consistently higher (Lombardo and Eichinger, 2000; Tornow and London, 1998).

A final issue in assessment is that the ratings must be reliable and valid (Leslie and Fleenor, 1998; Van Velsor, 1998). Participants deserve ratings that they can take seriously and use productively to create plans for change. If program facilitators cannot say with certainty that the scores are reliable and valid, then they do not know that the instrument or rating scale is constructed well enough to produce consistent, stable scores, and they do not know whether scores are measuring what they claim to be measuring or whether higher scores are really related to greater effectiveness. People have many reasons for rejecting tough feedback—the quality of the assessment tools should not be one of those reasons.

Self-Assessments: The Use of Personality Instruments

Personality-based preferences are one underlying source of behavior on the job and elsewhere, so a comprehensive assessment process should include data on these preferences. We typically collect these data through personality questionnaires completed in preprogram activities. These questionnaires focus on the person's preferred ways of interacting with the world. Although they have no right or wrong answers and no good or bad scores, the scores can be compared to norms from a large database of managers to show participants how their own preferences compare to those of other individuals.

The Myers-Briggs Type Indicator (MBTI) is a good example because it is probably the most widely used instrument of this kind (Myers, 1987). It assesses preferences in how people gather and process information, reflecting those preferences on four bipolar dimensions: extroversion (E) and introversion (I), sensing (S) and intuition (N), thinking (T) and feeling (F), and judging (J) and perceiving (P). Based on their scores on these four dimensions, people are assigned one of sixteen "types" (ESTJ, INFP, ENFJ, ISFP, and so on). When this instrument is used in the classroom, participants see the diversity of preferences in their group and recognize that each person brings to the group unique and valuable assets.

When multiple self-assessments are used, participants can begin to see patterns among the results and learn to apply new language to their preferences. The result is a deeper understanding of self and a foreshadowing of possible feedback from others. For example, one manager's strong preference for intuition (focusing on the big picture) on the MBTI might parallel feedback from others that she lacks attention to detail. The next section describes the various ways a person is assessed by others in an FIP.

Assessment of Skills and Behaviors

In a feedback-intensive program, the assessment of participants' skills and behaviors is accomplished in several ways: through 360-degree feedback, through formal activities with fellow participants, and through feedback from different assessment methodologies.

360-Degree Feedback. In recent years, 360-degree feedback has received a great deal of attention in the field of human resource development. Because this type of assessment is a relatively quick and easy method of providing managers with information on current leadership strengths and development needs, 360-degree feedback instruments have become quite popular. (For more on 360-degree feedback, see Chapter Two.)

In a feedback-intensive program, 360-degree feedback allows participants to compare self-perceptions of their leadership skills and behaviors to perceptions from back home—that is, how their boss, peers, direct reports, and clients view their leadership skills and behaviors. As we said earlier, it is sometimes the case that these viewpoints are quite different. Such data bring the reality of work in the organization right into the classroom.

Powerful feedback of this kind is fraught with potential for misunderstanding, so it is important that the facilitators provide the right context for receiving the data, explain how to read the report, and be available for questions and concerns. In an FIP, participants usually receive the data in a classroom setting, but they have the opportunity to review the data again in a one-to-one session with a trained facilitator. (See Chapter Two for guidelines on delivery of information from 360-degree instruments.)

Integrating the feedback from self-assessments and 360-degree instruments is a central feature of an FIP. The combination helps participants understand not only their leadership skills and behaviors as seen by others but also their needs, preferences, and values and how these lead to behaviors that influence other people's perceptions. For example, peers and direct reports may indicate that the participant rarely considers the opinions of others. Scores from the personality instruments may lead to some hypotheses as to why—for example, the participant may report a preference for low inclusion and high control. This preference for minimal involvement with others and for being in control of decisions may be leading to the behavior pattern of rarely considering others' opinions. It is this process of comparing 360-degree feedback to self-assessments that is so valuable in an FIP. Through the process, participants come to realize how their own needs and preferences lead to behaviors that are perceived as either effective or ineffective by others. By understanding the links between their behaviors and their preferences and needs, participants can understand more about what it will take to change behaviors. As a result, they can decide how to modify their leadership approach for a more effective outcome.

In addition to these two strong sources of information—360-degree feedback and self-assessment data—an FIP also uses observations of other participants and facilitators to continue strengthening the developmental experience.

Assessment from Fellow Participants. During a classroom experience, participants are sometimes assessed through formal activities in which peers give them wide-ranging feedback based on their experiences together during the program. Activities like these are especially valuable because peers bring a breadth of experience, have no hidden agenda in providing feedback, and have a sincere desire to help one another learn. (Later in the chapter, we will discuss how the format of a program—open-enrollment or custom—affects the issues involved in peer feedback.)

Two methods of peer assessment are peer observations and peer coaching. In peer observations, each participant is assigned to observe others throughout the course of the program. Then participants give each other constructive feedback on the impact of their behavior, both during classroom activities and outside of class, during evening activities. Participants are taught how to watch for patterns of behavior that might help their fellow participants understand more about the impact of their behaviors. These observations are consolidated and delivered, one participant to another, during a specific program module devoted to peer feedback. Peer observations often provide fresh behavioral examples of the feedback already received from self-assessments or 360-degree feedback, confirming and solidifying self-understanding.

Peer coaching is similar to peer observations, but in this case, the assessment and feedback are specific to a particular content area or exercise. For example, participants are given the opportunity to develop more effective coaching skills in a certain module. They are provided with a model of effective coaching, form groups of three, and are given the opportunity to play coach, learner, and observer throughout the course of the module. In playing these roles, the participants put into practice what they have learned about effective coaching, and they are assessed on how well they accomplished the goal of being an effective coach.

All forms of assessment—self-assessment, 360-degree feedback, and peer observations—can support and reinforce one another. Take the earlier example of the participant who is perceived as not valuing the opinions of others and has reported preferences for low inclusion and high control. His peer assessments may highlight a pattern of always choosing to lead an exercise and rarely giving control to others or asking their viewpoint. Because feedback received from fellow participants in the program often mirrors feedback from back home, the participant can begin to blend and integrate the data into a clearer understanding of self.

Other Assessment Methodologies. Other methods we use for assessing and feeding back data are individual reflection, participant observation of the group, videotaping, and staff-facilitated debriefing. Each of these methods helps individuals see the impact their behavior has on others and more clearly understand what it means to be effective in a group.

As the participant engages in an exercise, it is not uncommon for insights about one's behavior to be gained in the moment. Taking time for reflection immediately after a task can help participants identify the lessons learned. Participants assess themselves by asking, "How did I do?" and "What would I do differently?" Using a journal is a great method for capturing answers to their questions and providing personalized feedback about the experience. Such a learning journal can be used in many ways: at the end of each learning segment, following feedback from the group or from an assessment, or after a discussion. Sometimes after specific exercises, we give participants thought-provoking questions and instruct them to write out their responses. Or we might simply instruct them to summarize the event and write down what they were feeling as it unfolded. Journals are useful for discovering patterns of behavior, planning future actions, or simply working through issues. Using a journal also gets participants out of the "continuous action" mode. This is important because whenever people are asked to move out of their familiar ways of operating, they need time to step back, assess their effectiveness, and consider what they have learned.

Participant observation of group work is another assessment method often used in our programs. We ask individual participants to observe the group in action on a particular task, document what works and does not work, and then share their observations in a group discussion of the activity at its conclusion.

An exercise called Hollow Squares illustrates this use of group observation and discussion. Hollow Squares is an interactive team exercise in which the group is divided in two; one half is assigned a project that the other half must complete. The exercise reflects what occurs in a team when some members are responsible for planning an event they will not execute, while others must implement a plan they have not developed. Time constraints, untested assumptions about what information can or cannot be shared, somewhat ambiguous directions, and lack of communication all tend to get in the way of effective group problem solving.

Typically, the group members given planner roles focus intently on deriving the best plan for the implementers to carry out. Implementers, meanwhile, know only that they are waiting to be told about a task they need to complete under a tight deadline. They usually spend their time anxiously trying to figure out what is going on. Several participants are asked to be observers of the exercise. The observers are told to make note of behaviors and actions that help or hinder the group in accomplishing its task. They are asked to be charitable, remembering that they would probably make the same "mistakes" that their fellow classmates will make.

After the exercise, the facilitator provides a structure for debriefing the exercise. The observers are asked to summarize for the group what they saw, without identifying specific people by name. Because they were not involved in the exercise, the observers often see key behaviors that influenced the outcome. Having these observations come from a fellow participant rather than a staff member can make tough feedback easier to hear. Listening to the observer, each individual participant can reflect on how he or she might have behaved differently to achieve a more effective outcome.

Videotaping an exercise is another method for assessing skills and behaviors that we use. After completing the exercise, the participants are given a structure for reviewing the videotape. The type of structure depends on the purpose of the exercise. For example, participants are given the task of deciding a course of action for a business problem, presenting to their fellow group members, and persuading the group to choose their course of action. The overall purpose of the exercise is to view a person's ability to influence the group. Facilitators provide a structure for viewing the video, and participants discuss how they, as individuals, were effective or ineffective in their ability to influence. Participants gain insights from group dialogue as well as individual reflection.

When an exercise is not videotaped, as in a full-day simulation, a trained observer records the actions and behaviors of the individuals participating in the simulation. The assessment of what participants did well and what they could do better comes from these observations. The simulation is followed by a series of facilitated debriefs during which the assessment is discussed with the participants.

In these facilitated small group discussions, participants receive feedback on individual and group performance from the staff observer, discuss their own views of how they did as individuals and as a group, and give each other peer feedback. These debriefings are fairly lengthy because it takes time to review important aspects of the simulation content, along with the interpersonal interactions and individual performance that took place throughout the simulation.

Elements of Challenge

In a feedback-intensive process, there are multiple sources of challenge. Assessment and feedback, by their very nature, provide one source of intense challenge: that of looking inward, the discomfort of being observed and rated by others, the fear of having weaknesses exposed. Other sources of challenge include structured exercises, engaging in unfamiliar activities, and encountering different ideas and perspectives.

Structured Experiences

Structured experiences are group activities that provide challenge through goal-directed, live-action, task-based interactions. The experiences may involve the entire class, or participants may form small groups that will act independently of one another or will engage in some way to complete the task. Unlike instruments, which display a person's strengths and development needs numerically on paper, structured experiences reveal strengths and weaknesses in real time. Three common types of structured experiences are leaderless group discussions, simulations, and targeted exercises.

Leaderless Group Discussions. This technique has a long history in assessment center research and practice. The basic idea is that a group of four to eight people is assigned a task, and the group as a whole, rather than an individual leader, is accountable for the outcome. Participants are given a time limit for completing the task and may be instructed to use a collaborative process, a competitive process, or a combination of the two. Staff members, trained to rate certain individual leadership behaviors, observe the group and rate participants on a number of variables, such as motivating others, leading the discussion, task orientation, interpersonal skills, and verbal effectiveness. These observations are compiled for feedback that is delivered later in the program.

One challenge implicit in leaderless group discussions is the challenge of being observed and assessed. The other challenge is working on an unfamiliar problem when information is sketchy and the directions are ambiguous. It is not uncommon, given the lack of familiarity with the task, for participants to feel insecure about their effectiveness. These challenges often lead participants to recognize there is still a lot they can learn about themselves.

What follows is one example of a leaderless group exercise. Participants are told to imagine themselves living on another planet, one without a designated leader. They must accomplish three tasks in a short period of time: (1) reflect on and create their own description or résumé for an ideal leader, (2) influence other group members that their candidate is the one best suited to lead on the planet, and (3) as a group, choose one leader among the candidates and rank-order the remaining ones. The challenge for participants is balancing the need to have their own candidate win against the group's need to have the best possible leader—a very common conflict between individual desires and group needs that most managers face in their own organizations.

Simulations. Simulations are exercises that in some way replicate aspects of people's real-life jobs, situations, or environments. The simulated task can be as small as managing a single manager's in-basket or as large as managing in a full-scale simulation of two organizations working together in a merger situation. In many simulations, individuals or teams are scored with respect to a "book solution" (for example, how many "correct" choices were made within a specified period of time) so that the individuals and groups can measure their performance against the "right answers."

In our larger simulations, which last from half a day to several days, small groups of people interact to solve a series of problems, such as finding a better way to respond to customer complaints, secure scarce resources, or retain high-potential employees. These simulations may involve twenty or more people. The participants are often asked to play the role of leaders in the top level of a large corporation or employees in two or more organizations that are in some sort of working relationship, such as customer and supplier or joint-venture partners. They take on roles in marketing, operations, or international human resources in their respective "companies," often complete with in-baskets, computers, e-mail, telephones, and fax machines. They are presented with a complex, realistic situation and a fairly intense timetable for solving the issues presented to them.

Simulations are challenging for participants in many ways. The process of being observed and rated on how quickly or how well they prioritize the information, communicate the critical information, respond to others' needs, and make good decisions is one challenge. Other challenges occur when participants take on roles in the simulation that are quite different from positions they have held previously. For example, in one simulation, the participants run a glass company for a day. A key role in this simulation is CEO, and the person in this role grapples with issues of strategy, global expansion, the acquisition of new businesses and the selling of less profitable ones, ethics, and multiple stakeholders. Challenges presented in other roles may include making sense of the financial reports, understanding the business process for a particular industry, and seeing the reality of the political landscape. Further challenge takes place when individuals must work closely with and rely on others they really do not know. When working to master the elements of the simulation, untested assumptions and lack of attention to relationships can lead to misunderstanding among group members. In an intense five-day program, the misunderstandings can grow if not thoroughly discussed and solved. We will discuss this issue further when we turn to the elements of support in an FIP.

Targeted Exercises. We also use short, experiential exercises in our FIPs to deepen participants' understanding of specific content or to continue the learning about a theme central to the program. Targeted exercises are not as extensive as simulations in replicating the actual work environment, but they facilitate working in real time on realistic projects and dilemmas. Targeted exercises usually focus on one or two specific aspects of a leader's responsibilities. Communication, planning and implementing, influence, negotiation, and challenging assumptions are common topics of targeted exercises.

Participants are challenged by targeted exercises in many ways. They are challenged to demonstrate strengths, try new behaviors, test their knowledge and experience, question their thinking, and work outside of their comfort zone. A large variety of lessons ensue. For example, managers learn that comfortable behaviors that have made them successful in the past may not serve them well in every situation. They learn that a group can usually perform better than any one individual alone and that the lack of involvement of implementers in planning a task leads to higher levels of dissatisfaction on the part of the implementers.

Programs can also incorporate the use of the outdoors in targeted exercises to help drive home some teaching points. Since most individuals have organizational roles that keep them indoors, the outdoor environment provides a new, challenging, and thought-provoking setting for examining organizational issues. The exercises we use range from small physical challenges (trust walks) to more intense experiences (orienteering exercises). Many people report that simply engaging in outdoor problem-solving activities as a group gives them a different perspective on learning than they might get in the indoor environment. They report feeling more permission to experiment with new behaviors, a heightened challenge in the problem-solving exercises, and a greater willingness to test out assumptions that are often present in organizational life, such as "Who has what information?" and "What are the rules?" and "How do we define quality?" Like simulations, the true success of any targeted exercise is in extracting what has been learned from the experience through effective debriefing and reflection activities. We will discuss effective facilitation of these exercises in the following section on support.

Engaging in Unfamiliar Activities

Structured experiences are designed to be challenging. They become more challenging when individuals are asked to engage in activities that fall outside their comfort zone. A good example is the use of artistic activities. A majority of business people tend to be hesitant about stepping out of a logical, business-oriented mind-set to engage in drama, drawing, clay sculpting, or collage making. These activities are often seen by participants initially as play and not relevant to their world of work. Yet these challenges take people out of their element, introduce a level of discomfort, and demand that they use untested skills and behaviors. For some, the exercises themselves are so disconnected from their daily life that they feel frivolous. However, it is often through the use of such creative activities that individuals discover insights not gained from more traditional pursuits. Some of the activities we use are dramatic movement, guided visualization, and collage.

Dramatic Movement. Dramatic movement can shed new light on troublesome situations. A participant in one CCL program talked about her difficulty in coping with multiple demands from her boss, coworkers, and family. She described herself as being pulled in too many directions at once. In a module involving dramatic movement, she asked several of her classmates to help portray her situation. She "sculpted" them into position, creating a frieze depicting the tugs she felt from these demands. She gave each of her feedback participants a phrase to say, and then she put herself into the picture. The purpose was to create a visual picture of her problem using the people in the room. The verbal and visual effect on the entire class was powerful. We suggested that she reshape the frieze as she would like her situation to be, again assigning short phrases to each character. The group members were then asked to reflect on and compare the two scenes without group discussion. From the change, the participant gained new insight into what she needed to do to change her situation. A few of the lessons were to learn to say no and to let go of the small things.

Guided Visualization and Collage. These are activities in which participants sit quietly, listening to the voice of a staff member who guides them through a series of images. We may play music in the background to stimulate thoughts. The objective of the visualization differs with its placement in the curriculum and its content. In one such activity, participants are asked to create a picture of where they want to be in five years. They are asked, "What does this person look like?" "What is he or she doing?" "How is the person feeling?" "What has changed in five years?" Then the participant takes the visual picture that has emerged and re-creates it in a drawing or a collage using various art materials.

These are but a few examples of nontraditional methods. Some participants, because of their learning style, may not find these types of exercises challenging. For others, they might be very challenging because they represent a creative or "right brain" approach, which is not typical of the methods used in traditional classrooms, boardrooms, and business settings. For participants who find the activities difficult or who are unwilling to engage for learning's sake, there is knowledge to be gained from exploring their reaction. What prevents them from engaging in these nontraditional methods? Is it a feeling of incompetence ("I can't draw")? Is it a need for perfection ("My collage doesn't look as good as the others")? Is it fear of change ("If I see my future, I may not like what I see")? The answers to these questions can have a powerful impact on these individuals.

Meeting Diverse People with Different Perspectives

The last source of challenge we will discuss here is the challenge people feel when they encounter others with ideas and perspectives different from their own. We build this type of challenge into our FIPs by maximizing racial, gender, and cultural diversity in the classroom. Challenge also comes from interacting with people who are different in terms of their functional, professional, or industry perspectives. Sharing personal feedback data during the program, from personality assessments such as the MBTI, also challenges people to see the diversity that is often hidden, even in a group that appears on the surface to be homogeneous.

Why is working with a diverse group of people challenging? For starters, most people are more comfortable working with individuals who share the same style, perspectives, values, and opinions. Studies of selection processes confirm that people promote or select people with whom they are comfortable (Sessa and Taylor, 2000). In an FIP, by working with a diverse group of individuals, participants often realize that there is more than one way to frame an issue, resolve a problem, or handle a situation. Having diversity of thought challenges mental models and gives participants the opportunity to offer—or to hear—an opinion that is radically different, fostering participants' courage, risk taking, and openness.

Another value of diverse perspectives in the classroom is that participants have the challenge of working with individuals who are different from themselves in terms of style. This enables them to gain another perspective on individuals back home who do not share their way of working. As they learn from the diversity in the program, participants begin to appreciate the diversity in their own workplaces and realize that they may need to capitalize more on these differences, rather than approaching them as a nuisance or point of conflict.

Diversity is a necessary but not sufficient condition for learning. Sometimes the conflict or tension that arises from differences stays under the surface and is never explored. This is particularly true when we move beyond discussions of personality differences to issues of gender, race, and ethnicity. The volatility of these issues in organizations and society at large makes them difficult to discuss in the classroom. A powerful FIP will provide opportunities to "speak about the unspeakable." Skilled facilitation (surfacing issues and modulating the conflict that arises) and the willingness of participants to engage in the exploration of differences are two critical aspects for effectively engaging in these discussions.

In sum, a well-designed and skillfully implemented feedback-intensive process provides challenge in several areas. The program moves from structured exercises, which are interpersonally and cognitively challenging, to 360-degree feedback, which challenges assumptions about self and others, to a diversity of participants, which provides the opportunity to see issues from different and enriching perspectives. To develop as leaders, people need both the challenge of the unfamiliar and the support of the familiar. The unfamiliar encourages them to stretch, while the familiar helps them stay open to new things by validating their strengths and reinforcing who they are.

Elements of Support

To foster effective learning, an FIP must take place in a safe and supportive environment. Such an environment is necessary for participants to appreciate their strengths, feel accepted and respected, view the feedback as relevant and useful, define what is important in their feedback, and develop a workable plan for the changes they want to make.

As we mentioned earlier, providing support in the classroom is essential for helping participants focus on the data honestly and openly. Getting feedback can provoke significant anxiety. Participants often lose sight of what they are doing well and focus on areas where they feel less competent and more vulnerable. Without adequate support, being challenged by unfamiliar or difficult activities can lead to overwhelming feelings of incompetence. This anxiety, if allowed to get out of hand, can prevent participants' full exploration of the data and thus inhibit their learning.

Creating a Supportive Environment

In an FIP, there are critical processes that staff must engage to create a climate of support, including facilitating participant learning, teaching to different learning styles, integrating participants' work into program activities, encouraging the sharing of perspectives, allowing time to practice new behaviors, and providing opportunities for consolidation of feedback.

Although the content of a program is important in helping people cognitively frame their feedback in a wider leadership context, the "process" side is what enables people to deal emotionally with their feedback and to connect it meaningfully to their work and personal lives. As program staff model behaviors that convey support, participants begin to enact these attitudes and behaviors with each other and the staff. As they become more open and candid, a bond of trust forms. This trust leads to the ability of program staff and participants to challenge each other's perspectives. As people learn that they each have the ability to help and teach others, the classroom becomes a true community for learning. The participants themselves become supportive threads in the elegant tapestry of their own program experience. It is the program facilitators, however, who are responsible for setting these processes in motion.

Facilitating Participant Learning. The program staff contribute more than solid knowledge of the content and facilitation of stimulating activities. Staff members consciously enact attitudes and behaviors that facilitate participant learning. To create a community where participants feel safe, attempt self-disclosure, and are willing to listen to feedback, program staff must do all of the following:

- Relate to each participant with personal authenticity
- Be comfortable with self-disclosure
- Sincerely understand and acknowledge each participant's situations and perspectives without passing judgment
- Be nonprescriptive in discussions with participants

For staff members, being authentic means having a strong sense of self yet not pretending to have competencies or knowledge one lacks or portraying oneself as good at everything. This is not easy for all potential program staff, and it is an important factor in choosing and developing people to staff an FIP. Although many people care intensely about providing a good experience, for some, this may mean having to know all the answers. Experienced program leaders freely admit when they do not know something and use the opportunity to ask others to share their opinions. This attitude is crucial to creating a good learning environment for participants, because it sets a tone that it is acceptable not to know everything, thereby allowing participants to feel free to take the risks that lead to learning.

Throughout the program, appropriate self-disclosure is another important staff behavior. Done in the right measure, self-disclosure by staff helps pave the way for participant self-disclosure. This reciprocal vulnerability allows participants to more fully discuss the challenges they are facing and the feedback they are receiving.

To create the best possible learning experience for each individual, program staff must also be willing and able to ignore their own needs, values, and expectations and respectfully meet the participants wherever they are, developmentally and emotionally. To meet participants' need to feel accepted, respected, and cared for, facilitators must find a way to connect personally with each individual. In the classroom, a staff member makes eye contact with each participant, acknowledges the contributions made by each, recognizes when a participant may not understand the material or has a question, remembers which person asked a particular question or made a specific contribution, and takes whatever time is necessary to ensure that each participant is having a valuable learning experience every day. This means taking the time to get to know the participants, their unique ways of looking at the world, and their special areas of expertise.

Finally, to support the participants' need to feel accepted and respected, staff must project a sincerely nonjudgmental attitude about each individual's way of understanding self and others. This nonprescriptive stance is also important in helping participants take responsibility for their own development, which is a key ingredient for long-term success in behavior change. For example, when participants examine their personality profiles or feedback from back home, they frequently ask, "What's the best way to be?" The best answer for the staff to give is to say there is no one best way to be, although certain ways may be more effective than others in some situations and with some people. This kind of response can be hard for people to hear, especially those who are in the midst of turbulent change (either in their external environment or within themselves) and who are seeking some solid ground on which to stand. When participants insist on getting the "right" answer, staff must guard against the temptation to want to be "helpful" by providing seemingly definitive answers. In fact, providing answers for participants is probably the least helpful thing staff can do. The role of staff is to facilitate the process whereby participants themselves come to decide what the feedback means to them, what their development needs and issues are, and how best to go about tackling them.

Teaching to Different Learning Styles. If a program is to provide support in the learning process for participants, every individual must not only have challenges from which to learn but also should be able to learn in the ways that suit him or her best and at a rate that feels comfortable.

Each individual comes to an FIP with a set of preferred learning tactics (see Chapter Seven). Some may learn best by observing others, hearing what others say and seeing what they do in classroom discussions and exercises. Others may be most comfortable learning by taking action themselves, in exercises, simulations, and outdoor activities. Still others learn most easily in interaction with other people, by seeking advice from staff or discussing issues with peers in a group setting. And although many people are not comfortable with or used to reflection as a way of learning, most people need time to reflect on the information they receive if they are to integrate it properly into their thinking and their future behavior. To be most effective, an FIP needs to provide both learning opportunities for people with different ways of learning and opportunities for individuals to add to their ability to learn by trying out new and less comfortable learning tactics. For these reasons, program staff design FIPs to maximize the use of a variety of learning methodologies.

Integrating Participants' Work into Program Activities. In the most effective feedback-intensive process, staff learn the details of the participants' situation back home, such as industry or market issues, and make that information an integral part of the program content. This enables the participant to more readily translate program content for back-home use. Good facilitators do their homework, reviewing biographical information on all the participants, along with the pre-program questionnaires and scored feedback reports. They also read about the latest issues the participants' organizations are facing. Once the program begins, they listen and watch closely for clues about the participants' interests, concerns, and differences. They stay alert for comments that reveal the issues and challenges the participants bring with them. As the program progresses, they are quick to use opportunities to weave appropriate pieces of this information directly into the program as examples or as prompts for group discussion while being careful not to violate individuals' confidentiality.

Encouraging the Sharing of Perspectives. Participants bring with them a wealth of experience and knowledge. Skilled facilitators look for ways to pull that expertise into the discussions so that the larger group can benefit from shared information.

To stimulate the sharing of perspectives, facilitators might ask participants to describe how the content is connected to their experiences, to brainstorm ways of using the content, or to talk about their opinions on a particular issue being discussed. This sharing of perspectives and expertise helps participants understand that their experience is of value to others and that each person has something to learn from the others, no matter how different they seem to be. This is an important norm in each of our programs and works to enhance the climate of support in the group.

Practicing New Behaviors. It is important that an FIP go beyond the delivery of data to enhance self-awareness of strengths and development needs and to provide participants with the opportunity to try on new behaviors during the course of a program. Given the feedback they receive, participants need a firsthand experience of using a new approach in a safe environment that has no consequences. They need to be able to fail, make mistakes, and feel the discomfort of engaging in behaviors at which they are less competent. Experiencing this discomfort prepares them for what they will experience back home when they are attempting change; it gives them time to discuss with others how to manage the feelings associated with change. Finally, they have an opportunity to receive additional feedback on how their small experiments with behavior change went without fear of negative consequences from colleagues they work with on a regular basis.

Providing Opportunities for Consolidation of Feedback. As we have said throughout this chapter, an FIP is an information-rich experience. By the second or third day, people have been given multiple pieces of feedback from a variety of sources, and this onslaught of data can be overpowering. To support the person in focusing on the key elements of the data, we provide many opportunities for individuals to consolidate the feedback.

One process we use is an extension of the journaling process. Participants are provided with a template outlining the topics covered during the program (360-degree feedback, MBTI, outdoor exercises, and so on). Under each topic, the participant captures the learning or highlights they have gleaned from each experience. After reviewing these together in one place, participants can begin to see the themes that are emerging in their data and discussions. This theme building helps narrow their attention to the data points that are most important to them.

Another process that is very effective and highly valued by participants is the use of feedback coaches. In highly interactive, confidential sessions, the participant and the coach work one-on-one to learn as much as they can from all the accumulated feedback the participant has received throughout the program—from preprogram assessments, classroom experiences, observations during exercises, discussions, simulations, and personal observations from staff and fellow participants. Together, the two explore the implications, settle on some possible areas for change, and discuss various action plans for change. It is an integration activity designed to be an exciting process of discovery, confirmation, and action.

The Outcomes of a Feedback-Intensive Program

Over the course of more than two decades of research, we have learned a great deal about the impact of feedback-intensive programs. Key elements of the research are summarized here; a more detailed discussion of how impact can be assessed can be found in Chapter Eight.

There are potentially five main areas for development and growth as a result of participating in a feedback-intensive program: knowledge acquisition, self-awareness, transformational perspective change, goal attainment and reframing, and behavior change. Some kinds of change begin during the program itself; others are not likely to occur until much later.

Knowledge Acquisition

Participants in our programs report that they learn significant new information about such topics as the human elements of strategy, influence, leadership skills and competencies, conflict, and coaching. Participants report different degrees and types of knowledge acquisition, depending on the content presented and their level of knowledge prior to the program.

Self-Awareness

Enhanced self-awareness is the most frequent and most powerful result of a feedback-intensive program. People who felt less than competent often become aware that they are reasonably good managers. Some gain awareness of skill deficits or of how they are viewed by different groups of people. Some gain personal insights about how they see themselves or learn more about their own needs.

Often an increase in self-awareness is sparked by a discrepancy between how participants view themselves and how others view them. In one study of a five-day leadership program (Van Velsor, Ruderman, and Phillips, 1992), only 10 percent of the managers saw themselves as others saw them on all the dimensions measured by a 360-degree feedback instrument. Forty-five percent had a significant discrepancy, and most of those in the 45 percent tended to rate themselves higher than others rated them. Yet when asked to rerate their leadership capacities soon after the program, the vast majority of people (80 percent) revised their self-view to be more in line with feedback they received in the program. Participants thus appeared to have significantly improved their self-awareness as a result of the program.

Transformational Perspective Change

Perspective change is similar to awareness building in that it refers to a change in attitude or outlook rather than a change in observable behavior. It differs from self-awareness building by referring not to a changed view of self but to new understandings about others, about the challenges people face, or about other significant aspects of the context in which people live and work. Some examples of this kind of change in thinking are "One can view change as opportunity," "It is possible to manage an organization without becoming a technical expert," "I am now viewing my sensitivity toward others as a strength rather than something that I should avoid in the workplace."

Perspective change, like self-awareness change, can be the result of knowledge acquisition and insight. For example, the person who realized that it is possible to manage an organization without becoming a technical expert may have come to that perspective by acquiring more information about what management involves— that it is essentially focused on getting the work done through other people.

A striking and powerful change resulting from an FIP is this combined change in awareness and perspectives that causes many a participant to report feeling that he or she has become "a different person." A distinguishing feature of this type of change is that participants who report such changes do not attribute them to any single lesson or component but to the program experience as a whole. It is important to note that these kinds of reported changes are highly consistent with the values espoused in the program and its stated goals and purposes, as discussed at the beginning of this chapter.

Goal Attainment and Reframing

Over the years, our follow-up on the goals participants set has shown that three to twelve months later, most people either are still working on their goals or have accomplished them. We also know that people are more likely to achieve their goals when they have adequate postprogram support or when they are participating in an FIP that extends over a period of time.

We took an in-depth look at how participants approach goal setting in an FIP and found that there are at least three approaches (Young and Dixon, 1996). The first is traditional, characterized by the view that a person sets goals and tries, in a fairly linear pattern, to carry them out. If obstacles to goal attainment arise, they are overcome, or the person abandons the goal and fails to attain it. Whether the person succeeds in these goals or fails, he or she considers the exercise closed after that. This approach is similar to that taken by many program evaluations, which seek only to confirm whether the goals set have been achieved.

A second approach views goals as visions or ideal outcomes, with the path to achieve them subject to change as events unfold. This more flexible approach takes a longer view of goal accomplishment and allows the participant freedom to create new strategies for goal attainment as circumstances change and obstacles arise.

Finally, a third group of participants in this study took what was described as a process view of action planning. They appeared to set out on a journey leading them through a series of goals and action plans, success or failure, each culminating in some learning and a resetting of goals. This group probably got the most from the goal-setting or action-planning process, since participants tended to set and achieve many goals and learn from both successes and failures.

Behavior Change

Simple behavior change may take place as a direct result of new awareness gained during leadership development assessment or other kinds of feedback. Some examples might be that one decides to stop interrupting others, to set aside time for meetings with staff, or to spend more time with family. More complex behavior change, such as collecting more data before making a decision or fully allowing the perspectives of others to influence one's own, take longer amounts of time and a higher motivation to achieve.

More extensive behavior change was found over time in the Young and Dixon study (1996) of a program with an extended design and significant follow-up. This feedback-intensive program spanned six months and included two classroom sessions three months apart, extended work with process advisers between classroom sessions, back-home partners in change, and on-the-job learning projects. In this program, alumni were seen by coworkers as having made change in thirteen of the fourteen areas measured. Participants rated as having changed in a particular area were also rated as more effective as a result. Compared to the results of a control group of managers who did not participate in the program, this was still impressive, as program participants showed significantly more change than control group members in eight of the fourteen areas assessed.

When and How to Use a Feedback-Intensive Program

The practical challenge for human resource practitioners is to know when a feedback-intensive program is the appropriate developmental experience and when another experience might be more useful. In addition to the very real constraints of budget, an FIP would be recommended only after looking at the totality of a situation. How central is the person's role in the organization? What are the new role demands? How severe is the difficulty? How significant is the future potential? We have, unfortunately, no formula to answer this question, but there are certain guidelines we can suggest.

Organizations can create a strong leadership line by selecting and developing people for their next leadership step when they are effectively working at the level to which they are currently assigned (Charan, Drodder, and Noel, 2001). An FIP is an effective procedure for priming future leaders by helping them plan for their own development, coaching them, and measuring the results of those efforts. Research shows that an FIP is particularly useful for people who have recently taken on management responsibilities, have had a significant change in the scope of their responsibilities, or are facing significantly different job or personal demands because of other organizational (or life) changes (Van Velsor and Musselwhite, 1986).

In general, circumstances that appear to call for an FIP include the following:

• When developing the careers of people identified as high-potential. Organizations often feel that full and complete assessment of the strengths and weaknesses of their future leaders is a worthwhile investment.

• At a time of career transition, either to a new organization or to new responsibilities in the present job. Integrating feedback from many sources can help a manager recognize that new challenges require additional skills and new behaviors.

• When someone shows signs of potential derailment. Being passed over for promotion, faltering in performance in normally strong areas, and interpersonal difficulties are all signs pointing to a need to take stock with the sort of comprehensive assessment that an FIP provides.

• When the organization is attempting to blend or change the culture, shift the organization's strategy, or work with a merger or acquisition and there is a need for understanding differences, thinking in different terms, and driving change effectively.

Another factor to consider when deciding on the use of an FIP is whether to use a public, open-enrollment program or a customized, organization-specific program.

Open-Enrollment and Organization-Specific Programs

When considering feedback-intensive programs, organizations can select from different formats. Open-enrollment programs are composed of individual managers from different companies; the public programs held at CCL are an example of these. This format is the obvious choice if only a handful of managers is being considered for participation. FIPs can also be offered as organization-specific programs developed and run for a single organization by a vendor (such as CCL) or by the organization itself.

Whether the participant group is made up of individuals from various organizations or people from the same organization is a significant issue from the point of view of impact. Each kind of program offers benefits; each has its drawbacks.

In an open-enrollment program, people have access to the diversity of perspectives and concerns of other participants and learn that issues are very often similar across different organizations. A benefit of this environment for participants is that everyone has access to the breadth of experiences and best practices occurring in a number of organizations. For a fair percentage of participants, the interactions do not end at the close of the program, as people tend to stay in touch with each other for an extended period of time. Further, in an open-enrollment program, there is often a greater sense of trust and confidentiality than can be achieved in an organization-specific program, and the ability to learn increases because of the variety of viewpoints and diminished sense of vulnerability in discussing ideas and feedback.

An organization-specific program, by contrast, can afford greater leverage in effecting organization-level change because it can be targeted to specific organizational issues. When people from the same organization experience a program simultaneously and develop a common language, the impact on the overall organization can outweigh sending a few people at a time to FIPs over an extended period. The organization-specific program is effective when the intent is to increase communication and team building, as with an organization that is geographically dispersed. It is also effective with an identified high-potential group, where the intent is both to develop each person and to enable all individuals as a group to develop a network, learn more about their organization, and develop more effective relationships among themselves.

There is a significant difference between the classroom environments of open-enrollment programs and organization-specific programs. In an organization-specific program, there is an elephant in the room—the current culture of the organization—and it exerts an enormous influence on what is learned and how. For example, one participant in a CCL program worked for an organization that had just been through a major reorganization. She arrived feeling confused, overloaded, frightened, and frustrated. In her organizational culture, no one addressed issues directly; hallway conversation about them was rampant, but during meetings, no one dared bring them up. In the program classroom, the participants behaved the same way. Between sessions, private grumbling could be heard, but when the facilitators asked people to talk about their organization and what might need to change, not one person would acknowledge the elephant. They were all in the program because of their high potential in future leadership roles, but before individual or group development could begin to happen, an intervention was required that allowed them to address their organizational issues honestly and openly.

Exhibit 1.1 summarizes additional guidelines for selecting or designing an FIP, based on our assessment, challenge, and support model of what constitutes effective leader development.

What Managers and HR Practitioners Can Do to Enhance FIP Impact

Finally, there are several actions a manager or human resource practitioner can take before and after a feedback-intensive program to enhance its impact for participants. Prior to the program, be clear about the desired outcomes for the persons attending the program; establish clear expectations, goals, and a plan to put what is learned into practice; ask about content and its relevance to the leadership level of the persons attending; ask whether assessment tools have known reliability and validity; and find out what the facilitators do to create and maintain a safe learning community in the classroom.

When people return from a program, encourage discussion, coaching, and ongoing development planning between each participant and his or her manager; allow for mistakes as the participant begins to try new approaches. You can create networks or alumni groups and identify other mechanisms your organization has in place to continue and expand each participant's learning, and you can integrate the face-to-face classroom experience with technology-based tools and processes to maximize the effectiveness of the impact. Finally, you can help people devise long-term development plans that incorporate the FIP assessment by linking their development goals to next-step developmental experiences, such as skill-based training or a developmental relationship.

Conclusion

Feedback-intensive programs play a critical role in the development of effective leaders throughout their careers. Assessment, a variety of challenges, and developmental support—the key ingredients for continuous individual leader development—must be present in good measure in any effective feedback-

EXHIBIT 1.1. GUIDELINES FOR SELECTING OR DESIGNING A FEEDBACK-INTENSIVE PROGRAM: WHAT TO LOOK FOR OR BUILD IN.

Assessment
- Use of multiple assessment methodologies (for example, personality instruments, 360-degree leadership instruments, peer assessments, participant observation)
- Variety in sources of assessment data (self-ratings; feedback from boss, peers, direct reports, customers, fellow participants, program staff)
- Integrity in assessment processes (for example, reliability and validity of assessment methods, confidentiality for participants, anonymity for raters)
- Program methods and experiences that surface participants' leadership strengths and development needs in real time

Challenge
- Teaching methodologies and experiences that address various learning styles (for example, lectures, structured experiences, one-on-one discussions)
- Use of unfamiliar activities (art, drama, music)
- Diverse participant mix
- Program content that is based on real issues that participants face

Support
- Program staff who understand participants' learning and support needs
- Structure in which development needs and goals are defined with participant learning needs in mind, rather than prescribed by program content or staff
- Program staff who have the process facilitation skills necessary to link program content to feedback and feedback to action planning in a way that protects confidentiality and promotes openness and learning
- Ways of extending the participants' learnings about self beyond the program, for individual benefit and for better coaching and development of others
- Processes for program follow-up through goal report forms, telephone calls, or other methods of support, encouragement, and assessment of development and change over time
- Organizational development systems to support learning

---

intensive program. We have discussed the various mechanisms and underlying principles of this particular development process, discussed how the ACS model plays out in the design and implementation of a feedback-intensive program, and presented some guidelines for practitioners. It is important to stress that in addition to effective teaching and assessment methodologies, support must extend beyond the classroom and come from the participant's organization. Linking the developmental FIP experience to the work environment through projects, dialogues with bosses, and ongoing feedback provides a powerful framework for leveraging this investment in leader development.

CHAPTER TWO

360-DEGREE FEEDBACK

Craig T. Chappelow

Of all the recent trends in the field of leader development, perhaps the most remarkable is the popularity and growth of using 360-degree feedback instruments in organizations. In 1977, a team of researchers at the Center for Creative Leadership set out to write a comprehensive review of all multirater assessment instruments in use at that time (Morrison, McCall, and DeVries, 1978). After an exhaustive search of the psychological and business literature, they could not find enough instruments to form a critical mass. They expanded the search by making contact with numerous client organizations to solicit samples of any multirater instruments developed and used within companies. The final strategy the research team used was a review of the catalogues of major test publishers. The three strategies together yielded a total of only twenty-four instruments—some were fairly primitive, and others were only used once or twice by the developer before being shelved.

Now, more than twenty-five years later, a research team taking on the same task would be overwhelmed by the hundreds of multirater assessments in use, and a comprehensive review would be nearly impossible. Atwater and Waldman (1998) have called the proliferation of multirater assessment one of the most notable management innovations of the 1990s. Nearly all Fortune 500 companies either currently use or have plans to use some form of 360-degree feedback (Antonioni, 1996; London and Smither, 1995; Yammarino and Atwater, 1997).

When a methodology becomes as popular as 360-degree feedback has become, interest in best practices runs high, and so do concerns about misuse. The aim of this chapter is to summarize the lessons we have learned about effective use of 360-degree feedback instruments over the past quarter century, through research and practice at CCL as well as through other practitioners and researchers. As such, it is not a comprehensive review of the professional literature on 360-degree feedback. (Readers interested in such a review should consult Bracken, Timmreck, and Church, 2001; Fleenor and Prince, 1997; Lepsinger and Lucia, 1997; or Tornow and London, 1998.)

The chapter is organized into four major sections. The first section examines the role of 360-degree feedback in the leader development process. The second investigates the impact of 360-degree feedback, and the third provides an overview of the steps involved in implementing a 360-degree feedback process. The final section provides insights into 360-degree feedback initiatives that go wrong and investigates ways of increasing the odds that a formal feedback initiative will succeed.

The Role of 360-Degree Feedback in Leader Development

What we call "360-degree feedback" is a method of systematically collecting opinions about a manager's performance from a wide range of coworkers. This can include peers, direct subordinates, the boss, and the boss's peers, along with people outside the organization, such as customers, suppliers, and in some cases even family members.

Typically, the person being assessed (the "participant") selects a number of coworkers ("raters") to participate in the feedback process. Working individually, the raters and the participant complete surveys designed to collect information about the participant's specific skills or behaviors that are deemed important to managerial or leadership effectiveness within the organization. (Exhibit 2.1 shows a sample page from a rater survey.)

After the raters complete the surveys, they return them to a centralized location for scoring. A report is printed and, ideally, delivered to a feedback facilitator. (Exhibit 2.2 shows a sample page from a feedback report.) The participant and the feedback facilitator then meet and review the results. The facilitator, usually someone who has experience with the particular instrument being used, helps the participant understand what the various scores mean. The participant then uses this feedback to establish a development plan geared toward increasing his or her effectiveness.

EXHIBIT 2.1. SAMPLE PAGE FROM A 360-DEGREE RATER SURVEY.

	Strength	Development Needed

Getting Information, Making Sense of It; Problem Identification

1. Seeks information energetically . . . . ○   ○
2. Probes, digs beneath the surface, tests the validity of information . . . . ○   ○
3. Creates order out of large quantities of information . . . . ○   ○
4. Keen observer of people, events, things . . . . ○   ○
5. Defines problems effectively; gets to the heart of a problem . . . . ○   ○
6. Spots problems, opportunities, threats, trends early . . . . . . ○   ○
7. Logical, data-based, rational . . . . ○   ○

Communicating Information, Ideas

8. Adept at disseminating information to others . . . . ○   ○
9. Crisp, clear, articulate . . . . ○   ○
10. Good public speaker; skilled at performing, being on stage . . . . ○   ○
11. Makes his or her point effectively to a resistant audience . . . . ○   ○
12. Strong communicator on paper; good writing skills . . . . ○   ○

Taking Action, Making Decisions, Following Through

13. Action-oriented; presses for immediate results . . . . ○   ○
14. Decisive; doesn't procrastinate on decisions. . . . . ○   ○
15. Troubleshooter; enjoys solving problems . . . . ○   ○
16. Implements decisions, follows through, follows up well; an expediter . . . . ○   ○
17. Carefully weighs consequences of contemplated action . . . . ○   ○

Source: SkillScope®, copyright © 1997 by the Center for Creative Leadership. Reprinted with permission.

EXHIBIT 2.2. SAMPLE PAGE FROM A 360-DEGREE FEEDBACK REPORT.

SKILLSCOPE for Managers

KEY TO SYMBOLS
- ● Strength
- ■ Development Needed
- ○ Strength ⎫
- □ Development ⎬ Boss's
   Needed ⎭ feedback

RESULTS

PAT SAMPLE		
SELF	8 Others	
	Strength	Development Needed

KNOWLEDGE OF JOB, BUSINESS

	●●	■■	70. Shows mastery of job content; excels at his or her function or professional specialty
	●	□■	71. A good general manager
■	●●	□■	72. Effective in a job with a big scope
	○●	■■	73. In a new assignment, picks up knowledge and expertise easily; a quick study
■		■■	74. At home with graphs, charts, statistics, budgets
■	●	■	75. Understands cash flows, financial reports, corporate annual reports

ENERGY, DRIVE, AMBITION

	●●●●		76. Good initiative; continually reaches for more responsibility
●	○●●●●		77. High energy level
●	●●●●●		78. Ambitious; highly motivated to advance his or her career
●	○●●●●	■	79. Goal-directed, persistent; driven to achieve objectives

TIME MANAGEMENT

■	●	□■■■	80. Sets priorities well; distinguishes clearly between important and unimportant tasks
●		□■■■■■	81. Makes the most of the time available; extremely productive
■	●	■■■■	82. Deals with interruptions appropriately; knows when to admit interruptions and when to screen them out
■	●	□■■■■	83. Avoids spreading self too thin

Clearly, 360-degree feedback is an assessment process; thus much of its power as a leader development experience comes from the strong element of assessment embedded in it. But a 360-degree feedback experience also provides particular challenges for the participant and if optimally designed also creates support for development.

Assessment

The assessment data generated from 360-degree feedback have two important characteristics that make them particularly rich: they are formal, and they come from multiple perspectives.

Formal Feedback. In the life of a busy organization, people often find themselves feedback-starved. Two factors play into this. First, people get caught up in day-to-day pressures and responsibilities and fail to pick up the cues from others that provide one source of ongoing feedback. While waiting for the elevator after a tough meeting, a manager gets a pat on the back from a colleague for handling a presentation well. The next day, someone lets her know that her reaction to a sensitive question was unnecessarily defensive. At the end of the week, one of her team members cautions her that her instructions to their assistant sounded patronizing. These small bits of data—informal feedback—float around managers all the time, largely unheeded in the rush of business concerns.

Formal 360-degree feedback provides some things that informal feedback seldom does: a structured means of collecting and compiling data and an opportunity to reflect on this valuable information. It may be the only time many leaders consciously stop to take stock of their performance effectiveness.

Second, giving and receiving feedback can be threatening activities for many people, and they may not think that doing either is worth the risk. This is particularly true the higher up in the organization one moves, and senior executives often receive the least feedback of anyone (Kaplan, Drath, and Kofodimos, 1985). In the modern organization, much lip service is paid to the need to increase communication in all directions; at the same time, many people are reluctant to give performance feedback to coworkers, especially to their superiors. When they ask themselves, "What do I have to gain by telling my boss about his development needs?" they struggle for an answer.

Formal feedback helps reduce the interpersonal threat of face-to-face feedback for both parties. The formalized structure and the neutral character of the instruments serve as a medium of objectivity. As one participant in a leader development program stated, "Normally, the thought of having someone give me job feedback is like going to the dentist. Even though I'm glad I did it after it's all over, I have white knuckles the whole time I'm in the chair. Using a 360-degree feedback instrument makes the process easier to take because it is broken down into specific manageable pieces. I can reflect on my data privately and then talk with someone who knows how to help me understand them."

Multiple Perspectives. "If one person tells you that you remind him of a horse's backside," the wisdom goes, "you can ignore him. If ten people tell you the same thing, you probably ought to go ahead and get fitted for a saddle." There is strength in numbers. Managers receiving 360-degree feedback can be jarred to attention about their shortcomings by agreement among their raters.

The other benefit of collecting data from different rater groups (bosses, peers, and direct reports) is that the participant gets to see a panorama of perceptions, presenting a more complete picture than that afforded by any one group. For example, in many cases, subordinates and peers are in a better position than the immediate boss to evaluate certain competencies, such as interpersonal behavior (Bracken, 1996). Or different people may simply have different expectations or values, which in turn create differences in perceptions about the participant's skills or performance.

Challenge

Even though 360-degree feedback is strong on assessment, the process itself can be a source of challenge. As a *Fortune* magazine article put it, "What your boss, your peers, and your subordinates really think of you may sting, but facing the truth can also make you a better manager" (O'Reilly, 1994, p. 93). The 360-degree feedback process forces managers to examine the perspectives other people hold of them. For some participants, taking part in such a process is the first opportunity they have had to seriously examine their strengths and weaknesses. This exposure to other views and the resulting self-examination can create disequilibrium, causing people to question the adequacy of their skills or perspectives.

This was very true for an individual I worked with recently at a large aeronautical manufacturing company. Phil, a young engineer, had been identified early on as a high-potential employee and was placed on his organization's fast track. He had impressive intellectual capacity and was known for getting results. One of his brightest moments came when he solved a problem that no one else, including some senior engineers, had been able to fix. This was a high-stakes problem for the company, and solving it gave Phil's career a substantial boost.

Over the years, Phil was progressively given more responsibility. There was no question in Phil's mind that he was being groomed for a senior leadership position in this organization, and that was precisely what he wanted. However, a pattern was emerging. Phil noticed that despite the technical successes he was having, no one seemed eager to work with him. The ultimate blow came when he was passed over to lead the team that was developing a high-visibility space exploration project. This was a wake-up call for Phil, to say the least. He consulted with a senior engineer in the company whom he respected. The senior engineer suggested that Phil collect anonymous feedback from a variety of his coworkers by using a multirater feedback instrument.

When I met with Phil to review his feedback, he was shocked at what he found in his report. Phil viewed himself as smart, focused on problems, and above office politics. By comparison, his coworkers saw him as arrogant, clueless about the people issues, and naive about how decisions are made. The difference between how he perceived his behavior and the way the others perceived him was startling for Phil. Normally, he would have dismissed the data as just plain wrong, but in this case there were eight people clearly agreeing that Phil's interpersonal shortcomings were causing problems. It was, for him, a blind spot that he wanted desperately to eliminate. Phil was motivated to improve his interpersonal style. He had to, for the writing on the wall was clear: change or become derailed.

A 360-degree feedback instrument can provide challenge in a second way also. It can help make participants aware of what skills and behaviors are valued in their organization. In other words, it holds up a model of what it takes to be high-performing in the organization, and the assessment data show how the participant measures up to that standard.

The simple process of completing the survey—reading and answering the specific questions on the feedback instrument—puts these described behaviors out in front of the participant and triggers discussion of them. For example, a large European insurance company decided that the key to its survival was to be less bureaucratic and more entrepreneurial. The company searched for and found a 360-degree feedback instrument designed to specifically measure behaviors known to exist in successful entrepreneurial environments. The company has now implemented the use of this 360-degree feedback instrument with its senior managers and is preparing to introduce it more broadly to its mid-level managers.

Another example comes from the era of deregulation in the telephone industry. One service provider decided that as a market edge, it was going to pursue excellence in customer service. Most of the company's managers had been hired at a time when telephone customers did not have options and were forced to live with the service they received. This company started a major initiative that included conducting internal customer service workshops, individual coaching, pushing decision making downward in the organization, and completing 360-degree feedback to focus on decisiveness, customer focus, and responsiveness. As a result, it was able to help the managers see where their skills did or did not match the organization's valued behaviors.

Other aspects of the 360-degree feedback process can call out the value an organization is placing on new ways of working. This sort of feedback is particularly useful in supporting three types of organizational values: open communication, valuing employee input, and setting expectations that people should take charge of their careers. Here are some illustrations:

• A major urban hotel group wanted to encourage open communication among the six co-owners of the company. One part of the hotel's approach was to initiate a regular 360-degree feedback process in which each of the six participants was a rater for all the others. This served to contain the feedback within this particular group. This process and the ensuing discussion helped establish an environment of open conversation among the co-owners. By asking others to complete the survey, these leaders indicated that they are amenable to performance feedback. They were, in a sense, establishing a norm for communication as well as establishing a common language (as used in the survey) to discuss performance-based feedback in the future.

• One organization became particularly interested in using a 360-degree feedback instrument as part of its efforts to enhance employees' sense of participation and empowerment. The process of multirater assessment is inclusive; soliciting participation from diverse rater groups indicates that the organization is interested in their perspectives.

• An international consumer products company encouraged its managers to actively plan their career progression from the day they are hired. The company used 360-degree feedback to put data in the managers' hands and responsibility for career planning on their shoulders.

Support

To maximize the developmental potential of 360-degree feedback, elements of support need to be designed into the experience. Support helps people handle the potential growing pains and challenges often associated with personal development. Let's return to the earlier example of Phil. He initially received support when entering the 360-degree feedback experience (a respected colleague had encouraged him). He had support when he received his feedback (a trained feedback facilitator helped him understand his data). But support doesn't stop there. Phil was motivated to improve his interpersonal style. He knew it was probably not possible for him to change the combination of genetic coding and early life experiences that combine to make up his personality (and besides, that is not what Phil's coworkers were asking him to do). What he could—and did—change were some specific behaviors he used with some coworkers. Phil accessed two sources of support to make that change: He worked with a mentor to structure a development plan for himself, and he asked his coworkers for encouragement and to be patient with him as he tried out some behaviors that were awkward for him at first.

Strategies for building support into 360-degree feedback will be discussed in more detail throughout the chapter, but to summarize briefly, support is enhanced in 360-degree feedback by the following actions:

- Establishing a systematic and safe learning environment by maintaining the confidential nature of the feedback data
- Giving participants access to a trained feedback facilitator for clarification about the data and for guidance in putting together a development plan
- Involving superiors, to gain buy-in for the participant's development plan
- Allowing the participant and immediate boss to meet beforehand to discuss their goals for the process
- Offering organizational support for the kinds of assignments that are known to contribute to effective development of leaders
- Strategizing with the participant about how to receive ongoing feedback after the formal 360-degree feedback process is over
- Structuring an organizational norm for following up periodically on the development plan

Administrative Versus Developmental Use

An ongoing debate within the community of 360-degree feedback users is whether the feedback should be used only for the development of the participants receiving the feedback or whether it should also be used for administrative purposes (see Bracken and others, 1997). When feedback is used for development purposes, the data help the participants set in place a plan to increase their effectiveness in the organization. (All of the examples used so far in this chapter have represented developmental use.) Administrative purposes, by comparison, involve using 360-degree feedback results to make decisions about hiring, promotion, or compensation.

A critical difference between these two approaches is ownership of the data. In assessment for administration, the participant's organization owns the data. The final assessment might be shared with the participant, but it is also used by the boss, human resource representative, or others in the organization for administrative decisions. In assessment for development, the individual participant owns the data. Although the participant may be encouraged to share some of the data and the development plan with his or her boss, the feedback report itself is confidential to the participant. He or she alone decides if, with whom, and how to share the completed report data and what action to take, if any.

In our work at CCL, we use 360-degree feedback for development purposes only. There is increasing pressure in some organizations to tie assessment to administrative uses, but sufficient evidence shows that rater responses change when they know the resulting data will be made public (London and Smither, 1995). In general, raters tend to score people more leniently if they know it could affect their salary or promotion opportunities. Such data are less accurate and therefore not so helpful to people who want to make changes. Ultimately, if the participants own the data, the organization places the primary responsibility for personal development squarely on the participants. That does not mean, however, that a participant's feedback report should go from the hands of the participant into a black hole, never to be discussed. Effective use of a 360-degree feedback instrument means that the individual uses the confidential feedback results as a springboard to establish a development plan that should be shared with his or her manager, for example. In the long run, the organization benefits by allowing the report to be confidential but expecting the participant to act on its content.

Because the focus of this handbook is on the development of leaders and because CCL's experience is in using 360-degree feedback for development purposes, the feedback processes and practices described in the rest of this chapter assume that the 360-degree assessment is for development.

The Impact of 360-Degree Feedback

A number of studies indicate that multirater feedback can have a positive impact on individuals (Atwater, Roush, and Fischthal, 1995; Avery, 2001; Bernardin, Hagan, and Kane, 1995; Hazucha, Hezlett, and Schneider, 1993; Hegarty, 1974; Johnson and Ferstl, 1999; Reilly, Smither, and Vasilopoulos, 1996; Smither and others, 1995; Walker and Smither, 1999). Many of these studies focus on the impact of upward feedback (from the subordinate to the manager). Empirical research on the impact of 360-degree feedback has focused on two types of evidence: (1) the degree to which self-ratings become more congruent with ratings from others, which serves as an indication of an increase in individuals' awareness of how others view their skills and behaviors, and (2) the degree to which behaviors are changed in useful ways.

A consistent finding in longitudinal studies of impact (when participants are rated on the multirater instrument two or more times) is that the most improvement in performance following feedback occurs in managers initially rated moderate to low (Atwater, Rousch, and Fischthal, 1995; Avery, 2001; Johnson and Ferstl, 1999; Reilly, Smither, and Vasilopoulos, 1996; Smither and others, 1995). Only a few studies have inspected other moderators of the feedback-improvement relationship. Hazucha, Hezlett, and Schneider (1993) found more evidence of changed behaviors following 360-degree feedback among managers who obtained input from coworkers on their development plans, reviewed their plans and progress regularly, and received ongoing coaching and feedback. Walker and Smither (1999) found that managers who met with direct reports to discuss their upward feedback improved more than other managers.

Assessing change in individuals has always been a measurement and evaluation challenge, and linking those changes to organizational improvement is complex (see Chapter Eight). Also, isolating the impact of 360-degree feedback can be difficult because it is often used as part of multifaceted development programs or coaching interventions. Bracken, Timmreck, Fleenor, and Summers (2001) suggest that ultimately the organization has to determine whether the 360-degree feedback initiative creates focused and sustained behavioral change and skill development in a sufficient number of people so as to result in increased organizational effectiveness.

Designing a 360-Degree Feedback Process

The process of using a 360-degree feedback instrument in a way that maximizes the organization's investment and leads to the best opportunity for the participant's continued growth and development is complex. The steps outlined here—many of which occur long before the first survey is filled out by a rater—can help the organization get the most from its investment.

Step 1: Identify the Purpose

At the most basic level, human resource professionals setting out to design and deliver a feedback intervention must be clear up front on these questions: Why is this needed? Whom is it for? What outcomes are expected? (Dalton and Hollenbeck, 1996). One common mistake that organizations make is to commit to an assessment activity without clearly defining what they hope to gain from it and without connecting it to specific business needs. Choosing a feedback instrument involves first identifying the business purpose and the target population for the 360-degree feedback.

The business purpose should drive the decision about what kind of instrument to select. A manager's performance is defined within the context of a business strategy—and so should the selection of the feedback instrument. All too often, one particular 360-degree feedback instrument is chosen simply because an HR executive or consultant has an affinity for it and tries to use it in all cases. You are better off, however, clearly identifying why the assessment activity is needed and then finding the best instrument for that purpose. If the purpose of the feedback intervention is to focus the participants on organizational competencies, the instrument should ask questions that connect to the particular competency model.

Step 2: Identify the Audience

Once the business need for the assessment has been defined, identify the target population. This is essential for choosing the right instrument. People at any level can benefit from 360-degree feedback, but care should be taken to ensure that the instrument is appropriate for the participants' particular situation. For example, an instrument containing many questions about managerial skills would probably not work well with lower-level staff or individual contributors.

Managers need different kinds of feedback at different times in their careers. Early on, they might use 360-degree feedback to help define what skills are important. Later in their careers, they need to know how their strengths and weaknesses affect others, to make any changes needed. As they continue to move higher in the organization, it may be critical to use 360-degree feedback to evaluate their ability to set and implement a vision for the company's future success.

Step 3: Choose an Instrument

It is not my goal here to provide a detailed guide to selecting from among the scores of 360-degree feedback instruments on the market. A comprehensive source for that purpose is *Choosing 360: A Guide to Evaluating Multi-Rater Feedback Instruments for Management Development* (Van Velsor, Leslie, and Fleenor, 1997). I will describe some basic steps, however, that can help guide your search.

The first step in narrowing your selection is to find an established tool with psychometric integrity. It should be professionally developed and adequately tested. Is the instrument valid? Does it really measure what it claims to measure, and are the resulting scores empirically related to effectiveness on the job? Is the instrument reliable? Is it stable over time? Do the items within a scale measure the same construct? Is there agreement within rater groups? The vendor should be willing to answer these basic questions and provide you with supporting information.

When selecting an instrument, be a savvy consumer. Ask the vendor for a summary report of the research foundations for the instrument. Obtain samples of the survey and feedback report. The individual items should make sense to you, and they should reflect behaviors that are valued by the organization.

Other things to investigate include accompanying materials and vendor support. Is there a developmental planning guide to help participants sort their data and set a workable plan for change? Does the organization have adequate resources to respond to questions or problems encountered in using the instrument? Organizations have a choice of using a preexisting standardized assessment instrument developed by a vendor (sometimes called an "off-the-shelf" instrument) or having one custom designed specifically for a particular organization's use. Unfortunately, there is no such thing as the perfect instrument, and there are advantages and disadvantages to both types.

A primary advantage to using an existing instrument is cost; it is usually less expensive to use an existing feedback instrument than it is to hire someone to design and develop an instrument, scoring program, and supporting materials to accompany it. Also, an existing 360-degree feedback instrument can provide extensive normative data so that participants have the opportunity to compare their scores to many other managers in other organizations.

An advantage to creating a customized instrument is that the questions can be tailored to measure the specific competencies your organization considers important. At first glance, this may seem the best route to follow. Organizations are like families: they all like to think that theirs is unique—the best or the most unusual—and hence no existing instrument could capture the essence of their particular situation. It is usually not difficult for an organization to draw up a list of behaviors and outcomes, generally called competencies, it deems essential or desirable. The difficulty comes in designing the survey, scoring program, and supporting materials to test for these competencies.

More important than the logistical challenge of creating a customized instrument is carrying out the validity and reliability studies to ensure that the instrument is psychometrically sound. Some organizations do not care if the instrument does not meet these standards and therefore never conduct these studies so long as they are able to use their unique list of competencies. This is a shortsighted approach. If the organization is asking participants to be open to the feedback and to make changes in their behavior based on the results, it should ensure that the feedback is valid.

A third approach is to customize an existing instrument. This allows you to tailor the content and length of the instrument, selecting competencies from existing individual development instruments and combining them to create an instrument that closely reflects the competencies of interest to the organization. One advantage to this approach is that it ensures the organization of valid and reliable questionnaire items.

In the end, many organizations realize that there are good standardized instruments that already measure the majority of competencies or behaviors that they have identified as important; they conclude that the logistical and cost factors involved with customizing an assessment are not worth it. Now that so many 360-degree feedback instruments are available, most organizations should be able to find a good tool that matches the business need and works for the particular population being assessed.

Step 4: Internal Communication

Each person involved in the assessment and feedback process should be adequately prepared for his or her role. The purpose for the activity and the expected outcomes should be explained fully, and it should be made clear how the feedback will be used. I recently worked with a regional electric utility that did this particularly well. The company held a half-day session to kick off the assessment phase of the development program for upper managers. The participants who were to receive feedback, their bosses, and their raters attended this session together. The president of the company addressed the background and goal of the overall program. A senior human resource executive then introduced the 360-degree feedback instrument and discussed its purpose. She presented raters with instructions intended to reduce rating errors, identified deadlines, and distributed all materials on the spot. The bosses or coaches of the participants attended an additional afternoon session that helped them understand how to best support the participant's future developmental planning process.

Step 5: Collecting the Data

Once an organization selects the best instrument for its use, it must provide the proper structure to help the participants collect the best data possible.

Rater Selection. The participant typically collects feedback from his or her boss, peers, and direct reports. The instrument vendor usually suggests the optimal number of raters for each group; a typical distribution is one boss, five peers, five direct reports, and miscellaneous "others." The most accurate responses come from raters who have had a chance to observe the manager using a wide variety of behaviors over time. Therefore, it is most beneficial for the participants to select raters who have worked closely with them over time.

Some organizations prefer to control distribution of surveys by selecting the raters for the participant. A possible disadvantage to this approach is that it could deter buy-in by the participant being assessed. Most organizations let the participant select the raters (Farr and Newman, 2001).

Rater Anonymity. The sensitive nature of personal feedback data requires that care be taken to protect the privacy of the raters. If the raters suspect that their feedback is not anonymous, they may be reluctant to participate in the process or may answer the questions more favorably than they would if their responses were protected (Van Velsor, 1998).

Feedback reports should be constructed so that participants have no way to tell "who said what." This is typically done by requiring a minimum of three respondents in each rater category and presenting these data in aggregate form. If fewer than three people in one category return surveys, the participant's report does not include item-level feedback in that category. A common exception is with the boss's feedback. These data are frequently identified separately. In this case, the materials should give the boss clear notice that his or her responses will not be anonymous.

Some instruments provide a way for raters to add written comments, expanding their feedback to include data that the instrument does not capture. Having these more extensive comments can be an advantage, but it comes with a potential disadvantage: loss of anonymity. The participant may be able to identify the rater's handwriting or communication style. Thus simply requiring the raters to type their comments offers only partial protection, as open-ended questions and verbatim comments make it harder to protect rater anonymity.

The other downside to using verbatim comments is the possibility of a "verbatim bias." Anecdotal experience resulting from the individual feedback sessions has shown that participants often give more attention to written comments than numerical or graphical scores. No matter what the scores on the standardized part of the assessment, people often tend to focus on and remember the written comments more. As a result, verbatim comments that are inconsistent with the numerical results can unfairly skew the participant's interpretation of the data. Feedback facilitators need to help participants keep verbatim comments in perspective.

Data Confidentiality. The data collected through 360-degree feedback instruments belong to the individual participants and should not be viewed by anyone else without the participants' consent. Breaches of confidentiality and rater anonymity, even if accidental, can jeopardize the feedback process, compromise the integrity of the human resource group, and lead to a lack of trust in any subsequent assessment activities. Take the utmost care throughout the entire feedback process to protect these data.

Step 6: Feeding Back the Data

How the feedback is delivered to participants varies, depending on the type of instrument being used and the organization's plan for its implementation. The three most common approaches are a one-on-one session, a group session, or a combination of the two.

In the one-on-one approach, the participant has an individual session with a facilitator that includes an introduction to the background of the instrument, an interpretive session about the participant's data, and further assistance with developmental planning.

The second approach involves participants' going through the feedback experience at the same time in a group setting. They receive an introduction to the instrument, get their individual feedback data, and participate in development planning activities as a group. (They have individual time to read and interpret their own data.) This approach is less staff-intensive and affords the opportunity to use small group activities, when appropriate, to enhance learning. The disadvantage is that the participants do not have an opportunity to speak privately with a facilitator to discuss their data.

Combining a group session and individual one-on-one sessions often provides optimal outcomes. In this scenario, the general presentation is made once in a group setting, but the individuals meet one-on-one with a facilitator to discuss their personal data privately.

Even instruments that are fairly simple and straightforward are enhanced by a private consultation with a facilitator who has experience using the tool. This is particularly true for participants receiving 360-degree feedback for the first time. They typically appreciate the opportunity to open up and discuss their feedback, good or bad, with a dispassionate third party.

One large pharmaceutical firm maintains a pool of eight independent consultants to deliver instrument feedback as part of its leader development program for middle managers. The company finds that this gives the process additional credibility, since the organization is investing in these "experts." It also reinforces the confidential nature of the data, since no company employees (even those in human resources) see the participants' reports.

It is helpful if the participants have ample time to analyze their data before the one-on-one session. For the sake of efficiency, it is tempting to hand participants their report, give them a few minutes to digest the data, and then shuttle them off to their one-on-one. When this happens, participants arrive for the feedback session still trying to understand what the numbers, graphs, or tables mean. With no time to reflect on the feedback, they will probably not be ready to consider the full implications of the data when they come to the individual session.

It is ideal to give participants an overnight break between receiving the feedback and having the one-on-one session. If they have a chance to sleep on the data, they usually understand the details better, have time to come to terms with any emotional reactions, and are fresher for the meeting. But feedback does have a shelf life. Ideally, the one-on-one session should occur within four days of delivery of the data, while the information is still fresh in the participant's mind.

Step 7: Interpreting the Data

Beyond the absolute value of the numbers and graphs displayed on a participant's feedback report, there is a great deal to be learned by the level of agreement among raters on both competency and importance ratings.

Are Importance Ratings Important? Many 360-degree feedback instruments ask the raters to identify a limited number of competencies that are particularly important for success in the participant's position or organization. The data are tabulated and presented in the feedback report. The participants can then compare their perceptions of which competency areas are most important to the perceptions of their raters and use those similarities and discrepancies to prioritize development goals (Dalessio and Vasilopoulos, 2001).

These importance ratings are typically welcomed by the participants, who feel that the ratings give them a way to focus on whatever feedback appears to be most important. For example, Joe received negative feedback from his raters on the scale that measures "managing relationships." However, out of eight raters, none indicated that "managing relationships" was one of the five most important competencies. As a result, Joe ignored this feedback and concentrated on other areas for improvement.

The problem is that the accuracy of importance ratings has not been established on most 360-degree feedback instruments. Even for instruments that have sound psychometric properties for items and dimensions, the importance ratings may not have been subjected to the same scrutiny. Therefore, it would be prudent for Joe's feedback facilitator to encourage him not to completely discount his relationship feedback. It could be that every single rater thought that there were six critical competencies for Joe's job, but the limitations of the instrument forced them to pick five. If that sixth most important item in Joe's case is managing relationships, he has missed a major part of his feedback. In addition, it could be that Joe's raters do not know what is really important for success in his job, either because they do not know his job well or because they are mistaken about the real selection criteria used within the company.

Self-Rater Agreement. Participants tend to pay close attention to the degree to which their own ratings of their performance agree with the ratings from others. In general, there tends to be closer agreement between peers and supervisors than with either self and peer or self and supervisor (Harris and Schaubroeck, 1988). This would suggest that self-perception of strengths and weaknesses is more out of alignment than the collective perceptions among raters. Does that matter? Besides, who is right?

It can matter a great deal. In their study on executive derailment, McCall and Lombardo (1983) found that when many executives derailed, it was because they had blind spots. They were unaware of or ignored the fatal flaws that had led to termination or missed promotions. Using a sound 360-degree feedback instrument can be a first step in reducing or eliminating these blind spots.

As to who is right, people need to consider whether a discrepancy represents inaccuracy on their part or merely a difference of opinion. Campbell and Nilsen (1993) suggest that when it comes to predicting job performance, the other raters are more accurate than the participant. Dunnette's analysis (1993) suggests that in some cases self-scores are more accurate.

Also, does a discrepancy mean that a person is unaware of strengths and weaknesses? Fleenor, McCauley, and Brutus (1996) believe that a self-other discrepancy does not necessarily represent low awareness. Their findings suggest that it could be a reflection of either arrogance (on the part of those who rate themselves higher than others rate them) or modesty (by those who rate themselves lower than others do). That is, overraters or underraters may understand how they are perceived by others but choose not to believe it.

Even though a divergence of opinion might make the feedback harder to interpret, it does represent the real environment in which people must do their work. One implication for the feedback facilitator is that it is important to hear the participant's reaction to any self-rater disagreement on the report and to use that response to frame a context for the feedback.

When Raters Disagree. Unanimous agreement, even if less than complimentary, would be easy to understand, but it occurs only rarely. It is far more common for people to be perceived differently by different rater groups. This variance can cause considerable confusion for the participants unless they are able to think the reasons through. Helping participants with this analysis is one of the functions of the debriefing session with the feedback specialist.

There are many valid reasons why feedback is not uniform (Moxley and McCauley, 1996). It may be that the participant behaves differently with the various rater groups. The amount of exposure that someone has with different groups also explains variations in perception. Perhaps one rater group has more opportunities to see the person using the behavior being rated than another rater group does. Also, the raters' expectations come into play. The rater groups may have differing expectations about how the participant will use the specific behavior when interacting with them, and so they have their own opinions as to whether the behavior, or its absence, is a problem. Finally, two observers can interpret the same behavior very differently. For example, consider a manager who is blunt in his interpersonal interactions. One observer might interpret the behavior as direct, efficient, and precise. Another observer might see the same behavior as abrupt or even rude.

Even though interpreting their significance sometimes takes work, obtaining multiple perspectives on performance is an improvement over the traditional assessment approach in which only the boss evaluates performance (known as the "top-down" approach). Multiple views of a 360-degree process are preferable for a number of reasons:

- They reflect a more comprehensive representation of a manager's reality, in which a multiplicity of views need to be taken into account. A typical manager today may supervise double or triple the number of staff members than was typical ten years ago.
- They reduce the potential for bias (London and Beatty, 1993).
- The boss often does not observe the individual's behavior daily, especially if the two are located in different buildings, regions, or even countries—conditions that make it very difficult to maintain an accurate, ongoing assessment.
- The increase in team-based work has dictated the need for collecting and synthesizing other team members' feedback.
- Previously untapped sources of feedback can be included. Some leaders are in a position of being judged for their effectiveness by how well they work with people outside the organization, such as customers, suppliers, or clients.

Step 8: Creating a Development Plan

The process of collecting data and reading the feedback report is not, by itself, developmental. Development is what happens after the participant begins to digest, understand, and, most of all, plan to change his or her behavior. Feedback interventions are more effective when they are accompanied by goal-setting activities (De Nisi and Kluger, 2000). To adopt a 360-degree feedback process without defining the development goals of the process leaves the participants to fend for themselves, and they tend not to follow through on the identification and pursuit of development goals or action plans (Antonioni, 1996). Quality developmental planning is more than just an exercise in goal setting. It is a thorough blueprint for achieving and sustaining behavior change by using a variety of strategies proven to enhance learning.

When using 360-degree feedback as a springboard for setting a development plan, the participant should ask the following three questions about his or her goals:

1. Does the goal motivate and energize me?
2. Will achieving this goal help me be more effective in my current position?
3. Will my organization benefit from this goal?

If the answer to any of the questions is no, the individual may not be focusing on the right goal.

Once an appropriate goal has been identified, the individual should use a variety of strategies to achieve it. For example, most workshop leaders or feedback facilitators have had this experience: An eager participant, sincerely motivated to make behavioral changes as a result of a formal feedback event, sets out to plan for personal change. The first question he asks is, "Can you recommend a good book (or workshop) on this subject?" By using this approach only, the individual is closing himself off to the richest developmental activities at his disposal. One study indicates that reading and classes account for only 6 percent of the events that teach the key managerial lessons (McCall, Lombardo, and Morrison, 1988). It would be much more effective to set a development strategy that takes into account a broad variety of experiences:

• *New job assignments.* When practical, new jobs with different duties—starting something from scratch, fixing something gone wrong, moving from a line to a staff job, or accepting a broad change in scope and scale of responsibilities—can teach a wide variety of important lessons. (See Chapter Five for more on job assignments.)

• *Existing jobs.* There may be tremendous potential for development in someone's present job. By becoming aware of the challenges in their current role, and how these challenges can teach critical lessons, people are in a better position to capitalize on them and address development needs quickly.

• *Ongoing feedback.* A critical component of any development plan is to build in progress checks. This feedback may be formal or informal, but the plan should provide for collecting it regularly.

• *Role models.* An excellent developmental opportunity is to watch someone else do something well. For example, if a participant decides to work on delegating more effectively, she should identify someone she knows who does it well. Then she should go out of her way to observe that person in action and try to discover what makes him effective. It would also help to engage that person in ongoing conversations about this subject. (See Chapter Three for more on developmental relationships.)

• *Training and reading.* As mentioned earlier, this constitutes a small part of the sum total of developmental learning, but it can be an important one for some individuals.

Web-Based Advances in the Implementation of 360-Degree Feedback

The most significant change in the administration of 360-degree feedback has been the development of computer-based assessment tools. The number of computer-based assessment vendors has increased as many internal human resource processes look to outside vendors and software applications. Evidence of this phenomenon is clear when one walks through the vendor exposition area at professional conferences geared toward the HR professional. The presence of computers in the vendor booths creates the atmosphere of a high-tech expo.

Successive advances of technology have simplified the administration of this inherently complex process (Summers, 2001). The vehicle of choice has evolved from floppy disk to CD-ROM to intranet to the vast majority of organizations using electronic 360-degree instruments via the Internet. These systems typically make efficient use of e-mail notification and Web-based survey collection systems. Participants can set up their rater groups by entering raters on a password-protected Web site. Raters receive an invitation e-mail with a link to the Web site embedded in the e-mail.

Although there are clear advantages to a Web-based system, there are trade-offs involved in using technology for 360-degree feedback administration.

Advantages. The attractiveness of an Internet-based system over a paper-and-pencil system is primarily speed of administration and user convenience (Huet-Cox, Nielsen, and Sundstrom, 1999). Cost, accuracy, and ease of linkage are other advantages.

The convenience to the organization lies in two areas. First, Web-based applications eliminate paper surveys and the inherent hassle of distribution, tracking, and collection. The second convenience lies in the ability to log on to a Web page to check the status of assessments currently in process. Any raters or participants who have not yet returned surveys can easily be reminded by e-mail.

Speed is improved because the total time for deploying an assessment activity can be reduced by eliminating the shipping time. My experience with client use of online 360-degree feedback instruments (versus paper-based ones) is that the total turnover time savings is approximately 30 percent for a domestic user and more for global users. The individual raters save time as well. In one pilot program, participants with a basic level of Web navigation skills took approximately twenty minutes to complete the online version, compared with thirty-five minutes for the paper-and-pencil version.

The obvious way organizations can save money by using an online 360-degree feedback instrument is through the elimination of all or almost all shipping charges. Because completed surveys are commonly shipped by priority carriers at premium cost, the cumulative effect of hundreds of surveys being returned for scoring adds up. Again, this is particularly true for multinational initiatives. If the final surveys are made available to the participants electronically and not on hard copy, there are virtually no shipping costs involved in the initiative. The instrument purchase price might be lower as well. Some vendors are able to sell assessment services at a lower cost as a result of less investment on their part in stock.

Web-based implementation can also improve the accuracy of the feedback data. With most systems, the participant gets to select the raters and identify the rater relationship before the rater logs on to complete the survey. This is an improvement over the paper-and-pencil approach, which usually dictates that the rater identifies the relationship with the participant. When raters identify the rater relationship, they will sometimes identify themselves differently than the participant would. For example, a rater might consider herself a "superior" and identify herself as such on the returned survey, even though the participant might consider that rater a "peer" and expects to see that person's feedback appear in the peer category on the feedback report.

Finally, by name and by function, the Web is an entry point easily linked to other places. As such, an individual's feedback report can provide links to a developmental planning process. More sophisticated systems can customize the participants' developmental planning process to their feedback results. For example, the scoring system might be programmed to identify a participant's lowest feedback scores from all raters and automatically print out a list of suggestions for development in that particular area.

Potential Disadvantages. The responsible use of a quality Web-based 360-degree feedback system has many advantages, but it does have some disadvantages as well. Of most concern are potential technology issues and privacy issues, both of which should be addressed prior to an organization's investment in an online system.

For a Web-based system to work effectively, each person in the process must have an individual e-mail address and relatively private access to a computer with the correct Web browser software. Many organizations have internal security systems such as firewalls that serve to protect their physical and intellectual property. Settings must be adjusted so that participants and raters can access the vendor's

Web sites and receive the e-mails involved. If raters are completing surveys from home or while traveling using a dial-up modem, the bandwidth required by the assessment could make the process excruciatingly slow.

If the individual feedback report is ultimately going to be made available to the participant and feedback facilitator electronically, it opens doors for control problems. For example, any time a file is e-mailed from one location to another (for example, from the scoring location to the facilitator and then on to the participant), a copy of that report has likely been saved at each stop. Users must establish a process regarding the deletion of electronic copies of the report.

Why 360-Degree Feedback Initiatives Fail

I believe that conscientious use of a 360-degree assessment initiative is a cost-effective way to encourage leader development in an organization. To achieve the maximum return on what is typically a $100- to $400-per-person investment, it is wise to avoid some of the common mistakes people make when using a 360-degree feedback instrument.

Mistaking an Assessment Activity for a Development Process

Savvy HR executives understand that a 360-degree feedback activity is not a stand-alone event. The feedback by itself probably does not have a long-lasting effect or lead to behavioral change. In fact, providing assessment without developmental planning and follow-up almost guarantees that the organization will not get its money's worth. As one senior manager from a large bank noted, "We have access to some of the best 360-degree feedback instruments on the market through our human resource office. The problem is, nothing happens afterward. You are on your own to try to guess how best to carry on. Your boss may even hold you back. We even have a name for it; we call it 'drive-by assessment.'" The way for an organization to realize a return on the money and effort invested in a 360-degree feedback instrument is to make the feedback event part of a larger, ongoing development process.

Not Getting the Boss's Support

To achieve a developmental target, participants should solicit the buy-in and support of their bosses or, as an alternative, an executive coach. Managers who have bosses who support these changes are more likely to achieve the changes in the end (Hazucha, Hezlett, and Schneider, 1993).

An international pet food company follows a simple model of boss-participant meetings that work well for this purpose. Before completing the assessment forms, the participant meets with his or her boss or coach to discuss how to use the information collected by the assessment (for example, to get a promotion, to work more effectively with subordinates, or to identify the next logical job challenge). They then agree on a date for a second meeting to take place after the participant receives the feedback report and has a one-on-one consultation with a feedback facilitator.

After the participant receives feedback and has had an opportunity to identify development goals, he or she meets with the boss or coach to discuss the goals identified and to elicit the buy-in and support of the effort from the boss. A secondary purpose of this meeting is to allow for any clarification (in a nondefensive manner) the participant might need regarding the boss's feedback. This would apply only when the 360-degree feedback instrument has the boss's scores broken out separately.

The participant and boss meet again after six months to discuss the progress made toward the development goals. The goals can be refined or redirected by the participant, if necessary. The two then set a date and time for another progress check in six months.

Starting with the Wrong People

Some organizations have learned through experience not to start a 360-degree feedback initiative with the participants at the lowest level, the ones with the greatest resistance, or the ones who need to be "fixed." If the assessment process is to be spread across different levels of the organization, it can be difficult to decide where to start. The recommended approach is to start at a high level in the organization and move downward.

A security equipment manufacturer I worked with had success using this "cascading" approach. The company identified a need to become more action-oriented and decisive. It hoped that having a more entrepreneurial approach would result in shorter delivery cycles. Every individual in the organization was required to participate in a 360-degree assessment process that measured these and other behaviors. This initiative was set in a sixteen-month developmental process within the organization. The president of the company and three vice presidents were the first to complete the assessment and receive feedback. The activity was then delivered to the directors and so on down through the company, until all 250 employees were included.

The organization reported that using this particular approach had two clear benefits. First, starting with the top executives demonstrated their buy-in to the process and modeled openness to feedback. The second benefit was that all employees had the opportunity to complete the survey as a rater for someone else before having the assessment done on them. This helped them become familiar with the kinds of questions being asked and helped demystify the process in general. Starting the process as a rater, in turn, helped them not dismiss other raters' data on them when their turn came.

Ignoring Individual Readiness

It is sometimes easy to overlook the importance of the individual's readiness and willingness to take part in a 360-degree feedback event—particularly when it is part of a larger organization initiative that has already developed momentum. For a 360-degree feedback process to be effective, "a participant must first be willing to accept feedback as relevant and useful and be open to change" (Day, 2000, p. 590). When is the best time for people to receive feedback? When are they most open to hearing feedback and motivated to make behavioral changes? In CCL's experience, a person in the midst of a career transition, such as a significant increase in the scope and scale of his or her job, is usually more motivated to consider 360-degree feedback than someone who is continuing with business as usual. People who sense a need to break out of a rut are often particularly open to performance feedback if they think it will help them make a transition. Finally, people who are being sent messages from the organization that they must change or face derailment may be the most motivated of all.

Shoddy Administration

Even a well-planned 360-degree feedback initiative can fall short if the many small details, which make up the administrative process, are overlooked. To ensure a smoothly administered process, be sure to do all of the following:

- *Insist on process integrity.* This effort should be the best work of which the organization is capable. It is crucial to maintain the integrity of the process through confidential handling of sensitive material.
- *Commit to 100 percent accuracy.* Implement administrative checklists to ensure that all raters have the correct materials and know how and when to return them.
- *Anticipate what will go wrong.* Plan for unexpected events: slow mailing systems, raters on vacation, program materials being held up in customs, and so on.
- *Start small.* An organization's first 360-degree intervention should start with a small pilot group, to work out the kinks before rolling out a large initiative.

- *Make administration user-friendly.* Find ways to make it simple for people to participate. Plan ahead, give plenty of lead time, and use postage-paid return envelopes. Publish the name and contact information of the process administrator in all materials.

To protect the confidentiality of the raters, most 360-degree feedback instruments require that a certain minimum number of instruments (typically three) be returned from each rater group. It is important, therefore, for each rater to complete a survey and return it on time. Announce the schedule with deadlines well in advance. Monitor the survey return status. Use e-mail or telephone reminders to contact any nonrespondents as the deadline date approaches.

Ignoring Organizational Readiness

Check the timing of the event, and be sensitive to what else is going on in the organization that might get in the way of successful implementation. Midway through a downsizing is not the best time to conduct this activity, nor are heavy vacation periods. Are there other survey-intensive activities occurring at the same time? If so, reschedule the 360-degree feedback activity to avoid survey fatigue.

The increased popularity of 360-degree feedback with intact teams means larger workloads. In these cases, the boss is likely completing surveys for each person in his or her group, and the group members are all rating each other. At twenty to fifty minutes for each form, this can become an overwhelming time commitment. The best way to avoid this problem is to allow the participants as much lead time as possible to spread the task out and to inform the participants in advance of how long it takes to complete one survey.

Confidentiality and Anonymity Problems

Quality implementation requires keen attention to protecting the anonymity of the raters. It is important to note that the boss and possibly other superiors are often exceptions to the anonymity rule, and their feedback is often displayed in isolation. If this will be the case, they should be advised of this ahead of time in the survey instructions. The sponsoring organization should also make the survey return process a secure one. A process that permits direct return to the scoring organization gives a greater perception of rater anonymity. The integrity of the instrument and the feedback process also depend on complete confidentiality of the participant's feedback report data. Ideally, the participant and the feedback facilitator, if applicable, should be the only ones to receive a copy of the participant's feedback report. Confidentiality of results should be clarified before planning the event.

Finally, have a sunset clause on data. What is the shelf life of an individual's report data? This varies from person to person, but a reasonable rule of thumb is not to use data that were collected more than a month earlier.

Conclusion

There are many reasons for using a sound 360-degree feedback instrument as part of an organization's leader development efforts. Feedback from such an instrument provides people with formal assessment data from multiple perspectives and challenges them to set development goals. Given an organizational context that supports efforts to work toward those goals, the outcomes include increased bench strength in the organization and increased effectiveness in leadership roles.

An effective 360-degree feedback instrument is more than simply a tool; it is a process to foster focused, sustained behavioral change and skill development. This chapter identified and explored the eight areas critical to the development of an effective 360-degree feedback process: identifying the purpose of the feedback within the context of the organization; identifying the target population; choosing the appropriate 360-degree instrument; internal communication; data collection; feeding back the data; interpreting the data; and devising a development plan.

Organizations will enjoy better results if the feedback is embedded in a long-term development process. They will also do well to safeguard against the common mistakes organizations make when implementing 360-degree feedback initiatives. This can be done by giving careful attention to organizational and individual readiness, proper administration, managerial buy-in, and confidentiality and anonymity safeguards. By using the information presented in this chapter, organizations can enhance the benefits of using 360-degree feedback instruments and avoid many of the common problems associated with it.

CHAPTER THREE

DEVELOPMENTAL RELATIONSHIPS

Cynthia D. McCauley
Christina A. Douglas

A sk someone to describe the people who have influenced his or her personal development, and you can expect a long conversation. Beyond all the stories about parents and grandparents, there are favorite teachers, classmates, teammates, siblings, and coaches. Then there is the first boss, the great boss, the horrible boss, special coworkers, mentors, spouses, and children. And don't forget the people who influence from afar, through their writings, their art, or their activities as reported by the media.

That relationships shape people's lives is both a commonly held notion and a phenomenon widely studied in the social sciences. Two broad topics in particular have received a great deal of attention in the psychological literature: social learning theory, a framework for understanding how people learn by observing others (Bandura, 1986), and socialization, the process by which individuals internalize the norms and values of the groups they become part of (Van Maanen and Schein, 1979).

In addition, research-based advice on almost any topic related to learning and development also entails a relationship strategy:

- How do schools increase learning in the classroom? Allow students to work in cooperative learning groups (Johnson and Johnson, 1989).

- How does a workplace support the development of new knowledge? Build relationships and community around the work (Institute for Research on Learning, 1993).
- How can people enhance their career development? Seek a mentor (Zey, 1991).
- How can people learn to cope better with stress? Develop a social support network (Aldwin, 1994).

Within this larger framework of learning through others, we focus in this chapter on relationships in work settings that are particularly developmental, that is, relationships individuals point to as their key sources of assessment, challenge, and support. We begin by describing the various roles other people play in the leader development process and then suggest how people can maximize their use of these relationships. The remainder of the chapter is devoted to organizational strategies for enhancing access to relationships for leader development.

The Role of Other People in the Leader Development Process

When asked to reflect on the most important learning experiences in their careers, about a third of managers and executives will describe how they learned from other people (Douglas, 2003; McCall and Hollenbeck, 2002; McCall, Lombardo, and Morrison, 1988; Morrison, White, and Van Velsor, 1992). The "other person" was most likely a boss; but mentors, peers, and short-term interactions with others are also mentioned. In the Corporate Leadership Council's 2001 Leadership Survey of over eight thousand managers, leader development activities that were grounded in feedback and relationships (mentoring, executive coaching, and interaction with peers, for example) were rated as more effective for development than job experiences and education. About two-thirds of executives report having had at least one mentoring relationship in their career (Roche, 1979). Nine out of ten employees who receive mentoring report that it is an effective developmental tool (McShulskis, 1996).

Why are relationships experienced as important for leader development? Relationships can contain each of the elements—assessment, challenge, and support—in the leader development model described in the Introduction. To better understand how relationships serve these functions, let us examine the various developmental roles that people in relationships play for one another. These roles are grouped by the major elements of the ACS model in Table 3.1. Note that although each role represents just one aspect of a relationship, most developmental relationships are made up of multiple roles. At the end of this discussion are

TABLE 3.1. ROLES PLAYED BY OTHERS IN DEVELOPMENTAL RELATIONSHIPS.

Element	Role	Function
Assessment	Feedback provider	Ongoing feedback as person works to learn and improve
	Sounding board	Evaluation of strategies before they are implemented
	Comparison point	Standards for evaluating own level of skill or performance
	Feedback interpreter	Assistance in integrating or making sense of feedback from others
Challenge	Dialogue partner	Perspectives or points of view different from own
	Assignment broker	Access to challenging assignments (new jobs or additions to current one)
	Accountant	Pressure to fulfill commitment to development goals
	Role model	Examples of high (or low) competence in areas being developed
Support	Counselor	Examination of what is making learning and development difficult
	Cheerleader	Boost in own belief that success is possible
	Reinforcer	Formal rewards for progress toward goals
	Companion	Sense that you are not alone in your struggles and that if others can achieve their goals, you can too

illustrations of how roles are combined to form different types of developmental relationships.

Assessment

Assessment, the formal and informal processes for generating and delivering data about an individual, is an important element of an effective development process. One key developmental role in assessment is that of *feedback provider:* a source of day-to-day, ongoing feedback on how a person is doing in seeking to learn new skills or perspectives. An in-depth feedback-intensive program or data from a 360-degree feedback instrument might provide the impetus for taking on particular development goals (see Chapters One and Two), but it is the continuous feedback that people receive as they work to achieve those goals that becomes critical.

Someone acting in the role of feedback provider observes a person who is working to improve and provides in-the-moment feedback. For example, after getting feedback that she dominated meetings, Melissa set a goal of giving others an opportunity to share their views and influence the group. She asked two coworkers who were often in meetings with her to give her feedback on how well she was achieving this goal. For the next six months, she checked in with them after each meeting to get feedback and any suggestions they had for improvement.

People also need feedback on strategies and ideas before they are implemented. In other words, they need *sounding boards*. People bring their ideas to a person acting as a sounding board for reactions and fine-tuning: What should I do in this situation? What would be the likely consequences if I took this action? Which of these three options is the best? George, a manager of a nonprofit organization, was about to lead his board in a strategic planning process for the first time. He contacted a manager in another organization who was considered an expert in strategic planning and asked for help; the two met regularly to debrief and plan next steps. For George, engaging in a new challenge while having access to a knowledgeable sounding board made the experience a particularly developmental one.

People also gain informal assessment data by comparing themselves to others. In this type of relationship, the other people take the role of *comparison points*. There are two types of comparison points: comparing oneself to someone who is seen as a model or expert (How do I compare to the best? How do I compare to someone who is doing what I want to be doing?) and comparing oneself to people in similar situations (Am I doing as well as others? Have I been able to achieve as much as others?).

Comparing themselves to a model helps people see how they measure up and where improvement is needed. After spending several days shadowing a top executive in a major organization, a younger executive running a smaller company noted that although her own work required tackling problems that were just as big, a major difference was the number of problems the other executive had to juggle at once. She realized that this skill of managing multiple problems and finding their interconnections was what she needed to develop if she ever hoped to occupy a similar position.

Comparing themselves to others in similar circumstances gives people insights about how well they are doing. A small group of employees who are going through a yearlong leadership development program get together periodically to update each other on their progress toward development goals. These meetings serve as a sounding board for addressing the obstacles they are encountering, but they also serve as a context for judging how well each person is accomplishing his or her goals relative to the others.

Finally, other people serve in the role of *feedback interpreter*. As such, they usually do not provide assessment information directly but instead help people make sense of the feedback they receive. In one feedback-intensive program, all participants spend half a day with a feedback specialist who helps them (usually in a private meeting) discover themes in their data, connect those themes to their current context, and begin thinking about next steps. Many organizations that use 360-degree feedback provide recipients with access to a professional who can help them interpret the feedback. This role, however, does not have to be a formal one; people often turn to a trusted colleague to help make sense of feedback received informally from a boss or direct report.

Challenge

Challenge—pushing oneself or being pushed beyond the normal comfort zone—is another important element of a development process. One way other people push individuals beyond their comfort zone is by challenging their thinking. We refer to people in this role as *dialogue partners*. They expose people to different perspectives and help each other explore these differences by questioning, prodding, and reflecting on underlying assumptions. This exploration of different perspectives is often the first step in developing more complex and adaptive frameworks for understanding and acting in the world. For example, members of a cross-functional team addressing a major business issue discovered that in the process of digging beneath their differences and learning together, they shed some of their functional biases and developed more of an integrated perspective on the problem.

Other people also play important developmental roles when they provide individuals with assignments that stretch their capacities; we call this role *assignment broker*. These assignments can be new jobs, new responsibilities added to the current job, increased decision-making latitude in the current job, or temporary assignments outside of a person's normal job responsibilities (see Chapter Five).

Another way that people motivate others to learn and grow is by holding them accountable for the development goals they have set; this is the role of *accountant*. Bosses are often expected to play the roles of assignment broker and accountant simultaneously. For example, as part of many performance management systems, employees decide with their bosses on development goals for the coming year. Part of the boss's responsibility is to find the challenging experiences that help move the employees toward those goals and then monitor their progress in the assignment.

Individuals are also challenged when they attempt to emulate *role models*. They step outside of their comfort zones, trying new or more complex skills and behaviors. Rita, a high-potential manager who had been assigned a mentor as part of a leader development program, observed a style of supervision in her mentor that was different from her own. The mentor used a style Rita termed "hands-in" (auditing a subordinate's work), while Rita herself tended toward a hands-on approach (looking over subordinates' shoulders while they are doing the work). She was attracted to her mentor's style, but trying it out was a stretch for her.

Support

People need support to help them effectively deal with the struggles of a developmental experience. That support often comes from other people, who play a variety of support roles for one another.

One is the role of *counselor*, providing emotional support during the difficulties of the learning process. Counselors encourage people to explore the emotional aspects of the learning situation: fear of failing, anxiety about leaving the familiar behind, stress in trying to learn and change while carrying a heavy workload, frustration at not making progress, or anger with others who do not support development.

In a relationship with a strong counseling component, people can vent frustrations and negative emotions without feeling judged. They know that there is someone they can turn to if they need to, and this alone can give them the confidence to take risks or try new things. Michael had a tendency to redo the work of subordinates if the work did not meet his standards, rather than giving them feedback and coaching. He lived in a constant state of frustration and finally shared those feelings with a trusted and more experienced colleague. The colleague helped Michael see that he was contributing to his own frustration by his perfectionist tendencies and his fear of giving negative feedback. With a better understanding of his emotions and a colleague who cared enough to help him reach this understanding, Michael felt he could begin trying to change his behaviors.

Support is also provided by people who play the similar developmental roles of *cheerleader* and *reinforcer*. Cheerleaders are on the sidelines, encouraging learners, expressing confidence in them, and providing affirmation. Reinforcers reward people for making progress toward development goals. Julie, an R&D project leader, shared with her mentor her desire to become more assertive and forceful with her ideas. Knowing Julie's reserved nature, her mentor knew that the change would require a long and sometimes difficult learning process. So she became Julie's cheerleader, helping her celebrate small wins along the way and assuring her that the changes she was making in her attitude and behaviors were indeed valued by the organization. As Julie improved, her mentor reinforced the changes, giving her opportunities to represent the organization at several important external forums and writing a letter to her divisional vice president that praised Julie for the progress she had made and pointed out the resulting positive benefits for the company.

There is a final role that provides valuable support to the learner, albeit a more passive form of support. We refer to this role as *companion*. These are people who are struggling with the same challenges and thus can empathize with each other. People find great comfort in connecting with others facing similar challenges, realizing that they are not alone. Members of a network focused on managing innovation in organizations cited this type of support as a major reason for remaining in the network. Back in their companies, they often felt alone, struggling to make innovation a priority. However, connecting with like-minded people during network meetings left them reinvigorated to face their challenges again.

Companions can also provide people with the living proof that they can learn to master the challenges of the journey. Seeing others who are similar to themselves doing it, people believe they can do it, too. Brad, a school superintendent who was working hard to be more delegating and to give his direct reports authority to make major decisions, got an unexpected boost from Jack, another superintendent he knew well. While they were both away at a national convention, a crisis arose back home in Jack's district. Assuming that Jack would rush back home to handle the crisis, Brad offered to take over his friend's remaining responsibilities at the convention. To his surprise, Jack replied that he had touched base with the key leaders back home and was confident they could handle it, so he would be staying at the convention. Brad suddenly felt renewed in his own development efforts: if Jack could delegate the responsibility for handling a crisis, surely he too could learn to delegate and trust the decision-making capacities of others. Not only did Jack serve as a role model, but because Brad saw Jack as someone in the same job experiencing the same types of demands as he did, Brad felt more strongly that he could succeed, too.

From Roles to Relationships

Each developmental relationship in a person's life provides a mixture of roles. A boss might be both accountant and assignment broker. A former colleague might act as both sounding board and companion. A spouse may play many roles at different times: role model, counselor, accountant, dialogue partner. Note that these kinds of relationships provide differing developmental roles. There is no prototypical developmental relationship, no one role or combination of roles that have to be present in order to make it developmental.

Some relationships, however, are more developmental than others. At least two factors seem to be at work here. First, some relationships are more developmental because they provide more such roles. Mentoring relationships, for example, are usually long-term, and the two individuals develop a personal closeness. Over time, mentors are likely to play a number of roles: sounding board, counselor, feedback provider, assignment broker, cheerleader, reinforcer, role model. Bosses are also often in the position to play multiple developmental roles.

Second, a relationship can be especially developmental because it provides just the right role that the person needs at the time. Having someone in a counseling role may be particularly developmental during a hardship experience (see Chapter Six). Someone to provide feedback and encourage from the sidelines may be exactly what a person needs the most as he or she tries to change an ingrained habit. The lesson is that at various times, depending on the development need, different types of relationships are seen as the most essential.

Of the various relationships that contribute to leader development, mentoring relationships have been studied and written about the most. However, bosses and developmental networks have been emphasized in recent years. We shall briefly review some of the highlights from this literature.

Mentors. A mentoring relationship is typically defined as a committed, long-term relationship in which a senior person (mentor) supports the personal and professional development of a junior person (protégé). In understanding how mentors influence the development of protégés, scholars distinguish between functions that facilitate and enhance career advancement (sponsorship, coaching, and providing challenging assignments, for example) and ones that support psychological and social development (such as counseling, acceptance and confirmation, and role modeling) (Kram, 1985; Noe, 1988). The benefits of having a mentor, particularly early in one's career, have long been espoused by adult development and career theorists (Hall, 1976; Kram, 1985; Levinson, 1978). Research indicates that receiving support from a mentor is associated with higher performance ratings, more recognition, greater compensation, more career opportunities, and more promotions (Burke and McKeen, 1997; Chao, 1997; Dreher and Ash, 1990; Fagenson, 1989; Orpen, 1995; Scandura, 1992; Turban and Dougherty, 1994; Whitely, Dougherty, and Dreher, 1991).

Mentoring continues to be a topic of high interest among scholars and practitioners. From 1986 to 1996, more than five hundred articles on mentoring were published in popular and academic publications in business and education (Allen and Johnston, 1997). Research has focused on the phases of mentoring relationships; the roles served by mentors; the benefits for protégés, mentors, and the organization; mentoring issues and obstacles for diverse employees; and the individual and organizational factors that affect the cultivation of mentoring relationships (Hegestad, 1999; Russell and Adams, 1997). Recognizing the value of mentoring, organizations have increasingly experimented with formalizing these relationships as part of their management development strategy. We will return to this practice later in the chapter.

Bosses. In the Center for Creative Leadership's original study of key events in executive careers (McCall, Lombardo, and Morrison, 1988), about 20 percent of the events featured another person. Most of these people (90 percent) were the manager's immediate boss or another superior that the manager was working closely with. This general pattern was found in extensions of the research to more diverse samples (McCall and Hollenbeck, 2002; Morrison, White, and Van Velsor, 1992), although white female executives reported a higher proportion of boss-relationship key events than white males or African American managers did (Douglas, 2003; Van Velsor and Hughes-James, 1990).

There is additional evidence that the boss-employee relationship is a central one for development. Managers report receiving more mentoring when their mentor is their direct supervisor than when he or she is not (Burke and McKeen, 1997; Fagenson-Eland, Marks, and Amendola, 1997). And supervisor support has consistently been linked to greater employee participation in development activities (Hazucha, Hezlett, and Schneider, 1993; Noe, 1996; Tharenou, 1997).

Bosses are in the unique position of working directly with a manager, having regular contact, feeling responsible for the manager's continued success, and having the power to access organizational resources for the manager. Thus bosses have the opportunity to play many of the roles that provide assessment, challenge, and support. It is important to note, however, that not all of the relationships with bosses that were reported as key events were positive; about a third of the bosses were experienced as having few redeeming qualities. In these situations, rather than enjoying the benefits of a developmental relationship, managers learned what not to do and how to persevere in adverse conditions.

Developmental Networks. There is a growing realization that individuals do not rely solely on single mentors or their current boss for development. Rather they have a network or "constellation" of relationships that they rely on for developmental assistance and support (Higgins, 2000; Higgins and Kram, 2001; Kram, 1985; McCauley and Young, 1993). These relationships can be lateral or hierarchical, within an organization or spanning organizations, ongoing or specific to a particular job transition, and job-related or career-related (Eby, 1997). Higgins and Kram (2001) suggest that the structure of the network will influence the developmental consequences for the protégé. Networks with stronger relationship ties spanning more diverse subgroups will have more developmental power.

"Build informal networks" has long been a staple of advice for managerial success. Yet the stated reasons for these networks has highlighted increased ability to access others for information and expertise, resources, and cooperative action—what might be regarded as the more instrumental functions of a network. Given the changing context of work (for example, increased mobility, flatter and more team-based structures, more diverse employees), long-term relationships for development are becoming more unattainable and connections with a wider array of colleagues more probable. This context creates the impetus to look beyond the instrumental value of networks and see them as sources of support and development (Eby, 1997; Higgins and Kram, 2001).

Individual Strategies for Using Developmental Relationships

To capitalize on the developmental power of relationships, how might people approach them? What steps should they take? If you are involved in helping people in your organization plan their development, here are some strategies you might suggest to them.

1. *Regard the boss as a partner in development.* As noted, bosses are in a unique position to provide various developmental roles or access to other development resources. Make development a topic of discussions with the boss. Bosses and employees should develop a mutual understanding of what each can expect from the other in terms of developmental effort and support. Often these expectations are tacit and not explicitly discussed, thus increasing the possibility for misunderstanding, misguided efforts, and missed opportunities.

2. *Seek out multiple relationships for development.* It is unlikely that one person can provide all of the roles needed in ongoing leader development. There are just too many diverse roles for one person to handle them all, and no one person should be burdened with all those expectations. Even if a person has a close relationship with a mentor, the mentor is unlikely to meet all the development needs of the individual. Instead, people should cultivate a range of relationships across a variety of settings. Exposure to a breadth of viewpoints and experiences is important, and overdependence on one individual can actually limit a person's career progression (McCall and Lombardo, 1983).

3. *Figure out which roles are needed to help with current development goals, and find the right people for those roles.* What is actually needed, a role model who can demonstrate the skills and behaviors this person wants to develop? Encouragement, to stay motivated? Ongoing support to change an ingrained habit? A dialogue partner to move the individual beyond accustomed ways of looking at issues?

Once needs have been clarified, the question becomes, Who can best meet these needs? As with all human capacities, people excel in different developmental roles, perhaps because of their innate gifts. For example, certain people seem naturally meant for a coaching relationship. They are motivated to teach others; they may be keen observers, enabling them to give clear and specific feedback; they know when to give stretch assignments and how to encourage without pressuring. Others are much better in the role of counselor. They are good listeners, sense the personal issues underlying development problems, and are comfortable with close relationships in the work setting.

Other differences are due to the nature of formal roles in organizations. For example, bosses are often in a better position to provide stretch assignments, hold individuals accountable for development, and reinforce learning through the formal reward system. Peers in a work group might be the best source of comparison points; people in other functions or even outside the organization might be the best source of fresh perspectives.

The point is to strive to understand which people—because of their personal strengths or the nature of their relationship—have high potential to fulfill particular developmental roles. Table 3.2 presents a series of questions that help people reflect on the roles they might need and the kind of person who could best play those roles for them.

4. *Make full use of lateral, subordinate, and external relationships.* People often look upward in organizations for the developmental relationships they need. A more senior manager can provide important forms of assessment, challenge, and support, but the hierarchy gets narrower toward the top, and higher-level managers are often difficult to access. An experienced colleague, a peer in another division, or even the retired executive who lives down the street may serve your development needs just as well. Learning partnerships can also develop with subordinates (sometimes referred to as "reverse mentoring"); a supervisor coaching a direct report in one area could easily receive coaching in another area in return.

5. *Do not assume that relationships need to be long-term or intense to be developmental.* As a result of the dominance of the mentoring concept, most people have a certain type of relationship in mind when they think of learning and development. They might miss or underestimate the opportunities to learn from relationships involving only modest contact. We have found that people can learn a great deal from shadowing a role model for several days, from working on a short-term project with a cross-functional team, from bosses that they were not particularly close to, or from colleagues they see a couple of times a year. Instead of focusing on the length or depth of the relationship, the real question is whether the experience with the person brings a different perspective, new knowledge, willingness to engage, belief in one's capabilities, insight, or talent for keeping people motivated.

6. *Be especially aware during times of transition.* It is particularly important for people to reassess their development needs during times of transition; this includes reassessing the kinds of developmental relationships they need. Going through a transition is challenging in and of itself and may require special advice and support from others. Developmental relationships become more important during times of restructuring or downsizing, for example, because they act as an antidote to the stress (Kram and Hall, 1989). Also, being in a new situation puts new and different demands on people, which is likely to require development in new areas. This in turn calls for new role models, new sources of support, and people with expertise connected to the challenges in the new setting. For example, managers

TABLE 3.2. QUESTIONS FOR EXPLORING POTENTIAL DEVELOPMENTAL RELATIONSHIPS.

My Development Goal:

_____

_____

_____

What developmental roles do I need as I work on this goal?	Who could serve in this role?
Feedback provider: Will I be practicing new behaviors that need to be refined based on feedback?	Who is in a position to observe me practice these behaviors?
	Who is good at observing and assessing the impact of behaviors?
	Whom do I trust to be straightforward with me?
Sounding board: Will I encounter dilemmas and choices that I need to think through before acting?	Who is good at thinking out loud and considering alternatives?
	Who has faced these same sorts of choices before?
	Whom am I willing to share my uncertainties with?
Comparison point: Would it help to gauge my progress against others?	Who would be a relevant comparison point?
	Who would be willing to share his or her progress with me?
	Whose successes would be easy for me to see?
Feedback interpreter: Will I need someone else to gather feedback for me and help me make sense of it?	Who is good at making sense of complex data?
	Whom am I willing to share feedback with?
	Whom will others trust as a gatherer of feedback for me?

Dialogue partner:

Do I need to understand new and different perspectives?

Who has a perspective different from my own?

Who is good at engaging in dialogue and examining underlying assumptions?

Who is good in the role of devil's advocate?

Assignment broker:

Will I need help in gaining access to stretch assignments?

Who can sponsor me when certain jobs become available?

Who can help me add needed challenge to my job?

Who can help me find stretch opportunities outside the workplace?

Accountant:

Am I more likely to succeed if someone holds me accountable for making changes?

Should my boss hold me accountable in some way for achieving this goal?

Are there others who want me to achieve this goal?

Role model:

Do I need to closely watch someone who is already very skilled in the area of my development goal?

Who would be a great role model for me?

Whom should I watch or talk to, to get strategies for achieving my goal?

Whose ability in this area inspired me?

Counselor:

Will this goal be very difficult for me? Will I likely encounter a personal frustration?

Who can be my confidant as I struggle with this goal?

Who can be both empathic and objective?

Who understands me enough to see through my excuses and procrastinations?

Cheerleader or reinforcer:

Do I need a lot of encouragement and reinforcement to succeed?

Who is always able to make me feel competent?

Whom can I share my small successes with?

Who is in a position to reward me for success?

TABLE 3.2. (*Continued*)

Companion:	
Will this be easier if I can connect with others in the same boat?	Who would understand what I'm going through?
	Who are my peers in this situation?
	Who would be good company on this journey?

in expatriate assignments need role models for how to work in the new culture and advice to help them interpret and make sense of their new environment.

Creating Developmental Relationships in Organizations

Shelley is a manager in the marketing department of a large organization. She's known as a consistently high performer. She works well with people throughout the organization, and she's extremely bright, quickly learning new technical and business information as she takes on new projects. Her boss sees her as an asset to the company and wants to encourage her continued development. Earlier in the year, the two of them had a long discussion about her development goals. They identified two specific areas for her to work on: learning to be more comfortable making decisions amid ambiguity and developing a broader organizational perspective.

When Shelley's boss heard that the vice president of public relations was looking for someone to work with her on a short-term assignment, he secured the assignment for Shelley. He felt that the assignment would stretch her in ways that would help her develop in the areas they had identified and that the vice president would be a good role model. As Shelley was planning for this temporary assignment, she thought of a fellow member of the international group (an informal network in the organization that meets monthly) who had previously worked for this particular vice president. She asked if he would be willing to act as a confidant and sounding board for her during this assignment, and he agreed.

Shelley's boss was also able to get her into one of the organization's formal programs for high-potential managers. As part of this yearlong program, she was assigned to a learning triad with two other managers at her level but from different functional areas. The three worked together on various tasks and exercises given as part of the program and debriefed their experiences together, but there was an additional mandate: each person brought to the group a problem he or she was struggling with at work. The threesome coached one another as they worked on their problems throughout the year.

Shelley works in an organization that is rich in developmental relationships. The richness is not just in the number of relationships and the roles they play for Shelley but also in the various ways they came about. We might say that the developmental relationship with her boss evolved naturally. It was part of his role as a manager: he saw her development as part of his responsibility. Other relationships—with the vice president of public relations and with her former subordinate—were more intentional. They were consciously sought out to fill a development need. Finally, the peer learning group was brought about by a formal organizational initiative. The organization created the structure that brought these three people together for the primary purpose of learning and development.

There are, then, three bases for developmental relationships: some arise naturally, some are intentionally sought out by the individual, and some are structured by the organization. We use this framework to think about how organizations enhance access to developmental relationships in the workplace, employing three proactive strategies:

1. Enhance the developmental power of natural relationships within the organization.
2. Encourage employees to intentionally seek out the developmental relationships they need.
3. Create formal relationships for the purposes of learning and development.

Enhancing the Developmental Power of Natural Relationships

Organizations pursuing this strategy work to develop the mind-set that making the most of the organization's people resources is a manager's responsibility (Waldroop and Butler, 1996). They spell out the payback to managers for spending time developing their subordinates: they get stronger teams that deliver better results, become magnets for talent, and—as subordinates move to other positions in the organization—develop a network of support (Peterson and Hicks, 1996). Most important, these organizations hold managers accountable for the development of direct reports through their performance review and reward systems.

To make this work—to give managers responsibility for developing others and then hold them accountable—organizations also have to develop managers' skills in this area. Many organizations have framed these as "coaching" skills. (Although related, these should not be equated with the skills of a professional coach, described in Chapter Four.)

Being a good coach means being competent in many of the roles described earlier in the chapter: giving feedback, acting as a sounding board, providing the right kind of developmental assignments, and providing encouragement and reinforcement for learning. Managers may need help here, because enacting these roles sometimes runs counter to typical behaviors (Waldroop and Butler, 1996). The manager must adopt the attitude of a teacher, not a competitor; must be willing to explore ideas and issues rather than make quick evaluations and judgments; must think long-term rather than about the immediate task at hand; and must slow down enough to develop a relationship rather than work with subordinates in frantic sound bites. Resources available to managers on developing and coaching employees have exploded in recent years (see, for example, Chiaramonte and Higgins, 1993; Evered and Selman, 1989; Geber, 1992; Goldsmith, Kaye, and Shelton, 2000; Hargrove, 2002; Hendricks and Associates, 1996; Hunt and Weintraub, 2002; Kinlaw, 1993; Mink, 1993; Peterson and Hicks, 1996).

Just like any other leadership competency, coaching skills are best developed using a multiple-strategy approach: feedback on coaching behaviors, skill-based training, opportunities to practice coaching in work situations, and access to others who can give advice and support. In addition, a focus on improving these skills is most likely to meet with success if it is part of a larger development effort. One organization developed a five-day coaching skills program for managers as part of a sales force improvement initiative (Graham, Wedman, and Garvin-Kester, 1993). Sales managers completed the program and were expected to use the skills as part of their role in the improvement process. The course material was tailored specifically for coaching salespeople and included tools (such as a behavioral checklist for observing interactions with clients) that managers would begin using in their jobs.

Similarly, a division of Mobil Oil implemented an on-the-job development program for its engineers in which supervisory coaching was a key component (Cobb and Gibbs, 1990). All the supervisors attended a coaching workshop with one of their engineers. They were introduced to effective coaching practices and engaged in skill development as a pair. Together they developed a plan for the supervisor to coach the engineer in a work assignment after the workshop. The two also worked together to implement coaching between the supervisor and other members of the work group who were not at the workshop. The lesson here is the critical importance of integrating any formal program on coaching with the real work of coaching in the organization.

Some organizations have carried this strategy of enhancing the developmental power of existing relationships one step further. They see developing others as a shared responsibility across the organization, not just a managerial responsibility. They want staff members to know how to develop not only subordinates but peers and superiors as well. In other words, they want the skills of developing others to be a part of the skill repertoire of all employees.

One financial organization has launched an initiative to develop more of a "coaching culture." As one part of this effort, the company identified employees who are particularly good coaches and set out to understand the mind-sets and skills of these people, the tools they use, and the impact they have on "coachees." They are using this knowledge to develop a coaching model and a workshop to teach the skills of coaching to others throughout the organization.

Another organization expects each manager and his or her direct reports to be a work team and also serve as a "learning group," sharing responsibility for giving feedback and supporting the development of each member of the group (Palus and Rogolsky, 1996).

Encouraging Employees to Intentionally Seek Out Needed Developmental Relationships

The first strategy, enhancing the developmental power of relationships, focuses on creating more people who have the skills and motivation to develop others in the workplace. This next strategy focuses on the other half of the relationship equation: creating more people who want to access others as part of their development efforts.

The most straightforward way of implementing this strategy is in the development planning process. As employees are setting development goals and steps for reaching them, they should be educated about the role of other people in learning and development and encouraged to include relationship strategies as part of their development plan. The questions in Table 3.2 can help. In our earlier example, Shelley felt she would need a sounding board as she took on the special assignment with the VP of public relations, but not just any sounding board—someone who had worked with this VP before and could give her particular insights. She intentionally sought out someone who could play this role.

Once the need for a developmental role has been established and a potential candidate identified, the next step is to explore whether the person is willing to serve in the role. Sometimes the candidate is someone the individual already knows well and can informally approach on his or her own. If not, an introduction from a third party may be best, or the person might need to set up a formally recognized developmental relationship with the chosen candidate, such as asking that person to serve as a formal adviser to a project or as a mentor in a special assignment.

However formal or informal the resulting relationship, clear expectations, time frames, and intended outcomes should be discussed. A strategy for working together needs to be established, and the need for confidentiality must be acknowledged. Potential obstacles or downsides to the relationship should also be explored.

An additional tactic to use in developmental planning is to ask employees to examine their network of relationships and the implications of these patterns on their development. Brutus and Livers (2000) describe such an exercise used in a leadership development program for African American managers. Participants are asked to draw up a list of the people with whom they network and the reasons why and frequency with which they network with these people. They transform this list into a graphic that denotes the hierarchical levels, gender, race, and emotional intimacy of the people who comprise their network. After reflecting on these patterns, participants share their network graphs with others and strategize ways to strengthen their networks.

Another way that organizations encourage employees to seek out developmental relationships is to intentionally broaden their access to other people, particularly people who might help them in their development efforts. One technique is to solidly support the formation of networks. Some organizations have created networks for women managers or for particular ethnic or racial groups (Barclay, 1992; Morrison, Ruderman, and Hughes-James, 1993). Others have created networks to link people at similar levels across functions. An emerging practice is the cultivation of "communities of practice," informal groups made up of employees from across the organization who have common expertise and interests. With organizational support, these communities develop processes and strategies for sharing knowledge, learning from one another, and putting their shared expertise to use in solving organizational problems (Wenger and Snyder, 2000).

Some networks extend across organizations, providing a forum for people with similar responsibilities to connect with each other. For example, the Association for Managers of Innovation (AMI) is a network of people from different organizations who are responsible in some way for innovation within their company. They learn from each other using a process they label "beg, brag, and what if." This means that a large part of the agenda is devoted to individual members' bringing problems to the group that they would like input on, sharing a successful initiative or project with the group, or engaging the group in exploring future scenarios.

An additional way of broadening people's access to others they can learn from is to designate special developmental roles within the organization. For example, after defining its core competencies (the areas of expertise that are crucial to the success of the business), one company designated particular individuals as mentors in each of those areas. These mentors were highly skilled and knowledgeable in a particular core competency and were given the responsibility of keeping the organization at the forefront of that competency. Then if employees needed to develop more expertise in a certain core area, they immediately knew whom to seek out for coaching and guidance.

Creating Formal Relationships

A more direct strategy for enhancing access to developmental relationships is to create them intentionally—to formally match people for the purposes of learning and development. Why do organizations do this? From the organization's perspective, there are times when people need extra developmental attention. Formal relationships are most often created for the following purposes:

- Socialization of new managers
- Preparing high-potential employees for more responsibility
- Developing women and people of color
- Meeting development needs of senior executives
- Organizational change efforts

We have found that about 20 percent of organizations with five hundred or more employees have at least one initiative that makes use of a formal developmental relationship (Douglas and McCauley, 1999). These initiatives were found in many kinds of organizations, with different geographical locations, employee size, sales volume, and types of product or service.

Socialization. Starting a new job or a new assignment is typically a stressful time for a manager. From the organization's perspective, getting new managers acclimated quickly is vital to productivity. Formal relationships are a very effective solution. In one large manufacturing organization, people who are promoted to a management position are routinely assigned to an experienced peer (called a peer coach) in a similar managerial role to facilitate their transition. These assignments typically last about six months and include shadowing, advising, and weekly meetings. Peer coaches are nominated for these assignments by a committee of senior managers; they receive bonus pay through the company's performance appraisal system.

High-Potential Employees. Many organizations frequently find that high-potential, fast-track managers need some extra developmental attention to facilitate their rapid progression through the management ranks. Formal developmental relationships provide that attention, in the form of support, exposure, and developmental opportunities. Generally, a senior manager is matched with the high-potential employee for one-on-one mentoring as part of a multiyear formal development program that includes training, rotational assignments, workshops, action learning, and broad exposure to strategic issues.

Developing Women and People of Color. The number of women and people of color in management positions has been steadily climbing over the past twenty-five years, but this upward progression through the organization is still a struggle, and the number of women and people of color in the top echelons of U.S. companies remains small. Informal mentoring relationships, frequently identified as a key source of development and support for people seeking higher levels of leadership responsibility, are less available to women and people of color because of the small number of suitable potential mentors within the executive ranks (Douglas, 2003). Therefore, organizations have turned to formal developmental relationships as a strategy for members of these groups. For example, a large financial corporation has implemented a one-year program for African American managers that includes formal mentoring relationships and structured networks. All African American managers in the middle-management ranks are asked to participate in the program. Each participant is assigned to a network of seven to nine other African American managers, and each network meets monthly to discuss career issues and to provide mutual support. In addition, each participant is also assigned to a formal mentoring relationship with a senior manager from a different function or division. (The benefits and limitations of formal developmental relationships for women and people of color are discussed in greater detail in Chapters Nine and Ten.)

Meeting Development Needs of Senior Executives. Organizations frequently find that top executives require extra developmental attention to address specific needs, involving perhaps specific skills, performance issues on the job, or broader changes in behavior (Witherspoon and White, 1997). Because of their level and the nature of their jobs, these executives often have difficulty developing and maintaining developmental alliances. Therefore, organizations often create formal developmental relationships (frequently, executive coaching relationships) to provide these executives with that extra developmental attention when attempting to remedy a particular skill deficit or address a broader development goal. (Chapter Four provides a more in-depth look at how formal coaching is used in leader development.)

Organizational Change Efforts. Finally, formal relationships are sometimes created during times of organizational change to help managers develop the skills and behaviors they need to facilitate the transition. For example, a large manufacturing company underwent a major reorganization that included setting up self-managing work teams. Each work team was assigned a sponsor, a senior manager nominated for the role by an executive committee. The sponsor provided support and coaching to the work team and to each individual on that team. The sponsor also worked closely with the team's immediate supervisor, to formalize development goals for the team and its members. This sponsorship process contributed to the subsequent success of the self-managing work teams.

Types of Formal Developmental Relationships

In addition to having a range of purposes, formal developmental relationships also vary in form or structure. The examples we have cited so far illustrate this variety. These variations, however, can be grouped into five basic, common types:

- One-on-one mentoring
- Peer mentoring
- Formal coaching
- Mentoring in groups
- Action learning teams

When should an organization opt for a particular type of formal relationship? What are the potential problems associated with each type? These questions are addressed in the descriptions that follow, and guidelines are summarized in Table 3.3.

One-on-One Mentoring. A one-on-one formal mentoring relationship typically entails assigning a junior manager to a senior manager outside of the direct reporting line. This type of formal relationship is usually directed toward a particular group of junior managers (high-potential employees, new managers, people of color) in the hopes that these relationships will provide some of the same important career and personal development supports as informal, long-term mentoring relationships do. By formalizing the process, the organization is ensuring that all of the identified junior managers have equal access to a mentor, and it focuses the mentoring effort within a specified time frame. One-on-one formal mentoring relationships should be considered by organizations if junior managers need additional exposure to the perspectives and job demands of senior managers and if senior managers have particular experience and expertise to share with junior managers.

A national restaurant chain uses a formal mentoring program to train and socialize new managers. Every new store manager is assigned to a senior manager (at another store) for a yearlong mentoring relationship. The mentor is expected to spend at least six hours per week in the new manager's restaurant, providing coaching and support. The mentoring role has been integrated into the company's

TABLE 3.3. TYPES OF DEVELOPMENTAL RELATIONSHIPS.

Relationship Type	When to Use It	Potential Problems
One-on-one mentoring	When senior managers have time, experience, and expertise to share with junior managers	Lack of integration with other management development strategies in organization
	When junior managers need exposure to perspectives and job demands of senior managers	Senior managers may not have skills or motivation to teach others
		Potential for role conflict between boss and mentor
		May narrow opportunities for other developmental relationships
		May cause resentment for managers who have not been asked to participate
Peer mentoring	When individuals need familiarity with issues and perspectives in other functions or parts of the organization	Development needs of the targeted managers may not complement each other
	When individuals need coaching to get up to speed in a business knowledge or technical area	Organizational climate may not promote open communication between colleagues
	When improved cross-group communication is desired	Managers may feel resentful at being asked to develop and assist other managers
	When peers going through similar experiences need opportunities to learn from and support one another	Managers may not have the time or motivation to participate
Formal coaching	When a manager has no peers or boss who can serve as coach	Experience and skills of coach may not meet needs of executive
	When the expertise of a professional skilled in behavioral change strategies is needed	May be too expensive
		Boss may be skeptical or not supportive
	When a concentrated period of coaching on a particular skill or development goal is desired	

Mentoring in groups	When potential mentors are in short supply	Some managers may need more individualized developmental attention
	When it is anticipated that peers can learn and benefit from each other	Potential mentors may lack skills, time, or motivation to mentor group
	When increased cohesion among group members is desired	Requires a fair amount of time and planning to be effective
		Potential for conflict between group mentor and supervisors of participants
Action learning teams	When cross-functional teamwork is needed on strategic projects	Pressure to deliver results can undermine learning experience
	When opportunities to apply content knowledge from a training program to work problems are desired	Requires projects to be real work
		Requires skilled facilitators for the teams

performance appraisal system, and each mentor is held accountable for the protégé's store performance.

Although one-on-one formal mentoring provides junior managers with wonderful opportunities for learning and development, there are also some cautions to be considered before making the decision to implement such a program. For one, formal mentoring relationships, if they are to be effective, need to be integrated into the larger management development strategy and clearly linked to business strategies and personnel practices (Kram and Bragar, 1992; also see Chapter Seven).

Another caution concerns the people selected to act as mentors. Not all senior managers have the time, motivation, experience, and expertise to share with junior managers. It is also important to assess the potential for role conflict between the mentor and the junior manager's boss. Other potential drawbacks include creation of a climate of favoritism, resentment by nonparticipants, and negative experiences (Kizilos, 1990; Kram and Bragar, 1992; Murray and Owen, 1991; Noe, 1991).

Finally, formal mentoring programs should not be viewed as a substitute for informal mentoring. Although protégés report positive outcomes from formal mentoring relationships, the benefits are often not as strong as those experienced in informal mentoring because the mentor may not be as committed to working with the protégé or the relationship is not as intense or long-lasting (Chao, Walz, and

Gardner, 1992; Fagenson-Eland, Marks, and Amendola, 1997; Ragins and Cotton, 1999; Scandura and Williams, 2001).

Peer Mentoring. In peer mentoring, an employee is paired with a colleague at the same level within the organization. This form of mentoring is based on the assumption that peer relationships are important vehicles for learning and growth (Douglas and Schoorman, 1987; Kram and Bragar, 1992; Kram and Isabella, 1985). Common in educational settings, as with peer mentoring among teachers or principals, it has been gaining popularity in corporate settings in recent years.

Peer mentoring is typically used to help people develop specific skills in their current positions. One organization, citing poor communication between functions, instituted a peer mentoring program in which each employee was matched with a colleague in another function; they were to share information, help each other develop skills, and support one another. National Semiconductor has instituted a development process in which managers receive 360-degree feedback and then form a "performance partnership" with a peer, a partnership for new behavior and enhanced personal productivity (Peters, 1996). The partners attend a workshop together and create a contract for their collaboration.

Peer mentoring is called for when employees need familiarity with issues and perspectives in other functions or parts of the organizations, when they need help getting up to speed in a particular skill or knowledge base, or when cross-group communication needs improvement. An organization considering a peer mentoring initiative has to take the time to fully understand the development needs of the potential participants and their ability to help each other with those needs.

There are some potential drawbacks to a peer mentoring program. There may be times when the development needs of the targeted individuals do not complement each other. The organizational climate may not promote open communication between colleagues. Some people may feel resentful at being asked to help others. Some people may not have the time or motivation to participate in the peer mentoring program if they do not see any career or personal benefits.

Formal Coaching. Formal coaching is usually used to help managers increase their effectiveness in the workplace and develop capability for future challenges. The managers are teamed up with internal or external coaches (professionals specializing in coaching), who work with them on an identified agenda. Chapter Four focuses on this type of formal relationship.

Mentoring in Groups. Group mentoring typically involves a learning group of four to six individuals who meet regularly and are assigned to a senior manager.

The senior manager's role in the group is to act as a learning partner by helping the managers understand the organization, guiding them in analyzing their experiences, and sharing knowledge with them. The senior manager strives to create an environment wherein participants can learn from each other as well as from the senior manager (Kaye and Jacobson, 1995). Group mentoring was designed to address some of the problems of formal one-on-one mentoring, such as limited numbers of senior managers to serve as mentors and the uncertainties of the matching process.

But group mentoring also has potential drawbacks. Some managers need more individualized attention than group mentoring can realistically provide. Finding the right senior manager is also a concern. Group mentoring requires a great deal of commitment from a senior manager and skills different from those for mentoring a single individual (for example, group facilitation skills and an understanding of group dynamics). Potential mentors might lack the necessary skills, time, or motivation to mentor a group. The participants' immediate supervisors may also feel resentful toward the group mentor. Finally, group mentoring requires a fair amount of time and planning by all participants.

Action Learning Teams. Action learning projects are being used more and more in leadership development initiatives (Dotlich and Noel, 1998; Marsick and O'Neil, 1999; Vicere and Fulmer, 1998). Typically, under the sponsorship of a senior manager, teams of five to eight managers work on a project related to a strategic organizational issue (such as movement into new markets, the opportunities afforded by new technology, or decentralization). Team members are from different functions or units, and the project represents work beyond the participants' day-to-day job responsibilities. Learning is an explicit goal of the project, so time is devoted to meet as a team, usually with a facilitator or adviser, to discuss the dilemmas the team is encountering, to examine the theories and concepts team members are applying to the project, and to discover new ways of thinking or creative alternatives to accomplish their objectives. Action learning teams have the opportunity to learn from the project itself, from each other, and from their efforts to collectively examine their work.

One of the tensions experienced by action learning teams is balancing the action and the learning. If there is more felt pressure to focus on the task and to deliver tangible results, processes to enhance learning will be marginalized. By contrast, if the work of the project is "made up" and not really strategic for the organization, teams are less likely to engage in the work at the deep level needed to stimulate learning. Action learning teams also need skilled facilitators to encourage learning from both collective action and reflection.

Key Characteristics of an Effective Formal Relationship Initiative

With all the shapes and forms that formal relationships take, how can organizations be sure the ones they are considering will be effective? The literature on this subject cites numerous characteristics or components of successful initiatives (Hegestad, 2002; Kram and Bragar, 1992; Murray and Owen, 1991), but they all seem to cluster into five overarching themes (Douglas, 1997):

1. Organizational support for the program
2. Clarity of purpose, expectations, and roles
3. Participant choice and involvement
4. Careful selection and matching procedures
5. Continuous monitoring and evaluation

Organizational Support. Organizational support is defined as the degree to which an initiative is encouraged and supported by the organization as a whole. Specifically, it means that the program should be integrated with strategic business needs, organizational systems (performance appraisal process, reward systems, communication systems), and other management development efforts. There should be visible support from top management and a supportive organizational culture. In fact, support of top management is probably the most frequently mentioned success characteristic in the literature. Finally, adequate resources need to be available.

Clarity of Purpose, Expectations, and Roles. The program goals and objectives must be clearly defined, and the choice of program must be driven by those objectives. The goals and objectives need to be fully communicated to everyone involved—program participants, potential mentors, top management, nonparticipants, program coordinators, and others—so that they have realistic expectations of what the program can and cannot achieve. They should also receive, in an orientation session or similar format, a clear description of their roles and responsibilities. Finally, participants in the program should clarify their expectations with their partner in the match.

Choice and Involvement by Participants. The more participants feel they have decision-making control over their involvement in a program, the more effective it is likely to be. In particular, people need to feel that they have something to say about how the process is structured and about their individual roles in it.

Careful Selection and Matching Procedures. Selection and matching are thoughtful and predetermined processes for identifying and pairing participants in relationship-based initiatives. If the effort is to succeed, the program needs participants who are committed to its goals and motivated to participate wholeheartedly. This means that the participants need to be carefully selected on the basis of the program objectives and a predetermined set of criteria. Then they must be matched with their relationship partners through procedures that are well thought out and consistent with the goals of the initiative. The procedures should address both how the matching happens (through voluntary matching, matching by a committee, matching by a program coordinator, and so on) and what criteria are used (similar interests, accessibility, position, functional areas, strengths, and so on).

Continuous Monitoring and Evaluation. Effective relationship-based programs typically have established processes for monitoring the programs while they are under way, assessing their effectiveness, and making improvements. The strategies used for monitoring should be worked out while the program is being designed—well before it is actually implemented. Periodic assessments can be made through focus groups, interviews, or surveys (Kram and Bragar, 1992). The choice of strategy may depend on existing mechanisms in the organization's human resource area, but it is important to make sure that the chosen strategy assesses both process and outcome variables and links to business strategies.

Formal Developmental Relationships as Part of a Development Process

Two promising trends we see in formal developmental relationships are assigning people to more than one relationship and linking the relationships with other leader development strategies. These practices help integrate formal relationships into an overall development process.

One such program is being implemented in a regional financial organization. The goal is to prepare fast-track employees for key management positions. Participants must apply for the program and go through an extensive screening process by top management. Those who are accepted spend their entire time focusing on learning and development; during the program, they are actually employees of the organization's corporate university. Over the next nine months, they take formal training classes and are involved in rotational assignments. They are also assigned to a business mentor—a senior manager who provides business, technical, and political advice. While participants usually have just one business mentor, they may have more than one if the required exposure to expertise cannot be met through a relationship with a single individual.

Participants also have a formal developmental relationship with the university's director of trainees, who provides them with ongoing feedback. The director garners input from the various supervisors on each participant's rotational assignments and from each business mentor and then feeds these observations and impressions back to the participants and helps them plan changes and improvements based on the feedback.

A second example is the two-year executive development program sponsored by the Council of Jewish Federations (CJF). The council is an association of 189 Jewish federations, local organizations that raise money to help each Jewish community respond to people in need and populations at risk. The CJF helps strengthen the work of its member federations by developing programs to meet changing needs, providing an exchange of successful community experiences, establishing guidelines for fund-raising and operations, and leading joint efforts to meet local, regional, and international needs. Their executive development program was designed to develop high-potential professionals who are projected to attain the most senior positions in major federations throughout North America. The program is funded in large part by the Mandel Associated Foundations in Cleveland, and participants are called "Mandel Fellows."

Over the course of two years, Mandel Fellows engage in a variety of development activities. They begin the program with a weeklong feedback-intensive program (see Chapter One). They also spend a two-week period in Israel, working with emerging Israeli leaders to understand various issues in the Jewish community worldwide. Throughout the program, there are several two-day meetings focused on particular managerial issues, as well as opportunities to engage in distance-learning events focused on Jewish history and philosophy.

The Mandel Fellows are assigned to two formal relationships during the program: they are matched with an "executive mentor," and they choose one or more "leadership coaches." The executive mentor is a successful, large-city federation president. The major purpose of this relationship is to help the fellow see the issues and challenges faced by a senior leader in a major federation (the type of position the program is preparing them for) and the strategies used to lead such organizations. The relationship is built around a visit by the fellow to the mentor's organization. A typical visit consists of shadowing the mentor during normal work activities, debriefing and discussion time with the mentor, meeting with other staff and getting their views of the mentor's leadership behaviors and styles, and being included in the mentor's nonwork activities. The connection could also foster an ongoing informal relationship, one in which the fellows get advice and input as their careers progress.

The leadership coaches are recognized leaders in each participant's own local community, usually leaders in corporate or public sector organizations. These relationships are intended to help the fellows understand the leadership complexities, dynamics, styles, and strategies in a markedly different institution. The expectation is that they will be exposed to new perspectives of effective leadership in a large-scale organization. In addition, fellows often look for leadership coaches who are particularly strong in an area in which they want to learn and improve.

The pairs engage in a wide variety of activities. Coaches are shadowed (a role-modeling activity), are used as sounding boards, or serve as consultants on a project the fellow is working on. They share with the fellow their experiences, philosophies, leadership models, things they have read, and other knowledge. Coaches open up their organizations to the fellows for observation and discussions with staff members. Coaches are asked to observe activities in the fellow's organization or to share their expertise with a particular group in the organization. The type of activity depends on what the individual fellow wishes to get out of the relationship.

In addition to these two one-on-one relationships, the program also engenders valuable relationships among the participants. They learn from one another by sharing their experiences, soliciting and giving feedback, and providing advice. They are also sources of support for each other, thus strongly fulfilling the companion role. Because of the length of the program and the intensity of many of their shared experiences, these relationships are likely to continue once the formal program is over.

An Evolving Context for Developmental Relationships

Virtual relationships are ones that are maintained at a distance, with the majority of connections occurring through e-mail, intranets, videoconferencing, phones, and other communication technology. Internet or online technology in particular allows individuals who are geographically dispersed to communicate more regularly, quickly, and cheaply—thus supporting the maintenance of a relationship. This is good news for developmental relationships. Relationships can be maintained even when one individual moves to a new location. Geographically dispersed networks can have more frequent exchanges. Individuals in assigned formal relationships have additional methods for communicating and sharing information.

The major question, of course, is whether these new methods of connecting with others can be relied on for maintaining developmental relationships. Cohen and Prusak (2001) point to the following problems with "virtuality":

- None of the technology of virtuality can currently carry a fraction of the whole range of communications that people use to relate to one another.
- Virtual connections tend to be brief and intermittent, and building durable social connections takes time.
- Virtual connections tend to have clear, specific purposes (usually information exchange) and limited participants, while social connections are more likely to grow from chance encounters and broad-ranging conversations and chat.

- Virtual communications (such as e-mail and videoconferencing) may actually distract people from what is going on around them so that they are "neither here nor there."

The emerging view is that virtual connections and communication are helpful but not sufficient for the cultivation of relationships (particularly those that are intended to be developmental). Some face-to-face interaction is needed to maintain the richness and breadth of what is shared. Some developmental roles, such as sounding board or feedback interpreter, are likely more easily provided at a distance than others. In addition, leaders will need to learn new communication and interaction skills as their work becomes more virtual. Having the opportunity to practice these skills in the context of a development initiative that requires some virtual connections with peers, facilitators, and coaches will accelerate this learning (Pulley, Sessa, and Malloy, 2002).

Conclusion

Developmental relationships are an important strategy for enhancing the leader development process. They are a source of assessment information and a resource for interpreting and understanding that information. They challenge an individual directly or provide access to challenging assignments. And they are a primary means of support for development.

Some people seem naturally to turn to others in their efforts to learn and grow, and some people are natural coaches. Generally, these people tend to find each other without much organizational intervention. However, organizations that want informal developmental relationships to occur regularly for more people need to develop coaching skills in the organization and reward people for using those skills, encourage people to seek out the developmental relationships they need, and provide ample opportunities for people throughout the organization to meet and to develop relationships.

In addition to creating a context in which informal developmental relationships are likely to flourish, it is often appropriate for organizations to create formal relationships directed toward specific development agendas: developing employees new to their roles, preparing high-potential managers, developing women and people of color, meeting the development needs of senior managers, and supporting organizational change efforts. These relationships can take the form of one-on-one mentoring, peer coaching, executive coaching, coaching in groups, and action learning teams.

Successful formal initiatives are those that have organizational support; clarity of purpose, expectations, and roles; choice and involvement by participants; careful selection and matching procedures; and continuous monitoring and evaluation. Formal initiatives are most effective when they are integrated into a larger process of leader development.

CHAPTER FOUR

FORMAL COACHING

Sharon Ting
E. Wayne Hart

Perhaps you can remember a time when a "coach" was somebody with a whistle who told you and your teammates how to win games. Today, the picture's not that simple. Twenty-first-century coaching is applied across a broad spectrum of circumstances, serving personal, relationship, fitness, career, business, and executive needs.

Definitions of coaching vary as widely as the purposes to which it is applied. Virtually all current definitions capture the notion of a coach relating with a coachee to facilitate the coachee's accomplishing something in the future (Douglas and Morley, 2000; Hargrove, 2002; Hudson, 1999; International Coaching Federation, 2003; Whitmore, 1996; Witherspoon and White, 1997). And coaching can take many forms beyond one-on-one, including multiple coaches with a single coachee, multiple coachees with a single coach, or coaching integrated with other developmental experiences.

This chapter examines one facet of that broad tapestry: formal one-on-one coaching for individual leader development. We define coaching as a practice in which the coachee and coach collaborate to assess and understand the coachee and his or her developmental task, to challenge current constraints while exploring new possibilities, and to ensure accountability and support for reaching goals and sustaining development.

Of course, anyone can act informally as a coach at any time, in the course of a personal, supervisory, or developmental relationship. Sometimes this is a good idea. At other times, that approach may be unwelcome. We think of coaching as "formal" when the coachee and coach enter into a written or verbal agreement or have an express contract between them that coaching will occur. They mutually and explicitly understand, endorse, and commit to the goals, actions, and timeline of the process and to their respective roles and responsibilities.

This chapter focuses on formal coaching delivered by an external coach in an organizational setting, to senior leaders, executives, mid-level managers, and emerging leaders. We begin by examining the framework, or conceptual model, we apply in our practice and the principles that guide our coaching work. Then we examine several aspects of the coaching process.

A Framework for Coaching

The Introduction to this book offered a model for leader development. The first part of that model explained that for an experience to be developmental, three elements—assessment, challenge, and support—must be present. Here we will discuss how the ACS model fits into our coaching framework.

Our coaching framework has three aspects:

1. *Relationship,* the context within which the coaching occurs
2. *Assessment, challenge, and support* (ACS), the core elements of the leader development model
3. *Results,* the visible outcomes that the coaching process is focused on achieving

The three parts of this framework are synergistic. Relationship building, leader development, and results typically occur concurrently. Accordingly, each aspect informs and triggers new activity or perspectives in the others.

The dynamic of these aspects working together for a common end is illustrated by the following case. Through multirater feedback used in the context of his coaching, Marc learned that he was not viewed as very approachable. His development goal was to be more open and accessible. He initiated several behavioral changes to build more bridges to his peers and direct reports. He replicated behaviors his coach used with him, such as asking more open-ended questions, checking for understanding before stating his views, and expressing genuine interest in others' work. With encouragement from his coach, he also modified his behavior of eating lunch in his office and began to join others for lunch. He got results. One measure of his success was that more information flowed to him about how others were feeling and functioning, so he was able to monitor and maintain performance and morale more easily. An added benefit was that more feedback about Marc's leadership style flowed to him, specifically that his reliance on a few direct reports was viewed by others as playing favorites and displaying disinterest in the development of the "outsiders." As a result, Marc set new goals that focused on these perceptions.

Through formal assessment, Marc was able to focus on a particular goal—being more accessible and open. Through the coaching relationship, Marc was able to see his coach model openness and was challenged to try unfamiliar behaviors to achieve his goals. He achieved his desired outcome, and a by-product of his new openness was additional informal assessment data regarding perceptions about his relationship with direct reports. Marc, in working with his coach, came to understand the new challenge this posed and used his coaching relationship to continue his development and to work on this new goal through continued application of ACS.

Throughout this coaching experience, Marc and his coach were building a relationship by assessing, addressing challenges, and assuring sufficient support for Marc to achieve desired results. Through processing multirater instrument and ongoing person-to-person feedback with his coach, Marc identified behavioral changes that were challenging (such as asking open-ended questions, checking for understanding, socializing during lunch, and distributing responsibility throughout the team). Concurrently, Marc's coach provided encouragement and modeling and served as a sounding board in support of Marc's identification of new behaviors and development of new habits. Collectively, these efforts produced the results of more productive and enjoyable interaction with his reports.

The ACS elements of the leader development model interact and manifest throughout coaching. Balancing the time and effort spent between and within each of the three aspects (relationship, ACS, and results) is as important in formal coaching as is mixing the right quantities of ingredients in cooking. Our experience confirms what intuition might suggest: that focusing too much or too little on any one component can result in a diminished or, worse yet, adverse impact. Even if all the components listed in a recipe are blended together, if the ingredients are not mixed in the proper proportions, the bread may not rise or the chili may be too bland. In the sections that follow, we discuss how this might occur with each aspect and element of formal coaching and comment on some of the potential impacts.

Relationship

Many features characterize an effective coaching relationship. Our experience suggests that three broad characteristics are particularly important for coaching success: rapport, collaboration, and commitment.

Rapport. Rapport is at the heart of a good coaching relationship. This harmonious state occurs when the coach and coachee connect, understand each other's perspectives, and appreciate each other as people. The coach has primary responsibility for developing rapport with the coachee and recognizing her uniqueness as a person. Satisfied coachees describe their coaches as trustworthy, open, respectful, caring, straightforward, empathic, reciprocal, nonjudgmental, and holding confidences. However, the coach cannot do it all. In the best coaching relationships, the coachee reciprocates these rapport-building behaviors and exhibits appreciation of and openness to the coach as a person.

Collaboration. While rapport connects the hearts of coach and coachee, collaboration connects their minds. Collaboration occurs when coach and coachee work together as equals, with mutual respect, exchanging thoughts and ideas for the purpose of generating new information, options, and solutions. They share a belief that each of them has had relevant experiences, holds important knowledge and perspectives, and brings essential expertise (the coachee about himself and his context and the coach about leadership development and behavioral change processes) that are needed to achieve the purpose of the coaching relationship.

Hart and Kirkland (2001) describe an important area of opportunity for the coachee to assert herself in collaboration (as well as rapport building). They note the importance of the coachee's taking initiative in structuring the coaching process in ways that will promote her success—for example, the types or modalities of coaching meetings (face-to-face, telephone), scheduling, and assurances of confidentiality.

Commitment. Commitment is the bonding agent that supports and potentiates rapport and collaboration within the relationship. Coachee and coach mutually pledge to follow a course of action to fulfill their respective responsibilities in the coaching relationship, persevere through setbacks, and celebrate successes. This commitment is demonstrated through simple behaviors, such as being timely and prepared for scheduled appointments and implementing action plans between meetings. It also takes more complex forms, such as the coach's pushing and probing when the coachee appears to be losing momentum and the coachee's not throwing in the towel when the going gets tough.

Mary and Ron's coaching relationship exemplifies these components and how quickly they come into play. Mary began coaching Ron on his style of leadership, which others had labeled as domineering and micromanaging. She spent their initial two-hour meeting getting to know Ron and listening to him. Without judging or commenting on whether his view was correct, Mary demonstrated an understanding and empathy for Ron's perspective and feelings by accurately paraphrasing his situation and by expressing appreciation for his views about his behaviors. After she sensed that they had established rapport and the beginnings of trust in the relationship, she asked him about his personal life and specifically if he had challenges around similar issues in his personal relationships. Ron became somewhat subdued and revealed that there were severe problems occurring between him and his wife. After listening to Ron's challenges in his marriage, Mary broached the possibility of seeking professional counseling to address the marriage issues. She also explored the impact of and connection between those personal issues and his leadership. In this case, Ron's willingness to open up so quickly about his personal relationship and the way in which Mary responded allowed them to establish a bond based on empathy and compassion. At the same time, Mary's limited venture into the personal arena also served to build further trust in the relationship and open an important avenue for discussion around the impact of Ron's leadership style.

Building the coaching relationship is fundamental, but it is not the end goal. The relationship is a vehicle for facilitating ACS in order to achieve results. If the relationship becomes the primary focus of time spent together, or if the coach does not use the relationship to turn the coachee's attention toward personal development, the coachee may make little progress, achieve minimal results, or not be sufficiently challenged on substantive issues. If the coach becomes overly invested in maintaining a harmonious relationship or the relationship becomes too personal, the coach may find himself reluctant to challenge the coachee, or the coach may be infringing on boundaries that exceed the scope of the coaching relationship.

Assessment, Challenge, and Support

In formal coaching, assessment, challenge, and support are used throughout the process to shape the dialogue and activities of each coaching event. We recognize three levels of work that help people change: behavioral, underlying drivers, and root causes. An important feature of ACS is the depth at which we apply it to the coaching process.

Depth of Coaching Work. At the behavioral level, ACS focuses on observable actions and strives to answer the question, How can one act differently to get more desirable results? Most observers can easily identify behaviors that are having an undesirable impact, and coachees find it easy to be conscious of the behaviors once they have been pointed out. Working at this level to help people modify their less effective actions and behaviors is an essential part of coaching as well as other developmental relationships. In fact, much of the formal coaching described in contemporary literature and delivered by a wide range of vendors today focuses on this approach.

A host of internal forces, however, can significantly influence a coachee's behavior. These factors include personality characteristics, defense mechanisms, and historical points of reference, among many others. Sometimes these forces are so powerful that despite a conscious desire to behave differently, individuals are unable to modify their behavior; they make initial strides but eventually lose momentum and revert to old behaviors. In these situations, the ability to make lasting change may depend on the coachee's managing forces within himself differently. Reflecting on and addressing these internal forces characterize the next two levels of coaching work.

To address underlying drivers, ACS focuses on the coachee's thoughts and feelings that occur before or during his observable behavior. These inner processes are understood as "driving" or triggering the observable behavior. By applying ACS at this level, coaches establish links between internal and observable factors by seeking answers and solutions to the question, What thoughts and feelings cause you to act like that? Working at this level involves integrating quality self-assessment questionnaires, observer feedback, and coachee disclosures about key work and life experiences through skilled facilitation and interpretation by the coach. This level of work is extremely reflective and works with content that the coachee can easily recognize and remember.

Finally, there is the level of root causes. Treatment of these issues typically involves considerable effort to identify the coachee's beliefs, reactions, or historical events that are not easily accessible to her conscious thought and awareness. Work at this level tends to answer the questions, Where do these thoughts, feelings, and behaviors come from and why are they there? Once identified, these factors are typically associated with resistance to change. Working at this level requires using clinical methods to examine the origins of behavior; it sometimes entails reliving events or healing of wounds caused by early-life experiences, which occurred before the individual had a broad frame of reference for making sense of events. We do not see coaching as working at the level of root causes. This type of deeper-level work is usually a lengthier process, has different goals, and requires that the coach have clinical expertise.

We do encourage working at the second level of underlying drivers and engaging in a limited exploration of the coachee's internal and historical world as a means for understanding his external behavior and its impacts on the external world. We characterize this approach as an "inside-out" process as distinguished from an "outside-in" process.

The inside-out process starts with an internal focus on the coachee's developing self-awareness about his thoughts and feelings, what observable behaviors they are likely to trigger, and the impacts of those behaviors on others. Self-management strategies start with a focus on one's internal thoughts and feelings. This process is grounded in the same theories as analytical and psychodynamic psychology. The outside-in process assumes that internal shifts in outlook and orientation can occur through the implementation of repetitive and consistent behaviors that the coachee, over time, internalizes as new habits that become "second nature." This process is grounded in the same theories that support behavioral and cognitive psychology.

While our practice uses both approaches, our preference for the inside-out process assumes the coachee will be more capable of self-directing and building his own learning infrastructure for sustained development if he uses driver-level self-awareness to help effect observable changes in his behavior.

However, it is important to note that to the extent a coach employs the inside-out approach, he engages the gray area of differentiation between coaching and psychotherapy. We do not consider root-level work to be within the realm of leader development coaching. If a coachee is unable to apply behavioral and driver-level coaching strategies and realize growth, he may have what Hart calls "a diagnosable condition" (1997a, 1997b). This is the point at which internal processes and historical factors become the province of psychotherapy, and referral to a mental health professional for assessment and treatment at the root-cause level may be appropriate.

While an in-depth discussion of the differences in coaching, other developmental relationships, and therapy is beyond the scope of this chapter, we assert that the greatest potential for blurring the boundary between coaching and psychotherapy lies in decisions about how directly to work with internal factors and how deeply to probe them. To avoid exceeding the boundaries of coaching, we limit the extent to which we delve into internal causes while applying the inside-out approach, recognizing that psychotherapy often works at a deeper level than our coaching. Having examined the depth at which we apply assessment, challenge, and support, we now turn our attention to the application of each of these elements in our coaching framework.

Assessment. Assessment can function as an "unfreezing" experience that enables a coachee to see herself differently or become more aware of how she affects others. Having a full picture of the coachee's current skills and perspectives, from her own view and from the perspective of others, is crucial to helping her decide what goals she wants to set. The coachee can obtain a rich assessment through a number of avenues that will be discussed later in the chapter.

Through the assessment element of the framework, the coach and coachee work toward clarity by reconciling various perspectives. This is emphasized during the data-gathering phase of the coaching program and repeatedly surfaces throughout coaching interactions as coach and coachee seek to learn from experiences. The coach's skills at interpreting, analyzing, summarizing, and distilling assessment data, in collaboration with the coachee, is critical to leveraging the power of this element.

The coachee is a key contributor to the assessment process. Prior to the first coaching meeting, the coachee may engage in structured interviews, complete written surveys, participate in structured activities, and engage in more open-ended dialogue with the coach. While information gathered from others can identify behaviors on which the coaching might focus, the coachee herself holds the knowledge about underlying drivers and motivations even if she may not always be aware of the links between inward drivers and outward behaviors.

Consider the case of Monica, whose employer engaged a coach to enhance her leadership skills. Her company was one of the premier global banking firms, considered within the industry as highly discriminating in both its client base and its employee hires. This organization took pride in cultivating an elitist culture with an "up or out" development approach. Though the company highly valued Monica for her intellectual prowess, one particular attribute the company felt she needed to learn was how to convey more "executive presence." The company saw this skill as especially critical because the current economy was tight and the business environment was unusually competitive for high-quality clients. Upon completion of the assessment stage and during their discussion of the feedback, the coach asked Monica to expand on what "executive presence" meant and looked like to her and how her perceived lack of it was affecting her leadership and career aspirations. As Monica began to answer the question, two issues emerged. First, the issue of executive presence seemed related to Monica's discomfort with being in the spotlight and her inability to command attention and respect when in a room of her peers. Second, she had difficulty articulating her career goals. She expressed ambivalence about aspiring to higher levels. Her reasons were, in part, because of life balance trade-offs and also because she equated achieving that higher level with learning to become more aggressive and less collaborative; that is, she interpreted "executive presence" negatively. Monica had not recognized the impact of her discomfort and unfavorable belief on her behavior.

When assessment is discussed in an individual leadership and coaching context, people usually think of collecting data about the person. While the coachee is the primary target for assessment, assessing the coachee's context is also essential. Contextual factors can greatly affect what leadership styles will thrive, be tolerated, or derail individuals. As became evident in Monica's case, the organizational norms, culture, business environment, and current work conditions and challenges played a significant role in the perceptions of Monica's leadership style. It also became an important topic of discussion within the coaching relationship as Monica struggled to reconcile her personal values with the organization's values and expectations.

It is possible to use too much or too little assessment. Underassessment takes three primary forms: insufficient or poor quality data, overinterpretation of a few data points, and inadequate review of data (moving to a conclusion too quickly). The impact of underassessment can be that the coachee's effort is misguided toward a goal less meaningful to her long-term development or that she does not fully buy into the coaching process. In either case, the coach will be unable to get traction with the coachee around meaningful goals. Therefore, coaches and coachees are cautioned not to perform a superficial assessment or move through the process of assessing the coachee or her context too quickly.

For example, from all levels, Lina received extensive feedback that she was micromanaging. She did not feel she was doing so, nor did she understand the behaviors that caused her to get this label. Staff reported that when giving an assignment, she always gave extensive instructions on how to accomplish the task, constantly checked on their progress, and sometimes even took over the work. Through a deeper assessment of her personality style and life experiences, Lina concluded that she was an excessively action-oriented individual and someone who did not easily trust. Had the coach relied solely on observer assessment data, these two underlying drivers would not have been identified as behaviors that caused others to conclude that Lina was micromanaging. What Lina eventually learned was that giving instructions was OK and even welcomed when the staff needed more direction or were stuck. She learned to ask first what they needed from her, to trust what they said, and to measure accomplishment not through detailed actions but more by outcome.

Overassessment can occur when too many assessments or too many assessment methodologies are used simultaneously. It is possible to have an abundance of riches—the benefits of more and richer data can reach a point of diminishing returns. What constitutes "too much" data depends largely on the individual's need for and comfort with data, her ability to absorb and integrate different views, and her resilience. It also depends on the level of organizational support available to assist the coachee in addressing the perceived gaps during the coaching program and after it formally concludes.

The possible impacts of overassessment, especially negative feedback, can be that the coachee becomes paralyzed or demoralized, loses motivation, or even becomes temporarily depressed. Worse yet, if inadequate follow-up support is offered, a further impact might be cynicism on the part of the coachee and others. The coach can help manage and calibrate the amount of feedback both at the onset, when decisions regarding how much and what data to collect are made, and during delivery, based on how the coachee is responding to the data shared.

This is illustrated by the case of Rich, a data-hungry executive. In his business context, data were king, and he desired the same approach in his coaching program. His coach, Joan, administered the standard series of assessments. After receiving feedback on two sets of data, however, Rich was visibly subdued. While the feedback was more negative than positive, it was within the norm of what other executives receive. Rich's response to it, though, was more pessimistic. Joan made a decision to hold back the remaining data, since they reinforced the earlier feedback and on some dimensions were even more critical.

In this case, a small degree of exposure caused a "fast thaw" and potentially a meltdown. Sometimes more is *not* better. The key is to monitor the coachee's response and energy level and calibrate the quantity of data according to need and receptivity. To the extent that initial and ongoing assessment provides useful feedback about the coachee's behaviors, the inner drivers for those behaviors, and the impacts of the behaviors, coachee and coach have valuable points of reference for identifying and engaging developmental challenges.

Challenge. As described in the Introduction, challenges come in many forms and have one thing in common: they create disequilibrium. That state, which is usually described as uncomfortable, represents the opportunity for learning and change as the coachee engages in actions for self-development.

In a formal coaching program, challenges are generated in a number of ways and take different forms. Most often, coachees find it challenging to review assessment information where perceptions of respondents may not fully align with their own perceptions and those of the coach.

Challenging experiences also result from the new and different behaviors or assignments that the coachee undertakes in the workplace. Often called action plans or developmental action plans, these are typically deliberate choices to practice different behavior. Sometimes these choices are not deliberate but are instead driven by the need to adapt to circumstances in the work context that occur during the coaching program, such as a new assignment, a reorganization, or a business goal. New behaviors are often uncomfortable for the coachee. Since they involve reaching beyond the familiar, they are sometimes referred to as stretch assignments, suggesting the challenge of stretching beyond one's comfort zone.

Obstacles can also contribute to challenge. They come in two types, external and internal. External obstacles are environmental factors like limited resources, market conditions, regulatory restrictions, or oppositional direct reports, peers, or bosses. Internal obstacles are factors like fear or lack of self-confidence. This is where our inside-out approach, focusing on drivers, can accelerate development.

Last, challenging experiences in a formal coaching program can be created through the coach's direct interaction with the coachee. This may come in the form of questioning the coachee's interpretations, conclusions, choices, and goals or, once goals have been set, holding the coachee accountable for meeting commitments to specific actions and behavior changes.

Finding the right amount of challenge is a balancing act because different individuals need differing amounts of challenge to feel motivated to grow and change. Overchallenge can occur as a result of a number of conditions. When an assessment is too negative, when the gap between the current state and the desired state is beyond the coachee's immediate capability, when too many goals are set, or when the coach pushes too hard, the coachee may feel overwhelmed. If she is unable or unwilling to articulate this, she may attempt to achieve the goals and fail—either because she cannot sustain focus on the many goals or because the stretch was too great and not broken into more manageable, shorter-term targets. When stretching fails, a loss of energy or diffused effort can occur, and old behavioral patterns will dig in and remain unchanged. Another response to overchallenge is the relentless effort to achieve all the goals set within a short period; burnout is a natural consequence of that dynamic. Resistance is a third response: the coachee finds reasons to deny the assessment, avoid setting goals, and avoid following through on commitments to actions.

Conversely, without enough challenge, the coachee may have little reason or motivation to change and grow. Underchallenge can occur when assessment information is superficial or unenlightening, when set goals do not require the development of new skills or behaviors, when results are measured in inputs and activity rather than outcomes and progress, or when the coach does not probe the coachee's assumptions and choices.

Even with an optimal balance of challenges, in pursuing the process of formal coaching, an individual takes on more than the usual workload and makes efforts to overcome old habits. This typically adds to stress and fatigue. An individual's chances of success are increased when a suitable level of support is received.

Support. A supportive environment facilitates development. Support is needed even more if challenge knocks a coachee off center; in that event, support enables the coachee to right himself and perhaps find a new center of balance. However, what feels like support varies for different people. Accordingly, in a formal coaching program, the coach needs to be prepared to offer support in a way that meets the coachee's particular needs.

Coaches meet these needs by helping the coachee in three key ways: to identify motivators that will sustain his commitment to growth and sustain him through the sometimes uncomfortable learning process, to recognize small wins and manage setbacks or lulls in growth, and to identify and access resources and tactics necessary for success.

Helping the coachee stay aware of his personal and professional goals and aspirations can sustain the momentum that builds from the insights the coachee garners through assessment—and it can jump-start him if his growth begins to languish. If aspirations begin to shift because of changes in context or life circumstances, the coach can assist in rethinking goals. And as necessary, the coachee may set new or modified goals. Regardless of outcome, the coach assists the coachee by ensuring his growth process aligns with his ideals.

Second, coaches help place small achievements and setbacks in perspective. Too often leaders focus on hitting home runs and neglect to celebrate the hits to first, second, and third base. The cumulative impact of small successes leads to desired outcomes just as surely as major achievements do (Kram, Ting, and Bunker, 2002), but executives often miss this lesson and, if unsuccessful in making significant change quickly, give up or get distracted. The coach helps the coachee see movement, even if only in small increments. And if the coachee strikes out, the coach facilitates the process of learning from experience by reminding the coachee that unsuccessful efforts are inevitable, helping him evaluate what went wrong as well as what went right, and applying this learning in preparation for the next at-bat.

Last, support involves knowing what resources to access and which tactics to employ to succeed. Often a coachee sees limited possibilities and options or has not thought through what he will need to succeed and how to gain support of the organization in accessing those resources. The coach can help the coachee move past obstacles and find the path of least resistance to needed resources. In addition, the coach can help the coachee employ his dominant learning tactics strategically, as well as employ underutilized learning tactics that can facilitate or deepen his growth (see Chapter Seven).

When there is insufficient support, a coachee may find the learning curve too steep to climb or get discouraged along the learning path. He may have initial successes but be unable to sustain the change. He may even resist engaging fully in the process early on if he does not sense adequate support will be forthcoming when he experiences the greatest challenges.

With too much support, a coachee may not assume full responsibility for her learning and may become too dependent on the coach or others for drive and motivation. She may develop a false sense of assurance, lose sight of her goals, and even misinterpret the support as "I don't need to change." The coach can assist the coachee in recognizing this possibility and guard against perpetuating or creating false reassurance by overempathizing or functioning solely as a cheerleader.

Results

When the right balance of ACS exists in the context of a trusting relationship, coachees achieve results. In our coaching practice, results tend to focus on three areas:

- *Behavioral change:* exhibiting more of, less of, new, or different behaviors as perceived by others in the organizational environment, to achieve more effective leadership
- *Personal and professional development:* identifying and engaging in long-term strategies and short-term tactics to enhance the individual's development as a leader, professional, and person, consistent with her values, vision, and goals
- *Learning agility:* developing an increased ability to learn and to direct that learning independently; this includes knowing how to perform self-assessment, employ a variety of learning tactics, and develop a sustainable learning infrastructure

Work-related behavioral changes are most common in and expected by organizations because these changes can occur immediately and can be observed. The other two forms of results may take longer to achieve and may be less visible to others. All three forms of results can be measured by qualitative and quantitative means. Informal qualitative measurements involve the coachee's self-assessment (based on internal or more personal measures, such as the extent to which she feels more capable and competent on a certain leadership dimension). They may also include informal feedback from selected individuals. More formal qualitative measurements may involve reinterviewing respondents for feedback on the specific goals set or verbatim feedback on a written survey. Quantitative measures typically take the form of written assessment surveys.

As with effective assessments, using multiple means to review results offers a more complete view of the coachee's accomplishments. An overreliance on one or two sources of feedback or evaluation may result in new blind spots because the coachee has no alternative feedback loop to serve as a reality check or verify that perception. Also, if the coachee overrelies on highly contextual feedback, he runs the risk of adapting his leadership style to a particular situation or to a narrow audience.

For example, imagine a coachee who has received feedback that he needs to give more attention to and fully meet the needs of his work group. He does that but then begins to neglect his relationship with peers or becomes blind to others' perceptions that his work team is not meeting the needs of internal customers. If he relies only on the personal feedback from his team without monitoring his effectiveness with other stakeholder groups, he may miss important signals that he has overcorrected or neglected other skills.

At the other extreme, an overreliance on quantitative measurements of results may not fully capture what the coachee has learned or may cause the coachee to focus on too narrow an aspect of his development. There is also a growing tendency for companies to want to measure leadership development in the same ways it measures business success and to demand tangible proof of a direct link to business results because quantitative measures are needed to justify the investment of development dollars. We would caution companies from overstating the need for proof of causality with business results because many factors, in addition to leadership, contribute to business success.

Our caution about what and how to measure results should not be interpreted as inconsistent with our belief that measuring results is crucial. "Keeping score" enables the coachee to know when he has achieved success and to examine its impact. In the absence of that information, he may not realize when it is time to practice desired behaviors more, reevaluate his tactics, try new approaches, celebrate success, or set new goals.

The coaching framework we have described provides a context for the activities performed in the course of the coaching process, which we will describe shortly. Before moving to that section, however, we acknowledge the principles that constitute the foundation of our coaching framework.

Coaching Principles

We have developed certain principles that guide our coaching. These rules of action ensure that our knowledge of leader development is applied across a wide variety of effective coaching styles and coachee needs.

For example, some coaches use humor or sarcasm, and some do not; some coaches are dramatic and expressive, while others are low key; and some coaches refer extensively to the business and developmental literature, while others focus more on the coachee's experience and context. Coachees also differ with respect to the coaching style that works best for them. Some respond better to one personality type than another, and some respond well to a variety of types. Coach behaviors that irritate one coachee might motivate another.

It is beyond the scope of this chapter to examine the range of coaching styles and coachee needs; however, we offer six principles that define the character of our coaching and are imbedded in all the styles used by our coaches.

1. *Create a safe but challenging environment.* It is the coach's responsibility to create a safe environment in which the coachee can take risks and learn. In the coaching process, the ability to live this principle depends on the coach's skill at balancing challenging and supporting behaviors. Regardless of what the coach believes may be true or right for the coachee, she must ensure that the coaching process does not damage the coachee's sense of self or open wounds that are not easily healed.

2. *Work with the coachee's agenda.* The learning experience is, first and foremost, for and about the individual leader. The coachee is responsible for driving the process and directing his own learning. He decides which goals to work on and how to go about it. While others (such as his boss) have a strong stake in the process and outcomes, their role is to influence the agenda, not set it.

3. *Facilitate.* A fundamental feature of our approach to coaching is to make it easier for the coachee to implement ACS rather than directing the coachee in what to do. Facilitation is a key aspect of the collaborative nature of our work. Although a coach typically possesses considerable knowledge and expertise, she does not act like an expert. She should not become preoccupied with disclosing personal reactions, telling her own stories, advocating her preferred theories and techniques, making recommendations, or giving instructions. The coach should be very selective about such directive actions, doing so only to the extent that it is clearly relevant to the coachee's needs and agenda and only when more facilitative methods will not work as well. The coach is not there to lecture, opine, or pontificate. And although the coach may suggest options, the ultimate decision rests with the coachee.

4. *Advocate self-awareness.* Knowing one's strengths and development needs is a prerequisite to leader development. By learning to better recognize his own behaviors and understand the impacts they may have, the coachee is better able to analyze or predict the outcomes of his interactions with others and take steps to achieve desired results.

5. *Promote sustainable learning from experience.* Most individuals have the capacity to learn, grow, and change, given readiness and the right set of experiences. Reflecting on those experiences is a powerful method for identifying personal strengths and development needs as well as opportunities and obstacles. We encourage the coachee to think about events from the perspective of what worked well and what did not work so well and to use the findings of this process to chart a course to enhanced leader capabilities. The coach supports that process by modeling use of the ACS elements to leverage learning. Ultimately, the coach should recede from the coachee's life. By that time, the coachee should understand her best learning processes, and she should be able and motivated to practice the ACS elements for herself.

6. *Model what we coach.* It is the coach's responsibility to exhibit the emotional competencies (such as self-awareness, self-management, social awareness, and social skills; Goleman, 1998) that the leader is trying to develop. It can be challenging for the coach to apply this principle. For example, in order to model effective, in-the-moment feedback, the coach might face the challenge of describing the negative impact that the coachee's behavior is having on him.

The Coaching Process

While the coaching framework offers an understanding of how and why coaching is developmental, this section offers a practical guide to enacting a formal coaching program. To this end, we will describe a formal coaching program as a structured, one-on-one learning process delivered by an external coaching vendor comprised of a group of coaches and that has an articulated coaching philosophy and methodology.

A formal coaching program has three phases: preprogram, program implementation, and postprogram. Each phase has a series of key activities.

- *Preprogram activities:* assessing need and readiness, matching coachee and coach, designing the program
- *Program implementation activities:* getting started, evaluating the current state, reviewing the feedback and facilitating awareness, constructing a personal learning agenda, implementing the plan, measuring outcomes, transitioning from coaching
- *Postprogram activities:* evaluating program and coach effectiveness

Preprogram Activities

Taking time with the preprogram activities before making a final decision to engage in formal coaching pays dividends once the program is under way. When done thoughtfully, these activities increase the likelihood of a successful outcome.

Identify Client Need. The first activity is to understand the client's need. There are four basic questions that help clarify need and will influence the program's design:

- What reasons drive the inquiry or request for coaching?
- What are the desired outcomes?
- What is the impact if the outcomes are not achieved?

- What causes the client to believe that a formal coaching program is the appropriate development activity?

The responses to these questions enable the coach to determine if she is facing a "fix-it," in which the leader has an identified gap in skill and might derail, or a situation in which the leader is ready for a rich developmental experience to prepare him for future challenges. The coach will also learn if she is dealing with a specific behavioral issue or a broader development agenda and if the client organization is looking for specific behavioral changes or general growth. These are some examples of the types of information that should become known through the initial discussion of need.

When a client organization initially presents its need, it is reasonable to assume that the organization has accurately assessed formal coaching as the appropriate developmental experience. However, this may not always be the case; the organization may not have fully considered the range of developmental opportunities. Coaches therefore have the added role and professional responsibility during these initial discussions to ensure that coaching is the appropriate learning option for the expressed need before they proceed to match coach and coachee or design a program. Some individual development issues may benefit more from a group learning setting or may be a team or organizational issue too narrowly diagnosed as an individual development problem. So even though the prospective client may enter with a declared coaching need, the coaching vendor should probe sufficiently to satisfy itself and the client that a formal coaching program is the preferred response.

Assess Organizational and Coachee Readiness. A close cousin to need is readiness. There are two levels of readiness: individual and organizational. At the individual level, there are also two aspects of readiness: the first is psychological, and the second is environmental.

Psychological readiness includes motivation, capability, willingness to proceed, and commitment to candid assessment and action-oriented follow-through. Prospective coachees enter coaching in different states of psychological readiness. Sometimes they desire coaching and initiate the process. At other times, they engage it in collaboration or compliance with another key person who has urged them to proceed. Or they are sentenced to coaching, as if it were a diversion program offering one last chance before dismissal or reassignment to a position where less harm can be done. Regardless of what brings him to coaching, a coachee should meet a minimal threshold of psychological readiness to offer any opportunity of success: a willingness to make time, to fulfill coaching meetings and program elements, and to keep mind and heart open to the process.

Environmental readiness has more to do with external factors such as time, resources, relevance, and compatibility with one's current work situation. For instance, Jorge was actively involved in leadership development opportunities and was looking forward to receiving coaching, which was offered to individuals at his level. As he was enrolling, the organization asked him to assume a "turnaround assignment" that required him to quickly acquire new technical skills, become familiar with a new group of direct reports, and use his known strengths in building teams. Jorge and the potential coach concluded that the "hard skills" learning curve on the job was steep and would require immediate and intensive devotion. Jorge knew he could do that quickly by accessing knowledge within the current team and at the same time learning more about their skills and interactions. He felt that the real challenge to his leadership skills, and therefore the point at which he could benefit most from coaching, would emerge once he became familiar with the new operations and people. Jorge and the potential coach agreed to postpone the start of their work together until Jorge had had a chance to assess the situation, the extent of challenge he faced, and the type of support he needed going forward. At that point, he could also obtain early feedback from his new direct reports about his impact on them and the business. In Jorge's case, he was psychologically ready but the conditions needed ripening before he could make optimal use of the coaching opportunity.

In addition to individual readiness, organizational readiness is an important factor. Experience teaches that while the coachee is ultimately responsible for and most influential in determining the success of coaching initiatives, the nature of outcomes is not determined solely by the coachee or even by the coachee and the coach together. The organization's commitment to and participation in the process are also critical.

Organizational readiness for coaching initiatives can be demonstrated by a wide range of actions, including removing roadblocks to the coaching process or goal achievement, implementing systems that facilitate the coaching process, influencing organizational culture to support coaching, and ensuring that developmental learning is in alignment with organizational priorities by checking on the goals and progress of the coaching process.

For example, the attitudes toward coaching initiatives of both the coachee and others (peers, managers, direct reports) can either facilitate or undermine the coaching process. Consider the implications if employees get the general impression that coaching is being provided to just a favored few or only when the coachee is perceived by managers as "broken" and on the path to derailment. Either scenario is bad for morale and the coaching relationship. It is the organization's responsibility to set the tone for the role of coaching in the organization. If this is done well and with sincerity, the organization can facilitate readiness in the individual by building a strong organizational platform for coaching.

Jim's situation illustrates this point. He was shaken by an allegation that he committed gender discrimination. Previously, he had terminated Laura based on poor performance. Laura claimed she was fired because of being female. A subsequent review of documents revealed ample evidence, over a significant period of time, that Laura's performance was substandard and that she had not improved significantly, notwithstanding several interventions by the organization. Although the case was dismissed, the organization recognized that the ordeal had taken its toll on Jim, so it arranged formal coaching for him. Jim mistakenly believed that the organization still doubted his integrity and consequently hired a coach to "find him out" or "fix him." The organization and Jim put very different frames on the same picture. Had the organization been more successful in representing to Jim that the coaching was for support and empowerment, Jim might have entered the coaching relationship with more psychological readiness.

Another way organizations display readiness for coaching is through their ability to clearly and realistically articulate anticipated outcomes. When expected outcomes are not communicated well, organizations run the risk that coaching will change behavior, but not in the ways organizational leaders had in mind when they approved the coaching program. Another possible consequence of inadequate direction and momentum is that little or no behavioral change may take place.

In general, organizations with a high degree of readiness are able to do all of the following:

- Determine the purpose of the coaching initiative and clearly communicate it to the appropriate people
- Promote the coaching initiative in alignment with the organization's vision and values, as an integral part of strategic plans, and as a means to develop talent and sharpen the competitive edge of both the individual and the organization
- Make greater use of coaching as a developmental rather than a rehabilitative process
- Clearly identify, adequately and consistently communicate, and reinforce the behavior it wants from employees
- Recognize and respond favorably to new desired behaviors
- Tolerate performance dips that occur during the learning process
- Monitor progress and outcomes and reward behavioral changes

Sometimes the organizational context is not ideal for coaching. The boss may be insufficiently involved or skeptical or may make demands that continually preempt the coaching work. The organization itself may not be ready: senior leaders may be in conflict over the value and role of coaching, what the organization says it values in leadership may not be congruent with what it rewards, or there may be mixed messages about coaching. With support from the coach, the coachee needs to decide how the extent of organizational readiness will affect what she is trying to accomplish. However, even with marginal organizational support, the coachee who is ready can still achieve some success.

In many cases, it will be appropriate for the coach to discuss such contextual issues with appropriate persons. All discussions must respect the confidentiality of information shared between the coach and coachee, as well as other ethical considerations. (A full discussion of this point lies beyond the scope of this chapter.)

Compile Data. As part of the needs and readiness assessment, the coach or coaching vendor should begin to compile data on the coachees. Not only does this information contribute to understanding need and readiness, but it also provides valuable information in preparation for the next steps, matching the coachee with a coach and designing a program. Typical data include the following:

- Basic contact information, such as name, title, mailing addresses, phone numbers, and e-mail addresses of the coachee, the coachee's supervisor, and the coachee's HR professional or organizational sponsor
- A brief description of perceived strengths and weaknesses
- Easily accessible and releasable personal information, such as biography, background information, interests, and résumé
- Inventory of relevant preexisting assessment data (both personal style and multirater inventories)
- Preferences for coach selection, such as background, experience, and content expertise
- Organizational background information such as products and services offered by the organization, current state and challenges of the organization in its business sector, general organizational structure, nature of the organizational culture, and role of each prospective coachee in the organization
- Objectives for the coaching process

Once need and readiness have been clarified and both parties agree that undertaking a formal coaching program has merit, the final two preprogram activities—matching and refining the program design—will occur before the formal process begins. The sequencing of these steps is less important than ensuring that each occurs with a maximum level of input from the coachee wherever possible. Often when an organizational broker handles the request, the program design and identification of potential coaches will be well under way by the time the coachee becomes involved. We recommend, even with systemic efforts, that some flexibility and decision making be reserved for the coachee, to enable her to feel ownership in the coaching process.

Match Coachee and Coach. Ideally, an organization has several coaches or coaching vendors from which to consider matches for the coachee. Matching involves two stages: a process that identifies possible suitable coaches and a "fit conversation" between the coachee and coach for final selection.

A good match, or fit, involves alignment between the coachee's needs, style, beliefs, and developmental challenges and the coach's skills, style, and previous experience. In addition to using the demographic data captured at the initial intake, the following are factors to consider when matching a coachee with a coach:

- Compatibility in behavioral preferences, personality, interpersonal needs, and work style
- Commonalities in personal, educational, and work backgrounds, as well as areas of interest
- Level of coach background and experience in the coachee's sector and function
- Capabilities of the prospective coach in dealing with any special problems or challenges noted when collecting coachee identification data

Note, however, that alignment does not equal likeness. In some cases, having similar behavioral preferences or personality profiles will be desirable to facilitate rapport and communication. In other cases, a difference of preference or personality profile will be desirable to stretch the coachee in learning to work with differences. For example, some CEOs will be served best by a coach who has functioned at that level (though such a coach may be hard to find). Other CEOs will benefit most from an expert in behavioral change or relationship and reputation management.

A well-planned and organized matching process will yield promising pairings, but no matter how good a match looks on paper, the final test is how well a pair "connects," either over the phone or face to face. Good fit is an essential part of the relationship aspect of the coaching framework.

"Fit conversations" should last twenty to thirty minutes and should clarify whether sufficient rapport exists on which a relationship can be built; whether the coach has the skills, content knowledge, and experience to meet the coachee's needs; whether coachee readiness is sufficient; and whether the two generally concur on program goals and design. This last task will be repeated in greater detail once the coachee and coach actually begin the coaching program. Coachees can find valuable guidelines for deciding whether the coach is a good fit in *Choosing an Executive Coach* (Kirkland Miller and Hart, 2001).

An added benefit of the fit conversation is to help build momentum and create continuity between the initial coachee-coach discussion and subsequent coaching contacts. It also transitions the commitment to coaching from the coachee's company and coaching entity to the coachee and coach.

Refine Program Design. Appropriate program design is largely a function of coachee needs and organizational resources. Accordingly, the scope and design of coaching programs varies widely and will evolve, starting with a schematic, usually negotiated at the organizational level, and growing into a fuller, more detailed design once the coachee and coach begin their work.

The most important factor in influencing program design harks back to our initial discussion about need. The coaching client and her needs are paramount in selecting a program design. Good designs have the common components noted earlier in our discussion of program implementation; however, the depth, breadth, and delivery modality for each component can vary significantly.

A number of baseline decisions should be made. For example, is the program for a single individual or a group of individuals? John might receive coaching in preparation for a promotion, or Beverly might receive coaching to improve her abilities to influence without authority. On the group level, members of the senior management team might receive one-to-one coaching for better collaboration across functional boundaries, or new hires and promotions might receive coaching to assist transition to new responsibilities and reporting structures.

A second question is whether the organization should use a generic design for many coachees or allow individuals to customize the program to fit their needs. Regardless of whether a customized or standardized design is selected, decisions about the following design elements need to be made:

- *Duration.* How long will the coaching engagement last?
- *Modality.* What combination of in-person and telephone meetings will be used? How might other electronic communications be used?
- *Frequency.* How often will the contacts occur?
- *Confidentiality.* With whom and how will information be shared, and what formal and informal roles will other key individuals have in the program? Typically, the coachee initiates all content information sharing.
- *Assessment tools.* In general, the type and depth of assessment to be done and how outcome measurement will be handled must be determined. (Specific assessment decisions are discussed in greater detail in the section on program implementation.)

• *Coaching tools.* Although the decision on coaching techniques to be used is mostly a function of the specific relationship and coachee needs during the actual coaching, some discussion of possible approaches is important for both coachee and organizational understanding of the range of approaches that might be employed. For example, the most common approach, collaborative dialogue, may be supplemented with other techniques, such as role playing, story writing, mind mapping, and visioning.

• *Delivery system.* Though our discussion of formal coaching is focused on a program in which the entire developmental experience is delivered through a relationship with a single coach, in fact there are a number of other delivery mechanisms that should be considered. One approach involves having one coachee work with two coaches. This design is best suited for top-level executives. Approaches may also include integrating the coaching with other developmental experiences—for example, combining one-to-one coaching with a classroom leadership program or with specialized training in a hard skill such as strategic thinking, speech making, or finance.

When all these considerations have been addressed, it is customary for the organization and the coaching vendor to execute a written contract that defines the nature and scope of services, fees, confidentiality policies, and other matters common to such documents.

Program Implementation Activities

The preprogram activities set the stage for this next phase, program implementation, in which the coaching occurs. By this point, responsibility for the coaching process has been fully transferred to the coachee and coach. The client organization and coaching vendor assume the secondary role of support to the process.

Getting Started. The climax of the preprogram phase is the execution of a contract for services, which usually occurs near the end of that stage. The first step in the program implementation phase also involves an agreement, only this is a verbal contract between the coachee and coach. The discussions that occur as part of this contracting will cover some of the same ground discussed during the preprogram phase but will be done in greater depth. These conversations are important because, in addition to building the relationship aspect of the framework, they help create a shared mind-set and establish the ground rules for the coaching process.

The coach should take this opportunity to clarify his dual responsibility. His first responsibility is to the coachee—for finding the most effective way to work with each other, honoring the coachee's learning style and helping her to achieve her goals. His second responsibility is to the organization, for executing the coaching contract with due diligence and facilitating outcomes consistent with the established expectations.

As part of the relationship building and continuation of the fit conversation, the coach will learn more about the coachee by using an informal, conversational approach. Once the two are comfortable, they may move into a more structured interview process. Through these questions, the coachee's uniqueness as a person emerges as the coach learns about the environment in which the coachee functions and the current state of her work and personal life (Hart and Kirkland, 2001). This last point reflects one aspect of our distinctive form of coaching. We believe that coaching functions at its maximum effectiveness when it considers the "whole person." This means asking about and listening deeply to understand the aspects of a coachee's personal life that she considers significant. Often events and relationships in the coachee's personal arena have an impact on her behavior at work. However, until the coach has an opportunity to talk in-depth with the coachee, he has a limited view of the situation generated largely by the coachee's organization.

Coaches should also share enough information about themselves to put the coachee at ease and make a connection. The individual style and needs of the coachee will determine how much and what type of information (professional and personal) the coach and coachee will share with each other.

The coachee and coach should each share their understanding of the purpose of the program to assess the degree of alignment in their perspectives. Often the coachee has very sketchy or general information about the purpose of and goals for the coaching engagement. Sometimes a coachee will have personal beliefs about the "real reason" for coaching, as Jim did in the example presented earlier. The coachee may have strong feelings about how the coaching opportunity came about. She may not see it as a positive opportunity but as a sanction. However, she may not be comfortable sharing her true feelings during the fit conversation, not knowing how the coach will react or if the coach will judge her.

When the coach shares his understanding, he should be forthright even if the information may be viewed as challenging. What the coach shares and how he shares his understanding becomes part of the ongoing relationship-building process. This is typically the first opportunity for coaches to build trust by modeling open, honest, and nonjudgmental behaviors.

In addition to comparing notes about the whys of the engagement, the verbal contracting process allows the coach and coachee to set mutual expectations for going forward. This is the time to discuss what they each expect to accomplish from their work together. They will set general goals for the coaching program and ensure alignment with any stated organizational expectations. These will evolve as the coachee identifies better-defined goals through the assessment process.

The coach and coachee should also talk about boundaries for the relationship and the range of topics that might be discussed. Where they set these limits depends on a number of factors. The provisions of the program contract are most important. Note that this chapter focuses on coaching done by someone external to the organization. So here we are discussing setting boundaries for external coaches. More and more, organizations are using their own staff as internal coaches, and we believe that boundary setting is different and more complicated when internal coaches are used. However, that discussion is beyond the scope of this chapter.

In addition to setting boundaries, the coach and coachee will also want to establish ground rules for managing various aspects of the coaching program. This is an early opportunity for the coach to experience at first hand the coachee's working style and preferences and learn how she might need to modify her own style to best work with the coachee. This also gives the coach and coachee the opportunity to further customize the process to meet the client's needs, albeit within the framework established by the contractually agreed coaching program. These issues may seem basic, but having an agreement in place is an important foundation for a smooth working relationship.

Because the coachee operates within a context, she should discuss with the coach who the significant people are in her work and personal life and how they may be involved in the coaching program. Examples include boss, human resource staff, and the boss's superiors. We advise coaches not to become go-betweens in these other relationships. Whenever possible, any insights and data the coachee wants to share with the coach or others should be done directly by the coachee. Conversely, it is also preferable that the coachee be the one to seek informal feedback from these individuals, rather than having the coach intervene. The coach may, however, serve as a facilitator in such discussions if so desired by the coachee.

From the start, the coachee and coach should anticipate potential obstacles that may negatively affect the coaching program. This is a challenge that they face and can address together. They should develop counterstrategies to keep the work on track when these obstacles arise. Common obstacles we have encountered in our work with clients include limited time, lack of support from others, extreme work demands, ambivalent motivation, and inadequate resources.

Evaluating the Current State. Gathering and analyzing high-quality data enables the coachee to gain a clearer picture of herself. This stage consists of planning and implementing a process of data collection and preliminary analysis.

In many cases, assessment instruments are specified ahead of time during the program design phase. In that case, this part of the coaching process involves clarification and consideration of modifications to the plan.

Often, though, the program design envisions the general type and form of assessment, such as using 360-degree surveys, personality inventories, and structured interviews conducted by the coach, but not the specific instruments or the exact number of interview questions. In these situations, the coach and coachee have more decisions to make regarding what data to collect. They can begin by reviewing the quality and availability of existing data. Typically, because written surveys have a shelf life and anecdotal data may be skewed if they come from limited sources and observations, the coach and coachee will choose to gather new and current data. Table 4.1 lists different types of data with their benefits and considerations. As noted earlier, we recommend a blend of formal and informal data. Written surveys offer quantitative and normative data, and interviews offer highly contextual and customized feedback. Organizational and coachee expectations should drive the depth and comprehensiveness of assessment.

Once the assessment tools have been agreed on, the coachee selects respondents for multirater surveys. Typical respondents include direct reports, peers, superiors, coworkers outside the immediate hierarchy, and internal stakeholders. Less typical but potentially valuable respondents are suppliers, customers, spouses or life partners, other family members, friends, and community members.

Coachees often look to the coach for guidance on whom to include. Although there is no set formula, we recommend that coachees select respondents who offer diverse perspectives and possess one or more of the following attributes:

- They have the opportunity to observe the coachee directly.
- They are in the coachee's immediate work group.
- They have a substantial impact on the coachee's work life.
- They have seen the coachee in a variety of settings.
- The coachee values their judgment.
- They may have had a conflict with the coachee but need to maintain an ongoing working relationship.
- They may have a different style from that of the coachee.
- They will be candid.
- They know the coachee well.
- The coachee depends on them for achieving certain business goals.

If the coaching program uses both written surveys and interviews, the coachee has the luxury of casting a wider net by asking respondents to participate in only one or two of these feedback activities. Although comprehensive data are good to have, we offer two cautions in addition to our earlier caveat about overassessing: obtain the data within a short time frame so that they are fresh, and avoid overloading any individual respondent.

There is one activity that occurs prior to reviewing the feedback data with the coachee that is one of the few times when the coach does not collaborate with the coachee. The coach, who should be highly skilled in analyzing and interpreting

TABLE 4.1. FORMS OF ASSESSMENT.

Type of Data	Benefits	Considerations
Hard		
Feedback surveys: multirater and 360-degree individual, team, and organization	Easily administered Quantifiable Permit norm comparisons Anonymity Time-efficient	Information about context is minimal Reliability and validity of instrument should be verified
Personality style surveys	Supplement current-state feedback with underlying orientation Can help explain behavioral feedback	Not designed to address context Not a measurement of effectiveness
Soft		
Biographical inventory, work history, and background; personal history and background; self-descriptors	Offer insights from client's perspective Often anticipate and reinforce other data	Time to complete more comprehensive surveys
Interviews	Clear context Personalized information More elaborate and detailed descriptions Richer data Provide coach with a keener sense of organization and context	Time-consuming (though can be done by phone) Less anonymity Do not permit norm comparisons
Shadowing	Enables coach to form a perspective based on direct observation and without intervening filter Enables coach to offer direct feedback Provides coach with a richer sense of organization and context	Most time-consuming
Verbatim feedback on surveys	Rich supplement to quantitative survey	Instrument-dependent

data, will spend time reviewing and preparing for the data-sharing meeting. Exhibit 4.1 presents steps for aggregating, organizing, sorting, analyzing, integrating, and interpreting the data. Taking these steps will enable the coach to develop some solid theories about the coachee's leadership style and underlying motivations; nevertheless, the coach should go into the meeting with the coachee prepared to engage again in a collaborative process and hold his own perspective loosely while the coachee fills the gaps in the coach's "theory" with her own perspectives and understandings.

Reviewing Feedback and Facilitating Awareness. During this process, the coachee and coach collaboratively review and analyze the collected data. The desired outcome is for the coachee to better understand how others see her and to develop key themes and patterns about her leadership style, including strengths and development needs.

The way in which the coach "feeds back" the data can vary. The data are tools, keys to unlock closed arenas of awareness, or if blind spots are numerous, the data can function as a loud wake-up call. In any event, increased insight and awareness on the part of the coachee is the first return on the investment for the time and energy the coach has devoted to developing the relationship and doing a quality assessment.

The coach and coachee will determine the order and way in which the data are shared. There are a variety of options in sequencing the flow of data. The learning style, openness, and readiness of the coachee are primary determinants; so is the coach's sense of which data contain the most vital and powerful messages.

For example, Franco, a recent coaching client, expressed feelings of tentativeness as he approached his feedback review meeting. The coach suggested starting with self-report data (primarily personality and work style surveys), moving on to the written 360-degree surveys, and tackling the verbatim interviews last. At the conclusion, Franco thanked the coach for choosing a delivery method that eased him into the tougher data.

The assessment process typically used in a coaching program is likely to deliver the most comprehensive and in-depth feedback a coachee will ever receive. As such, this experience of reviewing feedback can be very draining, and the coachee may feel vulnerable and exposed. The emotional nature of reconciling differences in perspectives, receiving feedback that may feel hurtful or unfair, or seeing gaps in skills that feel like chasms is very challenging. It is therefore useful for the coach to think ahead and consider ways to support the coachee through this part of the process. The coach should monitor the coachee's responses continuously to ensure that she is not becoming overwhelmed by the data. Regular check-ins with the coachee during the meeting on how she's thinking and feeling

EXHIBIT 4.1. DATA PREPARATION AND ANALYSIS GUIDELINES FOR COACHES.

One of the most important components to an effective coaching relationship is to understand the person whom you are coaching. The following are some preferred and nonpreferred approaches to use as you compile, sort, and analyze data.

Step 1. Aggregate

To obtain the most comprehensive and meaningful information about your coachee that is reasonable and appropriate.

Dos
- DO be inclusive rather than discriminating.
- DO make sure that multiple sources and perspectives are represented.
- DO make note of rate of return and quality of responses; these are also data.

Don'ts
- DON'T discard or dismiss any data at this point.
- DON'T assume that you have the full picture, regardless of the amount of data you've collected.

Step 2. Analyze: Organize and Integrate

To sort and categorize the data in ways that will help you make sense of it. To discern patterns and themes across the data.

Dos
- DO organize each data set by strengths and development needs.
- DO look for gaps in the data.
- DO take note of questions that emerge from the data.
- DO note seemingly discrepant data points.
- DO review the data more than once using a different "lens" each time.
- DO identify themes and patterns (as a general rule, look for three concurrent data points).

Don'ts
- DON'T prejudge the data.
- DON'T make assumptions about the relative validity of the data.
- DON'T dismiss discrepant data.
- DON'T dismiss data from any source.

Step 3. Interpret

To form reasonable hypotheses about your coachee's strengths and development needs, style, and orientation. To then link those to hypotheses about how that style affects others. This process provides a starting point for your assessment discussion.

Dos
- DO embrace the tension of healthy skepticism and solid faith.
- DO get a feel for the individual as a whole person.
- DO consider how the patterns might affect "fit" with current positions along the lines of interests, skills,

Don'ts
- DON'T draw any conclusions about the meaning of the data.
- DON'T overinterpret data; each data source has limitations.
- DON'T solve the coachee's problem before the two of you have explored the data and options.

values, and natural challenge areas; be prepared to ask the coachee to self-assess "fit."

- DO consider ways in which you can enhance the coachee's understanding of specific feedback.
- DO develop possible reasons why seemingly discrepant data might nevertheless be accurate.
- DO be prepared to bring new data forward from your discussion with the coachee.
- DO prepare lots of questions for the coachee to help you both make sense of the data.

- DON'T make pronouncements about "fit" within the organization on the basis of expressed preferences or style.
- DON'T allow the coachee or yourself to use the data as an "excuse" for behavior.
- DON'T label the coachee's development issue.
- DON'T fall into the trap of summarizing the data for the coachee.

---

are advisable. Encouraging breaks and short walks for a change of scene can help the coachee digest the data. The coach should also ask for feedback, from time to time, on both the process and the coach's delivery.

Constructing a Personal Learning Agenda. Once the data have been thoroughly reviewed, discussed, and understood, the coach helps the coachee craft goals and identify actionable steps to achieve those goals. This process usually begins on the same day that the data are reviewed and concludes at a subsequent time after the coachee has had time to sit with the data.

The coachee decides how she wants to translate her awareness into action. She will map her strengths and development needs to her aspirations and the organization's and her boss's expectations. Through that process, she will identify areas of strength to maintain and build on and gaps where she will need to grow in order to achieve the skill level desired. The challenge aspect of the ACS model reemerges and dominates at this stage as the coachee wrestles with how large a developmental "stretch" to take on.

In selecting goals, the coachee will need to answer some key questions: What am I motivated to work on? How much challenge can I add to my plate? What can I afford not to address? What goals will offer the greatest leverage for my existing leadership strengths? What does the feedback suggest I need to improve? What do I feel is important? Are there personal goals that I want to work on but don't want to disclose to others?

Sometimes the goal selection process opens up subjects for discussion that were not anticipated at the time the coaching program was undertaken. It is not uncommon in our experience, for example, that a coachee concludes after reviewing the data that she is ill-suited for her current position or for the company or that her devotion to work is having an undesirable impact on her home life. The coachee may choose to set a goal around such issues, particularly if she feels it is critical to her well-being and values. Typically, organizations do not expect a coachee to make this type of goal public; however, the coach should confirm this understanding at the start of the program. Depending on the pervasiveness of these issues and their impact on the coaching program, the coachee may need to renegotiate expectations with the organizational sponsor.

The outcomes from this process of creating a personal learning agenda (Kram, Ting, and Bunker, 2002) are a set of goals, which are usually developmentally focused, realistic, measurable, aligned with program expectations, and challenging and motivating enough to cause the coachee to want to stretch and learn. Finally, the coach should assist the coachee in translating her goals into behavioral language. For instance, it is more difficult to develop specific actions, monitor, and measure achievement for a goal such as "Improve leadership" than for "Develop a more participatory leadership style: listen first to others' ideas before presenting my own; incorporate and acknowledge others' contributions to solutions." Without specificity, it will be difficult and perhaps frustrating for the coachee to receive meaningful feedback when ultimately assessing achievement.

A well-designed developmental action plan contains a realistic number of goals, is constructed in behavioral terms, and contains some key action steps and means of measuring progress. Beyond that, how detailed the plan is depends on the coachee's need and style. Some coachees prefer a structured, detailed action plan that outlines specific strategies, actions, time frames, and steps. Coachees with this preference need to be careful that they do not confuse completing activities with making developmental and behavioral progress. For example, Elyse set a goal of expanding her network beyond her immediate business unit. Her action steps were joining a cross-functional task force and volunteering to teach a technical course for the division. Elyse completed these tasks. However, it was still unclear whether as a result of her participation, she had developed new relationships that would be beneficial to her part of the business and her own professional growth.

Others prefer a more organic plan that has clear outcomes but in which interim steps are more fluid and dependent on development opportunities that emerge from current situations. The caution to these coachees is that they not lose sight of their goals and the daily opportunities to make movement. In both cases, the coach serves as one reality check.

Part of developing a workable learning agenda involves extensive exploration before committing to steps and activities. One of the challenges during this phase is enabling coachees to see new solutions and possibilities. The natural tendency is for coachees to consider options that are known to them. Often these are easily identified—they have been tried already. Yet often the comfortable options have a lower likelihood of success. Each coachee has a predominant style and way of looking at the world. That naturally causes them to narrow their choices—to presort and gravitate to options that suit that style—when in fact what might reap the greatest improvement would be trying something different. The downside of having a strong style is that it can work like psychological blinders that prevent the coachee from seeing or considering other approaches. The coach is responsible for challenging the coachee's assumptions and perspectives.

In choosing options, the coachee and coach assess the personal and environmental resources needed to execute action plans and strategize how to attain them. Personal resources can include knowledge and skills as well as inner strengths. In other words, strengths can be used to address their development needs. For example, Marina's goal was to focus more on staff development and be more direct and honest with negative feedback to her direct reports. She understood from the assessment process that being liked and preserving harmony were important needs for her, and she received very positive feedback on being viewed as caring, considerate, friendly, and compassionate. Her coach encouraged her to use those strengths in a different way: to enable others to receive developmental feedback more easily from her.

Environmental resources can include time and money for additional training to gain skills, as well as understanding and support for the development process. The coachee and coach should identify individuals in the organization who can approve funds and influence assignments and schedules. Equally important is identifying the individuals who will, through informal coaching, provide real-time support through the learning curve, during the coaching process, and particularly after the formal coaching has concluded. These individuals will frequently perform the roles described in Chapter Five. These other kinds of developmental relationships can be found in the coachee's work or personal life.

Implementing the Learning Agenda. During the implementation of the coachees' learning agenda, the coaching relationship encompasses the hard work of helping the coachee execute the plan she has constructed, practice behavioral changes she finds desirable, and apply the insights she has gained.

The coachee and coach should regularly review the goals they've set to ensure they are congruent with the coachee's personal values and professional aspirations. They should be prepared to rethink and modify goals if there have been significant changes in the coachee's work environment, personal life, or in her thinking about her developmental path.

Ingrid, a female executive with a start-up technology firm, had set greater work-life balance as a goal. During the subsequent six months of coaching, Ingrid's company was hit hard by an economic slump and was forced to downsize and reorganize to better reflect market demand and stay competitive. As a result, Ingrid's duties increased and her span of control grew as the company sought to streamline management levels. It became apparent to Ingrid and her coach that her goal of balance would require redefinition and that new goals would need to be set.

Sustaining momentum is a constant challenge during implementation because behavioral change is an extended process. For that reason, the coach and coachee should look for small successes to celebrate and be heralded as milestones on the path toward achievement. Recognizing these small wins is an important task of coaching because coachees often set difficult goals toward which movement comes slowly. For coachees who are used to quick and tangible results, the experience of making behavioral change can be frustrating and demoralizing.

Take Henrik, whose goal was to demonstrate understanding of others' views by asking questions and paraphrasing their thoughts before offering his own. Henrik reported to his coach that in a meeting with his boss, he was so taken aback by his boss's presentation of a reorganization plan that he reacted strongly and in the moment. It was not till the next day that Henrik reapproached his boss and asked clarifying questions to gain a better understanding of the intended outcomes. Henrik thought he had failed miserably. His coach helped him see that his ability to self-assess and then self-correct were important achievements, even if he was unable to enact them in the moment. Surfacing and celebrating the ways in which a coachee is moving forward are important supports for development.

People need support for a variety of reasons in a coaching process. The coachee often gets stuck, reaches a plateau, or has a setback. At these times, the right balance of support and challenge can help facilitate movement and recovery. In a setback, the coach can help the coachee see small gains and derive learnings from the hardships (see Chapter Six).

When stuck or at a plateau, the coach may need to challenge the coachee's thinking and assumptions that tend to lock her into old patterns and solutions that have not worked or that result in defeatist thought patterns, undermining her own efforts or causing her to give up too quickly. Sometimes being stuck or set back challenges the coachee to move out of her comfort zone and take risks. For leaders and managers, this is particularly discomfiting because although they may be used to taking risks in a business environment, in the behavioral and emotional world, they may be less comfortable with risk.

Entering into a problem-solving mode can be good support as the coachee seeks to find ways to overcome obstacles. In a problem-solving mode, the coach is more proactive and directive. The coach may offer a series of options to stimulate the coachee's thinking rather than rely wholly on a questioning mode to pull ideas from the coachee. The coach may also work through a particular situation in the workplace as a means of modeling the use of new skills. The challenge for the coach is to identify when problem-solving techniques can help create movement and then, when movement begins, to seamlessly move back into a questioning, pulling, and probing mode in order to facilitate the coachee's accessing her own skills and knowledge.

Measuring Outcomes. The coach and coachee should be measuring outcomes on a continuous basis and at defined points. The continuous measurement allows the coachee to see incremental change and occurs informally each time the coach and coachee meet. A simple scaling question such as "On a scale of 1 to 10, where were you at the start of this program on this behavioral goal, and where do you think you are now?" helps the coachee self-assess and note whether she is on or off track. These smaller movements serve as milestones on the way toward the larger stated goal and make goal attainment seem more accessible. This assessment also enables the coachee and coach to monitor program effectiveness and also to modify learning strategies as needed.

Progress on goals can also benefit from a more structured measurement process. As noted earlier in the chapter, this more formal assessment can take a qualitative (interviews and informal feedback) or quantitative (written reassessment surveys) form.

The coachee should continue to have discussions with her boss periodically during the coaching program and upon completion of a reassessment or progress survey, to share learnings, provide updates on goal progress, and discuss current alignment of goals with organizational needs.

Transitioning from Coaching. Eventually, the coaching relationship will need to shift into a less active mode. In a formal program, the contractual endpoint is generally well defined as a point in time or as completion of a certain number of coaching meetings. In these situations, the coach and coachee can anticipate and plan for program closure, which is typically signaled by the reassessment process. We recommend that time be reserved after the outcome assessment or progress survey to review accomplishments, plan for continued work on existing or new development goals, discuss ways to self-manage the development process going forward, assess adequacy of support structures and strategies to strengthen them, and determine the ongoing role, if any, of the external coach. In most cases, the coach will recede from the coachee's world. At other times, the coachee may choose to retain access to the coach and even contract for booster coaching services.

It is helpful and sometimes contractually required for the coachee (with support from the coach) to share highlights from her outcome assessment or progress report with her boss or HR sponsor. Some areas that this briefing may cover are what was learned and accomplished, business metric outcomes, a postcoaching action plan to address developmental issues where capability growth is desired, and a synopsis of how the organization can best leverage the coachee's skills and talents.

Postprogram Activities: Evaluating Program and Coach Effectiveness

An important and usually closing step in the coaching program is to turn the lens on the coaching vendor. While the coach should be asking for feedback on an ongoing basis, it is good for the coach to undergo a formal assessment by the coachee. Measures might include how effectively the coach enacts the framework: how he builds relationship (rapport, collaboration, commitment); facilitates assessment, challenge, and support; and assists in achieving results. In addition to feedback on the coach himself, the coachee should be invited to assess the coaching process. Measures might include ease of administration of assessments and contractual provisions, relevance and adequacy of program elements in meeting desired outcomes, and overall value. The coachee's organization will not be in a position to evaluate the content of the coaching or the interaction between coachee and coach; however, their feedback should be sought for issues such as ease of working with the coaching vendor and coach, responsiveness to the organization as well as the coachee, adherence to agreed expectations, and the organization's perception of outcome success.

Conclusion

This chapter presented an in-depth look at CCL's practice of formal coaching for leader development. It demonstrates how our work is rooted, first and foremost, in previous CCL learning about leader development: that leadership can be learned and that optimal learning comes from experiences that include assessment, challenge, and support.

Our formal coaching framework for leader development consists of the core elements of developmental experience (assessment, challenge and support) occurring within the context of a coaching relationship. This relationship strives to produce the primary result of leader development and secondary results of personal and organizational performance.

We have presented our coaching process as a practical guide for others working to enact a coaching program. We believe that by using this framework and this process, one can create a "best practice" coaching experience—one in which there is a collaborative assessment and understanding of the coachee and her development task, in which current constraints are challenged and new possibilities are explored, and in which accountability and support for reaching goals and sustaining development are ensured.

CHAPTER FIVE

JOB ASSIGNMENTS

Patricia J. Ohlott

Take a few moments to reflect on your career. Try to identify at least one job (or an assignment that was part of a job) that you think was an important developmental experience for you as a leader, a job experience from which you learned a great deal. It was probably a job from which you learned more than just new business content; something about this experience changed the way you lead. Ask yourself what it was about this job that was so difficult or challenging for you:

- Was it a promotion or a move to a different part of the business?
- Did you have to deal with difficult customers or clients?
- Did you have to manage something with which you were unfamiliar?
- Did you have to build an effective team from scratch?
- Were you responsible for a downsizing?
- Was there a great deal of risk involved?
- Was it a high-visibility task?
- Did it require you to work with people whose values seemed to be radically different from your own?

Now ask yourself what you learned from this experience. What do you do differently today because of your experiences in that job or assignment? Perhaps you learned about persuading others, strategic thinking, perseverance, delegation, or coping with ambiguity.

Did you realize you were learning at the time? Was it planned? Was it difficult? Do you think you could have learned these things in a classroom?

Job assignments are one of the oldest and most potent forms of leader development. They give leaders the opportunity to learn by doing—by working on real problems and dilemmas. However, systematic and deliberate use of job assignments for development purposes is a more recent phenomenon in most organizations. Until the 1980s, most organized leadership development efforts focused on classroom education and training. The goal of this chapter is to describe the types of job assignments from which people learn, the kinds of learning that typically result from various assignments, and how organizations can better leverage assignments for development purposes. I begin, however, by looking at the growing awareness of the importance of job assignments for leader development.

Importance of Job Assignments for Development

A number of research studies conducted at the Center for Creative Leadership and elsewhere in the 1980s and 1990s support the notion that many managers consider job experiences the primary source of learning (see, for example, Broderick, 1983; McCall, Lombardo, and Morrison, 1988; Morrison, White, and Van Velsor, 1992; Wick, 1989; Zemke, 1985). Although the studies are based primarily on retrospective accounts and are therefore subject to all the biases associated with memories, these studies are noteworthy in that their conclusions are drawn from actual stories related by successful executives. Executives were asked to identify crucial events in their development as leaders. Their stories showed that they felt they learned more from influential people at work and from the challenges inherent in their jobs than from formal training programs and other nonwork experiences. The original studies have been replicated extensively by CCL and by other individuals and organizations, not only in the United States but also in other countries such as the Netherlands and Japan.

These findings have begun to influence how organizations practice leadership development. Although formal training and development programs are still important, organizations are becoming more aware that systemic use of on-the-job experiences is crucial if they are to develop executives who are effective and adaptable. This increasing awareness is clearly illustrated in the Conference Board's assessment of the efforts of leading-edge companies to develop sufficient leadership bench strength to meet their competitive needs of the future. They asked the questions "What are the primary business challenges that leaders will face in 2010?" and "What leadership practices are considered most effective in developing the leadership competencies required for success in that environment?"

The Conference Board surveyed 150 companies regarding their development practices, interviewed members of these companies as well as experts working in the field, and solicited input from members of a working group that supported the study (Barrett and Beeson, 2002). They identified leadership skills that would become most critical for businesses in 2010, including communication and talent development, team building, and quick decision making in the face of pressure and ambiguity. Most of the respondents expected these skills to become more important than technical skills and industry knowledge. Most companies felt their current leadership capacity could not adequately meet these future business needs, yet most of them were not doing much to actively develop future senior leaders. One of the best practices identified by the Conference Board emphasizes experiential learning; it includes detailed career planning for future leaders to provide them with a range of job-related assignments and experiences tailored to each individual's particular strengths, development needs, and career potential.

For example, Johnson & Johnson identifies as one of the seven critical factors in successful leader development "Leaders are developed primarily on the job" (Fulmer and Goldsmith, 2000, p. 117). Despite its decentralized philosophy, Johnson & Johnson has realized that movement throughout the organization is crucial for leader development. As part of its appraisal, development, selection, and reward process, an executive committee identifies high-potential candidates and plans for their development. These plans include sharing talent across business lines. The company further encourages managers to explore opportunities in other regions and operating companies with the goal of improving their skills and broadening their perspectives.

Other notable examples include leader development programs at Citicorp, General Electric, and Kodak. At GE, an important factor in executive appointments is considering who will benefit the most from the experience in terms of their development (Sherman, 1995). Citicorp tries to place high-potential managers in jobs for which they are no more than 60 to 70 percent prepared, thus giving them the new challenges they need to continue development (Clark and Lyness, 1991). At Kodak, the manager of its Image Science Development Program coordinates job assignments with sponsors from its various business groups to meet not only the work assignment needs of the various businesses or functional units but also the development needs of individual managers (Kodak, 2002).

It is important to note that the trend toward using assignments for development purposes is not limited to corporations; it is taking root in government, educational, and other not-for-profit institutions. For organizations that may not have much in the way of resources to spend on extensive training programs, job assignments can play a critical role in developing future leaders. The U.S. Department of Housing and Urban development, for example, has the Mid-Level

Development Program to develop the managerial and leadership skills of high-potential, mid-level supervisors in its Office of Administration. Developmental job assignments are a key part of the sixteen-month program.

Johnson & Johnson, Citicorp, GE, Kodak, and HUD are somewhat unusual in their practices. In most organizations, the ideal candidate for a position is someone who already has the skills to do the job and can hit the ground running, not one for whom the assignment is developmental. One reason assignments are not often systematically used for development purposes is that organizations do not really understand why and how to do this. The remainder of this chapter is devoted to filling some of this knowledge gap.

What Constitutes a Developmental Job Assignment

I use the expression "job assignment" because it can refer to an entire job, such as opening a new facility or redesigning a system, or an aspect of a job, such as dealing with a difficult employee or serving on a temporary task force to solve a particular problem. A new assignment can be an entirely new job (via a promotion or transfer), or it can mean responsibilities added to an existing job, such as working on a short-term project team while continuing the day-to-day work of one's normal job.

An important distinction is that assignments are not necessarily work someone is "assigned" to do; a person may seek out and volunteer for assignments, such as heading up a task force to study the efficacy of a new software package, handling a negotiation with a customer, or serving as liaison with a community group.

What makes a job assignment developmental? Essentially, it must be something that stretches people, pushes them out of their comfort zone, and requires them to think and act differently. It may involve roles that are not well defined, and it usually contains some elements that are new to the person. These assignments place people in a challenging situation full of problems to solve, dilemmas to resolve, obstacles to overcome, and choices to make under conditions of risk and uncertainty.

Thus the key element in a developmental job assignment is *challenge*. By tackling unfamiliar tasks and seeing the consequences of their actions, people learn from the challenges in their assignments. This learning may produce changes in how managers make decisions, take actions, handle risks, manage relationships, and approach problems.

Although developmental assignments are, first and foremost, challenging, the job assignments that are most developmental also incorporate assessment and support—the other elements of the leader development model presented in the

Introduction. New assignments provide assessment data if they reveal strengths or deficiencies in someone's current skills. Until leaders face situations that call for a particular competency, they may not know to what degree they possess that competency. For example, a manager who is in charge of building a new team discovers for the first time how good (or bad) she is at it. This points her toward areas where she needs to improve. If the context is feedback-rich as she tries different strategies and if she gets multiple sources of input on how well she is doing, her learning in this new assignment will be enhanced.

Being given a developmental assignment in and of itself can be experienced as supportive. Such an assignment is a signal that the organization believes the person can successfully handle the challenge and learn from the experience. This boost to self-confidence motivates the person to learn. The challenges of an assignment, however, can be particularly difficult, requiring additional support from others as the work unfolds (I will return to this point later in the chapter).

Challenges Inherent in Developmental Jobs

Research into what makes a job developmental has identified five broad sources of challenge related to learning:

1. Job transitions
2. Creating change
3. High levels of responsibility
4. Managing boundaries
5. Dealing with diversity

Within these broad categories are a number of specific challenges, characteristics of assignments that have been found to be particularly developmental (McCauley, Ruderman, Ohlott, and Morrow, 1994; McCauley, Ohlott, and Ruderman, 1999). These challenges, summarized in Exhibit 5.1, stem from the roles, responsibilities, tasks, and context of the job.

This section describes how and why the five sources of challenge affect learning and suggests specific types of jobs that are likely to present these challenges. Exhibit 5.2 provides other specific examples of job assignments.

Job Transitions. A transition involves a change in work role, such as a change in job content, level of responsibility, or location. Specific job transitions that have been shown to be particularly developmental include changes in level, function, or employer (Nicholson and West, 1988); vast increases in the scope of the assignment (McCall, Lombardo, and Morrison, 1988; Valerio, 1990); and moving from a line job to a staff job (McCall, Lombardo, and Morrison, 1988).

EXHIBIT 5.1. SOURCES OF CHALLENGE IN JOB ASSIGNMENTS.

Job transitions	1. *Unfamiliar responsibilities:* The leader must handle responsibilities that are new, very different, or much broader than previous ones.
Creating change	2. *New directions:* The leader is responsible for starting something new in the organization, making strategic changes in the business, carrying out a reorganization, or responding to rapid changes in the business environment.
	3. *Inherited problems:* The leader has to fix problems created by a former incumbent or that were preexisting in the job.
	4. *Problems with employees:* Employees lack adequate experience, are incompetent, or are resistant to the leader's initiatives.
High levels of responsibility	5. *High stakes:* Clear deadlines, pressure from senior leaders, high visibility, and responsibility for key decisions make success or failure in this job clearly evident.
	6. *Scope and scale:* The job is large and includes responsibilities for multiple functions, groups, products, or services.
Managing boundaries	7. *External pressure:* The leader must manage the interface with important groups outside the organization that affect the business, such as customers, unions, or government agencies.
	8. *Influence without authority:* Getting the job done requires influencing peers, people in higher positions, external parties, or other key people over whom the leader has no direct authority.
Dealing with diversity	9. *Work across cultures:* The leader must work with people from different cultures or with organizations in other countries.
	10. *Work group diversity:* The leader is responsible for the work of people of both genders and different racial and ethnic backgrounds.

Source: Adapted from McCauley, Ohlott, and Ruderman, 1999.

Transitions place people in new situations where the responsibilities of the job are to some degree unfamiliar and where the usual routines and behaviors are no longer adequate. Transitions require people to find new ways of thinking about and responding to problems and opportunities. In addition, people who have been moved into dramatically different assignments are motivated by having to prove themselves all over again to an entirely new group of coworkers.

The extent to which a job transition is developmental is person-specific; that is, it depends on how similar the new job is to previous jobs. A job amounting to a great stretch for one person may be developmental, but the same transfer would not be so for someone who has already held a job with similar responsibilities and tasks. A job move is likely to be less developmental if there are few new elements

EXHIBIT 5.2. DEVELOPMENTAL CHALLENGES AND EXAMPLES OF ASSIGNMENTS WHERE THEY MAY BE FOUND.

Developmental Component	Examples of Assignments
Job transitions	Being the inexperienced member of a project team Taking a temporary assignment in another function Moving to a general management job Managing a group or discipline you know little about Moving from a line job to a corporate staff role Making a lateral move to another department
Creating change	Launching a new product, project, or system Serving on a reengineering team Facilitating the development of a new vision or mission statement Dealing with a business crisis Handling a workforce reduction Hiring new staff Breaking ground on a new operation Reorganizing a unit Resolving subordinate performance problems Supervising the liquidation of a product or equipment
High levels of responsibility	Managing a corporate assignment with tight deadlines Representing the organization to the media or influential outsiders Managing across geographic locations Assuming additional responsibilities following a downsizing Taking on a colleague's responsibilities during his or her absence
Managing boundaries	Presenting a proposal to top management Performing a corporate staff job Serving on a cross-functional team Managing an internal project such as a company event or an office renovation Working on a project with a community or social organization Negotiating with a union Managing a vendor relationship
Dealing with diversity	Taking an assignment in another country Managing a work group made up of people with racial, ethnic, or religious backgrounds different from your own Managing a group of employees from a different generation who seem to be motivated in different ways than you are Training in your organization's diversity program Leading an organizational effort to revise policies around harassment and the development of people of different genders, races, sexual orientations, and so on Managing a group that consists largely of expatriates from other countries

in the job (Davies and Easterby-Smith, 1984; McCauley, Lombardo, and Usher, 1989; Nicholson and West, 1988) or little increase in the amount of discretion the manager has to define the job (Brett, 1984) or if differences from previous positions go unnoticed by the incumbent (Brett, 1984; Nicholson and West, 1988).

Listen as one manager describes his first key transitional assignment:

> I was considered one of the best electricians at the site. Most of the guys and managers were coming to me when they needed answers, and the crew was rather close. They knew me and knew how I functioned. One of the guys I even went to high school with. Then I was promoted to electrical foreperson. When I got the job, it was like I had to re-prove myself. The guy that surprised me the most was the one I went to high school with. He expected that because he was my friend, he should receive special treatment. I learned that there is a transition period when you move from the labor force into management. The testing that goes on from below and above is a feeling-out process to determine boundaries, not only for them but also for me. At the time, I didn't understand what was happening to me and took the actions as an attack on my authority.

Another example of a transitional assignment is moving from a line job to a corporate staff role. Line managers assigned to staff roles must often relocate to corporate headquarters and report to executives they have not worked with before while struggling to master technical areas that are new to them. A line-to-staff move challenges people to learn to think strategically as well as tactically. It can also teach important relationship lessons about what top leaders are like and how to work effectively with them. In summary, this particular assignment provides opportunities to learn how to influence those over whom one has no direct control.

In 2001, the Corporate Leadership Council (CLC) surveyed more than fifteen thousand leaders from a diverse set of organizations to assess their views on the importance and effectiveness of various leader development strategies. The survey included eight on-the-job activities. The leaders surveyed identified transition-related challenges such as working in a new functional area, a foreign city, or a new line of business as important for leader development, more powerful than the more commonly used strategies of people management seminars or courses in business and technical skills.

Creating Change. Jobs that require a leader to create change call for numerous actions and decisions in the face of uncertainty and ambiguity. A leader with a mandate to create change may be responsible for starting something new in the organization, carrying out a reorganization, fixing problems created by a predecessor, or dealing with problematic employees. Often the assignment has a clear goal, such as reducing the workforce by 20 percent, but the role itself is not clearly defined and the leader has some freedom to determine how the goal should be achieved. The more uncertain and complex the changes are, the bigger the learning challenges of the job.

Starting a business from scratch and turning around a business in trouble are classic examples of this type of developmental assignment. These two types of assignments were also identified as important developmental experiences by leaders in the CLC study. Although the two assignments are very different in focus and can teach some distinct lessons, they both hold opportunities to learn some of the skills important to effectively create change. Among other things, leaders in such assignments often learn important lessons about setting agendas, such as decisiveness and shouldering responsibility for their own actions. They also learn more about relationships with employees, such as how to lead, motivate, and develop others, as well as how to confront those who are problematic.

One manager gave us an example of an assignment in which she was required to create change:

> I was assigned to manage a brand that needed to be repositioned. I worked with my boss on a new campaign that capitalized on our research and development findings as well as our consumer research data. I assembled a core team of members from the majority of areas to share the brand's objectives and how they could achieve those goals. Within the first year, we reversed a five-year decline and grew volume by 35 percent. From this experience, I learned that when people feel a part of a process or decision, there is greater team effort and positive end results. The key was to listen to what they were saying and then empower them to act on the information. I also learned to truly set clearly defined goals that are measurable and achievable. Once people feel valued and appreciated, they are willing to go the extra mile for the project or the manager.

High Levels of Responsibility. Leadership assignments with high levels of responsibility have greater breadth, visibility, and complexity; they also expose the individual to pressure and high-stakes decisions. Moving to a job with a high level of responsibility may involve a leap in the scope of the job, larger budgets, more people, and more diverse responsibilities, as with different functions, groups, or areas. With a higher level of responsibility can come higher stakes and greater business diversity. There may also be a danger of overload because the job requires a large investment of time and energy.

Jobs of this sort provide potent opportunities for learning such lessons as resourcefulness in knowing how to adapt to changing and often ambiguous circumstances, being able to think strategically and make good decisions under pressure, and building and mending relationships with subordinates, coworkers, higher management, and external parties. Dealing with broader and more complex problems provides a setting for learning about integrating different perspectives, prioritizing, and making trade-offs.

Leaders in high-level jobs are in a position to have significant impact on the organization. At the same time, they do their work with greatly increased visibility. The combination of having the opportunity to make a difference and being in the spotlight may encourage people to work harder to enhance their leadership skills and abilities. There is also evidence that when the actions people take in a significant context are successful, learning is reinforced and supported (Kelleher, Finestone, and Lowy, 1986; Wick, 1989).

Here is one manager's account of his company's innovative use of a developmental assignment with a high level of responsibility:

> The CEO specifically requested me to work with him to develop a strategic plan to curb the drug problem in our metropolitan area. I worked closely with him and with an executive director in the community. They taught me how CEOs think, process information, and view success. I worked closely with impoverished communities: gathering information, identifying their issues and needs, and working with them to accomplish real tasks. This assignment strengthened my strategic planning skills and polished my interpersonal skills, from one [socioeconomic] extreme of people to the other.

The 2001 Corporate Leadership Council study strongly supports the use of an assignment with high levels of responsibility as a developmental challenge. The CLC systematically analyzed the views and needs of thousands of leaders who asserted that the most important on-the-job experience for their development was the amount of decision-making authority they wielded during the assignment. They suggest that leaders need the power, leeway, and freedom to take action on their own in order to best develop their leadership skills.

Managing Boundaries. Most leaders are accustomed to managing downward. When they find themselves in situations where they must work across lateral boundaries, either externally or within their own organizations, they encounter a new source of challenge—the need to work with people over whom they have no formal or direct authority. In these situations, they are managing the interface between their work and the demands of external groups, such as clients, vendors, regulatory agencies, or joint-venture partners, or among internal groups, such as teams in different locations, different functional groups, or managers at different levels. Leaders in these situations learn a great deal about building relationships, handling conflict, and being straightforward with others. To get all parties to work together effectively, leaders have to learn new skills in effective negotiation, communication, and conflict management.

Among the most common examples of assignments that challenge leaders to manage nonauthority relationships is leading or participating in a cross-functional project team or task force. As organizations become flatter, make greater use of cross-functional teams, and rely more on alliances and partnerships to accomplish their work, this type of assignment is increasing.

One executive told us about his experience and what it taught him. In addition to his normal managerial role, he was selected to work with the company's complaint department to find a better way to handle customer problems. To identify the different types of calls and decide who would handle them, he had to work with people who did not formally report to him. There was constant finger pointing and disagreement between departments as to who should handle which types of calls and who should pay for overtime or incentives for improved performance. From this experience, he reported learning how to build and sustain relationships in other departments, how to deal professionally with people who had different management styles, and how to disagree while maintaining professional respect for one another.

Dealing with Diversity. A fifth type of developmental opportunity derives from the contextual features of the job. Most organizations are experiencing rapid and substantial increases in diversity, not only in the domestic workforce but also in the demands of operating in the global arena. These changes require leaders to work with and manage people who are not like themselves—people with different values, different experiences and backgrounds, and different workplace needs and desires. To effectively manage these differences, leaders are challenged to move beyond their own beliefs and perspectives to understand personal, business, and workplace issues from perspectives that may differ greatly from, and sometimes even conflict with, their own. This is true internationally as well as domestically.

A Hong Kong Chinese executive in McCall and Hollenbeck's extensive study of global executives (2002) described his experience working in Thailand as transformational. He could not speak the language and experienced severe culture shock. He had to learn Thai to eat. Working with people from different parts of Asia challenged his assumptions—he learned that Singaporeans differed substantially from Malaysians, for example. Managers in their first global assignment are surprised when their assumptions about the lifestyle, motivation, or values of people in other cultures turn out to be wrong. Tried-and-true approaches may no longer work, and new behaviors and skills must be learned and practiced.

Here is another manager's story:

My second job in the organization was an overseas assignment. I had never been outside the United States. I was given a special assignment in production control to improve the efficiency and effectiveness of production scheduling. I had no prior experience in scheduling and was trying to solve problems in a culture that did not place the same value on efficiency and speed as I did. What interested and motivated my work team seemed completely different from what I had experienced as an American working in the United States. The language difference presented an additional challenge; I was just learning the local language, and miscommunication often complicated matters.

During the course of this extremely challenging assignment, this leader learned the importance of showing genuine interest in others and exhibiting sensitivity to their needs. She found that learning to work effectively in these diverse conditions forced her to surface her own assumptions and biases and to learn new ways to communicate and connect with others. Only by making the effort to understand the diverse needs and perspectives of her team could she begin to fathom how to direct, motivate, and provide appropriate developmental opportunities to her staff. She also learned to take different perspectives into account to generate new solutions to problems as well as different ways to manage conflict.

Learning from Assignments

Talking about assignments for development purposes begs the question, "Development for what?" What kinds of things can people learn from the challenges in a developmental assignment? In a word, developmental assignments teach practical knowledge and skills that enhance and expand the ability to be effective. Burgoyne and Hodgson (1983) call this type of development "natural managerial learning" because it requires people to draw conclusions independently on the basis of their own experiences and to apply those lessons to help meet current and future challenges.

The Center for Creative Leadership has conducted extensive research into the challenges inherent in developmental assignments and the types of lessons they teach. The initial study of 191 managers and executives by McCall, Lombardo, and Morrison (1988) identified thirty-three important lessons executives reported they had learned from challenging experiences. These lessons do not reflect qualities such as intelligence or common sense; rather, they reveal fundamental leadership skills and ways of thinking. Although derived from a study of executives, these lessons are important for all kinds of leaders, as they represent a wide range of skills, abilities, insights, knowledge, and values. Over the years, these lessons have been grouped in different ways, and a few new categories have been added to reflect new research findings (Center for Creative Leadership, 2002a; Douglas, 2003; McCauley, Lombardo, and Usher, 1989). Our current thinking is that the lessons are most easily understood and applied when grouped into three thematic areas: meeting job challenges, which involves managing the work; leading people, which involves managing relationships with a variety of people; and respecting oneself and others, which has to do with knowledge of oneself and the principles that guide one's life as well as one's career. Each category further contains several subcategories (Center for Creative Leadership, 2002a; Douglas, 2003). These categories are also somewhat fluid; accomplishing tasks in one category is often related to skills and perspectives inherent in the other two.

"Meeting job challenges" captures the drive, energy, attitudes, and resourcefulness needed to cope with the demands of a leadership position or management job. The types of lessons that enhance a leader's ability to meet and manage job challenges involve finding alternative solutions to problems, structural and systemic design skills, business and technical knowledge and skills, accepting responsibility for the direction one sets, and strategic thinking. Other lessons that fall into this category include acting in the face of ambiguity, facing adversity, and seizing opportunities. Lessons about managing change—sharing information, building consensus, overcoming resistance—are becoming more prominent now than they were in the original research. Resourcefulness is the key.

"Leading people" encompasses a variety of lessons about working with other people who may have different ideas, outlooks, and agendas. These people include other people in the organization as well as the specific group of individuals for whom the leader is responsible. Central to this skill is the ability to understand other people's points of view. The lessons in this category reflect the recognition that different skills may be required for dealing with all types of people in varying situations. Examples include how to handle political situations, understanding the perspectives of others, delegating and encouraging, and motivating and developing others. In the past few years, more items relating to managing and valuing diversity have been added to this category.

"Respecting oneself and others" are the underlying principles that guide leadership behavior. New values may be formed, and established values tested and shaped, by organizational experiences. Examples of these lessons include understanding the importance of credibility, learning how to treat people with respect, being sensitive to people's needs, and acting with integrity. Respect for oneself evolves from an increasing self-awareness and a heightened awareness of the importance of learning about oneself. The most effective leaders are self-aware, and a lack of self-awareness is strongly related to derailment. Knowing what they want to achieve helps leaders identify opportunities for growth in that area. Knowledge of their own strengths, weaknesses, and goals helps them recognize further areas of development while maintaining the confidence to withstand the feedback and criticism entailed in achieving their goals.

A key finding common to all the studies is that assignments with different challenges teach different types of lessons, although the relationships are not unique. That is to say, each challenge has the potential to teach multiple lessons, and the same lesson may be learned from any number of different challenges. For example, while working on a task force where a key challenge is to influence others without formal authority, a person is likely to learn important lessons about resourcefulness, building and mending relationships, and putting people at ease. From a turnaround assignment where a reduction in workforce is required, a leader can learn more about how to confront problem subordinates and how to build and mend relationships.

Individual Differences in Learning from Job Assignments

The participants in our initial studies were almost exclusively white men, reflecting the demographics of the executive workforce in the early 1980s. In response to changing workforce demographics and in attempts to better understand the experiences of previously underrepresented groups in organizations, CCL has continued to collect information about challenging experiences and the lessons they teach. Not only do leaders experience different challenges, but they may value developmental assignments differently.

Morrison, White, and Van Velsor (1987, 1992) replicated the initial study with a comparable sample of 176 female executives. They found many similarities, but they also discovered that women faced additional contextual challenges such as prejudice and differential treatment. The Corporate Leadership Council (2001) found that male leaders placed a higher value on job experiences as a form of development, while women valued coaching, mentoring, development plans, and people-management courses. Thus educational preferences, which may differ between men and women, may also affect the impact of a developmental assignment.

Recently, CCL conducted a similar study comparing African American and white managers (Douglas, 2003). Regardless of their race or gender, managers emphasized the value of job assignments in their development as leaders. White managers, however, reported more challenging assignments than African American managers, and male managers reported more challenging assignments than females—particularly assignments that involved changes in scope. Many of the key challenging assignments reported were similar to those in the initial studies (for example, creating change, transitions), but in the new study, responsibility for implementing downsizing efforts emerged as a significantly greater challenge than in the original research. In addition, contextual features of the job, in particular the impact of race and gender dynamics, became important. For many leaders, being the first woman or African American manager in their position presented additional challenges; in other cases, managers personally observed or experienced injustice resulting from racial prejudice or discrimination.

Similar to the research on differences between male and female managers, our research uncovered that the same assignment might be experienced differently by white and African American managers. What is a developmental opportunity for a white manager may more often be a proving ground with a different set of pressures and objectives for an African American manager; research consistently shows that women and African American managers must repeatedly prove themselves in order to get the same opportunities as their white male counterparts. (These challenges are discussed in further detail in Chapters Nine and Ten.)

The use of challenging assignments for development purposes is also affected by culture. The degree to which particular job assignments are challenging and whether their challenges convey key learnings can vary across cultures. Research in Japan and the Netherlands replicating CCL's "lessons of experience" framework demonstrates this. These studies confirm the types of experiences that produce learning and note some differences. In the Netherlands, there is much more emphasis on power and politics, as well as on personal events outside the workplace that contribute to development, such as a leadership role in a community organization or growing up in an immigrant family (Brave, 2002). Researchers in Japan have also successfully applied the CCL framework explicating sources of challenge and the lessons they teach. Many of the same types of challenging assignments found in the United States also occur in Japan; however, there are some striking differences in the frequency with which these assignments occur. For example, switching from a line to a staff job is much more common in Japan than in the United States, reflecting a culture in which horizontal shifts are more acceptable (Works Institute Recruit Co., 2001). Japanese managers find rich opportunities for learning in such shifts, including understanding different parts of the business and solving different types of problems. Japanese managers also more often cited early work experiences as key developmental events than U.S. managers. One possible explanation for this finding is the difference in educational emphasis between the two countries. Japanese students tend to receive a generalist education at university and gain practical knowledge once they begin working, whereas American college students often take business courses in school. Finally, the idea of increasing the scope of one's job takes on a new meaning in Japan, where individuals often occupy several positions at the same time.

Despite cultural differences, international executives report learning many of the same types of lessons as U.S. domestic executives (McCall and Hollenbeck, 2002). The most striking difference was in terms of the cultural lessons learned by international executives that were not mentioned in the earlier studies of U.S. managers. Whereas U.S. managers reported significant learnings about managing subordinates and other relationships, global executives learned more about big-picture strategies and how to work across cultures. Both U.S. and international executives learned similar lessons about self and career, but the global managers seemed to learn them more deeply and broadly as a result of the complexity within which they operated.

The foregoing discussion considers just a few of the potential individual differences that may affect the experience of a developmental assignment and the lessons learned from it. Other possibilities abound. For example, we know that high performers place a higher value on on-the-job experience, that senior leaders develop more from on-the-job training than managers at lower levels do, and that personality, learning style, individual growth needs, and level of aspiration, self-confidence, and self-esteem may all influence the way a developmental assignment plays out for an individual.

Increased understanding of the role of individual differences in learning from job assignments has important implications for individuals who would take a developmental perspective when placing people in assignments. Issues such as prejudice, discrimination, and differential preparation may affect the assignments members of different groups have access to, as well as how they experience the job and what opportunities they see for learning from it. For example, a manager who places a strong value on learning from relationships may need to be encouraged to take a developmental assignment and may also need to work with a mentor or learning coach for support throughout the assignment in order to derive maximum benefit from it.

Further, it is critical that the organization ensure that its policies and practices are universally applied to provide developmental assignments for all managers and that hiring bosses are not just picking their closest colleagues (who tend to be others demographically similar to themselves) for the plum assignments. One way to do this is to insist that behavioral ratings are included in the selection system and that decisions are based on factual information about the candidates.

Finally, organizations operating in the global environment need to recognize that the challenges of a developmental assignment in the United States may look very different from the challenges of a developmental assignment in Europe or Asia, where cultural differences add another layer of complexity to individual differences. Managers in international assignments may need different kinds of preparation, encouragement, and support than their colleagues in similar jobs in their home countries. McCall and Hollenbeck (2002) emphasize that to increase the probability of success and to maximize learning from an international assignment, organizations need to carefully deliberate the kinds of support and intervention that enhance learning and provide them at the appropriate times and that this can be done only by closely monitoring the manager's progress.

Leveraging Assignments for Development Purposes

To systematically use assignments for development, an organization needs to focus on five tasks:

1. Creating a shared understanding of how assignments can be developmental
2. Helping individuals see the learning opportunities in their current jobs
3. Using development as a criterion in giving assignments to individuals
4. Maximizing individual learning during a developmental assignment
5. Tracking developmental assignments over time

The following section discusses these tasks in greater detail and includes examples from a few organizations that are more systematic and intentional in their use of assignments for leader development than the typical organization tends to be.

Creating a Shared Understanding

To be active partners in their own development process, people need to understand which competencies contribute to effectiveness in their organization and which job assignments help develop those competencies. There are a number of techniques organizations can use to identify these assignments.

One strategy is to use existing, published general resources, which have become increasingly abundant in the past several years. *The Lessons of Experience* (McCall, Lombardo, and Morrison, 1988) provides valuable tools, including checklists, tables, and summaries, that may be helpful in linking assignments with potential outcomes. The authors provide a particularly useful matrix of types of job challenge and the management lessons most often associated with them. McCall and Hollenbeck (2002) provide linkages between international experiences and lessons. Lombardo and Eichinger (1989) offer eighty-eight developmental experiences that can be added to existing jobs—for example, represent concerns of nonexempt staff to higher management, deal with a business crisis, do a competitive analysis, design a training course, carry out a project with another function, supervise outplacement, and run the company picnic. Eichinger and Lombardo (1995) offer strategies for developing leadership in staff managers. The book *Grow Your Own Leaders* (Byham, Smith, and Pease, 2002) includes a chapter on growth through job assignments, which contains a list and discussion of some key questions to ask when making assignments for development purposes.

Organizations also conduct informal, internal "developmental audits" to determine where developmental assignments tend to occur and what kinds of things people typically learn from them (White, 1992). For example, a human resource manager can survey current and former job incumbents and their coworkers to see what they perceive to be the job's major challenges. White also suggests interviewing senior managers to determine which assignments they feel have been most developmental for them and what they learned from those assignments. Valerio (1990) used this strategy to customize a taxonomy of developmental assignments for NYNEX, the communications company that is now part of Verizon. In addition to asking about key developmental assignments, she presented the managers with the thirteen competencies used by the company to assess managerial performance and asked them to describe on-the-job and off-the-job tasks that contributed to the development of each competency.

From this type of information, a few organizations have created their own unique matrix of developmental assignments and learning outcomes. Such a matrix can be part of career development information shared with employees. NCR Corporation (1992) provided this information to its engineers and engineering managers in a career development manual. The manual explains the levels and types of jobs in various career paths for engineers within the company, the competencies needed in these jobs, and which key assignments help develop these competencies. The key assignments are fairly specific and are tailored to the organization. For example, "working on a customer hotline" and "serving on a quality deployment team" are among the assignments that help develop negotiation skills.

A few innovative organizations systematically collect information about the challenges in their job assignments and what individuals are learning from them and make that information widely available in their organization through an online database. As part of a special assignment or before moving on to a new job, people complete a computerized questionnaire that asks about the tasks of the assignment, the challenges faced, and what they learned or in what ways they have grown. Tasks, challenges, and lessons learned are categorized in a framework that is available to others throughout the company. Thus a leader who needs to expand the ability to build a team could go to the database and see in which jobs or special assignments others in the company reported learning a great deal about team building and then look for similar opportunities.

Helping People See the Learning Opportunities in Assignments

People are more likely to learn from their current job assignment if they are aware that the potential exists to do so. Most people recognize that they learn a great deal on the job, but when asked to plan for their own development, they tend to think more about training and education programs. They need to be encouraged by bosses, mentors, coaches, and human resource staff to think about the challenges in their jobs and to see the potential learning opportunities.

To approach these challenges as opportunities sometimes seems unnatural. The things that are challenging in jobs may also be particularly stressful, and people's first reaction may be to avoid them. Thinking about jobs as developmental requires a change of mind-set. Sometimes this attitudinal change can be achieved simply through a discussion with a boss, mentor, coach, or human resource person. At other times, however, it is difficult for people to think about an assignment in terms of development because they are more focused on meeting deadlines, completing tasks, and accomplishing goals. Often a formal approach is necessary.

Organizations wishing to take a formal approach to conversations about developmental opportunities can use a survey instrument, such as the Job Challenge Profile (JCP) (McCauley, Ohlott, and Ruderman, 1999; Ruderman, McCauley, and Ohlott, 1999). The JCP can be used to assess the developmental aspects of existing jobs. This short questionnaire asks people to what extent specific challenges are present in their jobs, using the framework of job transitions, creating change, high levels of responsibility, managing boundaries, and dealing with diversity presented earlier in this chapter. Some sample items:

> You have to manage something, such as a function, product, technology, or market, with which you are unfamiliar.

> You have to carry out a major reorganization as a result of a merger, acquisition, downsizing, or rapid growth.

> This job is a dramatic increase in scope for you (managing significantly more people, dollars, sites, functions, and so forth).

> You have to coordinate action across dispersed sites over which you have no direct authority.

> You have to get people from different racial, religious, cultural, or ethnic backgrounds to work together.

JCP feedback improves individuals' overall understanding of how jobs contribute to development. It also helps them recognize the specific developmental opportunities in their own jobs and encourages them to take advantage of and learn from these challenges.

Maria's experience provides an example. Her new assignment brought both changes in job responsibilities and a new boss. Before the new job, Maria had for several years reported to the same vice president, a hands-on kind of person who was heavily involved in all aspects of her work. Her new boss was exactly the opposite. This gave Maria the freedom to independently manage the activities of her area. At first, this independence was frightening. Not only was she managing in a less familiar area, but now there was no one looking over her shoulder to catch mistakes. In a conversation about the new assignment, Maria's boss pointed out that mastering the unfamiliar parts of her assignment and working more independently were the developmental challenges in her job. This learning orientation provided Maria with a new level of enthusiasm toward the job. She developed new insights about how to effectively manage in the new area and gained confidence in her decision-making ability.

Looking back on her assignment some time later, Maria told us, "I gained a renewed appreciation for the value of change and the exposure to new challenges. Now the importance of job rotation and change is a more common element in planning my career and that of my staff." This positive experience encouraged Maria to seek out further challenges and also led her to emphasize challenging assignments with her staff.

Using Development as a Criterion in Giving Assignments

To make the most of developmental assignments, organizations need to ensure that development considerations are included at all levels of the staffing process. At the individual level, leaders can use assignments in planning for their own development or for developing their subordinates. Organizationally, the developmental potential of assignments should be given careful consideration in charting succession plans and in planning development of high-potential managers.

Encourage the Use of Assignments in Individual Development Plans. Increasingly, people are taking more responsibility for their own development. As you help aspiring leaders with their development planning, encourage them to set development goals based on feedback they have received about their strengths and weaknesses. The development plan should focus on directing their improvement efforts within a few domains. Sun Microsystems is one company attempting to create individualized development plans. The company uses a self-developed tool, the Survey of Executive Experience (SEE), which identifies twenty-three experiences that are beneficial for managers aspiring to the director level and above. Managers use the SEE to provide detailed career histories and descriptions of experiences in their current and prior assignments and articulate career preferences and skills. The tool provides a springboard for manager, boss, and human resource coach to discuss career goals and possible developmental steps (Barrett and Beeson, 2002). Thus once career aspirations and areas for improvement have been identified, you can work together with these employees to develop individualized action plans to meet their development goals.

Assignments can play a key role in an action plan, although the plan may also include other elements such as coaching, coursework, and regular feedback. Encourage people, when outlining their plan, to think about the types of challenges they need to help them reach their goals. If those challenges are not present in the current job, help them strategize ways to gain access to some of the needed challenges, such as through new assignments or adding responsibilities to their current job. McCauley and Martineau (1998) provide a valuable guide for pursuing development goals that includes helpful discussion and tools for individuals seeking challenging assignments. Absent this emphasis on assignments as a development strategy, many people think about development only in terms of training opportunities.

Leaders at all levels can be educated about how to use assignments in development planning for their subordinates. The process used by one national retail chain is a good example. A task force worked along with senior managers to identify leadership competencies that are important to success in the organization. To help managers develop these core competencies, a review board consisting of business directors, human resource staff, and members of the executive committee creates a detailed development plan for each of them. The plan includes the development issue, learning objectives, and expected outcomes of the assignment for the organization (such as a new sales initiative or better financial performance). It encourages the managers and their bosses to consider such questions as these:

What are the individual's learning and development needs?

What are three to five leadership challenges in each job?

How can the learning need be matched with the appropriate challenge?

How can assignments be structured to make them more developmental?

In addition, as part of the organization's performance management system, bosses are evaluated on how well they develop others (Sutter, 1994). They are encouraged to take an active role in helping their direct reports meet their development goals.

Use a Developmental Perspective in Succession Planning. Traditional approaches to succession planning attempt to fit the most highly qualified candidate with the job in the hope that candidate then carries out the responsibilities of the job most efficiently and effectively. Currently, a pitfall of many succession-planning systems is that they focus primarily on identification and assessment of talent and pay less attention to development. What results is a list of candidates who might fill particular positions should they become vacant, with less consideration as to what experiences the candidate might need to be prepared for the job or how the job itself might fit the individual's development needs.

However, organizations today are becoming increasingly aware that it is important to incorporate developmental considerations into job placement decisions. In one study, 31 percent of executive promotion decisions were developmental in nature (Ruderman and Ohlott, 1994). In these promotions, executives were being prepared for further advancement, groomed for specific key positions, or given the opportunity to improve in order to prevent derailment. Other research suggests that incorporating individual development needs into succession planning decisions is related to improved organizational reputation and financial performance (Friedman, 1986).

The recent experience of one organization illustrates the value of this approach. A critical executive position in this organization—head of a rapidly growing division—was opening up within the next nine months. At about the same time, because of retirement and transfers, a number of key people were moving out of the division, so one of the challenges for the new executive would be to put together a new management team for the division. The team charged with selecting the new leader followed the company's basic philosophy of succession planning, asking: Who is most likely to learn from the assignment? Of the potential candidates, who has not had the opportunity to deal with some of the challenges in this assignment? Whose talents can be further refined by the assignment? Who has development needs that can be addressed by the assignment?

Three potential candidates were reviewed, all of them with outstanding strengths. For one candidate in particular, however, the job would clearly be developmental. Her last several job assignments had involved fixing parts of the business that were in trouble, and now she needed an opportunity to work in a growing business that would allow her to build and expand rather than downsize. In particular, she needed to learn how to size up talent and hire a team of people who could complement each other and work together. This assignment would provide just the experience she needed to continue growing as a leader.

Identify and Target Key Assignments for Employees of High Potential. Organizations often identify key competencies needed by their leaders for achieving the organization's strategic goals. For example, an increased emphasis on international markets calls for leaders who can work across cultures. Or a focus on creating new products requires leaders who foster innovation. Key assignments for developing these competencies should be identified, and people with a high level of leadership potential should be targeted for those assignments.

For instance, a company that wants to compete globally may decide that it is important for its future leaders to have international experience early in their careers. The company then pinpoints specific overseas assignments that can develop the necessary skills. One company that has exemplified this strategy is 3M (see Seibert, Hall, and Kram, 1995). Knowledge of international operations has been identified as an important skill for 3M's future leaders. To this end, the company uses international experience, in the form of managing a subsidiary in a foreign country, to develop its high-potential managers. These international assignments are especially designed to encompass appropriate experiences deemed necessary for advancement within 3M.

Another example comes from Citicorp (Clark and Lyness, 1991). The organization was growing rapidly, becoming flatter, and facing intense competition. As part of the response to these organizational challenges, Citicorp identified interpersonal and strategic skills as important competencies to develop in people targeted for senior-level jobs. A major component of the development process for high-potential managers is to undertake two assignments of three or four years each. One assignment involves a major strategic challenge, and the other exposes the manager to intense people management challenges.

Implementing a system that targets key assignments for high-potential managers requires significant organizational investment and a commitment to individual development by top leaders, who realize that the policy can yield organizational benefits as well. Involvement at every level of the organization and tight collaboration between the human resource department and top management are critical success factors (Clark and Lyness, 1991; Cobb and Gibbs, 1990).

Maximizing Learning from Assignments

As we have discussed, just because the opportunity for learning is present in an assignment does not mean an individual can or will take advantage of it. Preparation and support are important steps organizations can take to increase the chances the desired learning will occur.

Prepare People for Learning from New Assignments. Telling people who are chosen for a developmental assignment that they are being given the assignment as an opportunity to learn often motivates them to take advantage of the opportunity.

One way to prepare people for a developmental assignment is to have them complete a checklist for learning (Dechant, 1990, 1994). Such a checklist includes questions about what strengths and limitations the individual brings to an assignment, what aspects of the job and its context might prove to be particularly challenging, and what learning outcomes may be expected. A sample checklist is presented in Exhibit 5.3.

Whether or not an actual checklist is used, thinking about such questions helps raise people's awareness of themselves as learners and helps them make the most of new opportunities. Setting development goals, providing access to coaches, and

EXHIBIT 5.3. QUESTIONS TO ASK TO FACILITATE LEARNING FROM A DEVELOPMENTAL ASSIGNMENT.

About yourself	1. What strengths do I bring to this job? What will help me? 2. What are my development needs? What might hinder me from being effective and successful? 3. What aspects of this job may be particularly challenging for me, given my background, experience, strengths, and development needs? For example, is the role clear or ambiguous? Will I have the formal authority to do what I need to do? Are there obstacles, and if so, how might I overcome them? 4. What can I learn from this job? What do I want to learn? 5. What do I need to know to be able to do this job effectively? 6. What might make it difficult for me to learn? 7. What kind of help or advice am I likely to need? 8. What are my career goals? How can this job help me move toward them?
About the assignment	1. What are the organization's objectives for me in this job? 2. What are my own personal objectives in this job? 3. How does this job fit with the organization's mission, values, and goals? 4. What do I know about this job? What are the tasks, responsibilities, and requirements? What are the key leadership challenges? 5. What are my subordinates like? 6. What is my boss like? 7. Am I likely to encounter any resistance? What steps might I take to overcome it? 8. Who can help me? Where can I turn to for support? 9. What other resources do I have available to me? 10. Is there anything I would like to change about this assignment?
During and after the assignment	1. How can I monitor my learning progress? (For example, should I keep a journal? Find a learning partner? Seek formal or informal feedback? Do other things?) 2. What am I learning? Is there anything I did not expect? 3. What am I not learning that I thought or hoped I would? Why? 4. How will I know I have learned what I wanted and needed to learn? 5. What was the most challenging part of this assignment for me? 6. How did I behave and what did I do when I felt particularly challenged? What were the consequences or results of my behavior? 7. What will I do differently if faced with a similar situation in the future? 8. What mistakes have I made? What have I learned from them? 9. What was my greatest success? What contributed to it? What did it teach me? 10. What are my next steps? How can I take better advantage of the learning opportunities in my next assignment?

scheduling regular feedback on developmental progress are other ways organizations can help people prepare for learning.

Support Individuals Throughout the Developmental Assignment. Perhaps the most important success factor is organizational support. People in developmental assignments are placed in situations in which some of their abilities and skills may be deficient. Support boosts their confidence in their ability to learn, increases their sense of permission to experiment, and relieves the stress that can inhibit learning. Support for learning can mean the difference between failure and success.

Support takes a variety of forms: an outlet for stress relief, a sense of collegiality with coworkers, understanding that one has permission to fail, endorsement of one's ideas and actions, and acceptance and approval from others. Models or mentors who have experienced similar challenges themselves can help guide people through their new assignments. In a job-swapping program at Greyhound Financial Corporation, for instance, managers are coached by the previous jobholder (Northcraft, Griffith, and Shalley, 1992). Support may also come in the form of compensation and other means of public recognition.

People learn more effectively when they have support and encouragement from above. Bosses have a positive impact on development through their special abilities or because of the relationships they form with their employees. Supportive bosses can foster development in a number of different ways: giving subordinate managers the latitude to try things on their own, providing visibility and recognition, opening doors, giving advice, buffering their people from the system, providing useful feedback, and delegating exciting and challenging tasks.

Support plays an especially important role in helping overcome obstacles. For example, 3M pairs senior, U.S.-based executives with managers in overseas assignments to help provide ongoing support and advice throughout the assignment (Seibert, Hall, and Kram, 1995). (See Chapter Three for an in-depth discussion of the importance of relationships for development.)

One important form of support is follow-up. At some point during the assignment, human resource staff should work with the individual to assess whether the assignment actually contains the requisite developmental challenges. This assessment serves as the basis for a discussion with a coach or boss about whether the assignment is working out as planned, unexpected challenges have arisen, there is enough support for learning from the assignment, and the right balance between using existing talents and stretching has been achieved. For example, one organization's development guide emphasizes follow-up on the development process by including timetables for reports and review meetings with the boss.

Central to the process of supporting the individual is providing specific ways of capturing what he or she learns from the assignment. Many of the methods of support discussed here also provide avenues for reflection. Research into the adult learning cycle of planning, doing, and reflecting emphasizes that when lessons are learned in active learning experiences such as job assignments, they have deeper, more practical, and longer-lasting meaning.

Tracking Developmental Assignments over Time

Human resource information systems should track the kinds of developmental assignments people are given and how they respond to these challenges. In terms of job assignments, human resource functions normally track only changes in job titles, organizational levels, business units, or locations. This type of information provides little insight into the developmental history of the individual. In contrast, organizations such as State Farm incorporate job assignments as part of the development planning process. Individuals reflect on what their experiences have taught them, and their learnings are captured in the development plan. Possible next positions are identified, as well as potential types of developmental experiences that may be beneficial for the manager. Tracking developmental assignments and what is learned from them provides decision makers with a way to assess whether they are providing people with a breadth of challenge over their careers, insight into which individuals are particularly effective learners and thus have high potential for continued development, and in-depth knowledge of how to create assignments that are effective for developing certain capacities.

In particular, organizations should monitor the developmental track records of women and minority managers, because succession plans have been less successful in advancing them than in advancing white males (Curtis and Russell, 1993). Limited variety in career assignments is one explanation for the career blockages encountered by nontraditional managers. Chapters Nine and Ten provide detailed discussions of the role of challenging assignments in developing nontraditional managers.

Some Issues in Using Assignments for Development

This chapter has touched on some of the issues inherent in using assignments for development purposes. Here we investigate these issues in greater depth by examining questions frequently asked by human resource practitioners grappling with the idea of an assignment-based development system.

On Whom Should Organizations Focus Developmental Assignments?

Admittedly, some of the most powerful developmental assignments, such as major start-from-scratch or turnaround jobs, have limited availability. Who receives a developmental assignment depends partly on the organization's strategy for leadership development. Organizations with traditional approaches limit developmental opportunities to a select group of people, such as those who are considered to have high potential. These are people who have been carefully identified and selected as candidates for future top leadership positions. Current leaders closely follow their careers, and developmental assignments may be allocated to them as the organization deems necessary. It is advisable that these organizations search broadly and deeply for their talent and reassess people often, to lessen the possibility of overlooking talent.

Other organizations choose to create a range of developmental opportunities and make them more widely available. They investigate ways to add some developmental elements to existing jobs as well as systematically place selected individuals in highly developmental jobs (such as starting up a new business or revitalizing a poorly performing existing business).

Finally, as previously mentioned, significant tension exists between finding the "right" person for the job and finding the person who will learn the most from the job. McCall and Hollenbeck (2002) characterize this tension as finding the balance between maximum performance and maximum development. Every assignment, no matter how small or insignificant it seems, has the potential to be developmental for someone. Clark and Lyness (1991) caution decision makers to differentiate smart from dumb risks when deciding who receives a developmental assignment. A smart risk has two components: the manager has most of the competencies and skills to help him or her succeed in the job, and the stretch is not overwhelming. Learning is undermined if the challenging part of the assignment is too great a challenge.

How Can Organizations Use Assignments Developmentally While Downsizing or Restructuring?

People often equate a developmental assignment with a move to a position with higher levels of responsibility. Most organizations, however, lack enough big developmental assignments to adequately develop all the future leaders they need. As organizations downsize and become flatter, they are no longer able to rely on promotions and high-visibility assignments to meet all their development needs. To compensate, the developmental component framework presented in this chapter can be used to identify opportunities in assignments other than promotions and to add developmental opportunities to existing jobs without moving people around.

A lateral move, for instance, can be just as developmental as a promotion, provided some aspect of the job is challenging to the new incumbent. Lateral moves still involve transitions if they are moves to a different function, business, or product. Consider this example described to us by one manager: "I was on the threshold of being promoted into a sales and proposal-writing role in one of the most successful businesses in the investment area. Instead, I was transferred to HR, at a level that was really a lateral move for me. I learned that you can make lemonade out of lemons. I took the job and redefined it into one of the most influential positions in the organization."

Other avenues for development when high-level assignments are few and far between are redesigning jobs to include more developmental features, giving special task force or project responsibilities, creating joint projects across functions, and giving special troubleshooting assignments (Baldwin and Padgett, 1993; Lombardo and Eichinger, 1989; Sutter, 1994).

Lombardo and Eichinger (1989) also list a number of small developmental assignments that can be added to existing jobs. The five types of job challenges defined earlier in this chapter can readily be added to existing jobs, as in assigning a manager to lead a cross-functional project that involves people over whom the project leader has no direct authority.

Finally, a few organizations are moving beyond today's best practices and experimenting with new approaches that expand our perspective on developing from experience. One potential new experimental approach involves positions or projects outside the organization. Byham, Smith, and Pease (2002) suggest that vendor and customer organizations can also provide assignment opportunities. In this way, the manager can gain experiences that may not be available within the organization. A classic example is the United Way's "loaned executive" program, in which executives on loan from local companies work as full-time staff members of the United Way for a given period of time. Loaned executives work with volunteers to manage employee campaigns in businesses, government organizations, and professional firms. They organize employee informational meetings, make presentations, obtain pledge commitments, make sales calls, and oversee a variety of accounts. In addition to benefiting the United Way, these assignments provide developmental experiences for the loaned executives. My own research suggests that managers can learn valuable lessons about leadership from roles they play outside the workplace. For example, a leadership role in a volunteer organization can teach valuable lessons that can be applied at work, further suggesting that organizations may need to expand their perspective on what constitutes a developmental assignment (Ruderman, Ohlott, Panzer, and King, 2002).

Aren't Some Jobs Too Important for Developmental Assignments?

Yes. Some assignments are too critical to the continued success of the organization to risk entrusting them to people who might not be able to handle them. The business risks of the candidate's failure are usually easy to identify: the business will lose money or customers, for example. However, to err on the side of caution has its risks too. An organization that does not place people in challenging assignments where they can learn and grow never develops its executive bench strength.

A large oil company, for example, relied on one man as its specialist in oil field start-ups. The company never allowed him to do anything else and never allowed anyone else to open a new oil field. Eventually, the employee felt stifled and left to take a job with another company that offered him opportunities to broaden his skills. The oil company was left with no one who was even partly competent to open a new oil field.

In contrast, a consumer products organization purposely holds on to a small area of the business that is not profitable. The company continues to fund the business because it is headquartered overseas and provides a valuable international assignment used to help develop potential senior managers, with relatively small risk.

How Do You Find the Right Amount of "Stretch"?

Most development professionals agree that there is a fine line between a challenging assignment and an overwhelming one, and the location of that line varies by individual. Byham, Smith, and Pease (2002) suggest two general rules of thumb for making developmental assignments: (1) the greater the change in responsibility, the greater the learning; and (2) the larger the scope of the responsibility of the position, the greater the learning. Determining just how much stretch an individual can handle is complicated. Bank of America has developed an elaborate and well-thought-out system for making developmental assignments and for assessing the alignment of talent in critical areas. In its consumer and commercial business, it has created "complexity profiles" for key leadership positions with multiple incumbents. Using the Job Challenge Profile as a framework, the bank's leadership development professionals worked with finance partners and core business leaders to create job complexity profiles that include subjective measures of scope and challenge (for example, "high stakes" and "external pressure") as well as several objective measures of "scope and scale" such as financial and operational data. Leadership development professionals at Bank of America recognize that jobs with the same title may not be all that comparable across different operating areas. For example, the challenges of an executive role in an area where income, number of clients, and number of employees are high and the unit's performance is critical to the overall success of the company are likely to be greater than the challenges of the same role in an area of the business that is more tangential, has fewer employees and clients, and generates less revenue. Using this system helps the bank determine which assignments might be too much of a stretch for a given individual and which might be a good fit. The bank reviews individual managers' skills, abilities, and backgrounds to see if they have had the appropriate experiences to prepare them for particular assignments. If it will be an individual's first time in a particular type of job, for example, it is less risky but still developmentally beneficial to take on a role in a smaller, less critical business unit. These profiles also play a central role in ongoing talent management, which includes moving high-potential talent into stretch assignments and ensuring that top talent is aligned to the most challenging and complex roles.

McCall and Hollenbeck (2002) also emphasize the importance of considering the manager's background; for example, the experience of an expatriate who speaks the local language will be qualitatively different from that of one who does not, and thus different people may be more or less challenged and may learn different lessons from the same assignment. Some organizations even try to quantify the amount of risk they are willing to take and will only consider people with a certain degree of preparation for an assignment. Finding the right balance of challenge requires a careful look at the individual's skill level in terms of critical competencies identified by the organization; other individual characteristics such as temperament, emotional intelligence, and career goals; the organization's needs; and available support mechanisms (Byham, Smith, and Pease, 2002).

How Long Should Someone Stay in a Developmental Assignment?

This is a controversial subject in many organizations. If people are kept in jobs too long, they experience few opportunities for learning and become bored. At the other extreme, if people are moved too quickly, they lose the opportunity to complete an assignment, as well as the chance to reflect on, consolidate, and refine what they have learned from their experience. To optimize learning, people need to remain in an assignment long enough to be able to see the consequences of their actions and decisions. They need to remain long enough that they learn to cope with the issues, dilemmas, and problems that confront them—only then will they truly learn and develop.

John Gabarro's research (1987) suggests that it can take three and a half years for a person to glean the important lessons from a developmental assignment. At first, managers tend to deal with the most familiar problems, as when those with financial backgrounds concentrate on the numbers. Then they begin to learn other aspects of the job, and eventually new problems surface that were not apparent in the initial assignment. Gabarro also found that managers did not learn at a deeper level until after the first eighteen months in a job.

Conclusion

Job assignments provide many of the developmental opportunities in today's organizations. Unfortunately, these potent sources of leader development are often ignored or used haphazardly. This chapter can serve as a framework for using assignments for development purposes.

Once an organization has identified its potentially developmental jobs and the strengths and weaknesses of the people it wants to develop, there are several ways it can proceed. At one end of the spectrum, where organizational involvement is minimal, it can provide people with information about developmental opportunities in their current jobs and allow them to take charge of their own development, including seeking out the challenges they believe they need.

Other organizations choose to develop a systematic program of job rotation, in which they identify future leaders and their strengths and development needs and then devise a development plan in which the individuals are given particular jobs intended to improve their skills and abilities. The organizations may decide to systematically expose early career managers to a variety of key assignments or look at specific individual development needs and attempt to address them by one assignment or a series of assignments. Some organizations choose to conduct assignment-based development on a small scale, or they choose an informal rather than a formal system. They may encourage widespread developmental opportunities or limit opportunities to a select group of people.

We at CCL believe that rather than limit developmental assignments to select groups, it is important to keep in mind that most jobs with leadership requirements can be shaped to increase their developmental potential so that more people encounter developmental aspects in their work (McCauley and Brutus, 1998). Thus assignments can be used to grow future senior leaders or to provide opportunities for solid performers who are not being groomed for top-level positions to stretch and grow nevertheless.

Challenging job assignments are perhaps the most potent form of leader development that exists. However, learning from challenging assignments is much more difficult than learning from a typical leader development program. Simply because an opportunity for development exists does not guarantee that learning will happen. Developmental features of jobs are not objective; whether or not they provide learning depends on how they are experienced by individual managers, who have varying backgrounds and experiences, interpret jobs differently, and even shape their own jobs.

To further complicate matters, development for its own sake is seldom the primary objective when organizations place a manager in an assignment. Enhanced performance and goal accomplishment are justifiably the primary outcomes desired from assignments in most organizations. But if used properly, with the appropriate attention given to matching individual needs with the developmental aspects of the proposed assignment, organizations might be better able to maximize both performance and development. It may not be appropriate to place people in developmental assignments when the stakes are very high because the costs of failure are too great. However, using job assignments for development purposes provides an additional benefit beyond achieving task objectives and may even result in competitive advantages for the organization. Leaders can learn essential practical skills and perspectives that help them function more effectively.

Organizations in the Conference Board study (Barrett and Beeson, 2002) recognized the risk of stretch developmental assignments to both the organization and the individual. Leading-edge companies recognize and manage the risks by devoting time to carefully identifying future leadership talent and intentionally placing future leaders in assignments that stretch and challenge them while reducing the risk of failure by providing ongoing feedback and support to individuals in those positions. Providing individuals with stretch assignments at lower levels of responsibility tends to entail less risk with a potentially great payoff. The most successful companies take care to plan developmental assignments so that they are not solely for the sake of general experiences or to satisfy an employee's desire to keep moving. Instead, learning objectives are clearly articulated, and the experiences are clearly translated into learning that can then be applied.

In an organizational environment where the structure of the employment relationship is changing and lifetime employment is no longer a given, providing employees with a variety of developmental opportunities to round out their repertoire of leadership skills is one way organizations help their people remain employable, even if their business should experience a downturn. It also helps ensure that they always have a core group of competent leaders to count on.

CHAPTER SIX

HARDSHIPS

Russ S. Moxley
Mary Lynn Pulley

Sitting around a conference table at a beautiful resort in Manchester, Vermont, executives of a large consumer products company were asked to reflect on their careers and identify one or two significant events that had changed the way they managed. The president sat quietly, very pensively, while his colleagues talked about the critical incidents they had encountered and what they learned from them. They described many of the experiences detailed in other chapters of this book: challenging assignments, difficult bosses, their first job as a supervisor, training courses they attended.

Suddenly the company's chief legal counsel, realizing that the president hadn't spoken, turned to him and said, "Jim, what do you have on your list?" Jim demurred. "The items on my list are different," he said. "They're not like yours." The attorney persisted, gently nudging Jim to share his experience.

Finally Jim spoke. "Sometimes I guess you really have to get your nose bloodied before you learn. I've had a great career. Lots of good jobs, and on each of them I've done fairly well. Along the way I developed a lot of confidence in my ability, to the point that I pretty much thought I always knew what needed to be done. So I didn't delegate very well, didn't rely much on the other members of the team. Then I had a heart attack. It was like running into a brick wall. I realized that I was finite, that I couldn't do it all. It was a humbling experience. It was only then that I realized that I'd better learn to delegate, to really trust the experience and expertise of people like yourselves. I think I've been a different kind of leader since then, not so much of a one-man band."

Jim's story is a good example of the sort of lessons people can learn from life's curveballs. From the challenging and important assignments Jim completed during his career, he learned self-confidence, among other things. He learned to trust his own judgment and have confidence in his decisions. These are important lessons for a leader to learn. But as is true with every other strength, if self-confidence is taken to an extreme, it becomes a weakness. Self-confidence that goes unchecked becomes arrogance, and by his own account, Jim had become arrogant. He thought he could do it all. He didn't need to delegate; he didn't need a team of strong subordinates.

What's the best antidote for arrogance? Often it is a hardship. After his heart attack, Jim learned to balance self-confidence with humility. In the process, he became a more well-rounded leader. He was able to act with flexibility, maintaining confidence in his own judgment but also relying on the judgment of others.

In this chapter, we will discuss why hardships are a different kind of developmental experience and the relationship between hardships and resilience. We will explore the types of hardships along with specific examples of lessons that can be learned from them. Following this, we will address how individuals, human resource professionals, and line managers can use hardships to promote development. Finally, we will show how hardships relate to the leader development model.

A Different Kind of Developmental Experience

One of the surprising findings in the Center for Creative Leadership's research is the extent to which hardships are important to the development of well-rounded leaders. The last time CCL replicated its research on lessons of experience, men and women mentioned hardships more than any other experience as a key event in their development.

The reason that hardships are important is clear: learning is not random. Specific experiences teach specific lessons, and hardships offer lessons not attainable elsewhere—not from challenging assignments, not from feedback-intensive courses, not from mentors or coaches, and not from any other developmental experience discussed in this handbook. We will say more about these lessons a bit later in this chapter.

But hardships are not a different kind of developmental experience only because the lessons learned from them are different. It is more fundamental than that. One reason that hardships are different is that they are not intentional on the part of either the individual or the organization. People encounter them, ready or not, during the course of their careers and their lives. Another reason why hardships are different is that the lessons they teach are usually learned in retrospect, after people have gotten through the experience and had time to reflect and gain perspective on it. Finally, hardships are different because the challenges embedded in them are different.

Most of the challenges described in other chapters of this handbook derive from people or experiences that are external to the individual: a tough assignment, a difficult boss, a challenge built into a training program. Although challenges such as these may have a personal aspect to them, hardships as described in this chapter are events experienced in an intensely personal way—challenges such as losing a job or having a heart attack—such that the experience is internalized as part of oneself. The common element in hardship challenges is that they involve a sense of loss. By facing the loss and dealing with the adversity related to it, these challenges provide the opportunity to develop resilience.

Hardships and Loss

As just noted, at the core of any hardship experience is a sense of loss—of credibility, control, self-efficacy, or identity. Jim, the executive mentioned at the start of the chapter, told his direct reports that with his heart attack he lost a sense of his own invincibility, that he realized he was human and finite. Such loss provokes confrontation within oneself, and with appropriate support, unique learnings can emerge from it.

The experience of loss is key to understanding the power of hardships, because loss elicits a questioning of meaning, and meaning is the crucial organizing principle for human behavior (Kegan, 1982, 1994; Marris, 1986). Meaning integrates one's purpose, feelings, and behavior. It allows people to make sense of their actions by providing reasons for them.

Often a deep sense of loss causes people who usually live in an outer world to turn inward. Managers and executives who have been successful primarily because of their ability to operate in the external world—a world of empirical data and rational decisions, of strategies built on marketplace and competitive analyses, of bottom lines and return to shareholders—are suddenly forced to go on an inner journey, a journey of introspection and reflection. The sense of loss provokes a confrontation with the self: What does this mean to me? What did I do wrong? Do I not measure up? What could I have done differently? Could I have done anything to prevent this from happening? It is a time of taking stock, reflecting on strengths and weaknesses, considering what's important in life and work, and perhaps giving up an old identity while transitioning to a new one. By taking this journey, people have the opportunity to develop resilience.

Hardships and Resilience

Hardships are also a different kind of developmental experience because they are inextricably intertwined with the development of resilience. Resilience is associated with the ability to bounce back from adversity or hardship. It is a multidimensional concept like leadership, intelligence, or athletic ability. Therefore, there is no single definition of resilience, and resilient people cannot be easily categorized (Pulley, Wakefield, and Van Velsor, 2001). There is a large body of research on the topic, however (Anthony, 1987; Masten, 1989).

Resilience consists of a set of individual characteristics that can be developed at any time in a person's life. It is an active process of self-righting and growth that helps people deal with hardships in a way that is conducive to development. There are four key characteristics of resilience: purpose and meaning, cognitive strategies, improvisation, and social support.

One of the fundamental characteristics of resilience is that it permits people to weave the difficult experiences of their lives into a larger sense of purpose and meaning. For instance, when experiencing a serious loss (such as facing a life-threatening illness), resilient people use the experience as an opportunity to learn, often by constructing a renewed sense of purpose. More important than what happens to people is how they think about what happens and how they derive meaning from it.

Cognitive strategies are the ways that people think about their experiences. For instance, a common belief is that resilience stems from an optimistic nature. This is true only so long as optimism does not create a distorted sense of reality (Coutu, 2002). Resilient people see things as they are and deal with reality in a constructive way. For instance, we spoke with a manager who had a strong track record in the high-tech industry. He told us that several years ago, he left his job to join a new company because he wanted to improve his work-life balance. Unfortunately, he soon discovered that the new job was not what he expected. In the new work culture, there was tremendous pressure to perform, a very confusing management structure, and a highly charged political environment. He also realized that direct confrontation to address differences was not acceptable as a cultural norm, so he needed to pay close attention to unspoken nuances. Initially he tried to bring about change in the new organization, but it was met with resistance. Within two years of joining the company, this manager knew that he was becoming sidelined, and the stress of the new environment began to affect his health. He told us that he kept a quotation on his desk that read, "The biggest mistake you can make is to believe that you work for someone else." He evaluated what was and what was not within his realm of control. He realized that he was not a good fit with this organization. He made a decision to go into business for himself. Rather than remaining stuck or beleaguered in an untenable work situation, he believed that he had many options and was not afraid to make a change.

A third characteristic of resilience is the ability to improvise, to respond creatively in the moment with whatever resources are at hand. We heard a poignant example of this shortly following the tragic attack on the World Trade Center towers on September 11, 2001. One executive was in charge of his company's office on the ninth floor of the second tower. Immediately after the first tower was hit, he ran into the hall. He was told by a security guard to stay in the building. He did not believe that this was the best course of action, so instead he quickly gathered all the staff on his floor and led them down the stairs. He had successfully evacuated everyone in his office when the second tower collapsed. In this case, the most significant resources that this executive relied on were his own judgment and his ability to coordinate a fast evacuation in the moment.

A fourth characteristic of resilience is social support. Resilience is enhanced by the ability to cultivate a large network of relationships, ranging from the intimate to the professional. When people have a sense that the important people in their lives will support them through good and bad times, it provides a sort of safety net so that when they stumble, they do not fall too far.

There is an interaction between these resilient characteristics and the lessons learned from hardships, as shown in Figure 6.1. As people encounter hardships, they draw on these resilient characteristics, which deepens the lessons they learn and develops their ability to successfully face hardships in the future.

FIGURE 6.1. RELATIONSHIP BETWEEN HARDSHIPS AND RESILIENCE.

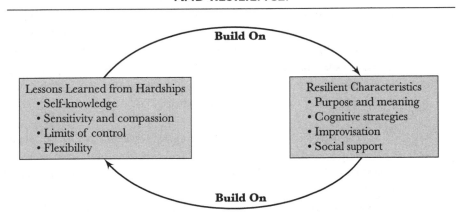

Types of Hardships

Through several research projects conducted at CCL, we have identified six types of hardship events and the particular lessons that leaders can learn from them: mistakes and failures, career setbacks, personal trauma, problem employees, downsizing, and situations in which race mattered. Of course, this is not an exhaustive list of the hardships people experience, but it is fairly representative. Other hardships usually fit in with one or another of these types.

Mistakes and Failures

According to IBM legend, in the early days of the company, a young engineer made a mistake that cost the company thousands of dollars. Embarrassed and afraid, the engineer approached founder and president Tom Watson, told him of the mistake, and offered to resign. Watson is reported to have said, "Resign? I can't afford for you to resign. Look how much I have already invested in your development."

Like that young engineer, all managers and executives make mistakes. Contracts are negotiated poorly, business deals go sour, opportunities are not seized, a relationship with an important client is mismanaged, the boss does not get what she wants when she wants it. The question is not whether mistakes are made and failures experienced but whether people see them as opportunities to learn, grow, and change. More agile learners use all experiences, including hardships like mistakes and failures, as opportunities to learn important leadership lessons; "blocked learners" do not; they are often demoralized or even defeated.

The sense of loss that often accompanies mistakes and failures involves a loss of self-efficacy—a loss of confidence in doing a particular thing—and a loss of the confidence of others at work. When people lose their sense of self-efficacy, their ability to learn from experience also decreases (see Chapter Seven for a more complete discussion of this). When people help others "save face" after a mistake, they are trying to make sure that they do not add to the sense of loss already being experienced.

Leaders are more likely to learn from their mistakes if three conditions are present (McCall, Lombardo, and Morrison, 1988):

1. *The cause and effect are very clear to the individual involved.* If people are unsure of their responsibility for the mistake or feel they could not have done anything to prevent it, few lessons are learned. But if the cause and effect are clear, if people know they are culpable, and if they take responsibility for the mistake, the chances that they will learn are greatly enhanced. A person who says "I blew it" or "I had a part in it" is in fact signaling an openness to learning.

2. *The mistake is openly acknowledged.* It is easy to downplay mistakes, to pretend they did not happen, and to deny their consequences. It is much harder to put a mistake on the table, discuss it openly, and pull learnings from it. But discussing mistakes honestly and openly is the best way for managers and executives to assess their contribution to the mess and learn from it and the only way to encourage broader organizational learning.

3. *The organization's position on how mistakes are treated must be clearly understood.* The best possible way to view mistakes is as an opportunity for learning. Many organizations proclaim that they encourage appropriate risk-taking behavior as a way of becoming more innovative, but few have clearly defined how they will help individuals learn when risks are taken and the inevitable mistakes are made. Likewise, companies often encourage high-potential men and women to accept stretch assignments (jobs for which the individual is not fully prepared), but if mistakes are made, the company's response is often punitive, providing a disincentive for other high-potential employees to take risks. The best way for companies to show that they really mean what they say is to implement a "mistake system." Like a reward system, an organizational mistake system specifies what support employees can expect if they take appropriate risks but do not succeed, such as moving into difficult assignments and making mistakes or agreeing to test untested skills in managing a difficult employee and not handling it adeptly. We discuss mistake systems in more detail later in this chapter.

If the three conditions just described are met, the lessons that can be learned from mistakes are quite potent. We turn now to discuss these lessons in more detail.

Mismanaging relationships is a frequently cited mistake, and learning how to better handle such relationships is one of the most important lessons. This includes learning more about what senior-level executives are like and how to work with them, how to deal better with direct reports on issues such as delegation and decision making, and in a general sense, how to understand other people and their perspectives better.

A second lesson often learned from mistakes is humility. Mistakes have the capacity to teach people about their flaws and limitations. One executive told us the story of doing a poor job of negotiating a contract with a major international client that cost his company thousands of dollars: "I didn't ask for help. I didn't think I needed it. I learned very quickly how much I didn't know. I learned it the hard way." Another executive put it like this: "I believe that if at least once every five years you don't put yourself in a position where you feel truly stupid, you're not learning. If I don't do it every five years, I get out of the habit and begin to feel comfortable and forget that learning can be painful and hard, and it takes repetition and work and requires changing behavior."

Finally, making mistakes and learning from them teaches the very important lesson of how to handle them. There appears to be a real difference in how leaders who succeed and those who don't succeed handle mistakes. People who try to cover up or whitewash their mistakes, who blame others when mistakes surface, and who do not warn others that the consequences of a mistake might affect them are candidates for derailment. Conversely, people who acknowledge their mistakes, take responsibility for them, and warn others who might feel the consequences are seen as effective. The difference is not that one group makes mistakes and the other doesn't. All leaders make mistakes. The difference is in how the mistakes are handled.

Career Setbacks

Jan had been identified as a high-potential manager in her organization. She rose very quickly, completing one challenging assignment after another. She was on a fast track. Then it happened: a promotion that she expected went to someone else.

Calvin was moved from his line job to a corporate staff position. He was told that his new job in long-range planning was important; he was not told that it was intended as a developmental experience for him and that there were particular leadership skills he could learn in this new assignment. Calvin eventually hated the new job; he felt he was on the sidelines looking on while others were making important operational decisions. He believed he had been marginalized.

Helena was put in a new assignment that entailed a significant change in scope and scale. For the first time, she was managing people who had more technical expertise than she had, and many were older than she was. The company knew it would be a stretch assignment for her, that she was going to be in over her head at first. They thought she could do it, but she couldn't—it was too much of a stretch. After a year of struggle, Helena was demoted. But she also received a lot of support so that after having time to catch her breath, she got her career back on track.

These stories illustrate three types of career setbacks: missed promotions, unsatisfying jobs, and demotions. Being fired is an obvious fourth type.

Where is the sense of loss in a career setback? For some, the setback represents a loss of control, especially control over their careers. For others, it is a loss of self-efficacy, the sense that they might not measure up in certain critical skill areas or the realization that they do not have all the capacity they need to be effective leaders. For still others, especially those who have been fired, it is a loss of professional identity. One executive described how the loss and recovery of his professional identity served as a catalyst for significant personal development (Pulley, 1997, p. 37):

I had to come to the realization of who I was and that there's a difference between who I am and what I do. In my previous job, I *was* what I did. I was the zone manager. I had the car and I had the clothes and everything that went with it. I became consumed with the position. It was my identity—it's what I drew everything from; it fed my ego. After I left and all that was stripped away, I had to deal with who am I? Having done that, the job I do is no longer who I am. Yes, it feeds the ego somewhat, but it's not the total me. There's more to me than that. Looking back, when I was assigned to be zone manager I would've thought my next move was vice president. At that time if someone had told me that in three and a half years you're going to be terminated, I would've thought that would be the end of my life. Because it was the end of my identity. I had to discover a new identity.

Whatever the sense of loss, career setbacks are usually wake-up calls. They offer people a chance to learn others' perceptions about themselves. Executives who experience a setback may already know that they have weaknesses, but now they learn that others also recognize the weaknesses and that the weaknesses matter. They learn that without significant change in their skills and perspectives as leaders, they can derail—if they haven't in fact already done so. For people who are open to learning, career setbacks are challenges that are unfreezing experiences, opening them to new insights about their strengths and limitations and enhancing their readiness to learn from other developmental opportunities.

Not all setbacks, we hasten to add, result from limitations of the individual. Reorganizations, reengineering, and mergers and acquisitions all lead to less than desirable opportunities for otherwise outstanding performers. Sometimes events conspire and individuals experience setbacks through no fault of their own. It is easy at times like these for people to become cynical and blame their situation on organizational politics. Our key point is that development happens when people are able to see career setbacks—whatever their origin—as opportunities to learn.

Another lesson that leaders can learn from career setbacks is what kinds of jobs they like and do not like. The reality check that comes with the setback often leads people to take stock of themselves. As they do, they learn about what type of work is satisfying and meaningful, and they decide to take more responsibility for managing their careers and choosing work that is meaningful.

Learning positive lessons from career setbacks is aided by the right balancing of the challenging experience with support from significant others in the organization. If wounds are to be healed, an appropriate intervention, one that includes lots of listening and sorting of feelings, is crucial. Someone needs to work with the person, someone who is willing to take on the role of counselor or coach (see Chapter Three for more on developmental relationships).

Unfortunately, in most organizations, it is exactly at such times that an effective intervention is least likely to happen. The managers of individuals who have experienced a setback are often unable or unwilling, or perhaps lack the emotional intelligence, to help the wounded through their experience of loss.

Personal Trauma

One powerful developmental experience that people continue to report to us is personal trauma: illness, death, divorce, children in trouble. Although personal trauma is never something that people would choose, they find that they often learn powerful and enduring leadership lessons from the experience.

One CEO told us that her deepest learning experience was when she was diagnosed and treated for cancer:

> I can look back now and say it was one of the defining experiences in terms of my life and career. It taught me several lessons: It taught me that I had more strength and resilience than I thought I had. It taught me the value of being in the present—of not being so concerned about next year but taking advantage of every moment and opportunity because who knows what's going to happen in the future. And it taught me that it's important to rely on other people. It taught me that I don't have to do everything myself. When I had cancer, I had no choice. But I learned to draw on the support and help that others gave me, which is not something that I feel comfortable doing. I grew up learning how to be self-reliant. And it was important for me to learn how to accept help.

Another executive told us how reality broke through his years of denial when he realized that his teenage son was an alcoholic. When the boy was arrested for driving under the influence and a police officer asked if he wanted to call his father, the son answered bitterly, "He probably isn't home, and if he is, he won't care." Stopped dead in his tracks, the executive was able to admit to himself that he had spent too little time being a father and a husband. He also realized, once this experience started him on a journey of introspection, that work was not bringing the kind of meaning and satisfaction for which he longed. The result: he eventually created a better balance between his work and his personal life and, in a long and tough process, rebuilt a relationship with his son.

These are just two examples of personal trauma, but there are myriad variations on this theme. Studies of individuals who survive extreme trauma show that the essence of their ability to endure and bounce back is creating meaning from the experience and maintaining their self-esteem and dignity, a sense of group belonging, and a feeling of being useful to others (Fine, 1991; Frankl, 1984; Lifton,

1988). The key point is this: their response to the experience is far more significant than the experience itself.

Problem Employees

Difficult employees come in many guises. The most obvious—people guilty of theft or fraud or deceit or whose work is clearly below standard—are not the hardest to deal with. Company policies and common sense provide a ready solution for handling those. The hardest to manage are situations involving employees in which the decision about what to do is not clear-cut.

Take, for example, the employee whose behavior is inconsistent. When he is "on," he is one of the best workers in the company, charming and competent. But when he is "off," he is serious trouble: deceptive and manipulative, doing things he knows are wrong and then trying hard to cover his tracks.

What should his manager do? Here's a talented employee with important skills and abilities that the company needs. Most managers would like to develop him and shore up the downside, rather than fire him. So they spend an inordinate amount of time talking with him, influencing, coaching, and even cajoling him. They keep thinking that if they just work hard enough, well enough, and long enough, they can turn the situation around. Some executives report working with problem employees for years before moving them to a more suitable position or, as a last resort, firing them.

What can leaders learn from this situation? They can learn about the importance of standing firm and being forceful. And they can learn how to confront problem employees. This learning fits one of the overall themes of this handbook: leaders learn by doing.

Leaders also learn from the sense of loss they experience when dealing with problem employees. This loss is often the loss of an illusion—perhaps the illusion that the leader could in fact turn the situation around. From this disillusionment individuals learn humility—they learn something about their limits. Understood in this way, disillusionment is a good thing.

Downsizing

Sometimes events conspire. No matter how hard and well some people work to develop their capacities as leaders, no matter how much they try to meet the company's expectations, no matter how loyal they have been, there are times when none of that matters because they fall victim to corporate downsizing. They lose their jobs through no fault of their own, but knowing this does not lessen their sense of loss.

Because people so often identify themselves with the work they do, there is first and foremost a loss of identity. This is compounded by the loss of relationships and community and the loss of a sense of security. As much as with any other hardship, men and women who experience downsizing need an opportunity to work through their fear and insecurity, their frustration and anger, their sadness and their distrust.

Yet most organizations, and the people in them, are not prepared to help people work though the healing process following downsizing. As David Noer (1993) has pointed out, downsizings are done from the head, not the heart, of the organization's executives. Although some downsized individuals seek out professional counseling and others rely on support systems outside of work to help them sort out their feelings, almost none find the kind of support they need inside their organization. The element of the development process that we have called support is too often lacking exactly when it is most needed.

If support is available, either inside or outside the company, powerful lessons can be learned. People learn that they have the ability to cope with things beyond their control. One executive said to us of his experience of downsizing, "I learned that nothing is guaranteed. I decided to take advantage of every opportunity to maximize my marketability. I also learned not to be overwhelmed with anxiety, especially in situations where I have little or no control."

Being downsized is one kind of hardship; being responsible for a downsizing is another. One district operations manager told us, "Because of a reduction in the number of districts in our company, some 250 people were being displaced or laid off. I had the unpleasant duty of telling people how this reorganization affected people in my district. The hardest task was telling this one manager he was being laid off. He took the news extremely hard. I was not prepared for his reaction—he cried."

What did this manager learn from the experience? "This experience awakened me to the real world of management in dealing with people. I became more compassionate and gained more understanding of people's feelings. I think it made me stronger and better equipped to handle difficult situations when managing people."

Experiences When Race Mattered

The final hardship is something we call "race mattered." This hardship, along with downsizing, was added in 1998 upon completion of CCL's Lessons of a Diverse Workforce research project (Douglas, 2003). A race-mattered event is a situation or interaction where a manager either experiences or observes an injustice due to racial prejudice or discrimination or is the first minority to be hired at the management or executive level. In these situations, the direct experience of injustice is the hardship.

The sense of loss that results from these injustices is felt deeply and personally. Sometimes it is a loss of self-esteem or self-respect. At other times it is the loss of a sense of connectedness. But too often this hardship leads to a loss of a sense of self; one's identity is suffocated by the experience of injustice (see Chapter Ten for a detailed discussion).

Lessons Learned from Hardships

Our research has shown that the lessons learned from hardships tend to fall into four general themes or patterns. All focus on the important issues of personal awareness and personal attributes. These themes are self-knowledge, sensitivity and compassion, limits of control, and flexibility.

Self-Knowledge

Hardships often serve as a wake-up call, prompting people to decide what really matters, become more clear about their values and career aspirations, and develop more self-awareness. Individuals recognize, perhaps for the first time, that they have limits. They also become aware of their blind spots, what others have known about them but they themselves have not. Often hardships move people toward a more appropriate balance in their work and family life.

This happens only if people take the time to reflect on their experience. Most Western cultures—especially in North America—have a bias toward the external and active and a tendency to ignore the internal and reflective. Many people become busy with so many tasks that they do not stop to consider whether or why those tasks are important. Or if they have been through a painful experience, they avoid returning to it to consider the lessons for fear of reliving the pain. Yet without reflection, people get caught in an endless cycle of repetition, relying on the habits they developed yesterday to deal with the challenges they face today and will face tomorrow. With reflection and appropriate support, individuals can develop new levels of self-clarity from hardships—and this, our research and experience have shown, is a key attribute of effective leaders.

Sensitivity and Compassion

Being sensitive and compassionate is often seen as the "soft side" of leadership. Sensitivity and compassion are valuable attributes for everyone, in personal life and on the job. Yet many people, especially those who hold positions of power and authority, find them hard to express.

Occasionally we talk to executives who want to be seen as sensitive and compassionate and are surprised to learn they are not. They receive low ratings from direct reports, peers, or supervisors on the Sensitivity and Compassion scale in our Benchmarks instrument (Center for Creative Leadership, 2002a, 2002b). During private feedback sessions, it is often apparent that they are sensitive and caring people, and they wonder, "Why do other people not see this?"

Being compassionate is hard. The word *compassion* derives from the Latin prefix *com-* ("with") and verb *passire* ("suffer"), so its literal meaning is "suffering with" or "suffering together." This empathic suffering requires vulnerability and an openness to someone else's pain. Showing vulnerability in the workplace can be a frightening proposition precisely because it means that people must stop masking, denying, or avoiding their own pain or that of others. Even though leaders may feel compassion toward a person or situation, they mask these sensitive feelings due to the common belief that expressions of such emotions are inappropriate in the workplace. Often it is only when a leader experiences a personal hardship that he or she learns the importance of being sensitive to others, becomes more aware of the fears and hopes of others, and decides to be more vulnerable.

Limits of Control

The sense of having personal control over one's environment and one's destiny is generally associated with high motivation and achievement. This internal locus of control is the idea that the rewards people receive are contingent on their own actions or attributes. Yet events do conspire; no one can control everything. Hardships often teach people the limits of their control.

Several of the examples mentioned earlier in this chapter, such as illness or death of a loved one, are not a choice that anyone would make, nor are they within anyone's realm of control. From hardships, leaders can learn to determine more accurately what is and is not within their control and to recognize that everyone has limits to their control. They can also learn that their greatest realm of control is not in the situations themselves but in how they respond to situations or hardships as they occur.

Flexibility

The traditional view of a healthy personal identity is one that is characterized by stability and constancy. But today change is so omnipresent that constant personal identity is no longer as useful as having multiple involvements, images of self, and skills that allow adaptability to changing circumstances. This is one definition of flexibility. In addition, most individuals have often thought that they could only be either-or people: either tough or soft, either self-confident or humble, either a strong individual leader or a good team player. Another idea of flexibility, we have learned from our research, suggests that a key lesson individuals can learn from hardships is to be both-and people. They must learn that they can be both tough, stand-on-their-own-two-feet, forceful leaders and empowering, sensitive, and compassionate leaders.

Making the Most of Hardships

Even though people realize that they can learn positive lessons from these difficult experiences, they do not usually include hardships when they think of development. In fact, individuals usually try to avoid hardships. They work hard to avoid embarrassing gaffes, to minimize the possibility of failure, and to avoid derailment at all costs. Managers do not choose to hire difficult people just so that new skills can be tested. Executives do not always regard personal trauma (such as cancer) as relevant to work-related development, and they don't think of stressful situations as developmental. For all the right reasons, people seek to minimize the possibility of experiencing hardships.

Managers also tend to go out of their way to keep their direct reports from experiencing hardships. Even the worst ogre of a boss would not go to someone and say, "You need a good developmental experience that will teach you humility. I suggest a heart attack." Rather, managers are likely to structure work in a way that avoids hardship. They give their direct reports safe assignments, such as jobs they have proved they have the skills and abilities to handle. They promote people in small, incremental steps, usually in the same area of their technical specialty, so that they will not experience failure.

This is very human and very understandable but shortsighted. If managers want assignments to be developmental, they must understand that comfort is the enemy of growth. They must make sure that jobs or tasks stretch employees and force them to operate outside of their comfort zone to an appropriate extent. Assignments given for developmental reasons always involve some risk, and one of those risks is that the person doing the work might make mistakes or even fail.

Hardships, after all, are unavoidable; the trick is to make sure that the hardships that do happen are eventually perceived as opportunities to develop resilience and learn other leadership lessons. How does this shift in thinking come about? What can individuals, their bosses, and HR managers do to make sure that the lessons of hardship are not buried by the trauma?

What Individuals Can Do

There are several things that people can do for themselves to maximize the likelihood of learning positive lessons from difficult experiences. First, they must accept the reality that during the course of their careers and lives, hardships will happen. They are built into the fabric of life. Mistakes are made while learning the ropes in new and challenging assignments; employees occasionally make life difficult for others; plum assignments go to someone else.

Whenever there is a choice, people must be willing to embrace hardships rather than shy away from them. They must accept assignments that challenge and test them, even though chances are great that they will make mistakes. They must be willing to try out untested skills, such as the ability to confront a difficult employee, even though the process is uncomfortable. It is easier to avoid these challenges and the hardships that often accompany them, but that only ensures that people miss out on the leadership lessons they offer.

At the same time, it must be stressed that individuals can experience too much challenge. As mentioned earlier, challenge is but one element of a developmental experience; the other two are support and assessment. Too much challenge with too little support can be counterproductive. One organization we studied was known for taking bright M.B.A. graduates and "throwing them in over their heads." Those who survived were thought of as having the "right stuff." The problem was that many bright, talented people sank not because they did not have the real potential but because they received no support.

People must be intentional and purposeful about finding the constructive leadership lessons in hardship. Learning positive lessons is not automatic. It requires that people be willing to look inward and face whatever they find there. This kind of introspection goes against the grain for many people. Yet without reflection and careful attention, it is too easy to become cynical, to feel victimized rather than learn positive and enduring lessons. After his heart attack, Jim, the executive in the opening story of this chapter, confronted himself with the hard questions; only then did he find the positive lessons.

People must also learn how to move beyond the hardship. One difference between leaders who are effective and those who are not is that effective leaders learn to face up to their hardships, acknowledge the effect of the experiences, and then let go. They do not wallow in their situation or continue to berate themselves.

What Human Resource Professionals Can Do

There are at least five specific things that HR managers and professionals can do to help individuals and organizations use hardships developmentally: implement a mistake system, encourage stretch assignments, link developmental experiences, develop coaches, and intervene only when indicated.

First of all, as we have previously noted, HR managers can help the organization develop and implement a mistake system. Not all companies treat mistakes as opportunities to learn: "In some companies even the executives believe that 'one mistake and you're out.' . . . If managers are not given opportunities to learn from their mistakes, there would be no one left to manage anything more testy than the company picnic" (McCall, Lombardo, and Morrison, 1988, p. 109). As a first step, human resource managers can work to avoid the downside by seeing that people are not punished if they fail at a stretch assignment or if a decision known to involve risk does not quite work out. On the upside, they can build into their systems recognition (such as performance appraisal) for taking on difficult assignments or people, even if in the end a business mistake or failure results or the problem employee has to be fired.

Second, human resource managers can help ensure that hardships are not avoided. They can encourage line managers to add challenge to people's present jobs and occasionally select someone for an assignment based on what that person can learn, even though the assignment will be a real stretch and mistakes will be made. HR professionals can also work to ensure that other developmental experiences, such as classroom training, are designed to stretch the capacities of participants.

Third, human resource managers can help make sure that hardship experiences are linked to other developmental experiences. Hardships often provoke informal but intense self-assessment. The lessons learned can be enhanced from a formal assessment process, such as use of a 360-degree feedback instrument. (Other suggestions for linking hardships to other developmental experiences will be discussed shortly.)

Fourth, human resource managers can train other managers in the organization to be good informal coaches of others. Too often, organizations create formal mentoring relationships or encourage informal ones without providing any training for the mentors. At least one focus of this training should be the use of assessment, challenge, and support for the development of the skills and perspectives needed by the individuals being trained.

Finally, human resource managers can intervene when necessary. Left alone to stew in their own juices, people often do just that. Human resource professionals may have to step in at the right time and in the right way to give employees the support and encouragement they need and help them learn positive lessons from the experience. Willingness to suspend judgment, the ability to listen deeply, and the ability to facilitate learning are the skills most needed to help others in making sense of a hardship.

To be sure, there is a boundary issue that must be carefully considered. It is appropriate to intervene during a work-related hardship—after a business mistake has been made, during a downsizing, while an executive is struggling with a difficult employee—to offer the executive a chance to vent, reflect, and process learning. Intervening during or after a personal trauma raises the issue of boundaries. Personal experiences can be powerful forces for professional growth, but they are also, by definition, personal. Perhaps the best rule of thumb is for the HR professional to help an individual reflect on and learn from a personal trauma only when that person initiates the conversation.

What Line Managers Can Do

There are also specific things that line managers can do to help their employees learn positive lessons from hardships. First of all, they must understand mistakes and other hardships as opportunities to learn and not as failures or signs of a fatal flaw. Line managers must also make sure that they do not directly or indirectly punish people for making mistakes.

Conversely, line managers can help create the norms in an organization that reward people for good-faith efforts even if those efforts do not produce the desired results. They can create a holding environment that tolerates or even encourages individuals to learn from mistakes, setbacks, and failure.

For instance, we interviewed a very successful executive who founded, grew, and sold several companies in the computer industry. He told us that once he had a brilliant employee who became so depressed that the man could not perform his job. Evidently this employee was very much in love with his wife, but she left him, and he just could not focus on work. A traditional manager might have told this employee to pull himself together and to learn to separate his work from his personal life. But with greater wisdom than that, this executive sent the employee to Hawaii for a month, giving advice that boiled down, basically, to "chill out." He also suggested that the employee write his thoughts and feelings in a journal, and the executive phoned him several times each week. When the employee returned a month later, he was given a new position; once again able to focus and caught up in a new challenge, he went on to have a successful, productive career.

However, the executive added an important caveat to this story. He said, "Here's the coldhearted reality: the only reason I did this is because this guy was so talented. Otherwise I could not have justified it. So [in such situations] a business judgment must be made. What is this person's life calling? What does this person need to do to make a contribution? Because that is where the employee's talents will come forward, and that is when the business can justify being so accommodating. We did not do this because we were nice. We did this because we needed this man."

This is an unusual example of unfurling a safety net so that the employee could heal from his setback. In smaller ways, line managers might intervene at the right time and in the right way to help an employee learn the right lesson from a hardship. But in doing so, managers need to make sure that cause and effect are clear. Once an employee has made a mistake, he or she needs and deserves an honest and forthright discussion of the mistake and its effect. Likewise, someone who has suffered a career setback deserves an honest discussion of the reasons. Anyone having trouble with a direct report because of his own poor management must be shown how he is contributing to the problem. Putting the cards on the table is a hard but important task of the line manager.

Hardships and the Leader Development Model

The Introduction to this book identified the elements of an individual leader development system and set forth the idea that all developmental experiences are stronger if all three elements of the model—assessment, challenge, and support—are present. This is true even of hardships. Let us now look at how the elements of assessment, challenge, and support relate to hardship experiences and how hardships can be linked to other developmental experiences.

Perhaps more than any other experience, hardship causes people to stop and reflect, take stock of their strengths and weaknesses, and think about what is important personally and professionally. Intense, informal self-assessment comes with the territory; it is part and parcel of a hardship experience. For executives used to living in an external world, this type of introspection can be difficult and painful.

The challenge built into hardship is the challenge of adversity and loss. Adversity means being stretched in new directions. It means being uncomfortable in new and difficult roles, being tested by fire, learning by doing in tough and demanding circumstances. Loss, as suggested earlier, includes everything from the loss of self-confidence to the loss of identity to a profound loss of meaning.

Two kinds of support are critical if a leader is to learn the right lessons from a hardship: support from a boss or another significant person in the organization and support from the organization itself.

The first thing a company needs to do to help turn hardships into developmental experiences is to create a mistake system. As mentioned earlier, a mistake system encourages, reinforces, and even rewards individuals for taking on challenging experiences that are rich in learning but ripe for mistakes and failure.

The second type of support needed if people are to learn important leadership lessons from hardship is that from key individuals. The person from whom support is most needed is often the individual's manager, but a human resource professional or a designated coach or mentor can also provide helpful support. Specific suggestions for supportive actions were given earlier in this chapter.

Hardships Linked to Other Developmental Experiences

Learning from hardship can be enhanced when hardships are linked to other developmental experiences, such as formal feedback, classroom-based training, and coaching. For example, an executive passed over for a promotion and left to her own devices might glean the wrong lessons about herself. She might conclude that she does not have the right stuff, the right combination of strengths, for a more senior-level position. But if she asks her boss for feedback, she may learn that there is just one particular skill deficiency that stands in the way, a skill that can be learned from the challenges in her present job and from a skill-based training program. The career setback provokes intense self-assessment (which in turn starts the process of learning), the self-assessment is contrasted with more formal assessment from the boss, and the formal assessment leads to a combination of learning on the job and in classroom training.

Another executive is having difficulty with a problem employee. His perception, based on months of their working together, is that the employee simply is not up to the job. The manager participates in a feedback-intensive program and learns, among other things, that he is conflict-averse. He realizes that he has never had a clear, direct conversation with the errant employee about the unacceptable work. As one of his development goals, the executive decides to develop his skills at conflict and confrontation. He plans to do it by working with a development coach who is external to the organization and by seeking 360-degree feedback later. Once again, these developmental experiences link to enhance the learning that comes from the single event of a hardship. (For more on linking developmental experiences, see Chapter Seven.)

Hardships: A Final Word

It is important to remember that the goal is to develop well-rounded leaders who have the skills and personal attributes needed to adapt, act with resiliency, and combine what appear to be opposites: toughness and compassion, self-confidence and humility, individual strength and a team player mentality. The goal is not to develop ideal leaders of mythic proportions but rather people who have the ability to handle whatever is thrown their way in these times of "permanent whitewater."

Well-rounded leaders are developed by experiencing and learning from the diverse challenging experiences presented in the earlier chapters of this book and from the adversities discussed in this one. Having an appreciation for the important lessons learned from hardships can help individuals, human resource professionals, and line managers view them as opportunities for growth. Although they are unlike the developmental experiences described in other chapters, hardships are an important source of lessons that help develop better leaders.

CHAPTER SEVEN

THE LEADER DEVELOPMENT PROCESS

Ellen Van Velsor
Russ S. Moxley
Kerry A. Bunker

The preceding chapters of this handbook provide detailed information about specific experiences (assignments, developmental relationships, and the like) that develop the capacities of individual leaders. Each of these chapters illustrates how an experience can be made most developmental when well designed, using a framework of assessment, challenge, and support. That framework represented the first part of the leader development model, as explained in the Introduction. Yet we also believe that any one experience has greater developmental impact when three other things occur: when the experience is linked to other experiences, when we work to enhance the individual's ability to learn, and when these experiences are embedded and aligned in a supportive organizational context. This is the second part of the leader development model.

In this chapter, we elaborate on the second part of the model. We focus on the necessity for individuals to have a variety of developmental experiences over time, the ability to learn from those experiences, and an organizational context in which development and business systems and processes are aligned and in which individuals find support for their development.

We start our discussion of the leader development process by describing several shifts that have occurred in the thinking of human resource professionals in recent years. These shifts mirror the assumptions underlying the second part of our model. After reviewing these shifts in perspective, we focus on the importance of linking one developmental experience to another and on the ability to learn from experience. We describe what we mean by the ability to learn, discuss why it is often so difficult for people to learn from their experience, and provide suggestions for enhancing learning from experience, in oneself or in others.

Next, we examine how the ability to learn from experience enhances a person's capacity to engage in a variety of developmental experiences and how a variety of experiences can in turn build one's ability to learn. Finally, we turn to organizational context, the last component of this second part of our model. We focus on the importance of embedding the development process in the organizational context in a variety of ways. We conclude with stories from the field, actual examples of organizations moving in the directions suggested by this model.

Shifts in Perspective

In recent years, human resource professionals and the companies in which they work have developed richer, more complex ways of thinking about and approaching the development of individual leaders. People are changing the way they understand the processes by which individuals develop their effectiveness as leaders, the role the organization has to play in that process, and how systems can be designed to support it. Organizations are beginning to practice leader development more systemically. Underlying this change in approach are several significant shifts in perspective.

Development as a Process

The first shift is temporal, from practicing development as an event to supporting it as a process over time. The Center for Creative Leadership's research confirms organizational experience: no single developmental event, no matter how powerful, is enough to create lasting change in an individual's approach to the tasks of leadership. Leader development is a lifelong, ongoing process.

Yet in today's business environment, advocates of a long-term systems approach to development face a real challenge from colleagues with a bottom-line orientation. Today's environment creates, in many organizations, a sense of urgency to produce short-term results and hence short-term solutions. But the fact remains that development, by its very nature, occurs as a process over time. There is no such thing as a quick fix.

The Experiences That Develop

The second shift in perspective centers on the basic question of what kinds of experience are developmental. For some time, many organizations have believed that classroom-based training was the stuff of development and that the organization's role was to provide it. Organizations are now viewing training as but one component of the development process. They have expanded their portfolios to include targeted stretch assignments, developmental relationships, and 360-degree feedback—in short, the full range of developmental experiences described in this handbook.

Development Integrated with Work

A third perspective shift that has emerged seeks to integrate development into the daily work of the organization. In the past, development was viewed as something separate from the day-to-day work of the organization, something that required sending people to off-site workshops or seminars. Increasingly, however, organizations are finding rich sources of development under their own roof. They are creating developmental experiences within employees' regular, ongoing work, using such strategies as adding developmental challenges to people's present jobs, giving people special short-term assignments as developmental opportunities, and making selection decisions for new positions with an eye toward whom it might serve as an important developmental experience. Today, development does not mean taking people away from their work; it means helping them learn from their work.

Complexity of Development

A fourth perspective shift centers on the complexity of development. In an environment where businesses face continual change, rapid innovation, and increasing globalization, complexity has become the norm. People charged with managing in these complex environments have learning challenges that are frequent, steep, and multidimensional. Although clearly defined training objectives were the focus in the past, today's environment requires meeting development goals that are constantly evolving—an unstable mix of clearly defined benchmarks, ambitious stretch goals, and a broad set of competencies that will prepare a leader for an uncertain future.

Responsibility for Development

Finally, the perceived responsibility for development is shifting. With the decay of the paternalistic organization and the advent of the new employment contract, the issue of employee responsibility looms large. Gone are the days when employees abdicated active responsibility for their careers in return for the implicit agreement that the company would take care of them. Today, employees are being asked to shoulder greater responsibility for their own development.

But in some organizations, the pendulum has swung too far, to the point that employees are held responsible for their development in a virtual vacuum. Organizations with a systems perspective know that many individuals and functions—individual employees, their managers, senior executives, and the HR organization—must be closely involved with all aspects of development: planning and implementation; providing ongoing assessment, challenge, and support; and continuous evaluation of the chosen processes.

Linking One Developmental Experience to Another

Except in the rarest of cases, no single developmental experience, no matter how well designed, leads to substantial growth or change. Leadership lessons are learned best when one developmental experience is reinforced by other experiences. Change is hard and sometimes painful. People need to work on change through several developmental experiences over time.

Furthermore, learning is not random. For a particular individual, certain leadership lessons are easier to learn from some experiences than from others. To have opportunities to learn all the lessons needed to become a well-rounded leader over time, a person must be exposed to multiple developmental experiences that are linked together and reinforce one another.

To be sure, one does not need every potential kind of experience to meet a particular development need. For example, someone who needs to think and act more strategically might work on the change through an assignment that requires the use of these skills, with the help of a coach, and with some formal 360-degree feedback along the way. This person is on the road to developing a new skill through just three experiences. Yet most people have several development needs at any point in time, and one's needs for development change as one's challenges evolve.

Also note that developmental experiences do not have to be undertaken in a particular linear sequence. A person learning strategic thinking may use three experiences that are integrated but not done in a rigid sequence. An executive who gets passed over for a promotion (a hardship) may realize that it is time to take stock of her strengths and weaknesses and may decide to participate in a feedback-intensive program (FIP). After the program, she might solicit support from a development coach who can help her learn the skills she needs. The lessons of each experience are reinforced by the others.

Some people do report significant awareness change from a single event or experience because powerful developmental events can provoke startling self-insights. Most often, though, development that results in actual behavioral change happens slowly and over the course of a career; it happens when one experience is linked to another as part of a larger, more continuous process.

Yet even when these links are made well, some individuals do not learn to take on the new behaviors and perspectives that would enable them to be better leaders. While some people learn from the most minimal experience, others learn little even from the best-designed developmental experiences. In short, some individuals are more able than others to learn from their experience. As described in the second part of the leader development model, leader development outcomes are the result of the interaction between one's ability to learn from experience and a variety of well-designed developmental experiences. So in addition to providing an integrated set of experiences to each individual, an organization must also help many individuals improve their ability or their willingness to learn.

Learning from Experience

Learning new approaches, behaviors, and attitudes is no simple task. It is neither easy nor automatic. In fact, some management development experts contend that the payoff for trying to develop one's weaker areas is not worth the required investment in time, effort, and resources. These experts argue that the key to career success lies in identifying and capitalizing on one's strengths (Buckingham and Clifton, 2001). In our view, this would be a great strategy if the demands of our rapidly changing world would only cooperate by slowing down and allowing us to settle into our comfort zones and if we were not interested in facing new challenges by moving up, across, or between organizations. Certainly, capitalizing on strengths is a vital element of both career success and satisfaction in life, but like everything else, one can overdo it. Our research suggests that the price for doing so is often derailment.

Over the years, CCL research has shown that the failure to learn, develop, and change in the face of feedback or transition is one of the most frequent causes of executive derailment (Leslie and Van Velsor, 1996). Executives who remain successful and effective over time are those who can *learn* from their experiences and use that learning to *develop* a wider range of skills and perspectives so that they can adapt as change occurs and be effective in a wider range of situations.

Yet there is a huge conspiracy in life to keep a person doing what he already knows how to do. Conspirator number one is the person himself—because his immediate need for short-term success seems more assured if he simply sticks to what has worked for him in the past. This is also easier and less painful. Conspirator number two is everyone else, since most people are happier when they can assign someone to roles in which the person has already demonstrated the capacity to perform. Since everyone is trying to "do more with less," others are less likely to have the time, inclination, or incentive to place someone in a stretch assignment where she may need to be monitored and mentored as part of the learning process.

In actuality, it has been our experience that one rarely has to remind people to capitalize on their strengths. Indeed, most people are more likely to err in that direction quite naturally. And why not? It is easier, safer, and less risky to focus on challenges already encountered and to repeat strategies and tactics that have worked in the past. The real danger lies in getting stuck in the comfortable patterns that grow out of prior success experiences and personal learning preferences.

According to our research (Bunker and Webb, 1992), most managers are not active and continuous learners. Most people learn easily within their comfort zone but find it more difficult to learn when operating under new challenges. Most people prefer to stay with the behaviors that have made them successful in the past, even if the conditions of the past no longer apply. As a result, a type of inertia develops. We have come to call the experience of overcoming this inertia "going against the grain." To go against their grain, leaders must let go of proven strengths and comfortable ways of learning long enough to acquire new ones.

Significant learning events almost never come packaged *only* with positives such as success, pride, accomplishment, fun, challenge, reward, achievement, growth, and triumph. Indeed, when people are asked to describe how they felt during the pivotal learning events in their lives, they will almost always counterbalance the positives with the negatives they experienced along the way, such as self-doubt, fear, discomfort, uncertainty, frustration, hesitancy, anxiety, or feeling overwhelmed. So it is not surprising that the natural tendency is to shy away from significant learning challenges. In order to learn, people must be strong and secure enough to make themselves vulnerable to the stresses and setbacks in the learning process.

But there are people who are natural learners. By virtue of their personalities or early life experiences, they have the personal resources and skills to learn easily and almost effortlessly. Yet they are the exceptions. Most people require considerable support for their learning, whether on a continuous basis or just at certain times in their lives when growth and development have for some reason become more difficult (Van Velsor and Musselwhite, 1986).

The Ability to Learn from Experience

Learning from experience is a way of thinking about learning that is somewhat different from what most people are used to. People typically think of learning in terms of academic activities, like reading and listening to lectures. Although our research tells us that the majority of an individual's learning over the course of her career happens on the job or from life experiences outside the classroom (Douglas, 2003; McCall, Lombardo, and Morrison, 1988; Ruderman and Ohlott, 2000; Van Velsor and Hughes-James, 1990), people often do not consider current experience in thinking about how they best learn. People often do not consider how they could improve their ability to learn from experience, and it does not occur to most people to spend time reflecting on their experiences, to extract from them the lessons learned.

So when do people reflect? Usually when they have a failure; when something does not work, people try to dissect the experience to find out what went wrong. It is the rare person who regularly reflects on his or her successes—"what did I (or we) do that made that situation turn out so well?" Also, it is often easier to see what needs changing in the attitudes, behaviors, or approaches of others than it is to see one's own inclinations to get stuck in comfortable ways. People tend to collude with themselves in rationalizing away learning challenges that fall outside of their comfort zones.

In our view, the ability to learn from experience involves all of the following:

- Recognizing when new behaviors, skills, or attitudes are called for; this involves being able to see when current approaches are not working or when existing strengths are not enough
- Accepting responsibility for one's own development and continued effectiveness
- Understanding the important aspects of one's personality, preferences, values, and commitments; how they inform current strengths; and how they get in the way of easily taking a different approach
- Going against the grain—intentionally trying on behaviors or attitudes that do not feel natural or moving into areas where one's skills are not well honed so that one might be exposed to opportunities for development
- Being able to reflect on the process of learning in day-to-day life; monitoring daily experiences with an eye toward examining *how* one is attempting to learn what is needed to be successful
- Persisting with attempts to learn, grow, and change in the face of mistakes, setbacks, and temporary performance decrements
- Using a variety of learning tactics to understand what is required in a new situation and to facilitate the development of new capacities

These, then, are the components of the ability to learn from experience. We believe that each of these components can be developed in all individuals and that the ability to learn from experience can thereby be enhanced. We also recognize that for most people, this will not be easy.

Learning from Experience: What Makes It So Hard?

Learning from experience can be difficult for a variety of reasons:

- Everything else seems more urgent.
- Inertia and past success hold us back.
- Learning signals risk and triggers anxiety.
- Personal orientations and preferences get in the way.
- Support for learning is often missing or inadequate.

Everything Else Seems More Urgent

Time has become a precious commodity. People focus on devoting precious resources to urgent and high-priority tasks. Managing time effectively has become a critical skill for anyone with leadership responsibility. Although learning and development are often recognized as important, people do not often give them the attention or priority necessary to realize growth outcomes. People almost never direct enough attention to the process of their learning. While learning and performance outcomes are closely aligned in schools, they can become separated in the world of work, where learning and development often take a back seat to other types of performance. As a result, organizations invest little in understanding the extent to which people are learning as an outcome of their jobs or the nature of the processes by which people can learn from their experiences. Not surprisingly, people often struggle to learn from experience, feel stuck in their development, and often do not understand why they are stuck. Being able to see when new approaches are not working requires time to reflect and skill with reflection. People rarely feel that they can take the time to pause and reflect about learning except when they suffer a significant failure. Unfortunately, because learning from failure experiences often focuses on what went wrong, it has the potential to erode self-esteem and reinforce one's fear of taking risks in new and challenging situations.

When time is scarce, people are less likely to use the tools that support learning, such as keeping a learning journal. Although one may not have time in the course of a hectic day to sit back and reflect, using a journal to note observations, feelings, thoughts, and critical events can be a useful way of preserving these experiences to reflect on later. Capturing reflections in a journal and reading back through them over time can be a powerful way of learning about learning—that is, seeing oneself grow and change over time.

Other tools that tend to lose out in the competition for time are simple dialogue and storytelling. Rachel Remen (1996) talks about the importance of storytelling as a tool for triggering personal reflection and passing along the wisdom of experience to others. She points out that people tend to make time for stories only when life draws them up short and forces them to take a closer look at what is happening. Part of the power of storytelling is that it allows people to tap into the emotional elements that typically accompany powerful learning events. In sharing stories, people identify with each other's situations and personal foibles and consequently relate as whole human beings. People provide living examples of how learning to learn works by expressing both the benefits and the risks associated with venturing into potent learning opportunities.

Inertia and Past Success Hold People Back

Doing things the way one has always done them, using skills one already has attained, and continuing to see the world as one has always seen it is a comfortable way of being. People like to use their strengths, to continue to be rewarded for what they have been rewarded for in the past, and to continue to get positive feedback on their achievements. In addition to the comfort this approach can bring, relying on strengths and sticking with tried-and-true behaviors usually seems like it makes the best use of that scarce resource, time. Everyone operates on the basis of comfortable assumptions about how things work, what things are important, and how they personally fit in, even when these assumptions interfere with effective action. Learning new skills or developing new approaches takes time and comes with the threat of performance decrement, however temporary.

To make matters worse, there is an active tension in most organizations between producing bottom-line results (performance) and developing people (learning). Rather than give employees a developmental assignment where learning is accompanied by the possibility of failure, many organizations prefer to put proven performers in key roles, doing what they already know how to do well. This practice reinforces people's tendency to stay with what is known and comfortable because it is safer. In this way, the combined effects of the organization's need for performance and the individual's desire for comfort often cause people to become stuck in what they already know how to do.

All of these factors can add up to inertia for the individual, an inability to grow or change. This inertia can get worse the older people get, the more successful experiences they've accumulated, and the higher they go in organizations. When individuals have been successful, it is harder than ever to let go of what has worked. It is usually not until people face demands seriously out of line with their skills and perspectives that they can begin to admit that the old ways may not be working. It is sometimes only at this point that individuals are able to examine their assumptions and take a fresh look at how their skill deficits, interpersonal style issues, or competing commitments (Kegan and Lahey, 2001) may be getting in their way. But even at these times, opening oneself up to learning is not without risk and anxiety for most people.

Learning Signals Risk and Triggers Anxiety

Learning from experience can feel risky. Recognizing the need for new learning is stressful because it requires that people admit to themselves (and possibly to others) that what they are doing is not working, that their current skills are inadequate, or that the basic assumptions they are making are flawed or simply wrong. For most people, such an admission provokes some level of anxiety. No one wants to be perceived as weak or flawed in any way, and too often the need to learn is perceived as an admission of inadequacy or inexperience. In this context, it often seems easier to respond to negative feedback by shutting down, giving up, or denying the need for new ideas or behaviors.

As mentioned previously, every experienced individual has a characteristic set of skills and approaches that has worked for her for some time. Her skills and approaches are often closely aligned with preferences and orientations based in personality or early learning. We refer to these preferences and orientations as a person's "grain." To learn significant new lessons from experience, people must be willing to go against their grain. Behaviors and approaches that go against one's grain inevitably feel clumsy, unskilled, and confusing, and they may not produce results with the speed or quality to which others have become accustomed. So engaging in such learning is often an exercise in courage. A key element in the ability to learn from experience is understanding one's grain—the patterns of habit, personality, and early learning that underlie both strengths gained throughout life and areas for development. One reason that learning from experience is so hard is that these personal orientations and preferences can get in the way.

Personal Orientations and Preferences Get in the Way

Over the years, an extensive body of research has accumulated on personality and other individual differences related to learning. Although it is not our intent to provide comprehensive coverage of this literature, we touch briefly on several factors relevant to the way in which we use the concept of ability to learn from experience. It is worth mentioning that although some of these factors may be more or less "hard-wired" aspects of personality, we believe that some can indeed be influenced or enhanced through rich developmental experiences that are balanced in assessment, challenge, and support. We return to a discussion of how this can happen later in the chapter.

Intelligence, Cognitive Complexity, and Metacognition. We address intelligence first, not because it is the most important quality, but because it is the one that for most people comes to mind first in connection with learning. We believe that intelligence, as traditionally defined, plays a relatively small and indirect role in a person's ability to learn from experience in adulthood (Sternberg and Wagner, 1986).

Although many people think of only one kind of potential when they hear the word *intelligence*, contemporary experts in the fields of psychology and education have presented the case for multiple forms of intelligence, each in itself complex and each important in certain areas of life. Howard Gardner (1993), for example, defines seven intelligences: linguistic, musical, logical-mathematical, spatial, bodily-kinesthetic, interpersonal, and intrapersonal. What most North Americans mean by *intelligence* is a combination of the linguistic, logical-mathematical, and spatial intelligences defined by Gardner. Because of its long history in the U.S. school system, this combination is probably the first thing most people think of as "learning."

While a reasonable level of linguistic and logical intelligence is beneficial to learning from life experience, it is doubtful that superior power in these areas is a prerequisite for the kind of learning from experience important for long-term leadership effectiveness (Argyris, 1991). Very "smart" managers often derail because they are unable to recognize the need for personal change or new behaviors (Leslie and Van Velsor, 1996).

However, one type of personal intelligence, described by Gardner (1993), does seem likely to affect the ability to learn from experience and to be enhanced by leader development experiences. Intrapersonal intelligence is the ability to form an accurate model of oneself and to be able to use that model to operate effectively in everyday life. Intrapersonal intelligence is closely aligned with the concept of self-awareness. In fact, many formal leader development experiences (feedback-intensive programs and 360-degree feedback, for example) have enhancement of self-awareness as a key goal; that is, they work toward enabling people to form and then use a more accurate or more comprehensive view of self. If a leader is to effectively recognize when new skills, behaviors, or approaches are needed, she needs to be able to assess the fit between her current skills and perspectives and the challenges she currently faces. In that kind of assessment, the ability to form and to use an accurate model of oneself is essential.

Two other factors that are related to but different from intelligence also play a role in the ability to learn from experience: cognitive complexity and metacognitive ability. *Cognitive complexity* is the capacity to receive, store, and process information in a multidimensional fashion (Streufert and Streufert, 1978). Cognitive complexity is related to the ability to develop refined and highly complex knowledge structures and is proposed to foster the ability to make multiple and fine-grained distinctions and connections between concepts (Bader, Fleming, Zaccaro, and Barber, 2002). It seems, then, that higher cognitive complexity may facilitate one's ability to recognize subtle shifts in the demands of new situations and to put together numerous, diverse, and often subtle pieces of feedback, both formal and informal, from the environment.

Metacognition is both the awareness of and the ability to regulate one's own cognitive processes (Sternberg and Wagner, 1986). We often call this "catching oneself in the act of learning," a critical element of self-awareness. Metacognitive ability can be thought of as the voice of a wise observer looking over one's shoulder and offering provocative questions, astute observations, unbridled insight, and candor as one engages (or decides not to engage) in a potential learning situation. The observer's primary role is to raise questions for reflection: What am I thinking? What am I feeling? What lies behind these thoughts and feelings? Why am I focusing attention on this learning challenge instead of others? Are there alternative paths that I have cast aside, rejected, or avoided? Why? How is this approach like or different from what I typically do in these situations? What am I afraid of? What is holding me back? What would it take to get me to move in a new direction? Because how one is thinking can be an important part of what is getting in the way of learning from an experience, increased metacognitive ability can enhance the ability to learn, grow, and change.

Self-Esteem and Self-Efficacy.

Self-esteem can be defined in two ways, globally (feeling good about oneself in general) and specifically (feeling worthy in relation to a specific task or category of tasks). Specific self-esteem is sometimes referred to as self-efficacy. If someone is trying to learn from a particular kind of experience, say, a new kind of work assignment, self-efficacy may be more important than global self-esteem. That is, if a person believes he is generally a good and worthwhile person but an ineffective manager, that feeling of low self-efficacy will get in the way of learning from the new experience or perhaps even taking it on in the first place.

Self-esteem is a well-researched aspect of personality (Branden, 1998), although much of the research focuses on its impact on performance rather than learning. Research has shown that individuals with high self-esteem seek more feedback because they feel they have less to fear from it (Ashford, 1986). We also know that reasonably high self-esteem protects people from various kinds of stress and enables individuals to work harder in response to negative feedback, compared to people with low self-esteem. Yet research has also shown that people with very high self-esteem (overconfidence) may be less susceptible to influence by others or to cues from their environment (Brockner, 1988).

People with low self-esteem have different issues—they tend to be highly affected by feedback. They are more likely to be actively looking for information as to "what I may be doing wrong," may overestimate the degree to which improvement is needed, and may engage in "doom loop thinking." Doom loop thinking is a self-fulfilling prophecy of failure. If a person expects to do poorly or does not believe that his actions will make much of a difference in the outcome, he may invest less time and energy, thereby ensuring the very outcome he anticipated. This failure or poor performance then reinforces his original negative belief and leads him to lower his expectations the next time. Although people with low self-esteem may be likely to believe that they need new skills or approaches, they may also be making an inaccurate assessment based on doom loop thinking.

So what can we conclude about the effect of self-esteem or self-efficacy on the ability to learn from experience? It seems reasonable to say that having a strong sense of self-worth and a good measure of confidence in one's abilities helps people face the possibility that their familiar skills are no longer adequate for the new challenges they face. If a person believes she is a reasonably good manager (self-efficacy) and an intelligent and acceptable person overall (global self-esteem), these beliefs enable her to seek the feedback that can help her identify when new skills or behaviors are needed.

Like anything else, however, self-esteem can be overdone. If self-esteem is exceedingly high, it may get in the way of recognizing that old approaches are no longer working, that strengths are being overused, or that one's current set of skills is insufficient to meet new challenges. Overconfidence can be a serious stumbling block to learning, especially if a person has been rewarded over time for many successes and strengths. We believe that openness to feedback is a gateway to development; people with very high self-esteem may tend not to open that door wide enough on their own.

Openness to Experience. In the past couple of decades, researchers have come to agree that one of several stable factors in personality is "openness to experience" (McCrae and Costa, 1985, 1987). People who are open to experience tend to see life as a series of ongoing learning experiences, seeking out new experiences and relishing the opportunities they bring rather than dwelling on the problems. They appear to have a sense of adventure, to enjoy trying out new ideas, having novel experiences, or meeting new people.

Openness to experience has been found to be correlated with training proficiency (Barrick and Mount, 1991). A key component of success in training is the attitude of the individual going into the event, and people who score high on openness tend to have positive attitudes toward unfamiliar (learning) experiences.

In terms of the ability to learn from experience, then, people who are more open to experience are generally more willing to try new behaviors or attitudes (which may not at first feel natural or comfortable) and to move into areas where their competency is not well established. In our framework, people who are very open to experience are more able to go against their grain, while people who are less open to experience may feel more anxiety in new situations and need more support and encouragement to undertake the risks involved in new types of challenges.

Research has also shown that although openness to experience is important in seeking out new or unfamiliar learning challenges, openness alone does not account for an individual's ability to make effective use of that experience (Young and Dixon, 1996). In other words, openness to experience appears to be a necessary but not sufficient factor in learning.

Conscientiousness. In addition to openness to new experience, a learner needs to be willing to take responsibility for using the new information to modify his perspectives or behaviors. He must also have the persistence to work through difficult issues to accomplish the desired changes. This responsible persistence is accounted for by another stable personality characteristic, conscientiousness.

Conscientiousness relates to how likely a person is to seek out and accept responsibility for learning, work hard to learn as a result of feedback, and persist in the pursuit of difficult learning goals. Again, it is important to recognize that people with lesser orientations toward conscientiousness are not unable to learn from experience; however, they will likely need more encouragement to take responsibility for learning and more support to continue to learn in the face of mistakes, setbacks, and performance decline.

Support for Learning May Be Missing or Inadequate

Learning from experience can be difficult because it requires a level of support that many people do not have in their organizations. Support for the risk of learning (and failure) is one kind of support, but support also includes processes and relationships that help people receive and hear the information they need to hear, understand the meaning of that information, devise development plans, persist in their efforts to learn and develop new skills, and have the courage to change outmoded behaviors and attitudes.

How to Develop the Ability to Learn from Experience

With this understanding of the learning process in mind, the ability to learn from experience can be developed in the following ways:

- Enhancing self-esteem
- Enhancing self-awareness, which includes increasing opportunities to receive feedback from others
- Enhancing metacognitive abilities
- Developing learning skills and strategies
- Finding sources of support for learning
- Engaging in a variety of developmental experiences

Many of these factors operate together in a self-reinforcing loop. Self-awareness triggers and enhances metacognitive reflection, which in turn leads to openness to learning new skills and strategies. Succeeding in any of these efforts tends to enhance self-esteem, which further opens the door to self-awareness, and on it goes.

Enhancing Self-Esteem

Branden (1998) has outlined a program for enhancing self-esteem. This program is constructed around the premise that simply making time to reflect on the components of positive self-esteem as these relate to one's ongoing learning efforts enhances the likelihood that more of these elements will be acted on as time goes by. In Branden's view, there is no need to implement the plan, since the act of reflecting on it is the implementation. This is very compatible with our belief in the importance and power of journaling, and it is linked directly to the notion put forth by Remen (1996) that creating and telling stories is a powerful tool for personal and professional growth.

Both feedback-intensive programs and 360-degree feedback can work to enhance self-efficacy by affirming one's strengths. We know from our work in evaluating FIPs that a key benefit is enhanced confidence and self-esteem (Van Velsor, Ruderman, and Phillips, 1989; Young and Dixon, 1996). Therefore, it is often true that people who by virtue of personality or motivation may not seem ready for a developmental experience can benefit from feedback from a 360-degree instrument or a feedback-intensive program. The experience provides just enough support to motivate the person to dig deeper, set goals for improvement, and build interest in further development.

Enhancing Self-Awareness

By midlife, most people have formed a self-image that they may or may not be satisfied with but that they tend not to question most of the time. One's self-image, however, can differ greatly from the way one is seen by others. Because others interact with and react to a person on the basis of their perceptions of that person, gaining a more complete understanding of one's strengths and weaknesses—an understanding that includes not only one's own view but the views of others—is a valuable way to increase self-awareness and enhance intrapersonal intelligence.

New information about the self can come from participation in a feedback-intensive program, described in Chapter One, or from formal 360-degree assessments, described in Chapter Two. A key benefit of both FIPs and 360-degree feedback is that they improve the accuracy or comprehensiveness of people's views of themselves.

However, formal assessment and feedback opportunities such as these are not enough. Aside from an annual performance review on the job, most people do not have the opportunity to participate in these kinds of development activities on a regular basis. To know whether one's current skills fit well with current challenges, one needs various kinds of good information delivered in various forms, not just once, but continuously over time. Informal sources of feedback from colleagues, friends, and family members can fill the gaps. While some people are fortunate to have others who are willing to offer unsolicited feedback, it most often needs to be sought out on a regular basis. To maintain the flow of constructive feedback, one needs to be able to develop skills for receiving it graciously and using it well (Weitzel, 2000).

A powerful tool for enhancing self-awareness involves looking back at the "pivotal" learning events in one's life. These are the experiences that punctuated one's existence and shaped who an individual has become, as a person and as a leader. We offer the following questions to guide reflection on each pivotal learning experience:

- How did you get into the situation? What caused you to address the learning?
- What adjectives would you use to describe what you were feeling while you were immersed in the experience? Did your emotions change over time?
- What pearls of wisdom did you learn from this experience that you would pass on to someone else about to enter the same learning challenge?
- What was your learning process? How did you learn your way through this experience?

The goal of this exercise is to discover who you are as a learner and how you came to be that way.

We have found that people are not too effective at answering the last item. In general, people do not spend much time analyzing their preferred patterns for learning or identifying what processes they use for learning and, often more important, where their learning process could be improved. We often ask people to look for gaps, both in the challenges they have encountered or chosen and in the processes they have used to address these challenges. People find it easier—or perhaps safer—to see the patterns in the lives of others than to be objective about their own situation.

Enhancing Metacognitive Ability

Committing to ongoing reflection is one of the best ways we know to begin to understand more about how the learning process unfolds in real time. Making time each day to reflect on one's experience can be a good methodology for seeing one's "learning in progress," that is, to catch oneself in the act of learning. In this process, it is useful to ask questions like these:

- Am I going against the grain of my learning history?
- Am I tackling the issues that I have historically avoided?
- Am I using the new processes that I committed to, or am I falling back on methods that are already within my comfort zone?
- Am I getting stuck in the same patterns that usually trap me?
- What would it look like if I were truly going against the grain today?

Some people do quite well with a blank learning journal as their only tool for this reflection process. Others need a structured list of questions to which they respond. Some people have greater success if they can discuss their thoughts with a colearner rather than trying to write them down.

Developing Learning Skills and Strategies

People approach learning in different ways. Some people prefer to learn from direct experience, where action-oriented experimentation strategies can be employed; others are more comfortable learning from reflection, reading, conversations with other people, or classroom training.

In our research and practice, we have categorized the tactics people use when they are in a learning situation (Dalton, 1998; Dalton and Swigert, 2001). A self-assessment instrument, the Learning Tactics Inventory (Dalton, 1999), captures the variety of ways people approach learning. Our expectation is that if people have reference to a set of behavioral categories, they can use these to understand that how they currently approach learning is one of several possible ways. They then can expand their own repertoire of learning tactics and eventually master a greater variety of learning challenges. Implicit in this statement is the belief that particular challenges are best approached in certain ways and that people who use the greatest variety of tactics are the best learners.

The Learning Tactics Inventory categorizes tactics in four major groupings:

1. *Thinking tactics* are solitary, internal cognitive activities. These include recalling the past to search for similar or contrasting events, imagining the future through activities such as visualization, and accessing knowledge, facts, and wisdom through sources like the library or the Internet.
2. *Taking action* consists of the behaviors that focus on direct experimentation—jumping in with little hesitation to learn, in the moment, by doing.
3. *Accessing others* involves activities such as seeking advice and support, identifying role models and coaches, and seeking their help.
4. *Feeling tactics* are activities and strategies that allow people to manage the anxiety associated with trying something new so that they can take advantage of opportunities to learn.

In approaching an unfamiliar task—an opportunity for learning—people not only use a preferred approach to learning but also tend to move in a pattern, beginning with their most preferred tactic and moving to another tactic only if the first one does not work. For example, if an individual is likely to confront a new situation with a preferred tactic of taking action, she will do this even in situations where it would be better to read the directions (the thinking tactic) or ask for help from others. Once she becomes sufficiently frustrated, she might be motivated to reconsider her approach, choosing to look for someone who might provide help or advice. But she will probably go through this preferred sequence (action, then feeling, then accessing others) regardless of whether it makes the most sense to do so or not. It is all too easy to become stuck using one tactic, or one sequence of tactics, over and over, even if it is not working. In fact, "blocked" learners (Bunker and Webb, 1992) do just that, trying harder and harder without changing their approach.

The problem is that one's preferred approach is not always the most effective approach. It may be the one that people are most skilled in applying because they have used it the longest, but it may not be what is needed at the moment. Maximizing the ability to learn from a variety of experiences means learning to expand the variety of learning skills or tactics people are most comfortable with—or at least learning to work (for short periods) outside one's personal comfort zone. New skills and behaviors are often learned only by using different approaches to learning.

To illustrate, consider the case of Fred, who started his career during the early days of the "do more with less" wave that followed downsizing and reengineering. He has learned to be quick, opportunistic, and action-oriented. He can think and act on the fly. However, he has received feedback that sometimes he is perceived as slapdash, presenting uninformed and ill-conceived plans and favoring the tactical over the strategic. To develop as a leader, Fred needs to learn to be more thoughtful, reflective, solitary, and integrative. Yet his action-oriented style of working and learning does not lend itself to learning these skills. The "just do it" approach won't make Fred more reflective. Being more reflective probably does not appeal to him. It has not been important to his success in the past, and he may even have been frustrated in the past by reflective people, since he regards them as slow to make decisions. The first thing Fred has to do is deal with his feelings about what is being asked of him; then he needs to find a very different way of learning this skill.

In general, effective learners are facile in their use of all tactics. Once one has had an opportunity to assess one's preferred learning tactics, another useful approach to developing a wider repertoire can be to look for patterns in one's learning history. Finding examples of times when one's preferred patterns and processes did not work can be a powerful starting point for enhancing strategies for learning more effectively in the present. People should ask themselves, What would have worked more effectively? What got in the way of trying that avenue? If I had it to do over, what would I do differently? Who do I know who is good at the tactics I typically avoid? How might I get that person to help me with my learning?

Consider next the example of Sarah, who graduated with honors from an excellent school. She joined an organization where she established a record as an extraordinary individual contributor. She was thoughtful, reflective, thorough, and assertive. Unfortunately, in leadership roles, she was not good at spanning boundaries and working with others to accomplish a task. Having received consistent feedback that she was perceived as an abrasive loner—albeit a smart one—she set a personal goal of becoming better able to accomplish tasks with others in a group setting.

The "thinking" approach to learning felt natural to Sarah: reading and reflecting. So she set forth energetically on her goal by getting the best new books on leadership and teamwork. Once she felt she had read and thought about the problem enough, she took action, trying to apply what she had learned to her everyday interactions with people. Things did not go well. She soon realized that her old style of learning (reading and reflecting) would not be sufficient; she would have to learn from others how to work more effectively with others. That is, she would also have to use the "accessing others" tactic to complete her learning goal. She would have to share her goal with peers, find role models, and seek feedback on her attempts to change. Sarah realized that this would be a new and uncomfortable learning style; the mere thought of talking to others about her issues generated considerable anxiety. To be successful, she would also need to employ a "feeling" tactic to manage the anxiety.

The development of feeling tactics may be the most important step one can take in becoming a better learner, because facing new challenges—adopting new learning tactics to develop new skills—often causes significant psychological discomfort. Dealing successfully with this discomfort is a critical step in being able to go against the grain and learn from experiences.

Finding Sources of Support for Learning

With all its inherent difficulties—the need to go against the grain, the risk of exposing weaknesses, the fear of failure—learning is hard. Most people need support during the process.

Support constitutes one element of any good developmental experience, and it can take a variety of forms. If the developmental experience is a new assignment, the learner can be put in touch with a network of others currently working in similar assignments. He may also benefit from a supportive relationship with a senior manager who is a veteran of that type of work. With formally occurring developmental experiences, such as feedback from a 360-degree instrument, feedback-intensive programs, or formal coaching, support comes in the form of a well-designed process for administering and delivering the feedback (Tornow and London, 1998), competent specialists to interpret the results, and good development planning materials (Leslie and Fleenor, 1998).

People often think of support in the form of one-on-one relationships, and of course, this kind of support is usually essential for learning. Both formal coaching and mentoring and informal developmental relationships can provide support during stretch assignments or for extracting learning from failure and success. The positive effects of support can be seen regardless of a manager's organizational level, level of current performance, learning style, or personal characteristics. In fact, research shows that a supportive boss moderates the effects of low self-esteem on learning (Ruderman, Ohlott, and McCauley, 1996). In other words, for someone with lower self-esteem, support can mean the difference between learning from a challenging experience and withdrawing from that experience.

Engaging in a Variety of Developmental Experiences

We have now come full circle. The last on our list of ways to enhance one's ability to learn from experience is to engage in a variety of developmental experiences. Being able to take advantage of many different kinds of experiences presents one with different kinds of challenge, which will in turn require different learning tactics to master new learnings most effectively. So the variety of experiences maximizes the likelihood that a person will need to go against his grain not only to develop new skills and perspectives but also to enhance the portfolio of ways he is able to learn. Being able to learn from a wider variety of experiences will in turn help an individual get more learning from any one experience and will provide better support for those experiences that are most challenging.

Leader Development and Organizational Context

We turn now to another important component of the second part of our leader development model: embedding leader development in the context and systems of the organization. Our experience is that an organization can provide a variety of developmental experiences to an individual, each of which has the elements of assessment, challenge, and support, and can help the individual become a more agile learner. Yet that development system can still fall short of desired goals. The organizational benefit from individual leader development cannot be maximized unless the development system is embedded in the organizational context.

The Business Context

Development processes are not generic; they must support the strategic direction of an organization and in turn be supported by that strategy. Indeed, a developmental component is inherent to an organization's strategic priorities. To meet the challenges of the future, to achieve the growth and continuous improvement that most strategic initiatives call for, employees must stretch beyond their current capabilities.

Embedding leader development processes in the business context means two things: understanding the strategic direction of the company and identifying the behaviors and perspectives that individual leaders must develop if they are to support that direction effectively. A leader development process, and each of its components, must help individuals learn these behaviors and develop these perspectives.

A major oil and gas company makes a strategic decision to move aggressively from being a domestic producer of hydrocarbons to an international force in its field. Knowing that this is the strategic direction gives all individuals responsible for leader development a good sense of the skills and perspectives the company's leaders must learn: leading a geographically dispersed team, leading by remote control, maintaining a perspective that allows people to adapt and change, and being able to live with ambiguity and honor differences, to name but a few.

As another example, a large chemical company decides that its future requires it to become more technology-driven. As part of this shift in strategy, the company wants to make sure that its R&D scientists—the people "on the bench"—develop the skills and perspectives they need to be effective general managers. To help that happen, the company identifies the behaviors that the scientists need to develop to be effective as managers in a new and changing environment. They have to make the transition from managing projects to managing people and in the process learn a host of skills related to delegation, influence, confrontation and conflict management, and team development. They need to learn to think and act strategically and to make day-to-day decisions with the longer-term goal in mind. They must learn how to see organizations as systems. With strategic direction set and behaviors identified, the company is able to put together a leader development process that supports the strategy and is in turn supported by the strategy.

Target Population

An organization must decide whom to target for leader development. Is leader development for all employees? For managers and executives? For employees who have been identified, formally or informally, as high in leadership potential?

To be sure, most people at some time in their careers engage in many of the developmental experiences we have identified. They have a challenging job, get here-and-now, unsolicited feedback from a trusted peer, experience an unplanned hardship from which they grow and change, or participate in a training program where they learn new skills. Some people learn easily and naturally from these events, especially those who actively learn from any experience. For most people, though, leader development needs to be planned, and the learning process needs to be supported. The inherent challenge in many companies is that there are too many employees for all of them to be targeted for holistic and purposeful leader development. Most companies must decide whom to select for the developmental experiences described in this handbook.

A second reason companies must make these decisions is the practical consideration of availability. Consider job assignments, for example. Assignments are a powerful source of leadership lessons (see Chapter Five). People learn how to be leaders on the job. To be developmental, however, assignments have to be challenging, they have to push people out of their comfort zone, and they have to require people to develop new skills or at least try untested ones. This means there is at least some risk that an individual will not successfully navigate the new job. A consequence of this for organizations is that not all jobs can be used as developmental assignments; some are too important, with the risks from failure too great. For individuals, the consequence is that there are not enough stretch assignments for everyone. Similarly, practical considerations require that organizations selectively deploy other developmental strategies: identifying participants for a feedback-intensive program, the target audience for 360-degree feedback, candidates for developmental relationships, and so on.

For the important question of whom to target, there is no single answer. The answer will depend on the strategic direction of the company, the company's growth and its anticipated needs for future leadership, the developmental culture of the company, and the talent available in the labor market. Some organizations focus development processes on a select group of high-potential individuals; others focus on a broad range of employees.

Shared Responsibility for Development

To repeat what we said earlier, responsibility for leader development must be shared. Development, and the environment in which it occurs, is too complex to be sufficiently managed by the individual alone. Responsibility must be shared by the individual employee, the manager, the person's team, the people in human resources who help structure developmental experiences, and the senior executives of the organization, whose support for development is crucial.

Supportive Business Systems

Other organizational systems must support the leader development process. To be fully effective, a leader development process must be integrated with the organization's other processes: management planning, performance management, job selection, reward and recognition systems, and even mistake systems (how an organization handles mistakes and failures; see Chapter Six). The confluence of these processes determines the relative effectiveness of any one developmental activity.

If these processes are not woven into an integrated system, the effort expended will not be fruitful. For example, one organization's leader development program focused on helping people develop the skills needed to effectively operate in a flatter, more team-based environment. Yet the performance appraisal and compensation system put more emphasis on individual performance, thus undermining the goal of developing a team-based work environment. Other organizations understand, in theory, that assignments can be used developmentally, but they make selection decisions based on who already has the skills needed to hit the ground running. There is risk involved, but unless some selection decisions are made for developmental reasons, the organization misses an important opportunity. Of course, there is also risk involved in the "safe" course. Without the use of assignments as developmental experiences, organizations limit their ability to develop their bench strength.

Human resource accounting systems are also used to support the process of leader development. Organizations can define job assignments not only by title and job responsibilities but also by the challenges embedded in them. Ready access to such information helps in development planning discussions between employees and their managers. Knowing what challenges people have experienced in past jobs offers the employees, their managers, and HR professionals insight into which leadership lessons may have been learned and which leadership skills and perspectives may still need to be developed.

Even budgeting processes will support or undercut leader development. In general, budgets reflect organizational priorities; thus they either help build a development culture or communicate that development is not an important emphasis.

Imagine an organization where line managers see themselves as responsible for leader development and understand that one of their key roles is to be development coaches, where at least some assignments are made for developmental reasons, where individuals are not punished for making honest mistakes from which they can learn or for trying out new skills and behaviors, and where the skills and perspectives assessed during the annual performance appraisal process are in alignment with the skills and perspectives people need to be effective in their jobs. In this kind of organization, leader development is not just a priority but is understood and practiced systemically.

Stories from the Field

There is much to be learned from what other organizations are doing. A few organizations have already developed an overall systems approach to development; they have linked together several of the developmental experiences described in this book, integrated those experiences with other management processes, and used those experiences to develop individual leadership ability and accomplish business results. Other organizations are moving toward a systems approach by linking two or three developmental experiences, but they have not created a fully supportive development system by embedding the experiences in a business context.

We offer stories here to illustrate some of the ways in which organizations are moving toward a more systemic approach to leader development (pseudonyms are used).

"Retail Stores of America" (RSA)

RSA, best known by its chain of stores in shopping malls across the country, has implemented an entire system for developing its leaders.

A leader development process is more nonlinear than linear. But to understand more easily what RSA has done, let us list the component parts of the system the company implemented in a simple step-by-step way:

1. The executive vice president, who is primarily responsible for leader development and who designed the company's system, first made sure that leader

development at RSA was linked to the strategic needs of the business. In her words, the process had to be "need-driven," and the outcomes to the organization had to be clear and important. At RSA, leader development was seen not as extracurricular but rather as key to accomplishing business objectives.

2. Based on internal and external research, RSA knew what behaviors were needed to pursue the company's strategy; it created its own leader success model, with factors such as problem solvers, organizers and planners, achievers, team builders, communicators, and developers. These success factors were then weighted for each manager's job, based on the importance of the behavior to success on the job.

These first two steps created the all-important organizational context for RSA's leader development process. Specific experiences in the development process—assignments, developmental relationships, 360-degree feedback, and so on—could now be directed toward developing the skills, behaviors, and perspectives important to the company's business success.

3. A 360-degree instrument was developed to give feedback on the skills and behaviors already identified as important at RSA. With this feedback, individual executives learned how their profile compared to the profile for success at RSA and identified new behaviors they needed to develop.

RSA reinforced its system of leader development by linking it to performance, using the same success profile. One-half of the managers' performance appraisal was based on the content of their job: how well they met their goals. The other half was based on the success factors, or how they met those goals.

4. After conclusion of the 360-degree feedback process, a review board, composed of members of the executive committee, met for a day and a half to complete the management assessment process and to focus development for the next year. The purpose was to ensure that the right message and challenges were given to help leaders grow and that a major job challenge was matched to each individual's development need. The end result was that a measurable assignment was created for many managers, particularly those identified as having high potential.

What RSA called a "measurable assignment" is the same as what we describe as a developmental assignment (see Chapter Five). Three important aspects to what RSA did should be emphasized: the company understood the potency of jobs as developmental experiences, it was willing to make selection decisions about some jobs based on the development needs of its high-potential employees, and it individualized development by matching an individual's need to a measurable assignment.

5. Another important strategy in any leader development process is a developmental relationship. At RSA, members of the executive committee, the indi-

vidual's boss, and human resource professionals all saw themselves as providing developmental relationships. They played several of the roles described in Chapter Three: feedback giver, counselor, and coach.

Thus three developmental experiences were carefully linked at RSA: 360-degree feedback led to a measurable assignment, which was in turn supported by a developmental relationship. Each of these experiences reinforced the others, and all three were reinforced by other organizational systems and processes.

"Global Shipping, Inc." (GSI)

Global Shipping, a major international shipping company, began implementing its own development system. A snapshot of GSI taken a year earlier would have shown a company operating on traditional business practices severely in need of modernization. Cooperation between offices was lacking. Information technology was primitive. Customers were demanding world-class service, yet GSI had no formal quality system. Managers were well versed in the technology of shipping, but they were trapped in a rigid managerial hierarchy and seldom made any overtures toward leadership.

Into this situation stepped a new CEO. He was brought in from the outside and given an emphatic mandate for change. His background included extensive experience with organization development, and he used that experience to collaborate with his senior management team to build a new model for leader development. This model is shown in Figure 7.1.

The four cornerstones of the model are GSI's goals, the strategies for accomplishing them, the business factors critical for the company's success, and the values that are central to running the business. Each cornerstone provides part of the framework for GSI's leader development processes, but two of the core values, honesty and openness, provide the bedrock for the processes. The processes simply do not work unless these values are acted on.

In the middle of the diagram is the "toolbox." At GSI, leader development is designed to foster business results. The tools are intended to support the company's business goals, and the tools themselves are designed to be mutually supportive. Three of the tools relate specifically to individual leader development: coaching groups, employee dialogues, and the leader development program.

Coaching groups are work groups meeting in intense sessions so that members can provide each other with direct feedback related to working effectively. Every work group, and thus every employee in the company, meets with their group three times a year. This is learning in a public forum.

In these sessions, all the people on a work team are expected to give feedback to everyone else, including their boss. The values of honesty and openness are

FIGURE 7.1. GLOBAL SHIPPING, INC., MODEL FOR LEADER DEVELOPMENT.

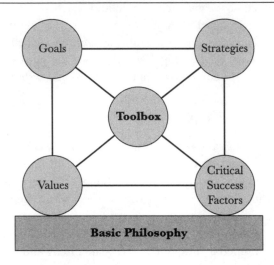

Source: Courtesy of Ingar Skaug; reprinted with permission.

particularly important. No one can be punished for flaws or weaknesses that are mentioned during these sessions, but an employee can be punished—even fired—for not participating or for not trying to improve a weakness.

One outcome of the coaching group sessions is that each participant puts together a clear and precise action plan each year. The action plan is a statement of what he or she will do differently because of what is learned during the sessions. Action plans are designed to improve individual performance and help meet business goals.

From the model put forth in this handbook, this developmental experience combines a version of 360-degree feedback with developmental relationships. The elements of assessment, challenge, and support give the experience impact.

Employee dialogues are an ongoing, one-to-one process between all employees and their supervisors. The two people discuss performance in the broader context of functional job descriptions, employee development, and career progression. Honesty and openness are demanded during the conversations, and the expected product is an individual improvement plan. In these conversations, the supervisor engages in several types of developmental relationship: feedback provider and interpreter, sounding board, assignment broker, and reinforcer.

At GSI, the coaching groups provide feedback that informs the action plans, and the action plans are then refined during these employee dialogues. The two experiences support and reinforce each other.

All managers from middle level on up attend an off-site leader development program. The program is a six-day residential public enrollment program, an example of the strategy described in Chapter One as a feedback-intensive program. During this intense experience, individuals get copious feedback from a variety of sources on their leadership strengths and weaknesses, and they develop a deeper awareness of the impact of their leadership style on others. A detailed action plan is generated at the end of the leader development program, a plan designed to increase individual effectiveness and to meet business goals.

"Delta Products"

Delta Products knew well the leader development pressures the company was facing. Demographic studies suggested that it would experience significant leadership turnover in the next five to ten years. Women and minorities were underrepresented in senior leadership positions. Supervisors and managers did not possess sufficient coaching skills to help develop the underrepresented employees. Employees did not have a good framework for managing their careers.

With the help of external consultants, Delta developed an architecture for development that included learning assignments, learning groups, and learning forums. It also established a process for selecting employees for development.

Delta decided to target its formal leader development on one particular group: high-performing learners. The first step, then, was to identify these learners. They were pulled from the pool of high-potential employees, which had already been identified. All were seen as potential leaders; they were perceived as active learners, and they were diverse in education, race, gender, function, and career interests.

Delta was also clear about the attitudes and abilities expected from these learners during the development process. They were to be willing to experiment, look for alternative ways of doing things, become more self-observing, move from knowing to learning, suspend judgment, and think and act with a global perspective. In short, Delta expected the participants in this process to demonstrate that they had the ability to learn from experience.

Delta used several types of assignments to help learners develop the skills and abilities they needed: in-place assignments that had significant challenge and thus important lessons to teach, plus rotational and cross-cultural assignments that offered different lessons.

To reinforce the leadership lessons that people were learning from their assignments, Delta provided the "learners" with two different types of developmental relationships: learning leaders and learning managers. Learning leaders were outside the individual's chain of command, two or three levels higher than the learner, and also diverse in background, experience, race, and gender. The learning leader played three of the roles described in the discussion of developmental relationships in Chapter Three by meeting with the learner to listen to frustrations (the counselor role), discussing what was being learned on the job and from other developmental experiences (dialogue partner), and when asked for advice, responding with a story from his or her own experience (companion). Each learning leader received four hours of training.

The learning manager was the supervisor of the learner; he or she offered day-to-day support and encouragement as the learners tried out new skills and behaviors. The learning manager played two of the important roles in developmental relationships: feedback giver and cheerleader.

In addition to the one-to-one developmental relationships, the learners got support from learning groups and learning forums. The learning group served as the equivalent of an organizational homeroom. Here learners met to debrief their experiences, chat face-to-face, and practice new behaviors. The emphasis was on learning from and with peers in a safe environment. While they were in the learning group, the learners agreed to promote openness and trust, encourage new perspectives, realize that all points of view are flawed, "listen between the lines," and seek understanding rather than agreement.

Learning forums, by contrast, were occasional gatherings in which all the learning groups came together for the specific purpose of storytelling. The stories dealt with acquisition, globalization, work-and-life balance, technical choices, and current events. The belief underlying the use of these learning forums was that the culture of Delta Products and important lessons of leadership were communicated through the stories told by its employees.

Who was responsible for the development system at Delta Products? The learner was responsible for a substantial degree of self-management, development of a learning plan, and execution of the plan. Top management was responsible for providing support and focus, as well as learning leadership. Line managers were responsible for on-the-job coaching, sponsorship, feedback, and being learning-minded managers. Human resources was responsible for implementing the development strategy and mobilizing resources.

In sum, Delta Products developed a reasonably sophisticated leader development process for a subset of its high-potential employees. Each experience of the process had the elements of assessment, challenge, and support. One developmental experience was linked to another, and the whole process was developed to meet the business needs of Delta and the individual needs of participants.

Conclusion

The good news is that people in organizations with the best leader development systems and processes are changing the ways that leader development is understood and practiced. People are seeing effective leader development as a process that must occur over time and that takes place through a variety of experiences, both on the job and outside of work. And people responsible for leader development in these organizations are beginning to create linkages between the content and processes of leader development and the organizational context and systems.

Yet even when these links are made well, some individuals are not able to keep pace with the increasing demands for their development as leaders. That is, some individuals have more ability than others to learn from their experience. So helping individuals improve their ability to learn from experience must be another key aspect of any leader development process. Taking advantage of a variety of developmental experiences that each contain elements of assessment, challenge, and support can enhance one's ability to learn, if one is able and willing to use the variety of experiences to build a flexible repertoire of learning tactics. Having a greater ability to learn will in turn allow one to take on a greater variety of challenges, as well as challenges of increasing complexity.

Practitioners can make a useful start by helping people assess their learning histories and how they learn and by helping people expand their repertoire of learning tactics through use of formal or informal coaching. Paying attention to the support and enhancement of self-esteem, as well as to other personal factors that affect learning, is important. Helping individuals understand their "grain," through assessment, can facilitate their ability to purposefully take on significant learning opportunities that go against their grain. Ultimately, the goal is to create a learning environment in which people get more regular and more informal feedback and have opportunities to take on additional challenge without undue fear of negative evaluation for short-term mistakes. By reviewing the leader development processes currently in place, in terms of appropriate linkage to business context and other organizational systems and in terms of shared understandings about those linkages, practitioners can work to create the systems and organizational environment in which both leaders and leader development thrive.

CHAPTER EIGHT

EVALUATING THE IMPACT
OF LEADER DEVELOPMENT

Jennifer W. Martineau

Many organizations today spend significant amounts of time and money on leader development, and they want to know whether these investments are producing the desired outcomes. As providers of leader development, we also want to know whether our programs are meeting clients' goals and how we can enhance the impact of our work.

At the same time, high-quality evaluation of leader development is difficult to master, for two primary reasons. First, it is often difficult to identify the most critical factors to evaluate. Second, isolating the effects of leader development from other forces that act simultaneously within and outside the organization is quite complex. Although this dilemma can also exist for other types of training and development, it is particularly salient to leader development because of the very nature of leadership. Leadership theorists and practitioners often disagree about what leadership is, how leaders behave, what makes a good leader, and what effective leader performance looks like. That lack of agreement undermines the extent to which we are able to evaluate the effectiveness of leader development initiatives. However, because leader development is a process in which organizations invest significant resources, it is absolutely critical that we be able to assess its impact and learn how to continuously improve the practice of leader development.

In this chapter, I present CCL's approach and review our experience in evaluating leader development initiatives—initiatives that focus on the development of individual leaders. Until the early 1990s, the bulk of our work in evaluating leader development had focused on testing the effectiveness of new or revised programs, determining the best time in an individual's life to participate in leadership development, and understanding the learning, skill, and behavior changes that occur in individuals as a result of participating in feedback-intensive programs, 360-degree initiatives, formal coaching, job assignments, or other significant job or personal events, as discussed in Chapters One through Six. All of these efforts have contributed to CCL's knowledge and expertise with regard to understanding the key components of high-quality leader development experiences for individuals.

In recent years, we have begun to learn about the effects of team-based developmental experiences on individuals, teams, and organizations. We have also learned about the effects of individual development on organizations. This extension of our practice has both challenged and broadened our knowledge and expertise. While this chapter focuses for the most part on individual leader development, it is with this growing understanding of *leadership* development that we share our experience with readers of this book.

The structure of this chapter parallels our process for evaluating leader development. The four main sections outline the critical steps necessary to prepare, design, implement, and use a quality evaluation. I discuss how to do the following:

1. Identify key stakeholders
2. Perform needs assessment, including identifying organizational challenges driving the need for leadership development, identifying associated leadership needs and targets, and identifying desired outcomes
3. Design the evaluation, including key questions to be addressed, appropriate method types, the evaluation plan, and the communication plan
4. Implement the evaluation

The evaluation processes described here are those we at CCL apply to the evaluation of all our leader development initiatives—feedback-intensive programs, 360-degree feedback, formal coaching, developmental relationships, and challenging assignments. Throughout the chapter, I will illustrate points using a client I will call "Oak City Schools," a public school system. In this leadership development initiative, a group of us at CCL worked with a portion of the schools in the whole system and the executive team responsible for the school system. In each school, we worked with a team consisting of the principal, several teachers, counselors, and parents. In addition to Oak City Schools, I will offer further examples from CCL's evaluation practice.

Identification of Key Stakeholders

The first phase in any evaluation is to identify key stakeholders. Key stakeholders are individuals or groups who have some sort of involvement in, responsibility for, or key interest in the leadership development initiative and its evaluation. They may belong to the client organization, the provider organization, or some external group, such as an external funding organization. The stakeholder group might include designers of the initiative, program trainers, other human resource staff, potential participants in the initiative, senior managers who have a stake in the outcomes, line managers whose staff will participate in the initiative, and funders of the initiative.

To identify specific key stakeholders, we begin by asking the key contact person a number of questions such as the following:

Who has a vested interest in the intervention?

Who has a vested interest in the evaluation?

Are there additional people whose support is required for the success of the initiative or the evaluation?

Who has decision-making authority with respect to both the initiative and the evaluation?

After identifying key stakeholders, it is then necessary to determine the best way to involve each of them in the needs assessment and design process. Since we are rarely able to gather all key stakeholders together for this process, we modify it to suit their needs. For example, when we can gather only half of the key stakeholders, part of their "homework" in preparation for the needs assessment is to gather crucial information from the remaining stakeholders. This serves three functions: it provides us with the information we need for the assessment, it promotes relationships among the stakeholders, and it gets them all on the same page in terms of information about the initiative.

Whatever the method, the important point is to gain a commitment from all key stakeholders to both the leadership development initiative and the evaluation, greatly improving the chances of success. With Oak City Schools, for example, the key stakeholders included program participants (teachers, principals, senior staff); other key system executives, such as the superintendent and associate superintendents; an outside foundation; and the program's designers, trainers, and coaches. Most of our face-to-face needs assessment took place with the principals from each of the schools and the program's designers, but we also sought information from the other stakeholders through surveys and other forms of indirect communication.

Needs Assessment

The process of evaluating leadership development necessarily begins at the beginning—with needs assessment. In our experience, when evaluation is considered only after a leadership development initiative has been designed or even when it is under way, the effectiveness of the evaluation (and possibly the initiative itself) is greatly diminished. When developing an evaluation, we use a process developed by CCL faculty called Leadership Development Impact Assessment, which emphasizes both the focus of leadership development on impact and the subsequent need to identify all critical components prior to delivering the initiative.

There are four critical components to needs assessment:

1. Identifying critical organizational challenges that drive the need for leadership development
2. Identifying the targets for leadership development and the leadership needs related to a client's business challenges
3. Identifying where change is needed to solve a business problem or meet an organizational challenge
4. Identifying specific, measurable outcomes of leadership development, including the level of mastery desired for these outcomes

Identifying Organizational Challenges

To meet the leadership needs of a group or an organization, leader development and leadership development must be linked to the critical challenges the organization is facing. It is important to know why the organization's stakeholders are willing to spend time and money on leadership development and what they hope to accomplish. Essentially, what is the challenge that is so compelling that they are willing to devote resources to it? This step is crucial to laying the groundwork for establishing clearly focused and well-aligned leadership development processes.

In our practice, we typically ask a group of stakeholders questions such as these:

What organizational issues keep you up at night?

What are the most critical issues addressed in your strategic objectives or by your CEO? (Note that the CEO is rarely part of the key stakeholder group, except when the organization is relatively small or the risk of the initiative is relatively large.)

What challenges stand between your organization and its success?

What are the consequences of not addressing these challenges?

The responses we hear from clients vary widely, but here are some examples of the types of challenges business organizations identify:

Reducing employee turnover.

Developing leaders to fill the leadership pipeline.

Creating a new postmerger culture.

Increasing revenue.

Creating high-performing teams in order to remain competitive.

Bringing quality services and products to market in a more efficient manner.

Once the key stakeholders have listed and defined their most critical challenges, we ask them to prioritize these challenges. Prioritization is necessary to provide greater focus for subsequent phases in the process. In the case of Oak City Schools, needs centered around meeting upcoming federal and state educational achievement guidelines within the required period of time, thus demanding an increase in achievement at the school and system levels.

Targeting Leader and Leadership Development

Leader and leadership development must be targeted in a way that supports an organization's critical challenges if it is to be truly valued in the organization. Development can be targeted at individuals, work groups or teams, or even the organization as a whole. Most feedback-intensive programs—our own leader development programs, for example—are targeted at individual leader development. In these programs, individuals receive feedback on their personal strengths and weaknesses in a classroom or coaching setting. Some feedback-intensive programs have team leadership as the focus but target the individual team leader for development. Team development programs, by contrast, often get the whole team in the room and target group development as the goal. In these cases, team actions, interrelationships, and performance are the focus, and the feedback is about the strengths and weaknesses of the group as a team.

Oak City Schools was a unique client in that its initiative needed to target both leader and leadership development. Because of the nature of the challenge and the client's inherent structure as a public school system, Oak City Schools needed to target individuals, teams, and sometimes whole schools for development. (I will say more about the importance of understanding the relationship between who is targeted for development and what outcomes are achievable as the chapter progresses.)

Identifying Leader and Leadership Needs

Once we have defined and prioritized critical issues, we turn our focus to leadership development needs. Needs assessment involves discussing and identifying with stakeholders where change is needed to solve a business problem or meet an organizational challenge: What do individuals or groups need to *do* differently? In what ways do they need to *think* or *interact* differently?

With the appropriate stakeholder group participating in needs assessment, the information gathered in this phase is usually extremely valid. However, there are times when it is more appropriate to assess the current skills of leaders or groups to determine their level of proficiency in the areas deemed critical to organizational success; this can be done using existing organizational competency or team development models. Regardless of the method used to identify leadership needs, these data provide an overall focus for all leadership development programs and processes.

We assess leadership development needs using questions such as these:

What three changes in individual or group leadership would address the organizational challenges, and why?

What are individuals or groups doing, or not doing, that prevents the organization from overcoming these challenges?

What are the consequences of not addressing these leadership needs?

Typical individual leader needs identified by our clients include enhanced ability to share decision making, to act with incomplete information, to know how to develop and motivate others, and to adapt to an environment of rapid change. Typical group needs are related to improved communication and collaboration within and across groups, making changes in the way groups focus on the organization's strategy in their work, and an enhanced ability to execute the group's work in a way that makes use of the strengths and talents of all group members.

In the case of Oak City Schools, leaders needed to work beyond the bounds of their traditional roles, integrating knowledge and expertise across their individual school or among schools in the system, and they needed to encourage and support others to do the same. They needed to identify more innovative solutions to long-standing challenges, such as providing additional help to children who are achieving below their grade level while still providing expected and needed help to all children, and they needed to be able to adapt to change more rapidly.

Identifying Desired or Expected Outcomes

Once we understand how development will be targeted and have established the leadership needs of the group or organization, the next phase requires identifying specific outcomes that should be evaluated. For any specific leadership need, there may be multiple outcomes. For example, if a leadership need is stated as "All individuals need to be able to coach their direct reports more effectively," the associated, desirable outcomes might be that individuals can

Recognize the need for coaching with all employees

Prepare coaching strategies for each employee according to need

Develop employees by providing challenge and opportunity

Develop strategies for appropriately increasing employee responsibility

Support a challenging climate to encourage employee development

In other words, outcomes are ways to operationalize the leadership need and are measurable in the evaluation process. They are the competencies on which we assess change over time—for individuals, in this particular example.

In addition to individual leader outcomes, challenges may call for changes in the leadership capacities of groups or teams. Outcomes at the team or group level should also be specified for these leadership needs. If, for example, stakeholders identify a group-level need for improved communication and collaboration across units in the organization, outcomes could be articulated that focus on increased frequency of contact between groups and that assess change in this area over time.

It is frequently the case, however, that organizations want group- or organization-level outcomes from initiatives targeted at individuals. It is important to surface these expectations through dialogue with stakeholders that focuses on a deep understanding of both their targets for development and their expectations for impact. For example, we often hear our clients hoping for an improvement in the organization's bottom line as a result of sending many of their managers through a leader development program that targets the individual. Although such a result is not impossible to achieve under some circumstances, it is unlikely to occur without extensive organizational support for individual development, such as action plans or coaching. And it is an outcome that is very difficult to track in an evaluation.

So the assessment of leadership needs and the articulation of outcomes for efforts that address these needs are both part of a process in which stakeholders must agree on three issues. Two of the issues are interrelated: the desired targets for development and the level at which outcomes are expected. The third issue, less obvious but important to understand, is what level of mastery is desired for each of the chosen outcomes. The stakeholders' expectations on all of these factors have important implications for how the evaluation should be designed and implemented. In the section that follows, I discuss outcome levels and how they relate to the targets for development before turning to the issue of mastery.

Outcome Levels. As stated earlier, whereas an initiative may target the individual, the group, or the organization level, the outcomes expected from an initiative may or may not be limited to the level of the target audience. For example, feedback-intensive programs focus almost exclusively on each participant's personal strengths and development needs—that is, they target the individual. However, this kind of program is often used by organizations with the intention of obtaining outcomes at the group or organization level as well as at the individual level.

At the individual level, participants may learn new leadership models and practices, gain new knowledge about their own strengths and weaknesses, or increase their ability to understand an issue from multiple perspectives. It is also possible that an initiative such as this may have group-level outcomes if the individual leader returns to the work setting and implements changes that affect the work team. In fact, some organizations use individually targeted leader development to foster outcomes in the groups for which a single leader is ultimately responsible. Relevant group outcomes might come in the form of changes in working relationships within the group; changes in the operations of the group; changes in the vision, mission, or strategy of the group; changes in the effectiveness with which the group interacts with other groups; changes in the way the group interacts with clients; and changes in the productivity of the group, however it is measured. Table 8.1 shows the possible combinations of intended targets and desired outcomes. So, for example, in evaluating a development initiative targeted at individuals and designed to achieve both individual- and organization-level outcomes, you would be working in the areas labeled A and C in this table.

TABLE 8.1. TARGETS AND OUTCOMES OF LEADERSHIP DEVELOPMENT.

	Outcomes		
Targets	Individual	Team	Organization
Individual	A	B	C
Group or team	D	E	F
Organization	G	H	I

When a team is the target for development, development work can focus both on the team as a functional entity and on the outcomes for which the team is responsible. Possible team-level outcomes include team cohesiveness, team effectiveness, and the accomplishment of the team's targeted goals.

A team development program, while having the group as the main target, might be expected to have outcomes for both the team and for individuals (D and E in Table 8.1). For example, by working together in an initiative targeted at the team, team members may learn more about their unique contributions to their team and their current behaviors that make them less effective within the team.

Finally, organization-level outcomes are also often desired from individual or team development initiatives (areas C and F in Table 8.1). These outcomes may include culture change, enhanced organizational climate, improvements in the challenges represented during the needs assessment, and improvements in the group or company bottom line. The likelihood of these outcomes increases substantially when an individual or team development initiative is targeted at the skilled performance level of mastery (more on this shortly), when leaders have set specific action plans related to the challenges of the organization, and when the focus of the initiative is on leadership development more broadly defined (see the Introduction).

Of course, the quality of individual and team leadership is only one factor playing into most organization-level outcomes. Organizational success results from a myriad of factors, such as a well-aligned strategy, financial stability, and quality products and services.

Because the intended targets and expected outcomes can differ, it is important to review them both with all stakeholders. In this way, one can design measures that are appropriate to the target audience and that assess all desired levels of outcome.

Oak City Schools, for example, targeted development for the most part at the individual and teams levels, with some work at the level of a whole school within the larger system. The desired outcomes were at all levels—individual, team, and organization (both school and school system). We found that being clear about the subtle differences between who was participating in the intervention and where the outcomes were expected was useful in coaching the individuals and teams, in designing the evaluation, and in interpreting and communicating the results to the stakeholders.

Levels of Mastery. It is not reasonable to expect the same kind or amount of learning or change from different kinds of development initiatives or from initiatives of different scope—programs of different length, single events, a series of integrated experiences. In addition to clarifying stakeholder expectations with respect to targets and outcomes, it is important to understand the level of mastery desired for each outcome. Levels of mastery can be thought of as how well the targets are able to apply the skills and knowledge they have acquired during the initiative.

In CCL's discussions with clients, we work to assign one of four desired levels of mastery to each outcome (see Exhibit 8.1). This progression describes movement from knowledge about content, self, or group to skillfully performing a new leadership practice. Each level provides a platform for further development to the next level of mastery. What is important about these distinctions is that as the complexity of the learning increases, the time required for acquiring that learning also increases. A number of factors determine the specific length of time necessary to achieve (and therefore to be evaluated on) each level of mastery; these factors include individual or group abilities and motivation, organizational commitment to leadership development, and access to high-quality leadership development resources.

The first level of mastery, critical awareness and knowledge, includes the acquisition of new knowledge, change in self-awareness, and what we call "transformational perspective change." New knowledge is acquired in almost any development event, from feedback-intensive programs and coaching relationships to action learning and job assignments. The knowledge people acquire through these experiences takes various forms. People gain new information about themselves or about how others perceive them. They learn new concepts about leadership itself, such as the components of strategic leadership, the cultural values on

EXHIBIT 8.1. LEVELS OF MASTERY.

Mastery Level	Accomplishments
1. Critical awareness and knowledge	Gains powerful new perspectives on self (impact of my behaviors, impact of others on me, interaction between myself and others); is acutely aware of the need to change in order to be more effective; remembers facts, terms, models, and methods pertaining to leadership and understands them.
2. Guided application	Practices new behaviors to solve problems and receives immediate coaching and feedback on performance effectiveness.
3. Independent application	Practices new behaviors and uses new knowledge in the work setting; analyzes their effectiveness and seeks feedback on their effectiveness from coaches, mentors, and peers.
4. Skilled performance	Utilizes new and more effective leadership behaviors as a part of one's everyday leadership repertoire; seeks periodic feedback to ensure that new behaviors are creating desired new perceptions.

which the most significant national differences rest, or the dimensions of personality that affect leadership style.

Increased self-awareness can be general ("I am a reasonably good manager") or more specific ("I am not seen as listening well to others"). After participating in a feedback-intensive program, some people report gaining personal insights about how they see themselves ("I judge myself too harshly") or about their own needs for inclusion, achievement, or acceptance ("I want to be involved, and sometimes my requests for involvement overload me" or "I need substantial issues to keep me driven") (Van Velsor, Ruderman, and Phillips, 1989). It makes sense to think that new awareness about oneself must precede any behavior change. In addition, new self-awareness often motivates an individual's development of new skills. (See Chapter Seven for additional information on the dynamics of learning from experience.)

Transformational perspective change is similar to increased self-awareness in that it is a change in attitude rather than an observable behavior, but it differs in its focus: instead of focusing on one's own strengths and weaknesses, attention is paid to insights about others and the environment in which one lives and works. Significant perspective changes usually happen more slowly than new self-insights, but they can occur as a result of a single powerful event.

The comments of a participant in one of our feedback-intensive programs reveal a transformational perspective change: "The program got me to thinking that people are different—and that they are motivated differently, their priorities are different—and to start looking for it. When I came back, I started analyzing the people who were working directly for me, and then I started managing differently— not just one big blanket 'Here it is, folks.'" Here the perspective change (that people are different from him and from each other) is prompted by new knowledge about situational leadership (the idea that people need to be managed with a style that matches their job competence). This perspective change, in turn, prompts new self-awareness ("I need to manage differently"). In our experience at CCL, critical awareness and knowledge are key initiators of the development process and can usually be accomplished in two or three feedback-rich days of intense experiential activity designed around the assessment, challenge, and support model.

The second level of mastery, guided application, is a more complex developmental task in that it involves comfort with the use of new insights and learnings in a structured, safe setting. A safe setting is one in which the individual or group will not be ridiculed or penalized for making mistakes, will receive supportive feedback from others regarding the use of new approaches or behaviors, and will have multiple opportunities to practice. Mastery of guided application is usually accomplished in two or three days in a classroom setting or simulated work environment, with a facilitator or coach providing feedback and guidance. Without guided practice, it is difficult for most people to move to the next level of mastery, which is attempted in the work setting itself, where mistakes may not be tolerated.

The third level, independent application, involves the use of new attitudes, skills, and behaviors in actual workplace situations without real-time guidance from facilitators or a coach. Independent application begins after a formal development experience has sparked individual or group awareness of the need for improvement and after the individual or group has had some opportunity for guided practice.

Independent application often takes time and exposure to multiple experiences. This is particularly true for skills that involve significant personal change in perspective or self-understanding, such as empowerment (Drath, 1993) or learning tactics (Dalton and Swigert, 2001). Skills that are dependent on learning a process, such as giving constructive feedback or conflict resolution, can be acquired more quickly. Although real-time guidance is typically not available at this level of mastery, independent application does require an opportunity to debrief how well a new practice is being received by colleagues and others. Individuals working toward this level of mastery often choose a trained coach or a trusted colleague to give corrective and supportive feedback and to help devise a plan for further improvement. Working with a coach or trusted colleague ensures that use of newly developed leader skills, behaviors, and attitudes is transferred from the laboratory setting of the classroom to the more challenging milieu of the workplace. Independent application can last from one month to one year, depending on the amount of time devoted to practicing and coaching.

Mastery peaks at the level of skilled performance, which is marked by "unconscious competence," the effortless and seamless integration of a new leadership practice into daily repertoires. When individuals and groups are functioning at the skilled performance level, we see that real behavior change has occurred. Work at this level involves continual practice and the ability to adapt newly developed skills and behaviors to new contexts and situations. Leaders working on skilled performance often rely on journaling, periodic meetings with coaches and others, videotaping, and formal and informal solicitation of feedback from colleagues for their development. Attaining skilled performance requires devotion to the continued refinement of newly developed practices over a period of several months and even years.

In working with stakeholders to define outcomes, we discuss each identified outcome in depth to determine whether the desired mastery level is critical awareness and knowledge, guided practice, independent application, or skilled performance. We use the levels of mastery framework to guide the design of development initiatives for both individuals and teams or groups.

The amount of time an organization invests in leader development initiatives and the types of activities they offer must match the level of mastery desired—and the evaluation design must incorporate measures suited to the level of mastery desired as well. The design of both the initiative itself and the evaluation must be in line with client expectations regarding the level of mastery of the outcomes. A stakeholder who expects a skilled performance level of mastery to result from a three-day development program will inevitably be disappointed. In addition, an evaluation that attempts to measure this level of mastery from this kind of program is bound to have poor results.

Defining the attainable level of mastery requires that key stakeholders carefully analyze the time and monetary resources they have available for leadership development and make sure they can support the amount of effort required to achieve the desired level of mastery. If their goal is to see their leaders seamlessly demonstrate new and more effective leader practices in the workplace, they must find the time and money to support longer-term, more intensive development efforts. If sufficient time and money are not available to support the development of skilled performance, expectations must be adjusted to a more modest goal.

In our work with Oak City Schools, individuals and teams were expected to reach a level of independent application or skilled performance on most of the desired outcomes. Individuals were to become skilled at having difficult conversations with colleagues to the extent that problems could be solved readily. Teams were expected to be able to enact change in their schools, with the support and coaching of their principal. To achieve these outcomes, we designed a multiyear, multisession initiative that included ongoing team coaching and action learning projects. Action learning projects allowed teams to apply new knowledge and pursue goals in the context of real work that met school objectives. Ongoing coaching provided the support needed to carry out the action learning projects successfully.

Evaluation Design

We usually incorporate evaluation design into the process of designing the leader development initiative itself. This is a crucial point: design of the initiative and the evaluation should ideally occur together so that each can be modified as necessary and so that the two pieces are integrated. Designing the initiative and the evaluation of that initiative is not a linear process but a dynamic, iterative one. In our experience, effective evaluation and leadership development designs are modified several times before reaching the final versions.

In cases where the evaluation has not been designed in conjunction with the initiative itself, however, all hope is not lost. It is still possible to determine the outcomes from the initiative, although the methods required to do so are often more costly and somewhat less robust. In addition, it is unlikely that the evaluation will function as an integrated part of the initiative itself, reinforcing and playing a role in what is learned during the initiative. Therefore, although it is possible to conduct a good evaluation after the fact, it is advisable to codesign whenever possible.

In either case, our guidelines for evaluation design are as follows:

1. Identify specific evaluation questions.
2. Identify potential methods of evaluation.
3. Determine the evaluation plan: how will the methods be applied during and after the development initiative?
4. Determine the communication plan: how will results be conveyed to stakeholders, participants, and all relevant parties?

Identify Specific Evaluation Questions

This step assumes that key stakeholders have been identified at the beginning of the needs assessment phase. To identify specific evaluation questions, we ask stakeholders to imagine that the leadership development initiative has been completed and to think about the specific questions they will be asked by their own constituents regarding what success of the initiative looks like. These questions, obviously, should tie in with the business challenges, leadership needs, leadership competencies, levels of mastery, and outcomes identified in previous steps. The questions derived at this stage of the process are high-level and will be refined in later steps.

Sample evaluation questions our clients have been asked include the following:

Were participants (individuals and groups) adequately prepared for their developmental experience?

Did each component of the initiative (classroom training, action learning, coaching, job assignments, and so on) adequately prepare individuals or groups to practice new skills, perspectives, and approaches at work?

Have the intended outcomes been accomplished?

Are individual participants engaging their managers in working on their development plans? Are groups engaging others to coach them along?

How have teams benefited from their participation in the initiative?
How has the organization benefited from development aimed at teams?

Were the organizational challenges addressed by the subsequent work of the participants?

Did individuals or groups encounter obstacles in their work on action plans or goals?

For each of these questions, we develop specific criteria to ensure the accuracy of measurement (details will be given later in the chapter). Each of these broad key questions is broken down to include critical details such as specific leader or group competencies to be learned and mastered, particular organizational challenges to be addressed, and specific examples of how participants or groups could have been prepared for their developmental experiences.

Identify Potential Methods of Evaluation

Once the broad evaluation questions have been identified, we work with key stakeholders to identify the methods by which data will be collected for each question. Different methods are more appropriate than others for certain types of questions, as well as for the types of data preferred by organizational stakeholders; for example, the value placed on quantitative data by the client can differ from the value of qualitative data. It is important to determine both the specific types of data that the stakeholders will accept as "evidence of impact" and the types of data collection that will be tolerated and supported by the organization.

Specific considerations at this step are the following:

• Make sure the methods chosen are logical, given the culture of the organization. For example, do not choose a survey method if survey data (as opposed to interview data or existing organizational data) are not valued by the organization. Similarly, do not select a method that will produce qualitative data (an open-ended interview) if the organizational culture does not recognize its value.

• Select the appropriate method to answer each question. Questions of frequency or magnitude lend themselves to surveys or instrumentation, whereas questions related to how and why lend themselves to more open-ended methods such as interviews or focus groups.

• Keep an eye on resources. Whatever methods are selected, ensure that you have secured the necessary resources (time, people, money) to manage both data collection and analysis. Some methods are more time-consuming than others, in both the collection and analysis phases. Interviews are a good example. Even though they may be the ideal method for a particular question, they take a long time to do right. Do not use them if the resources you need to conduct them properly are not available.

• Collect only what you will use. Do not collect data that will not be analyzed and reported. Leaving data unanalyzed is wasteful, in terms of both your time and that of the people who provided the data. Such wastefulness causes frustration and breeds resistance to participate in data collection the next time around.

• Prepare for data processing, storage, and analysis when selecting methods. Do not select methods that will produce data you do not know how to analyze or store properly (in databases or other appropriate means of storage).

• Be clear about confidentiality of data. If individual names and data will be shared, make sure that the individuals providing the data are fully aware of this. If data will be kept confidential, be sure you uphold this promise. Inform stakeholders that the greater the confidentiality and anonymity of the data, the more truthful and open people will be. Be clear with *all* stakeholders (including those who will be providing the data) about the overall data collection and reporting process, including specifics regarding the way the data will be shared.

The methods of evaluation most commonly used by organizations are interviews, focus groups, end-of-program evaluation surveys, 360-degree instruments, collection and analysis of existing organizational data, tracking of projects designed to have both developmental and organizational-impact outcomes (action learning projects), and direct observation or field notes regarding group interaction and application of skills and perspectives. These methods and others are discussed in more depth later in the chapter.

Determine the Evaluation Plan

After the methods for evaluation have been identified, a comprehensive evaluation plan can be put together. To begin this step, we create a matrix to chart the methods that will be used to address each evaluation question, the timing with which the methods will be used, and the groups from which data will be collected. A sample matrix appears in Exhibit 8.2. This sample plan was created to represent the evaluation for a development process with the following components:

January: A three-day, face-to-face feedback-intensive program

February to April: Executive coaching

March to November: Targeted action learning projects

With a visual map of the evaluation plan, it is possible to see ways in which the evaluation components can be integrated into the initiative itself, causing evaluation to become part of the learning and growth experience. For example, in our sample matrix, the survey administered in January can be completed by participants at the end of their face-to-face program. Thus the evaluation survey also becomes a reflective tool enabling participants to think about whether they have

EXHIBIT 8.2. A SAMPLE EVALUATION PLAN MATRIX.

Evaluation Question	Three-Day Training Program	Coaching	Action Learning Projects	
	January	April	August	November
Were learning objectives met?	Survey (P)			
How do participants intend to apply their learning and new skills?	Survey (P)			
Is there growth in competencies?		360-degree behavior change instrument (P, M, DR, Pe, O)		
Are participants receiving support for development and application of new competencies?		Survey (P) Interviews (P)		Survey (P) Interviews (P)
What changes are resulting in participants' groups?			Survey (P, M) Interview (P, M)	
How is the organization benefiting?				Analysis of organizational data (C)

Key to data sources: P, participant (individual, group, team); M, manager of participant; DR, direct report of participant; Pe, peer of participant; O, other party (client, customer); C, key organizational client contact.

learned what was intended and how they will use it when they return to their jobs. Using evaluation methods this way actually creates impact, encouraging additional growth on the part of individuals and teams.

Similarly, by administering a 360-degree feedback instrument in April to measure growth in leadership competencies, participants receive an individualized feedback report regarding their own growth, which becomes a new part of the intervention. This feedback helps them identify areas in which they have had significant growth, moderate growth, and little growth. By knowing this, they are able to refocus their developmental attention on areas of importance for their professional and personal lives, using the data as a guide.

Integrating evaluation methods into the interventions themselves can best be accomplished by designing the development initiative to capitalize on them. For example, a coaching session should ideally follow the receipt of an individualized 360-degree feedback report, giving both the coach and the participant the opportunity to discuss the feedback and work together on action plans for further development.

Determine the Communication Plan

One of the most serious mistakes that can be made in evaluation is in conducting a quality evaluation, producing informative reports and presentations, and then not doing anything differently as a result. The potential negative outcomes from a lack of communication planning include frustrated key stakeholders, wasted time and money, loss of credibility with key stakeholders, lack of organizational learning, and failure to make critical changes to the initiative.

From the beginning of the design process, evaluators should intend to share the learning from the evaluation with key stakeholders at critical points in time, providing the information most useful to them (Russ-Eft and Preskill, 2001). Therefore, the communication plan is a central part of planning—long before the evaluation itself is initiated.

Russ-Eft and Preskill's thorough treatment of communicating evaluation results (2001) reveals four critical components of communication: purpose, audience, format, and timing. I will discuss each of these in light of our own experience at CCL.

The critical purposes for communicating and reporting include the following:

- Keeping key stakeholders informed about and involved with the evaluation itself
- Providing evaluation data for key stakeholders that they can share with their own constituents

- Sharing data with initiative designers and delivery staff regarding midcourse corrections or adjustments to the initiative that would result in greater success in meeting its objectives
- Providing data illustrating the outcomes attributed to the initiative

Our communicating and reporting *audiences* include key stakeholders from the client organization, our own leadership development initiative designers and delivery staff, other critical stakeholders from our own organization, and in some cases, participants in the initiative.

The timing and format of our communicating and reporting varies by initiative, as determined jointly by CCL and the client organization. The most minimal reporting for key stakeholder audiences usually includes an interim written report and presentation near the midpoint of the evaluation process and another written report and presentation at its completion. In many cases, key stakeholders from both CCL and the client organization are also provided with oral or written updates on a monthly basis throughout the duration of the evaluation. These updates occur within the context of regularly scheduled joint meetings (either face-to-face or via conference call) that allow us to make continuous improvements to the initiative.

For other audiences such as participants and other critical stakeholders from our organization, the reporting is often less frequent and coincides with either significant findings or critical time periods in the evaluation process, such as the midpoint or conclusion of the initiative.

For all major evaluation communications, we usually prepare written reports and presentations. All reports include executive summaries and graphic presentations of our findings. For more informal communications, we make use of e-mail updates and conference call discussions as primary formats.

The specific content of our communications varies but in all cases aligns with the key evaluation questions identified earlier in the evaluation design. We use a combination of narrative text, quantitative tables, graphic figures, interactive discussions, and verbal presentations for the majority of our communications.

The specific communication and reporting plan used in the evaluation of a leadership development initiative differs with each initiative, but the important point is that a plan should be developed prior to evaluation implementation for maximum effectiveness and designed to meet key stakeholder needs.

Implementing the Evaluation

As you can see, a great deal of time needs to be spent in assessing needs and designing the evaluation to make implementation as smooth and effective as possible. When it is time to begin implementation, we begin by applying specific methods that are appropriate to the types of outcomes being assessed and the intended users of the evaluation findings.

In this section of the chapter, I will briefly discuss a variety of relevant implementation methods (for more detailed coverage of these methods, including samples, see Martineau and Hannum, 2003). There are many other resources available that provide thorough coverage of each of the methods discussed here. The intent of this discussion is to describe their use with regard to leadership development in particular.

Put Details to Methods

Once the basic scope of the methods has been identified, it is time to put details to the methods. By this I mean constructing interview and focus group questions and processes, survey items, identifying the appropriate instrument to use, identifying which organizational data to collect and how to collect them, and so forth. This step involves careful reference to the organizational challenges, leadership needs, targets for development, desired outcomes, and levels of mastery so as to produce a set of evaluation methods that precisely capture all features of the initiative.

For example, one of our clients identified a weak leadership pipeline as a key driver for leadership development. The company's intent was to build capacity in a key set of leaders who were in line for executive positions in the coming years. Part of the capacity it wished to build was in the form of leaders who would be willing and able to call on critical people from across the organization to resolve key issues in an effective manner. In this case, the evaluation methods we selected included surveys, focus groups, interviews, 360-degree instruments, and analysis of organizational data. The 360-degree survey allowed for analysis of changes in leadership competencies (at specific levels of mastery); surveys, interviews, and focus groups enabled assessment of business challenges and leadership needs; and analysis of organizational data supported the further examination of the extent to which the business issues were addressed.

Excellent advice is available on designing the content of targeted evaluation methods (see, for example, Henerson, Morris, and Fitz-Gibbon, 1987; Krueger and Casey, 2000; Martineau and Hannum, 2003; Patton, 1987; Phillips, Stone, and Phillips, 2001; and Preskill and Torres, 1999).

Measure Individual Outcomes

To assess individual-level outcomes (see Table 8.1), the methods we typically use include daily evaluations, final evaluation surveys, comparisons of expectations and benefits, interviews or open-ended questionnaires, learning surveys, tracking of action plans and progress toward goals, customized behavior change instruments, 360-degree retests, behavioral observation, and interviews with participants' coaches.

Daily Evaluations. In some leadership development programs, participants complete evaluation forms at the end of each day. These evaluations are usually comprised of open-ended questions, and their value is twofold. First, they give participants an opportunity to reflect on their experiences that day, further reinforcing their learning. Second, they provide program staff with formative feedback that enables them to make adjustments to the program the following day, thereby enhancing the effectiveness of the program.

Final Evaluation Surveys. Participants complete final evaluation forms at the conclusion of each separate component of an initiative, such as a face-to-face event or a coaching engagement. These evaluations should be designed to capture detailed data regarding the perceived value of the program to participants.

These surveys can use a variety of formats and rating scales, including open-ended questions or Likert-type rating scales. At CCL, we use survey ratings related to whether the outcome was met as well as the application value. We ask participants to evaluate each of the intended outcomes or objectives of the initiative, stated at the appropriate level of mastery.

Comparisons of Expectations and Benefits. A comparison of participants' expectations before an initiative and their perceived benefits after the initiative can be a useful way to get a quick reading on whether the benefits were in line with expectations or perhaps even exceeded them. When not much is known about the actual impact of an initiative (for example, for a pilot run of a particular program), the simplest way to design such a questionnaire is to use survey items that reflect targeted objectives followed by open space for participants to write in any other expectations or benefits they perceive.

Interviews or Open-Ended Questionnaires. Interviews provide an opportunity to question individuals one at a time about their experiences. Interview questions are typically open-ended and provide qualitative data. They can be conducted either face-to-face or by telephone. Interviews can help determine the level of knowledge, skills, and attitudes related to an individual's experience with a development initiative. Interviews can also be used to assess perceptions of the initiative from a stakeholder's perspective.

If resources do not allow for time to be spent on interviewing, interview questions can be presented in the form of an open-ended questionnaire to be completed by participants. The trade-off is that probing follow-up questions cannot be asked as readily with questionnaires as with interviews.

Learning Surveys. A survey can be designed to assess the extent to which participants have learned new content during the initiative. This method is valuable when participants in the development initiative are expected to retain factual information, such as leadership models, organizational competency models, organizational business policies or practices, and specific steps for implementing participant leadership responsibilities, such as giving feedback and coaching others.

Probably the best way to assess learning is to administer the survey at two points in time: once before the initiative and once immediately after it ends. The survey should require participants to use their cognitive abilities to answer targeted questions designed around the intended content of the initiative.

Tracking of Action Plans and Progress Toward Goals. To capture participants' goals and subsequent progress, we ask that they record their action plan for these outcomes at critical points during a development initiative. Action plan records should cover

- The goal itself (task or outcome)
- The strategies or steps necessary to achieve it
- Particular resources the participant will need to rely on in order to be successful on the job
- Specific barriers the participant expects to encounter
- The expected outcomes or benefits of the goal

At planned points in time, determined during the needs assessment process, we follow up with the participants to assess progress toward their goals. This includes looking at what has been accomplished, the barriers encountered, the strategies used to overcome those barriers, the resources that have supported accomplishment thus far, and any specific issues the individual has had in reaching the remainder of the goal. Finally, we assess whether the goal has been accomplished at a time that is deemed suitable for that purpose.

Customized Behavior Change Instruments. Customized change surveys are useful in assessing whether change has occurred as a result of an initiative. They are typically used to measure changes in participants' attitudes or behaviors specific to the initiative in question. A well-developed change survey should be based on what evaluators already know about the impact of the initiative and on the given objectives of the initiative. Ideally, survey questions should be pilot-tested for clarity and for reliability (see Leslie and Fleenor, 1998). Survey questions should be pilot-tested to ensure that they will provide the types of responses desired from the survey—there is nothing more frustrating than collecting what you expect to be critically important data, only to find that respondents didn't understand your questions and provided irrelevant answers.

The response scale used in a change survey should be one that facilitates the measurement of change (see Martineau, 1998). At CCL, the custom change survey designed for use with our programs is called Reflections. It is a 360-degree follow-up assessment instrument designed to measure change using a retrospective pretest-posttest design. It has two 9-point rating scales for each question, enabling an assessment of how someone performed in a particular area "before" an initiative and how the person performs "now" (both measures are taken at the same point in time, after the initiative is complete). It is administered three to six months after a critical point in the leadership development initiative has occurred (a pivotal classroom training experience, the conclusion of all classroom training, or the conclusion of multiple components, such as classroom training, an action learning project, and coaching). This instrument provides both feedback to individual participants regarding their own leadership growth and aggregate feedback for organizational clients and CCL regarding the impact of an initiative on a group of participants and their organization.

360-Degree Retests. Many leadership development initiatives make use of 360-degree instruments administered prior to the initiative as a way of providing participants with feedback about their leadership capabilities on entering the initiative. To measure change, it may seem best to readminister the same 360-degree instrument after the initiative. Although this process seems to make sense, it has several inherent problems. For example, although it is possible to compare and contrast 360-degree results from two different points in time, this must be done at a broad level (looking at themes and patterns) rather than a specific level (looking at item or scale differences) because 360-degree retests offer a second snapshot regarding effectiveness at another point in time but do not allow for interpretations of change or impact (see Martineau, 1998).

Behavioral Observation. Observation is a method of data collection that involves observing a set of activities, the people who are participating in those activities, and the environment in which the activities take place. Observations can produce qualitative data, in the form of field notes, or quantitative data, if the observations are noted as ratings, rankings, or frequencies.

Observation can be used prior to, during, or after an initiative takes place and can occur multiple times. It is useful as a means of providing evidence to support data collected from self-report methods such as surveys or interviews and allows for the interpretation of performance within the context of work.

On the downside, observation is very resource-intensive and requires a skilled, well-trained observer. Performance may be altered if people know they are being observed, resulting in less than accurate data collection. Finally, it can be disruptive to the work situation.

Interviews with Participants' Coaches. When participants are supported in their work and development by a coach, the coach is a rich source of data regarding the individual's development. Professional coaches have perspectives on development and progress that are informed by their knowledge of and experiences with best practices. Therefore, they can share their perspectives of a particular individual relative to others in a way that sheds light on critical stumbling blocks that person may be experiencing, successful strategies the individual has used in working toward his or her goals, and the status of the goals or outcomes themselves.

One critical caveat associated with interviewing coaches is that all principles of data integrity and confidentiality apply. Coaches should not be expected or asked to divulge any information that could compromise confidentiality agreements.

Measure Group and Team Outcomes

If an initiative has been targeted at individuals but group- or team-level outcomes are of interest, one can aggregate individual-level outcomes as a way of determining impact at the group level. For example, changes in individual-level behaviors measured via a 360-degree instrument can be aggregated into a group report representing all individuals at a certain organizational level in a particular work group, data from interviews can be summarized to show the ways in which the work of this group of individuals is being implemented differently, and individual-level survey data can be rolled up to the group level to indicate themes in how perspectives have changed in the group as a whole.

For outcomes unique to groups or teams, additional commonly used methods include focus groups, group dialogue, tracking of team action plans and progress toward goals, observation of team meetings, and interviews with the team coach about the progress of the team.

Focus Groups. A focus group is a method of interviewing six to twelve people at one time. Its primary purpose is to obtain qualitative information from a group of individuals or a team who have had a similar experience (for example, participation in a training program). At CCL, we usually conduct multiple focus group interviews as part of an evaluation. We use a well-thought-out interview guide to focus the discussion. Focus group interviews should be designed so that participants feel safe disclosing information about their attitudes and perceptions regarding what is being evaluated. The interviewer should be skilled in focus group techniques to employ this method effectively.

Group Dialogue. Group dialogue is a special kind of conversation in which people listen intently for the underlying meanings and assumptions in the conversation. In group dialogue, the evaluator can be relatively invisible, and the conversation takes place primarily among team members—imagine a "fishbowl" conversation where the evaluator is the observer outside the fishbowl. The value of group dialogue lies in how team members interact with one another, exploring their perspectives and insights more deeply than they may in a focus group.

Group dialogue is a conversation that balances advocacy (taking a stand on an issue) with inquiry (asking questions to clarify what the other person means). Dialogue is thus a strategy for exploring the breadth and depth of the meanings of what is being evaluated. Dialogue can be used in the formative evaluation process to understand the participants' differing perspectives regarding the leadership development initiative. Dialogue can also be used in the summative evaluation process to clarify the meanings of the data. (For information on conducting dialogue sessions, see Senge and others, 1994.)

Tracking of Team Action Plans and Progress Toward Goals. Similar to the individual-level version of this method, we ask teams to record their action plans for tracking purposes. The components of the plan and progress reports remain the same as described earlier, but with the appropriate focus placed on aspects unique to team work.

Observation of Team Meetings. Sometimes it is possible to observe team meetings to assess team interactions and team effectiveness in working tasks and goals. As with behavioral observation at the individual level, this method can produce both qualitative and quantitative results that allow for deeper interpretation of the work and outcomes of the team. Observation can take place before, during, and after a leadership development initiative. The downsides of behavioral observation are the time required by the evaluator to meet with teams to get a representative sampling of their interactions and the intrusiveness of being observed, which may have a negative effect on the team's interactions.

Interviews with Team Coaches. As with coaches of individual participants, team coaches can be a rich source of data regarding the team. Coaches' exposure to the work of teams provides them with insights into teams' critical stumbling blocks, team dynamics, successful strategies the team has used in working toward its goals, and the status of the goals or outcomes themselves. As always, coaches should not be asked to divulge information that would compromise agreements of confidentiality between the coach and the team.

Measure Organizational Outcomes

The specific types of organization-level outcomes targeted by leadership development initiatives often vary by sector. For example, in for-profit organizations, organizational goals are naturally centered on increased financial health and profitability. In not-for-profit and educational organizations, the ultimate outcomes are usually ones such as financial responsibility, service to clients, and academic achievement scores.

Some of the methods we at CCL use to assess organizational impact are climate and culture survey retests, assessment of organizational systems change, assessment of return on investment, workplace statistics, document analysis, and assessment of customer satisfaction.

Climate and Culture Survey Retests. When leadership development is a component in an organization's efforts to make significant improvements or changes to its work climate or culture, it is useful to examine the extent to which that climate or culture has changed over the course of the initiative. This is done by using surveys of climate or culture, making at least two assessments of the organization— one prior to the beginning of the initiative and one at an appropriate time after the initiative has ended. Stronger designs include additional assessments during the initiative.

Organizational climate is typically defined by employees' satisfaction with specific features of the organization, such as pay and benefits, leadership, and opportunities for development.

Culture in organizations is typically defined as the behaviors and values that pervade the organization. Culture determines whether a particular behavior is deemed appropriate or inappropriate in the organization. The culture of the organization is built by its people but is greater and more powerful than any one individual's values or behaviors.

As with other measures of organizational improvement, climate and culture change should be examined only when the leadership development initiative was designed to affect it. To effect such a large-scale change, the initiative should include a critical mass of appropriate organizational employees, be of a duration long enough to create change at the organization level, and be designed to encourage organization-level changes.

Assessment of Organizational Systems Change. At the organization level, one type of outcome to look for is the extent to which organizational systems and processes—aspects of the organization that have a direct impact on the employees themselves—have been positively affected.

Assessment of these systems is accomplished by analyzing data collected or generated by the organization as a part of day-to-day operations (for example, employee manuals and written procedures or guidelines) or through other methods such as surveys, interviews, or focus groups.

Many leadership development programs—especially those with components that enable teams to work together more effectively, enable individuals to understand others' points of view more readily, or stimulate individuals and teams to more effective and creative problem solving and decision making—will result in improvements to various organizational systems and processes.

Some systems and processes to consider for evaluation include operating procedures, learning processes, human resource policies, formal and informal communication structures, financial accounting processes, maintenance procedures, compensation practices, and reprimand practices.

Assessment of Return on Investment. Return on investment (ROI) has become a hot topic in the development and evaluation world in recent times. Using prescribed formulas, data can be analyzed to determine the extent to which the benefits of the development initiative outweigh the costs. Results show ROI in terms of percentages. For many organizations, these can be useful data in that they enable comparisons across a variety of interventions. For example, a computer skills training program could be compared to a leadership development initiative with such a formula, enabling stakeholders to identify which initiative has a larger ROI.

The field of ROI has become much more sophisticated in the past few years. A professional practice that includes both consultants and organizational evaluators, the ROI Network, has emerged, providing certification programs and a variety of support tools for anyone interested in using this technique. ROI methodology involves creating a formula relevant to the costs and benefits of a particular developmental experience, isolating its effects, and determining the relative ROI (Phillips, Stone, and Phillips, 2001). Using this formula, the result is reported as a percentage.

In our work with clients, however, we have found that the usefulness of this type of outcome is limited. Although many of our clients begin conversations about impact by using "ROI," we find that rarely are they defining ROI as a specific numerical result. Rather, they are using the term to represent all of the ways in which their investment in leadership development can pay off. As a result of the needs assessment process, we usually identify more salient methods to assess return on investment.

Workplace Statistics. Workplace statistics are data that organizations measure on a regular basis. These data can be obtained from the organization and analyzed in relation to the leadership development initiative and its objectives. Workplace statistics relevant to leadership development concern absenteeism, communication breakdowns, customer loyalty, customer satisfaction, grievances filed, employee turnover, employee loyalty, training program attendance, performance appraisal ratings, and new products and services developed. (See Phillips, Stone, and Phillips, 2001, for a complete list of workplace statistics.)

Before requesting and using workplace statistics in an evaluation of a leadership development initiative, we carefully determine which statistics are likely to change as a result of an individual's or team's participation in the initiative. The organizational challenges identified in needs assessment provide these important connections.

Document Analysis. Documents and records are written statements or other materials that attest to an event or provide an accounting of some activity. Evaluators who use documents typically wish to make inferences about the values, sentiments, intentions, or beliefs of the sources or authors. Documents and records often exist in plentiful supply and are a low-cost way to gather organizational data. They are less subject to an evaluator's bias than data collected from interviews or observations. Documents provide information regarding the history or background of a program or situation, the people and activities involved, and the frequency of occurrence of various situations.

Assessment of Customer Satisfaction. It is often useful to know the customer's perspective when determining the value of a developmental experience. Customer satisfaction assessments can be conducted most readily through surveys, interviews, or focus groups.

The relationship between training and customer satisfaction is easy to understand when the training is directly related to customer service (as with telephone techniques and claims processing) but is somewhat more elusive in the case of leadership development. Who is the customer? How might the customer be affected by an organization's use of leadership development?

One member of a client organization told us a story about the impact of his manager's individual leadership development on the customer. This manager had set a goal of running more efficient meetings so that more employee time could be devoted to customer service. Indeed, customers were said to be receiving more time from employees, thus improving the service they were receiving and subsequently improving their satisfaction with the organization.

As this story illustrates, the customer can be affected in many ways, as when the organization begins making better decisions, working more effectively internally, communicating better both internally and with customers, and better understanding the customer's needs. Although customer satisfaction may seem to be a "light" indicator of impact, consider the effect on the organization if customers are dissatisfied and take their business elsewhere.

Whether developing one's own survey or interview or working with a vendor, the following aspects of customer service are important to capture:

What type of work does the customer do with the organization?

What does the customer value in his or her relationship with the organization?

What does the customer expect in his or her relationship with the organization?

How does the customer describe past experiences (prior to the developmental experience) with the organization?

To what extent was the customer satisfied with past experiences with the organization?

How does the customer describe current experiences (after the developmental initiative) with the organization?

To what extent is the customer satisfied with current experiences with the organization?

To what extent is the organization meeting customer expectations?

Some challenges in assessing organization-level outcomes are worth noting. Traditionally, organization-level expectations of leadership development are likely to remain unfulfilled, for at least three reasons. First, most organizations take an "event approach" to leadership development, using only a single strategy rather than a longitudinal, multiple-component development strategy, or they string together a set of unrelated events.

Second, organizations typically target leadership development at individuals, rather than enhancing the connections between individuals or groups that share common work. This oversight prevents critical links from being established, preventing the achievement of outcomes that could significantly influence the health of the organization in a positive way.

And third, even if the productivity of organizations is improved by making managers better leaders (as individuals, groups, or teams), too many other factors are in play. No leadership development program can protect a company against economic downturns, shifts in the political or regulatory climate, changes or chaos in the financial markets, natural disasters that damage the supply of raw materials or production facilities, labor stoppages, or the fickle tastes of consumers. No leadership program can protect a school system from the impact of a lack of parental involvement or teacher shortages. And no leadership program can protect a service-oriented nonprofit from federal budget cuts or changes in government policies and regulations. The benefit of leader and leadership development is in boosting the capacity of individuals, groups, and teams to effectively manage and address these types of challenges, recognizing that they do not have full control over all aspects of them.

Nonetheless, there will always be interest in documenting impact on the bottom line—and rightly so, we at CCL believe. Toward that end, it is especially important to design developmental experiences that align with organizational strategy and to implement evaluation processes that permit such improvements to occur, to carefully assess the effects in all possible domains, to capture changes at the work group and organization level (in satisfaction, climate, culture, systems, and productivity), and to examine the reasons for change and lack of change at that level. This kind of evaluation tracks how individuals are developing and also sheds light on what other factors are influencing the achievement of organizational goals.

Measure Outcomes at Multiple Levels

In our work with Oak City Schools, we used a combination of methods to assess outcomes at the individual, team, and organization levels. Individual-level methods we used were daily evaluation forms, end-of-program evaluation forms, tracking of action plans and goals, customized behavior change instruments, and surveys of participants' coaches. To assess team-level outcomes, we used focus groups, tracking of action plans and goals, observation, customized behavior change instruments, and interviews with team coaches. We assessed organization-level outcomes using document analysis of organizational (school and school system) data and tracking of organizational systems change (in operating procedures and communication structures). In choosing evaluation methods, we paid attention to the needs identified, the types of data preferred by the stakeholders, and the levels of mastery targeted. Also, we focused on using evaluation methods that contribute to the positive effects of the initiative for individuals, teams, and schools. We wanted to minimize as much as possible the time required of team members to complete evaluation methods. We also wanted to ensure that we had as full an understanding as possible of the entire learning process each team experienced, creating a case study of sorts for each team. Finally, we recognized that the teams' coaches and other members of each team's school were significant sources of information regarding the developmental and applied efforts of each team. These goals demanded multiple methods that drew data from multiple sources and were implemented multiple times over the course of the five-year initiative.

Consider Outcomes Beyond the Organization

In some cases, an intended outcome of large-scale leadership development is on the organization's community. The community, in this sense, includes constituents external to the formal organization yet inherently dependent on it in some way.

Community-level outcomes include customer satisfaction, customer loyalty, and customer involvement in directly supporting the organization. Whereas satisfaction and loyalty are more obvious outcomes, involvement may not be. To illustrate, one of the desired outcomes for Oak City Schools was to increase parental involvement. Parents are needed to provide tutoring, media room assistance, and clerical assistance—all necessary tasks that would otherwise require the time of already overworked teachers and school staff. In school systems, both students and parents can be considered "customers" of the school. Students must be fully engaged in learning to be successful.

The team of leaders at one school in this system made several attempts to involve parents, trying different strategies until finding one that worked: instead of trying to attract parents to the school, the leadership team went out into the neighborhoods to meet with the parents, sharing important information about upcoming events and school requirements. After this successful outreach effort, parents felt more comfortable coming to the school for events. They also took on roles in their neighborhoods to help students. One neighborhood began holding a "homework night" at the local community center, inviting all neighborhood children to attend and to receive tutoring from parents and help with their schoolwork. To prepare, the parents took the initiative of contacting the school to obtain resources that would help them in assisting the students.

This simple example illustrates the potential for affecting the local community: the neighborhood surrounding one of Oak City's schools is now committed to the academic success of its children and will likely become involved in other ways at the school itself as time goes on. Admittedly, the relationship between a school and its community can lead to greater opportunities for improving customer involvement as a result of leadership development than in other organizational sectors; nevertheless, some version of involvement is possible for most communities and most organizations.

Using Evaluation Results

It is imperative that organizations use the evaluation results they gather. Evaluation is a crucial piece of organizational learning—by evaluating what we do and discussing the findings, we learn how leadership development works in organizations and can begin to have conversations about how to make it work better. Having evaluation results also informs conversations regarding other systems (such as reward systems, communication systems, and performance support systems) that are related to yet separate from leadership development in function. By doing so, we discover ways to improve the leadership development system itself, as well as how to integrate it more effectively with other systems and make improvements in those systems. The outcome of these conversations is organizational change in support of leadership development—all initiated through evaluation!

For example, our evaluation of Oak City Schools' initiative revealed that the participating teams did not feel a strong connection between their own leadership development, the work of their leadership team that resulted from the initiative, and the larger organization. Although they perceived their own work to be meaningful for their segment of the organization, they were concerned that the executives at the senior levels of the organization did not understand or value what they were doing and that the lack of interaction between the team members and the senior executive responsible for their segment of the organization was causing further disconnects. We shared what we learned with program designers, program trainers, and key stakeholders; as a result, the initiative was adapted to encourage the participation of each team's senior executive during several of the sessions held at CCL. The senior manager therefore became an integrated part of the leadership development solution, enabling the team to create a greater purpose for its work.

If these ideas seem too complex and too large to imagine, consider scaling back to focus on the development initiative itself. Even in its simplest form, using evaluation results to modify development programs and processes is quite powerful. For example, realizing that time could be used more efficiently and effectively during a face-to-face program and making subsequent modifications to its design will increase its impact. Understanding that participants feel confused about how to apply new learnings to their work can result in new follow-on components designed to provide the support they need at critical times. Learning that participants have a difficult time accessing a Web-based portion of the development process can reveal that the software requirements for that component are not compatible with the organization's computer systems, and attention can be focused on resolving that issue. The opportunities for using evaluation to enable further improvements are truly innumerable. They should be considered during the assessment and design phases so that organizational learning can be as intentional as possible.

Organizational Learning

Traditionally, most evaluation of development initiatives has taken the "report card" approach: evaluate the program to see how well it is meeting its goals. This approach, which is technically known as "summative evaluation," is often used to determine whether a program or process should be continued or discontinued. The knowledge that is gained through a summative evaluation is often applied only to the program in question: a decision is made based on the information, and that is the end of it. Whatever is learned from the evaluation is not considered generalizable to other leadership development initiatives.

"Formative evaluation," in contrast, focuses on finding out how the development event or system is working and how it can better meet its goals. In the spirit of continuous improvement, it attempts to discover what effects the current system or event is having and what can be improved to boost the positive effects even further. The central question is "What can we learn and improve?" rather than "How well did it do?"

A large-scale study of program impact can have both formative and summative phases. For example, evaluators may conduct a formative study during the pilot phase of a mentoring program and follow that with a summative approach once the program is up and running. Even so, the specific program is still the only focus of attention.

There are also ways to implement evaluation that push the organization toward broader benefits. A series of approaches variously called "participatory evaluation," "collaborative evaluation," "empowerment evaluation," and "evaluative inquiry" add value in promoting learning throughout the organization (Cousins and Earl, 1992, 1995; Fetterman, 1994, 1996; Preskill and Torres, 1999). These approaches are characterized by collaborative and participative relationships that empower program participants to contribute directly to their own learning and that of others. Through reflection, dialogue, and action planning, participants play a role in collecting evaluation data while increasing their own understanding of what they learned. For example, by debriefing the value of a particular component of an initiative, participants increase their understanding and awareness of both the competencies addressed by the component and the ways in which to apply their learning to work settings.

For an organization to learn, both individuals and the larger collective must continuously learn (Dixon, 1996). As evaluation, especially formative evaluation, is used regularly, people become used to asking, "What can we learn, and how can we improve?" Over time, this mind-set helps produce a learning orientation in the organization as a whole.

Taking this perspective to another level, it is possible to determine whether organizational learning has resulted from an evaluation. Most directly, one can assess the extent to which the results and recommendations of the evaluation have been used to make improvements in relevant programs and processes. More indirectly, it is also possible to assess the extent to which an organization's propensity to be a learning organization has increased. Do organization members reflect more regarding their work, their leadership capacity, and the role of the organization in supporting their leadership? Does the organization have a stronger learning culture that encourages the sharing of new ideas? Does the organization have processes in place to support organizational learning?

Conclusion

Evaluation of leadership development is a complex undertaking, yet there is no question that it must be done—and done well—to effectively support organizations in their efforts to improve human and organizational performance.

There are four essential steps in the evaluation process: (1) identify key stakeholders, (2) perform needs assessment, (3) design the evaluation, and (4) implement the evaluation. Each of these steps has additional components that were addressed in this chapter. In addition to being concerned with the evaluation process, evaluators must consider the role of organizational context in both leadership development and its subsequent evaluation. Finally, evaluators and the organization must make conscientious use of evaluation results.

Our experience at CCL has shown us that effective evaluation of leadership development must be customized for each initiative yet draw from a common set of methods and use the process outlined in this chapter to produce continuity across evaluations. Our experience has also shown us that this approach to evaluation of leadership development produces results that are highly informative for all key stakeholders, including those in the fields of evaluation and leadership development.

PART TWO

LEADER DEVELOPMENT IN CONTEXT

CHAPTER NINE

LEADER DEVELOPMENT ACROSS GENDER

Marian N. Ruderman

When the Center for Creative Leadership (CCL) first opened its doors in 1970, most managers attending our programs were white and male. Thus much of CCL's early work in leadership development was designed for this population. When we started our work in 1970, women made up a mere 16 percent of the management workforce. In 1983, their participation had risen to 40.9 percent, and by 1999, women held 49.5 percent of the managerial positions in the United States (U.S. Bureau of the Census, 2000; U.S. Department of Labor, 1983). As the gender profile of the managerial world changed, so did our client base. We began to wonder whether traditional leadership development methods designed for men addressed the needs of women managers. A review of the research literature confirmed what common sense suggested: leadership development practices reflecting only the experiences and careers of white men can place women and people of color at a disadvantage (Morrison and Von Glinow, 1990).

This chapter examines the suitability of a variety of leadership development practices for the development of women managers. In particular, it uses the lens of gender to examine 360-degree feedback, feedback-intensive programs, challenging assignments, developmental relationships, and recognition practices. I selected these practices for discussion because they are well-established and commonly used leadership development techniques.

History of Women's Leadership Work at CCL

CCL's first attempt to build a knowledge base about women leaders took place in the mid-1980s. It was a response to a key study on how American executives learn, grow, and change (McCall, Lombardo, and Morrison, 1988). The study found that executives develop from a series of increasingly challenging transitions, assignments, and experiences; these results highlighted the role of challenge as a key development strategy. However, the sample included in this study was virtually all white men because they constituted the vast majority of executives at that time. As this study of male executives was being completed, Ann Morrison, Randy White, and Ellen Van Velsor replicated it with female executives. They had to search extensively to find enough women executives to form the basis of a study. Of the seventy-six executives in their study, seventy-three were white and three were black. Their research culminated in the 1987 book, *Breaking the Glass Ceiling,* which demonstrated that the path to the executive suite for these women was both similar to and different from that for white men. They found that although many of the same challenging experiences that develop men also play a role in the development of women, the women faced additional barriers of prejudice and differential treatment. These barriers act as a glass ceiling above which it is difficult or nearly impossible for women to rise. This work brought considerable light to the subtle but pervasive barriers that prevent women from advancing to the highest levels in organizations. It helped draw international attention to the reasons why there were so few women in top management.

At CCL, this research led to the development of a new type of feedback-intensive program, a program just for women. We initially developed this program as a means of sharing the glass ceiling research, but when we began running it, we learned that it had tremendous value in its own right as a place where women managers could focus on their own development as leaders amid the fellowship of women in similar situations. This was the first program we created for a single demographic group (although we offered programs for particular occupational groups), and it created another opportunity for learning about the development of women managers.

With this as the beginning, our efforts to understand the leadership development process expanded to include managers from other demographic groups. Our work with women was the catalyst for broadening our understanding of the population of potential leaders. In 1988, we began collecting data for the Guidelines on Leadership Diversity (GOLD) project. This study looked at organizational practices for developing leadership among men and women of color—African Americans, Hispanics, Asian Americans—in addition to white women. Findings suggest that the glass ceiling applies not just to women of all races but to nonwhite males as well. Ann Morrison reported this research in *The New Leaders* (1992), which analyzes the corporate practices that are most effective in developing a diverse managerial workforce. The publication of *The New Leaders* fueled our interest in understanding what it means to have a diverse managerial workforce and laid the groundwork for our later focus on African American leaders, discussed in Chapter Ten.

These two large-scale studies were complemented by several others, smaller in scope, that dealt with specific issues: a comparison of the developmental experiences of white men and women (Van Velsor and Hughes-James, 1990), the different managerial job experiences of men and women (Ohlott, Ruderman, and McCauley, 1994), a conference on best practices for diversity (Morrison, Ruderman, and Hughes-James, 1993), promotion dynamics for men and women (Ruderman, Ohlott, and Kram, 1995), and the diversity of work teams (Jackson and Ruderman, 1995; Ruderman, Hughes-James, and Jackson, 1996). Collectively, these studies gave us a deeper understanding of particular aspects of the leadership development process.

In the mid-1990s, client needs made it clear to us that it was time for another major study of women managers. After running a program for women leaders for over ten years, we realized that the issues our clients were bringing to our attention were subtly changing. In the earlier years, participants were focused on breaking through the career-related barriers blocking women and figuring out how to fit in a male-dominated organization. They shared stories of blatant acts of sex discrimination and tips on how to succeed in a man's world. In 1995, we realized that the issues had to do more with how to be a woman leader rather than how to climb over obstacles. Women told us that they were at a crossroads: career models based on the experiences of male executives did not apply, but sadly, neither did the societal norms for how to be a successful woman. They lacked models for and an understanding of how to be a successful woman manager and still have a life outside of work. They felt that their career and leadership development experiences were distinctly different from those of men and did not want to simply adopt the traditional masculine model. Essentially, they were asking CCL to develop an understanding of life as a high-achieving professional that was an alternative to the existing male high-achiever model.

To address these issues, we launched a major study titled "The Choices and Trade-Offs of High-Achieving Women" in 1995. The purpose of this study was to describe what career pressures look like from the vantage point of a woman manager. The study was designed to improve our understanding of the dilemmas high-achieving women face in defining and shaping their careers. It examined the choices, trade-offs, and decisions about work and life that women in leadership roles typically confront. Patricia Ohlott and I report this research in *Standing at the Crossroads: Next Steps for High-Achieving Women* (Ruderman and Ohlott, 2002). The findings from this body of work provided content for a major revision to our Women's Leadership Program.

Thus over the years, various studies have contributed to the content of The Women's Leadership Program, and the program itself has served as a key source of information about the issues women leaders are experiencing.

Focus of This Chapter

This chapter highlights CCL's work with regard to the development of women leaders. It draws on our classroom experience and the published research as well as the work of others in the field. An important caveat is that most of our knowledge base comes from work with white women who work in large U.S. corporations. We recognize that although white and black women have many shared experiences in organizations, black women and other women of color face racial barriers in organizations that white women do not (Bell and Nkomo, 2001). We do not look at leadership in other sectors, such as education or volunteer organizations, where women leaders may be more common. In addition, the focus in this chapter is on the United States, where the influx of women into managerial positions is relatively recent. The current research agenda at CCL includes a study investigating the experiences of women managers in Europe.

This chapter is organized into three main sections. It starts with a discussion of the contextual issues that form a backdrop against which leadership development occurs. The next section reviews common leadership development practices. The final section summarizes and discusses implications of this line of work.

The Context

Leadership development does not happen in a vacuum. To understand the degree to which common and well-regarded leadership development strategies serve the needs of women leaders, it is important to understand the context in which women leaders operate. This includes both the forces shaping the careers of managerial women and the career-related obstacles they face.

Forces Shaping the Careers of High-Achieving Women

A key feature of the modern American organizational environment is that large corporations are designed around the historic needs of men. Career systems are built around the traditional notion of the married male with the stay-at-home wife.

Organizational systems of advancement and rewards are based on the life patterns of men and assume that managers can prioritize work above all other roles in life, especially caregiving roles. As a result, these systems are less than welcoming to the traditional life patterns of women, who have been the primary caregivers in the family. Meyerson and Fletcher (2000) have argued that gender inequity is a characteristic of modern organizations in which a particular (and perhaps outdated) view of masculinity shapes the career development systems and leadership norms.

To capture the types of pressures women leaders in organizations experience as they forge new paths, we conducted the study reported in *Standing at the Crossroads*, which identifies five themes that capture the issues faced by high-achieving women as they approach their careers and their lives: authenticity, connection, controlling one's own destiny, wholeness, and self-clarity. Understanding these themes helps in addressing the suitability of the typical techniques organizations use to develop women leaders. Developing a view of oneself as a leader is a complicated process, involving multiple stages of growth and development (Hill, 1992). This process becomes more complex if the leadership development practices and norms ignore the specific developmental expectations of adult women.

Authenticity. The first of the five themes looks at the degree to which daily actions and behaviors are in concert with deeply held values and beliefs. Someone who is authentic has a good understanding of her priorities and emotions. Authenticity is important to development because adults learn best when they feel they can be authentic in that setting. It is hard to develop as a leader if you feel you must hide your true values, styles, and preferences. One of the complaints we heard from women managers is that it is difficult to develop your own style in an organization that prescribes a particular style of leadership. In particular, some women who worked for organizations with a command-and-control style of leadership found it difficult if their own personal nature was more collaborative. For example, Ashley, a participant in The Women's Leadership Program, told us that she preferred a leadership approach that was very collaborative and had trouble getting this alternative approach for effectiveness rewarded by her organization. She favored enabling and nurturing others rather than commanding that they do something. Fletcher (1996), in her work with women, would call this a relational approach. She argues that effectiveness and growth come from empowering others.

The relational approach stands in contrast to the view, characteristic of hierarchical organizations, that effectiveness equates with individual achievements. In these organizations, a relational style is undervalued, making women who engage in these behaviors feel as if they are behaving counter to standard practice. Women who regard this as their primary leadership style have a hard time feeling both effective and authentic in traditional organizations.

Authenticity is an issue in other ways as well. Our research noted that authenticity also became a career-influencing force when the organizational environment changed over time. An environment that was once hospitable may have grown less so. An organizational environment may have changed as unethical executives joined and influenced the organization. Situations such as these have motivated women to rethink their participation in the organization.

Connection. In a general way, connection refers to our need to be close to other human beings—family, friends, community, and coworkers. Psychologists acknowledge this as one of two fundamental drives that motivate our behavior. Historically, relationships have been seen as a strength of women, and connection is very important to the development of women leaders. In fact, several psychologists argue that an inner sense of connection is the central organizing force in women's development (Jordan and others, 1991; Miller and Stiver, 1997). They argue that a key developmental task is to develop a self in relation to others. This stands in contrast to the more male-oriented theories of development, which emphasize independence and autonomy at the expense of relationships.

Agency. The third theme is the desire to control one's own destiny. This is one of the strongest needs of high-achieving women. Psychologists refer to this quality of acting assertively on one's own behalf as "agency" (Bakan, 1966). Traditional psychological models say that agency and connection are fundamental human drives. Historically, agency has been associated with the qualities traditionally considered masculine, while connection has been associated with qualities considered feminine. Leadership positions require both. However, sometimes a woman employing the behaviors of agency (assertiveness, self-promotion, or questioning practices that do not meet needs) is seen as inappropriately aggressive. A man using the same behaviors, however, is seen as powerful. This disparity is part of the backdrop against which development for women leaders occurs. It can be a challenge to develop effective agentic behaviors when others in the organization perceive this as unladylike and do not view the behaviors in the light in which they were intended.

According to Miller and Stiver (1997), the key to effectiveness for both men and women is to employ agentic behavior without sacrificing relationships. They argue that effective behavior rests on demonstrating agency and acknowledging interdependence with others.

Wholeness. The fourth theme influencing the development of women leaders is that of wholeness, the desire to feel complete and integrated as a full human being. According to Still (1993), integrating various life roles is a driving force in the behavior of many high-achieving women. The demands of the business world and the insensitivity of the business world to caregiving needs make this hard to achieve. Women strive to address the needs of multiple life roles to fulfill the desires of their personal and professional lives. Most organizations, however, are built on a male model from the 1950s that is based on the norm that the ideal worker gives work a higher priority than all other aspects of life. This prevailing norm makes it difficult for women professionals to address their other life needs.

Our own research suggests that despite the many ways organizations deter women from having a whole life, wholeness is beneficial both for the organization and its individual employees. It has been demonstrated that there is a relationship between multiple roles and managerial performance such that as commitment to nonwork roles increases, so does the effectiveness in the managerial role (Ruderman, Ohlott, Panzer, and King, 2002). Further, this is not the only positive outcome associated with a whole life. This same study found that commitment to multiple roles was also associated with psychological well-being in terms of life satisfaction and self-acceptance.

Despite women's desire for a whole life, it is well documented that most organizations are built on the assumption that work takes precedence over all else. It is within this context that leadership development occurs.

Self-Clarity. The fifth and final development need is the desire for self-clarity. The women leaders in this study (Ruderman and Ohlott, 2002) expressed a need to understand themselves within the context of the world in which they operate. They wanted to know more than just how others see their strengths and weaknesses—they wanted to see themselves in the context of the many ways organizations treat men and women differently. They struggled to understand how stereotypes and perceptions of women influence how these colleagues saw them.

The desire for self-understanding is important for both men and women. Self-clarity allows the individual to grow by enabling her to recognize her values so as to live authentically, improve her ability to connect with others, enable agentic behavior, and allow her to make choices that produce feelings of wholeness. Many women reported that it was difficult to develop self-clarity in an organization with a climate that is hostile toward women. Such an environment makes it hard for a person to get an accurate picture of how others see her because she will doubt the validity of the feedback. Without trustworthy feedback, it is difficult to plan or to understand how to be more effective.

Together these five themes form the developmental backdrop for the careers of high-achieving women. Understanding the suitability of common leadership development techniques for women managers rests on an understanding of these pressures. However, it is not sufficient to simply look at these factors that influence the choices and decisions women leaders make. It is also important to look outside women to the climate they currently face in large organizations. Despite the advances in knowledge about the characteristics of women leaders, organizations are still challenged in their efforts to effectively include women managers in the managerial and executive ranks. Women may now be in the pipeline, but the pipeline leaks—organizations are having difficulty advancing them to the top and retaining them. Turnover is a major problem as women are leaving large corporations to create their own environments as entrepreneurs (Catalyst, 1998; Moore and Buttner, 1997). Not surprisingly, women are leaving because they do not feel fully accepted by ambivalent corporate environments. The women who do stay in large organizations are moving up very slowly (Lyness and Thompson, 1997) as organizations are having difficulty embracing the full inclusion of women when this means moving them to the highest ranks.

Explanations for the Differential Advancement of Men and Women

There are several reasons why women have not achieved parity with men at the highest levels. The current thinking is that many of these reasons have to do with the organizational climate and culture. Features of the climate that have been singled out as explanations of this phenomenon include prejudice, differential opportunities, isolation, comfort dealing with one's own kind, and work-family conflict.

Prejudice. Prejudice was the barrier to advancement most frequently mentioned in *The New Leaders* (Morrison, 1992). Morrison defines prejudice as "the tendency to view people who are different from some reference group in terms of sex, ethnic background, or racial characteristics such as skin color as being deficient" (p. 345). In other words, prejudice is the assumption that being different from the majority group automatically implies an inability to perform.

Several other studies of career barriers have also found prejudice to be a major obstacle, including the report of the Department of Labor's investigation into forces that have blocked advancement of minorities and women in the private sector (Federal Glass Ceiling Commission, 1995). Catalyst, an organization devoted to understanding and monitoring the progress of women in organizations, also found that stereotypical preconceptions were a major obstacle (1996).

Many of these prejudices are passed on as prevalent stereotypes implying that women are unsuited for senior management. Studies of stereotypes have found that when managers are asked to describe women in general, men in general, and successful managers, the descriptions of men in general and successful managers are markedly similar. Both men in general and managers are described as forceful, having leadership ability, aggressive, desirous of responsibility, and able to get the job done. Women in general are characterized as deficient in these qualities. Virginia Schein first demonstrated this in the early 1970s, dubbing this dynamic "Think Manager—Think Male" (1973, 1975). Despite changes fostering the movement of women into organizations such as legislation, recruiting efforts, and diversity programs, a replication of this work in the late 1980s showed that this dynamic still held true (Heilman, Block, Martell, and Simon, 1989). In essence, men and women are stereotyped differently, with males seen as more competent, active, potent, emotionally stable, independent, and rational than their female counterparts. Recent international research by Schein (2002) replicates the "Think Manager—Think Male" study in Germany, the United Kingdom, China, and Japan and confirms the finding that men view women as less capable managerially.

The number and variety of investigations into gender stereotypes show how deeply rooted these stereotypes are in organizations. Further, the strength of these stereotypes suggests just how difficult it can be for women to be effectively agentic in organizations. These stereotypes limit the range of agentic behaviors women can use without violating societal norms. Women who use a more feminine style of leadership run the risk of being labeled as ineffective, and women who use a more masculine style may be criticized as well.

Stereotypes are important when leadership potential is evaluated or staffing assignments are made. Stereotypes can get in the way of making decisions based on merit or ability (Ruderman and Ohlott, 1990). Prejudice has an enormous impact, preventing supervisors and peers from seeing others as they really are. In the face of uncertainty, decision makers filling top positions are likely to select individuals with whom they feel more comfortable and thus choose those similar in gender (Powell, 1999).

Differential Opportunities. A second barrier to advancement identified in the literature is that of limited opportunity. Women get limited exposure to the mix of assignments, experiences, and relationships that prepare them for senior positions. Typically, men get more of the high-visibility, high-stakes line assignments that lead to advancement (Ohlott, Ruderman, and McCauley, 1994). Even at the executive level, women have less authority than men, as indicated by numbers of direct reports (Lyness and Thompson, 1997).

In addition, women are not offered relocation opportunities at the same rate as men, even though they are just as likely to accept such opportunities (Brett, Stroh, and Reilly, 1993). Relocation is significant because it offers the opportunity to take on high-profile, developmental assignments. This difference in opportunity structure makes it complicated for women to develop and demonstrate skills associated with agency. It is a challenge to become comfortable with power and to refine influence skills if you are not given the opportunity to do so.

Isolation. Essentially, this has to do with the pressures of being on a lonely journey in an organization. At the uppermost levels of organizations, women are greatly outnumbered by men, many of whom (intentionally or not) treat them differently. They are often left out of the information loop. To make matters worse, another consequence of this isolation is that many of those being left out feel they have no one with whom they can discuss career issues or solicit advice. This issue is especially pronounced for black women; they receive substantially less collegial support than white women do (Bell and Nkomo, 2001).

Along with isolation, the lack of role models also hinders the advancement of women (Morrison, 1992). Even with all the progress today, women who rise above middle management have few role models and mentors. In contrast, ambitious male managers have many leaders with whom to identify. These feelings of isolation and the lack of role models both contribute to the desire for connection.

Comfort Dealing with One's Own Kind.

The next barrier is the fact that people tend to find greater comfort in dealing with their own kind. People prefer to be with others who are similar (Byrne, 1971). Thus white men in the dominant business group may be less comfortable reaching out to dissimilar others and including them in the business elite (Kanter, 1977; Powell, 1999). Bosses take into account their comfort level with a direct report when making a promotion decision (Ruderman and Ohlott, 1994). People who do not fit the mold are informally excluded and denied access to opportunities because differences in gender, cultural background, and race make others uncomfortable. This phenomenon is often more pronounced in situations where the stakes are high. Powell (1999) explains that women are still seen as an uncertain entity in top management, and male executives seek to reduce this source of anxiety by sticking with their own kind.

Integrating Career and Family.

The final barrier women leaders encounter has to do with the challenge of integrating career and family needs. Even in dual-career marriages, women still take most of the responsibility for home and family (Morrison, 1992; Newman, 1993). Careers in senior management often require complete dedication. For many women, the childbearing years are the same ones as the career-building years (the time when organizations traditionally expect managers to prove themselves). Furthermore, elder care responsibilities can come at almost any point in a career. Many corporate policies are still based on the 1950s assumption that there is someone else at home to manage family responsibilities. Despite an increase in the numbers of women entering the managerial ranks, these policies were reinforced by the combination of significant global expansion in recent years and the downsizing phenomenon of the 1980s, both of which increased managerial workloads.

The difficulty of integrating career and family is not unique to the experience of women in the United States. According to a survey of women managers in the

United Kingdom by the Chartered Institute of Personnel and Development (2002), 27 percent of female managers point to family commitments as a career blocker. An article in the *Wall Street Journal* (Steinborn, 2001) points out that women in Germany do not even have access to a basic infrastructure containing quality day care, making it extremely difficult for women to have both a career and a family.

To succeed in the corporate world, many women give up the idea of having a family altogether. Generally, women executives are less likely than male executives to be married or have children (Brett and Stroh, 1999; Lyness and Thompson, 1997). Extreme devotion to career in combination with lack of a family life may exact a cost for the women who choose this lifestyle. They forgo the emotional and developmental benefits from having a family, and they grow differently from their colleagues on yet another dimension.

These barriers are important for our purposes here because they are outside the normal challenges of development. In their journey to the executive suite, women managers must deal with these obstacles in addition to traditional work challenges such as stretch assignments, mistakes and failures, and personal trauma. Furthermore, these added obstacles are particularly potent because they are not just a function of simple prejudices. Rather, they reflect a larger, complicated setting in the United States, where gender relations are embedded in the legacy of old-fashioned patriarchy (McBroom, 1992) and in which men historically held positions of dominance in business settings. These larger societal issues form part of the landscape in which women's leadership development occurs.

Leadership Development Practices

With this discussion of the development pressures on women and barriers to career advancement as background, we now turn to four key leadership development practices described at length in other chapters of this handbook: 360-degree feedback, feedback-intensive programs, challenging assignments, and developmental relationships. I selected these practices because they represent some of the best thinking with regard to leadership development. I examine how gender introduces complexities to these practices. I then describe one other practice that is critical for people historically underrepresented in management: recognition.

Formal Assessment: 360-Degree Feedback

In recent years, 360-degree feedback instruments have become popular (see Chapter Two). In many cases, they form the heart of management development efforts. In these structured processes, bosses, peers, direct reports, and sometimes even clients are asked to anonymously rate the effectiveness of an individual manager.

This assessment is then compared to self-ratings and shared with the individual. The comparative data help the manager understand where he or she is with regard to a set of behaviors that are linked to managerial effectiveness. This kind of assessment is important because it allows managers to compare how they see themselves to how others see them. It is particularly important to women managers because they tend to get less informal feedback than white men do (Morrison, 1992).

As is true of other management development tools, most experience with these 360-degree instruments is drawn from the largest pool of managers and executives available in the United States: white men. The success of these assessments hinges on the credibility and usefulness of the feedback. The career barriers described earlier, however, can compromise this credibility and applicability. In particular, if these instruments are used with a diverse population, four questions arise:

1. Is the content (the dimensions assessed) useful for this population of managers?
2. Is this instrument valid for populations other than white males?
3. Do the norms vary for different groups?
4. Are the ratings biased?

Appropriateness of Assessment Content. An important consideration in deciding to use a 360-degree feedback instrument is the origin of the questions used on the instrument (Van Velsor, Leslie, and Fleenor, 1997). For the feedback to be credible and useful, the questions need to reflect relevant and appropriate managerial competencies. The managerial competencies on most instruments are based on theories of effectiveness, practitioner experience, or some combination of the two, and this basis has in the past made them acceptable to managers at large. However, to be relevant to a diverse managerial population, the instrument must be based on data or theory reflecting a heterogeneous population.

Basing an instrument on only one segment of the managerial population leads to a limited view of effectiveness and competence; including other groups leads to an expanded definition. For example, in addition to demonstrating many of the individual competencies displayed by men in organizations, women managers are also known for taking a relational approach to professional growth and organizational effectiveness (Cooper and Lewis, 1999; Fletcher, 1996, 1999). Women place great value on enabling others, seeing projects holistically, empowering others, and achieving through others (Fletcher, 1996). These are the types of practices that modern learning organizations are calling for (Senge, 1990) as well as the very competencies required in developing emotionally competent managers (Goleman, 1995). Ironically, these are also practices that tend to be undervalued in traditional models of effectiveness (Fletcher, 1996). Including women's experiences in the content of an instrument therefore leads to an expanded sense of what is effective.

Validity. In addition to wanting the content of the instrument to be appropriate for a population, it is important that it also be valid for that group. In other words, scores on an instrument should be related to a measure of effectiveness for the target group. This is, of course, important for any population, but with a diverse population, it is vital to understand whether the relationship between the instrument scores and the effectiveness criterion is the same for different groups (Van Velsor, Leslie, and Fleenor, 1997). Does a high score on a particular dimension for group A have the same meaning as for group B? For example, does a high score on a measure of building relationships have the same relationship to effectiveness for men as it does for women? Does a high score on demonstrating influence have the same relationship to effectiveness for men as it does for women? This is known as comparative validity. For assessment information to be seen as credible and useful, the scores need to mean the same thing for managers of different races and both genders.

Knowledge about the comparative validity of different multirater feedback instruments is relatively sparse. CCL and other providers of these instruments have conducted studies with regard to gender and have found that particular instruments have similar relationships to effectiveness for men and women.

Differences in Norms. Most multirater instruments report assessment data in comparison to some standard or norm. This helps the recipient understand how she is doing compared to others, which in turn adds to the power of the feedback. Clearly, it is important for an instrument to use a normative group that is appropriate for the individuals being assessed.

Women may be interested in getting feedback on how they compare to other women as well as to managers at large. For example, there are some small differences in the norms for men and women on Benchmarks, a 360-degree evaluation instrument commonly used by CCL (Center for Creative Leadership, 2002b). On most dimensions, women score higher than men. This is not an unusual pattern in 360-degree evaluation instruments. In a sample of 5,300 leaders and 31,000 observers, Posner and Kouzes (1993) found that women outperformed men on two key scales on their 360-degree instrument. A *Business Week* article (Sharpe, 2000), reporting on numerous studies conducted by different vendors of 360-degree evaluation instruments, pointed to a differential in the skills of men and women favoring women. Perhaps the most in-depth work done to date (Eagly, Johannesen-Schmidt, and van Engen, 2003) is a meta-analysis of forty-five studies using the Multifactor Leadership Questionnaire (MLQ) (Avolio, Bass, and Jung, 1995). These researchers found small differences between men and women, with female leaders rated as more transformational than male leaders and male leaders rated as demonstrating greater levels of laissez-faire leadership and contingent reward behaviors. The implications of these studies are favorable for women: the areas in which women outperformed men have positive relations to effectiveness and the areas in which men received higher scores either have no relationship or a negative relationship to effectiveness.

However, this pattern, which suggests that women are more effective managers, is not always the finding. Kabacoff (1998) evaluated male and female CEOs and senior vice presidents in eighty-eight North American companies and found that men garnered higher ratings on some dimensions of leadership and women garnered higher ratings on others. All the dimensions are related to effectiveness. This pattern of differential effectiveness underscores the point that it is important to examine the norms of any assessment tools used for development purposes. Regardless of the instrument, differential norms should be shared so that women can put their feedback in context.

Everyone who uses a 360-degree feedback instrument—no matter its source—should pay attention to the normative database. It is important to understand what population the normative database is drawn from and whether there are different norms for various groups. Training manuals and support materials should include these norms.

Bias in Ratings. For feedback to have the desired effects, the recipient must believe that the data are credible, important, and useful (Dalton and Hollenbeck, 1996). Feedback that is seen as accurate and honest can be a catalyst for change; that is, after all, the point.

The expected response when managers receive positive feedback is that they see it as indicating an area of strength. The expected response for negative feedback is that managers see it as signaling a need for change. There is, however, the potential for this process to go awry should recipients believe negative feedback is shaped by prejudice and bias (Cox, 1993). Women managers face the added complexity of figuring out whether prejudice or discrimination has influenced their feedback. Managers are not able to learn from discrepancies between self-views and the views of others if they believe prejudice is involved. Thus whenever non-majority managers are included in the population being assessed, the potential for bias becomes an important consideration.

Whether there are actually differences in the ratings that can be attributed to bias is still an open research question. Little has been done to look explicitly at rater bias in developmental feedback. Numerous studies have been done on rater bias in general, but their findings are inconsistent.

One study worth noting is a meta-analysis of the literature on gender and evaluation of leaders by Eagly, Makhijani, and Klonsky (1992). This analysis looked across all the experimental studies of leader evaluations. The strength of these studies is that all characteristics of leaders except gender are held constant. Thus any differences in evaluation of male and female leaders can be attributed to gender. The downside is that these studies were conducted in laboratories with college students and not in organizations with experienced adult workers.

Examining sixty-one laboratory studies, Eagly and colleagues (1992) found that people evaluate female leaders slightly more negatively than male leaders with equivalent qualifications. This very small trend was magnified under certain circumstances: if women used an autocratic, nonparticipative leadership style (a style that is stereotypically male and currently out of favor), they were evaluated more negatively, and if the evaluator was male, the evaluation was even lower. This suggests that women get lower ratings from men if they act in a way thought to be typically male, inappropriate, or both.

Bowen, Swim, and Jacobs (2000) replicated this type of research using performance ratings taken from actual performance appraisals at work. They selected for the meta-analysis studies that were conducted in the field rather than in laboratory settings. Their study did not look specifically at leadership positions. Overall, they found little evidence of bias in these performance evaluations. However, similar to Eagly and colleagues (1992), they did find that men were rated more highly on masculine measures and women more highly on feminine measures. Furthermore, they found that when the raters were all male, males were rated more highly than females.

These meta-analyses provide a backdrop for understanding bias in ratings in general, but they reveal little about biases specific to 360-degree developmental ratings. Although evidence of bias in 360-degree developmental ratings is scant, the fact that many managers believe prejudice to be alive and well in organizations is well documented (Catalyst, 1996; Federal Glass Ceiling Commission, 1995; Morrison, 1992). The implication of this is that if your organization uses 360-degree feedback instruments with diverse populations, you should be equipped to facilitate discussions of how stereotypes may influence results.

What Can Be Done

Participants in 360-degree feedback programs may want to figure out to what extent their feedback is based on realistic performance evaluation so that they can sort out what to change and what not to change. Facilitators should help concerned managers probe and try to understand whether ratings are biased. They need to be prepared to discuss the relationship of behaviors to perceptions and how perceptions can be distorted.

A real challenge, however, is to conduct these discussions in a way that recognizes the reality of prejudice but does not provide an easy excuse for overlooking or ignoring negative feedback. It is also important to point out that the perceptions of coworkers are part of the reality at work, regardless of whether those perceptions are accurate.

Despite these difficulties in applying 360-degree feedback practices to women managers, it is important that women have access to such assessment. Especially where differences between people make informal communication difficult, facilitated formal assessment processes can help managers get more of the information they need, both for their own development and to improve performance on their jobs.

The Feedback-Intensive Program

One way to ensure that women get opportunities for assessment is through a formal feedback-intensive program (described in Chapter One of this handbook). Women managers have the option of attending traditional, heterogeneous programs or programs specially tailored for them, known as single-identity programs. CCL offers a women's leadership program. Like CCL's traditional mixed-group programs, the women's program focuses on issues of leadership development; however, it is conducted in a setting that encourages additional content having to do with identity issues and complexities in the workplace arising from the career barriers discussed earlier. They also help people capitalize on their special cultural and situational life experiences, which are a function of membership in that identity group.

As mentioned earlier, The Women's Leadership Program offered by CCL is built around the needs of women managers as addressed in *Standing at the Crossroads* (Ruderman and Ohlott, 2002). The content and practices featured in the program address the five development needs identified by the research: authenticity, connection, controlling your own destiny, wholeness, and self-clarity.

Although single-identity programs have many advantages, they remain a controversial environment for development (Ohlott, 2002; Ohlott and Hughes-James, 1997). The next section looks at the arguments for and against such training. These arguments are summarized in Exhibit 9.1.

Advantages of Single-Identity Feedback-Intensive Programs. Perhaps the biggest advantage of these programs is that they offer participants a validating experience. They give managers the opportunity to learn, through the sharing that takes place, that what they feel and experience is similar for other women and that they are not alone or imagining things (Ohlott, 2002). The words of one woman manager poignantly express this feeling of normalization:

EXHIBIT 9.1. ADVANTAGES AND DISADVANTAGES OF ATTENDING A SINGLE-IDENTITY GROUP FEEDBACK-INTENSIVE PROGRAM.

Advantages

- Validates the experience of being a minority manager in a majority organization.
- Offers a safe, supportive environment for sharing experiences, taking risks, and practicing skills.
- Provides an opportunity to be with others like oneself, in contrast to the isolation usually experienced; provides a source of peers and role models and a chance to rehearse one's culture.
- Pays attention to the appropriateness of feedback for the identity group: uses feedback-intensive instruments created for the population or provides feedback on traditional instruments with norms for the single-identity group.
- Helps managers determine what parts of feedback are valid versus what parts may be filtered through prejudicial lenses.
- Contains specialized content relevant for the identity group.

Disadvantages

- May highlight perceived differences, producing the stigma of deficiency.
- Training does not take place in the "real world"; generalizability of skills may be affected if not learned in a mixed-race or mixed-gender setting.
- Participation may suggest that managers are receiving favorable treatment or are conspiring against majority-group managers, creating the potential for backlash.

> This program was just so powerful, because I think I didn't realize how much angst I carried inside myself, that I just didn't have anybody to affirm it or validate it, so I just kind of went forward and carried it. Being there I found myself really emotionally touched, which I wasn't really prepared for. . . . I thought it would be more of a cognitive enrichment, but instead I was just overwhelmed at the emotional release that I had, and I just think it was a validation that my trip had been hard, it wasn't in my head. It was some real tough times.

A second benefit of these programs is that they offer a safe, supportive place to share experiences, doubts, fears, and successes, as well as the experiences of sexism. Participants work on issues that cannot be discussed in a mixed group.

Women, especially those who are the trailblazers in their organizations, are more likely to have their work and behavior scrutinized for mistakes and be held to higher performance standards (Federal Glass Ceiling Commission, 1995; Morrison, 1992). Given this, they must be cautious with certain behaviors, such as publicly exposing vulnerability. Single-group programs offer people space for taking risks, asking questions, making mistakes, and expressing feelings without fear of being labeled inferior or being ridiculed or reprimanded (Baskerville, 1992; Josefowitz, 1990).

In a program with similar others, managers can practice new skills and "let their guard down" in a safe and supportive environment (Ohlott, 2002). Women who might be hesitant to talk about certain issues in mixed company have found they can open up without worrying about reinforcing negative perceptions about the vulnerability of women.

A third benefit of such a program is that it is very nurturing and supportive. Many women, particularly those at the highest levels or in a male-dominated industry, are isolated in their organizations. They have no other women managers to learn from, get feedback from, or socialize with. The single-group experience gives them a roomful of peers and role models. The comfort-with-your-own-kind factor that contributes to white male managers' hiring other white male managers kicks in for these women managers. For many, it is the first time in their careers they have been surrounded by women facing similar corporate managerial challenges. For many, it is their first experience in a work-related setting of being in the majority.

This opportunity to be with others who are likely to face similar job situations can be extremely reinforcing for people who are relatively isolated in their own organization. But more than support, participants also receive and internalize solutions, ideas, and approaches that have worked for others as they share information about how to manage the workplace and their role in it. This setting helps address the need for connection among women who do not have similar others to use as reference points in their organizational setting.

Another advantage of single-identity feedback-intensive programs has to do with the actual feedback of data. These programs can use feedback instruments created just for the population or customized from traditional instruments. For instance, we modified a 360-degree feedback instrument for our feedback-intensive program for women. The instrument was changed to include questions for peers, direct reports, and supervisors about expectations for women in general in that organization. This information helps each participant understand the norms and values in her own organizational climate as they relate to gender. She receives her 360-degree data in the context of a general sense of how her organization evaluates women. Such data are extremely helpful in efforts to develop self-clarity, which requires the ability to apply one's self-knowledge to a specific organizational environment.

Women-only programs help the managers figure out which aspects of their feedback are unique to them and which are a function of being in a minority position. This happens through the discussion of feedback, the presentation of normative data for their group, and peer feedback from other managers in the program. If negative performance feedback is received, these managers must deal with the additional step of determining what is valid in the feedback from what may be filtered through prejudicial lenses. Single-identity programs help with this process because women can compare (predominantly male) feedback from back home to (all-female) feedback from classroom peers who observe them throughout the program in structured exercises and informal experiences. The feedback portion of the program not only helps the managers understand how others see them but also encourages them to do this in the larger context of understanding gender dynamics in organizations—in other words, to develop a sense of self-clarity. It helps women understand both when stereotypes may be influencing their feedback and when prejudice is used as a convenient excuse to deny the painful reality of poor performance.

Another key advantage of single-identity programs is the opportunity to tailor content to the audience of women. At CCL, our program addresses the five themes identified as key pressures influencing the choices and trade-offs of managerial women (Ruderman and Ohlott, 2002). For example, the program addresses issues of authenticity by helping women uncover their priorities and values. It deals with issues of connection by emphasizing the key nature of relationships both inside and outside of work; networking and support are specifically discussed. It also discusses the potential clash between how women value relationships and the likely devaluing of relationships by the corporate culture (Miller, 1986; Van Velsor and Hughes-James, 1990). In terms of agency, the program addresses strategies for understanding and recognizing influential and political behavior in organizations, since women have told us how difficult it can be to effectively influence others at the upper levels of management. An important part of the program deals with developing skills in exercising power. Wholeness is a key theme in the program; women are given a forum to talk about the difficulty of and strategies for managing a multiple-role lifestyle. The program helps women deepen their understanding of what they value and want out of life so that they can make choices that allow them to feel whole. Finally, as discussed before, the delivery of feedback allows for rich discussions of self-clarity.

Despite these benefits, single-identity programs remain controversial. There are many reasons why women may choose not to use them.

Disadvantages of Single-Identity Feedback-Intensive Programs. Among the questions raised is the argument that because they highlight perceived differences, single-identity programs prove detrimental in the long run. Heilman (1995) argues that programs designed only for women can inadvertently nourish stereotypical attitudes in men. According to this line of thought, if women have special needs, as the existence of a women-only program attests, they must be "different." These differences, in turn, draw attention to perceptions of deficiency and inferiority (Fondas, 1986; Langrish, 1980). Managers may choose to enroll in programs provided to their male counterparts because they do not want other people to think they are lacking in any unique way related to gender.

Then there is the "real world" argument (Ohlott, 2002). Proponents of this argument (for example, Langrish, 1980) believe that training should mirror the so-called real world, the workplace dominated by male managers. Single-identity group programs create an artificial environment for social interaction since majority managers are absent. The belief is that knowledge, skills, and experiences used in the workplace should be learned in mixed settings or else the generalizability of certain skills is affected (Fondas, 1986).

The potential for backlash is a third reason given to avoid single-identity programs. The feelings of togetherness that are so validating for single-identity program participants may be threatening to others. Participants in segregated programs may be seen as receiving favorable treatment (Harlan and Weiss, 1980), thus fostering resentment among peers and bosses. There is also the concern that women-only programs are designed to denigrate men. Our trainers report that in fact, very little, if any, such bashing takes place—no more so than in the mixed-group programs. Participants are highly focused on their own strengths and weaknesses; they do not spend time tearing apart other groups.

Which Is Better? Although I have described several possible reasons for managers choosing not to attend a single-identity program, I believe that the advantages far outweigh the disadvantages. The criticisms against these programs come primarily from the literature. Our classroom experiences at CCL indicate that the arguments may be concerns for the managers, but the strengths of these programs outweigh the concerns. Ultimately, the bottom line of this discussion is that managers must choose for themselves which type of program leaves them more comfortable. (For guidance in this decision, see the next section of this chapter.)

Both women-only and mixed-gender programs carefully provide feedback and support for growth and development. They both offer expert help in understanding one's strengths and weaknesses. Participants need to decide whether they prefer to take this journey of self-exploration in the standard way that has been used by the majority of executives or whether they prefer a customized approach in the company of others likely to be experiencing similar career barriers. Both choices are good ones. The important point is that people be given valid assessment feedback in an environment that is built on balancing challenge with support.

Selecting a Mixed-Group or Single-Identity Development Program: Questions to Consider. Managers must evaluate their own needs and reasons for attending a development program. The following questions may guide the decision as to which is more appropriate, a traditional mixed-group program or a program designed for women only (Ohlott and Hughes-James, 1997):

- Does the manager believe that gender is affecting her career?
- Is the manager more comfortable learning in a mixed group or in a group made up of women?
- Does she feel isolated and want a sense of connection and bonding with others who may be experiencing similar career issues?
- Does she want to try out and practice new skills and behaviors in an environment that mirrors her organization or in an environment made up of others like herself?
- Has the manager already attended a traditional development program?
- If the person's organization routinely sends its managers to a traditional leadership development program, would attending a women-only program make her feel left out?

Challenging Assignments

Challenging job assignments—job experiences that push people to do something new or different—are another key strategy for development. Challenging jobs are important to advancement because they offer the opportunity for learning to handle a variety of leadership tasks and positions (see Chapter Five).

Challenging jobs promote growth for all managers. Through studies conducted at different times, we have found that executives attribute much of their success to challenging experiences (McCall, Lombardo, and Morrison, 1988; Rogolsky and Dalton, 1995; Van Velsor and Hughes-James, 1990). There are, however, some noticeable differences in how challenges occur for men and women. Women don't always have access to the kinds of challenging assignments they need for development, and they must navigate additional challenges stemming from sexism that are not experienced by majority men.

A comparison of job experiences found that men report a greater variety of challenging job assignments than women (Van Velsor and Hughes-James, 1990). In particular, men reported greater exposure to start-up situations, fix-it situations, and switches from line to staff jobs—all of which are experiences fruitful for learning. Generally, compared to men at the same level of management, women experience their jobs as less critical and less visible to the organization (Ohlott, Ruderman, and McCauley, 1994). This suggests that although women and men may be promoted to similar organizational levels, men are actually exposed to more significant learning opportunities. This is a subtle form of prejudice in which men and women holding jobs at similar levels appear to garner different developmental opportunities.

Additional Challenges. In addition to less experience with challenges critical to development, women experience additional challenges that men do not (Morrison, White, and Van Velsor, 1987; Rogolsky and Dalton, 1995). These extra challenges stem from some of the barriers mentioned earlier: obstacles arising from prejudice, isolation, and the multiple demands made on women. Women pioneers in organizations argue that on top of the day-to-day press of business, dealing with discrimination and harassment is a significant barrier to accomplishment. Women who are the first to hold a position have to struggle to gain acceptance and then must continuously work to convince people they are capable. There is no mention of these types of challenge in the experiences of white male executives (McCall, Lombardo, and Morrison, 1988).

As a group, nonmajority leaders experience other sources of challenge in addition to the key events mentioned here. Many of these stem from the fact that they must do their jobs under different circumstances than what their white male counterparts face (Morrison, 1992). One additional burden carried by many of the managers is to act as a role model or to represent their demographic group. For example, in the name of "diversity," nonmajority leaders are sometimes called on to speak about their experiences to the media or others in the organization.

Janice, a white engineering manager, told us that she has been photographed over and over again for recruiting materials on college campuses. African American women managers are often sought out to be mentors for others and spokespersons for the black community. Successful women of all races are frequently asked to represent women's issues or mentor large numbers of more junior women. One of our program participants, an African American woman who was the head of a nonprofit agency and had several advanced degrees, felt it was incumbent on her to act as a role model in the community and thus took on substantial responsibilities working with African American teenagers who were or were about to become single mothers. Most women find it difficult to say no, yet these opportunities add another set of duties to all their other job obligations.

A further challenge comes from some of the contextual issues raised earlier. Many women leaders must balance career demands with outside demands. For example, women often have additional responsibilities for child care and elder care that men do not. African American women managers face the additional challenge of making and maintaining a place for themselves in the African American community.

Bell and Nkomo (2001) have described the bicultural life experience of black career women. They explain that these women live a bicultural existence that requires them to develop careers in the professional world (which tends to be white and male) while making a place for themselves in the black world. Out of necessity, these women learn how to be boundary spanners, continuously making transitions from one community to the other.

Given all this, it is often true that the level of overall challenge experienced by a woman is different from that of a man in a similar job. Even though women may not get as much challenge from stretch assignments, they may have an equal or greater level of overall challenge from all sources given the additional obstacles they face in getting their jobs done.

Implications. Morrison (1992) cautions that it is easy to misuse challenge in developing women. On the one hand, there is the danger of too much challenge. Extreme amounts of challenge, and the stress that comes with it, can make it difficult to learn at all. Some organizations are in such a hurry to get a woman into the executive suite that they try to rush development and give women managers key jobs before they are ready.

On the other hand, some organizations err on the side of too little challenge. Fearing that women may fail, executives and managers tend to be more cautious with promoting them (Ruderman, Ohlott, and Kram, 1995). It often takes more steps for women than men to advance to the same level of an organization because women tend to get more promotions of smaller scope (Flanders and Anderson, 1973). The danger is that such a cautious approach limits learning. Managers learn from taking on major responsibilities, dealing with risks, and handling novel situations; modest changes in job responsibilities create less opportunity to learn. Assignments low in visibility and responsibility make it difficult to demonstrate the skills of power and influence associated with the need for agency. This situation also creates a catch-22 for further career advancement. The lower the developmental value of an assignment a woman receives, the greater the rationale for bypassing her in future promotions (Auster, 1989).

A second implication of the different challenges experienced by various groups has to do with organizations' need to understand how they use challenges for leadership development. Meaningful job assignments are among the most potent forces for development. Some organizations are better at using challenge for development than others. If they are to develop potential executives from all backgrounds, organizations must look at how they use challenge in their setting and assess how developmental assignments are distributed to different groups.

Another means of helping organizations use challenging assignments for development has to do with the support given to the managers who take them on. Morrison (1992) has found that multiple sources of support help managers select which additional challenges to accept and then help deal with them. Among the many forms of support are collegiality, information, feedback, and stress relief.

Developmental Relationships

Pursuing developmental relationships—alliances that enhance a person's learning and development—is a successful strategy for fostering leadership development, but again, women face certain obstacles and complicating dynamics. Here I focus on the effects of gender in two specific types of developmental relationships: informal junior-senior mentoring relationships and informal networks.

Junior-Senior Mentoring Relationships. As important as mentoring relationships are in the development equation (see Chapter Three for a comprehensive discussion), they are especially important for women because such relationships can help women overcome key career barriers (Ragins, 1997a, 1997b; Wellington and Spence, 2001) and provide an additional source of power and resources (Ragins, 1999). According to research by Catalyst, 91 percent of female executives surveyed had a mentor (Ragins, Townsend, and Mattis, 1998). Mentoring relationships are important because they provide both career-enhancing effects and psychological support. Mentoring has been associated with several positive outcomes, including promotions (Dreher and Ash, 1990), increased income (Dreher and Cox, 1996), and enhanced career satisfaction (Ostroff and Kozlowski, 1993).

Although men and women report similar rates of having mentors, most mentors are men (Ragins and Cotton, 1999). This results in differences in the mentoring experiences, for women and men. In particular, women are likely to be involved in cross-gender mentoring relationships, which are known for some complicated dynamics (Clawson and Kram, 1984). Some men worry that supporting women may be seen as a threat to their next promotion—or even their job (Kram and Hall, 1996). Others may worry about the possibility that the relationship may be misconstrued as romantic (Clawson and Kram, 1984).

Ragins and Cotton (1991) identified several perceived barriers to women's obtaining a male mentor: women have less informal access to men, such as through sports or other social outings; women are reluctant to develop a mentoring relationship with a man because others may disapprove of the relationship; women fear that mentors or others may misconstrue it as a sexual advance; and potential male mentors are unwilling to engage in relationships with women. Several participants in our women-only program have also described complicated efforts to find male mentors interested in forming alliances because the senior males are reluctant to take the risk of working with a woman.

One advantage of cross-gender mentoring relationships is that male mentors may bring greater power to the relationship than female mentors, enabling their protégées to secure better rewards. In a study with M.B.A. graduates, Dreher and Cox (1996) found that junior managers or protégés earned more if they had a male mentor than a female one. Ragins and Cotton (1999) also found that both men and women with a history of male mentors receive greater compensation than protégés with a female mentor.

There is some support for the idea that women in a mixed-gender relationship are at a disadvantage in terms of the psychosocial components. Typically, mentoring relationships can provide psychosocial functions such as friendship, acceptance, role modeling, counseling, and an enhanced sense of effectiveness. Anecdotally, participants in the women's leadership program have told us that it is difficult to get these sorts of benefits from a mentor who is very different from oneself. The research data, however, are equivocal. Thomas (1990) reported that women protégées with women mentors receive more psychosocial benefits in the form of mutuality and trust than women in cross-sex relationships. At CCL's 1992 conference on workplace diversity, he explained that women in a cross-gender relationship may be at a disadvantage (Morrison, Ruderman, and Hughes-James, 1993). Further, Ragins and McFarlin (1990) found that protégés in a cross-gender relationship were less likely to engage in social activities with mentors after work. However, other studies have found no difference in the psychosocial outcomes of same-gender and cross-gender mentoring relationships for women (Ensher and Murphy, 1997). It is unclear why these differences exist.

Research on this topic is difficult because the limited number of available women mentors makes it complicated to study this phenomenon. However, given the growing numbers of women in the managerial workforce, we expect this to change. In the future, there will be greater opportunity to study women mentoring women and women mentoring men (O'Neill and Blake-Beard, 2002). The future should also help us better understand the interaction of gender with race when it comes to mentoring (Blake-Beard, 2001). Research from Catalyst (1999) suggests that women of color have less access to mentors than white women do. Similarly, Bell and Nkomo (2001) reported that the pioneering African American women in their study had few mentors. Catalyst (2002) suggests that the number of mentors is especially important for women of color and is in fact related to the number of promotions they receive.

Network Relationships. Like mentoring relationships, network relationships are important in the career development process (Ibarra, 1995). They provide support for managers who share similar issues and challenges; serve as informal organizational information channels; lead to sources of feedback on abilities, performance, and perceptions of others; and enhance organizational savvy (Morrison, 1992).

Two types of relationships are formed through networks: instrumental and expressive. Dan, a senior manager of a division that was growing, was posting a newly created position. He had been working on a special task force with Kathryn, a manager just beginning her career in the company. He thought the new position would be a good match for Kathryn, so he called her and told her about the job. That evening, Kathryn called Robin, a friend and confidante who had joined the company at the same time as she had, to share her excitement at Dan's interest in her career and to ask Robin's help in thinking through the pros and cons of applying for the new position.

Dan's relationship with Kathryn is an example of an instrumental relationship: one that provides job-related, career-enhancing benefits such as access to resources, exchange of information, expertise, advice, political access, and material resources. Kathryn's relationship with Robin is an example of an expressive relationship. Characterized by higher levels of closeness and trust than ties that are only instrumental, expressive relationships provide friendship and social support (Ibarra, 1993).

In some ways, formal relationship networks resemble an official organizational chart: they consist of work-related relationships such as subordinate-supervisor dyads, work groups, project teams, and committees. These relationships tend to produce instrumental relationships. Informal networks, by contrast, emerge naturally within the organization. They are usually broader than formal networks because they include relationships that are work-related, social, or both, and because they are more likely to produce expressive relationships in addition to instrumental ones. Another distinction between formal and informal networks is that informal networks are established by the individual, who thus creates a network as diverse or homogeneous as he or she wants. In this sense, informal networks can be used as a strategy for career advancement because they are determined by the manager. It is this type of network that the research literature has focused on in relation to sexual differences.

The strategic benefits of networks can be substantial. The composition of a person's network can determine her access to resources, her power, and her ability to implement her agenda (Ibarra, 1993). That is, the higher the organizational status of the people in someone's network, and the further out in the organization the network reaches, the potentially more powerful it is.

The problem, though, is that women managers of different backgrounds report limited access to informal networks (Kanter, 1977; Linehan, 2001). For example, in interviews with fifty European senior female managers, Linehan (2001) found that forty-three perceived a serious lack of networking opportunities for women. This exclusion resulted in less visibility and connection to people of influence, thereby reinforcing gender inequalities in organizations.

In a now-landmark study, Ibarra (1992) found differences in the networking experiences of male and female managers. She compared men and women of similar educational and experiential backgrounds and learned that men are more likely to gain access to the networks of key organizational players. Women tend to have two types of networks: one of women, characterized by expressive ties and used as a source of social support, and one of men, which provides more instrumental support. These differences occur because people develop networks of similar others because they are drawn to them for friendship. However, since other women are unlikely to be high-status individuals, women lose out on being friends with people in power and tend to have only instrumental relationships with them. Managing two different networks, one for expressive purposes and one for instrumental purposes, can be stressful and time-consuming. A second difference is that women tend to have to reach out further in the organization to find other women with whom to network. Due to the abundant supply of men, male managers tend to have narrower networks. Ibarra (1993) therefore argues that the context of modern organizations influences the type of network participation available to women and men.

Ibarra points out that the situation is even more complicated for women who are racial minorities than for women who are white. Women of color have an additional dimension of difference to work through and must look even wider into the organization to find similar others (see also Chapter Ten).

Implications. There are numerous actions that women can take to increase their access to relationships for learning. Attending a single-identity training program provides an excellent source of support in a safe environment. It also sets the foundation for networks and developmental relationships outside of one's organization. Many participants in CCL's programs maintain contact with one another long after the end of the program. For instance, in the women's feedback-intensive program, many of the women stay in touch with other participants after the program through round-robin letters and calls.

Another avenue for increasing access to developmental relationships with senior managers is an organization's formal mentoring programs. The company sponsors these programs, but the individual manager has to take the initiative to enroll. Individuals must also take the initiative to seek out mentors, look for natural learning opportunities in regular work activities, and avoid overrelying on one mentor by developing relationships with several. On the reverse side, becoming a mentor also has its payoffs. Research has shown that managers serving in mentor positions are colearners, too, and the "seniors" also receive important benefits from the relationship (Kram and Hall, 1996; McCauley and Hughes-James, 1994).

Likewise, if organizations offer employee associations or single-identity networks, women might gain by joining them. Such networks offer a place to develop a richer sense of what is going on in the organization. They are a setting in which women can get feedback, exchange information, and receive support.

Recognition

The developmental experiences I have described so far—360-degree feedback, feedback-intensive programs, challenging assignments, and developmental relationships—are significant for all managers. When combined into a well-thought-out system, these experiences interact to facilitate the growth of people in leadership positions. However, studies of the career experiences of women suggest that a critical piece is missing. The missing strategy is recognition (Morrison, 1992).

Recognition is important because it reinforces managers for their education, training, skills, risk taking, and capabilities. Rewards acknowledge a job well done. This in turn enhances managers' self-esteem and increases their commitment to the organization. Furthermore, rewards symbolize one's worth and value to the organization. Many organizations are reluctant to give women the same rewards that go to male executives because they doubt women's competence or commitment. Women receive fewer rewards and resources than they legitimately deserve. Women need the same rewards as men; the problem is that the rewards are less available to them.

One type of recognition reflecting a large differential between men and women is compensation. There is a great deal of evidence that white men lead the way in compensation even when women and people of color are comparably qualified. According to a recent study by the General Accounting Office (2001) on the status of women in management in ten selected industries, women earn between 55 and 91 cents for every dollar made by male managers. The difference in the differential depends on the industry, with the widest gap in the retail trade and the smallest in educational services. In every industry, women managers earned less than their male colleagues. Women are not receiving starting salaries comparable to those of men, and they do not receive equal salaries as they advance (Brett and Stroh, 1999).

Another significant form of reward is promotion, and here too there are differences in how decisions are made. Managers outside the mainstream usually carry the responsibility for a particular job before getting the formal promotion. One organization CCL worked with was reluctant to reward women with big promotions (Ruderman, Ohlott, and Kram, 1995) and often required them to become "acting manager" or fill "assistant positions" before they were promoted to the actual position. When they asked why, the women were told they were "not ready"—even though men with similar career histories were promoted directly to those slots without first serving in an apprenticeship position.

These small promotions create discrepancies in recognition. They make capable, competent managers feel devalued. Women often work under a double burden: they believe that they work harder than their male counterparts and yet receive less recognition. This may be compounded by additional challenges, such as being the first person other than a white male in the position and pressures to perform better than a man. This creates a feeling of imbalance that Morrison (1992) suggests leads to turnover or ambivalence about advancing in the corporation. Many women are leaving corporate life because they do not feel the rewards for investing in their career are there (Catalyst, 1996). To keep women with executive potential in the corporation and on track with their development, it is important that organizations reward them fairly and appropriately. This is a serious issue in terms of inclusion.

A different problem with rewards is that they can become overused. In an effort to make their diversity efforts highly visible, some corporations give out rewards to women before they are ready. For example, Linda, a white woman we worked with, had been promoted too fast and was struggling in a job she was not prepared for. This led many people—including Linda herself—to question the integrity of the diversity effort. For rewards to be used as a force for development, they must be seen as deserved.

One complexity in using rewards for development is that they have the potential to be misused through overapplication or underapplication. Overly positive, unearned rewards are as much of a problem as lack of recognition.

Although recognition as an element for development comes out of Morrison's work on the new leaders (1992), it seems to us that it is an important strategy for development for all potential leaders. Developing executive leadership skills requires an incredible investment of time, energy, and effort. Recognition for handling challenges well, taking risks, learning, and growing is essential and should be there for all.

Implications for Leadership Development

To foster development of a diverse group of managers, the individuals responsible for leadership development in an organization need to make some changes. The basic practices of 360-degree feedback, feedback-intensive programs, challenging assignments, and developmental relationships are as important for the development of women as they are for men. These experiences promote and sustain development and address the common needs of all employees. They improve everybody's leadership potential.

However, the harsh reality is that women of all colors have less access to these experiences than white males do. If women are to develop their full leadership strength and contribute fully to their organizations, this reality must change.

Companies must modify their development practices to ensure that they are accessible to all and appropriately applied. One other concern is that these strategies not be the only major forces for development in this population. Recognition of skills, efforts, and abilities plays a key role in the leadership development process and should not be overlooked.

What can human resource professionals do to make sure their development programs fully address the needs of women? Here are some ideas:

• *Increase the opportunities for informal assessment of women by dealing with their isolation.* Encourage development of formal employee associations or networks for particular identity groups. These homogeneous groups help managers share common experiences and concerns. They give managers the opportunity to form developmental relationships with each other. Such relationships provide support as well as opportunities for informal feedback.

We found that after attending our women-only leadership development program, many women went back to their organizations and either joined an existing group or created a new group for networking women. These groups serve as a place in which they can support one another, validate what is going on in their experiences, and get the informal feedback they often miss in a mixed environment. If the organization does not have its own networking group, it can support women who join professional or industry association groups that support women. In our research, for example, we heard several women speak of benefits they derived from the Society for Women Engineers.

• *Encourage women to take advantage of opportunities for formal developmental assessment.* Structured assessment and feedback, such as that offered through 360-degree instruments, can be part of a larger development program. Opportunities exist to get this feedback in a single-identity or mixed-identity group. One industry association CCL works with has arranged for large numbers of its managerial women to participate in feedback-intensive programs. This association sponsors a single-identity program for high-potential women from different organizations in the industry so that women can get support from each other and assessment data at the same time.

• *Educate facilitators and trainers in how to provide 360-degree feedback to a diverse population.* Make sure practitioners are aware of the norms for different groups. Prepare them to handle discussions about the impact of prejudice on perceptions. Make sure they select feedback tools based on samples with validity evidence for both men and women.

• *Help decision makers understand how to develop and create appropriately challenging assignments.* These should take into account the extra challenges experienced by women managers. Too little challenge results in little growth; too much challenge overwhelms the learning process. Decision makers need guidance in matching individual managers with developmental assignments; they may need training to understand the different sources of challenge and to identify them in assignments. They may need to rethink how they distribute relocation opportunities so that women get appropriate consideration.

• *Help managers learn from these challenging assignments.* Although challenging situations provide opportunities for development, they do not guarantee it. They only provide the data for possible learning. To help people extract learning from the experience, make sure the assignment includes some opportunity for reflection (Seibert, 1996). Learning journals are one way in which managers can keep track of what they are learning. The learning process is key, and it is important that managers engaged in developmental experiences have the opportunity to consciously reflect on their learning.

• *Educate majority managers on how to initiate and develop relationships with people who are different from themselves.* Relational competency is a key requirement for successful performance in the organizations of today and the near future (Fletcher, 1999; Goleman, 1995; Hall and Associates, 1996). People skilled in relationships with those different from themselves can use these skills broadly in organizations. A key competency for the future is the ability to lead across differences.

• *Examine the formal developmental relationships presently offered in your organization—* formal mentoring programs, mentoring circles, learning partners, and so forth. Are they genuinely accessible to managers not in the mainstream? These kinds of programs provide learning opportunities and support to everyone involved, but they are especially important for overcoming the extra challenges faced by women.

• *Review the types and levels of rewards distributed to women and men.* Specifically, compensation, promotion, and bonus levels need to be reviewed to assess whether or not there are disparities in gender. Such disparities undermine the best-laid plans for developing diversity. Softer forms of rewards, such as invitations to work with senior executives, lunch with executives, announcements of achievements, and awards, need to be examined as well.

A Systemic Approach to Leadership Development

Modifying opportunities and procedures for assessment, effectively using challenge, shoring up systems of support, and assessing the fairness of formal and informal rewards are important steps to take in developing the leadership abilities of women; however, these steps should not be considered in isolation from one another. It is important that these elements be considered interdependent parts of a larger system of development. They work in concert with one another: together they are more than the sum of the parts.

In considering the interdependencies of strategies of assessment, challenge, support, and recognition, it is important that these strategies be balanced (Morrison,

1992). For example, too much job challenge without recognition and support leads to problems. The extra challenges women experience can deter even the most ambitious of people unless they are mitigated by support and recognition. Organizations are losing some of their most promising talent because challenges are not counterbalanced with support, recognition, and assessment. In contrast, too much support without much challenge or assessment leads to superficial learning. Inappropriate recognition, such as continuously putting women in the limelight, can result in resentment from peers and overscrutiny of the managers.

Developing leaders require a balance of all of these forces. This issue of balancing assessment, challenge, support, and recognition can and should be discussed individually with women managers. This discussion, however, is even more appropriate at the organizational level, looking across groups of employees. Most methods of managing imbalance require organizational solutions as well as individual ones. The modifications discussed in this chapter offer ways to help balance these principles in an organization.

Organizational Strategies for Leadership Development for Women

In addition to examining how these elements of leadership development interact with one another, it is important to consider them in the context of the larger organizational culture and climate. To effectively develop women leaders, the whole organization needs to be in the picture. Providing women with opportunities for assessment, challenge, support, and recognition is a necessary but insufficient condition. The general organizational climate needs to be considered as well.

Leadership development efforts should take the goals and needs of women into account to develop a climate supportive of both genders. Meyerson and Fletcher (2000) point out that the "glass ceiling that's holding women executives back is not just above them, it's all around them, in the whole structure of the organization in which we work: the beams, the walls, the very air. . . . Most of the barriers that persist today are insidious—a revolution couldn't find them to blast them away" (pp. 127, 131). To develop the leadership capacity of an organization so as to capitalize on the influx of women managers we must understand the factors that influence the organizational culture and the insidious forces holding women back. Organizations interested in retaining their female talent would be wise to address the features of their culture that are incompatible with the advancement of women.

Even with all the research that has gone into investigating the glass ceiling and organizational climate, there still is no clear answer as to exactly what organizations should do. Goodman, Fields and Blum (forthcoming) have found that women are more likely to thrive in establishments that emphasize promotion and development and that have women in top management. The practices reviewed in this chapter—360-degree feedback, feedback-intensive programs, challenging assignments, and developmental relationships—go part of the way toward identifying factors that contribute to a climate of development. These developmental practices and other efforts, such as work-family programs that address the need for wholeness and other diversity initiatives, may help create a more inclusive environment in which organizations can gain a competitive advantage from the full utilization of the skills of managers of both genders.

Conclusion

Increasing gender diversity in an organization depends on more than a select few leadership development practices. To have the best chance at developing a diverse organization, all human resource systems need to be adapted so that they are inclusive of all managers. Full inclusion of women requires thinking about the development expectations of women. The leadership development practices discussed here are just part of the work. Succession planning, staffing, compensation, benefit policies, and other policies need to be modified as well. Above all, it is vital that the leaders at the top of the organization act as role models, demonstrating and supporting norms that encourage multiple ways to lead and advance in organizations. For guidance on the steps necessary to make such sweeping changes, several helpful resources exist (Cox, 1993; Jackson and Associates, 1992; Kossek and Lobel, 1996; Morrison, 1992).

CHAPTER TEN

LEADER DEVELOPMENT ACROSS RACE

Ancella B. Livers
Keith A. Caver

M eredith, white, middle-aged, and very competent, listened with growing surprise. As the HR director, she had prided herself for creating a color-blind organization, a place, she thought, where everyone had an equal chance at being developed as a leader. The company had a strong equal employment opportunity policy—one in which it believed. It dealt harshly with discrimination and harassment of any sort. And it had well-publicized procedures on what to do if someone were a victim of any kind of discrimination. Yet as she listened to Calvin, she realized that even with all of the precautions and regulations, he was leaving because he didn't think he could grow as a leader in this organization.

Calvin hadn't planned to actually tell the truth during his exit interview. Instead, he intended simply to say that he had found a great opportunity elsewhere and express how sorry he was to be leaving. As an African American, he had learned long ago to share only what needed to be shared and to keep the rest of his thoughts to himself. He hadn't planned to say anything until he sat across from Meredith, and it was clear that she had very little understanding of what he had experienced in this company. So in spite of the fact that he had always been warned not to burn his bridges, he decided to say some of what was on his mind.

Calvin started by telling Meredith that the organization's climate made it difficult for those who were not white to develop as leaders. Part of the problem, Calvin said, was the pervasive belief that the workplace was color-blind. In reality, however, the workplace was not color-blind at all. But because the culture supporting this notion was so strong, anyone who saw it differently was branded as a troublemaker or at the very least as misguided or ill-informed. Consequently, conversations that might have led to organizational culture and systems change toward a more inclusive environment never happened. The organization's leaders and members were so clear about their perception of race and leadership and how they believed those elements played out in the organization that they had never considered examining or challenging their own viewpoints.

Yet as he looked at the organization, Calvin saw very few people of color in positions of authority; neither had he noticed people of color getting challenging job assignments at the same rate as their white colleagues—experiences that could help them stretch and grow—nor had he seen many getting assignments to senior executives for mentoring or getting important opportunities for classroom-based leader development. Sure, people of color were in middle management, and maybe two or three were in the senior or executive ranks. In addition, one or two people of color were involved in true stretch assignments, but when he considered how few these opportunities were, compared to all that were available, he was less than impressed with his odds of becoming an organizational leader. If he were to be moved to a new assignment, he believed it would likely be to one of those areas that affected other people of color, such as district supervisor over employees who worked in the region that covered the black part of town. The joke among the people of color was that people went into those jobs and were never again seen in the broader organization. From Calvin's viewpoint, the people in those jobs certainly weren't seen as leaders. They never seemed to garner much experience, visibility, or influence. In fact, as far as Calvin was concerned, anyone who identified "too much" with his or her racial group—speaking up for black issues, being seen with other African Americans too much of the time, allowing the black experience to inform his or her understanding and judgments—wasn't given even small opportunities to grow. In terms of leadership roles, it was as if these people ceased to exist.

As Meredith listened to Calvin, she grew increasingly dismayed. She had believed that people of color would be most effective and most comfortable working in areas where their cultural expertise was needed, and she had believed those areas were working with and for other people of color. She also assumed that if people of color wanted broader opportunities, they would ask for them and not just wait for someone to make an offer. And to be honest, she had never considered the organizational climate to be stifling in terms of development for ethnic and racial minorities. Meredith was particularly stunned by Calvin's concerns about identity. He said that being African American was an integral part of who he was, including who he was as a leader. He added that to have to leave part of himself at home when he came to work every day meant that the company was not getting the full benefit of his life experience. Being white, Meredith had never consciously thought of her racial identity and the impact it had on her work. It wasn't so much that she disagreed with Calvin; it was that she had never considered this concept as a relevant issue, nor had she realized that people didn't feel free to be who they were at work. She believed in the color-blind workplace, and this was the first time she had heard that the oft-stated value might dampen discussions around difference rather than enhance equality.

Calvin shared many other things with Meredith, but they all ended in the same place: in his estimation, the organization was not a place where people of color could easily be developed as leaders, and he wanted to be recognized and developed. He felt that he was skilled, capable, and worthy of attention. So he was leaving, and she was surprised.

The story of Meredith and Calvin is a fictional account of real-life perceptions that occur daily in organizations. While executives in many companies believe they have created a workplace that is ripe for leader development, nontraditional professionals (in this case, people of color) may have a very different perspective on what is actually taking place. All may agree that organizations should set the climate for leader development, but they may disagree on whether that climate is being effectively set and managed. Indeed, we would argue that the dynamic created by the introduction of race in the workplace sunders the climate for leader development largely because race is often not taken into account.

This chapter focuses on the leadership development of people of color and the roles that difference and organizational context play in that development. Toward this end, we will first look at why difference matters in organizations; that is, how organizations react to people who are different and how that reaction can impede their leader development. Next, we will focus on the impact of miasma on the key elements of leader development: assessment, challenge, and support. *Miasma* is the climate created as a by-product of difference and the reaction to it. We will look at specific aspects of miasma for African Americans—identity, responsibility, networking, and mentoring—and consider how they affect the work lives of blacks and how, in turn, these individuals tend to respond to their environment. Finally, we offer suggestions as to what can be done to enhance the leadership potential of people of color and African American managers in particular.

Because organizations tend to respond similarly to any element of racial difference, we begin by looking at racial difference broadly defined. As we move through the chapter, we will narrow our focus to African Americans. Our reason for doing this is twofold. First, we have chosen black managers because the vast majority of our research regarding leading from a different racial perspective is on African Americans. Second, we believe that our own professional experience as African American managers in the workplace provides us with additional insight into the phenomenon we are discussing. While we realize that different racial groups have different forms of miasma, we do believe that one group can serve as a template to guide our thinking about the experience and treatment of other groups. Though it is our intent that generalizations be made from our research on African Americans to other racial groups in terms of identifying baseline issues, we recognize that any particular racial group will have specific issues unto itself. We hope that the types of issues we raise about African Americans will prompt others to consider the questions they need to ask to illuminate the specialized aspects of miasma for all people of color. Note that many of the examples used in this chapter reflect the real experiences of participants in our research, but all names have been changed.

The Organizational Context: Assumption of Similarity, Reality of Difference

Equality is an important espoused value in the United States. Because of this, people often make the assumption that everyone is really treated in the same way and that differences do not exist or are inconsequential. Yet what people in organizations often do not understand is that the different experiences some people are having in the workplace really do matter. Rather than try to directly explore and understand the implications of differences in the workplace, some organizations adopt a casually neglectful attitude toward issues of difference. The organizational hierarchy puts forth statements and policies of equality but takes little notice of ways in which people are perceived and treated differently, often inequitably, and does nothing to correct the situation. That is, they operate under an assumption of similarity while a reality of difference actually permeates the corporate environment—often stifling the nontraditional leaders' experience. This decision to operate under the assumption of similarity is most likely influenced by the strong cultural and organizational values placed on fairness and equality and by the discomfort most people feel examining behaviors and systems that are out of line with their espoused values. Nevertheless, this assumption of similarity works as a powerful, subtly hegemonic force, shaping the fiction that all employees are having essentially the same workplace experience.

We know from our research, however, that people do experience work very differently. The Center for Creative Leadership's Lessons of a Diverse Workforce study underscores the differences between white and black managers (Douglas, 2003). Managers taking part in the study were asked to identify the experiences in their career that were particularly important in their development. White managers in this study proportionally identified more challenging assignments than their African American counterparts did. Whites identified more assignments involving turning around an ailing business, project or task force assignments, and assignments requiring starting something from scratch than black managers did. All of these jobs provide fruitful learning experiences to which African Americans seem to be less privy than their white colleagues. Conversely, African Americans identified more hardship experiences as developmental than whites did.

These data suggest that white managers are benefiting more from structured learning experiences while blacks are learning in a very different domain. Blacks certainly report more racial situations than their white counterparts do— situations in which they learned that despite their early success in education and career, race still matters. Perhaps it is not surprising, then, that as a group, blacks appear to be more cynical about the workplace.

Remember Calvin's initial plan to keep his thoughts about his work experience to himself and his belief that few developmental assignments would be offered him? From Calvin's perspective, there was little value in trying to share with Meredith something she was unlikely and probably unwilling to see, and it made little sense to count on developmental opportunities he believed would never come. For Calvin, like many African Americans, the workplace is fraught with subtle examples that they are not full and equal partners in the business of the organization or the leadership development process.

In spite of these and other data on race in organizations (America and Anderson, 1996; Bell and Nkomo, 2001; Cox, 2001; Fernandez and Davis, 1999), many companies operate as if the *desire* to have a color-blind workplace is a self-fulfilling prophecy. This determination to believe in the existence of a color-blind workplace stifles conversation about the differences that people experience by making them undiscussable. As a consequence, it is almost impossible for nontraditional leaders to make others understand that the workplace can be very different for people who diverge from the norm racially or in some other way. Thus marginalized, nontraditional leaders must negotiate in an environment in which their experience may be denied and, for them at least, the fictive reality that everyone is the same is touted as the truth. This marginalization impedes the developmental opportunities people of color receive and thus can stymie their leader development.

When an organization does not embrace or acknowledge these issues of difference, nontraditional professionals can become further alienated as well as less willing to be acclimatized to the organization's environment. Integrating into these organizational conditions may come at a significant cost to their personal, racial, or cultural identity. Under these circumstances, people can lose a sense of connection to the organization, believe that they are not seen as vital and important contributors, and develop a decreased level of trust in others different from them.

Again, think of the situation of Calvin and Meredith and their different assumptions about the importance of racial identity. As a white woman, Meredith did not understand race as a central aspect of identity. For Calvin, race was central to his identity because this was the aspect on which he felt he was most harshly judged. A major part of his self-awareness had to do with the meaning of being black in a white society: he was conscious of how his race had influenced his life experiences so far, and those experiences had taught him lessons that informed his thinking. By denying his racial identity and the impact that race had in the organization, Calvin felt undercut—and unable to be as effective as his skills and experience promised he could be.

Assessment, Challenge, and Support for African Americans

One way to begin looking at African Americans and leader development is to see how being black affects assessment, challenge, and support (ACS), the elements of leader development. Being different can cause leaders or potential leaders to be assessed unfairly, according to stereotypical notions rather than demonstrated skills and actual behaviors. Being different can cause leaders to be overly evaluated, formally or informally, as their mainstream counterparts consciously or unconsciously expect them to be less than competent. Inaccurate assumptions about difference can overchallenge people as well when nontraditional leaders have to exceed expectations and work to overturn unflattering perceptions in order to succeed. Support for nontraditional leaders can also be affected. People of color often do not feel supported by their organizations, either through the emotional support provided by peers in their immediate work group or through organizational support systems such as formal mentoring. As a result, people of color often feel that they must take care of each other, providing both emotional and career support. This responsibility is an additional, unique challenge, since it is not formally recognized or rewarded in most organizations.

The next three sections look at each of the ACS elements and examine their unique characteristics for African Americans in the workplace.

Assessment

One aspect of assessment that can be a problem for African Americans is the fairness and validity of the measures used to assess them. Managers are often assessed with informal observation and formal feedback, through the organization's performance appraisal system or through use of a multirater feedback instrument (see Chapter Two). In any assessment process, the desire is for managers to see the positive feedback they receive as areas of strength, and negative feedback as a signal of some need for change. This process, however, can be badly subverted if those receiving feedback, whether for development or for performance review, believe that it has been shaped by bias and prejudice (Cox, 1993). Any time the validity of assessment data is in question, a manager's first reaction will be to reject the data. From a development standpoint, African American managers find it difficult to learn from discrepancies between self-views and the views of others if they believe that prejudice is involved. So whenever black managers are included in a population being assessed, the potential for bias becomes an important consideration.

We still don't know whether differences in the ratings can be attributed to rater bias. One study that looked at bias in the context of 360-degree feedback examined the question of whether raters give higher ratings to managers of their own race (Mount, Sytsma, Hazucha, and Holt, 1997). Working with a large sample of managers, the researchers found that some categories of raters (bosses, peers, and direct reports) do indeed assign higher ratings to managers of their own race. In their study, white bosses rated white direct reports higher than they did black direct reports. However, there was no significant difference in the way white direct reports rated black or white bosses. The findings about white ratings of black peers were mixed. The patterns of black raters, however, were different. All three categories of black raters (bosses, peers, and direct reports) rate blacks' performance higher than whites' performance.

The researchers posit several hypotheses for this finding. First, research indicates that people tend to rate those whom they trust more highly than those whom they do not trust. It is possible then that blacks may trust other blacks more than they do their white counterparts. And indeed, our research suggests that trust is an important issue for black managers (Livers and Caver, 2003). In addition, high ratings may be a result of friendship. Because there are fewer blacks in organizations, it is more likely the blacks who are rating one another are friends; this is not an assumption one can make about white colleagues. These positive ratings may also be related to the feeling blacks have about supporting each other in an otherwise hostile environment. It may also be that because of reduced opportunities and related factors, black managers are demonstrably stronger managers by the time they are given the opportunity to lead. Clearly, more research is needed to further explore these issues.

One implication for feedback is that black managers with white raters may want to pay the most attention to what their direct reports say, since they seem to be fairly equitable in their ratings. This research supports the use of an assessment method that provides a 360-degree view of a person and also raises questions about the value of getting feedback from a single source, such as a boss. Because of the research findings, black managers may find it helpful to get supervisor ratings from more than one source, including a black boss or senior manager, if one is available.

In addition to bias in assessment, overassessment can be an issue for nontraditional managers. Whether it comes in the form of collection and review of more data prior to a promotion or closer supervision when given a developmental assignment, excessive evaluation adds significant challenge as black leaders feel a need to exceed expectations and manage perceptions that are often not flattering.

Challenge

As we said earlier, CCL's research underscores the point that whites and blacks are having different developmental experiences (Douglas, 2003). White managers are more likely to report learning significant lessons from assignments, while black managers are more likely to report learning from hardship experiences. Both of these types of experience contain challenge. Although we cannot say that black managers are more or less challenged than white managers, we can say that they are challenged *differently* by what they encounter on the job.

The type of challenge embedded in difficult assignments is the challenge to master new knowledge, to build new skills, and to develop new perspectives. In challenging assignments, managers learn to motivate and develop others, to shoulder responsibility, to confront problem employees, to find new ways of thinking about problems and opportunities, to manage scope, to deal with ambiguity, and to prioritize and make trade-offs (see Chapter Five). Hardships, by contrast, teach different lessons to both white and black managers: lessons about humility, about other people's perceptions and organizational politics, about how to better handle relationships and understand people, and about how to handle mistakes and loss (see Chapter Six). For black managers, hardships include an event not experienced by whites: learning yet again that race matters.

"Race-mattered" events are the incidents of prejudice, stereotyping, and discrimination that African Americans experience throughout their careers. Examples include dealing with other people's perceptions that they received job assignments or promotions because of their race or having to confront a boss about racial tension in the relationship after receiving a negative performance appraisal. African American managers have described these race-mattered experiences as leading to lasting changes in their management style. "I learned that to succeed, my management competence would need to be clearly demonstrable to all," one said. Another added, "I learned that I will have to find innovative ways to break down some barriers I face."

For African Americans, challenge lies not only in job assignments and hardships but also in the overall organizational climate in which they have to work—what we term *miasma*. While the race-mattered events reported by managers in our research illustrate the impact of miasma in its most overt form, there are more subtle nuances in organizations that come into play. We have discussed the challenge that can come from being assessed far more often than white colleagues and the challenge of drawing meaning from assessments where one suspects bias may color results. The next section, on support, ties in to the issues of challenge. Many blacks take on additional responsibility for providing formal and informal support to other blacks in environments where formal organizational support is in short supply.

Support

Support can take many forms. It can be formal or informal. It can come from individual relationships or from organizational systems or practices. As it is for all leaders, support is a crucial part of the development and work experience of blacks. Yet many blacks feel unsupported by their organizations. This lack of support is closely related to the organizational culture issues described earlier. As long as the workplace is inaccurately assumed by the majority of members to be color-blind, the need for support in issues where race matters will not be forthcoming.

Yet even though African Americans may sometimes feel unsupported through formal means, they are often sustained informally by other African Americans. Through activities such as networking with and mentoring new blacks in an organization, African American managers show their support for each other and for those whom they feel might otherwise be alone or have difficulty acclimatizing.

The support blacks provide each other is often less about work and career needs than about personal needs. It is generally known that people feel most comfortable with others like themselves. Often similarity of experience allows people to communicate more freely and understand each other more readily. For many black managers, this is particularly important because they work in relative isolation from day-to-day contact with other black employees and so keenly appreciate the opportunity to be with someone with whom they can practice their culture and around whom they don't have to worry about being misinterpreted because of race.

One African American man in our research said he found socializing at work very difficult because no one asked him to lunch. Consequently, he said, he made up his mind to reach out to every black employee who came to work on his campus. They would all know, he said, "that there was a black person who would reach out and welcome them. . . ."

Blacks' search for support in an organization can become very poignant. For instance, many African American managers want support in the form of being able to make mistakes. They feel pressure to be perfect for fear that their mistakes will jeopardize other blacks' opportunities. A number of African Americans interviewed in a CCL study said they just wanted the organization to see them as human and as wanting the same things for the organization that their white and other nonblack counterparts do (Livers and Caver, 2003). For these people, support is simply a matter of being shown the respect that they are due but that they often feel they do not receive.

Another form of support critical to nontraditional managers is recognition: for a job well done, for educational achievements, or for the acquisition of new skills. Recognition can take many forms, from informal positive feedback in the moment to formal announcements and celebrations, from salary increases to promotions. Recognition helps establish a manager's credibility and reinforce his or her capabilities, skills, education, training, and the risk taking involved in learning. While recognition is a necessary form of support for the development of all managers, it is particularly important in the development of black managers in organizations because they tend to get little of it.

Take the experience of Dan Carroll, for example, an African American manager for a household goods company. After a particularly successful year, Carroll's manager called him at his office one night to congratulate him on his top sales figures. However, this same boss feted Carroll's white colleague, whose sales numbers were good but not as good as Carroll's, at the office during the day when others would be aware of the honor. Dan's situation was one in which a job well done was recognized in a private rather than a public way. Although he did receive recognition from his boss, this did not send a message to others about how his skills and achievements were valued.

In other instances, blacks may find recognition lacking when it comes to job promotions. African Americans and other people of color may spend more time in beginning-level jobs than their white counterparts. Later, they may be less likely to receive the benefit of the doubt when being promoted. What is seen as a developmental assignment for a white manager may be seen as too risky an assignment for a black manager. Rather than getting a full promotion to director, for example, a black manager may be more likely to be appointed to assistant director so that his or her skills can be assessed before being offered the director's job. Although this might seem reasonable as a developmental step for anyone, research suggests that white managers are less often required to take the assistant job before they are given the responsibility and status of a full promotion (Thomas and Gabarro, 1999). It is true that learning the ropes in an assistant role may help managers be more successful in their next move up, but this practice becomes a source of unfair advantage for whites if it is applied more frequently to African American managers than to white managers, who are exposed earlier to more challenging learning opportunities and better-paid positions. It also sends a message to the employee and to the organization at large about the organization's level of confidence in that employee.

In some organizations, African Americans may be able to supplement weak organizational recognition through participation in corporate-sponsored, single-identity networking groups and social gatherings. In these settings, people can be publicly acknowledged and honored for their accomplishments, as well as encouraged to find sources of social, emotional, and career support. Yet this more limited form of recognition cannot and should not replace recognition that is more widely visible to a manager's immediate work group and to the organization as a whole.

African American Leaders: A Closer Look at Miasma

Tina Williams, an African American psychotherapist, explained that when she talks to school children, she has to tell them that education may allow them to knock on opportunity's door but still may not let them in. "I have attained all that society said needed to be attained in order for doors to be opened and barriers to be taken down," she said, "and I still find them being put in my way—doors being closed and expectations that I should be the way others are and not be myself."

As explained earlier, miasma is what occurs when difference, and the reaction to it, is introduced to the workplace (see Figure 10.1). It is the murky atmosphere of misperception and distortion through which nontraditional leaders must work. This noxious atmosphere operates like a low-lying fog, creating additional challenges not directly related to the work itself, with which people of color must cope and for which most organizations provide little formal support. In this climate, initially benign elements of difference, such as identity, become flashpoints—areas that are rife with misinterpretation and misunderstanding.

In this section, we will take an in-depth look at the four areas we found most prominently contributed to the miasma of black managers (see Exhibit 10.1). Two

FIGURE 10.1. MIASMA AND HOW IT WORKS.

of these areas, identity and responsibility, have a largely internal focus: they speak to African Americans' views of themselves and the behaviors in which they believe they should engage for their own good and that of the larger black community. The issues of identity and responsibility are sources of added challenge for black leaders. The remaining two areas, networking and mentoring, have an external focus: they are strategies that can help blacks more effectively navigate the workplace. They offer useful support to help managers face the additional challenge.

Identity: Bringing One's Whole Self to Work

For most African Americans, being black is one of the most salient issues in their workplace experience. Although their racial identity grants them a sense of uniqueness, it often puts them in a position of disadvantage and even loss. That is, many black managers feel they cannot be themselves at work.

Our study revealed that more than 50 percent of black professionals surveyed believe they have had to give up some of their identity as African Americans in order to effectively perform their jobs. While blacks may feel that these sacrifices of self are necessary to succeed in organizations, they also find them difficult to make. Even if they have not given away so much of themselves that their behaviors and values are at odds, many blacks are aware that being black in corporate America can set their desired expressions of racial identity and their professional behavior at loggerheads. Identity issues affect black leaders every day, influencing everything from decisions about their personal dress to their professional strategies and activities. As a result, black managers may see themselves as caught in a continuing struggle to maintain their racial identity while advancing their careers.

The most unique facet of the issue of racial identity in the workplace is that it is not an issue for whites. Although identity issues such as ethnicity, gender, religious affiliation, and other cultural attributes are important for everyone, racial identity is not a problem for people who are in the racial majority. Expressions of

EXHIBIT 10.1. AREAS OF DIFFERENCE.

Additional Challenges
- *Identity:* bringing one's whole self to work
- *Responsibility:* being successful and looking out for each other

Useful Supports
- *Networking:* making meaningful connections
- *Mentoring:* a scarce but valuable resource

the majority group identity are already incorporated into the workplace culture. What is seen as acceptable corporate dress and behavior (hairstyles, clothing, manner of joking and expressing oneself) is based on a historically white, middle-class version of what is appropriate for the corporate world. In general, white professionals do not have to think about expressing their white identity because it is taken for granted—built into the style and norms of what it means to be a professional in America. They do not have to worry about losing their whiteness or leaving it at the door when they come to work. Because they are white, they "fit in" in a way that African Americans and other ethnic and racial minorities do not.

Because whites do not have to consider racial identity as they take on a professional identity, they are less likely to see the significant challenges for others who attempt to express their identity in the workplace—or to recognize the value and importance of what it means to be black, in this case, combined with what it means to be professional. This additional consideration by blacks or other nontraditional professionals helps create the often cumbersome environment we typify as miasma.

Responsibility: Being Successful and Looking Out for Each Other

For many African American leaders, the added challenge posed by responsibility comes in two forms: the need to look after other blacks in the workplace and the need to be successful for the sake of other black managers in the organization. Indeed, 95 percent of African Americans in our study said they felt responsible for helping other blacks at work. This idea of looking after other blacks is both a self-imposed notion and something that is often asked by the organizations. The self-imposed aspect stems partly from group identity and partly from the environmentally induced identity crises that many professional blacks share. Helping each other is often a black leader's way of compensating for an environment that may not be willing to assist or understand black professionals. Often organizations expect black managers to take on racial issues at work, to tend to the needs of other black employees, and to be role models in the community. The sense of responsibility that African Americans feel toward other blacks makes it hard to say no to the organization's request to take on formal mentoring relationships or sponsorship of activities intended to be of benefit to their black colleagues, regardless of the cost to them in terms of time or energy. As we have stated earlier, the weight of expectations on African American leaders can be enormous—expectations of the organization, of other black employees, of the black community, and of themselves.

The overwhelming affirmative response to our survey question regarding blacks' sense of responsibility is a testament to their commitment to one another. It is also a perfect example of how not only the organization but also African

American culture can place additional burdens on its members. This joint sense of commitment and responsibility leads many blacks to feel that their future success is dependent on what other African Americans do; they become elated, depressed, or embarrassed in response to the words and actions of black public figures.

Conversely, black leaders often believe that their mistakes are generalized to other blacks in the organization. Feeling personally and collectively invested in the performance and success of their black colleagues, black managers may maintain a hyperawareness about what and how they are doing in the organization. It is not unusual for black employees to keep track of how many African Americans work for the organization, what their general roles are, who is in management, how long they have been there, and what power or influence they have. The grapevine buzzes each time another black person has been hired, all the more so when something happens to one of its black managers, whether good or bad. In addition, once an African American is hired, some blacks on staff may begin assessing the new hire on job competence and attitude about being black: "Is this person 'black' by my standards?" "Do we share viewpoints and backgrounds?" "Is this person likely to help or hinder me and other African Americans here?"

When one considers the additional challenges associated with identity and responsibility for nontraditional leaders, it is not surprising that many black managers grapple with issues of trust. Perhaps because of historical baggage and current experiences, many African Americans do not feel as if they can or should trust their white colleagues or the organizations for which they both work. As one general manager said, "The only people I can truly trust are African Americans." An employee service manager explained, "I don't trust my peers that often. I'm very leery of them." Although not all blacks feel this way, this sentiment was not unusual in our research. This distrust of the workplace makes work a more stressful environment for people of color than it may be for white employees. It is exemplified by the feeling that one must work twice as hard as other managers and continually be on one's guard in organizations.

The perception of many African American leaders that they have to work twice as hard as their predominantly white coworkers is widespread. In their book *Soul in Management* (1996), America and Anderson disagree that this belief is a reality, but they acknowledge that it is pervasive in the black community. It comes up, they note, "in workshops, conferences, books, and casual conversation" (p. 8). We find that this issue arises routinely in CCL's African-American Leadership Program.

Although it has not been extensively researched, there are a number of studies that may indirectly support the idea that blacks and other people of color often have to work harder to receive the same consideration as their white colleagues. Gender pay equity studies, for example, suggest that black women get paid almost the same as white women, but to reach that pay level, they must have greater education (Fernandez and Davis, 1999).

Many African Americans feel as if they have to continuously keep their guard up when they are at work, for a number of reasons. For example, blacks often feel as if people are waiting for them to make mistakes, and if they do make mistakes, many African Americans believe that other blacks will suffer. The end result is that for some blacks, going to work every day is like preparing for battle. As the senior manager of an executive consulting firm said, "People don't see me as always having my battle gear on, but internally these things challenge me. I have to be more personally 'on.'" In talking about the impact on her life of always having her guard up, she continued, "I'm carrying all my gear. I'm tired."

Many of the African Americans we interviewed or surveyed discussed the composite stresses they felt at being black in corporate America (Livers and Caver, 2003). At each step, whether it is because they feel a lack of trust, believe they must work twice as hard, or sense they should keep their guard up, black leaders lament the stress these concerns add to their work life. Indeed, for African Americans, the effects of stress are not additive but multiplicative. Black managers say they do not simply feel a little stress when discussing the impact of identity and responsibility, they feel encompassed by it. The lesson that many blacks learn from work and other social experiences is that race always matters, and it always matters all of the time.

This, then, is the effect of miasma. Because they know they are being treated and seen differently than many of their coworkers, black managers experience added stress in an environment whose culture denies their experience and tells them that all is equal. Consequently, when asked what their organizations could do differently, many African American leaders said they want their companies to see them as unique human beings, full partners in an organization in which they, too, have a vested interest.

Networking: Making Meaningful Connections

Networking, the broad-based skills associated with working through others, can help blacks reverse some of the fragmentation created by the loss of identity, the burden of responsibility, and the other challenges associated with being black in corporate America. The process of networking, however, also poses special challenges for African American professionals.

We define networking as creating and maintaining relationships to enhance work opportunities and to secure social and emotional support. While this definition may apply to all professionals, we have found that lack of trust between blacks and whites in the workplace often hampers effective networking for African Americans. Many blacks perceive that whites may not always honor them as full and equal corporate partners or give them full access to opportunities and information. Such behavior creates significant barriers to networking.

The strategic benefits of networks can be substantial for all leaders. The composition of a person's network can determine his or her access to information, resources, and power, and the ability to implement his or her agenda (Ibarra, 1993). The higher the organizational status of the people in someone's network, and the farther out in the organization or into other organizations the network reaches, the more powerful it can be.

The networks of people of color are likely to be heavily white, because that is who they have most contact with in the organizational context. However, cross-race relationships are less likely to develop into close friendships and so are more likely to be used for professional advancement than for social and emotional support. Also, the networks of people of color are likely to include similar others of their race because that is who they are initially drawn to for camaraderie, support, and friendship (Ibarra, 1995) and for a sense of validation (Morrison, Ruderman, and Hughes-James, 1993). These are the relationships that yield close affiliation.

Yet because people of color are not prevalent in organizations, minority managers often have difficulty finding someone within their immediate work environment with whom they can bond, so they must reach far into the organization to establish connections that produce personally and developmentally close relationships (Ibarra, 1995). Though not traditional, these widespread networks often give people of color access to information throughout the organization while fulfilling their need for affiliation. This information can give people of color a better "feel" for the entire organization than those whose networks are primarily focused upward or are bounded by the lack of necessity to look further than one's own area of the organization for support.

Ironically, because of the many difficulties African Americans face in the workplace, networking is of paramount importance as an aid to maneuvering around obstacles. Networking is vital to gathering and sharing valuable information with colleagues and clients, learning about options and opportunities to enhance job effectiveness or satisfaction, learning about potential pitfalls and how to avoid them, increasing professional or social visibility, garnering opportunities to display professional prowess and build credibility, gaining appropriate support for individual and team efforts, and forging alliances with organizational power brokers and other constituents. Although these benefits are generally associated with networking for all professionals, they are particularly important for African Americans, for whom negotiating the corporate workplace can be particularly tremulous. Networking helps blacks gain the visibility and recognition they often lack. It can also help black managers identify and sidestep potential racial pitfalls in the organization or insulate them from a sense of racial isolation.

There are forces in the workplace that may deter and discourage blacks from networking effectively. Some result from the inherent tension between personal lifestyle requirements or desires and the need to be corporately bicultural—the dynamic created by straddling different personal and professional worlds. For example, Robert Stanley, senior vice president of a polling firm, explained, "We chose to live in the city because our family, friends, church, and everything we do is in the city. If I wanted to just further my career, I would live thirty miles north. It's a whole other take on work-life balance." Stanley said he tried to compensate for not living in the suburbs near work by scheduling lunches or breakfasts with his predominantly white colleagues. He knew that by choosing to live in the city, he was giving up invitations to informal affairs such as dinners and cookouts and consequently losing these opportunities to cement ties with these colleagues.

Other pressures spring from the perceptions and the standards of a traditionally white corporate workplace that does not understand or welcome difference and is sometimes threatened by it. For instance, many blacks discuss experiences where they have been told directly and indirectly not to gather too frequently or openly with other African Americans in the workplace. As one black journalist said, "Every time a few blacks would gather, one of the white editors would come over to see what we were talking about. They never did that when a group of white reporters gathered." Ironically, those African Americans who do network with other African Americans at a percentage larger than they are represented in the organization are seen as more effective leaders (Livers and Brutus, 2000). We speculate that this is because African Americans' black colleagues provide support, career, and racial advice about maneuvering in the corporate environment.

Mentoring: A Scarce but Valuable Resource

Mentoring is in many ways a refinement of the networking concept. Through mentoring, leaders use honed networking skills to partner with others for professional growth and development. Mentoring can be simply described as a purposeful developmental relationship, generally between two individuals. Mentoring relationships may be set up explicitly by organizations through formal programs, or they may develop informally between people over time. Mentoring relationships usually include an expressed or implied commitment between both people to the protégé's development.

Finding Mentors. For African Americans, the source and nature of mentoring often spring from the family rather than the workplace. At the beginning of our African-American Leadership Program, we ask participants to acknowledge those to whom they most credit their professional development and advancement. Overwhelmingly, participants credit family members for contributing to their success and their professional development. Perhaps because the numbers of blacks in the executive ranks are few or because many African American executives are still first- or second-generation professionals, family members have often served as important mentors (Livers and Caver, 2003).

Though such mentoring may seem to provide the same sage counsel any parents would give their children, we believe there is a twist. In our discussions with black professionals, embedded in the advice their parents doled out was hope—paired with strategic tactics and poignant encouragement. Many African American parents gave their children advice for surviving in an often hostile world mingled with the belief that "there will be better days," hope that those days would come in their children's lifetime, and sadness that the odds were against it. Telling black children born in the forties, fifties, and even sixties that they could be what they wanted to be and that they should never quit was both wishful thinking and sound advice.

The challenges associated with mentoring for African Americans are complicated by two additional issues. First, people tend to feel more comfortable with those who look like them or those with whom they share some other allegiance or commonality. Since most of the senior leaders in corporate settings in the United States are white males, the opportunities for black men and women to be identified or sought after as potential candidates for an informal mentoring relationship are often scarce. Similarly, since there are relatively few black senior executives that African American men and women can seek out as mentors, the very absence of blacks in the mentor pool becomes a second stumbling block. These situations leave minority managers in the uncertain position of relying on white males for mentoring, who are often not forthcoming.

Cross-race mentoring, when it occurs, can be very rewarding, but it faces its own challenges. Some whites worry that supporting people of color may be seen as a threat to their own next promotion—or even their job (Kram and Hall, 1996). As one executive for an international oil company said, "I had to prove myself first before they would take a risk and say, 'I am going to help this person.'" Other white mentors may be concerned about the scrutiny that such relationships may bring because of their rarity in the workplace. And some white mentors may be unable to set aside negative preconceptions and stereotypes and fully invest in their protégés. In these instances, mentors may not give protégés the benefit of the doubt. Black protégés who do not feel they have the full support of their mentors may not take risks because they fear that if they fail, they may be disproportionately punished (Thomas, 2001).

All these dynamics contribute to a lack of mentoring support for people of color. When mentoring relationships do occur, there are unique aspects to cross-race relationships that can affect the forms of support that people receive. For instance, in cross-race mentoring, people of color often receive career support (such as sponsorship, advocacy for promotions, feedback, and coaching), but they receive less psychosocial support (emotional, interpersonal bonding) than people in same-race relationships. This difference is likely due to a lack of understanding about racial issues and the difficulty of addressing them in such relationships. Yet the implication is profound; mentoring focused on career support alone does not help minorities succeed as effectively as mentoring that includes interpersonal bonding (Thomas, 2001).

Because professional mentoring opportunities are scarce for minorities, African Americans may also be implicitly challenged to expand their views about where to find mentoring relationships and to assume mentoring responsibilities themselves. For example, they may have to broaden the scope of their mentoring net. Their wide networks often help in this regard. African Americans may need to seek out opportunities to mentor and to be mentored through their community, church, or other social settings. In doing so, however, they must also realize that there are positives and negatives to such actions. While the church or other organizations may contain some very apt mentors, there may be others who, while well meaning, do not have the appropriate background to mentor on the requisite professional issues.

Becoming a Mentor. Mentoring another person can be a powerful experience—especially for African Americans and other nontraditional leaders. This is because the very nature of mentoring allows people to establish personal and professional relationships of great significance. Serving as a mentor may also be one of the few opportunities African American leaders have to showcase their knowledge and understanding of management and the organization.

Strictly speaking, blacks who serve as mentors have a greater opportunity to have white mentees or protégés. This is largely because of the numbers of blacks who could be mentors and the vastly larger number of whites who could be mentees. Such relationships, if formed, would be subject to all of the benefits and difficulties of any cross-race relationship.

While the possibility of black mentor–white mentee relationships is statistically more likely, the reality is that blacks usually find themselves mentoring black or other nontraditional protégés. Again, the dynamic of like people tending to come together, because of ease of communication and because of the responsibilities many blacks feel toward each other, helps spur same-race pairings.

However, these are not the only reasons blacks mentor other blacks. Organizations, too, may use blacks as mentors for other blacks to further organizational goals. While this is similar to the organization's use of any of its employees, being asked to mentor a black manager solely because you are black can be stressful.

One project manager for a major chemical company put it this way: "When you feel like it's expected of you because of your position of leadership or expected of you because of your stature with a network of people, you start asking, 'When did it become a burden instead of a task of joy?'" Some blacks find such assignments limiting, or they may feel particularly vulnerable if they make mistakes, because as mentors they may be highly scrutinized. Other blacks welcome the opportunity to formalize nurturing relationships and to be recognized for work they would have taken on informally anyway. In either case, blacks who mentor other blacks often struggle with multiple loyalties between what to tell their black protégés in order to help them succeed in the organization and what to keep to themselves out of loyalty to the organization. These potentially conflicting priorities place black mentors in stressful situations.

In addition, because the mentoring bond can be both strong and personal and because racial feelings can be very sensitive and intensely intimate, race can have a strong impact on the relationship. Although this is generally true of cross-race relationships, it is also true in same-race ones. Same-race pairings can be positive. They can be relationships in which people can be truly open and can obtain personal and professional support without having to wade through miasma. However, same-race relationships can also be very difficult if the people involved have a different sense of the role race should play in their relationship or at work or if one in the pairing feels threatened because the other is also black. White professionals may not recognize the extent to which blacks may be wary of working with other blacks in mentoring relationships. However, in our work with African American managers, few conversations about this dynamic are considered complete without an extensive dialogue extolling both the virtues and the potential challenges of blacks mentoring other blacks.

In essence, the four areas of miasma—identity, responsibility, networking, and mentoring—can affect an organization's leader development because each contributes to the ways individuals connect to each other and to the organization's culture and systems. When people believe the organization is placing unfair and unreasonable responsibilities on them, they may feel overchallenged, undersupported, and underdeveloped. Such perceptions can decrease both the ability to develop in one's roles and one's willingness to be connected to the organization. If such perceptions of the organization's behavior are true, they may increase the likelihood that the culture is not a developmental one for people of difference. And like Calvin at the beginning of this chapter, people under these circumstance usually move on to find other opportunities.

Reducing Miasma and Enhancing Development

An organization's response to racial difference can help shape the effect and density of the miasma that surrounds its nontraditional leaders. This response should first acknowledge that African American managers struggle with issues that are different from those of white managers and that they need particular kinds of recognition and support. It should also recognize the differences that exist in the developmental opportunities afforded to black and to white managers and then seek ways to reduce that difference. For example, organizations should carefully examine the ways in which developmental assignments, formal developmental relationships, and opportunities for classroom-based leadership development programs are assigned by race and other factors, to ensure equal access. Leaders of *all* races can be helped with classes and other interventions that focus on understanding unconscious views toward race and how those views affect judgments and decision making.

What African American Managers Can Do

As African Americans and other people of color consider their work environment, they may find that changing some of their own behaviors and assumptions will influence the organizational context in which they work. For instance, a person of color may benefit from becoming more assertive toward his or her own development. Rather than waiting to be recognized, a nontraditional manager may need to let people know he or she is ready to take on new assignments. Black managers, in particular, may need to expand their ideas about racial identity and activities in which they can engage. By stretching their own comfort zones or taking advantage of new opportunities, black managers may find that their views on racial identity grow as their experiences grow.

In addition, people of color need to be aware of the racism that exists in the workplace. The experiences that black managers share as well as numerous research studies have shown that conscious and unconscious racial bias infuses the workplace. By being aware of this reality, people of color can find ways to maneuver around racial situations, to protect themselves, and to eradicate the bias. Yet while nontraditional managers need to acknowledge that race matters at work, they cannot be ruled by this idea. Not every situation at work is racial, and not every racial situation is insurmountable (see Exhibit 10.2).

What Managers and Practitioners Can Do

While African Americans and other people of color have a responsibility to work on their own behalf, managers and practitioners of all races must also help create

EXHIBIT 10.2. WHAT AFRICAN AMERICANS CAN DO.

- Be assertive.
- Expand ideas of racial identity.
- Be aware of the reality of miasma.
- Know that not everything is based in race.

an organizational culture that fosters the development of diverse leaders. To do this, managers and practitioners should consider three broad areas in which to focus their efforts: self-development, education, and behavior.

Self-Development. Managers and human resource practitioners must first recognize that they may need to develop themselves if they are going to be successful at helping others. This means understanding their personal beliefs and assumptions about difference and considering how these ideas affect both *whom* they develop and *how* they develop them.

- *Understand that differences really do matter.* For leaders in the majority, understanding the dynamic that having an identity of difference creates in the workplace is the first step toward understanding the nuances of the unique challenges faced by black and nontraditional leaders. Although differences may not seem to be important for individuals within the norm, they are crucial to those who are not. Being different touches every aspect of the work experience. As one woman said, "I don't think that a day goes by that I'm not reminded that I'm black in this country." As a manager or practitioner, this means that if a black employee tells you that he or she has experienced something racist or unwarranted, you must be willing to entertain this idea rather than assuming that the employee has misinterpreted the event. Understanding that race matters may also mean that you actively try to make visible the invisible, rather than assuming that the workplace is equal and fair.
- *Be willing to be uncomfortable.* As a person who is responsible for helping others, including people of color, you have to be willing to push your comfort zone and to question long-held assumptions. Do you see any patterns in your own behavior? Are they connected with types of people? Do you ask more questions about the competency of members of one group over those of another? Examining what you routinely do can be a difficult task because people are rarely fully aware of their own actions and because people typically wish to see themselves in the best light. Yet pushing yourself in this way will better enable you to help all who come to you for aid.
- *Make every effort to avoid misreading situations.* Too often, whites tell blacks and other people of color that a situation could not have been as they interpreted it.

Constantly being told that one does not understand what has just happened is off-putting at best. Instead, try to determine if an event could have happened as the person reporting the incident says it did. This may mean pushing your comfort zone. If the facts truly do not support that person's version of events, say so. If they are accurate—or if they *could* be accurate—actively work to ameliorate the situation.

Education. People often believe that because they work with a group of people on a regular basis, they automatically understand the members of this group and their motivations. This is usually an erroneous assumption. To understand other groups requires purposefully learning about them. This means learning new information and perspectives, even if the information contradicts previously held beliefs or assumptions. As with self-development, becoming educated about other groups often includes stretching comfort zones.

- *Educate yourself about individuals as well as groups.* Although this chapter is focused on people of color and specifically African Americans, we do not mean to suggest that people should be considered only as group members. Each person is an individual and should be treated as one, even as visible areas of difference are taken into account. In fact, stereotyping or making assumptions about individuals as a result of general impressions about a racial group will only contribute to workplace miasma.
- *Learn about people of color and miasma.* Educate yourself about the experiences of people of color in corporate America. Talk with people of color in your organization; study the company's patterns of behaviors, promotions, and pay. Find out what issues, assumptions, and behaviors African Americans and others are having to contend with in your workplace. Before approaching any person of color to discuss race, you should be fairly confident in the depth of your relationship. Further, you should be sensitive to any signs of discomfort on the other person's part. If someone does not wish to take part in the conversation, do not force the issue.
- *Seek feedback about your own behaviors.* Recognize that you may be part of the problem. Ask African Americans and members of other nontraditional groups whom you believe will speak honestly about your own behaviors and actions. If they identify areas for development, consider their feedback with an open mind, and take corrective actions where necessary.
- *Understand others' expectations.* As a manager or practitioner, employees (including African American and other nontraditional employees) will have expectations about your behaviors and actions. Learn what those expectations are; correct them if they are inaccurate, and live up to them if they are accurate. Sometimes managers and HR practitioners discover that people harbor expectations about them that they do not have the ability or the authority to achieve.

Behavior. Although educating and developing yourself is a useful personal endeavor, it is useful to others only if it affects how you behave. As leaders, what you do has a profound impact on both the organization as a whole and on individuals within the organization.

- *Allow for differences.* Strive to see African Americans and other groups in their entirety. Do not make them fit into preconceived molds that deny who they are. Find ways to bring their full experiences to bear on the work that they do. While allowing for difference is critical, this does not mean people should see others only as racial beings. Allowing for difference may mean giving a person of color the leeway to have different views and behaviors than those commonly associated with people in their group.
- *Offer both heterogeneous and homogeneous programs.* CCL, for example, offers an African American leadership program. Like CCL's traditional mixed-group programs, this program focuses on issues of leadership development; however, it does so in a setting that encourages additional content related to identity issues and workplace complexities that arise from miasma. Single-identity programs help people capitalize on their special cultural and situational life experiences, which are functions of membership in their group, as well as provide unique support (see Chapter Nine).
- *Engage racial issues.* Dealing with racial issues is an admittedly difficult and sensitive task, but don't be afraid to engage them. If, for example, you believe that someone is racially oversensitive, check your assumptions with yourself and with others. It is important to check yourself against people who also share the racial group of the person to whom you must speak. If after honestly questioning yourself and others you believe your views to be accurate, approach the employee. Be willing to state your viewpoint and give examples, and be open to hearing an alternative explanation of events as well.
- *Support "average" nontraditional leaders.* Many times, "superstars of color" are adequately rewarded within organizational systems, but average nontraditional employees get overlooked. Make sure you recognize and develop people of color who are solid employees, even if they are not "stars." Because people of color who excel and those who plateau are often treated the same in the early stages of their careers, as practitioners you may be surprised to find that the employee labeled "average" has more to offer than you suspected (see Exhibit 10.3).

What Organizations Can Do

Beyond what leaders can do individually, senior management, in partnership with human resource and organization development practitioners, can significantly help promote and manage diversity and can create climates where leader development

EXHIBIT 10.3. WHAT MANAGERS AND PRACTITIONERS CAN DO.

- Understand that differences really do matter.
- Be willing to be uncomfortable.
- Make every effort to avoid misreading situations.
- Educate yourself about individuals as well as groups.
- Learn about people of color and miasma.
- Seek feedback about your own behaviors.
- Understand others' expectations.
- Allow for differences.
- Offer both heterogeneous and homogeneous programs.
- Engage racial issues.
- Support "average" nontraditional leaders.

takes place equitably. This means that as systems, organizations must be willing to change processes and practices. The following are strategies organizations can consider.

- *Link diversity management to consequences.* Organizations must demonstrate that diversity is important. Take an active stance on diversity issues. Engage in policies that have consequences for both positive and negative actions toward diversity— policies such as open-door policies, harassment policies, young leader mentoring programs, and goal achievement and reward policies. Be consistent in enforcing these policies.
- *Recognize that diversity issues do not lend themselves to a onetime fix.* Organizations must constantly monitor their diversity behaviors, regulations, and compliance. Because racial notions are embedded in the larger society, they have a way of reappearing in the workplace. Consequently, companies cannot assume that once they have put diversity measures in place, the organization is immunized for all time. For example, a single training event for executives or a weekend human relations seminar for managers will not create change. Change is an ongoing process. Genuinely changing the culture requires influencing collective and individual consciousness.
- *Link inclusiveness to business strategies.* True diversity is not about political correctness; it is about maximizing the effectiveness and productivity of the entire work group. Organizations that understand this concept can more effectively tie their diversity efforts to bottom-line results. From gaining a greater understanding of market segments to allowing unrestricted expressions of perspectives offered by nontraditional managers, difference is a valuable resource for organizations. Likewise, by reducing the miasma for nontraditional managers, organizations create a more conducive environment for contributions by all.

- *Recognize that diversity management needs to take place at all levels.* Take a top-down as well as a bottom-up approach. Although an organization's senior leaders must be committed to and lead diversity efforts, a top-down approach alone can provoke resistance. It is important for leaders to move beyond simply mandating and managing diversity initiatives to modeling the changes they wish to see in others. Failure to do so will make the initiatives seem both insincere and unimportant. Managers at all levels should create opportunities for work teams to explore and act on diversity issues. Allow work groups to become incubators for diversity practices.

- *Honor and promote difference by encouraging affinity networks.* Affinity networks are formal or informal homogeneous networking groups. These groups are often formed as a response to issues or concerns that have already been raised in an organization, as a preventive to help avert issues or concerns from being raised, or as an enhancement that is part of a larger organizational change. Of these three reasons, we recommend the final one for creating the most conducive environment for effective networks. Starting networks to deal with an existing issue is simply reacting to a problem without dealing with its antecedents. Setting up affinity groups solely for preventive reasons attempts to preempt problems without effectively understanding and dealing with underlying issues. However, creating affinity groups within a context of a larger organizational change can have numerous advantages because the groups are part of an evolving organization. For example, affinity groups can tie their charter to business objectives around personnel, profitability, or workplace inclusion. Network groups can also be used to honor and recognize individuals who may not be recognized by the larger organization; they can serve as arenas to enhance employee skill levels, as places where people can advocate for ideas and find ways to bring them to the organization's leadership, and as training grounds for networking (see Exhibit 10.4).

EXHIBIT 10.4. WHAT ORGANIZATIONS CAN DO.

- Link diversity management to consequences.
- Recognize that diversity issues do not lend themselves to a onetime fix.
- Link inclusiveness to business strategies.
- Recognize that diversity management needs to take place at all levels.
- Honor and promote difference by encouraging affinity networks.

Conclusion

As the nation's managerial workforce has become increasingly diverse, the need to understand and manage difference has also become increasingly important. This chapter has provided an overview of the organizational context in which people of color strive to be successful. We have described what we call miasma, the climate created as a by-product of difference and the reaction to it, and how miasma affects the three main elements of effective leader development: assessment, challenge, and support. Finally, we have suggested several implications for managers, human resource practitioners, and organizational strategy.

As the American workplace takes on greater diversity, these issues are becoming more important than ever before. The extent of—and opportunities for—increased interaction between black and white managers has grown considerably. Simply as a by-product of having a greater number of blacks and other people of color rise to higher levels in many organizations, the type and nature of these interactions has also changed as a seemingly new set of rules for racial politics has emerged. Where once the business hierarchy allocated power almost exclusively to white males, today the distribution of power is more diffuse. Increasingly, people of color are heading departments, branches, and even multinational organizations.

This changing environment invariably results in more opportunities for racial interaction, understanding, and misunderstanding. If managed poorly, these interactions can amplify workplace tensions and decrease organizational connectivity, resulting in greater communication problems and more organizational conflict. Unchecked, these issues can lead to diminished employee loyalty, underutilization of workers, and increased retention problems. Conversely, if well managed, a diverse employee base can bring an organization improved problem solving and decision making, greater creativity and innovation, increased organizational flexibility, enhanced long-term strategy, and a better use of human talent.

CHAPTER ELEVEN

CROSS-CULTURAL ISSUES IN THE DEVELOPMENT OF LEADERS

Michael H. Hoppe

Two colleagues in the human resource function of a well-known U.S.-based transnational corporation bumped into each other in the employee lounge on a Monday morning. One had just returned from conducting a leader development program at the company's European headquarters.

"How did it go?"

"It was murder. You know we had people from our offices in Paris, Berlin, Milan—from all over, right? From seven different countries in all. I've never been so frustrated in my life. It was like pulling teeth every single minute."

"What do you mean?"

"Well, we had to justify everything we did. They were always asking us why we wanted them to do this or that. Especially the guys from France. And the Germans! Instead of just doing a particular exercise or role-play and sorting things out as they went along, the way people tend to do here at home, they insisted that we first give them a rationale for every single activity. Man, am I ever glad to be home!"

Nearly everyone who has ever conducted a training program outside his or her native country recognizes the feelings expressed in this fictionalized exchange. Frustrations aside, most are likely to reflect on the experience and wonder, "Why did these people react this way? What could I have done differently to stimulate the discussion? Should I have lectured more? Why didn't they buy into my definition of leadership? Why did they always seem to challenge my expertise or authority?"

Asked more generally, these questions become, Are the models and practices of leader development that are being used in many U.S.-based organizations and development programs applicable in the cultures of all of the participants? If not, why not? What adjustments need to be made in methods, practices, assessment instruments, and philosophies so that they will work? In short, what should be done to successfully transfer U.S. leader development models and practices to other cultures?

The question is important not just for training organizations or consultants and not just for megacorporations. U.S. organizations of all sizes and types increasingly incorporate people from other cultures, either as direct employees or as international work partners. A majority of the leader development programs and products in such organizations, however, rest on a set of cultural assumptions about the meaning of leadership and how leader development is best achieved according to U.S. notions. When those programs and products are used with people from other cultures, whose assumptions may be markedly different, the results are often disappointing: puzzled participants, unreliable data, unsatisfactory outcomes.

This chapter aims to lay a foundation for improving the cross-cultural transfer of U.S. leader development practices. It is divided into three major sections. The first section discusses basic assumptions that underlie many U.S.-based leader development models and practices. It then describes some of the key values and beliefs in U.S. culture and locates them in "cultural space" by comparing them to the values and beliefs held by countries to which U.S. leader development products and practices are frequently being transferred.

The second section turns its attention to the first of the three key elements that fuel any successful development of individual leaders, as presented throughout this handbook: assessment. I use the specific technique of 360-degree feedback to illustrate some of the U.S. cultural values and beliefs that may help or hinder the cross-cultural transfer of U.S. leader development practices.

Finally, in the third major section, I address selected cross-cultural issues in regard to the other two elements of leader development: challenge and support. I conclude this section and the chapter as a whole with a summary of general recommendations to guide practitioners involved in cross-cultural work.

Definitions and Perspectives

First, I should define the terms, parameters, and assumptions that will be used in this discussion. The term *cross-cultural* refers to comparisons among societies—in fact, among the mainstreams of societies. However, this is not to deny the existence of multitudes of cultures within a given society, whether along ethnic, gender, or organizational lines. Implicit in this notion of societal culture is the claim that culture matters. Culture is seen as a set of shared values, beliefs, and preferred actions among the members of a society that largely determine, among other things, the boundaries within which leader development is possible. Once again, this does not diminish the influence of other variables, such as the availability of economic resources or the effects of past or current colonization.

It is assumed that every society is engaged in leader development of some sort. However, what the notion means, how it is practiced, and where, when, and through whom it is done may differ significantly among cultures. Yet the need for leaders and their development is universal. In fact, this contention is extended to the three basic elements of developmental experiences: assessment, challenge, and support.

I also note that because this chapter is part of a handbook about U.S. leadership development experiences and practices, the discussion of cross-cultural issues is pursued from an American vantage point. That is, cultural comparisons are made almost exclusively between the United States and one or more other societies. Moreover, the emphasis here is on *leader* development, the development of individual leaders, as compared to *leadership* development (see the Introduction), because of the focus that U.S. culture places on the study and practices of individual leaders. This choice, however, should in no way be construed to mean that U.S. leader development practices are to be considered the yardstick for other cultures. Any country, independent of its economic level and given its cultural make-up, can enrich the understanding of leader and leadership development around the world. I offer in-depth discussion of the values and assumptions that shape much of U.S. leader development here because U.S. management practices are so prevalent in the field.

Last but not least, I recognize that the term *leader*—or its equivalent in societies around the world—carries different historical, cultural, and political connotations that may influence the practice of leader development. For example, the term *chun-tzu* in ancient China described a supremely cultured and educationally accomplished scholar-administrator who, through extensive studies and rigorous exams in poetry, morality, philosophy, history, music, and calligraphy, had earned the privilege and duty to help run the country and its institutions. Remnants of the *chun-tzu* concept of the leader can be detected in modern China's distinction between the *ling dao* (leaders), persons of high administrative position and power, and the *gan bu* (cadres), people who work as staff members, managers in businesses, or as administrative personnel. Germany's experience under Hitler may serve as a more recent example. His adoption of the appellation *der Führer* (literally, "the leader") has greatly sullied the term *leader* in today's Germany.

U.S. Society in Cultural Space

"Cultural self-awareness," Stewart and Bennett (1991, p. x) write, "is not always easy, since culture is internalized patterns of thinking and behaving that are believed to be 'natural'—simply the way things are. Awareness of their subjective culture is particularly difficult for Americans, since they often interpret cultural factors as characteristics of individual personality." It is important, therefore, to first make explicit some of the assumptions that guide U.S. leader development practices.

Culturally Based Assumptions: U.S. Leader Development Practices

As described in the Introduction and other chapters throughout this handbook, leadership development is seen as the expansion of the organization's capacity to carry out the leadership tasks needed for collective work: setting direction, creating alignment, and maintaining commitment. To expand this capacity, organizations must develop not only individuals but also collectives. That is, the development of individual leaders is but one aspect, albeit an important one, of the entire leadership development process. Yet anyone who is familiar with the vast literature on leadership and the practice of leadership development in the United States knows that the prevailing view by far is that leadership is a property of the individual and leadership development is the training of individual leaders (Hoppe and Bhagat, 2001). Individual capacities to be developed in the individual leader typically include greater self-awareness, systems thinking, creativity, the ability to get along with others, learning to learn, and other capacities called for in leadership situations.

With this view tends to come a number of assumptions that inform U.S. practices of leader development. For example, development can occur and skills can be learned anywhere and anytime in a person's life, through formal or informal roles and in many kinds of activities, ranging from heading up a strategic task force to facilitating a meeting of peers or being actively involved in the neighborhood's battle against a rezoning ordinance. Additional assumptions include that leader capacities can be developed by everybody at every level; that change, growth, and lifelong learning are normal and desirable; that objective feedback is a prerequisite for successful development; and that taking action is essential.

In the United States, it would be hard to find a leader development specialist who does not share most of these beliefs. Yet people from other cultures may disagree with some or even all of them, based on their experiences and their cultural values. This is why, in thinking about leader development and leadership, culture matters; culture largely determines the boundaries within which leader development and leadership are understood and practiced. Thus while culture facilitates certain practices, it also tends to inhibit others, thereby limiting the behavioral options that its members consider important and relevant. One example is the aforementioned emphasis in U.S. culture on individual leader development largely at the expense of leadership development or structural, legal, or political interventions (Meindl, Ehrlich, and Dukerich, 1985). Another is that leader development in the United States tends to emphasize practical experience and deemphasize intellectual and theoretical qualities. Also, in U.S. theories of leadership, there tends to be relatively little discussion of the concept of power, and therefore less attention is paid to helping people understand the politics of organizational life.

Selected Values and Beliefs in U.S. Culture

Alexis de Tocqueville observed that ". . . the American has no time to tie himself to anything, he grows accustomed only to change, and ends by regarding it as the natural state of man" (Pierson, 1996, p. 119). Two contemporary writers offer complementary notions, that individual agency and practicality are uniquely American values: "The [American] idea that man can control his own destiny is totally alien to most of the world cultures" (Kohls, 1984, p. 23) and "To call an American 'impractical' would be a severe criticism" (Cavanagh, 1984, p. 20). What is it, then, in U.S. culture that accounts for its notion of leader development? What specific values and beliefs bring focus to certain aspects of leader behaviors and inattention to others?

The patterns of U.S. culture have received a great deal of attention from researchers. For example, Stewart and Bennett (1991) provide authoritative and easily accessible summaries of U.S. cultural patterns, which stand out from a cross-cultural perspective. These value patterns, derived originally in the work of such anthropologists as Hall (1966) and Kluckhohn and Strodtbeck (1961), were confirmed by large-scale empirical cross-cultural studies in recent decades. In all of these studies, U.S. mainstream culture is consistently described as being individualistic, egalitarian, performance-driven, comfortable with change, and action- and data-oriented (Hofstede, 1980, 2001; Hoppe, 1990, 1993; House and others, 1999; House, Javidan, Hanges, and Dorfman, 2002; Inglehart, 1997; Schwartz, 1994).

Exhibit 11.1 offers an overview of the values pertinent to the discussion in this chapter. A comparison of these values and the examples in this chapter of U.S. cultural assumptions about leader development makes several relationships immediately apparent. To think of leadership development primarily as individual and personal development neatly fits with the cultural value of individualism. The notion that leader capacities can be developed by almost everyone clearly reflects the value of equality, and the idea that skills are acquired by doing reflects an orientation to action. The assumption that objective, data-based feedback should be a mainstay of effective leader development mirrors the U.S. preference for empirical, measurable, and observable data. And the emphasis on change and self-improvement in U.S. culture parallels the importance of growth, development, and lifelong learning mentioned before.

Of course, this is not to say that members of other societies do not hold similar values. Many do. Sweden, for example, is also individualistic, egalitarian, and data-oriented. However, many cultures are more different from the United States than they are similar. Table 11.1 offers a framework (created by Wilson, Hoppe, and Sayles, 1996, and largely based on empirical findings by Hofstede, 1980, and Hoppe, 1990) that compares U.S. values and beliefs to those of nine other countries from around the world. The information in this table can be used to locate the United States in cross-cultural space and link its values (from Exhibit 11.1) and the earlier examples of U.S. assumptions about leader development.

U.S. Values and Beliefs in Cross-Cultural Perspective

Table 11.1 groups ten countries along six bipolar cultural dimensions: *individual-collective, same-different, tough-tender, dynamic-stable, active-reflective,* and *doing-being.* My colleagues and I (Wilson, Hoppe, and Sayles, 1996) selected these countries for two purposes: to illustrate the range of cultural differences along the dimensions and to represent a broad range of nations from around the world. In this table, countries that cluster near a pole of a dimension share the cultural assumptions that are described by that pole; by extension, they differ significantly from the countries near the other pole of that dimension. Countries in the midrange are culturally different from those near either pole of a dimension. For example, the United States, Australia, Sweden, France, and Germany are individualistic societies; China and Mexico are collectivist; and Japan, Iran, and the Arab countries have moderate degrees of individualism and collectivism relative to either pole of the *individual-collective* dimension.

EXHIBIT 11.1. SELECTED U.S. VALUES.

- *Individualism:* the right to the pursuit of one's own happiness
- *Equality:* existential equality among members of society
- *Work:* hard work and achievement as the basis for a good life
- *Change:* openness to change and self-improvement
- *Data:* preeminence of empirical, observable, measurable facts
- *Practicality:* preference for inductive and operational thinking
- *Action:* progress and taking action as individual duties

TABLE 11.1. CULTURAL VALUE ORIENTATIONS: A CROSS-CULTURAL COMPARISON.

Individual (individualism)	Same (equality)	Tough (live to work)	Dynamic (change)	Active (data/practice)	Doing (action)
• Leadership development is individual or personal development. • Leadership development is an individual responsibility.	• Everybody can learn to lead. • All people are existentially the same. • Privileges need to be earned.	• Challenging tasks are good. • Work and career are central. • Competition is good.	• Ambiguity and uncertainty are natural. • Openness to change is good.	• Leading is learning by doing. • Data and measurement are essential.	• Pursuing progress and improvement are natural. • Taking action is a personal duty.
United States Australia Sweden France Germany	Sweden Germany Australia United States	Japan Mexico Germany United States Australia	Sweden United States Australia	United States Sweden Australia	United States Germany Australia Sweden France
Japan Iran Arab countries	Japan China Iran	Arab countries China France Iran	China Iran Germany Arab countries	China Germany Iran	Mexico Japan
Mexico China	France Arab countries Mexico	Sweden	Mexico France Japan	Japan France Arab countries Mexico	China Iran Arab countries
• Leadership development is a group or organizational responsibility. • Leadership development is development of the group or organization.	• Privileges are granted by birth, name, or position. • Leaders existentially differ from other people. • Few are born to lead.	• Cooperation is good. • Solidarity and good relationships among people are primary. • Quality of all aspects of life is essential.	• Stability and continuity are good. • Ambiguity and uncertainty are to be avoided.	• Reflection and theory are primary. • Leading is learning by intellect.	• Living in harmony with the universe is essential. • Accepting one's place in life is an inner duty.
Collective (collectivism)	Different (inequality)	Tender (work to live)	Stable (stability)	Reflective (observation)	Being (acceptance)

Notes: Country locations on the first four dimensions are based on Hofstede (1980, 2001); locations on the remaining two dimensions are based on the literature but are more speculative. "Arab countries" are a composite of data from Egypt, Iraq, Kuwait, Lebanon, Libya, Saudi Arabia, and the United Arab Emirates. Most of the data on China are a combination of Taiwan and Hong Kong. The grouping of countries within each dimension either near the poles or in the midrange indicates noticeable cultural differences among these groups of countries.

The information in Table 11.1 is referred to throughout the remainder of this chapter. It is important to keep in mind, however, that culturally, there are no good or bad value orientations. The fact that the United States happens to be located near the "top" of each dimension signals its unique cultural orientation, not its superiority (or inferiority, for that matter). Instead, the table merely serves as a graphic illustration of the degree to which countries hold the values and beliefs described by the poles of each dimension and their relative similarity or dissimilarity to U.S. values. From these relationships, it is possible to quickly deduce how easy or difficult it is to transfer U.S. leader development models and practices to other countries.

On the six dimensions, the United States places near the *individual, same, tough, dynamic, active,* and *doing* poles. It is not surprising, then, that in the United States, leadership is largely viewed as an individual leader development activity that is accessible to everyone and that is rich in challenge, change, active learning, and self-improvement. Conversely, the Arab countries, Mexico, China, and Japan are culturally the most different from the United States on these dimensions. In those areas of the world, then, transferring U.S. models and practices might be most problematic.

Australia, Sweden, and Germany are most similar to the United States; in these countries, the U.S. models of leadership and leader development practices should transfer more easily. However, Sweden and Germany differ from the United States' cultural profile in some respects. Sweden is located close to the *tender* pole, and Germany is in the midrange of the *dynamic-stable* and *active-reflective* dimensions.

A few brief examples illustrate potential implications of these differences for leader development; they are drawn largely from Derr's research (1987) on the different ways in which organizations in selected European countries identify and develop their "fast-track" managers.

Sweden: Tender and Same Values. In Sweden, Derr reports, leader development opportunities are readily available and largely independent of the person's technical background or functional expertise. However, many Swedish managers find it less than desirable to be singled out, even as high potentials. It threatens to limit their time for self and family, and it isolates them from their coworkers by elevating them in status (values describing the *tender* pole). In addition, the increase in authority that tends to accompany higher levels of responsibility is considered a mixed blessing by many Swedish managers, since in a highly egalitarian society such as Sweden (the *same* pole), the managerial prerogative is curtailed by high expectations of participation and consensus building among the employees. In sum, considering the potential damage to personal time, quality of life, and good relationships with their coworkers, Swedes anticipate few rewards from becoming a manager.

Yet in one way this handbook's model of leader development is facilitated in societies close to the *tender* pole (Sweden, Denmark, Finland, the Netherlands, and Norway): the model focuses on the whole person—personality, intellect, competencies, personal aspirations, and family and community life—and not just on a career, as an expression of values (*tender* pole) that are almost countercultural in mainstream U.S. business culture. Stewart and Bennett (1991) describe this more holistic view of the individual as an orientation that "emerged as a cultural motif in the 1960s and assumes a dominant position in movements with sources in humanistic and transpersonal psychology and in growth theories in education" (p. 71).

Germany: The Importance of Technical and Administrative Competence. In Germany, leader development is typically understood as advancement of technical and administrative expertise, an emphasis that is reflected in the apprentice system and admiration for the *Meister* who has demonstrated technical expertise in the classroom and through years of experience. In fact, the highly technical fields of engineering and microeconomics have been primary gateways to the managerial ranks, and 25 percent of German CEOs have risen through the ranks of the apprentice system (Hill, 1994). Thus the leader development practices that would likely transfer well to Germany are those that recognize the role of technical and administrative competence in leaders' capabilities and that balance action orientations with a theoretical approach.

France: Valuing Authority, Structure, and Theory. France provides an altogether different challenge, located opposite the U.S., near the *different, stable,* and *reflective* poles. In other words, French culture highly values authority, status, rules, structure, and theory and intellect. It is well known that the main springboard for a French executive's career is a degree from the specialized universities known as the *grandes écoles.* As Barsoux and Lawrence (1997) observe, managers in France tend to feel "that their career had been mapped out for them on the day they completed their education. They could also foresee how their careers would unfold and where their promotional ceiling would be, irrespective of their career aspirations" (1997, p. 6). By the same token, French companies tend to eschew personal objectives for their leaders, resist strict performance reviews, and lack explicit career plans. This can largely be seen as an expression of France's location near the *different* pole, where power and status determine what happens in someone's career (d'Iribarne, 1994).

On the other hand, the individual in France is still the target of leadership development, although within an organizational hierarchy and only for the selected few. That is, for optimal transfer of U.S.-based models and practices of leader development to occur, leader development needs to stress authority and status as important parts of a leader's role and repertoire. In addition, models and practices must appeal to the intellect and theoretical bent of French executives.

The Other Countries. China, Iran, Japan, Mexico, and the Arab countries pose still other sets of challenges. Development in these countries, especially China and Japan, needs to emphasize the development *of* the group *by* the group. Although development of the individual remains desirable (as noted in the earlier reference to the *chun-tzu* and *ling-dao*), it needs to be placed within the context and service of the group. Furthermore, development programs in these cultures must place greater emphasis on hierarchy, seniority, organizational rules and structure, reflection, and acceptance of what life dishes out. That is, within the context of our distinction between leader and leadership development, there is a greater need for the latter.

The Element of Assessment in Cross-Cultural Perspective

The model of leader development presented in this handbook explains that the most potent developmental experiences have three elements: assessment, challenge, and support. It is likely that leaders everywhere can benefit from all three elements. How each element is implemented and practiced cross-culturally—and the degree to which it is seen as acceptable or developmental—may noticeably differ.

   This section explores cross-cultural issues surrounding the element of assessment. Though fully aware of the many different forms that assessment can take (see the Introduction and Chapter One), for the purposes of this discussion, I will focus on one particular type of formal assessment, the 360-degree feedback instrument. I do so because of CCL's vast experience with the practice of 360-degree feedback and its increasing use worldwide. Moreover, as a data-driven assessment technique, it mirrors the deeply held belief in U.S. society that quantification and "objective" measurement of human characteristics and competencies are critical for effective leader development (see the *active* pole in Table 11.1 and Stewart and Bennett, 1991). It is my intention that this discussion surfaces both difficulties and opportunities in cross-cultural transfer that are applicable to other U.S. data-driven assessment techniques.

Using Assessment Instruments in Leader Development Across Cultures

As described in Chapter Two, a 360-degree instrument asks many people who know the individual leader well to rate his or her performance or psychological characteristics by responding to multiple questionnaire items; raters may include superiors, peers, direct reports, family members, customers, and others. The answers of the raters are then aggregated and, together with self-ratings, fed back to the individual for purposes of individual development (see Tornow and London, 1998, for more in-depth discussion).

What happens, then, when 360-degree instruments and feedback processes developed in the United States are exported to other cultures? Five issues may be encountered in this transfer:

- The acceptance or appeal of the 360-degree assessment may be low in other cultures.
- The leader competencies assessed by the instrument may be culturally biased.
- Strategies for making the content of assessment instruments cross-culturally generalizable are complex and time-consuming.
- Assumptions about the assessment process may not transfer to other cultures.
- Interpreting the feedback may be problematic.

Cultural Differences in the Acceptance of 360-Degree Feedback

HR practitioners may encounter varying degrees of acceptance of 360-degree feedback in other cultures. The resistance may be due to lack of trust among people who would be expected to give each other feedback. For example, members of former communist countries or people currently living in one-person or one-party dictatorships may not be as open to soliciting and sharing information about themselves because of historical violations of trust. Take the experiences of members of the former German Democratic Republic (East Germany). After the Berlin Wall came down, more than five million people (out of seventeen million) learned that friends, colleagues, neighbors, and even family members had spied on them and passed their information on to the East German secret police.

Of course, obstacles to the acceptance of feedback data can occur anywhere. A history of mistrust, breach of confidentiality, ambiguity as to use of the data, or confrontational relationships between management and unionized employees may seriously undermine its practice even in this country. The United States nonetheless provides the most fertile ground for the use of 360-degree feedback. In Stewart and Bennett's words, "When faced with a problem, Americans like to get to its source. This means facing the facts, meeting the problem head on, putting the cards on the table, and getting information 'straight from the horse's mouth'" (1991, p. 96).

U.S. managers prefer to face facts head on, regardless of whether they are receiving positive or negative feedback. Indeed, in a study by Dorfman and others (1997) comparing managers and professionals from the United States, Japan, Mexico, South Korea, and Taiwan, the U.S. sample was the only one that responded positively to negative feedback (in terms of increased commitment to the organization), while positive feedback had a positive impact on employees in all five countries. In other words, feedback that is direct, honest, specific, and measurable tends to be welcomed in the U.S. workplace—whether it points out strengths or shortcomings.

Cultural Biases in the Content of 360-Degree Instruments

It is no secret that the "practice of psychology within the U.S. is dominated by Western thought, with significant emphases given to white, middle-class, male attitudes, beliefs, worldviews, and values" (Leach, 1997, p. 165). What happens when assessment instruments that were developed by U.S. psychologists and that reflect U.S. models of human behavior are exported to other cultures? How applicable is the content of these instruments beyond the original cultural sphere? This is the ever-present issue of generalizability.

Everything that has been said so far about cultural differences in values, beliefs, and thinking suggests that U.S. assessment instruments are reasonably applicable in some countries (for example, other Anglo-Saxon countries and Scandinavia) but questionable or more selectively applicable in others (China, Japan, the Arab countries). In the latter cultures, societal expressions and, by extension, leader behaviors with respect to power (*same-different* dimension), communication (*individual-collective* dimension), change and innovation (*dynamic-stable* dimension), and action (*doing-being* dimension) differ greatly from those in the United States. As a result, leader behaviors that are considered effective in Saudi Arabian culture, which emphasizes respect for authority and position, indirectness in communication with others, tradition, and religion, are less likely to be found in U.S. assessment instruments (Abdalla and Al-Homoud, 2001; Feghali, 1997).

There are also distinct differences in the priorities that countries assign to various leader competencies. For example, in a study by Yeung and Ready (1995) in which leaders selected the five most important capabilities for leaders (out of forty-five), the U.S. sample ranked "get results—manage strategy to action" as the most important. In contrast, the professionals from France, Germany, Japan, Korea, and Spain did not include this capability at all among their five choices. Furthermore, "empowering others to be their best" was selected among the top five choices by the executives and managers from Australia, Germany, Japan, Spain, and the United States, but it was missing from the list of the French, Italian, Korean, and British samples.

The issue of generalizability may be somewhat tempered by the effects of globalization, technological advances, and industrialization around the world. The emergence of the global market over the past three decades has led to the rise of large transnational organizations with similar organizational and managerial functions. Because these organizations face similar challenges no matter where they are located, they require largely similar leader competencies.

However, even if the global economy should result in the emergence of similar leader competencies across countries and organizations, the ways in which these competencies are enacted and interpreted may continue to differ. That is, the ways in which these competencies are expressed in various instruments may also differ. For example, making decisions is seen as a generic leader function everywhere. Yet in the United States, its effective practice tends to be defined as "quick and approximate rather than slow and precise," in France as "deliberate and precise, rather than quick and approximate," and in Japan as "consensual and long-term rather than unilateral and short-term."

Of course, these observations are part of the convergence-divergence debate among sophisticated practitioners of whether or not cultures and their practices will become more and more similar over time or remain different or even diverge. Summarizing the results of large-scale empirical studies of cultural values and beliefs over the last forty years, Dorfman, Hanges, Brodbeck, and Associates (2002) conclude that ". . . while we acknowledge that global communication, technical innovation, and industrialization can create a milieu for cultural change, a convergence of cultural values is by no means assured. In fact, cultural differences among societies may be exacerbated as they adapt to modernization while simultaneously striving to preserve their cultural heritage."

Strategies for Dealing with Issues of Cross-Cultural Generalizability

A good first step in dealing with these issues is to ascertain the cultural affinity, or lack thereof, between the United States and the society in which the instruments are to be used. To this end, Table 11.1 provides some initial guidance. For countries not included in this table, Figure 11.1 offers additional information. It clusters sixty cultures, based on the results of a large-scale empirical study on societal and organizational culture and leadership, known as the GLOBE study, by House and colleagues (2003). It is largely similar to the clusters identified by Hofstede (2001), Schwartz (1999), Inglehart (1997), and Ronen and Shenkar (1985).

As in Table 11.1, in Figure 11.1 cultural similarity is greatest among countries that constitute a cluster. Therefore, using U.S. assessment instruments in the countries of the Anglo cluster (and to a lesser degree the Germanic Europe and Nordic Europe) is warranted. Close proximity, however, does not preclude noticeable differences between two countries. For example, England, jokingly described as being very similar to the United States but separated from it by the same language, tends to place less emphasis on practicality and business experience (Hill, 1994). By the same token, the farther country clusters are from each other in Figure 11.1, the more the cross-cultural validity of any given assessment instrument remains in question.

FIGURE 11.1. COUNTRY CLUSTERS ACCORDING TO THE GLOBE STUDY.

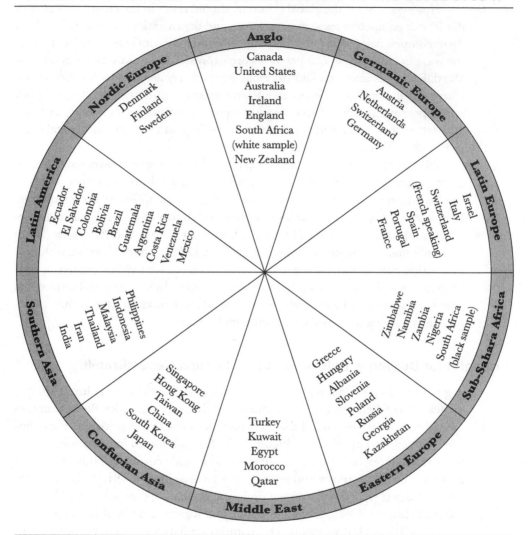

Source: Adapted from Dorfman, Hanges, Brodbeck, and Associates, 2002.

A helpful second step is to take into account GLOBE's empirical findings regarding each country cluster's preferred leader styles. GLOBE identifies six leader styles:

- The *performance-oriented* style, which stresses high standards, decisiveness, and innovation; seeks to inspire people around a vision; and creates a passion among them to perform
- The *team-oriented* style, which instills pride, loyalty, and collaboration among organizational members and highly values team cohesiveness
- The *participative* style, which encourages input from everyone, delegation, and equality
- The *humane* style, which is patient, supportive, and concerned with the well-being of others
- the *autonomous* style, which is characterized by independent, individualistic, and self-centric behaviors
- The *self-protective* or *group-protective* style, which emphasizes procedural, status-conscious, and "face-saving" behaviors

For example, in Table 11.2, the Anglo cluster values the performance-oriented leader style the most relative to the other styles and country clusters (see also Ashkanasy, Trevor-Roberts, and Earnshaw, 2002). Furthermore, it shares its preference for a performance-oriented leader style with the Germanic Europe, Nordic Europe, Southern Asian, Latin Europe, and Latin America clusters. It also highly values, together with the Germanic Europe and Nordic Europe clusters, a participative style and, with the Southern Asia, Sub-Sahara Africa, and Confucian Asia clusters, a humane style.

In contrast, the Middle East, Confucian Asia, Southern Asia, Latin America, and Eastern Europe clusters, in particular, are more accepting of a self-protective or group-protective leader style, an observation that is in line with the combination of their culturally more collective and different mind-set (see Table 11.1) and the importance of "saving face"—including saving the group's face as a whole. This is a leadership style that the Anglo cluster, together with the Nordic Europe and Germanic Europe clusters, prefers the least.

Overall, all ten country clusters prefer a performance-oriented, team-oriented, participative, and humane leader style over the self-protective or group-protective style. The autonomous leader style is viewed as having little impact on being seen as an outstanding leader in all clusters (for more information, see Dorfman, Hanges, Brodbeck, and Associates, 2002). In general, the applicability of U.S. leader style assessment instruments is likely to be greater in countries that share the U.S. preference for certain leader styles.

A third fruitful step in cross-cultural transfer is to identify leader characteristics that are universally viewed as either facilitating or impeding a leader from

TABLE 11.2. SOCIETAL CLUSTERS AND PREFERRED LEADER STYLES.

	Performance-Oriented[a]	Team-Oriented[b]	Participative	Humane	Autonomous[b]	Self-Protective or Group-Protective[c]
High	Anglo Germanic Europe Nordic Europe Southern Asia Latin Europe Latin America	Southern Asia Eastern Europe Confucian Asia Latin America Sub-Sahara Africa Latin Europe Nordic Europe Anglo Middle East Germanic Europe	Germanic Europe Anglo Nordic Europe	Southern Asia Anglo Sub-Sahara Africa Confucian Asia	Germanic Europe Eastern Europe Confucian Asia Southern Asia Anglo Middle East Latin Europe Sub-Sahara Africa Latin America	Middle East Confucian Asia Southern Asia Eastern Europe Latin America
Medium	Confucian Asia Sub-Sahara Africa Eastern Europe		Latin Europe Latin America Sub-Sahara Africa	Germanic Europe Middle East Latin America Eastern Europe		Sub-Sahara Africa Latin Europe
Low	Middle East		Southern Asia Eastern Europe Confucian Asia Middle East	Nordic Europe Latin Europe		Anglo Germanic Europe Nordic Europe

Notes: The placement of each societal cluster indicates the relative importance of that style compared to the other styles for that cluster. For example, the performance-oriented leader style is the highest in rank for the Anglo cluster, indicating that this style is more important to the Anglo cluster than any of the other five styles. In addition, when compared to the other country clusters, it is also seen as the most important. Societal clusters grouped together differ significantly from the other groups of clusters, using the Tukey HSD test; clusters within each group are not significantly different from each other.

[a]Called "Charismatic" by GLOBE.

[b]There are no statistically significant differences among societal clusters for this leader style.

[c]Called "Self-Protective" by GLOBE.

Source: Adapted from Dorfman, Hanges, Brodbeck, and Associates, 2002.

being perceived as outstanding. Once again, the GLOBE study provides some guidance. Exhibit 11.2 lists twenty-two universally desirable and eight universally undesirable leader characteristics, as well as thirty-five characteristics shown to be culturally contingent.

It would be tempting to conclude that the universal items would be perfectly suited for a cross-culturally valid assessment instrument. However, the same dilemma described earlier emerges: how does, for example, the characteristic of "trustworthiness" express itself in a given culture? What is "just" leader behavior? "Honesty"? "Decisiveness"? Without answers to these kinds of questions, successful leader development across cultures will remain difficult to achieve. Notwithstanding this difficulty, the two sets of universal items in Exhibit 11.2, coupled with a sound understanding of the values and beliefs of the countries in Table 11.1 and country clusters and leader styles in Figure 11.1 and Table 11.2, respectively, can serve as building blocks for a cross-culturally sound assessment instrument of leader attributes.

Of course, an alternative strategy is to look for existing 360-degree assessment instruments that have been cross-culturally validated. Unfortunately, as this discussion has highlighted, it is no small feat to make sure that questionnaires measure what is considered important across many societies and whose meaning and measurement are reasonably equivalent across these cultures (see Leslie, Penny, and Suzuki, 2001; Raju and others, 2001). As a result, there are still very few cross-culturally reliable and valid instruments on the market today, and many organizations are using instruments with no known reliability or validity outside of the United States. Leslie and Fleenor (1998) document translations of twenty U.S. leadership instruments into more than twenty languages, but they conclude that "much is unknown about the international validity and reliability of instruments developed and used in the U.S. and on no instrument so far has cross-cultural validity research done more than scratch the surface" (p. 18).

Even if cross-culturally validated assessment instruments should become more available, a basic difficulty remains: the uniqueness of each culture. As Tables 11.1 and 11.2 and Figure 11.1 illustrate, societies vary greatly in their cultural makeup. Any 360-degree instrument that attempts to capture this richness of diversity is bound to reduce it to some broad categories that have little to do with daily, hands-on, unique expressions of a leader's behaviors in these cultures. Furthermore, organizations and the communities in which they operate add layers of complexity that make it important to heed the following advice: "To be effective and efficacious, [leadership] capabilities need to be contextualized with each company's unique organizational cultures, histories, technologies, and socially complex interactions. To derive competitive advantage, it is clearly insufficient for corporations to simply benchmark from high-profile, successful companies. They must define, develop, and measure [leadership] capabilities based on their company-specific needs, challenges, and national cultures" (Yeung and Ready, 1995, p. 538).

EXHIBIT 11.2. UNIVERSAL AND CULTURALLY CONTINGENT LEADER CHARACTERISTICS.

"Universal" Leader Characteristics

Contribute to a Person's Being Seen as an Outstanding Leader[a]

Trustworthy	Motive arouser	Effective bargainer
Just	Confidence builder	Win-win problem solver
Honest	Motivational	Administratively skilled
Foresight	Decisive	Communicative
Plans ahead	Excellence-oriented	Informed
Encouraging	Dependable	Coordinator
Positive	Intelligent	Team builder
Dynamic		

Inhibit a Person from Being Seen as an Outstanding Leader[b]

Loner	Noncooperative	Ruthless
Asocial	Irritable	Dictatorial
Nonexplicit	Egocentric	

Culturally Contingent Leader Characteristics

Anticipatory	Habitual	Risk taker
Ambitious	Independent	Ruler
Autonomous	Indirect	Self-effacing
Cautious	Individualistic	Self-sacrificial
Class-conscious	Intragroup competitor	Sensitive
Compassionate	Intragroup conflict avoider	Sincere
Cunning	Intuitive	Status-conscious
Domineering	Logical	Subdued
Elitist	Micromanager	Unique
Enthusiastic	Orderly	Willful
Evasive	Procedural	Worldly
Formal	Provocateur	

[a]95 percent of all country means for each characteristic exceeded 5 on a 7-point scale *and* worldwide grand mean (N = 62) exceeded 6. GLOBE's definition of an outstanding leader is a person in an organization or industry who is "exceptionally skilled at motivating, influencing, or enabling you, others, or groups to contribute to the success of the organization or task."
[b]95 percent of all country means for each characteristic were less than 3 on a 7-point scale *and* worldwide grand mean (N = 62) was less than 3.
Source: Adapted from Dorfman, Hanges, Brodbeck, and Associates, 2002.

An ideal strategy for developing cross-culturally valid and reliable assessment instruments is to create them from scratch for each culture where the feedback is to be given. Although this approach would be particularly valuable in countries that differ significantly from the United States, such as China, Japan, or Saudi Arabia, it would not only be costly and time-consuming but also difficult to implement. For one thing, there is much less propensity in these societies for measuring people through assessment instruments. For another, the research infrastructure for developing measurements is significantly less extensive. For example, Triandis estimated in 1980 that only 20 percent of all psychologists who ever lived and were alive at the time were found outside the United States, and most of those were in Europe.

This is not to imply that no useful non-U.S. instruments are available, but it does suggest that the choice is still limited. It also suggests that those delivering the feedback may not be proficient in the language or the terminology of the instrument. Also, unless the facilitators and administrators are savvy insiders or knowledgeable expatriates, they may be unfamiliar with its implicit cultural meanings.

In the face of these problems with generalizing assessment instrument content, a few basic guidelines are helpful to avoid some of the pitfalls described here:

1. A good way to start is to become familiar with the vastly expanding literature on the global leader and intercultural competencies. Acquaint yourself with the leader capabilities that are seen as universally desirable, and begin to prioritize them for the culture in question (see Brake, 1997; Dalton, Ernst, Deal, and Leslie, 2002; House and others, 2003; Leslie and Van Velsor, 1998; Rhinesmith, 1993; Rosen, 2000; Yeung and Ready, 1995).

2. Next, as soon as a 360-degree instrument has been selected or is being developed, get help from knowledgeable practitioners and scholars from within the culture. Ask them if the leader scales and items on the questionnaire adequately capture the capabilities and behaviors that are regarded as effective in that culture.

3. Also, ask them to help identify leader capabilities that are not adequately covered, and have questionnaire items developed that measure them.

4. Another way to include areas otherwise neglected is to use an instrument that provides open space for soliciting additional leader strengths and development needs (and their meanings) directly from respondents. The questions in Exhibit 11.3 can help expand and refine the instrument over time.

5. Finally, make sure that the instrument reflects standard professional practices for validity and reliability.

Cultural Assumptions About the Assessment Process

Even if all the difficulties of generalizability of instrument content are overcome, there are some additional cultural assumptions about the assessment process that are worth examining. First, who owns the data? The efficacy of 360-degree

EXHIBIT 11.3. TEN QUESTIONS FOR TESTING THE ACCEPTABILITY OF A QUESTIONNAIRE OUTSIDE ITS CULTURE OF ORIGIN.

Rate each statement on a scale from 1 (strongly disagree) to 5 (strongly agree).

1. I enjoyed completing the questionnaire.
2. I found the questionnaire interesting to complete.
3. Many questions were difficult to understand.
4. The questions were relevant to my work.
5. All the questions were relevant to the culture.
6. I believe that the results of the questionnaire might help identify training needs.
7. I don't know how the questionnaire can detect relevant personality traits for personnel selection and development.
8. I was put off because the questionnaire was too long.
9. It is acceptable to ask these questions in the workplace.
10. An individual with a high score on these questions would be seen as an excellent manager in our company.

Source: Adapted from MacLachlan, Mapundi, Zimba, and Carr, 1995, p. 647. Reprinted with permission.

feedback for developmental purposes is greatly strengthened if the individual leader owns the data. Even though the employer typically pays for the assessment and typically also owns the data when they are part of a selection or performance appraisal process, it is not uncommon in the United States to allow the individual to determine how the data are used and with whom they are shared. Culturally, this practice is largely informed by the individualistic and egalitarian orientation of U.S. society. However, in a more collectivist environment such as China or Japan, individual managers may consider the data the property of the group. In societies with a stronger sense of hierarchy, such as France, Mexico, and Saudi Arabia, superiors are likely to consider it their duty to know everything about their employees and insist on seeing the data and storing them, even if the data were collected for developmental purposes.

This practice raises a second question: How good are the data when the people providing them (including the subject) know or suspect that their input will be shown to others? Research in the United States suggests that feedback data tend to be more accurate when raters believe that their input will remain anonymous (Leslie, Gryskiewicz, and Dalton, 1998). This, in turn, heightens the recipient's openness to and acceptance of the feedback.

If anonymity cannot be guaranteed (the boss's ratings are typically excepted), multiple scenarios arise. Peers in France may rate each other down because that is one way of gaining an advantage in the highly hierarchical and competitive French environment. Direct reports in China or Japan may inflate their ratings to please their boss. For example, Leslie, Gryskiewicz, and Dalton (1998) relate the story of a Chinese manager whose direct reports had given him perfect scores on all scales of an assessment instrument, having done so only because they believed their answers would not remain anonymous. Also, individual managers in the United States may boost their self-ratings, against their better judgment, out of fear that the data may be used against them, either to slow down their career or diminish expected salary increases.

Cultural Differences in Interpreting Results

In interpreting 360-degree feedback results, the participant tends to pay particular attention to the pattern of scores from various sources (self, boss, peer, subordinate) and to how his or her scores compare to those of other managers who have taken the instrument (norm groups). It is important that as part of this interpretation process, cultural differences are taken into account. It is hoped that the gap is meaningful, that it is not the result of inaccurate data or systematic response patterns that have little or nothing to do with the person being rated.

Moreover, it is well established that cultural response patterns among countries commonly show up in these ratings. For example, studies have repeatedly shown that relatively collectivist cultures such as Greece, Portugal, and Turkey significantly rate everything as more important or agree with it than more individualistic societies do (Hofstede, 1980, 2001; Hoppe, 1990), largely to avoid offending anybody or violating collective norms and expectations. Furthermore, there is some evidence that raters in Japan and China tend to avoid the extremes of a response scale, based on their cultural importance of maintaining harmonious relationships and "saving face," while Hispanics prefer to use them, partly due to their "tough" (see Table 11.1) cultural orientation. In the United States, self-ratings tend to be higher than those from supervisors or peers (Fleenor, McCauley, and Brutus, 1996); in Taiwan, they are lower, due in part to the two cultures' different emphasis on competition versus collaboration (*tough-tender* dimension). Therefore, "self-other gaps in the feedback may be larger for managers from some countries not because of their raters' inability to rate certain skills or abilities, or performance differences, but because of cultural influences in *rating patterns*" (Leslie, Gryskiewicz, and Dalton, 1998, p. 29).

Additional Suggestions

What can be done? Given the fact that 360-degree assessment instruments are in increasing use around the globe, it is essential to understand the tendencies of one's own culture as well as those of the recipient culture. Again, savvy insiders and knowledgeable expatriates are critical resources for information on the tendencies of the other culture. It is also advisable to educate raters ahead of time about the format and purposes of the instrument and to review instructions for answering the questionnaire.

Perhaps the most helpful solution is to begin any feedback discussion with an exploration of the various ways the respondents (self and others) may interpret both the instrument scales and the response format. This allows all available parties to gain insights into each other's cultural assumptions regarding possible answer patterns, and it sets the stage for an open and meaningful interpretation of the data and any changes to the instrument desired for the future.

A remaining issue concerns the question of which cultural norms to use to compare a person's ratings. For example, more and more work is being done in multicultural groups and organizations. Which group or culture's norm should apply? In multinational organizations that lack a distinctly national home culture, it may be more appropriate at times to develop and apply an organizational norm rather than a specific country norm. In such a case, the culture of the organization—its values, beliefs, practices, and desired leader competencies—would be viewed as the more relevant to guide leader development.

The question is somewhat less ambiguous if the instrument is transferred from the United States to just one other culture at a time. In this case, it is most appropriate to use that culture's instrument norm, if available. However, in a situation where people from just two cultures are expected to work together—individuals from the United States and Japan, for instance—it may make more sense to either apply the separate U.S. and Japanese norms or to create a single norm, perhaps the mathematical mean of both country norms. The decision of which of the two strategies to pursue will depend on the specific short- or long-term goals of the two cultural groups working together. In any case, the issue of cultural response bias, as discussed earlier in this chapter, needs to be kept in mind.

Challenge and Support in Cross-Cultural Perspective

As described and illustrated throughout this handbook, challenge is the component of leader development that stretches people beyond their existing levels of thought, skill, and expertise. Challenge can be generated by exposing people to novel, difficult, conflictual, or ill-defined situations. It can also come from exposing them to diverse perspectives, interactions with others, or new ideas. The element of challenge causes people to call into question current ways of thinking and acting.

The support elements in a developmental experience work to maintain self-esteem by letting people know that their current strengths have value. Support elements provide encouragement to people engaged in new experiences or change processes. Support comes from feedback that affirms the individual's skills and self-worth. Support in the form of encouragement is offered by family, friends, coworkers, and the organization, community, or society as a whole. It expresses itself through interpersonal encouragement, resources, or norms that value personal growth and development.

The Element of Challenge

There is sound empirical evidence that managers and professionals around the world value variety and challenging tasks and that they derive a sense of personal accomplishment from them (Hofstede, 1980, 2001; Hoppe, 1990). There are equally convincing findings that they consider experience, such as different job assignments or participation in task forces, as the best teacher for dealing with the complex challenges of their role (Smith and Peterson, 1995; Yeung and Ready, 1995). Thus the emphasis in leader development on varied, work-related developmental experiences, as promoted throughout this handbook, is likely to transfer well across cultural boundaries. Notwithstanding, questions remain: How do members of different cultures respond to the uncertainties and ambiguities that invariably accompany challenging experiences? What does challenge as a critical component of leader development look like in collectivist countries in which the organization or group tends to consider itself the primary target of the developmental effort? And what adjustments need to be made in our understanding and practice of challenge in leader development activities, here and abroad?

Differences in Tolerance for Uncertainty. On the whole, U.S. values and beliefs encourage Americans to engage in the types of developmental experience described throughout this handbook (challenging assignments, feedback-intensive programs, developmental relationships, and so on). For example, cross-cultural comparisons consistently find U.S. mainstream culture very open to experiences of change, personal growth, and lifelong mobility (the *dynamic* pole in Table 11.1). The entrepreneur as cultural hero, who may fail many times before succeeding, is one of the most visible manifestations of this observation (Hoppe and Bhagat, 2001).

Moreover, societies such as the United States where people are relatively comfortable with uncertainty tend also to be countries where people value learning by doing, since learning by doing (the *active-reflective* dimension) implies that the learner cannot know exactly what will happen next.

Cultural norms in Australia, Great Britain, and Sweden support a similarly active approach to learning. However, the same cultural preferences cannot be expected everywhere. For example, managers and professionals from France, Germany, Turkey, and Japan are noticeably more concerned with stability, continuity, and certainty. They tend to show less inclination to get involved in novel, ill-defined, and potentially conflictual situations that push them beyond their comfort zone. They find greater comfort in rules, structure, standard procedures, functional expertise, intellectual models, predictability, and job security (Hofstede, 1980, 2001; Hoppe, 1990; see Table 11.3). This helps explain, for instance, the greater emphasis on technical and administrative competence in Germany and on theory and intellectual development in France.

Primacy of the Organization or Group. Additional cultural dynamics come into play in the more collectivist cultural environments of China, Indonesia, and Japan, where organizational and group longevity and loyalty are important values. In these more collective cultures, employees understand that the purpose of their de-

TABLE 11.3. PREFERENCES AND BELIEFS IN THE WORKPLACE: NOT EVERYBODY THINKS THE SAME!

	Rank[a]					
Belief	United States	United Kingdom	Sweden	Germany[b]	France	Turkey
Variety and adventure at work are important.	2	1	3	4	5	6
A well-defined job is not important.	1	2	3	4	5	6
Security of employment is not important.	1	4	2	5	3	6
To get ahead, it is not best to stay with same employer.	3	1	2	6	4	5
It's all right for a manager not to have all the answers.	3	2	1	5	4	6
It's all right to have two bosses.	1	4	2	5	3	6

Note: Respondents were high-level managers and professionals in the private, public, and third sectors.

[a]Across each row: country ranked 1 agreed most with the statement, and country ranked 6 agreed least with the statement.

[b]German participants were from the former West Germany.

Source: Adapted from Hoppe, 1990.

velopment "is to create a lasting bond between employees and the company, rather than teach a set of transferable skills. . . . Training is called the 'professional ability development program' and is closely linked to organizational development" (Harris and Moran, 1993, p. 200). That is, developmental opportunities are decoupled from short-term advancements or greater marketability of the individual managers' skills. Over a person's career, developmental assignments are likely to be more incremental and designed to avoid failure, embarrassment, and discomfort. In addition, the development needs and aspirations of the individual are subordinated to those of the organization.

The emphasis on group belonging and loyalty also results in a markedly different approach to development. The group, instead of the individual, becomes the target for the developmental challenge. Elashmawi and Harris (1993) describe an incident in which a German technician attempted to train a group of Japanese, one at a time, in the use of a new machine. The manager of the group approached him at some point and said, "I am sorry, we are a group and expect to be trained together. Please, could you show us, as a group, how to use the machine?" (p. 38).

In other words, in these societies, learning, growth, and the accompanying experiences of stress and uncertainty tend to be embedded in the collective effort of the group and organization, as well as in a sense of belonging that is at the core of people's identity. In contrast and viewed cross-culturally, the expanding emphasis in CCL's work on organizational and group leadership capacities is largely fueled by a functional or instrumental concern with sustained individual, group, and organizational leadership. It remains anchored in a culturally individual orientation.

Need for Adjustment in Leader Development Activities. It is apparent from the foregoing discussion that what people consider challenging is to varying degrees attributable to cultural patterns. People with different cultural values also have different levels of comfort with challenging experiences. These differences suggest different kinds of approaches and activities, as U.S.-style leader development is transferred across countries.

For example, experiential activities with their built-in ambiguities and open-ended learning processes constitute a significant part of CCL programs. The majority of U.S. participants tend to approach them as an important and enjoyable learning opportunity. In contrast, participants from Germany or France frequently view them as "child's play" or "a waste of time," a reaction that largely reflects the location of these countries closer to the *stable* and *reflective* poles in Table 11.1, as compared to the location of the United States. To take these differences in the needs and expectations of participants into account, the assistance of savvy insiders is once again especially valuable in understanding (and justifying) what learning activities will be most appropriate in different cultural settings.

In addition, the notion of challenge as an essential element in leader development in U.S. society can greatly benefit from an increased emphasis on *leadership* development as described throughout this handbook, whether it occurs in the service of the individual, the group, or the organization as a whole. This last task is likely to be a difficult one, since the focus on the individual is so thoroughly ingrained in U.S. thought and action. However, success in meeting it may not only help develop and sustain an organization's leadership capacity but also buffer the individual from some of the stress or sense of overwhelming challenge and potential individual failure that individual leader development can entail. As a result, increased leadership development may become a significant source of support.

The Element of Support

The notion of support, among other things, encourages people, interpersonally or organizationally, to seek motivation for learning, encouragement, and advice as a balance to the challenges encountered in a developmental experience. Yet here again, culture plays a strong hand, both in the comfort that managers feel with relying on others for support and in the breadth of interpersonal and organizational sources of support available to them.

Differences in Level of Comfort with Supportive Relationships. Ironically, while U.S. managers have a variety of potential sources of interpersonal support, including bosses, peers, direct reports, human resource professionals, family, friends, and clients, the practice of actively seeking support from others does not come easily to them. This is due in large part to one of the most deeply cherished ideals in U.S. society: individual independence (*individual* pole in Table 11.1). Admiration for the self-made man or woman exemplifies this value. In fact, overdependence on a mentor or advocate was considered one of the ten fatal flaws in McCall and Lombardo's study of executive success and derailment (1983). Even though overdependence as a reason for derailment has disappeared in more recent research (Leslie and Van Velsor, 1996), perhaps because of today's faster pace of change in organizational alliances and work relationships, mainstream U.S. culture clearly views being dependent on others as undesirable. In Stewart and Bennett's words, "For many Americans, the search for autonomy, self-actualization, and personal growth has supplanted the mythic desire to save frontier towns single-handedly from outlaw bands. The social norm persists, however, as an avoidance of dependence. Since Americans can envisage few fates worse than dependence, they stress self-reliance" (1991, p. 137).

Members of U.S. society also tend to see success as something to be achieved in competition with others (the *tough* pole). Together, these cultural orientations create the image of the individual achiever who succeeds through his or her own talents, abilities, and efforts.

Paradoxically, by encouraging people to reach out to others for encouragement and advice, the notion of supportive relationships requires them to acknowledge to themselves that they cannot or should not do all the work alone. Many U.S. managers struggle with this realization. Yet there are numerous examples of fruitful relationships among U.S. managers involved in developmental experiences (Young and Dixon, 1996). Similarly, participants in CCL programs over the past ten years have shown an increased willingness and capacity to collaborate in challenging learning activities during which they used to compete. Their experience at work, with its greater degrees of volatility, complexity, and ambiguity, has taught them to rely more on each other.

Establishing supportive relationships may be significantly less problematic in other cultures, especially collective societies where "dependence on others is desirable, for it strengthens the relationship among people and affirms a broad definition of self" (Stewart and Bennett, 1991, pp. 137–138). For example, managers in China, Mexico, Japan, Indonesia, and Singapore consider it their duty to guide and counsel their employees. Similarly, the work group believes itself responsible for helping each member's professional development. Also, the organizational norms tend to support multiple layers of help from others. Moreover, emphasis on cooperation, solidarity, and good working relationships among organizational members in countries such as Denmark, Norway, and the Netherlands suggests a generally supportive environment for personal growth and development.

Availability of Sources for Support. By the same token, from an individual leader's point of view, opportunities for direct personal support can also be seen as more limited in some cultures outside the United States, particularly in those where the needs of the group or organization take precedence (the *collective* pole in Table 11.1) and where, as a result, supportive relationships outside of these circles may be discouraged. Moreover, in countries that combine collective norms with those of born leadership (the *different* pole)—such as Colombia, Indonesia, Mexico, and Singapore—the autocratic leader (such as the Mexican *patrón*) may be caring and supportive but, in return, expect loyalty and subordination. In those cultures, sources of personal support may be narrow and developmental relationships limited to the one between employee and superior. In short, while these societies, out of a deep cultural sense of obligation and collective identity, may consider it their duty to provide long-lasting developmental support to organizational members, the available developmental relationships may be more proscribed. In addition, as discussed earlier, their focus tends to be on creating a lasting bond between employees and the organization through ongoing professional development. However, U.S.

culture may offer more breadth and choice in supportive relationships that are available to individuals in leadership roles.

A Final Word on Support. As with the elements of assessment and challenge, the type and degree of support that individuals can expect for their own leader development is partly a function of the cultural norms that exist in their society. Therefore, U.S. practices must be adjusted when transferred to other parts of the world. Yet unlike assessment and challenge, establishing support may be culturally more in line with the values and beliefs of other cultures than with that of the United States itself and may therefore transfer well to some countries. U.S. practices of support can be enriched by practices in those cultures as it increasingly crosses national boundaries.

Conclusion

One thing is clear: culture matters. Leadership and leader development are profoundly steeped in the culture of origin—and the model presented here is no exception. Culturally, there is nothing particularly good or bad about this fact, as long as any given U.S. model or practice is used in its own cultural environment. Philosophical and practical questions arise, however, whenever the model is used outside the United States. The more philosophical questions touch on the dilemma that the transfer carries with it the risk of imposing U.S. cultural values and beliefs on the recipient cultures. The more practical questions concern the steps that need to be taken to make a successful transfer possible. Based on the discussion in this chapter and CCL's own experience, here is a summary of suggested steps for this type of cross-cultural work.

General Suggestions

- Know the cultural assumptions, values, and beliefs that inform your models and practices.
- Learn as much as possible about cultural assumptions, values, and beliefs of the recipient culture.
- Involve savvy insiders and outside country experts in designing and delivering interventions.
- As much as possible, use models and tools for development designed in the host country.
- Establish joint ventures with other providers who know the market you are entering.

- Assist host-country recipients in understanding your own culture's assumptions, values, and beliefs.
- Consider multiple solutions, scenarios, cases, and simulations for greater relevance in the recipient culture.
- Adjust names, dates, symbols, and so forth to those of the host country.
- Become a participant observer in the new environment.
- Encourage development of local capacities.
- Use Tables 11.1 and 11.2, Exhibit 11.2, and Figure 11.1 in this chapter for an initial check of cultural affinity between the host and U.S. culture and their preferred leader styles and behaviors.

Assessment

- Remember and apply as culturally most appropriate the rich variety of assessment methods described in this handbook: formal and informal, written and verbal, instrument-based and experiential, based on self and other assessment.
- Be aware of U.S. society's preference for objective, direct, measurable feedback.
- Whenever using assessment instruments, identify cross-culturally validated scales, and adjust them or add to them according to local needs.
- Discuss instrument scales, answer formats, operationalization of items, and other aspects of the instrument with the recipient.
- Use an instrument in the local language, if available, and only if you are confident in the quality of the scales and the translation.
- Use norms appropriate to the culture of the recipients and the purpose of the assessment.
- Check for threats to confidentiality, anonymity, and acceptance of data.
- Become aware of local feedback practices.
- Be clear on who owns the data, for reasons of confidentiality and practice of feedback.
- Check for possible cultural response patterns, and discuss them with recipients before the feedback session.
- Be aware of limited research data on the meaning of gaps between and among rater groups.
- Prepare for greater complexity of data collection and delivery in an increasingly global environment.

Challenge

- Keep in mind differences in the degree and type of challenge across countries, depending on their location on the *dynamic-stable* and *active-reflective* dimensions of Table 11.1.

- Check the role and responsibility of the individual, group, and organization as a whole in providing challenge.
- Be aware of the target for challenge: individual, group, or both.

Support

- Recognize possible ambivalence in U.S. culture toward the use of support (as indicated by the *individual-collective* and *tough-tender* dimensions).
- Keep in mind differences in degree and sources of support across cultures, depending on the location on the *individual-collective* and *same-different* dimensions.

There are no shortcuts in the successful transfer of leader development models and practices across cultures. The main reason is fundamental: leader development touches on the deepest layers of human existence—our values, beliefs, hopes, and fears. By definition, these are personal, communal, and cultural in nature. Although they are in many ways similar across cultures, they are also uniquely different. As a result, the challenge of cross-cultural leader development calls for a deep understanding of both the similarities and the differences—and in the process an openness to learning on the part of everyone involved.

CHAPTER TWELVE

DEVELOPING LEADERS FOR GLOBAL ROLES

Maxine A. Dalton
Christopher T. Ernst

The alarm goes off. It is 4:00 A.M. in Scarsdale, New York. John Smith jerks himself out of a deep sleep and walks into his study to prepare himself for a 5:00 A.M. conference call to Singapore, Tokyo, Mexico City, and London. John really dreads these meetings. He can adapt to the idiosyncratic style of each of his direct reports when he is working with them one at a time or face to face, but these monthly meetings with everyone on the phone at the same time are often fraught with confusion. Everyone has a different point of view and a different set of problems. In addition, Juan has a very strong accent, and the others have trouble understanding him. Kim rarely says anything even though John knows she has strong opinions and vast experience. Watanabe defers to John's every comment but does what he pleases in the marketplace, and Peter pushes back on everything. At 4:00 A.M., John has his doubts about the wonders of the global economy and his role in it.

In the first edition of this handbook, this chapter was based on an emerging and mostly theoretical literature; decades of studies on expatriates that included samples of missionaries, Peace Corps workers, and diplomats; and the author's sense of what comprised global work. In the intervening years, our understanding of the demands and requirements of global managerial work has increased tenfold. At least four major studies have been published, including our own (Dalton, Ernst, Deal, and Leslie, 2002; Den Hartog and others, 1999; Gregerson, Morrison, and Black, 1998; McCall and Hollenbeck, 2002). We now have the ability to describe the context of global work, the demands on global managers, the skills required to be effective in this work, and the developmental pathways of those aspiring to global responsibility. These topics will be the subject of this chapter.

What Is a Global Organization?

In the 1997 best-seller *One World, Ready or Not: The Manic Logic of Global Capitalism*, William Greider provides a vivid depiction of the world of work in the global organization. It is a world in which managers are required to process, integrate, and make decisions based on huge amounts of disparate information; negotiate with governments that have very different notions of how business should be done; interact with a complex web of organizational relationships in multiple and diverse countries; recruit and develop the best talent from anywhere in the world; and develop strategic alliances—even with competitors that operate with different models of capitalist systems. Stir all of these ingredients together and we get a sense of the expanded, diverse, and increasingly complex world in which global managers work.

Although there is no universally accepted definition of a global organization, there is general consensus that an organization evolves through distinct stages or forms as it globalizes. To illustrate, consider Adler and Bartholomew's organizational framework (1992), arranged along a continuum of increasing global interaction (see Table 12.1).

As an organization progresses through the various stages from domestic to global, there is an increase in the complexity of its structure, strategy, and systems. A key characteristic, as defined by Christopher Bartlett and Sumantra Ghoshal (1989) in their seminal book *Managing Across Borders*, is that global organizations operate across national boundaries, simultaneously achieving global integration while retaining local differentiation. To be globally integrated, structure, strategy, and systems must be determined by the task. Some activities of the organization may be organized geographically, some by function, and some by product line.

For example, a global organization whose product is sports apparel might design the clothing in the United States, source the fabric in China, manufacture it in Pakistan, and sell it through a chain of stores located in the United States, Canada, Europe, Singapore, and Japan. All of the activities of these organizations are planned, managed, coordinated, and led from a central office that may be located anywhere in the world; no activity is so permanently rooted that it cannot be shifted to another locale. If the political climate becomes too unstable in China, sourcing can be moved to Mexico; if labor costs become too expensive in Pakistan, manufacturing can be relocated to Bangladesh. Because time-to-market is

TABLE 12.1. FOUR ORGANIZATIONAL FORMS.

Organization Form	Description of Activities	Organization Focus
Domestic	Operates in home country only; serves only domestic market	Purely domestic
International	Engages in either exporting or developing assembly and production facilities in global markets	Domestic, but with a global component
Multinational	Integrates domestic and global operations into worldwide lines of business; services and products are largely standardized; major decision making takes place in home country headquarters	Global, but services and products are standardized globally, and decision making is local
Global or transnational	Integrates domestic and foreign operations into worldwide lines of business; products are mass-customized (tailored to individual country or cultural needs), and decision making and strategy are distributed across multiple headquarters in numerous countries	Global, but services and products are tailored to local needs, and decision making is global

of critical importance in the sports apparel industry, the company may have two factories, one in Pakistan and one in Bangladesh, each operating at half capacity, so that in the event of instability, one can be shut down and the other can take up the slack without missing a beat.

Multiply this example for every product the company has—shorts, golf shirts, bathing suits, baseball caps, sweat suits—each with the potential for a shared or different process of sourcing, manufacturing, distributing, and selling, and we see the world of the global organization. Extrapolate this to the work of an individual global manager like John Smith, and we find someone who is up a lot at 4:00 A.M., trying to manage and coordinate the work of his direct reports.

Stephen Rhinesmith (1993) emphasizes that this type of organization represents a wholly new paradigm for management. It requires organizational alignment along three broad dimensions: strategy and structure, corporate culture, and people. Of the three dimensions, the critical one is people, because it is through people that the strategy, structure, and corporate culture are enacted. No strategy, no structure, and no corporate culture can operate without people who can actually do the job. Succeeding in the global economy has risen to the top of many corporate agendas, and in increasing numbers, it is global managers who are ultimately responsible for leading the way.

What Is a Global Manager?

The rise of the global organization has occurred within the time frame of a single generation. These transformations have occurred so rapidly that there is no clear definition of what a global manager is. Recent writings offer colorful descriptions of global managers such as "cultural synergizers" (Adler and Bartholomew, 1992), "true planetary citizens" (Roddick, 1998), "cross-fertilizers" (Bartlett, Doz, and Hedlund, 1990), and "perpetual-motion executives" (Malone, 1994).

Another approach, taken by Ayman, Kreicker, and Masztal (1994), distinguishes between an international manager and a global manager. "*International* refers to an exchange across nations, whereas *global* represents a sense of unity across multiple borders. A global orientation is represented by a more collective awareness and inclusive perspective than is international, but international may be a precursor to global" (p. 64).

Bartlett and Ghoshal (1989), in contrast, suggest that the nature of global work is so complex that there is no such thing as a universal global manager. Rather, they define a global manager in terms of the work that must be done. Specifically, they recommend that organizations create three groups of global specialists—business managers, country managers, and functional managers—that should lead the organization in concert toward achieving its global strategy.

McCall and Hollenbeck (2002) describe a global manager as one whose work is cognitively and emotionally complex. "There is indeed no one kind of global executive; there are many. These global executives work across borders—borders of business, of product, of function, and of country. . . . Crossing country and cultural borders is the determining piece. Crossing business borders . . . is fundamentally different from crossing borders of country and culture. . . . The first is primarily a cognitive or intellectual task. The second is an assault on the identity of the person" (p. 22).

In pilot work conducted for our global research, Maigetter and Ragettli (1997) asked ten managers who had been in domestic jobs but who were now in global jobs (as defined by the corporation), "Now that your managerial responsibilities are global, how is your work different from when your responsibilities were domestic?" Maigetter and Ragettli summed up their interview responses as follows: "There is a need to work across time frames, time zones, and language. This requires patience, a different mind-set, a need to understand foreign culture, and a need to understand headquarters' perspective. Global work is more dynamic and more complex. Global managers face fundamental difficulties, the unknown, greater uncertainty. Information flow is more difficult. The global manager is always working with distant majorities."

The common theme across this discussion is that global managerial work is complex. In our work, we capture this central notion of complexity by identifying three dimensions—distance, countries, and cultures—across which global managers must work simultaneously:

- *Geographical distance.* Global managers must be able to deal with the inconveniences of time differences and the practical and psychological difficulties of not always being able to see the people with whom they work.
- *Country infrastructures.* Global managers must negotiate multiple and sometimes antithetical variations in political and economic systems, regulatory and legal frameworks, and civic and labor practices.
- *Cultural expectations.* Global managers must familiarize themselves and comply with a wide range of sometimes startling expectations in regard to behavior—their own and that of their colleagues, employees, customers, suppliers, and distributors—and the ways in which work should be done.

When we multiply each of these dimensions by the number of time zones, countries, and cultures in which a manager works, the complexity becomes more evident. When you schedule a teleconference, there is often a person in a different time zone at the other end of each of the lines. When you are sitting in a meeting—say, in Japan—you must be aware of the Japanese differences in currency exchange rates, corporate governance, political legislation, investment policy, and unions while also keeping in mind the country infrastructure of the multiple locations in which your company does business. When you get off a plane or log onto e-mail, there are a different set of cultural expectations waiting for you at the gate and the computer monitor.

The term *global manager* defines a manager by the context in which he or she works. As the foregoing discussion illustrates, the context of the global manager is one of increasing complexity, requiring managers to work simultaneously across borders of physical distance, country infrastructures, and cultural expectations. To meet this range of challenges, managers are required to develop a new set of capabilities. Managers who successfully acquire these capabilities and are supported in their efforts to develop these capabilities even further are less likely to become immobilized by this complexity.

What It Takes to Be Effective When the Work Is Global in Scope

At the Center for Creative Leadership, we wanted to learn whether managers with global responsibilities and those with purely domestic responsibilities needed different types of knowledge and capabilities to be effective. To find out, we conducted a study with 214 managers from thirty-nine countries working in thirty countries around the world. The managers' companies represented four industries and had headquarters in Sweden, Switzerland, and the United States. Half the managers had local responsibility, meaning that they directed operations within the borders of one country. The other half had global responsibility, meaning that they directed operations in multiple countries and across various cultures.

The managers completed a number of questionnaires constituting nearly one thousand items, and each manager's boss completed a questionnaire about the manager's job effectiveness. We then conducted a series of correlational analyses to determine the similarities and differences between domestic and global work. Our research has led us to understand that there is a set of *essential managerial capabilities* that are critical to good management, whether a manager is working in a local or global setting. An effective manager needs to do these things whether working with people in Barcelona, in Birmingham, or in both places. We also identified four *pivotal capabilities* that are uniquely related to the effectiveness of global managers.

Essential Managerial Capabilities

Some of the activities that managers have been doing for years in domestic settings are also critical when their work becomes global in scope. We characterize these essential managerial capabilities as "the same but different" because they are capabilities that managers need whether they are working within their own country or working across distance, countries, and cultures. There are five essential capabilities:

- *The ability to manage people.* This includes the skills associated with being an effective leader.
- *The ability to manage action.* This includes the skills associated with effective decision making, negotiating, and innovating.
- *The ability to manage information.* This includes the skills associated with serving as a spokesperson and communicator.
- *The ability to cope with pressure.* This includes the skills associated with being effective in a high-stress environment.
- *Core business knowledge.* This includes the day-to-day knowledge of one's own business.

The distinction within "the same but different" is that in a global setting, a manager plays the same roles (such as managing people), but the actual behaviors and the knowledge associated with the roles are different. For example, if you disagreed with your boss, would you state your disagreement in the same manner in Tokyo with Japanese coworkers as you would in The Hague with Dutch coworkers? Would you express your frustration with a coworker in the same way through e-mail as in person? We hope not. Although the point you desire to get across remains the same, how you convey it changes significantly in response to the types of behaviors that are considered acceptable in each of these countries.

This need to do the same things in different ways can be a real source of tension for the practicing manager. Managers are often promoted to complex global jobs because they are highly effective at what they do. However, without modifications for globally complex situations, the behaviors that lead to success in a domestic role will lead to failure in a global role. Global managers must learn to adapt their strengths and use them differently. To adapt to the challenges of the global context, managers must learn to nurture and attain four pivotal capabilities. These pivotal capabilities help managers adapt what they do successfully in their own country to other countries and other cultures and across multiple time zones.

Pivotal Managerial Capabilities

Imagine that you are a practicing global manager. You are standing in front of a globe. You locate your own country. You are already an effective manager in your own country because you have the knowledge, skills, and abilities you need—the essential managerial capabilities. Now imagine that the globe starts spinning. Distance, countries, and culture are now in motion. To be effective, you must be able to adapt what you know to this spinning globe. You must take what you know and do it differently again and again and again. Think for a moment about the axis on which the globe spins. Just as the axis allows the globe to spin, the pivotal capabilities allow you to adapt what you know to the situation at hand. The pivotal capabilities represent your motivation and ability to master the spin of a globally complex world. As a set, they provide the knowledge, skills, and abilities you need as an effective global manager to adapt and innovate as the context demands. The four pivotal capabilities are international business knowledge, cultural adaptability, the ability to take perspective, and the ability to innovate.

International Business Knowledge. To be effective, global managers must have a solid understanding of how business is conducted in each country and culture where they have responsibilities. On the big-picture level, international business knowledge means having a thorough grasp of your organization's core business and how to leverage that business within and across each country where your organization has markets, vendors, resources, and manufacturing operations. At the grassroots level, it means knowing the laws, histories, and customs of each of these countries.

Gaining international business knowledge involves taking classes, reading books, and talking with experts. Being sophisticated in the realm of international business not only gives global managers the savoir faire to behave appropriately and stay out of trouble, but it also guides them in developing a broad, long-range strategy and keeps them aware of how decisions at one location affect possibilities at others.

Intellectual knowledge, however, goes only so far. No matter how prestigious a manager's education and how thorough the data he or she receives from the organization's information technology, human resource, and legal departments, such knowledge is of limited value if that manager cannot use it to adjust his or her personal behavior to various business contexts. To capitalize on international business knowledge, global managers must pay close attention to the other pivotal capabilities.

Cultural Adaptability. Global managers must act on their knowledge of cultural differences and use that knowledge to help them interact effectively with people from different cultures. A large part of cultural adaptability is being able to deal with the stress and the perceptions of eccentricity and strangeness that can arise from global complexity.

For instance, a U.S. global manager who faces an important deadline on a project in Mexico may notice during a teleconference that the team members in Mexico appear unconcerned as they deliver an overdue status report. Cultural adaptability would allow the manager not only to know that Mexican business tends to be conducted under a different time orientation than is common in the United States (in Mexico, people take precedence over schedules) but also to act on that knowledge in an appropriate way. Similarly, cultural adaptability would allow a female global manager in Europe who is negotiating with a Saudi Arabian manager to use her knowledge of the role of hierarchy, class status, and gender in Saudi culture and to adjust her words and actions accordingly.

In an article published two decades ago, Indrei Ratiu of the global business school INSEAD was one of the first to examine the role of cultural adaptability in determining the success of global managers, or "internationalists" (1983). One characteristic of successful internationalists, wrote Ratiu, is that they begin with general knowledge, or prototypes, of cultures when first dealing with different cultures. As they get to know people from those cultures as individuals, however, successful internationalists let go of or adjust elements of their prototypes and gain a less stereotypical knowledge of the cultures and their people. Unsuccessful internationalists either don't start off with prototypes (and as a result interpret everything based on their own mental frameworks) or are unable to discard their prototypes despite evidence culled from their relationships with people from other cultures that ought to dispel these preconceptions.

Managers who are culturally adaptable, then, sign on to the notion that logic and truth are relative. Nancy Adler wrote, "In approaching cross-cultural situations, effective business people . . . assume differences until similarity is proven. They recognize that all behavior makes sense through the eyes of the person behaving and that logic and rationale are culturally relative" (1997, p. 71).

This view can create tensions for global managers, however, especially if they tend to approach the business world as a nuts-and-bolts environment of budget sheets and Pareto charts. To ease this tension, global managers need to develop the pivotal capability of perspective-taking.

Perspective-Taking. Everyone has a personal perspective—images of and beliefs about what things are and how they should be. But not everyone is adept at taking the perspective of others, seeing and understanding their views of what things are and how they should be.

There are several idioms used in the United States that give a sense of what is meant by perspective-taking: "Walk a mile in my shoes." "I know where you're coming from." "I see what you mean." All of these show that there is a large element of empathy involved in perspective-taking. In the case of global managers, it is *cultural* empathy—knowing, understanding, and acting in accordance with the deeply held values and beliefs of people from cultures other than their own.

Imagine that you and a friend are hiking up a steep, wooded slope. As you near the summit, you both stop to catch your breath and look back at the view. Your friend says she can see a town over the treetops. But she is ten yards ahead of you, and you can see only the trees. Because you and your friend are standing in different places, you literally have different points of view. To see what your friend sees, you must move to where she is standing, and vice versa. Of course, walking up or down a hill to see the view from a different perspective is easy. Understanding how to act, communicate, and lead while taking into account the perspectives of colleagues, direct reports, and customers from other cultures is not so easy.

Whether the context is global or is confined to a single culture, the processes and behaviors involved in perspective-taking are largely the same: listening to and absorbing information skillfully, recognizing that other people's view of a situation may be different from yours, understanding that other people's assumptions about what things are and should be may be different from yours, and understanding and accepting the limitations of your own point of view. Yet implementing these processes and practicing these behaviors can be especially difficult for managers operating in a global context because they do not have the luxury of working from a single, commonly understood cultural framework. The frame of reference held by each individual with whom global managers deal, and which they must strive to understand, changes from culture to culture.

An example of how fundamentally different perspectives can be was reported in the *New York Times* as the result of a study conducted with Japanese and American managers (Goode, 2000). Both sets of managers were asked to look at a picture and describe what they saw. The U.S. managers tended to talk about the people in the picture, whereas the Japanese managers were more interested in the setting of the picture. The study underscored how two people looking at the same thing will often focus on different aspects of it because of their cultural perspectives.

Developing the ability to distinguish the moods, temperaments, and intentions of people from other cultures requires a concerted effort, especially in the virtual environment in which global managers typically work. Global managers who interpret and label the behaviors of others based on their own cognitive and interpersonal frameworks will be more likely to make mistakes about others' motivations, and their own actions and reactions will be liable to leave other people shaking their heads. However, global managers who learn to take the perspective of others and can reorganize their own sensemaking frameworks will grow to see multiple perspectives as not incompatible but as all having potential for contributing to solid managerial decisions and action. Such managers will make sense to, rather than confound, the people from other cultures with whom they work.

Innovation. Global managers who add this final pivotal capability to the first three will have the tools not only to understand and adapt to the complexity of the global business environment but also to capitalize on that very complexity to achieve success for themselves, their teams, and their organizations.

For global managers, the role of innovation is integral to the other pivotal capabilities. Only through skill in innovation can global managers take their international business knowledge, understanding of cultural differences, and ability to experience diverse perspectives and leverage them in collaboration with others to create something new—a new policy, procedure, product, service, or practice that is greater than the sum of its parts.

In this respect, innovation is the most crucial of the pivotal capabilities. It takes managers beyond merely managing the complexity of global operations to turning that complexity to their advantage.

Building skill as an innovator is a step-by-step process of gathering information, learning to listen and pay attention, letting go of the need to always be right, and seeking out useful combinations. In the global context, someone who is skilled as an innovator can take the best of two or more cultures and create something that did not exist before. This capability does not represent a mechanistic bolting of one thing to another. It represents the creation of something new.

An example of innovation is found in the story of a British manager assigned to set up a manufacturing plant in an impoverished area of Africa. He had hoped to recruit a reliable and loyal workforce, but many employees were not showing up for work. In an attempt to solve the problem, he began offering free lunches to workers. But absenteeism continued to be rampant and was severely cutting into the bottom line. Unwilling to reconcile himself to a constantly revolving workforce, the manager brought into play his pivotal capability of perspective-taking and talked with local leaders to try to get a handle on the problem. He learned that the workers were concerned about coming to the factory because they were not certain that their families would be safe in the village if all the men were off at work. The manager innovated by moving the village within the protective view of the factory. The cost of this was more than offset by the fact that absenteeism all but disappeared.

How Do You Develop Global Capabilities?

We have introduced the notion that the capabilities of an effective global manager are the same but different. Effective global managers must be able to manage information, relationships, and action just as they have always done. They must be resilient, and they must know the business. But when the work is global, they must also be able to adapt how they do what they do to the interacting dimensions of distance, country infrastructure, and cultural expectations. It is our contention that managers who fail to adapt how they lead, negotiate, make decisions, or share information to fit the global context are more likely to fail.

We have also described and defined the pivotal capabilities—international business knowledge, cultural adaptability, perspective-taking, and skill as an innovator—that allow managers to adapt to the situation at hand. We want to concentrate now on the development of these pivotal capabilities. How can a person develop them?

This handbook is built around a model. The first part of the model illustrates the conditions that must exist for an experience to be developmental—assessment, challenge, and support. The second part of the model indicates that individuals on a developmental journey need to be willing and able to learn from a variety of experiences. This part of the model also illustrates that leader development needs to be embedded in and aligned with organizational systems and processes that will support it.

The remaining sections of this chapter will focus on the development of these pivotal capabilities. Specifically, in the section that follows, we will address development from the perspective of the individual manager. Because we have already described many of the challenges faced by global managers, we will focus next on assessment and support. We will then conclude the chapter by addressing the larger role that organizations can play in helping managers develop the skills needed to work effectively in complex, global business environments.

Assessment

In our research on global managerial effectiveness, we have learned that certain personality traits are covariant with certain pivotal capabilities. Therefore, a personality assessment may help a person who aspires to a complex global job determine which pivotal capabilities he or she might wish to work on, given natural preferences, and which capabilities the person might hope to discover in others. In other words, we do not mean to suggest that any manager will have all of these personality traits. That is highly unlikely. Nor do we mean to suggest that a given manager should aspire to master all of the pivotal capabilities. That is unrealistic and inappropriate, since no manager, no matter how competent, works alone. Rather, individuals who understand their own personality can be more realistic and intentional about setting personal goals while developing an appreciation of the need for interdependence with those who have different personalities and different strengths and weaknesses.

We take *personality* to mean a person's consistent and stable response to the world. Personality describes how we each prefer to deal with stress, with other people, with novel experiences, and with the demands of tasks and responsibilities.

In our global research, we found a statistically significant relationship between certain personality traits and each of the pivotal capabilities. Managers with positive scores on the trait of emotional stability—the ability to handle stress and provocation with aplomb and confidence—were more likely to have high scores on the capabilities of international business knowledge and cultural adaptability. They were also more likely to possess the trait of conscientiousness, meaning that they are dependable and orderly and aspire to success and achievement.

Managers with a personality that inclined them to be agreeable, altruistic, and interested in the welfare and concerns of others were more likely to have the ability to see the world from the perspective of others. Managers with the traits of openness to experience and extroversion (orientations toward persuading others to consider their novel points of view) were more likely to receive high scores on the capability of innovation.

Keep in mind that all of these relationships are correlational—they simply occur together—and not causal, which would mean that one thing *causes* the other. Our research does not permit us to say anything about causes. But the relationships we found suggest to us that a manager who aspires to global work and wants to develop global capabilities also needs to understand his or her own personality. For example, if the manager is, in the language of the personality theorists, strong on the traits of emotional stability and conscientiousness but weak on the traits of extroversion and openness to experience, he or she might find it easier to acquire the capabilities associated with international business knowledge and cultural adaptability and harder to acquire capabilities in the role of innovator. If the manager is weak on the traits of emotional stability and conscientiousness but strong on the traits of agreeableness, he or she might find it hard to acquire the capabilities of cultural adaptability but easy to acquire the capabilities of perspective-taking.

Support

As discussed in Chapters Three and Seven, all learning requires the support of others in the form of role models, opportunity brokers, and ongoing feedback. When a person's development goal is global in scope, he or she needs to seek out a particular type of support. Specifically, the person should identify role models who have had successful international experiences: opportunity brokers who can provide access to a variety of international experiences and culturally sophisticated informants who will provide feedback within a given cultural context.

Unfortunately, finding and maintaining these types of relationships can prove difficult for global managers. In working across the interacting dimensions of distance, countries, and cultures, global managers often find themselves operating in "boundary roles" that place them along the organizational periphery (Adams, 1976). In working across these boundaries, global managers tend to be more distant—both physically and psychologically—from others in the organization. They are often "caught in the middle" of numerous constituency groups both inside and outside the organization. These contextual demands can make it increasingly difficult for global managers to develop sustaining and ongoing mentor relationships inside their organizations.

Further, these challenges are compounded by the fact that many organizations lack systems to provide formal organizational support. When mentor relationships and role models are not readily available, aspiring global managers will be less likely to capitalize on their international experiences since they lack an understanding of what effective performance looks like. They lack a full appreciation of what they are supposed to be learning. And they are less aware of their impact on others.

We will provide some recommendations of what organizations can do to address these challenges in the last section of this chapter. We now turn to a detailed discussion of the role of developmental experiences.

Developmental Experiences

A manager who wants to learn a variety of skills must engage in a variety of experiences and must have the ability to learn from those experiences. In our global research, we found a statistically significant relationship between certain cosmopolitan experiences and all but one of the pivotal capabilities.

The managers in our study who were knowledgeable about international business and adept at adapting their style to the cultural expectations of others were more likely to have been expatriates and more likely to have lived in a variety of countries. Those who were skilled as innovators were also more likely to speak more than one language. While we are not necessarily sure how to interpret this last result, we know educational researchers report that bilingual children are more likely to obtain higher scores on tests of creativity later in life. It also makes sense to think about how language frames reality. A person who has more than one language frame—vocabulary, characters, syntax—has more than one mental scheme for viewing the world.

These statistical relationships suggest that people on a global manager career track need to extend the thinking laid out in Part One of this handbook to include a particular variety of experiences that will help them cultivate the skills they need to be effective. Consider the example of one man we interviewed, who is now a senior executive in his company with international responsibilities. When asked about the experiences—personal and work-related—that prepared him for his present job, he told the following story.

As a child, Robert visited several foreign countries, for his family liked to travel. When he was in college, he spent several summer vacations hitchhiking through Europe with his brother. Upon graduation, Robert joined a company with production facilities around the world. After some early success as a research and development engineer, he was assigned (because of his technical expertise) to headquarters as staff assistant to the vice president of operations for Asia. This vice president was an experienced international manager with the ability to get along with people wherever he found himself. In this position, Robert traveled throughout Asia with his boss and had the opportunity to observe how skillfully the man worked with people.

His next assignment was as a production manager. Then he learned through the grapevine about the formation of a new project team to develop a quality-control process that could be used in manufacturing plants in Bangladesh, the United States, Wales, and Malaysia. The team would be made up of people from all four participating countries. Because he had traveled in both the United Kingdom and Asia, he volunteered for the team.

At this point, Robert's organization, in the person of a human resource staff member, made a developmental intervention. As a young manager, Robert was told that in addition to the team goal—coming up with a quality-control process that could be successfully installed at all sites—he would also be expected to achieve an individual goal: learning how to be a more effective member of a cross-cultural team. So Robert was assessed on such skills as active listening, acting with integrity, seeing a situation from another's point of view (perspective-taking), and demonstrating appreciation of cultural differences. He was asked to set development goals based on this assessment before joining the team and was encouraged to share his development goals with the other team members. After the assignment, he was debriefed on the dilemmas of the task, what he learned, how he learned it, and how the organization could use what he learned in forming cross-cultural project teams in the future. It was a positive experience for him, so he continued to look for international opportunities.

Today Robert attributes his success to the fortunate happenstance of love for travel, experience outside the country, a good role model with international experience, and an HR professional who showed him how to leverage the learning from his experiences.

A manager who is interested in a global career should seek out such assignments as international business trips; membership on cross-cultural teams; management responsibility for a cross-cultural team; expatriate assignments; responsibility for products, services, or processes in more than one country; and opportunities to work with experienced global executives. Each of these assignments provides a different kind of stretch and the opportunity for both cumulative and differentiated learning (to be discussed shortly).

Business Trips and Long-Distance Multicountry Projects. Business travel and multicountry assignments afford exposure to cultural differences within a business context: people, money, laws, customs, language. Through these experiences, people develop the ability to listen, put others at ease, communicate orally and in writing across language barriers (perhaps through translators), and recognize that others make sense of events differently from one's preferred viewpoint. Experiencing, not just knowing, that differences in perspectives exist is an early step toward developing global capabilities.

Working as a Member of a Cross-Cultural Team. Serving as a member of a cross-cultural team gives people the chance to experience the simultaneous and multiple cross-cultural influences characteristic of senior-level global work. More often than not, the team is geographically dispersed, so the physical cues associated with words are absent. People learn to interpret meaning across time, distance, and culture, and they learn to trust.

An Expatriate Assignment. As when working on a cross-cultural team, accepting an assignment in a foreign country gives people the chance to learn what they do not know, practice perspective-taking, and increase self-awareness and interpersonal skill. They also have the opportunity to start noting the ethical dilemmas that are often embedded in culturally driven business practices, and they begin to appreciate what it is like to accomplish tasks in a different cultural context.

An Expatriate Assignment with Managerial Responsibilities. An expatriate managerial assignment provides the opportunity for a boundary-spanning role, explaining headquarters to the host country and the host country to headquarters. Depending on level and location, this assignment also provides the manager with an important external role: working to understand the framework of laws and politics in a foreign country and learning to negotiate within that framework, where ethical dilemmas may become more profound.

A Repatriate Assignment. Returning home provides an opportunity for people to teach others what they have learned abroad. The repatriate experience can be harvested to inform business strategy as well as administrative policies that support expatriate selection, preparation, and deployment. Ironically, in many U.S. companies, repatriates are at best ignored and at worst derailed because of their absence. Interviewers (Dalton and Wilson, 1996) asked sixteen senior-level repatriates in a Fortune 100 company, "How has the organization used what you learned during your expatriate assignment?" The unanimous answer was, "It has not." One interviewee commented, "You are the first person to even ask, and I have been back for two years." Another commented, "No one even asked to see my slides."

It is troubling that companies scramble to be globally competitive yet are so careless about developing the people they need. The biggest impediment to developing individuals for global work is poor treatment of expatriates. Unless this changes, talented people will not take the assignments, and in the long run, the organization will not thrive as a global entity.

Managing a Major Multicountry Project. This type of assignment provides the experience to work simultaneously in multiple cultures and across distance. Learning opportunities include creating and maintaining virtual teams, managing individuals whom one does not see very often, using the teams to leverage cultural differences in the service of innovation, and using the situation to develop the team members.

Assignments with Regional Responsibilities. Regional assignments involve working simultaneously in more than one culture, as in the Americas, the Pacific Rim, the Middle East, or Europe. Because the assignment is probably within a functional area such as sales, human resources, or finance, the influence of laws, foreign currency, and local custom becomes especially salient.

Global Responsibility for a Product. The true global assignment—managing across many cultures—calls on all of the skills previously acquired. Unlike project management, this assignment calls for long-term management of a product or process throughout the business cycle. This is the level of responsibility where strategic decisions that affect the life and future of the organization are made. The person chosen for this type of assignment is undoubtedly a senior executive with a background of substantial experience. Success in this role is largely dependent on the variety and intensity of experiences in the executive's career history.

Working with Experienced Global Executives. Threaded throughout their career assignments, managers who aspire to global work should have role models and mentors who themselves have had successful global careers and can provide advice, support, and feedback. Young managers who are interested in global work and have been identified as having high potential in this area are ideally given the opportunity to work within the sphere of these successful global executives at several points in their careers.

Finally, when international assignments are interspersed with domestic assignments, the learning from one should be reinforced and harvested during the other. For example, organizations can create opportunities for those returning from international assignments to orient potential expatriates, take part in planning discussions about a product launch in another country, or sit in on human resource discussions about developing policies or training programs for implementation in other countries.

How Organizations Develop Systems to Support the Development of Global Managers

As the story of Robert illustrates, the development of global managers is part individual initiative, part organizational intent, and part luck. In the current borderless economy, no organization has the luxury of leaving the development of managers with global responsibilities to chance. It was once sufficient to build international businesses by moving a limited group of employees overseas or to hire local nationals. Today, organizational structures are shifting from an international focus, with country or regional sales units, to a worldwide focus with global product development and manufacturing. Accelerating globalization, advanced technology, worldwide competition, and the rapidity of change are universal business drivers affecting individuals in all types of managerial roles. These trends dictate that senior management work collaboratively with the human resource group to ensure the development of a broad cadre of managers with a global, boundary-spanning perspective.

In this final section, we will address the critical role that organizations must play to develop managers for global responsibilities. Although today's organizations have developed advanced structures and strategies to be effective for global competition, they are much less sophisticated when it comes to developing systems to support individuals to be effective in global roles.

To illustrate, we recently heard a European with global responsibility, who works for an American-based corporation, groan that he did not know what to do about the Americans. Most members of the senior leadership team in his organization had never even been to Europe. Yet they made decisions and issued directives on a daily basis that adversely affected the growth of their business in Europe and around the world. These executives did not understand how the decisions made to the benefit of the business in one country worked to the detriment of the business in another country. We have heard similar complaints from Americans working for Dutch-based organizations and from the British when working for Japanese-based organizations. This problem of the country-centric senior executive appears to be a worldwide phenomenon, apparent at all levels.

An organization's development system needs to learn to produce people who are not like this! The development system needs to provide all its employees with the opportunity to learn how to see the world through a multifaceted lens. But the system also needs to have a specific development track for those who aspire to global jobs. The following discussion is meant to help you determine whether your organization has such a system in place.

Recruit and Cultivate People with International Experience and Interests

The individuals in the organization who are responsible for the global development track must be on the lookout for people both eligible for and interested in a career path leading to global responsibilities. A possible first step in the process is to identify people early in their careers. Look for those who show a liking for travel and international work, those who speak other languages, and those whose life experience includes time spent living or traveling extensively abroad. Recruiting and promoting individuals with these experiences and interests sends strong signals regarding the importance of openness to diverse cultures.

Informal mechanisms, such as providing opportunities to host foreign guests, a paid subscription to an international newspaper, or a stipend to attend a course on world history or geography, can further cultivate learning for these budding global managers. Such opportunities help build a solid foundation in preparation for more formal international assignments.

Recruit and Cultivate People Who Demonstrate Interest in Novelty, Learning, and Other People

In addition to hiring people with international backgrounds or a particular knowledge base, you also want to look for people who are open to learning, enjoy novelty, and relish difference but who may not have had the opportunity to travel or be exposed to other cultures. To identify those people, you will have to change the nature of your interview strategy. You must move away from simply asking people to recite accomplishments or report their college grade point average. You must ask them to compare and contrast, to describe activities that were challenging and tell you what they have learned from them, and to tell you what they have discovered while they worked, studied, and lived in the midst of people who were different. Look for people with the traits of agreeableness and openness to experience, traits that incline people to see the world as others see it and imagine things as no one else does.

Some people do not like to travel. Some people would never be willing to go on an international assignment. Some people demonstrate that they cannot or will not grapple with diversity even in their own country. Some people have life and work goals that conflict with the time demands inherent in global work. But there are those who have good potential and are simply unsure whether they would like to try an international assignment. These are the individuals that may grow into global leaders.

Provide Language Training for Employees Who Travel Abroad Frequently

There is a great debate in the field as to whether or not a global executive needs to speak more than one language. In our experience, those who do not speak another language think that English is sufficient, and those who speak a second language know that it is not. We believe that any manager who travels abroad should make the attempt to learn at least the local language, even if he or she never becomes proficient.

At one level, making the effort to speak another language indicates respect and appreciation for the manager's counterparts in other countries. On a different level, learning a foreign language helps managers develop an appreciation for different ways of expressing ideas. Just learning the basic grammar and syntax of another language opens up a window into a different way of thinking about the world. Moreover, attempting to learn a foreign language helps managers develop empathy for how difficult it is for others to speak to them in a second language. Each of these benefits has unique value, in addition to the primary value of developing a more multilingual and cosmopolitan organization.

Provide Support for Employees with Global Responsibilities

As previously discussed, providing traditional means of support, such as formal mentor programs, can be challenging when managers work across boundaries of distance, countries, and cultures. Typical norms of global work include such activities as handling dozens of e-mails daily, having face-to-face contact with subordinates once every six weeks, and working in airplanes and airports. Clearly, the press of global work creates additional challenges to global managers in their ability to develop meaningful and lasting mentor and role model relationships.

Organizations can address these challenges in a variety of ways. Advanced communication technology can be leveraged to allow managers and mentors to interact through videoconferencing or to establish electronic learning forums between a group of global managers and a learning coach. Modular networks can be established that cut across formal hierarchical lines and permit global managers to support one another on business challenges across regional units. Social ties can be formed by bringing global managers from different locations together to socialize and work on business issues. Approaches such as these can provide needed support to global managers while also promoting the type of trust that is essential to developing successful cross-cultural business teams.

Be Sure Your Talent Pool Reflects the Best and the Brightest

The image of the glass ceiling is often used to evoke the organizational structures that prevent women and people of color from moving above a certain level in an organization. Unfortunately, it is common knowledge that a country-based glass ceiling is experienced by many foreign nationals in international organizations. The outcome of this phenomenon is that we often see only people native to the organization's home country being promoted beyond the level of country manager. This outcome, whether unconscious or intentional, results in morale and retention problems around the world. The best and brightest members of your management talent are unlikely to remain with the organization if they know that they are trapped under a country-based glass ceiling. If they must watch an endless parade of expatriates from corporate headquarters take the plum developmental assignments, at a minimum, motivation will suffer, and at the extreme, they will take what they know to your competitor or start their own company—and become your most serious competition. You must therefore make sure that your internal talent pool includes the individuals with the highest potential, wherever they are located and wherever they are originally from.

Target Performance Capabilities That Are Multifaceted

Some organizations make the mistake of targeting high performers on the basis of capabilities that ensure success and achievement in their own country. Countries have different expectations of how effective managers should behave. In 1989, Derr and Laurent made the following observations: "German managers believe that technical creativity and competence is essential for career success. The French and the British view such managers as 'mere technicians.' The Dutch do not place high value on interpersonal relationships and communication. The British see the ability to create the right image and get noticed for what they do as essential for career success. Americans value entrepreneurs. The British and French view entrepreneurial behavior as highly disruptive. The French view the ability to manage power relationships effectively and 'to work the system' as critical to career success" (p. 296).

This suggests that organizations need to have a multifaceted and more culturally sensitive definition of what effective performance looks like. One way to do this is to build your effectiveness measures around your organization's core values. A set of deeply engrained and widely shared core values can serve as an integrating mechanism to define effective performance based on these values. Another approach is to develop a customized appraisal process built around a standard core. Measures that are responsive to varying country and cultural needs can then be added. A different approach, of course, is to adopt a standardized definition of performance required by all managers worldwide, with a standard format and set of defined steps. A strong recommendation, if going this route, is to make a significant effort to gain local commitment.

Whatever approach to defining performance is adopted in your organization, the key factor is to ensure that managers with the potential for global work be identified within the context of their home country. Then, as they mature and become more global, these managers will come to understand, from their own experience, what it takes to be effective in a variety of contexts.

Embrace and Leverage Diverse Points of View and Perspectives

Effective global organizations will have effective global people. These people will be able to work with diverse colleagues and leverage diverse points of view to create novel products, processes, and solutions. They will understand, for example, that seemingly appropriate decisions made in one location might have a negative impact in another location. Developing this mind-set combines awareness and openness to diversity across cultures with the ability to synthesize and integrate across this diversity. Managers in whom this mind-set is highly developed can play a crucial role in building bridges across complex boundaries of distance, countries, and culture.

Although there is no substitute for real international experience in the development of a global perspective, it is important to note that proper mind-set can be encouraged through numerous experiences in a manager's home country. Managing people of different gender, ethnicity, religious affiliation, or national origin is one way to develop the ability to see the world through other people's eyes. Other examples include making international news content available online, hosting international speakers, operating a "great books" club for foreign literature, and subsidizing tickets for international visual and performing arts events. Even for managers who will never learn another language or will not have the opportunity to become an expatriate or serve on a culturally and geographically dispersed team, it remains crucial in this era of globalization to provide and seek out experiences that challenge deeply held perspectives and offer opportunities to develop new ones.

Conclusion

We use the phrase "the same but different" to describe the skill set of an effective global manager. We would like to apply that same phrase to the development process that organizations need to build in order to develop people who are capable of managing complex global responsibilities. The way that human beings learn, grow, and change and the organizational support that is required to enhance the process are the same. What is different for managers in global roles is the context in which they do their work, the knowledge and capabilities that must be instilled, and the types of traits and experiences that are required. Returning to the story of John Smith at the beginning of this chapter, we realize that nearly all managers would share in John's dread for international conference calls at 4:00 A.M. In spite of the stress of travel and difference, however, we believe that for those so inclined, the developmental path of a global manager can be rich with novelty, excitement, and surprise.

CHAPTER THIRTEEN

A LIFELONG DEVELOPMENTAL PERSPECTIVE ON LEADER DEVELOPMENT

Ellen Van Velsor
Wilfred H. Drath

This chapter deals with leader development from the perspective of lifelong adult development, specifically using what has been called a constructive-developmental framework. This lifelong developmental framework is based on the work of Robert Kegan and his colleagues (Kegan, 1982, 1994; Kegan and Lahey, 2001). We believe that, as Kegan and Lahey suggest, the complex demands people face today, in both their work and their personal lives, call for forms of development that many people are only in the process of achieving. In a very real sense, many adults go about their lives feeling that they are "in over their heads." So in this chapter, we describe what it means for individuals to develop an enhanced capacity for dealing with increasingly complex challenge, whether on the job or in personal life.

Note that we neither assume that you are familiar with constructive-developmental theory nor seek to cover it in any depth in this chapter. You may wish to consult the original sources for more information on the framework and the assessment technique used by practitioners. To enhance accessibility for the lay reader, we use our own terminology for the developmental points of reference. Readers familiar with this framework will recognize the self-reading individual as equivalent to Kegan's stage three orientation, the self-authoring person as indicative of stage four, and the self-revising person as equivalent to stage five.

We will begin by telling the story of Milly, a typical manager whose experiences demonstrate the issues that arise for individuals within the lifelong developmental framework. We use the story of Milly to explain the developmental framework in such a way that no previous knowledge or understanding of constructive-developmental theory is necessary. Following Milly's story and the explication of the developmental framework, we turn to two categories of developmental experiences: job assignments and feedback-intensive experiences. We focus on job assignments because we have conducted research that examines job challenge using this developmental lens. We focus on feedback-intensive experiences because they form the core of current CCL leader development practice. While these experiences, and the lessons they teach, are covered in other chapters of this handbook, this chapter digs deeper into *why* and *how* these kinds of experiences are developmental for people as they grow and change over the course of their lives and careers.

We believe that understanding these experiences from the viewpoint of this lifelong developmental framework adds significant value for the practitioner and developmental power for the manager. We will focus on what practitioners can do to both challenge and support managers in their ongoing development by using this lifelong developmental framework.

The Story of Milly

You have probably known someone like Milly. After graduating from college with honors, she took a job working in her hometown in the local sales office of Campbell Enterprises, Inc. (CEI), and was successful from day one. In less than two years, she was managing the office, and within four years, she was a regional sales manager. Her early bosses all said the same thing about Milly: she was very smart, learned quickly, had creative ideas, and always met her goals and objectives. She was just the kind of person CEI identified early as a high-potential manager, and she was promoted through a succession of increasingly responsible jobs in the field. Within ten years from her first day on the job, Milly was considered ready to make the move to corporate headquarters.

From Milly's point of view, this was all pretty much the way she had dreamed it would happen. Both of her parents were successful in their chosen careers, and she admired them a lot and wanted to be like them. Her father used to tell her, "You'll do better than me or your mother, Milly, because you've got what it takes." Whenever the job got tough and she felt just the slightest bit tired or discouraged, she always told herself she could pull through because "I've got what it takes."

Working for CEI was also part of her dream. It was a huge international company that was mentioned in news stories along with other large and successful corporations. When the company made it into the Fortune 50, Milly felt as proud as if she herself had been given an important award. No matter how hard she had to work and how worn out she might feel at times, it always gave her a boost to be introduced to new people as a manager with CEI.

Her approach to management and leadership in those early years was, she thought, pretty effective, even if it was also pretty simple. "I don't expect anyone working for me to do anything I wouldn't do," she would explain to every new group of people she managed. "We're a team; we all pull our weight, and that starts with me." This approach worked wonders throughout her years in the field. In a succession of offices, she formed tight-knit teams of people who cooperated well, worked hard, covered for one another, and always met or exceeded expectations. She enjoyed being judged by her bottom-line performance, and she felt confident knowing exactly what she was responsible for and effectively carrying out every responsibility. During her first year at corporate, she often thought back on those days "in the field" when she had been the happiest.

After five years at corporate, in her private moments, Milly, who was now approaching forty, was married to a successful man, and had two great kids, would sometimes admit to herself that she was not nearly as happy as she had been in those early days. Life at corporate had been a kind of gradual awakening and disillusionment. Not that her winning streak had faltered. She was one of a handful of managers who had been identified as having high potential for reaching the executive level—vice president and maybe even beyond. During every performance review, she heard from whatever boss she had how much CEI appreciated her skills and efforts. She was sent away for training in marketing and finance and for leadership development. Clearly, Milly was destined for an important position with CEI.

Yet she felt like she was struggling. During her first year at corporate, she was pulled in every direction by the never-ending conflicts and politics she encountered. It didn't take her long to learn that work at corporate was never a matter of just "doing a good job" as spelled out by her boss. She might do just what the boss wanted, only to find out later that her efforts made the manager of some other area very unhappy. In fact, it seemed that she never had an unqualified success anymore. Every time she did something right in the eyes of one person, another person would criticize what she had done. She could often see why this was the case—Milly was smart enough to know that different people had different needs and interests and that she couldn't please everyone—but knowing why it happened did nothing to stop her from feeling that her work was usually just a washout. Every effort she made felt compromised. "Two steps forward and three steps back," she would mutter to herself. The very worst thing about this situation was that she no longer felt like she was an effective and successful manager.

In the past, Milly's job had been clearly defined. She had created or worked within given systems and processes that allowed her to monitor on a daily or weekly basis the progress of her team against goals. She got consistently excellent results, and a good performance review from her boss would put her on cloud nine. She would walk around for days, if not weeks, feeling a glow of self-respect and confidence. This feeling would sustain her through all kinds of discouraging and difficult problems until her next performance review, when she would get another infusion of esteem and confidence from her boss. What made her the proudest about this was that she didn't do this by being a "yes" person. She knew people who just tried to please the boss to get the good reviews, but that wasn't her. She knew that CEI wanted people who could stand on their own, so she always pushed back on her superiors when she felt it was warranted, and this was always mentioned in her good reviews. She had always walked away from a good review knowing that it was who she was, not just what she did, that was being appreciated.

Now, years later, all that had changed. At corporate, pushing back on higher-ups was not often appreciated. If you made someone look bad in front of some other higher-up, they would both think less of you—and your boss would warn you to exercise better judgment. This came out in her reviews. While she would be praised to the skies for most of her work, there was always a countertheme that spoke about her lack of finesse, interpersonal judgment, and political skill. As a result, Milly was not sure about herself anymore. Her self-confidence was slowly being undermined. Now she walked away from performance reviews feeling uncertain about the intended message. Just what was it they wanted from her? On the one hand, they said wonderful things about her work, but the criticism of her "political skills" confused and somewhat angered her. Everyone seemed to want something different from her, and it seemed impossible to get a sense of the organization's priorities. Milly finally concluded that they were trying to turn her into a "yes" person, and she didn't like it. That wasn't what a good leader was like. How often had her father told her to be true to herself? At first, she would call him to talk about this, and he would repeat his advice: Be who you are, Milly, and everything will work out. But recently she had stopped talking to him about this problem because, if the truth were told, after five years, her life at corporate was having an unmistakable and devastating effect on her: she was no longer sure about who she was.

Lifelong Leader Development

In one sense, this chapter is about Milly's struggle to find herself as an up-and-coming executive at CEI. It is also about the way that modern organizational life has grown ever more complicated in response to the increasing complexity of an interconnected and interdependent world and how this complexity is making new demands on all leaders. For example, many organizations now focus less on their own internal functional distinctions and more on satisfying customer needs in ever-changing markets. Often this means that hierarchical coordination and control are giving way to horizontal mutual adjustment. Managers in different functions and disciplines are called on to work together across the boundaries that used to divide them. This is more difficult and more complex than working within such boundaries. Also, there is often less supervision and monitoring. Managers are expected to take the initiative to create shared understanding and coordinate with people who may have different priorities and values. For many managers, these kinds of demands require more than an increase in competence; a basic shift in self-understanding is often called for.

So this chapter is also about the way in which the complexity of modern life is calling forth a qualitatively different mind-set about work and leadership, not just for Milly, but for CEI overall. It is a mind-set that recognizes the need for people to own their own work and take responsibility for their own performance; an approach that asks people to define themselves instead of relying on the organization to tell them who they are; an approach that seeks to make everyone responsible for leadership, not just a few top managers (Kegan, 1994). In our view, it is not an approach that can be taken on—either by an individual or by an organization—by making direct changes in behavior. This is not a superficial change in style: it is a profound transformation in the way people understand themselves, their relations, and how they enact leadership.

These changes in organizational life and this transformation of understanding are happening right now. What we aim at in this chapter is to help you understand the transformation better and to provide some practical suggestions for how people responsible for leadership development can challenge and support managers in making this transformation. With this chapter, we tackle the question, What is happening to Milly in the process of her lifelong development that is especially important for her development as a manager and leader? By "lifelong adult development," we refer to the development of assumptions Milly takes for granted about herself and her relations with others over the span of her working life. While much of her development as a manager and leader focuses on a variety of job-specific skills and perspectives, such as coaching others or delegating, her lifelong development as an adult who happens to be a manager and leader focuses on key underlying beliefs about herself and her world that she takes for granted as true. Milly, like everyone, continually constructs and reconstructs interconnected underlying assumptions—what we call "webs of belief"—that delineate her capacity to acquire new managerial and leader-specific skills and perspectives.

The ideas and examples presented in this chapter come partly from experience with our own feedback-intensive programs and partly from work we have carried out in recent years with school administrators, counselors, and teachers and with high-potential managers in a large corporate setting similar to Milly's. We engaged people in a reflective process aimed at helping them gain a new perspective on their assumptions related to their work as managers. We expected that in gaining a new perspective on what they had previously taken for granted as true, people would be challenged and supported in their lifelong development process with beneficial outcomes for their job-specific development as managers and leaders. In other words, we hoped that by using this developmental perspective with people like Milly, we would help them tap new capacities to learn managerial and leadership skills and perspectives and thus address the challenges—many arising from the increased complexity of organizational life—that they had been unable to effectively face before.

The Process of Reframing Assumptions

According to the theory that informed our work, people continue to develop in basic ways all their lives. Development is not confined to the childhood years, nor does it end after adolescence. Instead, people engage in a lifelong process of development that consists of an ordered series of insights into the assumptions and beliefs they hold as most basic to their sense of who they are and how they should live in the world. These insights often call unexamined assumptions into question. When this questioning process begins, personal beliefs take on new meanings. Beliefs that once triggered an automatic emotional or intellectual response are now evaluated, tested, and pondered. In short, the person gains more control over reactions to situations and contexts that previously called forth uncontrolled, reflexive responses.

Consider the very real fear a small child feels upon waking from a nightmare. It does little good for a parent to tell the child there is nothing to fear if she believes that dreams are real. As long as the child holds this belief in the reality of dreams, bad dreams will automatically trigger real fear. The child cannot "consider" that the dream is not real and cannot "reflect on" the nature of the dream world and how it is different from other aspects of life she also knows to be real. So the dream is real, it is scary, and the child is immediately frightened; she is *subject to* her belief in dreams, and there is nothing she can do about it—that is, not until she is able to call into question her belief in the reality of dreams. As soon as she is able to think about this belief *as an assumption* and not as the plain truth, she will gain a measure of control over the way she reacts to a bad dream. She may still feel fear for a time, but she now possesses a resource for controlling that fear in the form of the knowledge that dreams are not real. She can now take dreams *as an object* of knowledge, reflection, evaluation, and decision making.

The move from being subject to some assumption (assuming without question that a belief is true) to taking that assumption as an object (being able to evaluate and reflect on the truth of the belief) is basic to the process of lifelong development. This basic developmental movement is complicated by the fact that some assumptions and beliefs are more comprehensive than others. A child's belief in the reality of dreams is not very comprehensive. It makes no difference during the day when he is awake or at night when he is not dreaming. On the other hand, a belief that he is in himself the sum of what he needs and desires would affect him day and night and in all of his relations. In other words, believing that "who I am" is the same as "my needs and wants" is the kind of belief that would likely enter into nearly every action and interaction. In addition, it is the kind of belief that the child is not able to become aware of as a belief and can only be aware of as the way things really are. Only over a long period of time and with the help of many life experiences that cause him to doubt this assumption can a child finally come to question such a belief. Thus some beliefs are so comprehensive in their meaning that we say they create an "embedding context" to which a person is completely subject. A person who is embedded in some comprehensive belief is like a fish in water—unaware that water even exists.

The Book of the Self

In this chapter, we are primarily interested in three embedded webs of belief that are comprehensive and central to adult development. These sets of beliefs determine how adults form their sense of self and their sense of their place in the world. To illustrate these beliefs, we use the metaphor of the self as a kind of book that can be read, written, or continuously revised.

The first set of beliefs revolves around the assumption that a person's core identity is determined by what certain people and ideas—the people and ideas that are most important in his life—tell him about who he is. We say that a person with this set of beliefs "reads the book of his identity" in the responses and judgments of important others and in relation to certain important ideas and values.

The second set of beliefs revolves around the assumption that a person's core identity is determined by her own self-creating processes. With this belief, a person "authors the book of her identity" by her own lights, independent from the responses and judgments of others and independent of external ideas and values.

The third set of beliefs revolves around the assumption that a person's sense of self, because it is self-authored, is also subject to self-revision in the context of relations with other people, ideas, and values. With this belief, a person "continuously writes and revises the book of his identity" in relationship to his environment.

We call the first set of comprehensive beliefs *self-reading* because the person subject to this basic assumption believes that his sense of self is to be found in what he reads about himself in others. We call the second set of comprehensive beliefs *self-authoring* because the person subject to this basic assumption believes she

writes herself for others to read. And we call the third set of beliefs *self-revising* because a person subject to this basic assumption believes he continuously creates
himself while others are potential coauthors or editors who help him undertake
revisions.

These three sets of beliefs, related to how people compose the book of self, are
ordered sequentially. It is impossible in theory for a person to hold the self-revising
beliefs without having first held the self-authoring beliefs, which in turn presup-
poses that the person has already held the self-reading beliefs. And there is much
research to support this idea of the sequential ordering of development (Kegan,
1982, 1994). In fact, it is in the process of becoming aware of and questioning
the self-reading beliefs that a person becomes able to take on the self-authoring beliefs, and it is in the process of calling the self-authoring beliefs into question that
a person becomes able to take on the self-revising beliefs. Thus self-revising comes
after self-authoring which comes after self-reading. According to theory, and with
much empirical support, this is the developmental sequence adults go through to
form their sense of themselves and their place in the world. Table 13.1 summarizes
these three sets of beliefs about self, what each set of beliefs takes for granted as the
plain truth, and what each allows a person to reflect on and question.

Why and How People Reframe Their Beliefs

Why would people go through such a developmental sequence? Surely giving up
a set of beliefs that allows one to form a sense of self and adopting a new set of
beliefs is hard work. What is it that would make a person give up one belief and
trade it in for another belief? The answer is that a person will not in fact give up
on a belief *so long as that belief is working.* Thus for as long as Milly was able to create a secure sense of herself as a valuable and esteemed person, there was no reason for her to give up her beliefs about how her self was created. But when she
reaches the point, at a critical stage in her career with CEI, where she no longer
has a sense that she knows who she is, a new set of beliefs, a new set of assumptions about how she creates and maintains her self, are being called forth. This
brings us to the important idea of *developmental movement.*

So far we have made it sound like people hold one or the other of these three
sets of beliefs, that a person believes she reads the book of herself in others one
day and wakes up the next morning realizing that it would be much better to write
her own book of self. This is not the case, however. Development as it is actually
lived is less about holding sets of beliefs than it is about moving gradually from
one set of beliefs to another. This movement is brought about by changes in a person's life circumstances that cause the person, bit by bit, to discover the limits of
her beliefs.

TABLE 13.1. THREE DEVELOPMENTALLY ORDERED SETS OF BELIEFS ABOUT THE SELF.

Belief	Takes for Granted as True Beyond Question	Is Able to Reflect on and Call into Question
Self-reading	That identity can be understood by reading it in the way important other people respond	Childhood assumptions that the self is identical with one's needs and desires
Self-authoring	That one creates one's own identity according to self-generated standards	The role played by other people and important ideas and values in making a person who he or she is
Self-revising	That while being the author of an identity, one is responsible for continuously re-creating it in alignment with one's environment	The idea that a person can create a fully adequate identity once and for all from standards that are completely self-generated

As Milly moved from managing small teams of dedicated people in the field to the more ambiguous and politically charged atmosphere of corporate head-quarters, the context in which the book of herself was being composed changed significantly. At headquarters, she found that she was unable to feel a sense of self-esteem and value that she had been easily able to feel before. Since this loss of self-esteem was not related to her performance (she still got great reviews and was tapped for future promotion), we believe that this happened to Milly, and happens to many managers, because she ran into some definite limit in her way of making sense of herself and her world. In other words, the beliefs about how her self was created that had served her well throughout her early career no longer seem to be working.

In the specific terms of the beliefs about self that we have already laid out, Milly has arrived at a critical moment in her developmental movement. She is struggling at the painful cusp between the cherished and accustomed beliefs that she can read her self in the views of others—in her mother and father, in her bosses, in her husband and children, even in her relation to something as abstract as her idealized vision of CEI—and some newer, less well formed and therefore less trust-worthy beliefs about being the author of her own story. In short, Milly is moving through a wilderness of confusion between being self-reading and self-authoring.

Let's look at some examples of this in the story. In her earlier days, a good performance review was cause for elation—not just because she wanted to do well and the review was evidence that she had done so but also because a good review helped confirm her very identity. She read herself into being in her boss's reviews in the sense that his judgments of her played a formative role in her formation of her own self-image. And because the reviews were always excellent, the self she read was a worthy self, and she felt esteem for herself. Milly's ability to work hard and meet or exceed expectations was a complex mixture of her intelligence and talent and her reaping the benefits of being appreciated by important others. But it was all based on her unquestioned belief that a self could in fact be read in others.

At corporate headquarters, it did not take long for Milly to become disillusioned, although she could not be aware of why. To her it seemed that politics ruled the day. For every person who approved of some action or decision she took, there were others to criticize her. Because she understood herself mainly through the responses and judgments of others, she was confused about where she stood or how well she was doing. Because her self-reading belief was an unconscious belief, Milly could not reflect on it, and she felt stuck. For a long time, her only recourse was to blame her failing sense of self on CEI and the politics of headquarters. The only answer she could come up with was that who she was as a person was not right for the atmosphere at corporate, but yet they kept treating her as a high-potential manager. Even her father's familiar advice to "be who you really are" seemed impossible, because she could no longer say who she really was.

This does not mean that Milly's beliefs were poor beliefs or that she has been deluded about her "real" self for all these years. It only means that with sweeping changes in the context in which she lived and worked, there came a call for sweeping changes in *how* she went about creating a self. This is an important point: just because one set of beliefs comes earlier in a person's life does not make those beliefs less than or worse than beliefs that are developed later. Only the usefulness of applying beliefs in some specific context can make one set of beliefs better or worse than another. The question in development is always "better or worse *for what?*"

Why Leadership Development Depends on Lifelong Development

This confusion is not just happening to Milly. It is happening to managers in organizations everywhere. We believe that the increasing complexity in many organizations, related to the increasing interconnectedness and interdependence of the world, is making this movement from self-reading to self-authoring critically important in developing and enacting more effective approaches to leadership. In other words, the movement that Milly is trying to make from self-reading to self-authoring is a movement that many people in organizations will need to make in order to develop and enact more effective leadership.

More and more, modern organizational life is demanding that people take ownership of their own work and take responsibility for their own performance, without needing to be monitored. Organizational life is demanding that people define themselves and what it means for them to make an effective contribution in their workplace, as well as in their personal lives. People must develop a vision for themselves instead of relying on the organization to tell them who they are, what their contribution needs to be, or why their work is significant. Organizations are now holding more than just a few executives responsible for the overall leadership of the organization, so more and more managers will need to make the move from self-reading to self-authoring. This is because a person who is predominantly self-reading will likely lack the capacity to fully own her own work and to shape self-expectations independent of the expectations and judgments of important others. The person who is predominantly self-reading, as Milly was early in her career, will tend to see the organization and her bosses as the owners of the work and will see herself as fulfilling the expectations of important others. In the same way, a person who is predominantly self-reading will be unlikely to have the capacity to define herself and create a personal vision. The assumption that she could read her true self in the judgments of important others meant that Milly did not define herself, but signed onto an esteemed and valuable self that she "read about" in her relations with others.

Finally, a person who is predominantly self-reading will be unlikely to have the capacity to comfortably take responsibility for something on her own initiative. For Milly, leadership was something that had been bestowed on her by CEI and her bosses. Taking responsibility for more than that (such as taking responsibility for informal leadership in CEI overall) would have struck her as ridiculous at best or treasonous at worst, because she saw leadership outside her given boundaries as the responsibility of important others.

Reaching these kinds of developmental outcomes in organizations is not a matter to be addressed by improving the skills or changing the behavior of managers. Skills and behaviors can only be enacted within a framework of assumptions about the self. Such a framework creates definite capacities and places specific limitations on what a person can be skillful in doing. Developing individuals in complex organizations today is thus a matter of challenging and supporting development of the very beliefs that managers use to bring a sense of self into being. The movement that Milly is trying to make, from self-reading to self-authoring, is a movement that many people in organizations will need to make in order to continue to enact effective leadership as they face increasingly complex challenges.

The Story of Milly, Part Two

After several years, Milly was able to discern the outlines of her earlier struggle more clearly. Hindsight allowed her to see that her father's advice to "be who you really are" had been a good idea that she was unable to put into practice. In retrospect, it became much easier to see that it was the conflict between *wanting* to be who she really was and being unable to *know* who she really was that created her developmental movement. In time Milly came to see that the reason she couldn't put the idea into practice was because "who she really was" had been something she was reading about in the responses of others all her life. Only by taking the very brave step of taking her own story into her own hands—which meant taking it out of the hands of people like her favorite boss and even her beloved parents and her wonderful husband and children, as well as taking it out of the hands of CEI—could she even begin to think about being who she really was. Once she made this critical movement, life at corporate became no less political, no less ambiguous, no less complex and difficult—but it ceased to be the crucible in which her self was formed.

Once Milly had fully taken on the self-authoring web of beliefs, she experienced a sea change in her feelings and attitudes about herself, others, her work, and the shared work of CEI. She came to see that the most important thing for her now was less about meeting expectations and fulfilling the hopes others had for her and more about making her own meaningful contribution to the organization. What was critically different about this was that ultimately it was up to *her* to evaluate that contribution. Of course the judgments of her bosses and CEI management were important to her, and of course the ultimate value of her contribution depended in part on whether others recognized its worth. But the judgments and recognition of others did not determine her sense of contribution. In the end, it was her own standards that mattered the most to her. If, in living up to her own standards of what constituted a meaningful contribution, she was successful at work, so much the better. Milly came to see that CEI as an organization was less like a parent to please and whose expectations needed to be met and more like a partner who needed her to be her own best self. She came to see the creative role she could play as a manager in CEI: not just doing what was expected but shaping expectations; not just fulfilling the organization's hopes but helping it articulate its hopes.

It would be a happy (though unrealistic) ending if this sea change in Milly's life meant that her struggles at work were over. In making the move from self-reading to self-authoring, Milly did not move away from the complex challenges in her life; rather she moved toward new and even more complex challenges. In one sense, lifelong development is the process of encountering challenges at a new level of complexity.

Milly was promoted to vice president, and people talked about her as a viable candidate to one day be the CEO. Her performance reviews took note that she "stands by her convictions," "has a sure sense of herself," "does not blow in the wind and is not political," "is able to take charge of difficult situations without feeling undue pressure." All of these abilities are aspects of Milly's self-authoring belief system. But along with such newly formed abilities came newly formed challenges.

For one thing, Milly became increasingly impatient with those of her peers and superiors who she thought still looked to the organization for self-definition and who always tried to please others. She would fume for days over a peer who had committed to take a stand in a meeting and failed to do so, later explaining to Milly that he got cold feet after learning that his boss was opposed. She was often disgusted over what she saw as the wriggling and equivocating of her peers and even her bosses in the face of differing opinions and judgments rendered by the executives. She was sometimes gripped by a feeling of hopelessness about CEI, seeing it as an organization that would never be able to rise above petty bickering and maneuvering to gain favor. Whereas earlier in her career she felt herself pulled in every direction by the company's politics, now she saw herself as having risen above all that and was frustrated at the continuing immersion of others in it.

While this challenge was primarily on an emotional level, another type of situation arose for Milly that challenged her intellectually: How could she most effectively bring her unique perspectives on the organization and advocate for her sense of organizational priorities with her fellow vice presidents, many of whom had their own strong perspectives and priorities? How could she stand up for herself and at the same time work with others who held their own self-generated perspectives and priorities for the organization? Could they as a group have a clear sense of shared work? This was just the opposite of her other challenge. Instead of dealing with people who were always looking to please others, this challenge involved those people she worked with who, like herself, tended to stand on their own and work by their own standards of excellence. She had developed the capacity to be true to herself. Now the challenge seemed to be how to remain true to herself while allowing others to have an influence on designs or outcomes. How could she work on shared goals with others without giving up her hard-won sense of being the author of her own story?

As Milly continues to grow and develop in her work at CEI, she will find that self-authorship is not the end of her story. Already she is beginning to have a new good idea: being yourself means more than writing your own story. It means writing and rewriting that story based on experiences of interrelating with others and changing circumstances. Putting that new idea into practice—moving toward the beliefs we call *self-revising*—will be the work of Milly's most mature years.

The Difference Between Learning and Development

As may be obvious from Milly's story, *development*, as we use the word here, is quite different from learning. Milly has learned valuable lessons all of her life. For example, she has learned to manage increasingly large budgets, how to motivate subordinates, how to set goals and coach others for development. Yet these lessons were not necessarily transformational. Her learning about these tasks took place within her then-current way of understanding herself and her relationships to others. It was only when Milly began to move from understanding events (including learning) from a self-reading perspective to understanding them from a self-authoring perspective that transformation, or development, occurred. Developmental transformation is about a change in how all life events get understood—including events called learning. Development transforms the meaning of what one learns; it constitutes the basis on which learning is made meaningful. What a person can learn from an event depends on how the person constructs the event into a meaningful experience. Thus people can learn only what their current way of constructing meaning enables them to learn. Learning takes place within one's way of framing experience, within some generalized way of making sense of things, whereas development is the evolution and change of the way of making sense itself.

This difference means that *learning* and *development* are not interchangeable terms. In this chapter, when we speak of a person developing as a leader, we mean that he is changing the way he makes the events associated with being a leader meaningful; he is changing his whole way of understanding what it means to understand himself and others and what it means to be a leader. Obviously, a person can learn about leadership (what leadership is, the characteristics of effective leaders, what causes leaders to derail) and can acquire skills that will make him a better manager (how to give feedback effectively, how to set and achieve goals), and these lessons can lead to improvements in his abilities as a manager. But what he learns will be framed and limited by the ways in which he can make what he learns meaningful. Everything learned will cohere within that developmental framework—whether that framework is one of self-reading, self-authoring, or self-revising. Increases in the complexity of a person's leadership role, however, can require the person to change in ways that he cannot simply learn within the limitations of his current developmental order. This is when development is called forth. A change in the very way of making his life's events meaningful may be required, and this is qualitatively different from the ability to learn (see Chapter Seven).

The Power of Developmental Experience

This section focuses on two categories of developmental experience: job assignments and feedback-intensive experiences. As stated earlier, this chapter treats each type of experience using the lifelong developmental framework just described. In this section, we cover the question of *why* and *how* these experiences are developmental for individuals at each of the developmental transitions described earlier. To repeat: we believe that understanding these experiences from the viewpoint of this framework adds significant value for the practitioner and developmental power for the manager. In each of the sections that follow, we also focus on what practitioners can do to both support and challenge individuals in their ongoing development using this framework. So before we begin, it is important to revisit the ideas of challenge and support.

In the Introduction, support is described as elements of an experience that send the message that the individual will find safety and a new equilibrium on the other side of challenge and change. Support helps people handle the struggle and pain of learning and developing. It helps them bear the weight of the experience and maintain a positive view of themselves as capable, worthy, and valuable people who can learn and grow. Very much in line with the framework of this chapter, the Introduction goes on to say that support means different things to different people. For some, seeing that others place a positive value on their efforts to change and grow is a key factor in staying on course with learning goals. For others, having the resources and freedom needed to move forward on self-initiated goals is the needed support.

From our perspective in this chapter, support is specifically framed as an appreciation for a person's current way of making events meaningful, whatever that current way may be (self-reading, self-authoring, self-revising). Appreciation in this context means more than having empathy for a person's feelings in going through change and growth. It means more specifically gaining a keen awareness of what it will cost—what the person stands to lose—in changing and growing. Because we see development as the forming of a whole new way of understanding oneself and one's life, we recognize that development is not simply the acquisition of a new way but also the loss of an old and comfortable way of understanding. As such, it elicits both elation and grief.

The reason support is critically important is that this "developmental loss" (Kegan, 1982) is a key factor that can actually block development or cause the person to experience a sense of being "stuck" that can be frustrating or even debilitating. An understanding and acknowledgment, by the developing individual and by others hoping to support that development, of the inevitable losses incurred helps the individual endure and make best use of the developmental challenge he is facing. If the loss of meaning involved in changing the way one constructs certain events is not understood and acknowledged, the challenge of such change may be too great. We will return to these points, to better illustrate how to most effectively balance support and challenge for different individuals, as we focus on each of several kinds of potentially developmental experiences in the sections that follow.

Developmental Assignments

As described in Chapter Five, job assignments can be a powerful source of development. Whether we use the term *assignment* to mean an entire job or a piece of a job and whether the assignment is formal or informal, development happens because the assignment stretches the individual, pushes her out of her comfort zone, and requires her to think and act differently. In other words, challenge is a key element of job assignments.

For more than two decades, the Center for Creative Leadership has done research on the power of developmental assignments, what people learn from different kinds of on-the-job experiences, and how those lessons are learned (Douglas, 2003; McCall, Lombardo, and Morrison, 1988; Morrison, White, and Van Velsor, 1987). This research has shown us that there are five broad sources of challenge from which managers report learning important lessons: job transitions, creating change, high levels of responsibility, managing boundaries, and dealing with diversity (see Chapter Five). When managers face these challenges, they report learning critical lessons about themselves and about leadership, even more so when they have adequate support for their development. So we know what challenges people, and we know what they believe they have learned from those challenges. But we have understood less about *why* these assignments challenge people. What is it about a job transition or high levels of responsibility or dealing with diversity, for example, that challenges people and facilitates development? Why do some people struggle to develop in the context of certain challenging assignments, while others take the same assignments in stride?

Part of the explanation surely has to do with skills and behaviors acquired through previous experience. For example, a manager who has had one or two assignments in which dealing with diversity was involved will tend to be less challenged by such an assignment than another manager who has never experienced that kind of assignment. So the same assignment that at one point in a manager's career elicits significant development may, at another point, elicit none. There might also be gender, cultural, or other demographic differences in how people develop as a result of experience. It may be that some groups are more oriented toward development in the context of job assignments, while others tend to learn and develop more easily through relationships with other people (Van Velsor and Hughes-James, 1990). Yet we think that another key factor in understanding why people learn from particular experiences (specifically assignments) has to do with the *kind* of developmental movement they are making at the time of the experience, that is, whether they are fully embedded in the self-reading perspective at the time the challenge is faced, whether they are in transition from self-reading to self-authoring (and at what point they are in that transition), or whether they are fully embedded in the self-authoring frame of reference. This has been a less well understood aspect of CCL's work on the developmental power of assignments.

Until very recently, we have had no empirical data about the differences between what predominantly self-reading managers and predominantly self-authoring managers find challenging in their work. We also have had little knowledge about the developmental shifts from self-reading to self-authoring or from self-authoring to self-revising and how job challenge facilitates or blocks those transitions. Over the past several years, we have designed an extended interview and coaching process that employs a lifelong developmental framework to look at what kinds of experiences challenge working adults who are in the process of making these developmental transitions. Among the people with whom we have worked so far, 12 percent fall purely into our self-reading category, 36 percent are in developmental transition from the self-reading to the self-authoring stance, 48 percent appear to have completed the transition to self-authoring but not yet begun to move beyond it, and 4 percent have begun the transition from self-authoring to self-revising (see Table 13.2).

In understanding the ways in which assignments challenge people (as well as in understanding the challenge of the feedback experiences we will discuss later), we found it most useful to think about people as members of one of two groups: (1) people who most often use a self-reading frame of reference to understand work and life events and (2) people who most often use a self-authoring frame of reference to understand work and life events. We intentionally say "primarily" or "most often use" a particular frame of reference to emphasize that many people in our sample (36 percent), like many adults in the general population, are in transition between these two frames of reference. An individual who primarily relies on a self-reading frame of reference will occasionally experience, glimpse, or even use with some grace a self-authored stance in certain situations. Similarly, an individual who has come to primarily rely on a self-authoring frame of reference will occasionally return to the use of a self-reading stance in certain situations.

TABLE 13.2. ADULTS AGED THIRTY-FIVE TO FIFTY-FIVE AT EACH OF FOUR DEVELOPMENTAL POSITIONS.

Developmental Position	Sample of Managers and Teachers
Self-reading	3 (12%)
Transitioning from self-reading to self-authoring	9 (36%)
Self-authoring	12 (48%)
Transitioning from self-authoring to self-revising	1 (4%)

The transition from one developmental stance to another takes a significant amount of time and is not straightforward or linear. Individuals experience many leaps ahead, in terms of insights and capacity, often followed by returns to previous or more comfortable ways of knowing. So although for simplicity we will treat these two groups as if everyone in them is the same, that is truly not the case. Within each group, there is some variation among individuals in how they understand the significant challenges they face.

That said, we found that different elements of job assignments were in fact seen as challenging to people in these two groups (self-reading and self-authoring). Managers who most often used a self-reading perspective were more often challenged when the following elements were present in their assignments:

- Being in a role that is ill-defined
- Becoming a member of a more senior group
- Needing to take a minority position in a group or with a superior
- Presenting oneself authentically in stressful situations
- Facing competing demands from work and home lives

These are in contrast to the elements of job assignments that were seen as most challenging to managers who most often used a self-authoring perspective:

- Working with or respecting people (especially peers and superiors) who frame their experience primarily from the self-reading standpoint
- Needing to bring one's self-authored goals, viewpoints, or priorities into alignment with others' goals, viewpoints, or priorities, in the context of shared work

One thing that is immediately apparent is that self-reading managers seem to be finding a greater number of elements that create challenge in the context of their job assignments than self-authoring managers are. While this may be in part due to the fact that our sample so far is small and is drawn from a limited number of organizations, it is also reconcilable with the idea that today's work environments make demands on people that require the capabilities available to the group that we call self-authoring (Kegan, 1994). The demands that self-reading managers face in the context of their jobs may be at a level of challenge that is more intense for them and for which a higher level and a different kind of support is necessary. In fact, for some self-reading managers (perhaps those for whom little of the self-authoring perspective has emerged), the level of challenge may be beyond their current reach. As previous CCL research has shown, the inability to adapt during a transition is one of the key factors leading to executive derailment

(Browning and Van Velsor, 1999; Leslie and Van Velsor, 1996; McCall, Lombardo, and Morrison, 1988; Morrison, White, and Van Velsor, 1992).

In the next two sections, each of these sets of developmentally different challenges will be explored in more depth, with an eye toward helping practitioners understand what can be done to support self-reading managers facing what are essentially self-authoring demands and what can be done to support the ongoing development of self-authoring managers, some of whom may be facing, for the first time, a sense of diminished challenge in their jobs.

Elements of Challenge in Assignments for Self-Reading Managers

The managers we call self-reading have achieved mastery of many capabilities critical to effective management. They have internalized many points of view, can readily consider others' perspectives, and can use the perspectives of important others to understand themselves and to find personal direction and meaning. For self-reading managers, however, the perspectives of others are so readily considered and often given such weight that these managers cannot easily manage or prioritize complex work, particularly when these many important points of view and priorities come into conflict. Until a person makes significant movement beyond a grounding in self-reading, she cannot see the limitations of relying on others for her self-definition and direction and cannot subordinate those others' perspectives to one that she can fully call her own.

Remember Milly's struggle, during her first years at corporate, of never feeling she had an unqualified success? Despite doing just what her boss wanted, she was troubled to find that other important people would be unhappy with the actions she had taken or the decisions she had made. Looking primarily to the views of others for validation, she no longer felt successful or effective. Until she was able to "find herself"—that is, to shift more toward self-authoring than self-reading—she would not feel comfortable engaging in behaviors that are typical earmarks of taking ownership of and full responsibility for her work and the choices, behaviors, and feelings that play out there.

Being in an Ill-Defined Role. Being in a role that does not come with clear expectations or job requirements is our first example of a challenge that feels more or less overwhelming to the primarily self-reading manager. Such an assignment is likely to be seen by these managers not as an opportunity to invest the self in the creation of goals and structure (a likely self-authored reaction) but as a threatening situation where one can't know what to do because there has been inadequate (from the self-reading perspective) structure or direction given by important and relevant others, such as a boss, the HR function, or the executive team. When

Milly had a lead position in the field, her responsibilities and bottom line had been clear-cut, but when she got to corporate, it seemed there was no bottom line—no clear guideline for how to be effective, no day-to-day ways to know that she was being effective. So she floundered for some time, anxious about her own performance and frustrated by her own inability to figure it all out.

Because the self-reading manager often does not feel comfortable creating his own sense of direction and a structure to meet his needs, when he is in an ill-defined role he may feel paralyzed by his inability to act. He may continue to look for direction from others even when none is available and when others expect the job to be what he makes of it (which he is not likely to believe could be the case). Moving ahead without direction from an external guide is likely to feel unauthorized, risky, or a waste of time to the self-reading manager, since his belief will continue to be that direction should eventually be forthcoming and that any self-initiated action might be overridden or superseded by direction once it arrives.

When viewed from the perspective of a primarily self-authoring manager, this same situation is likely to be seen as an opportunity to exercise one's own sense of direction and priorities, to make one's mark on the organization, or to stand out by creating something important in the midst of ambiguity. The manager who has completed the transition to self-authoring will feel the needed comfort in making the role what he sees it should be, will tend to make use of the ambiguity to exercise his personal vision and goals, and will perhaps err on the side of asking for forgiveness rather than permission.

Moving to a Senior-Level Job. Of course, as one moves upward in almost any organization, roles and assignments become less well defined and less prestructured for the incumbent by the organization or by a boss. The farther a person moves up in an organization, the greater the expectation that she no longer needs guidance from external sources and that she will bring a personal vision and a personal sense of priorities—in short, a self-authored view of the work and her role in that work. As a result, senior-level positions can be especially challenging for managers who have not completed the transition to full comfort with a self-authoring frame of reference—and perhaps the more likely it is that an individual may derail at this level. We believe that moving up in an organization will be increasingly difficult if development from self-reading to self-authoring is not taking place, is taking place out of step with promotion, or is not adequately supported for the individual.

While a manager constructing experience fully from the self-authored perspective will tend to see the advantage of moving into a new level as an opportunity to have more personal authority, most people who move up are at a transitional point between self-reading and self-authoring. In our work, people who were somewhere in the midst of this transition were concerned with the fit or lack of fit between themselves and others already at this level—that is, those more senior people who would soon become their peers. These transitional managers tended to ask themselves whether they wanted the move, and they struggled with the question of whether they would need to be like "them" (their more senior-level colleagues) in order to succeed. Being "like them" could mean a range of things, from having no life outside of work to being a person who needs constant ego stroking (two not uncommon views of senior executives, from below). The questions these managers asked themselves were characteristic of people who have not fully achieved self-authoring—for example, "Can I still be me if I become a part of this group?" This question almost perfectly identifies the angst of transition away from the self-reading stage and the nature of the shift involved in further development.

In making the developmental transition from self-reading to self-authoring, people reach a place where they have moved beyond the stage of relying fully on others' views for self-definition to where they have begun to form a sense of identity that is partly self-authored and to which they have some access in certain situations. Yet part of what it means to be in this transition is that an individual has not fully realized the limitations of a self derived from others' views, nor has she reached a point where she can trust that her ability to self-author will remain with her in the context of a new group of peers who used to be superiors. In fact, it may or may not remain with her, as the tentative sense of self-authoring may seem to come and go for some time. Thus the question "Can I still be me?" becomes especially important. It is tantamount to asking, Will I be able to maintain the developmental ground I've gained so far in finding my own place to stand, and will I be able to do so in the face of this challenge of working with a new group of peers to whom I used to report and on whose perspectives I once based my views? It is, in fact, a good question for the person in developmental transition and one that relates to the need for support, which we will discuss later.

In contrast, the manager fully grounded in self-reading (and not in the process of transition) would not ask this question but instead would have his antenna up, waiting to see what the expectations of these important others would be for him at this new level. Because these "important others" would be his new peers, he might feel quite intimidated by the thought of working side by side with them. And the information he was waiting for regarding what their expectations may be would not be forthcoming in a way he would fully understand or be comfortable with. Instead, he might find out rather quickly that they expected him to come with his own point of view, his own clear vision, goals, and priorities. This would likely leave him anxious and confused. If this manager failed to develop (to begin the transition to a more self-authored posture) and instead continued to look to others as his guides, he might quickly be seen as slow to act or indecisive or could in some environments succumb to manipulation by self-authored and self-interested peers. So the challenges posed in moving up to a more senior management level can be perceived in three very different ways: as a threat to hard-won gains in one's development, as an important challenge against which to test those gains and further one's development, or as a setup for derailment. This is why we believe that support (in the form of a deep appreciation of the person's current way of framing her experience) is as critical as challenge (helping to call forth a new way of framing) to furthering an individual leader's development.

Taking a Minority Position. The primarily self-reading managers in our research also struggled with being comfortable in taking a minority position in a group or with a superior. This element of challenge often played out in situations in which it was important to be comfortable putting forth an opinion or a perspective that might not be welcomed by the recipient. When a manager grounding his experience from a self-reading perspective is in an assignment that demands that he bring a perspective that conflicts with the perspective of a large or powerful group, the psychological and emotional toll on the manager can be large. For example, in any organization, a group responsible for R&D can bring radical new ideas to the table, many of which may be less than feasible from a financial perspective. If this is the case, and if the new ideas have garnered support from senior levels, a person in a financial role will need to maintain what amounts to a minority view on the feasibility of those ideas over the long term. If this person constructs her experience primarily from a self-reading perspective, such a demand will present a significant challenge. Although she may, in fact, carry out her responsibilities quite well, and even with some interpersonal finesse, she will likely feel quite uncomfortable in this situation. This situation may contribute to a high level of stress and a sense of insecurity about how she is being perceived. However, if her perspective proves valid or if she finds she can present it without perceiving that others think less of her personally, the event can be one that assists her in her movement toward self-authoring—that is, in her ability to subordinate the views of others to a self view that can *comfortably* take a stand and stand alone.

Presenting Oneself Authentically. We found in our work that articulating "honest" views, that is, comfortably representing what one believes to be true, was in general a challenge with which self-reading managers tended to struggle. This issue with honesty generally played out in two types of settings. One situation has to do with needing to give honest negative feedback to a peer or a subordinate. In this situation, a self-reading manager will likely experience tension delivering the negative feedback effectively in the context of his fear that the other person will think less of him for having delivered it or for having delivered it awkwardly. The other type of situation has to do with the challenge of presenting oneself, often to a superior, in a way that feels honest, despite some fear that the "real you" will not be acceptable, and a feeling that it might be better to project a version of self one believes the other person wants to or needs to see.

In general, situations perceived as calling for honesty (honest feedback or honest presentation of self) can pose a challenge to people in developmental transition from self-reading to self-authoring because with movement toward self-authoring, articulating "where I stand" on an issue and presenting "my own view" begin to take on more importance to the individual. Yet while the need to make that articulation grows stronger during this transition, what may linger is a nagging feeling, originating in the self-reading capacity not yet fully left behind, that what one says or does will have some significant negative impact on the receiver and on the receiver's view of oneself—especially if the receiver is a superior or someone with whom one has a significant personal relationship. This tension reflects some self-reading assumptions about how one should present oneself to important others (in the way that one thinks the receiver would like) and about how one's honesty will be received (that it will in turn assert a strong claim on the receiver—which may in fact be the case if the receiver is also self-reading and thus strongly subject to the claims of others). If the person on the receiving end is a superior, the nagging feeling of the person in transition from self-reading to self-authoring may be that full presentation of one's own still-emerging self may not be entirely possible, may not be accomplished with grace, and may therefore create a negative impression in the superior's eyes. In other words, this hesitancy may reflect some lingering (and perhaps well-founded) uncertainty about one's ability to fully own a self-authored reality or to filter or contain the views of others within what is still only a tentatively and partially self-authored view.

Facing Competing Demands. Another element of challenge we found in the work lives of primarily self-reading managers was facing competing demands from work, home, and community—that is, from several groups of important others. Although the challenges inherent in "life balance" do not fit neatly within the category of challenge from job assignments, we cover them here because these are elements that definitely affect an individual's ability to handle the other challenges he may face on the job, and they are an important source of concern for many of the managers who attend programs at CCL.

Again, the perspective most often relied on by a self-reading manager can provide few, if any, resources for managing competing claims on his attention, because each claim "owns him" in the sense that he does not assume, as a self-authoring manager would, that the claims of significant others can and should be subordinated to a set of personally owned priorities and perspectives. Instead, the claims of each important other, when in conflict, can seem irreconcilable. So, for example, if a manager who is more or less self-reading perceives that her boss rewards and promotes people who are frequently willing to work late into the evenings and on weekends, while her spouse wants her to put more priority on time with him or time spent at home with children, the manager can easily feel completely torn and not know how to make the decision. This feeling of being torn has to do with the lack of having one's own place to stand, that is, the inability to manage competing commitments, to subordinate some claims of others based on one's own sense of self and priorities. In addition, because the self-reading perspective tends to orient a person toward the claims of others, she can become highly attuned to perceiving what these claims may be—even possibly making unfounded assumptions about what a boss or a spouse might want—and thus add unnecessarily to the chaos of conflicting expectations.

Elements of Challenge in Assignments for Self-Authoring Managers

Instead of relying on external guides for direction, understanding, and behavior, the self-authoring person has gained the capacity to guide herself in prioritizing and co-ordinating multiple demands or views. And again, we found that these managers typically reported different, and fewer, elements of challenge in their current jobs.

As individuals move through successive stages or phases of development, the perspective they most often have difficulty dealing with in themselves and in others is the one they are in the process of growing beyond. Even the slight hold of the previous stance can feel like a pull that threatens to throw one back or limit one to an increasingly ineffective range of behaviors and capacities—behaviors that the individual has struggled hard to surpass. Seeing others behave in ways or make assumptions that are somehow reminiscent of one's own prior perspectives can be especially annoying when one is struggling to maintain one's own developmental ground.

Respecting the Self-Reading Perspective. As managers approach and then gain a fully self-authoring perspective, we found it could become particularly difficult for them to work with people who had not gone far beyond the fully self-reading perspective. In our interviews, we often heard the self-authoring managers talk with frustration and even some disdain about direct reports who did not seem willing or able to act in an empowered way, initiate action, or make decisions on their own. This was part of Milly's frustration later in her career. Try as she might to pass on her vision of the work as something in which the team members share full accountability, she was reminded over and over again that the team members look to her for direction and feel rewarded mainly when they succeed in operating according to her standards or when they win her approval for their individual or collective actions.

Conversely, if a self-authoring person like Milly perceives self-reading assumptions in a superior, that superior is likely to be seen as an ineffective or weak leader lacking in personal vision. The self-reading manager will likely be seen by his more self-authoring colleagues as unable to make independent decisions or take an unpopular stand, potentially leading to morale problems when conditions call for change.

Aligning Oneself with Others in Shared Work. When a manager has achieved the ability to be self-authoring, has a place to stand that he can call his own, and feels clear about his stance or his priorities, it can be difficult to work in a way that brings his own goals, viewpoints, or priorities in alignment with those of others. He is moving toward, but has not yet achieved, the ability to use shared work and shared meaning in an ongoing process of reexamining and reshaping his views. This may be particularly challenging in a group of senior-level peers, many of whom may be as yet unable to see the limitations of their own self-authored stance. In our work with managers, serving on a high-level task force with an important and visible mission was an example of an assignment that held important elements of challenge for primarily self-authoring managers. The most challenging element of this assignment was the fact that such a task force was made up of peers representing different divisions and functions. Each manager had his or her distinct point of view about how to go forward with the task.

In one case, the team worked long and hard and was successful in hammering out a consensus plan. Weeks later, several of the organization's senior executives met with individual members of the task force to get additional information about the thinking of the group, and it was sometimes difficult for individual members of this team to reconstruct the rationale behind the group consensus. In other words, individuals tended to lose the ability to stand for the recommendations made by the whole group. Instead, individual team members could most clearly remember only their own point of view and the original rationale for that view. Although the group had worked together to create a plan that all could agree to (in other words, they had successfully reached consensus), they had not, as individuals, been able to see the limitations of their own individual views and use the experience of working in this group to change the way they created meaning for themselves individually. They had not been able to assimilate it or to assimilate themselves to the agreement they had achieved. Instead, the consensus was, as in many consensus situations, formed by cobbling together individual views into some kind of common architecture, with each individual then walking away essentially retaining his or her original piece of that architecture.

As in many group agreements, none of the members moved beyond their separate and unique ways of understanding the situation to create together a transformed way of understanding the shared work. It would be this new way of understanding one's own point of view in relation to the group view that would facilitate each member's ability to stand for the recommendations. This ability to work in a way that "cocreates" self and other ("my view and the group view") is a capacity established as one nears the self-revising stance. Working collaboratively from a self-authoring stance may be seen as working in a way that gets each individual's needs and goals met, not working in a way that includes each individual in intentionally transforming autonomous points of view to forge real common ground. The latter is an achievement that first becomes possible as one begins to move from a self-authoring to a self-revising perspective.

Feedback-Intensive Experiences

This section uses the lifelong developmental framework to focus on feedback-intensive programs (Chapter One) and 360-degree feedback (Chapter Two). We have chosen to focus on these leader development practices because they form the core of CCL's expertise. We believe that these are designed and implemented at CCL in a way that meets the needs of managers at all stages of development, yet the linkage of our practice to this lifelong developmental framework is not fully understood.

Both types of experience provide the individual with information about herself from a wide variety of sources. The distinction of 360-degree feedback is that it compares self-ratings to the ratings of one's boss, peers, direct reports, and sometimes other groups such as customers. In a feedback-intensive program, 360-degree feedback is used in conjunction with self-ratings on personality instruments and feedback from staff and fellow participants on a variety of experiential exercises, simulations, and targeted staff- and peer-feedback sessions. Given the challenges articulated by managers in the preceding section of this chapter, it is clear that classroom-based feedback-intensive developmental experiences can and do play an important role in supporting the necessary movement from the self-reading to the self-authoring perspectives. Feedback-intensive experiences can replicate the demands and developmental challenges being faced by managers moving between self-reading and self-authoring and can do so in an environment where psychological safety and support are key ingredients.

Intensive feedback saturates the individual with information from which she must draw out the meaning. Her most immediate task in a feedback-intensive experience is to make sense of the data—the information streaming in from multiple sources on multiple aspects of style and behavior. Yet in any type of feedback-intensive experience, the challenge is not just that the individual is confronted with personality, behavior, or performance data from many sources. On top of that, these data represent multiple views that often differ from one's self-view and one from the other. By presenting a participant with data from many people on many instruments, these experiences provide opportunities for the participant to make sense of both convergence of views (for example, feedback from fellow participants in a program may be similar to 360-degree feedback from back home) and to make sense of significant differences in views (for example, each rater group may see the participant differently on the back-home 360-degree feedback, or rater views may differ from self-view). Each of these challenges, with all of their possible outcomes, can be powerful and can have a different impact depending on whether the person tends to construct meaning through a self-reading, self-authoring, or self-revising perspective.

The experience of intensive, multisource feedback is likely to be most challenging for people who are in developmental transition. When a person is fully embedded in a particular way of constructing meaning, the perspectives typical of that developmental stance are unquestioned and unquestionable. For these people at this time in their lives, feedback (even intensive feedback) will tend to be experienced from within this unquestioned way of making meaning. For those people fully embedded in self-reading, feedback will tend to be quickly internalized and seen as something of a "report card," with all attendant positive or negative emotions, particularly if it comes from superiors or others whom the individual respects. On the other hand, people fully embedded in a self-authoring perspective may see feedback from others as a confirmation of what they already know about themselves, minimizing any apparent differences between self-views and others' views or seeing others' discrepant views as simply wrong. People who are comfortably ensconced in a self-authoring perspective may find that some aspect of their behavior needs tweaking. They will simply not feel the same need to use the data to reflect on themselves and will not be ready to consider the limitations of their current self-view. People who are in transition from one way of making meaning to another, however, are in the process of questioning their very way of making sense of experiences like feedback. For such people, intensive feedback can be a valuable opportunity for enhanced self-understanding—and a boost in their quest to achieve a new phase in their development.

Program participants who are moving from the self-reading to the self-authoring perspective are challenged differently by feedback-intensive experiences than participants who are fully comfortable with self-authoring or who are in transition from self-authoring to self-revising. Intensive feedback saturates the individual's experience with multiple views, some of which may conflict. Yet each has the potential to feel compellingly important to the participant who constructs his experience to some extent from a self-reading position. Because a primarily self-reading person does not yet feel comfortable authoring a view that can be used to coordinate the claims others make on him, each view seems to make a direct and separate claim on him. As such, the conflicting views of others will probably be a significant challenge, since he does not have a ready-made way of prioritizing or coordinating those claims. In fact, the conflicting views of others may be more of a challenge to a primarily self-reading individual than the fact that those others' views may also conflict with his self-view. Until one is fully comfortable with self-authoring, the self-view is, in a sense, tentative until the views of relevant others are known.

We often describe our feedback-intensive programs as holding up a mirror, or a set of mirrors, to the participant to help improve understanding of individual strengths and weaknesses. When we say that a feedback-intensive experience is like a mirror, that is almost literally true for self-reading participants. They will have difficulty filtering what they see in others' views, as these mirrored images are the material they use to create their self-view. If the views of others agree, the experience of these multiple mirrors can be quite powerful for the self-reading manager, whether the feedback is positive or negative. Seeing different versions of oneself in different mirrors, however, is likely to be disconcerting, especially when one assumes that others hold key elements of the "truth" that need to be taken in.

Feedback and the Transition from Self-Reading to Self-Authoring. Multisource feedback is developmentally powerful for managers in transition from self-reading to self-authoring because it usually presents the individual with conflicting views, which call for some resolution in order to make meaning of the feedback. For the manager who constructs meaning primarily through a self-reading lens, being able to sort the claims into some kind of hierarchy of worthiness may feel necessary. Questions from the perspective of this group often heard during a feedback session include "Which view is most important to pay attention to?" or "Why should I pay attention to any view other than my boss's?" The participant constructing her experience in this way, not feeling comfortable assigning the views of others to a designated place in a self-authored meaning system, wants to be reassured that there is one view that it makes the most sense to pay attention to, since paying attention to all of them seems like an impossible task—one that would pull her apart were she to try.

It is important to support the need this participant feels to prioritize the conflicting views so as to better manage the challenge of integrating the information. For example, with 360-degree feedback, as a practitioner or coach, one might point out to a participant that feedback from direct reports is probably more salient than feedback from peers in areas related to managing subordinates, while feedback from their peers in areas such as working collaboratively may have higher priority than the boss's views on those same items.

Yet development requires building a bridge that is well anchored on both sides, at both the self-reading and self-authoring ends (Kegan, 1994). Satisfying the need for prioritization is only one ingredient. The other aspect is finding ways to help the person get a glimpse, however small, of another way of understanding the feedback experience. For self-reading individuals, this may mean that a facilitator or coach would encourage the individual to articulate what he sees as important, to articulate a personal, independent point of view. Part of the magic of a feedback-intensive experience for self-reading individuals is that one's current self-view is elicited in a variety of situations and presented as separate from the views of relevant others, simulating the more self-authored orientation toward understanding self as separate and distinct from the views of significant others.

This process of movement from a self-reading way of making meaning of feedback to a self-authoring way is neither easy nor quick. It can be frightening, exhilarating, and extremely productive developmentally for people in transition. The experience of seeing one's self-view as possibly independent from others' views, combined with the seemingly impossible task of reconciling or prioritizing competing views, moves the individual one step further toward the realization that the only meaningful solution is to find a place to stand among the multitude of voices making conflicting claims, that is, to subordinate the claims of others to a new sense of self that can regulate those claims. This realization points toward a new way of making meaning of the differences, a self-generated meaning making that feels both empowering and facilitative of movement into a whole new realm of being and possibility. Therefore, in addition to supporting the need for prioritization of the competing perspectives, good facilitation of a feedback-intensive experience for managers making the developmental transition from self-reading to self-authoring (meaning most mid-level managers and some at more senior levels) will include multiple ways to point to the power and opportunity for self-authoring as a solution to the discomfort posed by multiple and competing views.

Feedback and the Self-Authoring Manager. Because people who are comfortable with self-authoring assume without question that they personally originate what is valuable and true, they will tend to understand feedback as something that needs no immediate or necessary reaction, since it represents understandable differences in perspective. Or they may feel that a response to feedback is important in order to enhance the probability of meeting their own goals. Because such a manager is self-authoring, he sees others' views presented in feedback as belonging to them and feels no particular need to be responsible for those, to own those, or to in any way allow those to claim him. This does not mean, however, that discrepancies between self-view and others' views will not facilitate development. For the self-authoring participant, discrepancies may be quite a surprise but will not be seen as a threat to the integrity of his self-view. He will tend to see discrepancies as understandable differences, or misperceptions to be cleared up. Participants taking this stance may seem to discount or minimize the meaning of others' ratings, or they may tend to see the impact of differences in views as something to more effectively manage in the future. The self-authored participant may reason, "If the boss sees me differently than I see myself, I need to better understand what I'm doing or what she is seeing that is causing her to have this view, and perhaps change my behavior or correct her perception so that she can come to see me as I see myself."

Feedback and the Transition to Self-Revising. To the extent that an individual is ready to begin the journey from self-authoring to self-revising—that is, to begin to examine the limitations of self-authoring itself—a feedback-intensive experience will be developmental in a whole different way. As people embark on this movement, they begin to see connections between the way others see them, or the self-other discrepancies, and the ways in which they feel ineffective. They begin to glimpse the way in which their self, the identity they worked so hard to discover at an earlier point in life, is now itself limiting their capacity to be effective in desired ways. They will begin to see that the self they have authored is not the only possible self they might author. As the generator of the self, they begin to see how they can also be the reviser of the self. More than that, they begin to see the self as it coexists in relation to others and not just as it stands alone. Thus instead of reading a self in others or authoring a self by one's own lights, a person undergoing this transition begins to have the capability to author a self in relation to others. At this point, feedback helps the person create and re-create a sense of self that feels both true and adaptable within the context of a community of others.

Before we move away from the topic of feedback-intensive processes, two other elements bear mention within the context of this chapter—simulations and structured experiences, and coaching sessions. Both of these are features we use often in our feedback-intensive leadership development programs.

The Power of Simulation. Simulations and structured experiences can foster the development of new ways of understanding self and others by replicating aspects of the environment that challenge people in developmental transition, whether from self-reading to self-authoring or from self-authoring to self-revising. Simulations and structured experiences can replicate organizational mergers, where participants are faced with bringing together different cultures, systems, and practices into one well-integrated unit. They can replicate the competing priorities and demands of different divisions within the same organization. They can present participants with decisions to be made in information-poor settings and ill-defined roles in a context of high ambiguity. They can present participants with unexpected and unwelcome change, ask them to function at a more senior level than they do at home, or challenge them to reflect on and see the limitations of their own visions, perspectives, or priorities. From a development perspective, a well-facilitated debriefing of such experiences will include both supporting the participant's current mode of constructing experience and pointing the way toward more complex ways of constructing experience that might serve one better given the challenges presented in the exercise.

Coaching Sessions. The staff coaching session in a feedback-intensive program can range in duration from one to four hours and is a tremendous support to this bridge-building process at any point in developmental transition. The intent of this portion of a feedback-based program or process is to help the participant integrate the feedback received during the session as a whole, create a synthesis that feels right for her, and begin to frame some development goals. The power of this experience for the transition from self-reading to self-authoring is that feedback staff do not, as a rule, tell participants what to do, nor do they present prescriptive explanations of the meaning of the feedback (to which the more self-reading participants may be inclined to pay too much heed), but rather they facilitate the participants' ability to journey on this road themselves. The potential power of the experience for the self-authoring individual who may be beginning to transition to more of a self-revising perspective is that the session is one in which the participant can, in the privacy of the one-on-one discussion, explore, perhaps tentatively and for the first time, the limitations of self and the possibility that the self-view, so useful at one point in life, is now inadequate to meet the need the individual feels to grow beyond it, perhaps entertaining the idea that the very structure on which he has depended may be on the verge of transformation. Although we have discussed coaching as part of a feedback-intensive program here, many of the same points apply to coaching as a stand-alone process (Berger and Fitzgerald, 2002).

Conclusion

There seems to be a commonly held belief that organizational life is becoming more complex, more stressful, and more demanding. Everywhere people are searching for the competencies that leaders need to answer this challenge. Certainly people do need greater skills and competencies. However, the most pressing issue, in our view, is the basic beliefs managers hold about the nature and source of the self. What beliefs about the self are most useful in today's organizational contexts? We think this question is a good guide for practitioners and line managers to use in thinking about developmental agendas and practices.

Perhaps fifty years ago, managers who were primarily self-reading were among the most effective people in an organization. At that time, the overall culture of organizations supported an environment in which the self-reading perspectives of the majority contributed effectively to a sense of organizational loyalty, chain of command, the creation of a single compelling organizational perspective, and even the meaning of leadership itself (Drath, 2001). It may be that a sharply vertical hierarchy supports people who are primarily self-reading more fully than people who are self-authoring at all but the most senior levels. Organizing by functions and disciplines may likewise be more supportive of people who are self-reading. Both of these contexts would seem to favor people understanding themselves and their work by taking in the responses, ideas, and values of those in authority and stated organizational ideals.

Much of this has changed dramatically in recent decades. Organizations are more concerned than ever with their capacity to act effectively in a global environment—in relation to changing markets, customer needs, and competitor surprises. Sharply vertical hierarchies are giving way to the realization that much work needs to be coordinated horizontally, calling on people in different functions and disciplines to work together across the boundaries that used to divide them. As we have said earlier, these changes call forth the need for people to be more responsible for their own work and to take responsibility for their own performance without looking solely to the standards and dictates of more senior managers. More and more work is required that is carried out by individuals and groups without close supervision and monitoring.

We believe this means that organizational environments are more developmentally challenging than ever before. Creating lists of competencies on the assumption that enough education and training can bring a person to the requisite level is probably a useless activity. Competence is an aspect of a person and the person's beliefs about himself. Some beliefs about the nature and source of the self make the learning of some competencies problematic. Think about the challenges that a strongly self-reading manager might face in trying to learn how to take an unpopular stand, work through conflicts with important peers, or be empowering while maintaining his authority with subordinates.

Organizations today need larger communities of managers who are self-authoring. People near the top of the organization are especially challenged to develop a self-revising perspective. If this is to happen, development practitioners will be required to understand three things: the nature of such development, what is happening in the organization that calls forth such development, and how they can make use of these challenges and support people whose very selves are, after all, our most important organizational resource.

PART THREE

LEADERSHIP DEVELOPMENT

CHAPTER FOURTEEN

ORGANIZATIONAL CAPACITY FOR LEADERSHIP

Patricia M. G. O'Connor
Laura Quinn

Modern organizations are facing increasingly ambiguous and complex challenges for which their existing resources, approaches, and solutions are insufficient. Take, for example, the case of an international world relief organization that is beginning to feel the limits of its existing strategy, which focuses on providing direct services to impoverished regions. The depth and breadth of the needs of the communities it serves continue to grow—a troubling case of demand far exceeding supply. Seeking new ways to expand its reach in the face of significant economic, social, and political complexity, the top management team decides that the organization must adopt a more systemic strategy for meeting the needs of the people the organization serves. The top managers elect to launch a shift toward a leverage strategy that is intended to increase the organization's impact through partnerships and advocacy rather than attempt to stem the tide of poverty on its own through direct services.

To craft and implement this systemic strategy, much more than a shift in the strategic objectives is required. For example, such a strategy will require the organization and its members to develop new technical knowledge and skills. It will require developing new kinds of external relationships and new organizational systems. Sustaining the new direction will also require creating an organizational culture that simultaneously respects the values of its multiple collaborators (the people in the various countries it serves and its partnering organizations) and enacts its own values. In other words, many aspects of the organization will need to change and develop.

The top management team believes that leadership is a key ingredient to the success of this organizational change effort. Leadership work—setting a clear direction, aligning the various aspects of the organization in support of that direction, and maintaining staff commitment—is critical and more complex during this time of transition. How will the top managers ensure that the organization has the necessary leadership capacity to carry out this work? As in most organizations, they have focused on enhancing the capabilities of their high-potential leaders. Through a needs assessment process, the organization identifies that to be more effective operating under the new strategy, its leaders need greater self-awareness and greater skills in the areas of systems thinking and contextual analysis, negotiating and influencing, building sustainable partnerships, and building capabilities for change. The plan is to develop these capabilities in existing staff and selectively bring in new staff who excel in these areas.

We believe that developing the capabilities of high-potential leaders and adding new talents to the management pool will indeed enhance this organization's leadership capacity—but only in a limited way. To significantly enhance its leadership capacity, the organization must develop more complex ways of thinking about and enacting leadership. These more complex ways include viewing leadership as a property of the whole organization (not just its top-level managers), involving more organizational members in leadership work, and enacting leadership with others who have equal power and authority (such as clients and partners).

The purpose of this chapter is to share a more inclusive framework for understanding organizational capacity for leadership. Traditionally, the science and practice of leadership development has limited its focus to the identification and development of individual leaders—that is, to enhancing individuals' capacity for leadership. We see the field of leadership development undergoing a shift from an exclusive focus on leaders to a more inclusive understanding of leadership (Day, 2000; Day and O'Connor, 2003; O'Connor and Quinn, 2002). This traditional leader focus recognizes leadership as the sole property of individuals (that is, an aptitude for or skill in leading) and is usually limited to individuals in formal positions of authority. From this perspective, the capability of the international relief organization to face the complex challenge of strategic change is highly dependent on its ability to develop and retain a relative handful of members (its high-potential leaders). On the other hand, if leadership is viewed as a property of the whole organization, success in facing complex challenges is dependent on the organization's ability to develop all aspects of the organization that contribute to leadership. From this expanded perspective, leadership development also includes developing elements other than individual leaders, such as the interconnections among organizational members and the organizational practices and systems that enable people to work together (Bal and Quinn, 2001; Liu and O'Connor, 2001; O'Connor, 2002).

To further articulate this concept of organizational capacity for leadership, we will address three central questions:

1. What does it mean for an organization to have capacity for leadership?
2. How does an organization enhance its capacity for leadership?
3. How does an organization assess how sufficient its leadership capacity is for the challenges it currently faces?

Leadership as an Organizational Capacity

As put forth in the Introduction, *leadership* can be understood as the collective activity of organizational members to accomplish the tasks of setting direction, creating alignment, and gaining commitment. All of these tasks enable individuals to work together effectively as a collective.

There are numerous ways in which organizations or other groups of people might accomplish these tasks. A common way for large organizations to accomplish leadership tasks is to make these tasks the responsibility of a management hierarchy, with each unit manager responsible for the tasks within his or her unit and with each higher-level manager responsible for ensuring that lower-level leadership is consistent with the larger organizational system. Other processes are used in different contexts. In an entrepreneurial start-up, the founder often does all the leadership tasks for the organization. To move into a new business arena, an organization might forgo the existing management structure and put together a special team drawn from experts from across the organization to lead the initiative.

The more versatility an organization has in how it can carry out leadership tasks, the more effective it will be. An assumption here is that organizations are healthy and thrive when they are capable of many responses to a given situation, and they become brittle and vulnerable when they are uniform and specialized (Sale, 1982). This concept of being able to choose among various ways of enacting leadership is central to the notion of organizational capacity for leadership. We maintain that organizations that are able to carry out leadership tasks in multiple ways have a higher organizational capacity for leadership than those with limited versatility in this area.

Consider the example of a product development team in a well-respected toy company. Team members have a good understanding of what the team is trying to accomplish and how their work supports the organization's overall objectives and strategy. In addition, each team member understands his or her role on the team, and the team uses product development processes to ensure that different aspects of their projects come together in predictable ways. The team has had success in the past, and its members are motivated to continue making important contributions to the organization.

For the most part, the work of the product team runs smoothly. When it does not, members rely heavily on their formal team leader. In the early stages of a project, when they have all kinds of questions about the desired outcomes of the project and how they will get there, they look to the team leader to clarify what the organization is hoping for and to suggest strategies for moving forward. When pieces of the project are not coming together as they should, they look to the team leader to diagnose the problem and get them back on track. When some other part of the organization is not providing the kind of support they need, they expect the team leader to plead their case and restore the support. The product team has an experienced and capable team leader who is able to clarify outcomes, solve problems, and gain the support of other groups—so it is no wonder that they rely on her for these tasks; it is in fact considered to be her job.

The product team works in an organizational context that is a major source of leadership for its day-to-day work. The organization's practices (for example, clarifying links between the work of teams and the organization's overall goals and objectives) and systems (for example, product development processes) contribute to the team's direction, alignment, and commitment. The team leader is a major source of leadership, particularly when questions or issues arise. The organization does indeed assign leadership responsibility to the team leader.

But what happens when the product development team faces a challenge it has never faced before? One of its products has been found to be defective and has led to the injury of several children. This is the first time the company has experienced the need for a recall. There are no organizational practices and systems in place to provide direction and alignment. The product development team, because of its in-depth knowledge of the product, is charged with handling the recall of the product. The team leader defines the team's top priority as finding out how the defect occurred and correcting the problem. This, after all, is her area of expertise, and determining the root cause of the problem appears to her to be the soundest strategy for facing the present challenge and preventing future defects from occurring. Several team members experienced in client relations, however, are concerned with the lack of attention being given to client perceptions of the situation. Other members, who have broad networks within the company, are learning that the product development function is losing respect in the eyes of its colleagues.

If this product team continues to enact leadership as it does during "normal" times, that is, to rely on established organizational practices and systems and on its formal leader, it will likely become paralyzed or overly narrow in its approach to the product recall—paralyzed because there are no established organizational practices or systems to handle this new situation, overly narrow because the formal leader is focusing on only one aspect of the challenge. However, if the whole team takes responsibility for creating direction, alignment, and commitment during this time of uncertainty, it will more readily draw on a broader, richer base of expertise and insights, thus finding ways to effectively navigate together through this unknown territory of product failure. In the former case, the team is limited in how it enacts leadership, whereas in the latter case, it demonstrates versatility and thus a higher level of organizational capacity for leadership. This degree of versatility will be in demand increasingly as groups and organizations encounter complex challenges with increasing regularity.

Shifts in the Understanding and Practice of Leadership

Carrying out leadership tasks in new ways requires changes in how people understand and practice leadership. In assessing the current understanding and practice of leadership, two things stand out for us.

First, organizations primarily rely on individuals or designated groups to carry out leadership tasks. Thus it makes sense that the view of leadership as an individual capacity predominates. Likewise, the primary focus of leadership development has been to develop individuals to do these tasks. From this perspective, the notion of an organization's leadership capacity is often interpreted as having a sufficient number of individuals in formal positions of authority who are capable of individually carrying out leadership tasks and having a pipeline of individuals in development for these positions. This is often referred to as having adequate "bench strength."

Second, because of the intense focus on individuals who have leadership responsibility, there is a strong tendency not to see that the larger context is actually part of the leadership task. For example, organizational members share belief systems about what constitutes effective leadership (O'Connor and Day, 2002). If individuals with leadership responsibility do not act in ways consistent with these belief systems, others in the organization will not respond in ways that yield effective leadership. Also, organizational systems and practices are a source of leadership in that they influence how leadership can be enacted. For example, when a work system is centralized in an organization, the management hierarchy is able to provide a great deal of alignment; with decentralized systems, more practices that encourage lateral coordination are needed to achieve better alignment. Organizations and their members do not often examine how their shared beliefs or organizational systems both shape and reflect how leadership tasks are carried out.

Let's now turn from the current understanding and practice of leadership to newer, emerging understandings and practices.

Organizations are increasingly finding themselves in situations that call for leadership tasks to be the shared responsibility of many people rather than the designated work of a few individuals or groups. These situations are characterized by complexity, ambiguity, and the need to develop new approaches. It is unclear how the organization should make sense of the situation or what responses it should consider. Individuals in high-level positions of authority find themselves in over their heads and cannot by themselves figure out how to move forward. It is in these situations that the multiple knowledge bases, beliefs, and practices that exist in the organization need to come together to create direction, alignment, and commitment. For example, the strategy of growth through mergers and acquisitions requires whole communities of people and sets of systems to be understood and integrated in novel ways. The perspectives and actions of a designated postmerger integration team cannot adequately address the complex task of creating alignment between two previously separate companies. To be successful, merging companies need to enlist a broad and diverse constituency of employees, customers, and other stakeholders in the integration task. Leadership in these situations shifts away from an exclusive reliance on individual members, teams, or systems and toward a more inclusive focus on the connections between these individual elements. This is a way of enacting leadership that is less familiar to most organizations.

Organizations that are able to add this new way of enacting leadership to their repertoire will increase their organizational capacity for leadership. This does not mean that all leadership work in the organization will take this new approach. It is a more complex way of enacting leadership—a form of leadership that is needed most when facing complex challenges. In dealing with routine, ongoing problems, organizations can continue to rely on more familiar ways of enacting leadership. Adding this new way of understanding and enacting leadership requires systemic development—that is, it requires more than the development of individuals; of groups, teams, and other communities within the organization; and of the beliefs and practices of the whole organizational system. It also requires the development of the forces that bring together—or separate—these organizational elements. We now turn to this issue of development.

Developing Organizational Capacity for Leadership

How can organizations develop more capacity for leadership? From our perspective, the degree of versatility in how an organization can carry out leadership tasks is strongly related to the patterns of connectivity that are resident within the organization. *Connectivity* is the relative interrelatedness of the members of an organization. Connectivity is important because it creates the means by which members can work together to collectively address the leadership tasks. In the words of Tom Peters (1992, p. 181), "Everyone has to be able to talk with [and] work with everyone else. . . . The web of relations *is* the firm." Of course, there are reasons why everyone cannot talk with and work with everyone else. An understanding of connectivity can help determine what those reasons are and how leadership is affected.

As members interrelate behaviorally, cognitively, and socially, connectivity can take both explicit and implicit forms. For example, a strategy process is an explicit form of connectivity that many organizations use to enhance the integration of disparate constituencies when attempting to set the organization's direction. The more implicit form of connectivity inherent to the strategy process is the congruence of individual members' aspirations. To what degree are members' hopes for the organization's future aligned? Group problem-solving processes are another explicit form of connectivity often used when organizations face complex challenges. The more implicit form of connectivity in this example is congruence in meaning. To what degree are members understanding and evaluating the complex challenge in similar or dissimilar ways?

When leadership is viewed as a property of whole systems, as opposed to solely the property of individuals, effectiveness in leadership becomes much more a product of these connections or relationships among the parts than the result of any one part of that system (such as the leader). Organizational capacity for leadership is expanded or developed by enriching the patterns of connectivity in order to overcome the limitations of an organization's current capacity. In a routine environment, in which challenges require technical solutions and established knowledge, existing patterns of connectivity are generally sufficient. In these instances, connectivity provided by such conduits as technology, designated processes, and reporting relationships usually suffice. In a nonroutine environment, in which addressing challenges requires innovation and learning, deeper, flexible, and more customized patterns of connectivity must be developed. In short, complex challenges require complex leadership responses, drawn from a broader array of choices, which are predicated on higher levels of connectivity.

So what determines the relative amount, quality, and utility of connectivity in a given organization? We will use the case of the research and development unit of a global pharmaceutical company called RDU to illustrate. Approaching the case as we would the diagnostic phase of a client collaboration, we first seek to understand the *complex challenge* that the organization or group is facing. The inability to adequately address complex challenges is what prompts organizations to recognize the limits of their approaches to leadership and ultimately invest in some form of development. Thus the presenting challenge is central to understanding RDU's relative capacity present to address it. We examine three factors that influence connectivity and hence leadership capacity: leadership orientation, breadth of targets for development, and valued organizational outcomes. We believe that developing a more systemic and inclusive leadership orientation, broadening targets for development, and valuing the integration of work and learning will increase an organization's leadership capacity.

RDU's Challenge

RDU is considered to have the best pharmaceutical R&D lab in the industry. Releasing new drugs based on breakthrough research has been the cornerstone of the company's stellar reputation and performance. RDU's most pressing challenge is one that many organizations are currently facing: trying to set the direction for the organization while understanding and addressing differing and often competing stakeholder demands. For RDU, these stakeholders include the Food and Drug Administration, with strict requirements governing drug development; interest groups lobbying for the development of drugs to combat certain diseases as well as those lobbying against certain types of research (using animals or stem cells); customers who demand easy and economical access to RDU's products; distributors, who argue for exclusivity and patent extensions to ensure high profit margins; and the scientific community, which values the importance of scientific discovery above all other factors. These stakeholders, with their multiple, competing demands, hand RDU a challenge in determining the direction of its research efforts for the next three years.

There are some additional factors that complicate RDU's situation further. Seventy percent of RDU's patents will expire within three years, and recent regulation has made it more difficult to extend the life of a patent through incremental improvements. Its two closest competitors are considering a merger to challenge RDU's position in the market. RDU has gone through two mergers in the past eighteen months in order to add more patents to its portfolio, but this has left the newly formed unit with two directors who are competing to head it up. The scientists who engage in the primary work of the unit have stronger professional interests in breakthrough research than in the introduction or economic value of new pharmaceuticals. These scientists most strongly identify and connect with the recognition and esteem of colleagues in the field of pharmaceutical research. So their time horizon for making an impact, taking into consideration the scientific rigor required for breakthroughs in this industry, is considerably longer than the unit's or the organization's.

RDU has not figured out how to deal with the increasing demands coming from so many different areas. They do not have a mechanism to enable a systemic view of this challenge, resulting in differing opinions among unit heads and scientists as to which stakeholders should have priority. This has fragmented the unit, driving groups in different directions as they try to appease various stakeholder groups at a time when the marketplace has become particularly unforgiving. If the challenge of setting a more inclusive direction—one that takes into account the perspectives of its various stakeholders—is not addressed, there is the real possibility that the fragmentation will weaken RDU's ability to maintain its competitive advantage, both in terms of attracting and retaining the industry's top talent and in being first to market with cutting-edge products.

RDU's Leadership Orientation

How do organizational members at RDU think about and enact leadership? One way to examine this question is to investigate the organization's "leadership constructs." Constructs of leadership, which exist in all organizations, are what individuals believe leadership to be. Constructs reflect assumptions of how leadership should be demonstrated and thus influence the way individuals and collectives operate in leadership situations.

What form of leadership does RDU believe to be most appropriate for facing its challenge? Does this form represent the status quo or a departure from leadership as usual in the unit? When the members were asked what type of leadership was needed to move the unit in the right direction, they almost invariably shared personal descriptors and examples of extending influence, often naming a specific director. For example, "We need someone who can communicate a single vision," "We need a motivational and persuasive leader," "We need someone who is comfortable being the head of the pack but also has the skill to bring the pack along," "We need someone who can influence the stakeholders to adopt our point of view on RDU's future, rather than having us adopt theirs," "We need someone who really knows this business—and can pull the right levers when the stakeholders are in conflict." At RDU, leadership is equated with personal attributes that are embodied in some individuals (directors) and not others (scientists), and the central purpose of leadership is to influence people and situations.

An Orientation Toward Personal Dominance. RDU is not unusual. The two most prevalent leadership orientations in modern organizations view leadership as either a personal attribute or as a social influence process. The former pertains to something (such as skills or knowledge) individuals called "leaders" have and then use. From this perspective, leadership is an almost immediately recognizable and agreed-on personal attribute. Leadership is equated with personal qualities that are attractive and compelling—that is, they attract the attention and positive regard of others. From this orientation, leadership is a property of a person, what we referred to earlier as a leader focus. An illustration of this is captured in the following statement made by one of the directors at RDU when presenting an overview of the previous quarter's dismal financial performance to the scientists: "Don't you worry about leadership. That's my job. I need you to worry about innovation." Because of the centrality of the person in a position of formal authority, this could be considered an illustration of a "personal dominance" orientation to leadership (Drath, 2001). This leadership orientation encourages relatively little connectivity in the organization because it requires little connectivity to enact, and vice versa.

An Orientation Toward Interpersonal Influence. An "interpersonal influence" orientation recognizes the inherent social aspect of leadership and views it as a highly instrumental process of negotiating influence (Hollander, 1964). From this perspective, an opportunity for social influence needs to exist in order for leadership (or the lack thereof) to be recognized, and there is generally some amount of agreement as to what constitutes exemplars in these situations. Although views on the most appropriate style to exhibit (for example, "soft sell" versus "hard sell" approaches) may differ, influence is still viewed as the core operator. Leadership is equated with being socially intelligent, influential, persuasive, or instrumental in a given situation. Leadership from this orientation is a property of a process and is illustrated in a comment made by a different director at RDU when discussing the launch of a new trial with his task force: "What do we need to do to get the lobbyists behind our new direction?" An interpersonal influence approach to leadership requires and encourages some amount of connectivity to be developed and in place.

An Orientation Toward Communal Meaning Making. A third orientation recognizes the creation of leadership through the "meaning making" in a community that shares work (Drath, 2001). From this perspective, leadership is considered a property of a community, as opposed to a person or a process. Leadership is recognized to exist when the tasks of leadership are addressed collectively, understanding of the tasks is deepened, and demonstrated efficacy in them is advanced over time. This orientation takes a more relational approach than the other orientations, recognizing the criticality of interrelatedness (dialogue). RDU showed no indication of this orientation. This leadership orientation requires and thus fosters relatively high levels of connectivity.

An Orientation Toward Systemic Differentiation and Integration. A fourth orientation recognizes leadership as a property of whole systems. Similar to the third orientation, a systemic orientation recognizes that leadership is something that is created through meaning making. How it differs is what the meaning making is in service of. Meaning must be brought not only to the shared leadership tasks that a community is responsible for but also to the context within which those tasks are carried out. In this way, the systemic forces that connect or separate communities within an organization and shape choices related to leadership tasks become what is important to bring meaning to. This orientation recognizes leadership as making sense of organizational complexity (Gharajedaghi, 1999; Marion and Uhl-Bien, 2001), not as an additional consideration or task but as a primary operator. There was no indication of this orientation at RDU. This leadership orientation requires and fosters the deepest levels of connectivity.

Thus leadership orientations shape how we make sense of and prioritize a variety of factors related to leadership:

- Whether leadership is embodied in a person, a process, a community, or a system
- Who participates in the leadership process
- What constitutes effectiveness
- What purpose leadership serves
- Whether leadership can be shared
- Whether leadership is a means to an end or an end in and of itself

The manner in which RDU addresses its multiple-stakeholder challenge will be fundamentally influenced by how leadership is understood at RDU. The existing reliance on the personal dominance of the two directors and the influence tactics used by both the directors and the stakeholders is beginning to feel its limits. The two directors, both highly competent and strong-minded individuals, are finding it increasingly difficult to share leadership or move away from their positions regarding which stakeholders are most critical to influence. They need the perspectives of both the scientists and the stakeholders to be more fully represented in the new direction, but they are not sure how to make this happen without appearing unprepared for the challenge.

Note that the orientations RDU needs to move toward—leadership as a property of the community and of the whole system—are more inclusive of multiple perspectives and thus are more complex. As we have discussed, facing more complex challenges calls for more complex ways of understanding and enacting leadership. This does not mean that RDU needs to carry out leadership tasks with a more inclusive orientation in all situations. Nor does this mean that complex challenges necessarily require more people to be included, although this is a common tactic for developing a more inclusive orientation. An alternative approach involves the same players bringing more or different parts of themselves to the leadership situation. Or it may involve recognizing, creating, or leveraging different connections in order to address the leadership task at hand more effectively. What is important to remember are the notions of versatility and choice: by expanding the ways in which leadership can be potentially carried out in the organization, the organization will have more overall leadership capacity.

What might help RDU experiment with a more inclusive leadership orientation? For one thing, the directors need to learn how to integrate their views on stakeholder prioritization. Their "either-or" assumptions about fulfilling stakeholder needs keeps pushing them into personal dominance and influence orientations, neither of which has helped them arrive at a solution. They need a process by which they can understand the various perspectives on the challenge without being owned or characterized by a given perspective—what Basseches (1984) calls "dialectical thinking."

To aid in developing such a process, an executive coach is brought in to coach the directors not as individuals but as a dyad, focusing on the communication patterns between them. The coach assists the directors in recognizing some of the defensive routines they use with one another and helps them develop greater objectivity about the positions they had previously held so strongly and so separately. As a result, the directors are better able to see how their positions are in some ways connected, and their strategies become more robust as their individual inputs are integrated.

For another thing, the directors need to determine how to broaden participation in leading the unit in the face of their challenge. They cannot make fullest sense of the challenge—and the array of responses to that challenge—without understanding the perspectives of the stakeholders and the scientists. The coach facilitates a dialogue with this broader leadership group in order to elicit the commonalities, rather than the differences, in their views on the new direction. In doing so, it becomes clear that individuals differ in leadership orientations. For example, one stakeholder with a strong personal dominance orientation toward leadership was initially confused by the invitation for a dialogue and then assumed that this invitation was a sign of incompetence on the part of the directors. He came prepared to tell the group what the priorities should be, only to find that the work at hand is to collectively develop the best response, not to evaluate prescribed responses that individuals brought to the table.

Targets of Development at RDU

To enrich connectivity in an organization, what elements or aspects of the organization need developmental attention? First, equipping individuals with the capabilities to work with others on complex challenges should not be overlooked.

The shift to understanding leadership as a property of the whole system does not negate the key role that individual development plays in leadership development. We believe that individual development is necessary but not sufficient for developing more connectivity in organizations and that organizations tend to narrowly focus on developing individuals.

This is certainly the case at RDU. A focus group representing a cross section of RDU employees revealed that the majority of members viewed the lack of certain skills and knowledge as the major factor limiting the organization's effectiveness in facing its complex challenge. They mentioned as critical such individual competencies as decision-making acumen, deep knowledge of the business, political smarts, and creative problem solving. This illustrates RDU's leadership orientation as primarily individually focused and concerned with the enhancement of the organization's *human capital*. In other words, RDU views developing the skills, knowledge, and abilities of individuals as the answer to enhancing the organization's capacity to address its challenges. Certainly, developing individuals is part of the answer, but other aspects of the organization need to develop, too.

Let us return to the assembled group at RDU. After making concerted efforts to integrate the individuals' views on stakeholder prioritization, they still feel a long way from resolving this challenge. There are still many unanswered questions about where various scenarios will take the company and whether the selected direction will be embraced by individuals not in the room. What other aspects of the organization might RDU consider developing in order for the members of this group to more effectively work together to face and resolve their challenge?

The coach asks the members of the group to think about what other resources they have available to answer, or at least better inform, their unanswered questions. One director suggests that she can make a call to a former colleague who faced a similar challenge at a different company two years earlier. A scientist offers that he has an in with a group of people at RDU who have been particularly vocal about their doubts about RDU's future viability. Might it be helpful to understand what those doubts are based on? It quickly becomes clear that every individual in the room has a network of relationships that can inform the group's challenge. It also becomes evident that the relationships in one person's network close a gap or hole in another's network (Burt, 1992). The coach then sets about engaging the group in a process that illustrates these connections and identifies the handful of critical nodes that hold real value in terms of informing this challenge.

Social Capital. What the RDU group is beginning to understand is that there are vast stores of *social capital* within the organization that have specific relevance to this organizational challenge. Social capital is the value embedded in social networks that enables collective action and takes at least three distinct forms:

structural, relational, and cognitive (Nahapiet and Ghoshal, 1998). The more forms the RDU group can understand and leverage, the more versatile it will become in facing the stakeholder challenge.

First, there is value in the formation of formal and informal networks that enable individuals to identify others with needed perspectives or resources; this is the *structural form of social capital.* In the case of the RDU directors, by essentially giving members of the assembled group a position in this newly formed network, they are able to access others for the perspectives and resources that they know they do not have at their own disposal.

While having a network of individuals is a critical part of developing social capital, equally important are the interpersonal dynamics between individuals within the network; this is the *relational form of social capital.* Through its shared approach to the leadership task of setting RDU's direction, the group now had a pragmatic venue through which to address the sometimes controversial or sensitive issues around trust, shared norms and values, obligations, and expectations regarding the stakeholder challenge.

Finally, the group, coming from distinctly different functional backgrounds, begins to strongly identify with the need for a common context and language; this is the *cognitive form of social capital.* Without a common understanding or "vocabulary," the group had struggled with recognizing the connections between the various perspectives on the stakeholder challenge. Now the group was learning that by developing social capital, the organization was enhancing its connectivity.

A social network analysis of the key players in the RDU situation, which is the tool RDU's coach used, served not only an instrumental purpose (it allowed the group to tap human capital outside the group) but also an important developmental purpose. The scientists, directors, and stakeholders are beginning to realize the limits of their personal networks to fully inform the challenge at hand, and so they are beginning to ask for and offer introductions to various people in other networks. These introductions are not in service of networking (which consists of broadening one's list of contacts to help advance individual career aspirations or agendas) but rather to help the group cross ideological boundaries. They realize that the existing patterns of social networks at RDU, which were primarily bounded by various functional interests—have actually fostered much of the chaos and division RDU has been experiencing. This has led to a question asked by one of the stakeholders: Why did these separate, exclusive networks form? What in the organization led to their creation?

Organizational Capital. What this stakeholder is beginning to recognize is that these networks did not develop randomly—there were forces shaping their creation. A dialogue ensues, exploring some of the possible explanations. A scientist shares that his network was formed, fairly exclusively, around scientific expertise. That is, the members of his network highly valued this form of expertise, almost to the exclusion of all other forms. "And besides," he offers, "the organization rewards that exclusivity. You said yourself that our job is innovation, not leadership. So that's what we do—and we know how best to do it by relying on our scientific expertise. Before today's discussion, I never saw any benefit in expanding my network. The work, as I understood it, simply didn't require it."

The assembled group is now beginning to recognize the *organizational capital* resident in RDU. Organizational capital is the value that lies in the culture and practices of a given company. For example, the scientific expertise at RDU is an obvious asset, embedded not just in the scientists themselves but in RDU's research practices. These shared research practices are part of what connects individual researchers. But those very same practices, and the cultural values that underpin them, limit the social networks that the scientists build. New values and practices will need to be put in place to broaden and enrich the networks that the scientists participate in.

One way to more clearly understand how organizational capital is a factor in RDU's situation is to examine the different formal and informal systems that characterize the company—the practices or routines and the culture. Developing these work and belief systems provides RDU with another avenue for enhancing its organizational capacity for leadership (O'Connor and Day, 2002; Salancik and others, 1975). RDU approached five work systems during this step: production, control, rewards, education, and communications.

The production system reflects the primary operative of the organization. For RDU, this is the researching and development of pharmaceuticals. This system influences the relative connectivity of members in that it defines the opportunities for work assignments and integration with other areas of the organization. The directors are increasing the connectivity in RDU's work system by bringing the scientists and the stakeholders into the work of addressing the stakeholder dilemma.

Another work system affecting connectivity at RDU is the control system, which focuses on the ways influence and power are played out within an organization. Control systems determine what gets measured or evaluated and thus (sometimes unintentionally) what is given some level of meaning. When the assembled group at RDU moves from stating positions of the stakeholder prioritization to developing a collective perspective, they shift the prevailing control system from one characterized by the power and influence of the directors to one characterized by the power of the ideas being generated. This focus on ideas rather than on the dynamics of policy or authority helps the group more strongly and personally identify with the work at hand. Enhanced identification creates deeper connectivity.

Reward systems are a third structure that communicates messages about the organization's norms and values. To this point, it was a norm at RDU that leaders got rewarded for making tough decisions but not necessarily shared decisions. This led the current directors to ignore the possibility of bringing others into the task at hand. Spending that kind of time and effort on decision making (which is how the problem was initially framed by both of them, that it was a decision to be made, not a challenge to be understood) was discouraged.

The education system outlines who has access to development opportunities and what those opportunities look like. RDU moved from formal educational opportunities (development programs and personal coaching) to opportunities embedded in the work when the assembled group took on the challenge as a collective. One could argue that the scientists received a more meaningful education on facing complex challenges by being engaged in this work, compared to gleaning such learnings from an off-site program.

The communication system at RDU also offers insight into the amount and type of information to which individuals in leadership roles have access. One form of communication system, the one embedded in the members' social networks, is explored by the group. The coach encourages them to examine other ways that information is shared (or not shared) within the company, based on some of the reporting practices. For example, do the directors encourage the sharing or the hoarding of information by various groups within the organization? What level of access to information were the various stakeholders given?

RDU's belief systems also hold implications for developing greater connectivity. Belief systems stem from the collectively held values of members of an organization. These systems are more embedded than work systems and hence more difficult to change. For example, the RDU directors are not going to change the values the scientists hold about scientific expertise, but they can develop a deeper understanding of how these values both help and hinder the organization's ability to resolve its stakeholder prioritization dilemma. The values of the organization serve as guidelines for leadership and set an expectation of how leadership will be enacted. Organizations that value innovation may expect some level of risk taking and exploration—for example, the exploration of new forms of leadership with which RDU experimented.

Often organizational values compete, causing leadership dilemmas. For example, RDU certainly values shareholder wealth and at the same time values breakthrough research. These two values compete in terms of time horizons: shareholders want value immediately and regularly, whereas research is a longer-term proposition. Understanding cultural values and how they play out is yet another key component of understanding why leadership has taken place the way it has at RDU.

RDU's Outcome Orientation

A final factor to understand about RDU is its outcome orientation. Organizations, by their very nature, are focused on outcomes; they differ, however, in how those outcomes are defined. How an organization understands outcomes exacts a powerful influence on members' leadership choices.

RDU is a victim of its own past success, in that there is a widely held expectation that high performance will be the outcome of any endeavor. Like many other organizations, RDU does not differentiate much among situations: it deems high performance the most important outcome of any given leadership task. Given the complexity of the stakeholder challenge it now faces, this expectation may be too limited, if not downright unattainable, at least in the short run. If by performance RDU means the expert handling of a situation, the company is not capable of performance because it has no expertise in handling this challenge. Furthermore, there is no definition of what constitutes expertise in this situation; there is no "right way" to handle competing demands from stakeholders. This would appear to leave the RDU group set up to fail. So what if RDU is more versatile in how it understands and evaluates outcomes in such leadership situations?

Action Learning. One could argue that a valued outcome of the group's work is not simply *what* work is accomplished (bringing differing perspectives into the room) but *how* that work is accomplished and the longer-term implications of applying more complex, sophisticated approaches to these complex challenge situations. The RDU group is making demonstrable advancements on the stakeholder task (performance) by trying new approaches (learning) that allow it to move toward more inclusive leadership orientations (development). In this way, the leaders are achieving performance, practicing learning, and experiencing development—a set of outcomes that they would not previously have considered viable in "normal" leadership situations.

What the RDU group is experiencing is a form of action learning, a process whereby a business dilemma is approached with a learning orientation (Revans, 1979). In this case, the group at RDU is intentionally integrating leadership work and organizational capacity development. The core requirements for action learning are action (for example, experimenting with new approaches to understanding the stakeholder challenge) balanced with reflective learning (for instance, inquiring as to the why, what, and how behind their traditional approaches to addressing complex challenges). The valued outcomes of action learning are more inclusive than traditional (performance-centered) approaches to leadership work. For RDU, along with the desired outcome of developing a response to the stakeholder challenge at hand, an equally valued outcome is the increased capability of the group to collectively address a future challenge. An additional outcome is the enhanced capability of members to transfer these learnings to other individuals and teams outside of this group by applying new approaches to the challenges being faced in different leadership situations at RDU.

The reciprocal relationship of learning through practicing collective leadership work and practicing collective leadership work with a learning orientation changes the meaning of what it means to be "outcome-oriented." A broader, more versatile outcome orientation begins to bring organizations like RDU closer to experiencing in real time some of the principles central to being a learning organization (Argyris and Schön, 1978). When collective leadership tasks are addressed in the service of more multidimensional outcomes (performance, learning, and development), they require and foster greater connectivity.

Assessing Your Organization's Capacity for Leadership

To develop the capacity for leadership, we suggest that organizations begin by examining their current status. Deciding that your organization needs to shift from a sole emphasis on leader development to one of building organizational capacity for leadership is only the first step in the journey. Recognizing that a change is needed is not enough to make the change happen. For many organizations, the shift to building leadership capacity will be quite extensive, requiring a good amount of thought and preparation. Due diligence is required up front and should address considerations in a number of arenas: clarity as to what the shift from leader to leadership development will mean for the organization, how extensive this change will be, the organization's commitment to this change, and how the shift in emphasis will fit with the current culture and systems of the organization. Of course, these are just a few of the factors to consider in your organization's overall readiness for change.

We offer the following series of questions to help you compose a snapshot of your organization's current situation and to identify opportunities for tapping greater capacity. Each series of questions starts at a different point: how your organization is facing complex challenges, how it is accomplishing leadership tasks, how it is approaching development, how it is managing outcome expectations, and how it fosters or limits connectivity. Given the relative urgency of the challenges your organization currently faces (the degree to which the sustainability of the organization or one of its key resources is threatened by the challenge), one series might be more useful than another. And each series will give you somewhat different insights, so addressing all the questions will generate the broadest perspective.

Complex Challenges

- What are the complex challenges facing your organization for which there are no ready solutions, tools, or responses?
- What leadership orientation characterizes the approach your organization is taking to address these challenges?

    Is top leadership expected to deal with the challenges?

    Are members throughout the organization trying to influence the adoption of certain approaches over others?

    Have cross-functional, cross-level groups come together to try to make sense of the challenge and collectively develop an approach?

    Have there been efforts to assess systemic factors within the organization that may be shaping the approach to the challenge?

- What is not working in the approach being taken? What are the limitations?
- Are there resources or perspectives not being brought to bear? Why?
- What evidence do you have that the organization is facing the challenge in ways that will help it learn and develop? How might it integrate more learning into dealing with the challenges?

Leadership Tasks

- How are setting direction, creating alignment, and maintaining commitment accomplished in your organization?
- Does your organization exhibit different leadership orientations for accomplishing this work in different contexts or situations (in the context of a new venture, addressing strategic versus operational issues, in time-pressured situations, and so forth)?
- Does this work happen similarly in different parts of the organization?
- How might your organization become more versatile in achieving direction, alignment, and commitment? What might that look like?

Targets for Development

- What forms of capital (human, social, organizational) do your practices tend to recognize as valuable and target for development? Why?
- Who in your organization has access to developmental opportunities?
- Who in your organization is most influential in determining which approaches to development will be supported? How are these determinations made?
- To what degree is development embedded in the leadership work?
- How might your organization develop more versatility in assessing and addressing relevant targets for development?

Outcome Orientation

- Has your organization articulated outcomes regarding the complex challenges it is currently facing? Are they primarily focused on performance? On learning? On development or change? On a blend of these?
- In what ways are outcome expectations in these situations influencing the approaches your organization takes to address challenges?
- To what degree are multiple outcomes understood, evaluated, and learned from in these situations?
- Do certain contexts or situations pit desired outcomes against each other? For example, are performance outcome expectations in conflict with learning outcome expectations? Why?

Connectivity

- How interconnected are members of the organization? Groups in the organization? The organization and its primary stakeholders?
- How is interconnectedness (or disconnectedness) demonstrated in your organization? What is happening or not happening when members address leadership tasks?
- Does your organization demonstrate greater connectivity while addressing some leadership tasks (setting direction, creating alignment, or maintaining commitment) compared to others? Why might this be so?
- Does your organization experience greater connectivity when involving certain individuals or groups compared to others? Why might this be the case?
- In leadership situations in which a high level of connectivity has been experienced, what were the resulting benefits?
- What kinds of practices and beliefs support connectivity?
- What kinds of practices and beliefs hinder connectivity?

Conclusion

We have recognized that organizations are facing complex challenges, for which traditional approaches to leadership and development focused solely on *individuals* are insufficient. In this chapter, we proposed an expanded way to address complex challenges through an emphasis on developing enhanced *organizational* capacity for leadership in such situations. Figure 14.1 illustrates some of the key drivers for organizational capacity for leadership, including a focus on enhancing connectivity, experimenting with more inclusive leadership orientations, ad-

FIGURE 14.1. BUILDING ORGANIZATIONAL CAPACITY FOR LEADERSHIP.

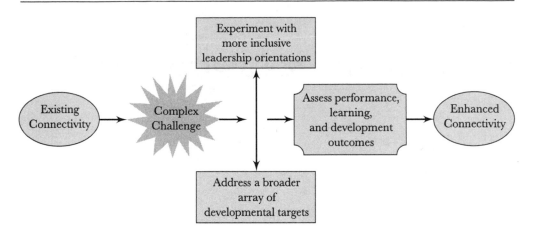

dressing a broader array of developmental targets, and taking a multidimensional view of outcomes.

As with the introduction of any new approach that requires a significant departure from existing practices, organizations are encouraged first to identify specific situations for which the approach is most suitable. A more inclusive approach to leadership and development is not required in every situation but in contexts where organizations are feeling the limits of their existing approaches. The proposed framework can serve as a guide to deepen the leadership versatility required to thrive in today's environment—and tomorrow's.

CHAPTER FIFTEEN

EXPLORATION FOR DEVELOPMENT

Charles J. Palus
David M. Horth

The challenges faced by organizations today are increasingly complex: volatile, multidimensional, and unprecedented. Leaders today find themselves facing challenges from all sides: an accelerating pace of scientific discovery, deregulation, mergers and acquisitions, shifting demographics, new business models, and a fluctuating economy.

Consider the following complex challenges:

- A cross-functional task team at Chemstar, Inc., a high-tech chemical products company, is formed to address a serious quality problem in the manufacture of its flagship product, a chemical analyzer. The team observes that the problem has been recurring in various forms for five years. It appears likely that fundamental limits to the underlying technology are driving Chemstar's customers to new products. There is a climate of fear in the organization—including fear that a root-level solution to this challenge will bring radical changes, ending the company as they have known it.

- Orion Research Center, the R&D department of an office solutions company, is seeking better ways to strategically select and prioritize projects. This team of scientists and technologists has been given the task of "picking winners"—high-return projects that match corporate strategy and capabilities. They feel an increased sense of urgency because Orion's competitors are picking winners at an accelerating pace. The team attempts to analyze all relevant data but runs into a wall: the inputs are too complicated and incomplete for clear decisions. To make matters more challenging, they have just been asked to help evolve the corporate strategy rather than simply apply it.

• Telco, the product of a series of mergers and acquisitions, is now a national leader in network and information services and a global contender in wireless communications. Different branches of the combined company come from quite different source cultures. Layers of differing legacy operating systems encumber all new work. Government regulations persist alongside deregulated sectors of the business. On top of this is the pressure for an essentially U.S. company to "go global." How can Telco provide seamless service when its origins, cultures, and environments are so fragmented?

Facing complex challenges requires leadership capabilities at the community level. Complex challenges are bigger than individuals. When one leader at a time takes on the challenges, these challenges are likely to be local in immediate scope, but what is needed for complex challenges is a whole-system response. Complex challenges also typically sprawl across the domains of multiple stakeholders invested in the resolution of the challenges. No single entity has the technical capacities for resolving the challenge, and no single entity "owns" it either. Leadership has to come from the community of stakeholders to integrate and apply their shared knowledge and expertise. Intelligent transformation, rather than only incremental change, is the expected result of community-level engagement of complex challenges.

The framework described in this chapter, exploration for development, enables leadership development at the level of the community and its interconnections while also fostering individual leader development. First we summarize the framework, and then we describe its elements. The rest of the chapter describes practical ways to implement the framework.

Exploration for Development

Exploration for development is a framework for enhancing organizational capacity for leadership (see Chapter Fourteen) that focuses on making shared sense and meaning in the face of complex challenges as the basis for committed action and transformation.

Complex challenges are situations or contexts that defy existing approaches or solutions. They are central in importance and demand decisive action. Yet because the organization, team, or individual does not know how to act, there is also a need to slow down and reflect.

Several criteria help identify these challenges:

- They defy existing solutions, resources, and approaches.
- They question individual and organizational assumptions and mental models.
- They demand individual and organizational creativity and learning.
- They require a reframing of the leadership perspective—the definition of what leadership is and how it is accomplished.

Typically, when a community first encounters a complex challenge, there is an initial lack of shared understanding as to what the challenge is and what it means. Because the complex challenge represents new territory for the organization and requires new ways of thinking and acting, there is no adequate language to describe it—or there are many languages, but each is wedded to discrete domains like finance or engineering (Heifetz, 1994; Hurst, 1995). "Making shared sense and meaning" refers to the process of bridging among the various positions and creating new shared perspectives and understandings. In a complex and turbulent environment, shared meaning about the work is vital to the leadership tasks of direction, alignment, and commitment.

Although individual leaders can describe complex challenges that arise in their particular contexts, there is also great value in articulating complex challenges as broadly shared in the organizational community. These shared challenges may be named by senior leadership and posed top-down, and they also may emerge from the grassroots level as a result of people seeing new connections within and across particular challenges. These two levels of seeing the challenge tend to meet and amplify in the middle of organizations, underlining the important place of middle managers in exploration for development (Oshry, 1999).

The metaphor of "exploration" refers to facing challenges in a way that inventories and mobilizes the community's resources, enters into and maps unknown territories, and thereby extends the community into new places and increases leadership capacity for facing future challenges. Exploration for development depends on able individuals coming together as a purposeful community, prepared for discovery and growth. Thus individual leader development and some group-level development are helpful precursors to the shared leadership processes described in this chapter.

In this framework, there are three primary leadership capabilities that communities need to mobilize to address complex challenges (see Figure 15.1): shared sensemaking, connectivity, and navigation. These capabilities are interdependent; for example, navigation benefits greatly from competent practices in sensemaking and connectivity. To more fully understand them, it is useful to consider the central features of each one.

Shared Sensemaking

In times of challenge, people need shared understandings about what they face and why. They benefit further if the understandings they share are accurate and effective and generate fresh perception and meaning. Where does this kind of shared understanding come from? Traditionally, it depended on one or more strong leaders, expert opinion, established wisdom, and the channels of culture. However, the increasing complexity and chaos in and among organizations severely strains these traditional sources. The exploration for development framework honors and works with these traditional sources but adds to them deliberate and competent sensemaking. *Sensemaking* is what people do in the rush of complex events to comprehend and anticipate what is happening to them (Kelly, 1955; Weick, 1995). Amid complexity and near-chaos, asking, answering, and reanswering "What is *this*? What is happening to us now?" is a key capability.

This kind of sensemaking is largely a social process. It is a matter of debating and sometimes agreeing about what is familiar and unfamiliar, of naming

FIGURE 15.1. LEADERSHIP CAPABILITIES FOR ADDRESSING COMPLEX CHALLENGES.

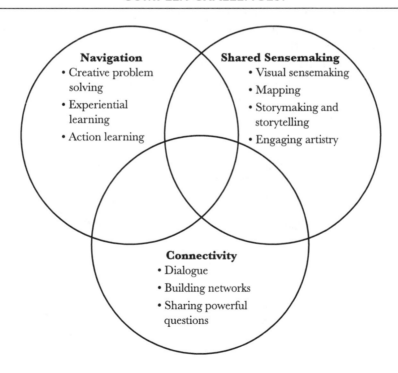

things, of discerning patterns. Competent sensemaking provides the foundation for committed action. In practice, it becomes a deliberate, participative process of shared leadership (Drath and Palus, 1994).

Sensemaking Competencies. In familiar situations, a tendency for automatic and reactive sensemaking can be effective. This tendency can be a liability, however, in unfamiliar and complex situations. In our research, we have identified six competencies for deliberately making sense of complex situations: paying attention, personalizing, imaging, serious play, co-inquiry, and crafting (Palus and Horth, 2002). How communities apply these competencies often proceeds in repeated cycles, each cycle following the "sensemaking loop," shown in Figure 15.2.

Paying attention is the selective use of multiple modes of perception when taking in a situation. Attention is a resource that can be harnessed and enhanced to see patterns in chaos and in complexity. Whole communities can suffer from forms of attention deficit disorder (Davenport and Beck, 2001). People come hurtling into a complex challenge loaded with assumptions and formulaic approaches. Paying attention begins a process of slowing down in order to be more deliberate about the encounter (Perkins, 1994).

Personalizing is tapping into life experiences, passions, and values in order to gain leverage on complex challenges. Great energies lie at the multichanneled confluence of avocation and vocation, of the personal and the organizational. Our identities are, for better and worse, powerful filters for our attention and for how people pursue their craft (Bateson, 1994). Competent personalizing requires conscious engagement, as well as conscious disengagement, of such personal experiences and filters to facilitate effective resolution of the challenge.

Imaging is the representation of evolving ideas and communication through the use of all kinds of images—pictures, stories, metaphors, shared displays, and

FIGURE 15.2. THE SENSEMAKING LOOP.

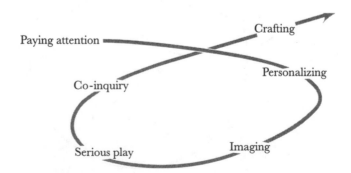

visions. Words by themselves are not enough for making sense, even though organizational habits often assume otherwise (Edwards, 1986). When something strange comes along, people need to ask, Is this an opportunity? A threat? A piece to a larger puzzle? At this time, an image or an animated series of images can be a very good way to take in the situation and make sense of it (Schwartz, 1991). Imaging is imagination with intent; imagination is playing with images.

Serious play refers to the generation of knowledge and new ways of doing work through free exploration, improvisation, experimentation, levity, and sport. One of the pitfalls of everyday sensemaking is that it can become too rigid. Making sense of what you may never have seen before requires play with a serious intent. Seriously playing is characterized by bending some rules, having fun—and harvesting what is learned in the process. Overcontrol is what people in authority do to keep the leadership all to themselves, a crippling stance when faced with complexity. Play is a dance between automatic and deliberate—a great place to get a not-too-tight handle on sensemaking processes (Schrage, 2002). Play becomes serious when it is contained within the purposes of co-inquiry (Gergen, 1991).

Co-inquiry is sustained dialogue in address of a challenge within and across the communities that have a stake in its reconciliation. The variety of the stakeholders and their issues is a source of much of the complexity of the challenges faced at all levels of society. It is also the source of much opportunity (Bray, Lee, Smith, and Yorks, 2000; Cooperrider and Whitney, 2002; Fisher, Rooke, and Torbert, 2000). Productive dialogue can take many forms, all of which encourage people to surface assumptions and share meaning making rather than confront each other with unrestrained advocacy (Dixon, 1998). At CCL, we often use the dialogue practice of "putting something in the middle," that is, sharing and recrafting artifacts such as pictures, scenarios, and prototypes as tangible, malleable embodiments of meaning (Palus and Drath, 2001).

Crafting refers to the synthesis of issues, objects, events, ideas, and actions into integrated, meaningful wholes. What is often missing in organizations is the recognition that artistry is needed to shape order out of chaos (Nissley, 2002). Aesthetics in this view is (or can be) more than a frill. Knowledge management in the face of complexity must become more like an inspired artistry of knowledge, including the best of people's passions, imaginations, and intuitions (Nonaka, Takeuchi, and Takeuchi, 1995).

Connectivity

The richer the connectivity in an organization, the greater the organization's capacity to respond to complex challenges as a whole system. To enhance connectivity, people working together in teams, groups, organizations, and communities need to better connect with each other around the work that they share. We invite people in the organizations we work with to explore the possibilities for enhancing the nature, quality, configuration, and number of connections throughout their organizational system, to ultimately build a well-integrated structure of leadership.

These ideas can be challenging if one is used to thinking of leadership in traditional ways, as something that arises from "within" the leader. If leadership is viewed as shared work, leadership can be seen as "between" whatever entities are involved: individuals, teams, groups, communities, organizations, systems of organizations, cultures large and small, industries, and so on. Enhancing the nature, quality, configuration, and number of connections between entities, then, can be viewed as leadership development. This means that leadership can never come simply and solely from within an individual but must be created in the relational spaces between persons, between groups, and so on (Drath, 2001). In our practice, we refer to this view as "connected leadership." Trait, situational, and transformative theories of leadership have, on the other hand, focused mainly on the individual leader traits and behaviors (Day, 2000).

Here are a few guideposts for beginning to develop a connected leadership perspective:

Think more, not less. It is a mistake to think of connected leadership as a reduction in authority and accountability or a reduction of the need for strong individuals who can make an impact. An important developmental principle of connected leadership is "Transcend and include": include the strengths of heroic, hierarchical leaders, but transcend the limitations (Wilber, 2000). This means that strong leaders need to become vulnerable in opening up to different ideas. It means developing a strong "loyal opposition" so that underlying assumptions can be surfaced and debated. It means developing a shared process for making sense of complex work so that authority and accountability can be negotiated and assigned in ways that are responsive to the community's or the organization's emergent needs.

Invent new forms of leadership. Leadership is traditionally thought of as a set of behavioral principles or individual characteristics that can be overlaid onto any situation. Connected leadership encourages the appreciation of such traditional models of personal leadership (include) but creatively reinvents them (transcend) according to the strange new worlds being explored. This kind of invention means holding lightly to what one already knows about leadership and experimenting with new ways of setting direction, creating alignment, and gaining commitment.

Invite people to participate in leadership. Leadership is a set of processes that people participate in and contribute to, in surprising varieties of ways, rather than simply "what leaders do." Even formal leaders must be aware of the modes of participation available to them in overlapping and evolving informal communities within the organization (Wenger, McDermott, and Snyder, 2002). Connected leaders try to be explicit about the processes, the means, and the expected outcomes of community participation—including the fact that it is being invented, tested, and modified along the way.

Navigation

Complex challenges are landscapes of possibility and constraint. The capability of navigating refers to effective ways of learning by doing amid uncertainty and change. Addressing the possibilities of this landscape requires imagination, and working with constraints requires creativity and disciplined experimentation. Navigating is about traveling this shared landscape flexibly yet wisely: How do we take the next step? How do we go in the direction we want?

Rather than one leader plotting an ideal course, the community tests its way forward using small wins and networks of connected leaders. The community applies various navigation skills and abilities: experimentation, improvisation, prototyping, successive approximation, invention of practical tools, mapmaking and map revision, and learning in public. The idea of a grand strategy thus gives way to that of emergent strategy. An ideal vision becomes less important than attention to a visible horizon. Communities that learn to navigate for themselves in such ways are well situated for future leadership challenges.

Navigation as a capability features two aspects that are in constant creative tension with one another: analysis and synthesis. On the one hand, navigation is goal-oriented and hence objective and analytical. *Analysis* is concerned with reducing wholes to parts, symbols, and formulas. Yet navigation is also emergent from experience and hence is subjective, intuitive, and synthetic. *Synthesis* is concerned with interconnections, contexts, and larger wholes—seeing them as well as making them. Later in this chapter, we discuss tools for deliberately interweaving analysis and synthesis in order to navigate effectively.

Practicing Exploration for Development: Tools and Techniques

There are a number of tools and techniques that we and others have found to aid in the practice of exploration for development. What these tools have in common is the combination of "doing real work" (addressing valid business objectives) while also developing leadership at the community level. Let us look at a few such tools, in terms of the three components of the exploration for development framework: shared sensemaking, connectivity, and navigation (see Figure 15.1). Keep in mind that each of these tools often draws on more than one of the components, but each tends to emphasize or highlight a particular component.

Shared Sensemaking

A variety of tools can be used to support shared sensemaking. What these tools do is help groups, as a collective, see their issues and challenges in rich detail. This includes seeing the diverse perspectives, assumptions, and experience bases through which the challenge can be understood; seeing where there are common, shared perspectives; surfacing lots of information for everyone to examine; looking for and testing patterns; putting private intuitions and hunches "on the table" for comparison and contrast; and thinking imaginatively about the work.

Visual Sensemaking. People are visual creatures living in a visual world. Yet organizations typically function with a narrow range of visual media and methods, such as text on screens or paper and talking heads in conference rooms. The digital revolution has brought some variety to this visual sparseness. The Internet and desktop graphics tools such as PowerPoint have opened fresh avenues for creating and conveying information. Yet the visual literacy required to be creative and effective in the visual realm is generally lacking (Stafford, 1994).

In our practice, we use various visually based methods designed to help organizational members make sense of complex challenges and point to options for action. We refer to this more generally as "visual sensemaking."

Visual Explorer (VE) is a tool to facilitate visual sensemaking based on our research on complex challenge competencies (Palus and Horth, 2002). VE provides a set of 224 images printed in color on standard-size paper. The images were selected because they were interesting, provocative, diverse, or ambiguous and lent themselves metaphorically or otherwise to the complex challenges of business and life.

Visual Explorer works well in activities designed to look at any sort of mutual question or issue. Telco used VE with a group of senior directors to visualize and wrestle with the challenge they faced. Having first done some thinking and discussion about their challenges, the directors came together and were instructed to browse the images (which were laid face-up in a hallway) and select two: "One that stands for the way your challenge is now, whether literally, metaphorically, emotionally, or intuitively, and another one that stands for what a positive path forward with your challenge will look like."

With selected images thus in hand, members gather in smaller groups of four or five to dialogue about their challenges, using the images as mediating objects. A volunteer goes first and starts by describing her first image in detail: What is the image? What are the details? What is mysterious or surprising? Then she describes the challenge itself and how it connects with the image. She repeats this with her second image. Then each person in the group responds to the images the volunteer has just described, first describing what they see in the image—especially if they see anything different. Then each person makes his own connections to the image in light of the challenge the volunteer has described. This is a key move in the process, and we suggest using language along the lines of "If that were my image, and if that were my challenge, I might connect them like this . . ." or "What I notice in that image is. . . ." Overt problem solving, advice, and criticism are temporarily off-limits. Finally, the originator of the image takes it back, sharing any new insights she has gained. Each person thus volunteers to place his or her images and challenges in the middle of the dialogue.

Visual Explorer creates shared sensemaking by using images as the starting place for dialogue. In ordinary conversation, people tend to revert to entrenched ways of thinking. The images selected by each participant to represent ideas she feels strongly about provide a way to publicly discuss difficult aspects of these ideas in a safe and inviting forum.

Telco used the Visual Explorer exercise with a variety of groups of senior managers over the course of their leadership development process. People often said something like, "I was doubtful at first about the pictures, but we were able to talk about our challenges in depth." One kind of comment gets at this idea of visual sensemaking: "People in our group tended to see very different things in the same image—and that was OK." For us this indicates *perspective taking*, which in typical discourse is a metaphor for what literally happens in the visual field. Another set of comments is along the lines of "It was fun. We laughed. The connections we made led to a lot of puns and jokes." Also common is this set of ideas: "We came up with metaphors we otherwise would not have. It seemed easy to tell stories to go with the images."

Collage is another visual sensemaking technique in which groups of people combine diverse images or artifacts. Collage is an excellent tool for assisting people in assembling diverse perceptions and crafting new ideas together.

For example, we worked with a director-level group at Telco as the participants formed action learning teams to address specific aspects of their common challenges. Before doing a step-by-step action plan, the group members synthesized their explicit and implicit knowledge into a collage, representing what the path forward for their team would look like.

We provided a stack of images clipped from various sources, a stack of trade magazines from their industry, glue, and scissors. They also had all the VE images they had used in a previous session. Working quickly, the group members produced a rich depiction of where they wanted to go—including vivid depictions of the difficulties. This led to a sober discussion of the politics they faced in working across boundaries and a frank appraisal of sponsorship possibilities among senior leaders. Working with this image in the middle of a rapid-fire dialogue, they then produced a detailed action plan.

Mapping Tools. Various methods are available to imagine, create, critique, and revise shared maps of a complex challenge. Complex relationships and patterns are more easily seen on a map than on a list. Exploratory maps that lay out the whole territory of the challenge can be crafted into formal models for creating new structures and action plans. Shared maps can be constructed and maintained in common work areas (including virtual spaces) and during group retreats.

The simplest mapping techniques uses "sticky notes" to capture ideas generated by brainstorming, which are then clustered into groups with common themes. For example, leaders at Orion Research Center create spreadsheet diagram cutouts, which they call "star maps," for each project in their pipeline, and then experiment with ways of mapping these projects against their strategy. Creating and rearranging these maps is a form of collaborative inquiry into the adequacy of their project portfolio as well as their strategy. Outliers in the maps, for example, sometimes point to holes in the strategy, ripe for debate.

Various software tools allow mapping to be done on a shared digital display (Conklin, 2002; Kirschner, Shum, and Carr, 2003; Selvin and others, 2001). The advantages of using software versus paper-based mapping include the ability to archive and recycle information for future use and to translate the maps into Web pages and text reports.

Storymaking and Storytelling. Stories are ways of creating shared meaning around some basic questions: Who are we? What happened and why? Who cares? Where are we going? (see Gargiulo, 2001; Simmons, 2000; Tichy, 1997). Stories are good ways of supporting shared sensemaking across boundaries. Peter Orton, a manager at IBM and former Hollywood scriptwriter, explains why stories are a powerful mechanism for teaching and learning: "Stories enhance attention, create anticipation, and increase retention. Stories use plot and character to generate conflict. They provide a familiar set of hooks that allow us to process the information that we hang on them . . . a protagonist the audience can empathize with, something important at stake, mounting jeopardy, a formidable antagonist" (Weil, 1998, pp. 38–39).

There are two basic kinds of stories to deliberately foster when a group conducts exploration for development: stories of the past and stories of the future.

Stories of the past deal with questions such as Who are we? What are we made of? How and why are we here? The past provides templates for the present and future—but the templates first need to be made visible as stories. The assumptions and perspectives of the past need to be honored but examined in fresh light.

Orion Research Center is a Pacific Rim organization whose one hundred employees speak thirty different languages or dialects. It turns out that, not surprisingly, many people on the leadership team did not know each other very well and were reluctant to contribute from their own work and life experiences on leadership questions. So they spent some time telling stories about critical learning experiences. Afterward there was more willingness in the group to speak up with opinions and culturally based points of view.

A technique we often use that elicits quite powerful stories of the past rather quickly follows these instructions: "Remember a situation or event with strong personal meaning that you experienced. Write the story in the present tense, from the perspective of a character or object within the situation other than yourself. You have just thirty minutes to write." The writing technique that supports this process is called *freewriting* (Goldberg, 1986). Freewriting is a process for writing quickly even in the face of writer's block. So we say, "Simply put your pen to paper, begin writing, and continue writing without stopping or editing—even if all you write at first is 'I can't think . . . I don't know . . . this stinks . . . .' Forget about rules like spelling. You will be surprised to find gems of ideas amid the gravel. With those gems as starting places, freewrite again: more gems, more gravel. Soon you will have a great deal of material that you can edit into a story." After freewriting, people tell their stories thus written. Almost always they are surprisingly compelling. The device of "through a character or object other than yourself" gives the writer imaginative license to take perspectives and make reflections that are otherwise difficult to talk about.

Imaginative stories about possible futures are commonly known as *scenarios* (Schwartz, 1991; van der Heijden, 1996). They can be used in support of strategic planning and creating shared vision. The exploration for development framework suggests that when deliberately facing complex challenges, it is important for groups and even whole communities to create their own scenarios.

Traditionally in organizations, only a few leaders imagined the future and turned those images into actions. In the face of complex challenges, the imaginations of a diverse array of people need to be tapped into. Tools for collaboratively making stories of the future are designed to involve more of the organization in the process of leadership. In doing so, critical differences in assumptions and perspectives can be surfaced and examined, greater awareness of the forces for and against positive change is fostered, and metaphors and symbols standing for a desirable future often emerge. Such stories then become a navigational aid for moving together into the future.

There are a variety of ways to seed the material for the scenarios. It is important to have high input of both facts and imagination. There are a variety of ways to accomplish this. You can ask the group to write headlines about their project or organization as it might appear five years in the future. You might have a number of industry experts, futurists, and mavericks talk to the group about trends and possibilities.

According to futurist John Petersen (1997), president of the Arlington Institute, "wild cards" are potential future events or circumstances with very low probability but extremely high impact that could drastically alter the way we live, do business, and think. As examples, Petersen lists human cloning, a large asteroid hitting the earth, and time travel. He believes that in the coming years, wild cards will be more frequent and unexpected and that people who recognize and learn to make sense of them will have a real advantage. Petersen offers several wild card questions for leaders:

What are the most important wild cards for my organization, my customers, and me?

What would really wipe us out?

How can I anticipate these things?

What are the early indicators?

What can I do about my wild cards?

A technique we use to have groups create and explore scenarios using all this variety of input is called *moviemaking*. The "movie" is a wall-sized collage of images and words that tell an imaginative story about where an organization might be headed or how certain challenges might worsen or resolve "someday in a place not too distant from here." The movie goes into the middle of a dialogue about possible futures as well as the nature of challenges currently being faced.

Engaging Artistry. Good leadership is infused with artistry. An understanding of this has recently moved beyond simple truism to yield robust insights, applications (De Ciantis, 1995; Mintzberg, 1989; Richards, 1995; Vaill, 1989), and theoretical frameworks (Edwards, 1986; Nissley, 2002). We have observed that shared sensemaking is at least partly aesthetic in nature (Palus and Horth, 1996). Practically everyone has some advanced capacity for the artistic aspect of shared sensemaking, but it tends to be expressed as what Booth (1997) calls "everyday art," more so than "fine art" or "genius art" (Bayles and Orland, 1993; Dewey, 1934). This sort of everyday art can be a strong basis for the creative work needed to face complex challenges.

In our own research and practice, we have spent considerable time with professionals, technologists, managers, and leaders—that is, artists of many descriptions. Here are some rules we have gleaned from them about engaging people's artistry:

• Creative potential increases when borders are crossed. Many artists thrive near the edge of chaotic borders. Others make their way by exploring niches in familiar territory. Artists make fresh connections.

• Art is social, "that solitary work we can only do together." Most artists work in a context of intense connections to others, even if some phases of the work are silent and solitary. People are different, yet potentially complementary, in their creative preferences.

• Artists are hot-wired to their passions. Call it your core, your genius, the Muse, inspiration, yearning, the Spirit, the live wire, or the uncensored source. Artists are connected to deeper wells, which they are seldom able to describe. Beware of uprooting your passion and replacing it with someone else's, to paraphrase the poet David Whyte (1996), beware of sleepwalking your way into someone else's life and mistaking it for your own.

• Artists move in the direction of discomfort. Artists engage in creative destruction, both within themselves and in their communities. Bateson (1994) describes "the double rhythm of pattern violation and pattern creation in the arts that must characterize any society undergoing change" (p. 224). Pattern violation can be incredibly disruptive; sugarcoating the dislocations of change is a shallow form of art.

• Artists practice the aesthetics of imperfection. Jazz musicians are adept at taking a mistake and building something interesting. Scientists have an "eye for the awry" and capitalize on experiments gone wrong.

• Art can take you far, fast. To grasp complexity often means slowing down for a bit, avoiding habitual shortcuts. But the reverse is also true: Art is hot. It strikes quickly. Imagination flies. The practiced artist or group can work at a white heat, with a high level of aesthetic competence.

• Artists see with fresh eyes and help others do the same (Perkins, 1994). A function of art is to help oneself and others break habits of seeing, thereby seeing something as if it were new. A corollary is that artists help people sustain improved habits of perception, seeing what has before been subtle or invisible.

Connectivity

Tools and techniques for connectivity are those that enrich the connections between entities within a system (individuals, teams, groups, or communities) as the system engages with its complex challenges. The idea is to create connectivity among people that can serve as what Sally Helgesen (1995) calls a "web of inclusion," a kind of flexible and evolving container for the complexities at hand.

Dialogue. Conversation is conducted atop layers of meaning. What people mean when they communicate, and what they think they understand of others, is both enriched and confounded by unspoken assumptions and the private textures of prior experiences. The more nonstandard and complex a topic is, the more confusion between organizational members is likely. When different people view the same situation, they may start with different assumptions, pay attention to different things, and form different interpretations. *Dialogue* occurs when people are able to temporarily suspend their certainties with each other, explore basic assumptions, and ask questions for which they do not already know the answers (Dixon, 1998; Isaacs, 1999). Dialogue in this sense can be understood as "meaning flowing through" a committed group of people (Bohm, 1996).

Dialogue is a form of skilled, searching, critical, supportive, open, and honest conversation that is sustained over time. It is not uncommon in high-performing groups such as scientific research teams or championship athletic teams; however, we have observed that it is rare in business organizations. Dialogue is particularly important in times of chaos and complexity because during these times organizations become more fragmented, and the fragments become disconnected. These fragments—split by function, role, geography, and culture—develop their own practices, languages, and assumptions. Specialization and focus are desirable, but leadership of the larger organization requires connection, awareness and appreciation of similarities and differences, and cultivation of shared understandings. These can be approached through dialogue.

Each group develops its own assortment of techniques and styles for engaging in dialogue. We encourage groups to experiment, improvise, and invent their own forms of dialogue—and to call it what they want. Others have called it skilled conversation, leadership council, forum, vision sessions, town meetings, "open kimono meetings," and Work Out (at GE). Effective dialogue incorporates feedback from organization members about both the process and the results. It takes practice to ensure that dialogue does not slip down into "discussion by percussion"—the usual verbal sparring. The following are guidelines and suggestions for starting a dialogue.

- *Designate a time.* Opportune times for dialogue are group retreats or when a team faces a new challenge. Make explicit your intention to have a different kind of conversation. Set a start time and an end time for returning to conversation as usual.
- *Create a space.* Rearrange the space to rearrange behavior. If you sit in the same chairs around the same table in the same room, you will have the same conversation. Sit in a circle without a table so that people can make eye contact without having to move. Not having a table decreases distance and enables the perception of body language.
- *Agree to norms.* Keep them simple. Post them. Agree to what kinds of information arising from the dialogue can be shared outside the room. If a norm is

broken, point out the violation and then decide whether to keep that norm or change it.

• *Consider using an outside facilitator.* The first few times a group tries to talk in these new ways, having an experienced facilitator can be helpful. Dialogue can be uncomfortable at first; a facilitator can keep people from simply reverting to old, comfortable habits.

• *Keep an open and curious mind.* Examine conflicting or polarized points of view that arise during the dialogue. Ask questions to surface the facts, assumptions, and emotions surrounding the various views. Don't smooth over differences; explore them.

• *Respect silences and softer voices.* Pauses in the talk, even long ones, can be constructive. At the same time, "quiet voices" should be given a chance to speak. "In and out chairs" is a move that we find works well: the dominant voices ("you know who you are") move their chairs one step back for ten or fifteen minutes while the quiet voices ("and you know who you are") have their say.

• *Let one person speak at a time.* Discourage interruptions, talking over others, and side conversations. Each speaker should have time to finish a thought.

• *Remember the intent.* State the purpose of the dialogue at the beginning of the session. Remind participants of this purpose if they stray. Check at the end to see if the intent was realized, and if not, determine why not.

• *Balance advocacy and inquiry.* Statements of advocacy and opinion should be balanced with searching questions. Sometimes it is effective to ask the group as a whole to alternate opinions and questions.

• *Affirm everyone's personal competence.* Disagree with ideas, not people. Create an environment in which people feel secure expressing unpopular thoughts.

• *Practice loyal skepticism.* Treat all points of view as hypotheses open to testing. Cynicism is poisonous, but doubt combined with commitment is healthy. At the same time, skepticism should not be used to undermine the inquiry. One manager we worked with expressed healthy skepticism with a simple statement: "Not proven, but carry on."

• *Legitimize intuition and emotion.* Hunches are valid. So are "what if" excursions of thought. Passion for the issues is positive. Interpersonal conflict should be acknowledged but taken offline.

• *Express chains of reasoning.* Inquire about the explicit reasoning that leads someone from the data to a conclusion.

• *Avoid the mechanics of problem solving.* Moving too quickly to problem solving and the giving of prescriptive advice are frequently symptoms of running away from the root issues.

• *Build shared meaning.* As the dialogue continues, try to integrate the various points of view into meaningful wholes. Often someone who stands apart from two opposing points of view is able to glimpse their synthesis. Sometimes the integration first appears in terms of an image or metaphor or a vision of how things could look in the future.

- *Shift attention.* Look at things from unusual perspectives. Pay attention to the periphery (Gryskiewicz, 1999). Pay attention to what is missing. Pay attention to the weak signals (Brown and Duguid, 2000).
- *Provide positive turbulence.* Invite the occasional guest in to stir the pot—a customer, partner, or someone with a radical point of view.
- *Debrief the dialogue.* Spend five minutes or so reflecting on how well the norms were kept, whether the process needs changing, and so forth.
- *Consider appointing a group reporter.* A nonparticipant reporter can be asked to take notes during the dialogue and write them up afterward. Make sure the group agrees to this first, however; individuals must have veto power over the recording and dissemination of their comments.
- *Continue the dialogue over time.* Reconvene on a regular basis. Improve the process. Assess the dialogue for progress on shared understanding of the challenges at hand. Supplement face-to-face dialogue with electronic forums such as e-mail, listservs, and intranet discussion rooms.

"Putting something in the middle" is a powerful way to learn dialogue and increase its effectiveness. The technique is simple: you place a tangible object in the middle of your group and focus dialogue on it. The object may stand for an idea but is something you can actually look at and touch. Objects we have used in our work include a video of a visit to a customer site, Visual Explorer images, a product prototype, a Web site projected on a large screen, and a competitor's product.

Why an object? Objects focus attention in a positive way. By describing their observations of an object rather than an abstraction, people become less polarized and argumentative. Objects also help people make personal connections. They provide images and invite metaphors and stories. They can be appreciated, played with, recrafted. The object "in the middle" becomes a symbolic vessel for holding the truths spoken by the group and transforms these into a collective meaning. Because the objects serve as media, we call this *mediated dialogue* (Palus and Drath, 2001). Techniques in this chapter that support mediated dialogue include Visual Explorer, collage, and moviemaking.

Dialogue can be risky if people are not prepared for it. For example, lack of mutual trust can result in heightened cynicism or abuse of openly shared feelings. Favorable conditions before conducting dialogue include the following:

- Prior team building with a self-and-others awareness component.
- Leadership development as individuals and as a group.
- The cultivation of well-founded trust.

- Analytical knowledge.
- Immersion in high-quality data appropriate to the challenge.
- A voiced challenge—the articulation of a shared and compelling challenge and the sense that it may be complex or chaotic.
- Maturity—if the group on the whole is emotionally young, then it is important that at least several of the members are mature and confident enough to serve as role models and anchor points.

After the dialogue, the following actions are beneficial:

- *Come to explicit closure.* If closure on the issues is not possible, be explicit about how you will continue to address them within or outside of the dialogue process.
- *Take action based on the meaning the group creates.* If the entire process ends with no tangible outcomes, your group may feel cynical—even though it may well be beneficial to defer action until considerable exploration of the issues has been accomplished.
- *Communicate salient parts of the dialogue to constituencies.* Beware of the appearance of being an elite group meeting secretly. But don't violate the trust of the group by going public with information and opinions expressed under assumptions of confidentiality.

Building Networks. Notable challenges in many organizations have to do with forming relationships across boundaries—of functions, cultures, nations, locations, merged entities, and so on. It can be hard to connect with other people. Digital means of connection do facilitate certain kinds of connection across boundaries, and improvement in their use is a positive part of this story; but digital tools have proved insufficient by themselves and even to stand in the way of trustful and open relationships. Fragmentation in relationships means fragmentation of connectivity.

Strengthening the web of interpersonal relationships across boundaries is called *networking.* No longer just an individual concern, building an organizational capacity for successful networking is a way of building connected leadership. This sort of capacity is built by actually designing repeated opportunities for boundary-spanning, dialogue-rich relationships into and around the work of the organization. A result of this kind of purposeful boundary-spanning networking can be a "web of inclusion" (Helgesen, 1995) in which leadership may emerge wherever it is needed in the network (Barabasi, 2002).

We worked with a group of peers in a division that had recently been involved in a merger. Most of these directors were near-strangers to each other at the outset of the program. One of the objectives was to network people around shared challenges they faced. Near the end of the program we conducted a "networking fair." Each person covered an easel sheet with his or her name, an updated challenge statement, a list of capabilities and resources the person could offer peers in the program, and a list of capabilities and resources the person might like to borrow from peers in facing and solving their mutual challenges. These sheets were posted on the wall. The group then spent about an hour networking amid this gallery, offering help, soliciting advice, writing their names as resources next to needs they might be able to fill, and generally building on the relationships started in the prior two days.

Sharing Powerful Questions. An important shift for leaders in recent years has been to broaden their role of answer finder to include that of question asker. One manager we worked with said, "For a long time, my whole frame of reference was that I had to have all the answers. Now I'm finding out that it's better to have the good questions." The next big shift is to move an inquiry mind-set into the organization at large.

How groups ask and answer questions together says a lot about how they are connected to each other and how well these connections function. Broader participation in leadership means inviting powerful questions from more people in the organization, as well as from customers, partners, competitors, and even chance encounters on the fringes of your usual business (Gryskiewicz, 1999).

Powerful questions typically have three characteristics: they invite exploration, they resist easy answers, and they provoke strong passions.

- *Powerful questions invite exploration.* They pull attention to unnoticed places. Powerful questions aim at the root of assumptions. Asking such questions can disrupt perceptual shortcuts to help people notice details, patterns, or movements that they have overlooked.
- *Powerful questions resist easy answers.* They slow down people's attention at crucial times so that they notice more. Such questions do not seek a final answer immediately but resonate over time in a way that feeds collaborative inquiry.
- *Powerful questions can call forth passionate responses.* They invite attention through our emotions. Heartfelt questions that take time to answer fully are at the core of learning communities.

As a community or organization, the key is to create contexts that invite and support both asking and responding to powerful questions. We see this being done in a variety of ways, including strategy retreats, peer coaching sessions, conversations with invited controversial experts, and impromptu brainstorming meetings. It can also be as simple as consistently asking, "Where could our work get blindsided?" and consistently listening to the responses as well as the negative spaces in the responses. One leader we know keeps a short list of the best, most provocative questions his team is grappling with and refers to these questions to get things moving when thinking gets stuck. It has become a point of honor on his team to be the first to pose a question that makes this list.

Here are some examples of powerful questions:

What are the patterns?

What is interesting, unique, beautiful, or unusual about this?

What is one hope we have going into this? What is one fear we have going into this?

What does our intuition tell us?

What is a metaphor for this?

What is the story behind this?

What questions are we neglecting to ask? What are we missing? What could blindside us?

How would a Martian describe this?

What if we deliberately tried to make this problem worse?

What would be the negatives if our dream came true? What would be the positives if we failed?

Navigation

In this section, we look at tools and techniques for developing the third capability of the exploration for development framework, navigation. We examine several useful domains of research and practice on the topics of creative problem solving, experiential learning, and action learning. Let's look at how these can be used within the broader objectives of resolving complex challenges and developing leadership at the community level.

Creative Problem Solving. At the messy day-to-day level of complexity, work (like the rest of life) is a tangle of problems in need of creative solutions. There is a danger, as we have discussed, of being trapped in technical problems, one at a time, and missing the leadership implications. Nonetheless, we have found great value for navigating messy landscapes of related problems in a set of theories and practices known as *creative problem solving* (CPS). CPS is ultimately based in the Osborn-Parnes Creative Problem Solving Model (Osborn, 1953; Parnes, 1992).

Creative problem solving embraces a set of useful principles, namely:

- All people have creative ability, probably much more than they think.
- Widely varying types of creative ability are nonetheless complementary.
- Creative problem solving consists of cycles of divergence (casting a wide net) and convergence (judging and focusing).

The basic model has six steps, each of which has a divergent phase and a convergent phase:

1. *Mess finding*—looking at the "mess" of interrelated issues and opportunities
2. *Fact finding*—exploring knowns and unknowns and looking for missing or needed information
3. *Problem finding*—identifying a specific problem on which to focus
4. *Idea finding*—generating diverse ideas relating to the problem
5. *Solution finding*—converging on a subset of ideas in preparation for synthesizing them into potentially useful solutions
6. *Action finding*—generating and refining action steps through acceptance and into implementation

Brainstorming, the nonjudgmental generation of a copious number and variety of ideas, is a standard tool of CPS. Often misused and then maligned, it is most effective when coupled with convergent techniques in the context of the rest of the model.

Another useful CPS-based technique is *reframing.* Reframing means asking, "Have we drawn the right boundary (frame) around this challenge or problem? Are we solving the right problem? What is the most advantageous way to frame this challenge?" People frequently spend enormous energy trying to solve the wrong problem. Facing complexity is partly a matter of applying a variety of frames: zooming in, zooming out, seeing this aspect or that aspect, and tying the smaller frames into a larger one. Some leaders have told us that the problematic part of their challenge "disappeared" upon shifting frames—what seemed to be an intractable problem was rendered either insignificant or temporary when placed in a different frame.

Here are basic steps we suggest in conducting reframing as part of small group dialogues. First, brainstorm alternative challenge statements. Use invitational question stems such as "How should we . . . ?" or "In what ways might we . . . ?" The offer of new challenge statements is a staccato conversation in which new perceptions and assumptions emerge about what the "real" problem is. The group will move toward consensus, selecting what participants view as the most advantageous one. One technique for isolating the reframed statement is for the group to gradually eliminate candidate statements, first by finding statements that rephrase or are covered by other statements. Some statements may be set aside as criteria or metrics ("We will know we have resolved the challenge when these statements are true"). At this point, realpolitik kicks in: Is someone in charge of addressing the challenge? If so, this person may well have the final vote. Are there a number of constituencies? Can they agree to one reframed statement?

Two important lessons for the leadership capability of navigating are to be learned from creative problem solving. The first is that challenges shift as you work on them and gain new insights. Working on challenges is a series of iterations and approximations. Don't work forever solving what turns out to be the wrong problem. The second lesson is that divergence of thinking and acting usefully follows convergence, and vice versa.

Challenges have a social landscape—"owners" of the various subproblems, champions, constituencies, and so on—that also must be mapped and navigated.

Experiential Learning. Successfully learning from experience, as well as learning how to learn from experience, is an important part of navigating complex challenges and, more broadly, human development (Bunker and Webb, 1992). There are many useful approaches and models for helping people individually and collectively learn how to learn in complex situations.

One model we have found to be especially helpful in designing challenge-based learning experiences is Bernice McCarthy's 4MAT learning model (McCarthy and Keene, 1996; see Table 15.1), which is in turn based in David Kolb's experiential learning cycle (1984). Four of the 4MAT steps invoke L-mode cognition, and four invoke R-mode cognition. *L-mode* is that part of thinking related to language, logic, sequential analysis, and stepping back from the flow of experience. *R-mode* is related to patterns (rather than symbols), nonverbal intuition, emotional and physical intelligence, and being immersed in the flow of direct experience (Springer and Deutsch, 1981). Both modes need to work in an integrated way for people to experience optimal learning. L-mode is typically dominant when organizations solve technical challenges. The developmental work in facing complexity thus often lies in surfacing and integrating the R-mode among leaders and leadership processes (Mintzberg, 1989). Visual sensemaking, for example, is heavily R-mode-oriented.

Consider the cycles of experiential learning in the Orion case introduced at the beginning of this chapter. This team of scientists and technologists had the task of picking "winners"—high-return projects that matched corporate strategy and capabilities. Strategic planning was integrated into the company's community of

TABLE 15.1. THE 4MAT LEARNING CYCLE.

Step	Primary Mode	Description
1. Connect	R	Make personal connections to the challenge by tapping into direct personal experience and by focusing and sustaining attention in a gut-level, intimate, and intuitive way.
2. Reflect	L	Step back and analyze what you see and the connections you have made.
3. Image	R	Create and explore images (metaphors, stories, pictures, scenarios) of the challenge based on your connections and reflections. Imagine future desirable states and the paths for getting there.
4. Conceptualize	L	Build (or borrow) and apply formal conceptual frameworks. Convert the metaphors to formal models.
5. Practice	L	Test the conceptual frameworks in a logical way.
6. Extend	R	Modify the frameworks and extend them into new realms by making imaginative connections, playful modifications, and intuitive leaps. This is the start of internalizing the new conceptual framework.
7. Refine	L	Refine the new knowledge by analyzing, assessing, critiquing, tightening, and formally expressing what has been learned.
8. Integrate	R	Incorporate the new knowledge into the broader systems of collective knowledge and practices (the organization) and personal knowledge and practices (self-identity).
Now repeat the cycle starting at 1 with this new level of integration.		The 4MAT cycle keeps repeating. It works simultaneously at different scales. It may, for example, be completed during a single meeting for one aspect of a challenge while taking a year for the whole of the challenge.

Note: For more information about 4MAT, go to http://www.aboutlearning.com

practice by inventing its own method of strategic mapping. Integration of this method into company practice started a round of fresh observation of the environment using the new, malleable "star maps" as foils to be revised in light of new learning. Documented results of these and related efforts included the halving of product development cycle time, a substantial increase in the value of completed projects, and a measured improvement in the climate for creative work.

What worked? Their deliberate practice of R-mode aspects of learning was one key (see Table 15.1). Some members of the Orion team remarked that they knew the value of R-mode from their work as inventive scientists, and this familiarity helped them use it in their work as strategists. Also, some team members saw their shared work at Orion as overwhelmingly analytical in nature but still welcomed R-mode for its complementary value, in what one called "a welcome synergy between science and artistry."

Of course, they had heard about R-mode, artistry, and shared sensemaking from us in a customized leadership development program we did collaboratively with them. Then they went back to work and uniquely adapted salient aspects of that experience to their strategy process. Thus they navigated their challenges by using the latter four steps of the 4MAT experiential learning cycle (see Table 15.1): testing and practicing, exploring and extending into new realms, analytical critiques and refinements, and integration of all kinds of new learnings into what they called "the big picture." The team members most acutely felt the leadership ramifications in their discernment of this big picture. What, for them, was in this picture? Their own culture, their corporate identity, their whole strategic portfolio of projects and resources, the picture of the changing markets, their own changing careers, and even, as a constant shade in the picture, their love of science.

Action Learning. Action learning is a set of organization development practices in which supported groups tackle important real-work projects with three kinds of objectives: delivering measurable results in service of the organization's work, learning and communicating lessons specific to a particular context, and developing individual and collective capabilities for learning and leadership more generally. The impressively broad scale of action learning usefully ranges from tacit, unfacilitated learning at work to focused and facilitated high-impact learning projects (including deliberately learning how to learn from experience and experiment) to transformations of people and organizations (Marsick, 2002). As a set of navigational tools, action learning taps the transformative possibilities inherent in the complex challenges now on the table. Action learning uses deliberate experiments coupled with reflection to facilitate moving from "where we are" to "where we are going." Action learning methodologies are well documented in theory and practice and are still evolving (see, for example, Argyris and Schön, 1978; Dotlich and Noel, 1998; Pedler, 1997; Revans, 1982; Rohlin, Billing, Lindberg, and Wickelgren, 2002).

Let's look at four important aspects of a facilitated action learning initiative— challenge, sponsorship, coaching, and integration—by continuing with the case of peers at Telco, who formed action learning teams during their leadership development program.

Exploration for development calls for the direct engagement of complex challenges rather than staying at the level of technical problems. The program at Telco spent time exploring the complex challenges the participants faced individually and collectively, including the current perspectives of the company's president.

Out of their own critical synthesis and mapping of the challenges, the program participants self-selected into teams, each focused on a project that was both practical and linked to higher-order challenges related to postmerger integration.

The participants were motivated by the potential to initiate profound changes in the ways they did their work. Any smaller challenge they denigrated as makework in their already too-busy work lives. Each team was sponsored by a member of the senior leadership team of the division. The sponsor's role was to guide the team and provide cover and feedback as members got out of their usual roles and started crossing boundaries within the company. Each team had a CCL coach, who helped as needed with issues as they emerged, including everything from basic team building to thinking through the political ramifications of the participants' activities. A main task of coaching, especially at first, was to help the team balance its action orientation with reflection in order to facilitate learning. Each team initially had two months to pursue the project before reporting its findings and results face-to-face to the senior leadership team of the division. The senior team tried to assimilate the most compelling of these findings into the work of the division.

The fullest use of action learning, however, is possible only with further integration of learning activities and strategic leadership initiatives. A powerful question for Telco is therefore "How can we make the peer network of directors an ongoing, strategic learning resource, rather than constraining it to special events like this leadership program?"

Cautions

Exploration for development is no silver bullet. In this or any form of human development there are pitfalls. Here is a summary of the main cautions we offer.

- Exploration for development can degrade to merely unearthing problems and placing blame. A fix-it mentality will preserve the status quo rather than transform it. A relentless focus on problems may yield short-term operational results, but it will stifle leadership development. An overly problem-focused mentality can be balanced by attention, dialogue, and inquiry into the strengths and dreams held in common within the organization (Cooperrider and Srivastva, 1987).

- Organizations are full of things that are rarely discussed in public: uncomfortable truths, deep-rooted conflict, maverick points of view. Chris Argyris (1990) calls these "undiscussables." People can interpret powerful questions as betrayal if there is not an honest commitment to open inquiry. It is too easy to interpret concern as resistance and doubt as betrayal. Protect the people who are paying attention and courting dialogue. Create safe places and methods to explore divergent perceptions.

- Dialogue, while collaborative in spirit and goal, is safely initiated in organizations by individuals with the authority to do so. Individuals without authority who initiate dialogue on issues that are contentious risk becoming lightning rods in any confrontation with authority (Heifetz, 1994). Realize that co-inquiry is long-term and exploratory, especially if you lack authority. Be patient, learn the territory, choose appropriate moments for expanding the dialogue, and evaluate the lessons of those moments once they are realized. Make sure you assess what is to be gained and lost, keeping in mind that risk avoidance is also the risk of lost opportunity.

- Strong communities are not the answer for all ills. Communities, even "better" ones, still reflect human strengths and weaknesses. The tasks of facilitating and navigating overlapping, newly constituted communities of practice can be overwhelming to members and managers (Wenger, McDermott, and Snyder, 2002). Exploration for development initiatives should start slowly enough to gauge the capacity of the system to handle complex, adaptive work (Heifetz, 1994). Knowing the rudiments of systems thinking and acting can help a lot (Oshry, 1999; Senge, 1990).

- Dialogue is rooted in language, but words often do not carry the knowledge we intend (Korzybski, 1941). Much of emotional intelligence, for example, is enacted nonverbally (Goleman, 1995). Therefore, cultivate shared sensemaking and connections by the kinds of things that complement language. For example, help members from different parts of the organization get lots of face-to-face time. Create opportunities for powerful common experiences. Make workspaces that help people visualize their common work and not just talk about it.

- Images complement language in exploring complex challenges, but images also can be misused. The scientist Richard Dawkins (1998) writes, "A brain that is good at simulating models in imagination is also, almost inevitably, in danger of self-delusion" (p. 282). Images have been used to impose tyranny. Hitler used the new media quite powerfully to construct a nightmarish vision and literally project it onto the senses of the population. "Visual capture" is what psychologists call the tendency of compelling sensory input to invade and hold our attention. Television, advertising, and architecture all take advantage of the power of the image to seize the imagination. Literacy in imaging, then, is a necessary complement to verbal literacy for participants in connected leadership.

Conclusion

The framework described in this chapter, called exploration for development, enables leadership development at the level of the community and its interconnections while also fostering individual leader development. The starting point is to see and name the complex challenges faced by a group or organization. The expected outcomes of such organizational leadership development are progress in resolving these specific challenges, appropriate transformations of the organization itself, and the development of new leadership capabilities at the community level. Exploration for development cultivates and applies three specific leadership capabilities: shared sensemaking, connectivity, and navigation. Exploration for development at its best enables a community-based artistry of leadership by coupling the analytical powers of an organization to its latent powers of synthesis and integration.

AFTERWORD

Ellen Van Velsor
Cynthia D. McCauley

This handbook presents much of what we at CCL have learned about leader development and are beginning to learn about the broader concept of leadership development. We ask, and answer, important questions about leadership development, and we hope we have done so in a way that is useful to you.

We realize that this handbook captures a view of leadership development at a particular point in time. Forces both internal and external to organizations are driving changes in how organizations are structured to get work done, in where and how the work is done, and in how leadership and leadership development are understood. As we move forward in our work over the next several years, new questions will continue to arise whose answers will deepen our understanding and broaden our perspective. Here is a sampling of the questions we are now asking:

AS ORGANIZATIONS FACE INCREASING COMPLEXITY IN THEIR EXTERNAL AND INTERNAL ENVIRONMENTS, WHAT ARE THE IMPLICATIONS FOR LEADERSHIP AND LEADERSHIP DEVELOPMENT?

Discussion of these implications began in the chapters in Part Three. However, we have much to learn about the range of strategies needed for effectively enacting leadership in the face of complexity. What are the alternative processes for setting (and resetting) direction, for creating alignment, and for maintaining commitment?

And what are the implications of using these alternative strategies? For example, does a more inclusive strategy for setting direction make a difference in how alignment gets created or how commitment comes about? Can we categorize leadership strategies and help organizations build flexibility in the use of those strategies? Is an organization that can employ a variety of leadership strategies more effective in facing a range of challenges, from the technical to the complex and adaptive? And to what extent does having a particular range of ways of enacting leadership enhance an organization's competitive advantage or mission effectiveness?

Similarly, new perspectives are needed to help groups build or strengthen the ties that are critical to effective interdependent work, both inside a single organization and between organizations that need to work in partnership. We are interested in expanding knowledge of the nature and implications of strong and weak ties, from the domain of individual leaders to the domain of group relations. We know that both strong ties (friendships) and weak ties (acquaintances) each have advantages for the individual leader, but we need a better understanding of the implications of analogous relationships for groups within organizations as well as ties between organizations.

Finally, our field needs a deeper understanding of the role of organizational culture and systems in leadership development. One aspect of an organization's culture is how leadership is understood and recognized. So one issue is how the culture in an organization in which leadership strategies are broad and diverse differs from the culture in an organization in which leadership is understood more narrowly and traditionally (that is, as the sole responsibility of individuals who are senior leaders). One might expect organizational cultures where inclusion is highly valued to be made up of organizational members who are either able to recognize and value more collective ways of enacting leadership or more open to and ready for the development of a wider array of processes for enacting the leadership tasks. Of all the ways one might work to change organizational culture, we are interested in learning about the relative power of an approach that starts with exploring how the enactment of leadership is recognized and understood.

Effective leadership in organizations today requires the development of leadership as a property of the whole system. We believe that enhancing sustainable leadership capacity in organizations is a product of both increasing the capacities within a wider population of individuals and of developing more and more robust connections between the parts of the organizational system (for example, between individuals and between groups). Surely the development of individual leaders will be enhanced when they participate in development that targets a collective of which they are a part or which enhances the connections between their group and other groups with whom they have interdependent work. We may, in fact, increasingly come to understand leader development as an outcome of group, organization, or "connection" development, rather than as a set of practices that stand alone. Or we may find that leader and leadership development are best done simultaneously.

Much of our research and development work over the next several years will be devoted to expanding our own capacity to offer leadership development practices, in addition to individual leader development, to help organizations build the connectivity and capacity for leadership strategy needed in a complex environment.

WHAT LEADERSHIP STRATEGIES ARE MOST EFFECTIVE IN PREVENTING OR MANAGING IDENTITY-BASED CONFLICT IN THE WORKPLACE WHEN THAT CONFLICT IS A SPILLOVER FROM THE SOCIETY AT LARGE?

Conflict between social identity groups is a major disruptive factor in nearly every country in the world. Although social identity conflict may not actually be on the increase, in the current climate of rapid communication, increasing globalization, nation creation, and political instability, it certainly appears to be. Daily, people read news stories about outbreaks of religious or ethnic enmity, sometimes ancient in origin, at other times precipitated by increased immigration or changing values.

The battles are usually over the symbols or markers of identity—English as the official language in Michigan, riots over the Miss Universe pageant in Nigeria, the use of headscarves by Malaysian women working in Singapore. But in fact social identity conflict is a battle for hegemony. It represents people's collective need for dignity, recognition, safety, control, purpose, and efficacy.

There is a rich legacy of efforts to prevent or mitigate the effects of social identity conflict in political systems and communities. But the workplace might be the ideal arena in which to address these deep-seated issues. Social identity groups tend to seek out their own in their churches, schools, and neighborhoods. But because human beings must make a living, the workplace may be the venue in a society in which people have the most contact with others who are not part of their social identity group. Furthermore, organizations have missions, policies, procedures, norms, reward systems, interdependent tasks, and a need to get the work done. These factors may serve as powerful levers for behavior change. Work itself can serve as a vehicle for increasing status and esteem—both precursors of successful intergroup contact.

Because the definition of effective leadership in a particular country is contingent on societal infrastructures (laws, freedom of the press, political systems), cultural values, and organizational context, it is important to understand which leadership strategies are most effective in preventing or managing identity-based conflict and to address this question in different cultures, different countries, and different types of organizations.

We expect, in the near future, to begin to make a significant contribution to understanding these effective leadership strategies and helping people develop their capacity for leadership in an environment of diversity.

WHAT ARE THE UNIQUE LEADERSHIP CHALLENGES FACING ASIAN ORGANIZATIONS, AND WHAT ARE BEST PRACTICES FOR LEADER AND LEADERSHIP DEVELOPMENT IN THIS AREA OF THE WORLD?

Most of the research and development work at CCL has focused primarily on North American managers, with a secondary focus on leaders in Europe. This Western focus is as true of the field of leadership development in general as it is of our work at CCL. The issue of cross-cultural generalizability of Western-based leader development practice was discussed in Chapter Eleven.

Yet Asian-based organizations are increasingly interested in U.S.-based, individually focused leader development interventions. We are experiencing a growing demand for individual leader development programs in Japan, China, and Singapore, for example. While it is important for us to meet the demand for our traditional products and services, it is also important to learn more about the strengths and limitations of these products and services in the various Asian environments and cultures. Do our feedback-intensive programs have the same impact in Asia as in the West? Should methods such as coaching and job assignments be implemented in the same way?

A broader question to ask is whether leadership is accomplished in different ways in Asian cultures. Our assumption is that in any culture, when groups of people need to work together in productive and meaningful ways, the leadership tasks of setting direction, creating alignment, and maintaining commitment are critical. Yet in Asian cultures, how much do groups and organizations rely on individual leaders to accomplish these tasks? In these more collectivistic cultures, are shared leadership models more common? Looking at how leadership is enacted in Asian cultures will broaden our understanding of the different ways in which leadership can be effectively accomplished.

WHAT ARE THE LEADERSHIP DEVELOPMENT NEEDS OF EMERGING LEADERS, THE PEOPLE IN YOUNGER GENERATIONS WHO ARE NOW BEGINNING TO FILL THE LOWER LEVELS OF OUR ORGANIZATIONS AND TO TAKE ON LEADERSHIP ROLES?

Members of Generation X are entering the ranks of management in increasing numbers, and members of Generation Y are beginning to enter the workforce. These individuals have grown up in environments quite different from those experienced by the baby boom generation that currently holds most senior positions in organizations. These younger people are generally more comfortable with technology, have traveled more at an earlier age, and are more likely to expect change as a normal part of organizational life. Although much has been written about how these younger generations differ from their elders, we have little hard evidence to back up many of these perceptions.

We know even less about the leader development needs of the members of this population. To what extent are their needs the same as the needs of any generation of new entrants to the workforce or new managers? And to what extent have they come to learn differently than their parents did, to understand leadership differently, and to want different things from their work lives, their lives outside of work, and their development? These are strategic issues for the practice of leader development, as most current practices (including those discussed in this handbook) were developed for a target audience composed primarily of baby boomers. The more we know about how to develop these new generations, the better we will be at creating sustainable leadership capacity for our future.

WHAT IS THE MEANING OF WORK-LIFE BALANCE IN AN INCREASINGLY COMPLEX WORLD?

Several aspects of work-life balance and its relationship to leader development are covered in this handbook. We know that dealing with the multiple and competing demands of a fast-paced career, personal relationships, family needs, community service, and taking care of oneself is a developmental task that all adults face. And the difficulty of this task is now exacerbated by ways in which technology seems to blur the boundaries between home and work. Given the increasing complexity and challenge in both business and personal environments, work-life "balance" seems unrealistic, if one understands that to be spending an equal or "correct" amount of time in each domain of one's life.

Getting beyond this understanding seems important, perhaps moving to a more holistic conception of life balance as the balance over one's whole life, of attention focused on the domains that are personally important. Understanding life balance as tied to one's sense of what it means to be successful and to have a full life seems important. How do we help people go beyond their current ways of understanding balance to one that is a better fit with the realities they face, both externally in their environments and internally on their own developmental paths? What are the individual and organizational benefits of approaching leadership development from a whole-life perspective?

We know that individual leader effectiveness is enhanced when people manage multiple roles at home and at work, but we need to know more about the organizational benefits and perhaps the benefits to family and community as well.

We need to understand what assumptions about organizational life are challenged by the idea of work-life integration. And we want to know more about what changes organizations need to make in order to facilitate greater work-life integration.

HOW CAN A BLEND OF FACE-TO-FACE AND TECHNOLOGY-BASED LEARNING TOOLS AND PROCESSES BEST BE USED TO ENHANCE LEADERSHIP DEVELOPMENT?

Advances in technology have changed the ways in which information and knowledge can be accessed and the ways in which individuals can communicate and share with one another. What impact does this have on the way leadership development interventions are delivered? Using technology-based tools and processes is attractive to organizations because they reduce the need for individuals to travel for face-to-face programs, they make learning opportunities readily available to a geographically dispersed population of leaders, and they allow individuals to access learning opportunities 24/7. Technology-based tools and processes also have attractive features for the leadership development practitioner: learning can be extended over time rather than limited to the time available in the classroom, online communication can facilitate the emergence and sharing of knowledge among participants, and technology opens up the opportunity for new learning strategies.

Our assumption, which is becoming widely shared in the leadership development field, is that technology-based tools and processes will not replace face-to-face learning experiences. Rather, blended learning solutions—the integration of face-to-face classroom and coaching experiences with technology-based tools and processes—offer the best opportunities to maximize the effectiveness of leader development interventions. Examples of technology-based tools and processes include online assessments, computer-based simulations, online modules teaching specific content, and online communication tools used by action learning project teams.

Despite their promise, blended learning solutions give rise to challenges and questions. Technology adds complexity to the design of a leadership development intervention, and content must be redesigned to deliver via technology platforms. What content is best suited for online delivery? Do well-established learning principles still apply with this new medium? How does technology affect the motivation to learn? Will the learner "find time" during a busy day to take advantage of the online portion of a blended learning program? As we experiment with integrating technology-based tools and processes and traditional face-to-face learning methodologies, we will also be studying their impact and efficacy.

At CCL, we work hard to turn ideas into action and action into ideas. This means we try to make sure that what we learn in our research expands our understanding of leadership and affects our practice of leadership development, and then we make sure that what we learn in our practice affects the research questions we ask. In one way or another, the beginning point of our learning is asking the right questions. Although this is the end of this edition of the *Handbook of Leadership Development,* the questions we have posed are the beginning of new learning for us and the seeds of our future.

REFERENCES

Abdalla, I. A., and Al-Homoud, M. A. "Exploring the Implicit Leadership Theory in the Arabian Gulf." *Applied Psychology*, 2001, *50*(4), 506–531.

Adams, S. "The Structure and Dynamics of Behavior in Organizational Boundary Roles." In M. Dunnette (ed.), *Handbook of Industrial and Organizational Psychology*. Skokie, Ill.: Rand McNally, 1976.

Adler, N. J. *International Dimensions of Organizational Behavior*. Cincinnati, Ohio: South-Western, 1997.

Adler, N. J., and Bartholomew, S. "Managing Globally Competent People." *Academy of Management Executive*, 1992, *6*(3), 52–65.

Aldwin, C. M. *Stress, Coping, and Development*. New York: Guilford Press, 1994.

Allen, J., and Johnston, K. "Mentoring." *Context*, 1997, *14*(7), 15.

America, R. F., and Anderson, B. C. *Soul in Management: How African-American Managers Thrive in the Competitive Corporate Environment*. Secaucus, N.J.: Citadel Press, 1996.

Anthony, J. "Risk, Vulnerability, and Resilience: An Overview." In E. J. Anthony and B. J. Cohler (eds.), *The Invulnerable Child*. New York: Guilford Press, 1987.

Antonioni, D. "Designing an Effective 360-Degree Appraisal Feedback Process." *Organizational Dynamics*, 1996, *25*(2), 24–38.

Argyris, C. *Overcoming Organizational Defenses: Facilitating Organizational Learning*. Upper Saddle River, N.J.: Prentice Hall, 1990.

Argyris, C. "Teaching Smart People How to Learn." *Harvard Business Review*, 1991, *69*(3), 99–109.

Argyris, C., and Schön, D. A. *Organizational Learning: A Theory of Action Perspective*. Boston: Addison-Wesley, 1978.

Ashford, S. "The Role of Feedback Seeking in Individual Adaptation: A Resource Perspective." *Academy of Management Journal*, 1986, *29*(3), 465–487.

Ashkanasy, N. M., Trevor-Roberts, E., and Earnshaw, L. "The Anglo Cluster: Legacy of the British Empire." *Journal of World Business*, 2002, *37*(1), 28–39.

Atwater, L. E., Rousch, P., and Fischthal, A. "The Influence of Upward Feedback on Self- and Follower Ratings of Leadership." *Personnel Psychology*, 1995, *48*(1), 35–59.

Atwater, L. E., and Waldman, D. A. "360-Degree Feedback and Leadership Development." *Leadership Quarterly*, 1998, *9*(4), 423–426.

Auster, E. "Task Characteristics as a Bridge Between Macro- and Micro-Level Research on Salary Inequality Between Men and Women." *Academy of Management Review*, 1989, *14*(2), 173–193.

Avery, K. J. "The Effects of 360-Degree Feedback over Time." *Dissertations Abstracts International*, 2001, *61*(8B), 4455.

Avolio, B., Bass, B., and Jung, D. I. *MLQ Multifactor Leadership Questionnaire: Technical Report*. Palo Alto, Calif.: Mind Garden, 1995.

Ayman, R., Kreicker, N. A., and Masztal, J. J. "Defining Global Leadership in Business Environments." *Consulting Psychology Journal*, 1994, *46*(1), 64–77.

Bader, P. K., Fleming, P. J., Zaccaro, S. J., and Barber, H. F. "The Developmental Impact of Work Experiences on Adaptability." Paper presented at the annual meeting of the Society for Industrial and Organizational Psychology, Toronto, Canada, April 2002.

Bakan, D. *The Duality of Human Existence*. Boston: Beacon Press, 1966.

Bal, V. V., and Quinn, L. "The Missing Link: Organizational Culture and Leadership Development." *Leadership in Action*, 2001, *21*(4), 14–17.

Baldwin, T. T., and Padgett, M. Y. "Management Development: A Review and Commentary." In C. L. Cooper and I. T. Robertson (eds.), *International Review of Industrial and Organizational Psychology*. Vol. 8. Chichester, England: Wiley, 1993.

Bandura, A. *Social Foundations of Thought and Action: A Social Cognitive Theory*. Upper Saddle River, N.J.: Prentice Hall, 1986.

Barabasi, A. *Linked: The New Science of Networks*. Cambridge, Mass.: Perseus, 2002.

Barclay, D. "Commitment from the Top Makes It Work." *IEEE Spectrum*, 1992, *29*(6), 24–27.

Barrett, A., and Beeson, J. *Developing Business Leaders for 2010*. New York: Conference Board, 2002.

Barrick, M. R., and Mount, M. K. "The Big Five Personality Dimensions and Job Performance: A Meta-Analysis." *Personnel Psychology*, 1991, *44*(1), 1–26.

Barsoux, J. L., and Lawrence, L. P. *Management in France*. London: Cassel, 1997.

Bartlett, C. A., Doz, Y., and Hedlund, G. (eds.). *Managing the Global Firm*. New York: Routledge, 1990.

Bartlett, C. A., and Ghoshal, S. *Managing Across Borders: The Transnational Solution*. Boston: Harvard Business School Press, 1989.

Baskerville, D. M. "Are Career Seminars for Black Managers Worth It?" *Black Enterprise*, 1992, *23*(5), 122–129.

Bass, B. M. *Leadership and Performance Beyond Expectations*. New York: Free Press, 1985.

Bass, B. M., and Stogdill, R. M. *Bass and Stogdill's Handbook of Leadership: Theory, Research, and Managerial Application*. (3rd ed.) New York: Free Press, 1990.

Basseches, M. *Dialectical Thinking and Adult Development*. Norwood, N.J.: Ablex, 1984.

Bateson, M. C. *Peripheral Visions: Learning Along the Way*. New York: HarperCollins, 1994.

Bayles, D., and Orland, T. *Art and Fear: Observations on the Perils (and Rewards) of Artmaking*. Santa Barbara, Calif.: Capra, 1993.

Beer, M. "How to Develop an Organization Capable of Sustained High Performance: Embrace the Drive for Results–Capability Development Paradox. *Organizational Dynamics,* 2001, *29*(4), 233–247.

Bell, E.L.J., and Nkomo, S. M. *Our Separate Ways: Black and White Women and the Struggle for Professional Identity.* Boston: Harvard Business School Press, 2001.

Berger, J. G., and Fitzgerald, C. "Leadership and Complexity of Mind: The Role of Executive Coaching." In C. Fitzgerald and J. G. Berger (eds.), *Executive Coaching: Practices and Perspectives.* Palo Alto, Calif.: Davies-Black, 2002.

Bernardin, H. J., Hagan, C., and Kane, J. S. "The Effects of a 360-Degree Appraisal System on Managerial Performance: No Matter How Cynical I Get, I Can't Keep Up." In W. W. Tornow (chair), *Upward Feedback: The Ups and Downs of It.* Symposium organized by the Society for Industrial and Organizational Psychology, Orlando, Fla., April 1995.

Blake-Beard, S. D. "Taking a Hard Look at Formal Mentoring Programs: A Consideration of Potential Challenges Facing Women." *Journal of Management Development,* 2001, *20*(4), 333–345.

Bohm, D. *On Dialogue.* Ojai, Calif.: David Bohm Seminars, 1996.

Booth, E. *The Everyday Work of Art: How Artistic Experience Can Transform Your Life.* Naperville, Ill.: Sourcebooks, 1997.

Bowen, C., Swim, J. K., and Jacobs, R. R. "Evaluating Gender Biases on Actual Job Performance of Real People: A Meta-Analysis." *Journal of Applied Psychology,* 2000, *30*(10), 2194–2215.

Bracken, D. W. "Multisource (360-Degree) Feedback: Survey for Individual and Organizational Development." In A. I. Kraut (ed.), *Organizational Surveys: Tools for Assessment and Change.* San Francisco: Jossey-Bass, 1996.

Bracken, D. W., Timmreck, C. W., and Church, A. H. (eds.). *The Handbook of Multisource Feedback.* San Francisco: Jossey-Bass, 2001.

Bracken, D. W., Timmreck, C. W., Fleenor, J. W., and Summers, L. "Another Angle on 360-Degree Feedback." *Human Resource Management,* 2001, *40*(1), 3–20.

Bracken, D. W., and others. *Should 360-Degree Feedback Be Used Only for Developmental Purposes?* Greensboro, N.C.: Center for Creative Leadership, 1997.

Brake, T. *The Global Leader: Critical Factors for Creating the World Class Organization.* Burr Ridge, Ill.: Irwin, 1997.

Branden, N. *Self-Esteem at Work: How Confident People Make Powerful Companies.* San Francisco: Jossey-Bass, 1998.

Brave, F. (chair). *Learning for Leadership: A New Look at Management Development.* Colloquium held at the Center for Creative Leadership, Greensboro, N.C., July 2002.

Bray, J. N., Lee, J., Smith, L. L., and Yorks, L. *Collaborative Inquiry in Practice: Action, Reflection, and Meaning Making.* Thousand Oaks, Calif.: Sage, 2000.

Brett, J. M. "Job Transitions and Personal Role Development." In K. M. Rowland and G. R. Ferris (eds.), *Research in Personnel and Human Resources Management.* Greenwich, Conn.: JAI Press, 1984.

Brett, J. M., and Stroh, L. K. "Women in Management: How Far Have We Come and What Needs to Be Done as We Approach 2000?" *Journal of Management Inquiry,* 1999, *8*(4), 392–398.

Brett, J. M., Stroh, L. K., and Reilly, A. H. "Pulling Up Roots in the 1990s: Who's Willing to Relocate?" *Journal of Organizational Behavior,* 1993, *14*(1), 49–60.

Brockner, J. *Self-Esteem at Work: Research, Theory, and Practice.* San Francisco: New Lexington Press, 1988.

Broderick, R. "How Honeywell Teaches Its Managers to Manage." *Training,* 1983, *20*(1), 18–23.

Brown, J. S., and Duguid, P. *The Social Life of Information.* Boston: Harvard Business School Press, 2000.

Browning, H., and Van Velsor, E. *Three Keys to Development: Defining and Meeting Your Leadership Challenges.* Greensboro, N.C.: Center for Creative Leadership, 1999.

Brutus, S., and Livers, A. "Networking Characteristics of African-American Managers: Empirical Validation and Training Applications." *International Journal of Training and Development,* 2000, *4*(4), 287–294.

Buckingham, M., and Clifton, D. *Now, Discover Your Strengths.* New York: Free Press, 2001.

Bunker, K. A., and Webb, A. D. *Learning How to Learn from Experience: Impact of Stress and Coping.* Greensboro, N.C.: Center for Creative Leadership, 1992.

Burgoyne, J. G., and Hodgson, V. E. "Natural Learning and Managerial Action: A Phenomenological Study in the Field Setting." *Journal of Management Studies,* 1983, *20*(3), 387–399.

Burke, R. J., and McKeen, C. A. "Benefits of Mentoring Relationships Among Managerial and Professional Women: A Cautionary Tale." *Journal of Vocational Behavior,* 1997, *51*(1), 43–57.

Burnside, R. M., and Guthrie, V. A. *Training for Action: A New Approach to Executive Development.* Greensboro, N.C.: Center for Creative Leadership, 1992.

Burt, R. S. *Structural Holes: The Social Structure of Competition.* Cambridge, Mass.: Harvard University Press, 1992.

Byham, W. C., Smith, A. B., and Pease, M. J. (2002). *Grow Your Own Leaders: How to Identify, Develop, and Retain Leadership Talent.* Upper Saddle River, N.J.: Prentice Hall, 2002.

Byrne, D. *The Attraction Paradigm.* San Diego, Calif.: Academic Press, 1971.

Campbell, D. P., and Nilsen, D. "Self-Observer Rating Discrepancies: Once an Overrater, Always an Overrater?" *Human Resource Management,* 1993, *32*(2–3), 265–281.

Catalyst. *Women in Corporate Leadership: Progress and Prospects.* New York: Catalyst, 1996.

Catalyst. *Women Entrepreneurs: Why Companies Lose Female Talent and What They Can Do About It.* New York: Catalyst, 1998.

Catalyst. *Women of Color in Corporate Management: Opportunities and Barriers.* New York: Catalyst, 1999.

Catalyst. *Women of Color in Corporate Management: Three Years Later.* New York: Catalyst, 2002.

Cavanagh, G. F. *American Business Values.* (2nd ed.) Upper Saddle River, N.J.: Prentice Hall, 1984.

Center for Creative Leadership. *Benchmarks Facilitator's Guide.* Greensboro, N.C.: Center for Creative Leadership, 2002a.

Center for Creative Leadership. "Gender Differences," in *Benchmarks Facilitator's Guide.* Greensboro, N.C.: Center for Creative Leadership, 2002b.

Chao, G. T. "Mentoring Phases and Outcomes." *Journal of Vocational Behavior,* 1997, *51*(1), 15–28.

Chao, G. T., Walz, P. M., and Gardner, P. D. "Formal and Informal Mentorships: A Comparison of Mentoring Functions and Contrast with Nonmentored Counterparts." *Personnel Psychology,* 1992, *45*(3), 619–636.

Charan, R., Drodder, S., and Noel, J. L. *The Leadership Pipeline: How to Build the Leadership-Powered Company.* San Francisco: Jossey-Bass, 2001.

Chartered Institute of Personnel and Development. *Working, Parenting and Careers*. London: Chartered Institute of Personnel and Development, 2002.

Chiaramonte, P., and Higgins, A. "Coaching for High Performance." *Business Quarterly,* 1993, *58*(1), 81–87.

Clark, K. C., and Clark, M. B. *Choosing to Lead*. (2nd ed.) Greensboro, N.C.: Center for Creative Leadership, 1994.

Clark, L. A., and Lyness, K. S. "Succession Planning as a Strategic Activity at Citicorp." In L. W. Foster (ed.), *Advances in Applied Business Strategy*. Vol. 2. Greenwich, Conn.: JAI Press, 1991.

Clawson, J. G., and Kram, K. E. "Managing Cross-Gender Mentoring." *Business Horizons,* 1984, *27*(3), 22–32.

Cobb, J., and Gibbs, J. "A New, Competency-Based, On-the-Job Programme for Developing Professional Excellence in Engineering." *Journal of Management Development,* 1990, *9*(3), 60–72.

Cohen, D., and Prusak, L. *In Good Company: How Social Capital Makes Organizations Work*. Boston: Harvard Business School Press, 2001.

Conklin, J. "Dialog Mapping: An Approach for Wicked Problems." CogNexus Institute, 2002. [http://cognexus.org/dmforwp.doc]. Retrieved January 22, 2003.

Cooper, C. L., and Lewis, S. "Gender and the Changing Nature of Work." In G. N. Powell (ed.), *Handbook of Gender and Work*. Thousand Oaks, Calif.: Sage, 1999.

Cooperrider, D. L., and Srivastva, S. "Appreciative Inquiry in Organizational Life." In R. Woodman and W. Pasmore (eds.), *Research in Organizational Change and Development*. Vol. 1. Greenwich, Conn.: JAI Press, 1987.

Cooperrider, D. L., and Whitney, D. *Appreciative Inquiry: The Handbook*. Euclid, Ohio: Lakeshore, 2002.

Corporate Leadership Council. *Voice of the Leader: A Quantitative Analysis of Leadership Bench Strength and Development Strategies*. Washington, D.C.: Corporate Executive Board, 2001.

Cousins, J. B., and Earl, L. M. "The Case for Participatory Evaluation." *Educational Evaluation and Policy Analysis,* 1992, *14*(4*)*, 397–418.

Cousins, J. B., and Earl, L. M. "The Case for Participatory Evaluation: Theory, Research, Practice." In. J. B. Cousins and L. M. Earl (eds.), *Participatory Evaluation in Education*. London: Falmer, 1995.

Coutu, D. "How Resilience Works." *Harvard Business Review,* 2002, *80*(5), 46–55.

Covey, S. R. *Principle-Centered Leadership*. New York: Simon & Schuster, 1991.

Cox, T. *Cultural Diversity in Organizations: Theory, Research, and Practice*. San Francisco: Berrett-Koehler, 1993.

Cox, T. *Creating the Multicultural Organization: A Strategy for Capturing the Power of Diversity*. San Francisco: Jossey-Bass, 2001.

Curtis, L. B., and Russell, E. A. "A Study of Succession Planning Programs in Fortune 500 Firms." Paper presented at the annual meeting of the Society for Industrial and Organizational Psychology, San Francisco, April 1993.

Dalessio, A. T., and Vasilopoulos, N. L. "Multisource Feedback Reports: Content, Formats, and Levels of Analysis." In D. W. Bracken, C. W. Timmreck, and A. H. Church (eds.), *The Handbook of Multisource Feedback*. San Francisco: Jossey-Bass, 2001.

Dalton, M. A. *Becoming a More Versatile Learner*. Greensboro, N.C.: Center for Creative Leadership, 1998.

Dalton, M. A. *Learning Tactics Inventory: Participant Workbook*. San Francisco: Jossey-Bass, 1999.

Dalton, M. A., Ernst, C. T., Deal, J. J., and Leslie, J. B. *Success for the New Global Manager: How to Work Across Distances, Countries, and Cultures.* San Francisco: Jossey-Bass, 2002.

Dalton, M. A., and Hollenbeck, G. P. *How to Design an Effective System for Developing Managers and Executives.* Greensboro, N.C.: Center for Creative Leadership, 1996.

Dalton, M. A., and Swigert, S. *Learning to Learn: The Relationship of Learning Versatility and Managerial Performance.* Unpublished manuscript, Center for Creative Leadership, Greensboro, N.C., 2001.

Dalton, M. A., and Wilson, M. S. "Antecedent Conditions of Expatriate Effectiveness." Paper presented at the annual meeting of the American Psychological Association, Toronto, Canada, August 1996.

Davenport, T. H., and Beck, J. C. *The Attention Economy: Understanding the New Currency of Business.* Boston: Harvard Business School Press, 2001.

Davies, J., and Easterby-Smith, M. "Learning and Developing from Managerial Work Experiences." *Journal of Management Studies,* 1984, *21*(2), 169–183.

Dawkins, R. *Unweaving the Rainbow: Science, Delusion, and the Appetite for Wonder.* Boston: Houghton Mifflin, 1998.

Day, D. V. "Leadership Development: A Review in Context." *Leadership Quarterly,* 2000, *11*(4), 581–613.

Day, D. V., and O'Connor, P.M.G. "Leadership Development: Understanding the Process." In S. E. Murphy and R. E. Riggio (eds.), *The Future of Leadership Development.* Mahwah, N.J.: Erlbaum, 2003.

Dechant, K. "Knowing How to Learn: The 'Neglected' Management Ability." *Journal of Management Development,* 1990, *9*(4), 40–49.

Dechant, K. "Making the Most of Job Assignments: An Exercise in Planning for Learning." *Journal of Management Education,* 1994, *18*(2), 198–211.

De Ciantis, C. *Using an Art Technique to Facilitate Leadership Development.* Greensboro, N.C.: Center for Creative Leadership, 1995.

Den Hartog, D. N., and others. "Culture Specific and Cross-Culturally Generalizable Implicit Leadership Theories: Are Attributes of Charismatic/Transformational Leadership Universally Endorsed?" *Leadership Quarterly,* 1999, *10*(2), 219–256.

De Nisi, A. S., and Kluger, A. N. "Feedback Effectiveness: Can 360-Degree Appraisals Be Improved?" *Academy of Management Executive,* 2000, *14*(1), 129–139.

Derr, C. B. "Managing High Potentials in Europe: Some Cross-Cultural Findings." *European Management Journal,* 1987, *5*(2), 72–80.

Derr, C. B., and Laurent, A. "The Internal and External Careers: A Theoretical and Cross-Cultural Perspective." In M. Arthur, D. T. Hall, and B. S. Lawrence (eds.), *The Handbook of Career Theory.* Cambridge: Cambridge University Press, 1989.

Dewey, J. *Art as Experience.* New York: Putnam, 1934.

d'Iribarne, P. "The Honor Principle in the Bureaucratic Phenomenon." *Organization Studies,* 1994, *15,* 81–97.

Dixon, N. M. *Perspectives on Dialogue: Making Talk Developmental for Individuals and Organizations.* Greensboro, N.C.: Center for Creative Leadership, 1996.

Dixon, N. M. *Dialogue at Work: Making Talk Developmental for People and Organizations.* London: Lemos & Crane, 1998.

Dorfman, P., Hanges, P., Brodbeck, F., and Associates. "Leadership Prototypes and Cultural Variation: The Identification of Culturally Endorsed Implicit Theories of Leadership." In R. J. House and others, *Cultures, Leadership, and Organizations: Project GLOBE: A 62-Nation Study.* Unpublished manuscript, 2002.

Dorfman, P. W., and others. "Leadership in Western and Asian Countries: Commonalities and Differences in Effective Leadership Processes Across Cultures." *Leadership Quarterly,* 1997, *8*(3), 233–274.

Dotlich, D. L., and Noel, J. L. *Action Learning: How the World's Top Companies Are Re-Creating Their Leaders and Themselves.* San Francisco: Jossey-Bass, 1998.

Douglas, C. A. *Formal Mentoring Programs in Organizations: An Annotated Bibliography.* Greensboro, N.C.: Center for Creative Leadership, 1997.

Douglas, C. A. *Key Events and Lessons for Managers in a Diverse Workforce: A Report on Research and Findings.* Greensboro, N.C.: Center for Creative Leadership, 2003.

Douglas, C. A., and McCauley, C. D. "Formal Developmental Relationships: A Survey of Organizational Practices." *Human Resource Development Quarterly,* 1999, *10*(3), 203–220.

Douglas, C. A., and Morley, W. H. *Executive Coaching: An Annotated Bibliography.* Greensboro, N.C.: Center for Creative Leadership, 2000.

Douglas, C. A., and Schoorman, F. D. *The Role of Mentoring in Career and Psychosocial Development.* Unpublished master's thesis, University of Maryland, 1987.

Drath, W. H. *Why Managers Have Trouble Empowering: A Theoretical Perspective Based on Concepts of Adult Development.* Greensboro, N.C.: Center for Creative Leadership, 1993.

Drath, W. H. *The Deep Blue Sea: Rethinking the Source of Leadership.* San Francisco: Jossey-Bass, 2001.

Drath, W. H., and Palus, C. J. *Making Common Sense: Leadership as Meaning-Making in a Community of Practice.* Greensboro, N.C.: Center for Creative Leadership, 1994.

Dreher, G. F., and Ash, R. A. "A Comparative Study of Mentoring Among Men and Women in Managerial, Professional, and Technical Positions." *Journal of Applied Psychology,* 1990, *75*(5), 539–546.

Dreher, G. F., and Cox, T. H. "Race, Gender, and Opportunity: A Study of Compensation Attainment and the Establishment of Mentoring Relationships." *Journal of Applied Psychology,* 1996, *81*(3), 297–308.

Dunnette, M. "My Hammer or Your Hammer?" *Human Resource Management,* 1993, *32*(2–3), 373–384.

Eagly, A. H., Johannesen-Schmidt, M. C., and van Engen, M. L. "Transformational, Transactional, and Laissez-Faire Leadership Styles: A Meta-Analysis Comparing Women and Men." *Psychological Bulletin,* 2003, *129*(4), 569–591.

Eagly, A. H., Makhijani, M. G., and Klonsky, B. G. "Gender and the Evaluation of Leaders: A Meta-Analysis." *Psychological Bulletin,* 1992, *111*(1), 3–22.

Eby, L. T. "Alternative Forms of Mentoring in Changing Organizational Environments: A Conceptual Extension of the Mentoring Literature." *Journal of Vocational Behavior,* 1997, *51*(1), 125–144.

Edwards, B. *Drawing on the Artist Within: A Guide to Innovation, Invention, Imagination, and Creativity.* New York: Simon & Schuster, 1986.

Eichinger, R. W., and Lombardo, M. M. *Twenty-Two Ways to Develop Leadership in Staff Managers.* Greensboro, N.C.: Center for Creative Leadership, 1995.

Elashmawi, F., and Harris, P. R. *Multicultural Management: New Skills for Global Success.* Houston: Gulf, 1993.

Ensher, E. A., and Murphy, S. E. "Effects of Race, Gender, Perceived Similarity, and Contact on Mentor Relationships." *Journal of Vocational Behavior,* 1997, *59*(3), 460–481.

Evered, R. D., and Selman, J. C. "'Coaching' and the Art of Management." *Organizational Dynamics,* 1989, *18*(2), 16–32.

Fagenson, E. A. "The Mentor Advantage: Perceived Career/Job Experiences of Protégés Versus Non-Protégés." *Journal of Organizational Behavior,* 1989, *10*(4), 309–320.

Fagenson-Eland, E. A., Marks, M. A., and Amendola, K. L. "Perceptions of Mentoring Relationships." *Journal of Vocational Behavior,* 1997, *51*(1), 29–42.

Farr, J. L., and Newman, D. A. "Rater Selection: Sources of Feedback." In D. W. Bracken, C. W. Timmreck, and A. H. Church (eds.), *The Handbook of Multisource Feedback.* San Francisco: Jossey-Bass, 2001.

Federal Glass Ceiling Commission, U.S. Department of Labor. *Good for Business: Making Full Use of the Nation's Human Capital.* Washington, D.C.: Government Printing Office, 1995.

Feghali, E. "Arab Cultural Communication Patterns." *International Journal of Intercultural Relations,* 1997, *21*(3), 345–378.

Fernandez, J. P., and Davis, J. *Race, Gender, and Rhetoric: The True State of Race and Gender Relations in Corporate America.* New York: McGraw-Hill, 1999.

Fetterman, D. M. "Empowerment Evaluation." *Evaluation Practice,* 1994, *15*(1), 1–15.

Fetterman, D. M. "Empowerment Evaluation: An Introduction to Theory and Practice." In D. M. Fetterman, S. J. Kaftarian, and A. Wandersman (eds.), *Empowerment Evaluation: Knowledge and Tools for Self-Assessment and Accountability.* Thousand Oaks, Calif.: Sage, 1996.

Fine, S. B. "Resilience and Human Adaptability: Who Rises Above Adversity?" *American Journal of Occupational Therapy,* 1991, *45*(6), 493–503.

Fisher, D., Rooke, D., and Torbert W. *Personal and Organizational Transformations Through Action Inquiry.* Boston: Edge/Work Press, 2000.

Flanders, D. P., and Anderson, P. E. "Sex Discrimination in Employment: Theory and Practice." *Industrial and Labor Relations Review,* 1973, *26*(3), 938–955.

Fleenor, J. W., McCauley, C. D., and Brutus, S. "Self-Other Rating Agreement and Leader Effectiveness." *Leadership Quarterly,* 1996, *7*(4), 487–506.

Fleenor, J. W., and Prince, J. M. *Using 360-Degree Feedback in Organizations: An Annotated Bibliography.* Greensboro, N.C.: Center for Creative Leadership, 1997.

Fletcher, J. K. *Relational Theory in the Workplace.* Wellesley, Mass.: Stone Center, Wellesley College, 1996.

Fletcher, J. K. *Disappearing Acts: Gender, Power, and Relational Practice at Work.* Cambridge, Mass.: MIT Press, 1999.

Fondas, N. "Single-Sex vs. Mixed-Sex Training." *Journal of European Industrial Training,* 1986, *10*(7), 28–33.

Frankl, V. E. *Man's Search for Meaning.* New York: Washington Square Press, 1984.

Friedman, S. D. "Succession Systems in Large Corporations: Characteristics and Correlates of Performance." *Human Resource Management,* 1986, *25*(2), 191–213.

Fulmer, R. M., and Goldsmith, M. *The Leadership Investment: How the World's Best Organizations Gain Strategic Advantage Through Leadership Development.* New York: AMACOM, 2000.

Gabarro, J. *The Dynamics of Taking Charge.* Boston: Harvard Business School Press, 1987.

Gardner, H. *Frames of Mind: The Theory of Multiple Intelligences.* New York: Basic Books, 1993.

Gargiulo, T. L. *Making Stories: A Practical Guide for Organizational Leaders and Human Resource Specialists.* Westport, Conn.: Quorum Books, 2001.

Geber, B. "From Manager into Coach." *Training,* 1992, *29*(2), 25–31.

General Accounting Office. *Women in Management: Analysis of Selected Data from the Current Population Survey.* Washington, D.C.: General Accounting Office, 2001.

Gergen, K. J. *The Saturated Self: Dilemmas of Identity in Contemporary Life.* New York: Basic Books, 1991.

Gharajedaghi, J. *Systems Thinking: Managing Chaos and Complexity.* Burlington, Mass.: Butterworth Heinemann, 1999.

Goldberg, N. *Writing Down the Bones: Freeing the Writer Within.* Boston: Shambhala, 1986.

Goldsmith, M., Kaye, B. L., and Shelton, K. *Learning Journeys: Top Management Experts Share Hard-Earned Lessons on Becoming Great Mentors and Leaders.* Palo Alto, Calif.: Davies-Black, 2000.

Goleman, D. *Emotional Intelligence.* New York: Bantam Books, 1995.

Goleman, D. *Working with Emotional Intelligence.* New York: Bantam Books, 1998.

Goode, E. "How Culture Molds Habits of Thought." *New York Times,* August 8, 2000, p. F1.

Goodman, J. S., Fields, D. L., and Blum, T. C. (forthcoming). "Cracks in the Glass Ceiling: In What Kinds of Organizations Do Women Make It to the Top?" *Group and Organization Management.*

Graham, S., Wedman, J. F., and Garvin-Kester, B. "Manager Coaching Skills: Development and Application." *Performance Improvement Quarterly,* 1993, *6*(1), 2–13.

Gregerson, H. B., Morrison, A. J., and Black, J. S. "Developing Leaders for the Global Frontier." *MIT Sloan Management Review,* 1998, *40*(1), 21–32.

Greider, W. *One World, Ready or Not: The Manic Logic of Global Capitalism.* New York: Simon & Schuster, 1997.

Gryskiewicz, S. S. *Positive Turbulence: Developing Climates for Creativity, Innovation, and Renewal.* San Francisco: Jossey-Bass, 1999.

Guthrie, V. A. *Coaching for Action: A Report on Long-Term Advising in a Program Context.* Greensboro, N.C.: Center for Creative Leadership, 1999.

Hall, D. T. *Careers in Organizations.* Pacific Palisades, Calif.: Goodyear, 1976.

Hall, D. T., and Associates. *The Career Is Dead—Long Live the Career: A Relational Approach to Careers.* San Francisco: Jossey-Bass, 1996.

Hall, E. T. *The Hidden Dimension.* New York: Doubleday, 1966.

Hargrove, R. A. *Masterful Coaching.* (rev. ed.) San Francisco: Jossey-Bass, 2002.

Harlan, A., and Weiss, C. *Moving Up: Women in Managerial Careers.* Wellesley, Mass.: Wellesley Center for Research on Women, 1980.

Harris, M. M., and Schaubroeck, J. "A Meta-Analysis of Self-Supervisor, Self-Peer, and Peer-Supervisor Ratings." *Personnel Psychology,* 1988, *41*(1), 43–62.

Harris, P. R., and Moran, R. T. *Managing Cultural Differences: High-Performance Strategies for a New World of Business.* (3rd ed.) Houston: Gulf, 1993.

Hart, E. W. "Bracing for the Storm: Protecting Autonomy of the Coaching Profession." *Being in Action, the Journal of Professional & Personal Coaching,* 1997a. No. 8, Fall 1997, 1–2.

Hart, E. W. "Bracing for the Storm II: Protecting Autonomy of the Coaching Profession." Keynote address presented at the Personal and Professional Coaches Association Conference, Atlanta, September 1997b.

Hart, E. W., and Kirkland, K. *Using Your Executive Coach.* Greensboro, N.C.: Center for Creative Leadership, 2001.

Hazucha, J. F., Hezlett, S. A., and Schneider, R. J. "The Impact of 360-Degree Feedback on Management Skills Development." *Human Resource Management,* 1993, *32*(2–3), 325–351.

Hegarty, W. H. "Using Subordinate Ratings to Elicit Behavioral Changes in Supervisors." *Journal of Applied Psychology,* 1974, *59*(6), 764–766.

Hegestad, C. D. "Formal Mentoring as a Strategy for Human Resource Development: A Review of Research." *Human Resource Development Quarterly,* 1999, *10*(4), 383–390.

Hegestad, C. D. "Development and Maintenance of Exemplary Formal Mentoring Programs for Fortune 500 Companies." Unpublished doctoral dissertation, University of Illinois, 2002.

Heifetz, R. A. *Leadership Without Easy Answers.* Cambridge, Mass.: Harvard University Press, 1994.

Heilman, M. E. "Sex Stereotypes and Their Effects in the Workplace: What We Know and What We Don't Know." In N. J. Struthers (ed.), "Gender in the Workplace" (special issue). *Journal of Social Behavior and Personality,* 1995, *10*(6), 3–26.

Heilman, M. E., Block, C. K., Martell, R. F., and Simon, M. C. "Has Anything Changed? Current Characteristics of Men, Women, and Managers." *Journal of Applied Psychology,* 1989, *74*(6), 935–942.

Helgesen, S. *The Web of Inclusion: A New Architecture for Building Great Organizations.* New York: Currency/Doubleday, 1995.

Hendricks, W., and Associates. *Coaching, Mentoring, and Managing.* Franklin Lakes, N.J.: Career Press, 1996.

Henerson, M. E., Morris, L. L., and Fitz-Gibbon, C. T. *How to Measure Attitudes.* Thousand Oaks, Calif.: Sage, 1987.

Higgins, M. C. "The More the Merrier? Multiple Developmental Relationships and Work Satisfaction." *Journal of Management Development,* 2000, *19*(4), 277–296.

Higgins, M. C., and Kram, K. E. "Reconceptualizing Mentoring at Work: A Developmental Network Perspective." *Academy of Management Review,* 2001, *26*(2), 264–288.

Hill, L. A. *Becoming a Manager: Mastery of a New Identity.* Boston: Harvard Business School Press, 1992.

Hill, R. *Euromanagers and Martians: The Business Culture of Europe's Trading Nations.* Brussels, Belgium: Europublications, 1994.

Hofstede, G. H. *Culture's Consequences: International Differences in Work-Related Values.* Thousand Oaks, Calif.: Sage, 1980.

Hofstede, G. H. *Culture's Consequences: Comparing Values, Behaviors, Institutions, and Organizations Across Nations.* (2nd ed.) Thousand Oaks, Calif.: Sage, 2001.

Hollander, E. P. *Leaders, Groups, and Influence.* New York: Oxford University Press, 1964.

Hoppe, M. H. "A Comparative Study of Country Elites: International Differences in Work-Related Values and Learning and Their Implications for Management Training and Development." Unpublished doctoral dissertation, University of North Carolina, 1990.

Hoppe, M. H. "The Effects of National Culture on the Theory and Practice of Managing R&D Professionals Abroad." *Research and Development Management,* 1993, *23*(4), 313–325.

Hoppe, M. H., and Bhagat, R. Leadership in the United States: The Leader as Cultural Hero." Unpublished manuscript, 2001.

House, R. J., Javidan, M., Hanges, P. J., and Dorfman, P. W. "Understanding Cultures and Implicit Leadership Theories Across the Globe: An Introduction to Project GLOBE." *Journal of World Business,* 2002, *37,* 3–10.

House, R. J., and others. "Cultural Influences on Leadership and Organizations: Project GLOBE." In W. H. Mobley, M. J. Gessner, and V. Arnold (eds.), *Advances in Global Leadership.* Vol. 1. Greenwich, Conn.: JAI Press, 1999.

House, R. J., and others. *Cultures, Leadership, and Organizations: Project GLOBE—a 62-Nation Study.* Unpublished manuscript, 2003.

Hudson, F. M. *The Handbook of Coaching: A Comprehensive Resource Guide for Managers, Executives, Consultants, and Human Resource Professionals.* San Francisco: Jossey-Bass, 1999.

Huet-Cox, G. D., Nielsen, T. M., and Sundstrom, E. "Get the Most from 360-Degree Feedback: Put It on the Internet." *HR Magazine,* 1999, *44*(5), 92–103.

Hughes, R. L., Ginnett, R. C., and Curphy, G. J. *Leadership: Enhancing the Lessons of Experience.* (4th ed.) New York: McGraw-Hill, 2002.

Hunt, J. M., and Weintraub, J. R. *The Coaching Manager: Developing Top Talent in Business.* Thousand Oaks, Calif.: Sage, 2002.

Hurst, D. K. *Crisis and Renewal: Meeting the Challenge of Organizational Change.* Boston: Harvard Business School Press, 1995.

Ibarra, H. "Homophily and Differential Returns: Sex Differences in Network Structure and Access in an Advertising Firm." *Administrative Science Quarterly,* 1992, *37*(3), 422–447.

Ibarra, H. "Personal Networks of Women and Minorities in Management: A Conceptual Framework." *Academy of Management Review,* 1993, *18*(1), 56–87.

Ibarra, H. "Race, Opportunity, and Diversity of Social Circles in Managerial Networks." *Academy of Management Journal,* 1995, *38*(3), 673–703.

Inglehart, R. *Modernization and Postmodernization: Cultural, Economic, and Political Change in 43 Societies.* Princeton, N.J.: Princeton University Press, 1997.

Institute for Research on Learning. *Reflections on Workplace Learning.* Palo Alto, Calif.: Institute for Research on Learning, 1993.

International Coaching Federation. "About Coaching." 2003. [http://www.coachfederation.org/aboutcoaching/index.htm].

Isaacs, W. *Dialogue and the Art of Thinking Together.* New York: Random House, 1999.

Jackson, S. E., and Associates. "Stepping into the Future: Guidelines for Action." In S. E. Jackson and Associates, *Diversity in the Workplace: Human Resources Initiatives.* New York: Guilford Press, 1992.

Jackson, S. E., and Ruderman, M. N. *Diversity in Work Teams: Research Paradigms for a Changing Workplace.* Washington, D.C.: American Psychological Association, 1995.

Johnson, D. W., and Johnson, R. T. *Cooperation and Competition: Theory and Research.* Edina, Minn.: Interaction, 1989.

Johnson, J. W., and Ferstl, K. L. "The Effects of Interrater and Self-Other Agreement on Performance Improvement Following Upward Feedback." *Personnel Psychology,* 1999, *52*(2), 271–303.

Jordan, J., and others. *Women's Growth in Connection: Writings from the Stone Center.* New York: Guilford Press, 1991.

Josefowitz, N. "Teaching Management Skills to Women: Why Women Learn Management Skills Better in All-Female Groups." *San Diego Woman,* April 1990, pp. 12–14.

Kabacoff, R. I. "Gender Differences in Organizational Leadership." Paper presented at the annual meeting of the American Psychological Association, San Francisco, August 1998.

Kanter, R. M. *Men and Women of the Organization.* New York: Basic Books, 1977.

Kaplan, R., Drath, W. H., and Kofodimos, J. *High Hurdles: The Challenge of Executive Self-Development.* Greensboro, N.C.: Center for Creative Leadership, 1985.

Kaye, B., and Jacobson, B. "Mentoring: A Group Guide." *Training and Development,* 1995, *49*(4), 22–27.

Kegan, R. *The Evolving Self: Problem and Process in Human Development.* Cambridge, Mass.: Harvard University Press, 1982.

Kegan, R. *In over Our Heads: The Mental Demands of Modern Life.* Cambridge, Mass.: Harvard University Press, 1994.

Kegan, R., and Lahey, L. *How the Way We Talk Can Change the Way We Work.* San Francisco: Jossey-Bass, 2001.

Kelleher, D., Finestone, P., and Lowy, A. "Managerial Learning: First Notes from an Unstudied Frontier." *Group and Organization Studies,* 1986, *11*(3), 169–202.

Kelly, G. A. *The Psychology of Personal Constructs.* New York: Norton, 1955.

Kinlaw, D. C. *Coaching for Commitment: Managerial Strategies for Obtaining Superior Performance.* San Francisco: Jossey-Bass/Pfeiffer, 1993.

Kirkland Miller, K., and Hart, E. W. *Choosing an Executive Coach.* Greensboro, N.C.: Center for Creative Leadership, 2001.

Kirschner, P. A., Shum, S.J.B., and Carr, C. S. (eds.). *Visualizing Argumentation: Software Tools for Collaborative and Educational Sense-Making.* New York: Springer-Verlag, 2003.

Kizilos, P. "Take My Mentor, Please!" *Training,* 1990, *27*(4), 49–55.

Kluckhohn, F. R., and Strodtbeck, F. L. *Variations in Value Orientations.* Westport, Conn.: Greenwood Press, 1961.

Kodak. "Careers at Kodak: Image Science Career Development. 2002. [http://www.kodak.com/US/en/corp/careers/index.jhtml].

Kohls, L. R. *Survival Kit for Overseas Living: For Americans Planning to Live and Work Abroad.* (2nd ed.) Yarmouth, Maine: Intercultural Press, 1984.

Kolb, D. A. *Experiential Learning.* Upper Saddle River, N.J.: Prentice Hall, 1984.

Korzybski, A. *Science and Sanity: An Introduction to Non-Aristotelian Systems and General Semantics.* Lancaster, Pa.: International Non-Aristotelian Library, 1941.

Kossek, E. E., and Lobel, S. A. (eds.). *Managing Diversity: Human Resources for Transforming the Workplace.* Malden, Mass.: Blackwell, 1996.

Kouzes, J. H., and Posner, B. Z. *The Leadership Challenge: How to Get Extraordinary Things Done in Organizations.* San Francisco: Jossey-Bass, 1987.

Kram, K. E. *Mentoring at Work.* Glenview, Ill.: Scott, Foresman, 1985.

Kram, K. E., and Bragar, M. C. "Development Through Mentoring: A Strategic Approach." In D. H. Montross and C. J. Shinkman (eds.), *Career Development: Theory and Practice.* Springfield, Ill.: Thomas, 1992.

Kram, K. E., and Hall, D. T. "Mentoring as an Antidote to Stress During Corporate Trauma." *Human Resource Management,* 1989, *28*(4), 493–510.

Kram, K. E., and Hall, D. T. "Mentoring in a Context of Diversity and Turbulence." In E. E. Kossek and S. A. Lobel (eds.), *Managing Diversity: Human Resource Strategies for Transforming the Workplace.* Malden, Mass.: Blackwell, 1996.

Kram, K. E., and Isabella, L. A. "Mentoring Alternatives: The Role of Peer Relationships in Career Development." *Academy of Management Journal,* 1985, *28*(1), 110–132.

Kram, K. E., Ting, S., and Bunker, K. A. "On-the-Job Training for Emotional Competence." *Leadership in Action,* 2002, *22*(3), 3–7.

Krueger, R. A., and Casey, M. A. *Focus Groups: A Practical Guide for Applied Research.* (3rd ed.) Thousand Oaks, Calif.: Sage, 2000.

Langrish, S. "Single-Sex Management Training: A Personal View." *Women and Training News,* Winter 1980, pp. 3–4.

Leach, M. M. "Training Global Psychologists: An Introduction." *International Journal of Intercultural Relations,* 1997, *21*(2), 161–174.

Leana, C. R., and Rousseau, D. M. *Relational Wealth: The Advantages of Stability in a Changing Economy.* New York: Oxford University Press, 2000.

Lepsinger, R., and Lucia, A. D. *The Art and Science of 360-Degree Feedback.* San Francisco: Jossey-Bass/Pfeiffer, 1997.

Leslie, J. B., Dalton, M. A., Ernst, C. T., and Deal, J. J. *Managerial Effectiveness in a Global Context.* Greensboro, N.C.: Center for Creative Leadership, 2002.

Leslie, J. B., and Fleenor, J. W. *Feedback to Managers: A Review and Comparison of Multi-Rater Instruments for Management Development.* Greensboro, N.C.: Center for Creative Leadership, 1998.

Leslie, J. B., Gryskiewicz, N., and Dalton, M. A. "Cultural Influences on the 360-Degree Feedback Process." In W. W. Tornow and M. London (eds.), *Maximizing the Value of 360-Degree Feedback: A Process for Successful Individual and Organizational Development.* San Francisco: Jossey-Bass, 1998.

Leslie, J. B., Penny, J., and Suzuki, M. *Assessing Individual Managerial Skill Across Cultures: The Influence of Language and Rating Source on 360-Degree Feedback.* Presented at the meeting of the Society for Industrial & Organizational Psychology, April 2001.

Leslie, J. B., and Van Velsor, E. *A Look at Derailment Today: North America and Europe.* Greensboro, N.C.: Center for Creative Leadership, 1996.

Leslie, J. B., and Van Velsor, E. *A Cross-National Comparison of Effective Leadership and Teamwork: Toward a Global Workforce.* Greensboro, N.C.: Center for Creative Leadership, 1998.

Levinson, D. J. *The Seasons of a Man's Life.* New York: Knopf, 1978.

Lifton, R. "Understanding the Traumatized Self: Imagery, Symbolization, and Transformation." In J. Wilson, Z. Harel, and B. Kahana (eds.), *Human Adaptation to Extreme Stress.* New York: Plenum, 1988.

Linehan, M. "Networking for Female Managers' Career Development: Empirical Evidence." *Journal of Management,* 2001, *20*(10), 823–829.

Liu, K., and O'Connor, P.M.G. "Leveraging Your Organization's Leadership Capacity." *Leadership in Action,* 2001, *21*(2), 3–6.

Livers, A. B., and Brutus, S. "Informal Networking and the African-American Manager." *Leadership in Action,* 2000, *20*(1), 1–3.

Livers, A. B., and Caver, K. A. *Leading in Black and White: Working Across the Racial Divide in Corporate America.* San Francisco: Jossey-Bass, 2003.

Lombardo, M. M., and Eichinger, R. W. *Eighty-Eight Assignments for Development in Place.* Greensboro, N.C.: Center for Creative Leadership, 1989.

Lombardo, M. M., and Eichinger, R. W. *For Your Improvement: A Development and Coaching Guide.* (3rd ed.) Minneapolis, Minn.: Lominger, 2000.

London, M., and Beatty, R. W. "360-Degree Feedback as a Competitive Advantage." *Human Resource Management,* 1993, *32*(2–3), 357–372.

London, M., and Smither, J. W. "Can Multi-Source Feedback Change Perceptions of Goal Accomplishment, Self-Evaluations, and Performance-Related Outcomes? Theory-Based Applications and Directions for Research." *Personnel Psychology,* 1995, *48*(4), 803–839.

Lyness, K. S., and Thompson, D. E. "Above the Glass Ceiling? A Comparison of Matched Samples of Female and Male Executives." *Journal of Applied Psychology,* 1997, *82*(3), 359–379.

MacLachlan, M., Mapundi, J., Zimba, C. G., and Carr, S. C. "The Acceptability of a Western Psychometric Instrument in a Non-Western Society." *Journal of Social Psychology,* 1995, *135*(5), 645–648.

Maigetter, J., and Ragettli, G. *Interview Summary: Domestic and Global Managerial Skills and Competences.* Unpublished manuscript, 1997.

Malone, M. S. "Perpetual-Motion Executives." *Forbes,* April 11, 1994, *153*, 93–98.

Marion, R., and Uhl-Bien, M. "Leadership in Complex Organizations." *Leadership Quarterly,* 2001, *12*(4), 389–418.

Marris, P. *Loss and Change.* London: Routledge, 1986.

Marsick, V. J. "Exploring the Many Meanings of Action Learning and ARL." In L. Rohlin, K. Billing, A. Lindberg, and M. Wickelgren (eds.), *Earning While Learning in Global Leadership: The Volvo-MiL Partnership.* Vasbyholm, Sweden: MiL, 2002.

Marsick, V. J., and O'Neil, J. "The Many Faces of Action Learning." *Management Learning*, 1999, *30*(2), 159–176.

Martineau, J. W. "Using 360-Degree Surveys to Assess Change." In W. W. Tornow and M. London (eds.), *Maximizing the Value of 360-Degree Feedback: A Process for Successful Individual and Organizational Development*. San Francisco: Jossey-Bass, 1998.

Martineau, J. W., and Hannum, K. M. *Evaluating the Impact of Leadership Development: A Professional Guide*. Greensboro, N.C.: Center for Creative Leadership, 2003.

Masten, A. S. "Resilience in Development: The Roots of Resilience as a Focus of Research." In D. Cicchetti (ed.), *Rochester Symposium on Developmental Psychopathology: The Emergence of a Discipline*. Vol. 1. Mahwah, N.J.: Erlbaum, 1989.

McBroom, P. *The Third Sex: The New Professional Woman*. New York: Paragon House, 1992.

McCall, M. W., Jr., and Hollenbeck, G. P. *Developing Global Executives: The Lessons of International Experience*. Boston: Harvard Business School Press, 2002.

McCall, M. W., Jr., and Lombardo, M. M. *Off the Track: Why and How Successful Executives Get Derailed*. Greensboro, N.C.: Center for Creative Leadership, 1983.

McCall, M. W., Jr., Lombardo, M. M., and Morrison, A. M. *The Lessons of Experience: How Successful Executives Develop on the Job*. San Francisco: New Lexington Press, 1988.

McCarthy, B., and Keene, C. *About Learning*. Old Barrington, Ill.: Excel, 1996.

McCauley, C. D., and Brutus, S. *Management Development Through Job Experiences: An Annotated Bibliography*. Greensboro, N.C.: Center for Creative Leadership, 1998.

McCauley, C. D., and Hughes-James, M. W. *An Evaluation of the Outcomes of a Leadership Development Program*. Greensboro, N.C.: Center for Creative Leadership, 1994.

McCauley, C. D., Lombardo, M. M., and Usher, C. "Diagnosing Management Development Needs: An Instrument Based on How Managers Develop." *Journal of Management*, 1989, *15*(3), 389–403.

McCauley, C. D., and Martineau, J. W. *Reaching Your Development Goals*. Greensboro, N.C.: Center for Creative Leadership, 1998.

McCauley, C. D., Ohlott, P. J., and Ruderman, M. N. *Job Challenge Profile: Facilitator's Guide*. San Francisco: Jossey-Bass, 1999.

McCauley, C. D., Ruderman, M. N., Ohlott, P. J., and Morrow, J. E. "Assessing the Developmental Components of Managerial Jobs." *Journal of Applied Psychology*, 1994, *79*(4), 544–560.

McCauley, C. D., and Young, D. P. "Creating Developmental Relationships: Roles and Strategies." *Human Resource Management Review*, 1993, *3*(3), 219–230.

McCrae, R. R., and Costa, P. T., Jr. "Openness to Experience." In R. Hagan and W. H. Jones (eds.), *Perspectives in Personality*. Vol. 1. Greenwich, Conn.: JAI Press, 1985.

McCrae, R. R., and Costa, P. T., Jr. "Validation of the Five-Factor Model Across Instruments and Observers." *Journal of Personality and Social Psychology*, 1987, *52*(1), 81–90.

McShulskis, E. "Coaching Helps but Is Not Often Used." *HR Magazine*, 1996, *41*(3), 15–16.

Meindl, J. R., Ehrlich, S. B., and Dukerich, J. M. "The Romance of Leadership." *Administrative Science Quarterly*, 1985, *30*(1), 78–102.

Meyerson, D. E., and Fletcher, J. *Toward a Psychology of Women*. (2nd ed.) Boston: Beacon Press, 2000.

Miller, J. B. *Toward a New Psychology of Women*. Boston: Beacon Press, 1986.

Miller, J. B., and Stiver, I. P. *The Healing Connection: How Women Form Relationships in Therapy and in Life*. Boston: Beacon Press, 1997.

Mink, O. G. *Developing High-Performance People: The Art of Coaching*. Boston: Addison-Wesley, 1993.

Mintzberg, H. *Mintzberg on Management: Inside Our Strange World of Organizations.* New York: Free Press, 1989.

Moore, D. P., and Buttner, E. H. *Women Entrepreneurs: Moving Beyond the Glass Ceiling.* Thousand Oaks, Calif.: Sage, 1997.

Morrison, A. M. *The New Leaders: Guidelines on Leadership Diversity in America.* San Francisco: Jossey-Bass, 1992.

Morrison, A. M., McCall, M. W., and De Vries, D. L. *Feedback to Managers: A Comprehensive Review of Twenty-Four Instruments.* Greensboro, N.C.: Center for Creative Leadership, 1978.

Morrison, A. M., Ruderman, M. N., and Hughes-James, M. W. *Making Diversity Happen: Controversies and Solutions.* Greensboro, N.C.: Center for Creative Leadership, 1993.

Morrison, A. M., and Von Glinow, M. A. "Women and Minorities in Management." *American Psychologist,* 1990, *45*(2), 200–208.

Morrison, A. M., White, R. P., and Van Velsor, E. *Breaking the Glass Ceiling: Can Women Reach the Top of America's Largest Corporations?* Boston: Addison-Wesley, 1987.

Morrison, A. M., White, R. P., and Van Velsor, E. *Breaking the Glass Ceiling: Can Women Reach the Top of America's Largest Corporations?* (updated ed.) New York: Perseus Books, 1992.

Mount, M. K., Sytsma, M. R., Hazucha, J. F., and Holt, K. E. "Rater-Ratee Race Effects in Developmental Performance Ratings of Managers." *Personnel Psychology,* 1997, *50*(1), 51–69.

Moxley, R. S., and McCauley, C. D. "Developmental 360: How Feedback Can Make Managers More Effective." *Career Development International,* 1996, *1*(3), 15–19.

Murray, M., and Owen, M. A. *Beyond the Myths and Magic of Mentoring: How to Facilitate an Effective Mentoring Program.* San Francisco: Jossey-Bass, 1991.

Myers, I. B. *Introduction to Type: A Description of the Theory and Applications of the Myers-Briggs Type Indicator.* Palo Alto, Calif.: Consulting Psychologists Press, 1987.

Nahapiet, J., and Ghoshal, S. "Social Capital, Intellectual Capital, and the Organizational Advantage." *Academy of Management Review,* 1998, *23*(2), 242–266.

NCR Corporation. *Developing NCR Engineers.* Dayton, Ohio: NCR, 1992.

Newman, M. A. "Career Development: Does Gender Make a Difference?" *American Review of Public Administration,* 1993, *23*(4), 361–384.

Nicholson, N., and West, M. *Managerial Job Change: Men and Women in Transition.* Cambridge: Cambridge University Press, 1988.

Nissley, N. "Art-Based Learning in Management Education." In C. Wankel and R. De Fillippi (eds.), *Rethinking Management Education for the 21st Century.* Greenwich, Conn.: Information Age Press, 2002.

Noe, R. A. "An Investigation of the Determinants of Successful Assigned Mentoring Relationships." *Personnel Psychology,* 1988, *41*(3), 457–479.

Noe, R. A. "Mentoring Relationships for Employee Development." In J. W. Jones, B. D. Steffy, and D. W. Bray (eds.), *Applying Psychology in Business: The Handbook for Managers and Human Resource Professionals.* Lexington, Mass.: Heath, 1991.

Noe, R. A. "Is Career Management Related to Employee Development and Performance?" *Journal of Organizational Behavior,* 1996, *17*(2), 119–133.

Noer, D. N. *Healing the Wounds: Overcoming the Trauma of Layoffs and Revitalizing Downsized Organizations.* San Francisco: Jossey-Bass, 1993.

Nonaka, I., Takeuchi, H., and Takeuchi, H. *The Knowledge-Creating Company.* New York: Oxford University Press, 1995.

Northcraft, G. B., Griffith, T. L., and Shalley, C. E. "Building Top Management Muscle in a Slow Growth Environment." *Academy of Management Executive,* 1992, *6*(1), 32–40.

O'Connor, P.M.G. "Building Sustainable Leadership Capacity." Paper presented at the Conference Board 2002 Leadership Development Conference, New York, April 2002.

O'Connor, P.M.G., and Day, D. V. "Tapping Your Organization's Leadership Reserve." *Leadership in Action,* 2002, *22*(1), 3–7.

O'Connor, P.M.G., and Quinn, L. "Explicating the 'Ship' in Leadership Development." *Mount Eliza Business Review,* 2002, *5*(2), 21–26.

Ohlott, P. J. "Myths Versus Realities of Single-Identity Development." *Training & Development,* 2002, *56* (11), 32–37.

Ohlott, P. J., and Hughes-James, M. W. "Single-Gender and Single-Race Leadership Development Programs: Concerns and Benefits." *Leadership in Action,* 1997, *17*(4), 8–12.

Ohlott, P. J., McCauley, C. D., and Ruderman, M. N. *Developmental Challenge Profile: Learning from Job Experiences: Manual and Trainers Guide.* Greensboro, N.C.: Center for Creative Leadership, 1993.

Ohlott, P. J., Ruderman, M. N., and McCauley, C. D. "Gender Differences in Managers' Developmental Job Experiences." *Academy of Management Journal,* 1994, *37*(1), 46–67.

O'Neill, R. M., and Blake-Beard, S. D. "Gender Barriers to the Female Mentor–Male Protégé Relationship." *Journal of Business Ethics,* 2002, *37*(1), 51–63.

O'Reilly, B. "360 Feedback Can Change Your Life." *Fortune,* August 1994, pp. 93–100.

Orpen, C. "The Effects of Mentoring on Employees' Career Success." *Journal of Social Psychology,* 1995, *135*(5), 667–680.

Osborn, A. F. *Applied Imagination.* New York: Scribner, 1953.

Oshry, B. *Leading Systems: Lessons from the Power Lab.* San Francisco: Berrett-Koehler, 1999.

Ostroff, C., and Kozlowski, S. W. "The Role of Mentoring in the Information-Gathering Process of Newcomers During Early Organizational Socialization." *Journal of Vocational Behavior,* 1993, *42*(2), 170–183.

Palus, C. J., and Drath, W. H. "Putting Something in the Middle: An Approach to Dialogue." *Reflections,* 2001, *3*(2), 28–39.

Palus, C. J, and Horth, D. M. "Leading Creatively: The Art of Making Sense. *Journal of Aesthetic Education,* 1996, *30*(4), 53–68.

Palus, C. J., and Horth, D. M. *The Leader's Edge: Six Creative Competencies for Navigating Complex Challenges.* San Francisco: Jossey-Bass, 2002.

Palus, C. J., and Rogolsky, S. R. "Development of and Within a Global, Feedback-Intensive Organization." Unpublished manuscript, 1996.

Parnes, S. J. (ed.). *Source Book for Creative Problem Solving: A Fifty-Year Digest of Proven Innovation Processes.* Buffalo, N.Y.: Creative Education Foundation Press, 1992.

Patton, M. Q. *How to Use Qualitative Methods in Evaluation.* Thousand Oaks, Calif.: Sage, 1987.

Pedler, M. (ed.). *Action Learning in Practice.* (3rd ed.) Aldershot, England: Gower, 1997.

Perkins, D. *The Intelligent Eye: Learning to Think by Looking at Art.* Santa Monica, Calif.: Getty Center for Education in the Arts, 1994.

Peters, H. "Peer Coaching for Executives." *Training and Development,* 1996, *50*(3), 39–41.

Peters, T. J. *Liberation Management: Necessary Disorganization for the Nanosecond Nineties.* New York: Knopf, 1992.

Petersen, J. L. *Out of the Blue: Wild Cards and Other Big Future Surprises: How to Anticipate and Respond to Profound Change.* Arlington, Va.: Arlington Institute, 1997.

Peterson, D., and Hicks, M. D. *Leader as Coach.* Minneapolis, Minn.: Personnel Decisions, 1996.

Phillips, J. J., Stone, R. D., and Phillips, P. P. *The Human Resources Scorecard: Measuring the Return on Investment.* Burlington, Mass.: Butterworth Heinemann, 2001.

Pierson, G. W. *Tocqueville in America*. Baltimore: Johns Hopkins University Press, 1996.

Posner, B., and Kouzes, J. "Psychometric Properties of Leadership Practices Inventory— Updated." *Educational and Psychological Measurement*, 1993, *53*(1), 191–199.

Powell, G. N. "Reflections on the Glass Ceiling." In G. N. Powell (ed.), *Handbook of Gender and Work*. Thousand Oaks, Calif.: Sage, 1999.

Preskill, H., and Torres, R. T. *Evaluative Inquiry for Learning in Organizations*. Thousand Oaks, Calif.: Sage, 1999.

Pulley, M. L. *Losing Your Job, Reclaiming Your Soul: Stories of Resilience, Renewal, and Hope*. San Francisco: Jossey-Bass, 1997.

Pulley, M. L., Sessa, V. I., and Malloy, M. "E-Leadership: A Two-Pronged Idea." *Training and Development*, 2002, *56*(3), 34–47.

Pulley, M. L., and Wakefield, M. *Building Resiliency: How to Thrive in Times of Change*. Greensboro, N.C.: Center for Creative Leadership, 2001.

Ragins, B. R. "Antecedents of Diversified Mentoring Relationships." *Journal of Vocational Behavior*, 1997a, *51*(1), 90–109.

Ragins, B. R. "Diversified Mentoring Relationships in Organizations: A Power Perspective." *Academy of Management Review*, 1997b, *22*(2), 482–521.

Ragins, B. R. "Gender and Mentoring Relationships: A Review and Research Agenda for the Next Decade." In G. N. Powell (ed.), *Handbook of Gender and Work*. Thousand Oaks, Calif.: Sage, 1999.

Ragins, B. R., and Cotton, J. L. "Easier Said Than Done: Gender Differences in Perceived Barriers to Gaining a Mentor." *Academy of Management Journal*, 1991, *34*(4), 939–951.

Ragins, B. R., and Cotton, J. L. "Mentor Functions and Outcomes: A Comparison of Men and Women in Formal and Informal Mentoring Relationships." *Journal of Applied Psychology*, 1999, *84*(4), 529–550.

Ragins, B. R., and McFarlin, D. B. "Perceptions of Mentor Roles in Cross-Gender Mentoring Relationships." *Journal of Vocational Behavior*, 1990, *37*(3), 321–339.

Ragins, B. R., Townsend, B., and Mattis, M. "Gender Gap in the Executive Suite: CEOs and Female Executives Report on Breaking the Glass Ceiling." *Academy of Management Executive*, 1998, *12*(1), 28–42.

Raju, N. S., and others. "Measurement Equivalence of a 360-Degree Feedback Assessment Across Four Rating Sources, Two Language Translations, and Two Racial Groups." Paper presented at the annual meeting of the Society for Industrial and Organizational Psychology, Atlanta, August 2001.

Ratiu, I. "Thinking Internationally: A Comparison of How International Executives Learn." *International Studies of Management and Organization*, 1983, *13*(1–2), 139–150.

Reilly, R. R., Smither, J. W., and Vasilopoulos, N. L. "A Longitudinal Study of Upward Feedback." *Personnel Psychology*, 1996, *49*(3), 599–612.

Remen, R. *Kitchen Table Wisdom: Stories That Heal*. New York: Riverhead Books, 1996.

Revans, R. W. "The Nature of Action Learning." *Management Education and Development*, 1979, *10*(1), 3–23.

Revans, R. *The Origins and Growth of Action Learning*. London: Chartwell-Bratt, 1982.

Rhinesmith, S. H. *A Manager's Guide to Globalization: Six Keys to Success in a Changing World*. Homewood, Ill.: Business One Irwin, 1993.

Richards, D. *Artful Work: Awakening Joy, Meaning, and Commitment in the Workplace*. San Francisco: Berrett-Koehler, 1995.

Roche, G. "Much Ado About Mentors." *Harvard Business Review*, 1979, *57*(1), 14–28.

Roddick, A. *Body and Soul*. New York: Crown, 1998.

Rogolsky, S., and Dalton, M. A. "Is That Still True? Women Recall Career-Shaping Events." Unpublished manuscript, 1995.

Rohlin, K. B., Billing, K., Lindberg, A., and Wickelgren, M. (eds.). *Earning While Learning in Global Leadership: The Volvo-MiL Partnership.* Vasbyholm, Sweden: MiL, 2002.

Ronen, S., and Shenkar, O. "Clustering Countries on Attitudinal Dimensions: A Review and Synthesis." *Academy of Management Review,* 1985, *10*(3), 435–454.

Rosen, R. *Global Literacies: Lessons on Business Leadership and National Cultures.* New York: Simon & Schuster, 2000.

Rost, J. C. *Leadership for the Twenty-First Century.* New York: Praeger, 1991.

Ruderman, M. N., Hughes-James, M., and Jackson, S. E. (eds.). *Selected Research on Work Team Diversity.* Washington, D.C.: American Psychological Association, 1996.

Ruderman, M. N., McCauley, C. D., and Ohlott, P. J. *Job Challenge Profile.* San Francisco: Jossey-Bass, 1999.

Ruderman, M. N., and Ohlott, P. J. *Traps and Pitfalls in the Judgment of Executive Potential.* Greensboro, N.C.: Center for Creative Leadership, 1990.

Ruderman, M. N., and Ohlott, P. J. *The Realities of Management Promotion.* Greensboro, N.C.: Center for Creative Leadership, 1994.

Ruderman, M. N., and Ohlott, P. J. *Learning from Life: Turning Life's Lessons into Leadership Experience.* Greensboro, N.C.: Center for Creative Leadership, 2000.

Ruderman, M. N., and Ohlott, P. J. *Standing at the Crossroads: Next Steps for High-Achieving Women.* San Francisco: Jossey-Bass, 2002.

Ruderman, M. N., Ohlott, P. J., and Kram, K. E. "Promotion Decisions as a Diversity Practice." *Journal of Management Development,* 1995, *14*(2), 6–23.

Ruderman, M. N., Ohlott, P. J., and McCauley, C. D. "Developing from Job Experiences: The Role of Self-Esteem and Self-Efficacy." Paper presented at the annual meeting of the Society for Industrial and Organizational Psychology, San Diego, April 1996.

Ruderman, M. N., Ohlott, P. J., Panzer, K., and King, S. N. "Benefits of Multiple Roles for Managerial Women." *Academy of Management Journal,* 2002, *45*(2), 369–386.

Russ-Eft, D., and Preskill, H. *Evaluation in Organizations: A Systematic Approach to Enhancing Learning, Performance, and Change.* Cambridge, Mass.: Perseus, 2001.

Russell, J.E.A., and Adams, D. M. "The Changing Nature of Mentoring in Organizations." *Journal of Vocational Behavior,* 1997, *51*(1), 1–14.

Salancik, G. R., and others. "Leadership as an Outcome of Social Structure and Process: A Multidimensional Analysis." In J. G. Hunt and L. L. Larson (eds.), *Leadership Frontiers.* Kent, Ohio: Kent State University Press, 1975.

Sale, K. *Human Scale.* (2nd ed.) New York: Putnam, 1982.

Scandura, T. A. "Mentorship and Career Mobility: An Empirical Investigation." *Journal of Organizational Behavior,* 1992, *13*(2), 169–174.

Scandura, T. A., and Williams, E. A. "An Investigation of the Moderating Effects of Gender on the Relationships Between Mentorship Initiation and Protégé Perceptions of Mentoring Functions." *Journal of Vocational Behavior,* 2001, *59*(3), 342–363.

Schein, V. E. "The Relationship Between Sex-Role Stereotypes and Requisite Management Characteristics." *Journal of Applied Psychology,* 1973, *57*(2), 95–100.

Schein, V. E. "The Relationship Between Sex-Role Stereotypes and Requisite Management Characteristics Among Female Managers." *Journal of Applied Psychology,* 1975, *60*(3), 340–344.

Schein, V. E. "Psychological Barriers to Women's Progress in Management: An International Perspective." Paper presented at the annual meeting of the Academy of Management, Denver, August 2002.

Schrage, M. *Serious Play: How the World's Best Companies Simulate to Innovate.* Boston: Harvard Business School Press, 2002.

Schwartz, P. *The Art of the Long View.* New York: Doubleday/Currency, 1991.

Schwartz, S. H. "Beyond Individualism/Collectivism: New Cultural Dimensions of Values." In U. Kim and others (eds.), *Individualism and Collectivism: Theory, Methods, and Applications.* Thousand Oaks, Calif.: Sage, 1994.

Schwartz, S. H. "A Theory of Cultural Values and Some Implications for Work." *Applied Psychology,* 1999, *48*(1), 23–47.

Seibert, K. W. "Experience Is the Best Teacher, If You Can Learn from It: Real-Time Reflection and Development." In D. T. Hall and Associates (ed.), *The Career Is Dead—Long Live the Career: A Relational Approach to Careers.* San Francisco: Jossey-Bass, 1996.

Seibert, K. W., Hall, D. T., and Kram, K. E. "Strengthening the Weak Link in Strategic Executive Development: Integrating Individual Development and Global Business Strategy." *Human Resource Management,* 1995, *34*(4), 549–567.

Selvin, A. M., and others. "Compendium: Making Meetings into Knowledge Events." Paper presented at the Knowledge Technologies 2001 conference, Austin, Texas, March 4–7, 2001.

Senge, P. M. *The Fifth Discipline: The Art and Practice of the Learning Organization.* New York: Doubleday, 1990.

Senge, P. M., and others. *The Fifth Discipline Fieldbook: Strategies and Tools for Building a Learning Organization.* New York: Currency/Doubleday, 1994.

Sessa, V. I., and Taylor, J. J. *Executive Selection: Strategies for Success.* San Francisco: Jossey-Bass, 2000.

Sharpe, R. "As Leaders, Women Rule: New Studies Find That Female Managers Outshine Their Male Counterparts in Almost Every Measure." *Business Week,* November 20, 2000, pp. 75–84.

Sherman, S. "How Tomorrow's Best Leaders Are Learning Their Stuff." *Fortune,* November 1995, pp. 90–102.

Simmons, A. *The Story Factor: Secrets of Influence from the Art of Storytelling.* Boulder, Colo.: Perseus, 2000.

Smith, P. B., and Peterson, M. F. "Beyond Value Comparisons: Sources Used to Give Meaning to Management Work Events in Twenty-Nine Countries." Paper presented at the annual meeting of the Academy of Management, Vancouver, Canada, August 1995.

Smither, J. W., and others. "An Examination of the Effects of an Upward Feedback Program over Time." *Personnel Psychology,* 1995, *48*(1), 1–54.

Springer, S. P., and Deutsch, G. *Left Brain, Right Brain.* New York: Freeman, 1981.

Stafford, B. M. *Artful Science: Enlightenment Entertainment and the Eclipse of Visual Education.* Cambridge, Mass.: MIT Press, 1994.

Steinborn, D. "Career Progress Is Slow for German Women Execs." *Wall Street Journal Online,* March 1, 2001. [http://www.careerjournal.com/myc/workabroad/globalmanage/20010319-steinborn.html].

Sternberg, R. J., and Wagner, R. K. *Practical Intelligence: Nature and Origins of Competence in the Everyday World.* New York: Cambridge University Press, 1986.

Stewart, E. C., and Bennett, M. J. *American Cultural Patterns: A Cross-Cultural Perspective.* Yarmouth, Maine: Intercultural Press, 1991.

Still, L. V. *Where to from Here? The Managerial Woman in Transition.* Sydney, Australia: Business and Professional Publishing, 1993.

Streufert, S., and Streufert, S. *Behavior in a Complex Environment.* New York: Halsted Press, 1978.

Summers, L. "Web Technologies for Administering Multisource Feedback Programs." In D. W. Bracken, C. W. Timmreck, and A. H. Church (eds.), *The Handbook of Multisource Feedback.* San Francisco: Jossey-Bass, 2001.

Sutter, S. "Making Management Development an Organizational Reality." Paper presented at the annual meeting of the Society for Industrial and Organizational Psychology, Nashville, Tenn., April 1994.

Tharenou, P. "Organisational, Job, and Personal Predictors of Employee Participation in Training and Development." *Applied Psychology,* 1997, *46*(2), 111–134.

Thomas, D. A. "The Truth About Mentoring Minorities: Race Matters." *Harvard Business Review,* 2001, *79*(4), 98–107.

Thomas, D. A., and Gabarro, J. J. *Breaking Through: The Making of Minority Executives in Corporate America.* Boston: Harvard Business School Press, 1999.

Thomas, K. M. "The Impact of Race on Managers' Experiences of Developmental Relationships (Mentoring and Sponsorship): An Intra-Organizational Study." *Journal of Organizational Behavior,* 1990, *11*(6), 479–492.

Tichy, N. M. *The Leadership Engine: How Winning Companies Build Leaders at Every Level.* New York: HarperBusiness, 1997.

Tornow, W. W., and London, M. (eds.). *Maximizing the Value of 360-Degree Feedback: A Process for Successful Individual and Organizational Development.* San Francisco: Jossey-Bass, 1998.

Triandis, H. C. "Introduction." In H. C. Triandis and W. W. Lambert (eds.), *Handbook of Cross-Cultural Psychology.* Boston: Allyn & Bacon, 1980.

Turban, D. B., and Dougherty, T. W. "Role of Protégé Personality in Receipt of Mentoring and Career Success." *Academy of Management Journal,* 1994, *37*(3), 688–702.

U.S. Bureau of the Census. *Statistical Abstract of the United States.* Washington, D.C.: U.S. Government Printing Office, 2000.

U.S. Department of Labor. *Handbook of Labor Statistics.* Washington, D.C.: U.S. Government Printing Office, 1983.

Vaill, P. B. *Managing as a Performing Art: New Ideas for a World of Chaotic Change.* San Francisco: Jossey-Bass, 1989.

Valerio, A. M. "A Study of the Developmental Experiences of Managers." In K. E. Clark and M. B. Clark (eds.), *Measures of Leadership.* West Orange, N.J.: Leadership Library of America, 1990.

van der Heijden, K. *Scenarios: The Art of Strategic Conversation.* New York: Wiley, 1996.

Van Maanen, J., and Schein, E. H. "Toward a Theory of Organizational Socialization." In B. M. Staw (ed.), *Research in Organizational Behavior.* Vol. 1. Greenwich, Conn.: JAI Press, 1979.

Van Velsor, E. "Designing 360-Degree Feedback to Enhance Involvement, Self-Determination, and Commitment." In W. W. Tornow and M. London (eds.), *Maximizing the Value of 360-Degree Feedback: A Process for Successful Individual and Organizational Development.* San Francisco: Jossey-Bass, 1998.

Van Velsor, E., and Hughes-James, M. W. *Gender Differences in the Development of Managers: How Women Managers Learn from Experience.* Greensboro, N.C.: Center for Creative Leadership, 1990.

Van Velsor, E., Leslie, J. B., and Fleenor, J. W. *Choosing 360: A Guide to Evaluating Multi-Rater Feedback Instruments for Management Development.* Greensboro, N.C.: Center for Creative Leadership, 1997.

Van Velsor, E., and Musselwhite, W. C. "The Timing of Training, Learning, and Transfer." *Training and Development Journal,* 1986, *40*(8), 58–59.

Van Velsor, E., Ruderman, M. N., and Phillips, A. D. "The Lessons of Looking Glass: Management Simulation and the Real World of Action." *Leadership and Organization Development Journal,* 1989, *10*(6), 27–31.

Van Velsor, E., Ruderman, M. N., and Phillips, D. A. "The Impact of Feedback on Self-Assessment and Performance in Three Domains of Management Behavior." Paper presented at the annual meeting of the Society for Industrial and Organizational Psychology, Saint Louis, Mo., April 1992.

Vicere, A. A., and Fulmer, R. M. *Leadership by Design.* Boston: Harvard Business School Press, 1998.

Waldroop, J., and Butler, T. "The Executive as Coach." *Harvard Business Review,* 1996, *74*(6), 111–119.

Walker, A. G., and Smither, J. W. "A Five-Year Study of Upward Feedback: What Managers Do with Their Results Matters." *Personnel Psychology,* 1999, *52*(2), 393–423.

Weick, K. E. *Sensemaking in Organizations.* Thousand Oaks, Calif.: Sage, 1995.

Weil, E. "Every Leader Tells a Story." *Fast Company,* June 1998, pp. 38–40.

Weitzel, S. *Feedback That Works.* Greensboro, N.C.: Center for Creative Leadership, 2000.

Wellington, S. W., and Spence, B. *Be Your Own Mentor: Strategies from Top Women on Secrets of Success.* New York: Random House, 2001.

Wenger, E. C., McDermott, R., and Snyder, W. M. *Cultivating Communities of Practice.* Boston: Harvard Business School Press, 2002.

Wenger, E. C., and Snyder, W. M. "Communities of Practice: The Organizational Frontier." *Harvard Business Review,* 2000, *78*(1), 139–145.

White, R. P. "Job as Classroom: Using Assignments to Leverage Development." In D. H. Montross and C. J. Shinkman (eds.), *Career Development: Theory and Practice.* Springfield, Ill.: Thomas, 1992.

Whitely, W., Dougherty, T. W., and Dreher, G. F. "Relationship of Career Mentoring and Socioeconomic Origin to Managers' and Professionals' Early Career Progress." *Academy of Management Journal,* 1991, *34*(2), 331–351.

Whitmore, J. *Coaching for Performance.* London: Brealey, 1996.

Whyte, D. *The Heart Aroused: Poetry and the Preservation of the Soul in Corporate America.* New York: Doubleday, 1996.

Wick, C. W. "How People Develop: An In-Depth Look." *HR Report,* 1989, *6*(7), 1–3.

Wilber, K. *Integral Psychology.* Boston: Shambhala, 2000.

Wilson, M., Hoppe, W. H., and Sayles, L. R. *Managing Across Cultures: A Learning Framework.* Greensboro, N.C.: Center for Creative Leadership, 1996.

Witherspoon, R., and White, R. P. *Four Essential Ways That Coaching Can Help Executives.* Greensboro, N.C.: Center for Creative Leadership, 1997.

Works Institute Recruit Company. *"The Lessons of Experience" in Japan: Research Report.* Tokyo: Work Institute Recruit, 2001.

Yammarino, F. J., and Atwater, L. E. "Do Managers See Themselves as Others See Them? Implications of Self-Other Rating Agreement for Human Resources Management." *Organizational Dynamics,* 1997, *25*(4), 35–44.

Yeung, A. K., and Ready, D. A. "Developing Leadership Capabilities of Global Corporations: A Comparative Study in Eight Nations." *Human Resource Management*, 1995, *34*(4), 529–547.

Young, D. P., and Dixon, N. M. *Helping Leaders Take Effective Action: A Program Evaluation.* Greensboro, N.C.: Center for Creative Leadership, 1996.

Young, D. P., and Hefferan, J. "LeaderLab Program Feedback Report." Unpublished manuscript, 1994.

Yukl, G. A. *Leadership in Organizations.* (3rd ed.) Upper Saddle River, N.J.: Prentice Hall, 2002.

Zemke, R. "The Honeywell Studies: How Managers Learn to Manage." *Training*, 1985, *22*(8), 46–51.

Zey, M. G. *The Mentor Connection.* New Brunswick, N.J.: Transaction, 1991.

NAME INDEX

SUBJECT INDEX

A

Abilities. *See* Competencies and capabilities

Ability to learn, 204–205, 208–223, 233; anxiety and, 213; barriers and challenges to, 211–217; coaching and, 128–129; components of, 210; developing and enhancing, 16–17, 217–223; from experience *versus* classroom, 208–223; importance of, 16–17, 208–209; inertia and, 209, 212–213; leader development and, 4–5, 204–205, 208–223; learning tactics and, 210, 220–223; metacognitive ability and, 214–215, 220; personal orientations and, 213–217; self-awareness and, 210, 214, 215, 218–220; self-esteem and, 215–216, 218; self-management and, 13, 207–208; support and, 217, 223; time constraints and, 211–212; transformational development *versus*, 395–396

Accessing-others tactics, 221

Accountant role, 87, 89, 97

Accuracy, rating: of importance ratings, 74; of Internet-based 360-degree feedback, 79; in 360-degree feedback programs, 74, 79, 82. *See also* Reliability; Validity

ACS (assessment, challenge, support) framework: for African American leader development, 309–314; in coaching, 117, 118, 120–128; depth of coaching and, 120–122; in developmental relationships, 86–91; in feedback-intensive programs, 16, 27, 29, 32–34, 57; for global leader development, 371; hardships and, 201–202; in job assignments, 154–155; purposes of, 5; in 360-degree feedback, 62–66; for women's leader development, 301–302. *See also* Assessment; Challenge; Leader development; Support

Action finding, 458

Action learning: to develop navigation capability, 461–462; example of facilitated, 461–462; in feedback-intensive programs, 34; as organizational outcome orientation, 433–434

Action learning teams, 107, 109, 461–462

Action management skills, 366

Action orientation: challenge and, 353–354; cross-cultural comparison of, 336–340, 353–354; of U.S. culture, 335–336. *See also* Doing-being cultural dimension

Action plans and planning: in coaching, 125, 145–147; in feedback-intensive programs, 53; job assignments in, 171; with 360-degree feedback, 77–78; tracking progress on, 255, 258. *See also* Development plan and planning

Active-reflective cultural dimension, 336–340; cross-cultural differences on challenge and, 353–354; cross-cultural

ABOUT THE CENTER
FOR CREATIVE LEADERSHIP

The Center for Creative Leadership (CCL®) is an international educational institution devoted to leadership research and training. Its mission is to advance the understanding, practice, and development of leadership for the benefit of society worldwide.

Since its founding as a nonprofit educational institution in 1970, CCL has grown to become one of the largest and most respected organizations devoted to leadership in the world. Over the course of three decades, more than four hundred thousand individuals from thousands of private corporations, nonprofits, and governmental agencies have participated in CCL programs. Five campuses span three continents: Greensboro, North Carolina; Colorado Springs, Colorado; and San Diego, California, in North America; Brussels, Belgium, in Europe; and Singapore in Asia. In addition, nearly two dozen Network Associates around the world offer selected CCL programs and assessments.

CCL draws strength from its nonprofit status and educational mission, which provide unusual flexibility in a world where quarterly profits often drive thinking and direction. We have the freedom to be objective, wary of short-term trends, and motivated foremost by our mission—hence our substantial and sustained investment in leadership research. Although our work is always grounded in a strong foundation of research, we focus on achieving a beneficial impact in the real world. Our efforts are geared to be practical and action-oriented, helping leaders and their organizations more effectively achieve their goals and vision. The desire to transform learning and ideas into action provides the impetus for our programs, assessments, publications, and services.

Capabilities

CCL's activities encompass leadership education, knowledge generation and dissemination, and building a community centered on leadership. CCL is broadly recognized for excellence in executive education, leadership development, and innovation by sources such as *Business Week,* the *Financial Times,* the *New York Times,* and the *Wall Street Journal.*

Open-Enrollment Programs

Fourteen open-enrollment courses are designed for leaders at all levels, as well as people responsible for leadership development and training at their organizations. This portfolio offers distinct choices for participants seeking a particular learning environment or type of experience. Some programs are structured specifically around small group activities, discussion, and personal reflection, while others offer hands-on opportunities through business simulations, artistic exploration, team-building exercises, and new-skills practice. Many of these programs offer private one-on-one sessions with a feedback coach.

For a complete listing of programs, visit http://www.ccl.org/programs

Customized Programs

CCL develops tailored educational solutions for more than two hundred client organizations around the world each year. Through this applied practice, CCL structures and delivers programs focused on specific leadership development needs within the context of defined organizational challenges, including innovation, the merging of cultures, and the development of a broader pool of leaders. The objective is to help organizations develop, within their own cultures, the leadership capacity they need to address challenges as they emerge.

Program details are available online at http://www.ccl.org/custom

Coaching

CCL's suite of coaching services is designed to help leaders maintain a sustained focus and generate increased momentum toward achieving their goals. These coaching alternatives vary in depth and duration and serve a variety of needs, from helping an executive sort through career and life issues to working with an organization to integrate coaching into its internal development process. Our coaching offerings, which can supplement program attendance or be customized for specific individual or team needs, are based on our ACS model of *assessment, challenge,* and *support.*

Learn more about CCL's coaching services at http://www.ccl.org/coaching

Assessment and Development Resources

CCL pioneered 360-degree feedback and believes that assessment provides a solid foundation for learning, growth, and transformation and that development truly happens when an individual recognizes the need to change. CCL offers a broad selection of assessment tools, online resources, and simulations that can help individuals, teams, and organizations increase their self-awareness, facilitate their own learning, enable their development, and enhance their effectiveness.

CCL's assessments are profiled at http://www.ccl.org/assessments

Publications

The theoretical foundation for many of our programs, as well as the results of CCL's extensive and often groundbreaking research, can be found in the scores of publications issued by CCL Press and through the center's alliance with Jossey-Bass, a Wiley imprint. Among these are landmark works, such as *Breaking the Glass Ceiling* and *The Lessons of Experience,* as well as quick-read guidebooks focused on core aspects of leadership. CCL publications provide insights and practical advice to help individuals become more effective leaders, develop leadership training within organizations, address issues of change and diversity, and build the systems and strategies that advance leadership collectively at the institutional level.

A complete listing of CCL publications is available at http://www.ccl.org/publications

Leadership Community

To ensure that the Center's work remains focused, relevant, and important to the individuals and organizations it serves, CCL maintains a host of networks, councils, and learning and virtual communities that bring together alumni, donors, faculty, practicing leaders, and thought leaders from around the globe. CCL also forges relationships and alliances with individuals, organizations, and associations that share its values and mission. The energy, insights, and support from these relationships help shape and sustain CCL's educational and research practices and provide its clients with an added measure of motivation and inspiration as they continue their lifelong commitment to leadership and learning.

To learn more, visit http://www.ccl.org/connected

Research

CCL's portfolio of programs, products, and services is built on a solid foundation of behavioral science research. The role of research at CCL is to advance the understanding of leadership and to transform learning into practical tools for participants and clients. CCL's research is the hub of a cycle that transforms knowledge into applications and applications into knowledge, thereby illuminating the way organizations think about and enact leadership and leader development.

Find out more about current research initiatives at http://www.ccl.org/research

For additional information about CCL, please visit http://www.ccl.org or call Client Services at (336) 545-2810.

HOW TO USE THE CD-ROM

System Requirements

Windows PC

- 486 or Pentium processor-based personal computer
- Microsoft Windows 95 or Windows NT 3.51 or later
- Minimum RAM: 8 MB for Windows 95 and NT
- Available space on hard disk: 8 MB Windows 95 and NT
- 2X speed CD-ROM drive or faster
- Netscape 4.0 or higher browser or MS Internet Explorer 4.0 or higher
- Microsoft Word 97 or higher

Macintosh

- Macintosh with a 68020 or higher processor or Power Macintosh
- Apple OS version 7.0 or later
- Minimum RAM: 12 MB for Macintosh
- Available space on hard disk: 6MB Macintosh
- 2X speed CD-ROM drive or faster
- Netscape 4.0 or higher browser or MS Internet Explorer 4.0 or higher
- Microsoft Word 98 or higher

NOTE: This CD also requires the free Acrobat Reader. You can download these products using the links below:

http://www.netscape.com/download/index.html

http://www.adobe.com/products/acrobat/readstep.html

Getting Started

Insert the CD-ROM into your drive. The CD-ROM will usually launch automatically. If it does not, click on the CD-ROM drive on your computer to launch. You will see an opening page. You can click on this page or wait for it to fade to the Copyright Page. After you click to agree to the terms of the Copyright Page, the Home Page will appear.

Moving Around

Use the buttons at the left of each screen or the text at the bottom of each screen to move among the menu pages. To view a document listed on one of the menu pages, simply click on the name of the document. Use the scrollbar at the right of the screen to scroll up and down each page. To quit a document at any time, click the box at the upper right-hand corner of the screen. To quit the CD-ROM, you can click the Quit button on the left of each menu page or hit Control-Q if you are a PC user or Command-Q if you are a Mac user.

In Case of Trouble

If you experience difficulty using this CD-ROM, please follow these steps:

1. Make sure your hardware and systems configurations conform to the systems requirements noted under "Systems Requirements" above.
2. Review the installation procedure for your type of hardware and operating system. It is possible to reinstall the software if necessary.
3. You may call Jossey-Bass Customer Care at (800) 274-4434 between the hours of 8 A.M. and 4 P.M. Eastern Standard Time, and ask for Jossey-Bass Product Support. It is also possible to contact Product Support by e-mail at techsupport@ JosseyBass.com.

Please have the following information available:

• Type of computer and operating system
• Version of Windows or Mac OS being used
• Any error messages displayed
• Complete description of the problem

(It is best if you are sitting at your computer when making the call.)